REALIZING THE POTENTIAL OF IMMIGRANT YOUTH

The well-being and productivity of immigrant youth have become one of the most important global issues of our times as a result of mass migration and resettlement. In this unique volume, leading scholars from multiple nations and disciplines provide a state-of-the-art overview of contemporary research on immigrant youth and delineate the most promising future directions for research on their success, suggesting implications for policy and interventions that will benefit host societies as well as immigrant youth.

The contributors to *Realizing the Potential of Immigrant Youth* include many of the leading international experts on migration, acculturation, intergroup issues, and immigrant youth development, with contributions from the fields of child development, demography, economics, education, immigrant mental health, social psychology, and sociology.

Ann S. Masten, Ph.D., Distinguished McKnight University Professor in the Institute of Child Development, University of Minnesota, is internationally known for her research on competence, risk, and resilience in human development. She is currently president of the Society for Research in Child Development and a member of the Board on Children, Youth, and Families of the U.S. Institute of Medicine/National Academies. She directs the Project Competence studies of risk and resilience, including studies of normative populations and high-risk children exposed to the stress of migration, homelessness, war, and natural disasters.

Karmela Liebkind, Ph.D., is Professor of Social Psychology at the University of Helsinki, Finland, and a well-known authority on intergroup relations. Her areas of expertise include the ethnic identity and acculturation of minority youth as well as contact and prejudice between minority and majority members. Professor Liebkind has pursued large-scale international comparative research and published extensively on these topics. She is also regularly consulted by international bodies as an expert in intercultural contact, immigrants, racism, and xenophobia.

Donald J. Hernandez, Ph.D., is Professor of Sociology at Hunter College and The Graduate Center, City University of New York, and Senior Advisor at the Foundation for Child Development. He conducted the first national study documenting reasons for the enormous changes experienced by children since the Great Depression in parental education and work and in family composition, income, and poverty. He directed the U.S. Institute of Medicine/National Academies study on the health and well-being of children in immigrant families. He currently directs studies on income, race-ethnic, and immigrant disparities in child well-being and on family, education, health, and neighborhood environments that foster children's educational success.

THE JACOBS FOUNDATION SERIES ON ADOLESCENCE

Series Editors
Jürgen Baumert
Marta Tienda

The Jacobs Foundation Series on Adolescence presents state-of-the art research about the myriad factors that contribute to the welfare, social productivity and social inclusion of current and future generations of young people. Sponsored by the Swiss Jacobs Foundation, the series offers readers cutting edge applied research about successful youth development, including circumstances that enhance their employability, their respect for and integration with nature and culture, and their future challenges triggered by global economic and technological changes. Contributing authors are internationally known scholars from a variety of disciplines, including developmental and social psychology, clinical psychology, education, economics, communication, sociology and family studies.

REALIZING THE POTENTIAL OF IMMIGRANT YOUTH

Edited by

Ann S. Masten
University of Minnesota, Twin Cities

Karmela Liebkind
University of Helsinki, Finland

Donald J. Hernandez
Hunter College and The Graduate Center,
City University of New York

CAMBRIDGE
UNIVERSITY PRESS

CAMBRIDGE UNIVERSITY PRESS
Cambridge, New York, Melbourne, Madrid, Cape Town,
Singapore, São Paulo, Delhi, Mexico City

Cambridge University Press
32 Avenue of the Americas, New York, NY 10013-2473, USA

www.cambridge.org
Information on this title: www.cambridge.org/9781107019508

First published 2012

Printed in the United States of America

A catalog record for this publication is available from the British Library.

Library of Congress Cataloging in Publication data
Realizing the potential of immigrant youth / [edited by] Ann S. Masten,
Karmela Liebkind, Donald J. Hernandez.
    p.   cm. – (The Jacobs Foundation series on adolescence)
    Based on the Jacobs Foundation conference, Capitalizing on Migraion: The Potential
    of Immigrant Youth, held at Schloss Marbach, in Germany, on Apr. 22–24, 2009.
    Includes bibliographical references and index.
    ISBN 978-1-107-01950-8 (hardback)
    1. Children of immigrants – Social conditions – Congresses.   2. Children of
    immigrants – Economic conditions – Congresses.   3. Children of immigrants –
    Education – Congresses.   4. Assimilation (Sociology) – Congresses.   5. Group
    identity – Cross-cultural studies – Congresses.   I. Masten, Ann S.   II. Liebkind,
    Karmela, 1949–   III. Hernandez, Donald J. (Donald James), 1948–   IV. Jacobs
    Foundation.
    JV6344.R43   2012
    305.235086'912–dc23   2012001485

ISBN 978-1-107-01950-8 Hardback

This volume is dedicated to the memory of

Klaus J. Jacobs

(1936–2008)

Visionary founder of the Jacobs Foundation

and

champion for realizing the potential of all youth

Contents

Contributors

Audrey N. Beck is a postdoctoral Fellow in the Center for Health Equity Research and Policy at San Diego State University. She recently published a paper with Sharon Bzostek titled "Familial Instability and Young Children's Physical Health" in *Social Science and Medicine*.

John Berry is Emeritus Professor of Psychology at Queen's University, Kingston, Canada. He has been awarded honorary doctorates from two universities (Athens and Geneva) and recently became an international Fellow of the Centre for Applied Cross-Cultural Research, Victoria University, Wellington, New Zealand.

Edmond P. Bowers is Research Assistant Professor in the Eliot-Pearson Department of Child Development and Director of the Thrive Foundation for Youth's GPS Project at Tufts University. He was selected to participate as a Fellow in the 2011 NICHD Summer Institute on Applied Developmental Science.

Xenia Chryssochoou is Professor of Social and Political Psychology at Panteion University of Social and Political Sciences, Athens, Greece, and currently the secretary of the European Association of Social Psychology.

Miles Corak is a full professor of economics with the Graduate School of Public and International Affairs at the University of Ottawa. His coauthored paper "Economic Mobility, Family Background, and the Well-Being of Children in the United States and Canada" received the 2009 Award for Research in Comparative Policy Analysis from the Association for Public Policy Analysis and Management.

Radosveta Dimitrova is a researcher in the Department of Cross Cultural Psychology at Tilburg University, the Netherlands. Currently she is editing a book on cultural and contextual influences on the well-being of immigrant families in Europe, Africa, Asia, and North and Central America at Springer, the international publisher.

Andrew J. Fuligni is Professor in the Departments of Psychiatry and Psychology at the University of California, Los Angeles. He is a Fellow of the American Psychological Association and Association for Psychological Science and is currently an associate editor of the journal *Child Development*.

Eugene E. García is Professor and Vice President for Education Partnerships at Arizona State University. He chaired the National Task Force on Early Education for Hispanics and received an honorary doctorate from The Erikson Institute in 2011 for his contributions to the field of child development.

Cynthia Garcia Coll is a Robinson and Barstow Professor of Education, Psychology, and Pediatrics. In 2009, Professor Garcia Coll was the recipient of the Society for Research on Child Development's "Cultural and Contextual Contributions to Child Development" award, and her current research is focused on documenting and explaining the immigrant paradox in education and behavior as evidenced by U.S. children and adolescents.

Jonathan Israel Gershuny is Statutory Professor of Sociology in the Oxford University Department of Sociology and a Professorial Fellow of St Hugh's College. At Oxford, he is the Director of the Centre for Time Use Research.

Taveeshi Gupta is a doctoral candidate in the Applied Psychology Department at New York University. She is currently conducting a three-year longitudinal study in India.

Donald J. Hernandez is Professor of Sociology, Hunter College and The Graduate Center, City University of New York. He recently completed research on an alternative poverty measure for the United States and a study assessing how socioeconomic disparities versus cultural differences account for low early education enrollment among children in immigrant and native-born families. In 2006 he received a Presidential Citation awarded by the American Psychological Association to recognize and commend distinguished contributions to the health and well-being of immigrant children and their families.

Gabriel Horenczyk is an associate professor in the School of Education at the Hebrew University of Jerusalem. His main areas of interest are psychological aspects of collective identity, identity and adaptation of immigrants, and the school acculturative context.

Inga Jasinskaja-Lahti is Professor at the University of Helsinki and has done extensive research on immigrant youth, particularly those immigrating from the former Soviet Union. Her most recent INPRES research project investigated the impact of the premigration stage on immigrants' postmigration acculturation and adaptation.

Ciğdem Kağitçibaşi is a professor at Koc University, Istanbul, and a founding member of the Turkish Academy of Sciences. She recently delivered a keynote address at the 12th European Congress of Psychology in Istanbul (July 2011).

Yoav Lavee is Associate Professor and Head of the Center for Research and Study of the Family, Faculty of Social Welfare and Health Sciences, University of Haifa (Israel). His research generally focuses on roles and relationships in families, family dynamics and interactions under stress, and cross-cultural comparison of family patterns in Israeli society.

Jacqueline V. Lerner is Professor of Applied Developmental Psychology at the Lynch School of Education at Boston College and scientific director of the 4-H Study of Positive Youth Development. She recently edited a thematic volume on positive youth development in the series *Advances in Child Development and Behavior* (with Richard M. Lerner and Janette B. Benson).

Richard M. Lerner is the Bergstrom Chair in Applied Developmental Science at the Eliot-Pearson Department of Child Development and Director of the Institute for Applied Research in Youth Development at Tufts University. He has edited both the 2006 *Handbook of Child Psychology*, 6th edition (with William Damon) and the 2009 *Handbook of Adolescent Psychology*, 3rd edition (with Laurence Steinberg).

Selva Lewin-Bizan is a research associate at the Institute for Applied Research in Youth Development at Tufts University. She recently authored an article on developmental cascades in a special issue of *Development and Psychopathology*.

Karmela Liebkind is Professor of Social Psychology at the University of Helsinki. She has published extensively on ethnic identity and acculturation of minority youth as well as on contact and prejudice between minority and majority members.

Tuuli Anna Mähönen focused in her Ph.D. research at the Unit of Social Psychology, University of Helsinki, on intergroup contact and social norms as predictors of the outgroup attitudes of majority and minority youth. Her research interests also include intergroup relations and acculturation.

Amy Kerivan Marks is an Assistant Professor and the Director of Undergraduate and Graduate Studies in Psychology at Suffolk University. Her second book, co-edited with Cynthia Garcia Coll, provides an in-depth exploration of the immigrant paradox and is currently in production at the American Psychological Association Press.

Ann S. Masten is Distinguished McKnight University Professor in the Institute of Child Development at the University of Minnesota. She directs the Project Competence studies of risk and resilience and is currently president of the Society for Research in Child Development and a member of the Board on Children, Youth, and Families of the U.S. Institute of Medicine and National Academies.

Andrea Michel is a doctoral Fellow at the Jena Graduate School "Human Behaviour in Social and Economic Change" (GSBC) and the Center of Applied Developmental Science at the University of Jena (Germany). Her dissertation deals with the psychological adaptation of adolescent immigrants.

Frosso Motti-Stefanidi is Professor of Psychology at the University of Athens, Greece. She recently became a Fellow of the Association for Psychological Science and president-elect of the European Society for Developmental Psychology.

Brian Nolan is Professor of Public Policy and Principal of the College of Human Sciences at University College Dublin. He recently co-edited the *Handbook of Economic Inequality*.

Andrea Patrico is a student at the Warren Alpert Medical School of Brown University. She is concentrating in advocacy and activism and intends to practice as a pediatrician.

Flannery Patton is a graduate of Brown University and past research coordinator for the Center for the Study of Child Development in Providence, RI. She has worked with immigrant groups in Rhode Island since 2003 as an ESL teacher, researcher, and public programming coordinator.

Jean Phinney is a visiting scholar at the University of California, Berkeley. In the past year, she has been an invited speaker at international conferences on immigration in South Korea and Austria.

Karen Robson holds a Ph.D. in applied social and economic research from Essex University in England and is Associate Professor of Sociology at York University in Ontario, Canada.

Abraham (Avi) Sagi-Schwartz is Professor of Psychology, Center for the Study of Child Development, the University of Haifa (Israel). His main research interests are in the area of attachment and socioemotional development across the life span and across cultures, as well as parenting and socioemotional development under extreme life circumstances, especially the effects of the Holocaust.

David Lackland Sam is Professor of Cross-Cultural Psychology at the University of Bergen, Norway, and recently gave a Ph.D. workshop on acculturation during the IACCP congress in Istanbul, Turkey.

Rainer K. Silbereisen is currently Professor of Developmental Psychology, Center for Applied Developmental Science, at the University of Jena (Germany) as well as Adjunct Professor of Human Development and Family Studies at Pennsylvania State University (United States). His research is mainly on behavioral development across the life span, with emphasis on cross-national differences and the role of social change.

Selcuk R. Sirin is Associate Professor in the Applied Psychology Department at New York University. He is directing Bahcesehir Research Methods Workshops in Istanbul.

Timothy M. Smeeding is Distinguished Professor of Public Affairs and Economics at the Lafollette School and Director of the Institute for Research on Poverty at the University of Wisconsin-Madison.

Christiane Spiel is Professor of Bildung-Psychology and Evaluation at the University of Vienna, Faculty of Psychology. She recently received the Grand Decoration of Honor in Silver for Services to the Republic of Austria.

Dagmar Strohmeier is Professor of Intercultural Competence at the University of Applied Sciences Upper Austria. She currently edits the special issue "Evidence Based Bullying Prevention Programs for Youth" for the journal *New Directions for Youth Development*.

Gloria A. Suarez is a doctoral student in the Combined Program in Education and Psychology at the University of Michigan. She recently received the Rackham Merit Fellowship from the University of Michigan.

Moshe Tatar is Associate Professor in the School of Education at the Hebrew University of Jerusalem. His main areas of interest are school psychology counseling, help seeking among immigrant adolescents, and the school acculturative context.

Eva H. Telzer is a doctoral student in Developmental Psychology at the University of California, Los Angeles. She recently received a National Research Service Award from the National Institutes of Health and a Doctoral Dissertation Improvement Grant from the National Science Foundation.

Marta Tienda is Maurice P. During '22 Professor of Demographic Studies and Professor of Sociology and Public Affairs at Princeton University. She is coordinator of the Princeton Global Network on Child Migration and editor of a Future of Children volume about immigrant children in the United States.

Peter F. Titzmann received his Ph.D. at the Friedrich-Schiller-University, Jena (Germany) and is currently a research associate in the Department of Developmental Psychology in Jena, Center for Applied Developmental Science. His general research interests focus on adolescent development, cross-cultural comparisons, and processes of acculturation.

Maykel Verkuyten is the academic director of the European Research Centre on Migration and Ethnic Relations (Ercomer) and a professor at the Faculty of Social and Behavioral Sciences at Utrecht University in the Netherlands.

Coady Wing holds a Ph.D. in public policy and administration from the Maxwell School at Syracuse University and is currently a post-doc working with Professor Tom Cook at Northwestern University.

Rui Yang received her bachelor's degree in psychology from Yale University and is now a Ph.D. candidate at Brown University. She also serves as Chief Director of the Psychology Unit at Beijing Genomics Institute, China.

Introduction

Ann S. Masten, Karmela Liebkind, and Donald J. Hernandez

The success and well-being of immigrant youth has become a global concern for many stakeholders at multiple levels, including individuals, families, schools, neighborhoods, local and national economies and governments, and international organizations. Millions of young people live and grow up in countries where they or their parents were not born, often as a result of families moving to find a better life or fleeing disastrous circumstances. Because of this migration and resettlement, ethno-cultural diversity is rapidly becoming the rule rather than the exception in many nation states and communities of the world, particularly in wealthier host nations. As noted by Hernandez in Chapter 1 on the demography of immigration, immigrants represent the fastest growing segment of the population in many affluent countries. Consequently, the economic and social futures of multiple nations depend on the success of immigrant children and youth. Moreover, immigrant families are transforming the neighborhoods and societies in which they settle. Recent migration has brought immense changes, challenges, and opportunities to host and sending nations, as well as the individuals and families who migrate.

This volume is based on the Jacobs Foundation Conference, "Capitalizing on Migration: The Potential of Immigrant Youth," held at Schloss Marbach in Germany on April 22–24, 2009. The Jacobs Foundation, strongly committed to the support of science, practice, and policy pertaining to productive youth development, sponsored this conference in response to growing international interest in the migration and well-being of immigrant youth. Leading international scholars in demography, human development, economics, social psychology, education, immigrant mental health, and sociology gathered to address urgent questions about the current status and

1

future potential of immigrant youth. The chapters of this volume reflect the diverse perspectives of the contributors and provide an overview of current leading research and its implications for practice and policy. The chapters point to promising directions for future research on the development and well-being of immigrant youth and how to facilitate their potential. Given the growing number of immigrant youth in many host nations, understanding the processes leading to the success of immigrant youth has tremendous potential to benefit national economies and societies, as well as individual young people and their families, both in the near term and for the foreseeable future.

In European Union countries and the United States, there has been a rapid recent increase in the numbers of first- and second-generation immigrants over the past two decades due to immigration and births in immigrant families. As a result, the proportion of children living in immigrant families with at least one foreign-born parent has increased dramatically in many nations. For example, recent data indicate that the proportion of all children (aged 0 to 17) with one foreign-born parent is 40% in Switzerland, 23% in Germany, 22% in the Netherlands, and 23% in the United States (Hernandez, Macartney, & Blanchard, 2009). Insofar as many arrive from non-Western developing countries, this surge in immigration is leading to large increases in cultural and ethnic diversity in the European Union and the United States. The U.S. Census Bureau projects that by the year 2030 fewer than one-half of all children in the United States will be non-Hispanic whites and more than one-half will belong to ethnic minorities (U.S. Census Bureau, 2004).

For the purposes of this volume, *immigrant youth* refers to first- and second-generation youth (those born outside the country and native-born children with at least one immigrant parent). There also is reference in the volume to third- or later generation youth descended from immigrants (native-born children of native-born parents). Age of migration is a focus of some discussion (e.g., see Chapter 4 by Corak), contrasting earlier and later ages of arrival, although this issue is not discussed explicitly in terms of the "1.5 generation" (referring to immigrant children who arrive early in life and therefore grow up largely in the new country; Rumbaut, 1994).

Not only first-generation but also second- and third-generation immigrants born in receiving countries may be viewed – and treated – as "second class" citizens, while at the same time individual immigrants and families may thrive and prosper. Attitudes toward immigrant youth vary widely within and across receiving countries. Displacements from war and disaster, as well as changing labor markets, may attract diverse immigrant workers and their children to communities previously homogeneous in ethnicity or religion. Consequently, public schools in many receiving communities are increasingly charged with educating young people from many cultures with varying degrees of fluency in the language of the education system, which is typically the host country's official language. Schools are asked to prepare these students for future labor markets and responsible civic engagement. In this dynamic context, the adaptation, integration, and development of immigrant youth and their families are important issues with profound implications for receiving and sending nations.

While the adaptation and productivity of immigrant youth are clearly issues of global concern engaging a wide array of scientific disciplines, a successful scientific conference and volume require a more delimited focus. The 2009 Jacobs Conference and consequently this volume were organized around a set of key questions (delineated in the following section) that are central to the core goal of realizing the full potential of immigrant youth for the sake of host societies, global well-being, and the immigrants themselves. Although it included research and discussions about a variety of host nations, the conference emphasized research on immigration to Europe and North America. This emphasis was chosen because of the large scope of migration to these regions, the rising concerns in these two regions about the extent of migration, and the preponderance of current research and researchers that have focused on migration to nations in these regions.

Recognizing that nations, employers, and those charged with educating and promoting the potential of immigrant youth cannot wait for definitive answers to all questions posed at the conference, there was a commitment in the conference to discuss not only the findings and shortcomings from the best available research, but also the implications of findings to date for policy and practice. There was a strong consensus at the conference on the importance of active cooperation and collaboration among researchers and policy makers to improve the opportunities for immigrant youth in society and to ease the processes of integration and acculturation, both for immigrants and the receiving population.

Consequences of migration include growth, change, and conflict at many levels of human life, from individual development and adaptation to integration at the level of nations and international global politics. The success of immigrant youth is undoubtedly shaped by complex interactions among systems at many levels. These include the characteristics of receiving and sending cultures, the nature of the contexts in which immigrant youth live, learn, play, and work (families, peer groups, schools, and neighborhoods), and individual development.

Many aspects of context are examined in the chapters of this volume, ranging from government policies to the ethnic composition of school classrooms, and from language spoken at home or at school to intergroup attitudes. Perceived and observed discrimination are critically important aspects of context for the adaptation of immigrant youth. Human development itself is an important context for understanding immigrant youth as they interact with other people in their host communities and in their own cultures and families. Expectations for youth vary by age or development, as well as by gender, ethnicity, and local or regional culture. These expectations can influence attitudes held by self and others about one immigrant individual or about groups of immigrant young people.

Many of the chapters in this volume embrace a dynamic and developmental systems view of human adaptation in the context of migration, characterized by interactions and change among many groups and systems that together shape the adaptation of individuals, families, schools, communities, and larger systems of human life (Bronfenbrenner, 1979; Ford & Lerner, 1992; Gottlieb, 2007; Kağitçibaşi, 2007; Verkuyten, 2005). Thus, immigrant youth shape the families and communities in which they live while, simultaneously, individual youth development is itself shaped by interactions (both their own and their families') with communities and various ingroups and outgroups. In many of the chapters that follow, authors emphasize that immigration is transforming receiving cultures at the same time that receiving cultures are influencing immigrants over time and generation. A bidirectional and dynamic view of acculturation is prevalent across the volume, with immigrant cultures and host cultures both undergoing change (Berry, 2006; Sam & Berry, 2010; Schwartz et al., 2010).

Organization of the Volume

The volume is organized around the three primary questions posed at the Jacobs Conference:

- *Who migrates and how do they fare?*
- *Who succeeds and why?*
- *What works to promote the potential of immigrant youth?*

In the first section of the volume, which emphasizes sociodemographic perspectives, multinational data on migration are presented along with data on the poverty, living conditions, and receiving contexts of immigrant youth. Some authors summarize findings from important immigration research projects, such as the eight-country study described by Hernandez in Chapter 1, while others present results of new analyses (see Chapters 2, 3, and 4 by Beck and Tienda, Smeeding et al., and Corak). Hernandez provides descriptive data from eight affluent countries on the prevalence, diversity, and well-being of immigrant youth. The data underscore the importance of success among these youth for the future economic vitality of these nations and the significance of policies and practices that influence the extent to which immigrant youth are supported in that success.

Beck and Tienda in Chapter 2 provide illuminating data on the living arrangements and quality of context for migrant youth in six developed nations, drawing on the International Public Use Micro-data Samples (IPUMS) of census data. Their analyses link context features in these countries to school enrollment, a key marker of adaptation available in the data. In Chapter 3, Smeeding and colleagues draw on data from 14 nations, available from two sources (Luxembourg Income Study and European Statistics on Living Conditions), to examine cross-national variation in policies and successes relevant to poverty and immigrant youth. Their analyses support the provocative conclusion that the country where one lands matters more than one's native or immigrant status.

Corak also analyzed original census data, in this case from Canada, to examine the relation of age of arrival to success of immigrant youth, testing the role developmental timing may play in the complex processes involved in the development and adaptation of immigrant youth. The results he presents in Chapter 4 are compelling in suggesting that early age of arrival (prior to adolescence and secondary schooling years) is very important for school and economic success, but also that the match is crucial between language experience in the child's history (or the sending context) with the language of the host country. When there is continuity in language, it is not surprising to find that age of arrival matters less.

The second part of the book examines questions about "who succeeds," with an emphasis on developmental, social-psychological, and sociocultural perspectives. This section is focused on theory and research pertaining to processes that may account for differences in adaptive or developmental success among individual immigrants, among different groups of immigrants in the same communities, or among immigrant youth from similar origins that end up in different contexts, including schools or countries. In Chapter 5, five leading investigators who study immigrant youth from three distinct perspectives present a unified framework for research on this population. This collaboration grew out of a 2008 Summer School on the interplay of development and context cosponsored by the Jacobs Foundation and the European Society for Developmental Psychology, held in Syros,

Greece. Motti-Stefanidi, Berry, Chryssochoou, Sam, and Phinney present the key conceptual contributions from research on development, social psychology, and acculturation of immigrant youth, followed by their integrative framework for linking theoretical and empirical findings across these fields to understand the adaptation and development of immigrant youth. Their model offers a way forward for future research concerned with the well-being of immigrant youth to bridge key areas of investigation, while at the same time it may serve as a bridge linking investigators from varying disciplines that typically have proceeded without the benefit of ideas and methods from other important perspectives.

In Chapter 6, Garcia Coll and her colleagues review the evidence on the "immigrant paradox," which refers to the observation that in some domains of well-being, recent immigrants show better adaptation than contemporary native peers and later generations of the same immigrant group. It is a complex topic with many possible explanations. These authors draw on diverse findings to document the paradox and offer possible explanations. Among their intriguing suggestions is the idea that immigrant families may bring important values and human and social capital with them to the host country that are subsequently lost in future generations. Sustaining these resources throughout the processes of acculturation and across generations may be a priority for preventive interventions. Garcia Coll and colleagues close their chapter with a set of questions to guide future research on this important and perhaps not so paradoxical theme.

In Chapter 7, Fuligni and Telzer focus on the contributions of immigrant youth to their families and the processes by which these roles may help or hinder their own adaptation as well as successful acculturation by families and receiving societies. Their chapter addresses a neglected theme in the discourse on immigrant research by emphasizing the key role that children and youth of immigrant families may play as cultural brokers, assisting communication between hosts and families, as social capital for the economic success of families, and also as economic contributors to families and thereby communities. The authors consider the benefits and costs of these various roles to the immigrant youth and the underappreciated contributions of these youth to the receiving societies. They present data from a large longitudinal study that included daily diaries kept by young people to document these family roles and conclude with comments on ways to appreciate and affirm the contributions of these youth without exploiting them.

The three other chapters in the second part of the book (Chapters 8, 9, and 10) focus on the processes and significance of different aspects of identity formation and development for understanding and guiding efforts to promote successful adaptation in immigrant youth and their receiving contexts. These chapters emphasize different factors relevant to identity processes during the developmental period of adolescence, a time in the life course when identity exploration deepens and intensifies.

In Chapter 8, Liebkind, Jasinskaja-Lahti, and Mähönen emphasize the central importance of harmonious intergroup relations for multicultural societies and for immigrant youth in those societies. They examine the challenges facing immigrant youth as they resolve cultural and national identities. In particular, these authors underscore the reciprocal nature of social identities and intergroup attitudes as communities and immigrants adapt to each other. They delineate the evidence on bidirectional influences of intergroup attitudes and perceived or experienced discrimination and describe effective strategies for reducing prejudice. Liebkind et al. discuss the convergence of evidence from social psychology and acculturation literatures suggesting that positive subgroup identities for each interacting subgroup (e.g., ethnic identity) combined with a common superordinate identity (e.g., national identity) provides the most adaptive resolution for harmonious intergroup relations. They also emphasize the point that interventions need to be directed at the majority cultural group as well as the minority or immigrant subgroups.

In Chapter 9, Verkuyten also emphasizes the significance and potential of strong ethnic identity for positive intergroup attitudes and behavior, and therefore the importance of positive ethnic identities for the well-being of multicultural societies and the individuals within them. Verkuyten describes the key theories that have contributed to our understanding of identity in immigrant and other youth in developmental, acculturative, and social-psychological sciences. He also makes a strong case for the multidimensional study of ethnic identity, underscoring the importance of ethnic behavior in actual interactions with ingroup and outgroup members where ethnic selves are enacted and/or change.

In Chapter 10, Sirin and Gupta focus on identity and adaptation in Muslim American youth living in a post-9/11 world. They provide an overview of three studies of Muslim students in the United States, highlighting the challenges and successes in forging a cohesive identity at a difficult point in history. They report findings from a large group of students who "happily reside on the hyphen," adapting to challenging experiences with impressive resilience. Their research opens a window on the strengths and needs of these youth, many of whom are immigrants. Their data are consistent with findings from very different situations (see Liebkind et al., Chapter 8), suggesting that perceived or experienced discrimination reduces the likelihood of positive dual identities (ethnic and national combined).

The third part of this volume is focused on the key question of "What works?" and evidence-informed strategies for promoting the potential of immigrant youth, given the knowledge to date. In Chapter 11, Kağitçibaşi presents her theory of the autonomous-related self and discusses the success of a prevention program she developed that is now widely used in Turkey and European countries. The program was designed to enrich the early education of children from families migrating from rural to urban centers, with beneficial effects observed in childhood and sustained into adolescence and early adulthood. Results are congruent with other international research supporting a high return on investment in high quality early childhood education for diverse groups of high-risk children, including immigrant children. The theme of early enrichment to promote the success of immigrant children is echoed in other chapters of this volume (e.g., Chapters 4 and 16 by Corak and García).

Kağitçibaşi points out that contemporary international migration often takes the form of migration from societies that value relatedness and interdependence (both material and emotional; sometimes called "collectivistic" societies) to those that value autonomy and independence (often termed "individualistic" societies). Kağitçibaşi asserts that humans have basic needs for both relatedness and autonomy and that these two goals are compatible when one distinguishes between the autonomy of "agency" and the idea of separation. She argues that the best resolution for both immigrant and nonimmigrant youth can be achieved by blending the values of relatedness and autonomy to support educational and economic success along with interpersonal support and closeness.

In Chapter 12, Lerner, Lerner, Bowers, and Lewin-Bizan discuss the general framework of Positive Youth Development (PYD) in relation to immigrant youth. PYD, grounded in developmental systems theory, emphasizes the strengths and potential of all youth for the societies in which they live. The authors highlight the resources young immigrants bring to their host communities, including their bilingual and bicultural skills. This aspect of their chapter echoes points made by Fuligni and Telzer in Chapter 7 on the contributions of immigrant youth. In the PYD framework, a fundamental developmental task for immigrant youth is to manifest positive development in the new context. In addition, however, this chapter examines the idea that a fundamental responsibility of societies in which immigrant youth live and develop is to afford opportunities and supports to facilitate the process and thereby gain human capital from the successes of these youth.

Chapter 13 by Silbereisen and colleagues provides an example of research on the positive development of immigrant youth based on the PYD conceptual framework. The study of "Migration and Societal Integration" is an ongoing effort involving Germany and Israel with the goal of comparing the adaptation of immigrants in diverse contexts to examine the role of transitions in psychosocial development. The adaptive criteria of interest are framed in the "5 Cs" of PDY: Competence, Confidence, Connection, Character, and Caring (Lerner et al., 2005). Chapter 13 focuses on the German findings to date, highlighting the idea that adaptation during key formal and informal transitions in the life course can foster advancement in the 5 Cs, including the transition into kindergarten, the first romantic relationship (usually in early adolescence), and the act of moving in with a partner (later adolescence or emerging adulthood). The chapter emphasizes the similarity between immigrant and native youth in the effects of the transitions but also points out differences between cultural groups in levels of adaptation, regardless of transitions and resources.

Three chapters in the third section of the volume highlight the importance of education and the school context for promoting the success of immigrant youth and thereby building the human capital of host communities and nations. In Chapter 14, Horenczyk and Tatar discuss school as a key context for adaptation in immigrants with respect to both development and acculturation, a broad theme echoed in many other chapters of this volume. They propose a multilevel (school, classroom) and multifaceted conceptual framework for understanding the school acculturative context. They assess multiple aspects of school climate, like visual signals, norms, values, and assumptions. They also assess the perspectives of immigrant students compared to other students, and emphasize that the attitudes, expectations, and behaviors of both national and immigrant classmates and teachers affect the acculturation and adaptation of immigrant students. Peer relations between immigrant and national peers, including friendship, are discussed as key contexts for reciprocal acculturation. Their discussion underscores the importance of school orientation (assimilationist versus multicultural) and the potential afforded by this important context for promoting cultural change, cultural understanding, and development.

In Chapter 15, Spiel and Strohmeier focus their discussion on peer relationships, with illustrative findings from research in Austria and other European countries. Research on the role of peer relations in acculturation and intervention research with schools that have immigrant students is surprisingly scarce given the well-documented significance of peer relations in adaptation and development (Gest et al., 2006). The authors focus on positive and negative aspects of peer relationships, with friendship serving as the example of the former and bullying/victimization as the example of the latter. They find, as expected, that homophily (attraction based on similarities) is characteristic of friendships in immigrant youth. In addition, their research underscores the effects of ethnic composition of schools and classrooms on immigrant friendships, a finding consistent with the hypothesized role of opportunity for intercultural friendships. In regard to bullying, one interesting difference observed between immigrant and native youth concerns the function of this behavior. In two different countries, immigrant boys were found to bully others in order to feel affiliated, while native boys appeared to bully others to feel dominant and powerful.

Spiel and Strohmeier suggest strategies for promoting positive peer relations in multicultural schools, based on evidence from basic and applied research. They present examples from two evidence-informed programs in Austria that targeted the whole school in an effort to improve peer relations and thereby the well-being of immigrant and native youth. They also note the counterproductive effects that "tracking" can have on intercultural friendships in schools when it segregates youth by ethnic group.

In Chapter 16, García discusses what can be done to address the achievement disparities for disadvantaged minorities in American schools, a goal that he and others at the conference viewed as vital to promoting success among immigrant students. As noted previously, growing evidence supports the value of high quality child care and education for disadvantaged children (Heckman, 2006). García highlights the themes of early enrichment, bilingual language development, and the value of preschool education for later success. García focuses specifically on Latino children in U.S. schools, with an eye toward lessons gleaned from prevention research for promoting the potential of immigrant youth. He also emphasizes the role of dual language access for child development and parent involvement in child education.

Language skills play a crucial role in early school success, and language development was one of the salient themes emerging in discussions at the 2009 Jacobs Conference. The participants at the conference agreed on the value in promoting the acquisition of the dominant host society language for success in that context while preserving the cultural capital represented by multilingual capabilities of parents and children. Bilingual education can be viewed as an investment in the language literacy of a society, enhancing the "linguistic capital" of a country by promoting the acquisition of the dominant, unifying language of the society at the same time that skills in different languages are preserved in subgroups and immigrants and promoted in the native population. Recent evidence on the possible role of bilingual learning for brain development and the acquisition of executive function skills offers additional support to the case supporting multiple language learning in children (e.g., Carlson & Meltzoff, 2008).

The third section of the volume closes with a suitably broad commentary by Nolan in Chapter 17 on the challenges and opportunities of understanding "what works" for promoting success in immigrant youth and implementing successful changes in practices and policies to impact youth success. Nolan offers a framework for organizing findings and policies pertinent to this multifaceted agenda without oversimplifying the complexities of contextual, developmental, and individual differences. Nolan concludes that both general and targeted strategies to promote the potential of immigrant youth are needed and serve different purposes, offering a strong rationale for both approaches. General programs that support educational attainment and healthy development in disadvantaged children and families living in poverty will impact immigrant families, who fall disproportionately into these segments of the population. Targeted programs that address specific barriers and issues of immigrants, such as language needs for education, unique health issues related to international migration, or housing discrimination are also important. Nolan supports the availability of "second chances" for reentry and training in the education system and the labor market. His framework encompasses the issues of family, housing, health, psychology, and education presented in many earlier chapters, along with economic strategies.

Conclusions

Throughout the conference and this resulting volume, major themes emerged regarding the challenges of and opportunities for promoting the potential of immigrant youth. It was clear that there are numerous barriers and questions that remain to be addressed, including important limitations in the quality of research available. At the same time, there are converging and compelling conclusions on how to move forward despite these challenges. The following summary points illustrate the counterpoints of challenges and opportunities recurring across this volume.

- Immigrant youth can be a vital source of future human and social capital for their host nations, but one of the barriers to developing and benefiting from this potential is that immigrant youth may not be perceived this way in receiving communities and nations.

- Additional obstacles remain to fulfilling the promise of immigrant youth, including discrimination and lack of access to adequate education, health care, or housing.
- Many promising strategies are available to address these barriers, although few strategies have strong experimental evidence to support their efficacy with immigrant youth.
- Additional research designed to inform strategic practices and policies is needed.
- Better methodology and international collaborations would serve to advance the knowledge base and the application agenda to benefit immigrants and the nations that receive and send them.
- Immigrant youth face many challenges but often succeed in ways that foster the well-being of their families and host nations.
- Language skills are a key component of adaptive success in contemporary affluent societies.
- Investing in bilingualism and bicultural (ethnic and national) identities yields benefits for societies as well as individuals.
- Addressing perceived discrimination is crucial to harmonious intergroup relations.
- Harmonious intergroup relations are central to the well-being of individual multicultural nations and have fundamental roles to play in global well-being.

The chapters of this volume highlight the contributions and the as yet unrealized potential of research on migration, acculturation, and the development or adaptation of individuals, families, and nations in the context of migration. Migration and pressing international economic issues are drawing attention to the importance of understanding the interplay of culture and development of individuals, families, communities, and nations, not only with respect to fostering productive youth development, but also for the much broader agenda of informing science or policy and promoting positive interpersonal and intergroup relations at many levels of human affairs.

At the same time, it is clear that there is much work to be done. In particular, high quality research on what works to promote the success of immigrant youth in the near and far future remains quite limited, particularly given the numbers of immigrant youth in many communities and nations around the world and the importance of their success for many stakeholders. Collaborative, translational, and multidisciplinary research, designed to inform policies and practices as well as theory in diverse fields, has an essential role to play in understanding and promoting the potential of immigrant youth.

REFERENCES

Berry, J. W. (2006). Contexts of acculturation. In D. L. Sam & J. W. Berry (Eds.), *The Cambridge handbook of acculturation psychology* (pp. 97–112). Cambridge, UK: Cambridge University Press.

Bronfenbrenner, U. (1979). *The ecology of human development: Experiments by nature and design.* Cambridge, MA: Harvard University Press.

Carlson, S. M., & Meltzoff, A. N. (2008). Bilingual experience and executive functioning in young children. *Developmental Science, 11*, 282–198.

Ford, D. H., & Lerner, R. M. (1992). *Developmental systems theory: An integrative approach.* Newbury Park, CA: Sage.

Gest, S. D., Sesma, A., Masten, A. S., & Tellegen, A. (2006). Childhood peer reputation as a predictor of competence and symptoms 10 years later. *Journal of Abnormal Child Psychology, 34*, 509–26.

Gottlieb, G. (2007). Probabilistic epigenetics. *Developmental Science, 10*, 1–11.

Heckman, J. J. (2006). Skill formation and the economics of investing in disadvantaged children. *Science, 312*, 1900–2.

Hernandez, D. J., Macartney, S., & Blanchard, V. L. (2009). *Children in immigrant families in eight affluent countries. Their family, national, and international context.* Florence, Italy: UNICEF Innocenti Research Centre.

Kağitçibaşi, C. (2007). *Family, self, and human development across cultures: Theory and applications* (2nd ed.). Mahwah, NJ: Lawrence Erlbaum Associates.

Lerner, R. M., Lerner, J. V., Almerigi, J., Theokas, C., Phelps, E., Gestsdóttir, S., Naudeau, S., Jeličić, H., Alberts, A. E., Ma, L., Smith, L. M., Bobek, D. L., Richman-Raphael, D., Simpson, I., Christiansen, E. D., & von Eye, A. (2005). Positive youth development, participation in community youth development programs, and community contributions of fifth grade adolescents: Findings from the first wave of the 4-H Study of Positive Youth Development. *Journal of Early Adolescence, 25*(1), 17–71.

Rumbaut, R. G. (1994). The crucible within: Ethnic identity, self-esteem, and segmented assimilation among children of immigrants. *International Migration Review, 28*(4). *Special Issue: The New Second Generation,* 748–94.

Sam, D. L., & Berry, J. W. (2010). Acculturation: When individuals and groups of different cultural backgrounds meet. *Perspectives on Psychological Science, 5*, 472–81.

Schwartz, S. J., Unger, J. B., Zamboanga, B. L., & Szapocznik, J. (2010). Rethinking the concept of acculturation: Implications for theory and research. *American Psychologist, 65*, 237–51.

U. S. Census Bureau (2004). U. S. interim projections by age, sex, race, and Hispanic origin. <http://www.census.gov/ipc/www/usinterimproj/> Internet release data: March 18, 2004.

Verkuyten, M. (2005). *The social psychology of ethnic identity.* London: Psychology Press.

Part 1

WHO MIGRATES AND HOW DO THEY FARE?

Sociodemographic Perspectives

1 Resources, Strengths, and Challenges for Children in Immigrant Families in Eight Affluent Countries

Donald J. Hernandez

Introduction

The integration of immigrants, a long-standing concern in countries of mass immigration such as the United States and Australia, has become a prominent public issue in most Western European nations as recent decades brought increasing, and often unprecedented, rates of immigration. Much of this immigration is from low- and middle-income countries, and many of the immigrants and their children differ in appearance, language, religion, and culture from nonimmigrants. Responding to these trends, the European Union recently began to vigorously pursue issues of immigrant integration with a view toward fostering social inclusion and social cohesion.

This chapter discusses new results from an eight-country study that for the first time compares the lives of children in immigrant families to those in native-born families regarding various aspects of their integration related to language, civic participation, education, employment, and housing. These dimensions reflect resources and strengths available to, and challenges confronting, children of immigrants and their families. Thus, this chapter provides important information for affluent countries experiencing rapid immigration as they consider public policies aimed at promoting the integration and well-being of children in immigrant families to help ensure that these children effectively participate in and contribute to the societies and broader economies of the countries where their parents have settled.

The Eight Study Countries

The eight settlement countries studied here include five of the largest original 15 European Union countries – France, Germany, Italy, the Netherlands, and the United Kingdom. The sixth country – Switzerland – shares borders with three of these countries (France, Germany, and Italy). The remaining two – Australia and the United States – were settled mainly by mass migrations from Europe that covered centuries. Five of these countries account for nearly one-half of the 11 countries worldwide that have the largest numbers of immigrants. The United States has more immigrants than any other nation, while Germany ranks third, France ranks fifth, the United Kingdom ranks ninth, and Australia ranks 11th. Somewhat lower in the list, Italy, Switzerland, and the Netherlands are ranked at 16th, 25th, and 27th, respectively, among nations around the world in the number of immigrants within their borders. All together, these eight affluent countries account for nearly 40% of all persons not living within their own country of birth, a total of 76 million international immigrants.

Results are presented and discussed for these eight affluent settlement countries based on data from the most recent population census (Australia, Italy, Switzerland, the United Kingdom, and the United States), the population registration system (Netherlands), or a large sample survey (France, and for Germany the "micro-census"). The new results pertain mainly to years 2000 and 2001, or in the case of Germany 2005, and are drawn from the first report to develop internationally comparable statistics from these sources for children in immigrant and nonimmigrant families (Hernandez, Macartney, & Blanchard, 2009). Results by detailed country of origin are available at www.albany.edu/csda/children.

The Origins of Children in Immigrant Families

Children aged 0–17 are classified in this chapter as living in an immigrant family if they have at least one foreign-born parent, that is, at least one parent who was born in a country other than the settlement country. These children are classified as first-generation if they are themselves foreign-born, and they are classified as second-generation if they were born in the settlement country but have at least one foreign-born parent. All other children in this age range are classified as third- or later generation, and they have parents who all were born in the nation where they live. Near the end, the chapter also focuses briefly on adolescents aged 15–17, distinguishing the foreign-born (first-generation) from the native-born (second-, third-, and later generations). The primary focus of the chapter is on children with origins in low- and middle-income countries, as identified by the World Bank (2007).

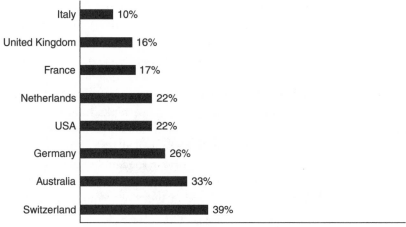

Figure 1.1. Children in all immigrant families as percent of all children.
Source: Prepared by Donald J. Hernandez from UNICEF-IRC project on children and immigrant families (Hernandez, Macartney, & Blanchard, 2009).

Because immigrants typically move to their adopted homelands during early adulthood, not only do many bring one or more children along when they immigrate, they also often bear additional children after arriving in the new settlement society. As a result, the proportion of children with one or both parents who are foreign-born can be much higher than the proportion of the overall population that is foreign-born. At least one of every 10 children, and as many as four of every 10 children, in the study countries live in immigrant families with one or two foreign-born parents (Figure 1.1). Focusing specifically on children in immigrant families, among these children the proportion with origins in low- or middle-income counties is as low as 10%–13% only in Germany (Figure 1.2, a range of estimates is presented for some countries because more precise results are not available), but this rises to one-third to one-half in Australia, and to between about one-half and three-fourths of children in immigrant families living in the other six study countries. These children often are from Africa, Asia, Latin America and the Caribbean, or Oceania and may also differ in physical appearance from the nonimmigrant population, making them potentially subject to racial or ethnic discrimination in school or the labor market.

For each of the eight countries studied here, between one-fifth and two-thirds of children with origins in low- and middle-income countries are

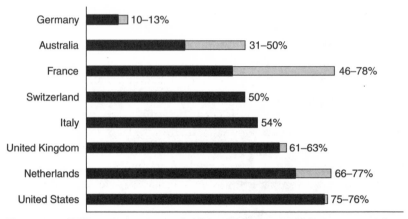

Figure 1.2. Children in immigrant families with low- or middle-income origins as percent of children in all immigrant families.
Source: Prepared by Donald J. Hernandez from UNICEF-IRC project on children and immigrant families (Hernandez, Macartney, & Blanchard, 2009).

accounted for by just two countries of origin. These concentrations often reflect the colonial history of the settlement country, for example, immigrants from Morocco and Algeria in France and from Pakistan and India in the United Kingdom, or long-standing needs for labor from nearby countries, including immigrants from Morocco in Italy and the Netherlands; immigrants from Turkey in the Netherlands, Germany, and Switzerland; and immigrants from Mexico in the United States (Hernandez et al., 2009). Despite substantial concentrations of immigrants with specific origins in each of the settlement countries, however, all of the settlement countries studied here have significant numbers of children in immigrant families from a large number of countries spread across the globe.

The Importance of Children in Immigrant Families

The growth of these immigrant populations has important implications for Western nations, in part because these affluent countries have rapidly aging populations with rates of natural increase well below the rates of natural increase experienced by many immigrant populations. As a result, recent population projections indicate that the proportion of the total population that is non-Western will roughly double between 2000 and 2050. For example, the proportion of the total population with "non-Western" origins is projected to jump from 7% to 18% in Germany, from 9% to 17% in the

Netherlands, from 9% to 25% in England and Wales, and from 31% to 50% in the United States (Coleman, 2006; U.S. Census Bureau, 2004).

Non-Western immigrants and their children often differ in appearance, language, religion, and culture from nonimmigrants. Yet it is immigrants and their children who are driving these population projections. The well-being and development of children whose parents are immigrants will, therefore, have important consequences, because as these children become adults they will represent an increasing share of the labor force, the political community, and the next generation of parents. It is important to emphasize that these enormous increases may bring profound changes, especially in European countries that historically have had populations with a high level of homogeneity, both racially and culturally.

For most of the countries in this study, at least 10% of children live in immigrant families, often from non-Western countries. As these children enter the labor force, at least one in 10 new workers will have grown up in an immigrant family, many with origins in a low- or middle-income country. The success or failure of these children in adapting to life in the eight rich countries studied here will depend greatly on the extent to which they are welcomed and integrated into the culture, the schools, and the other institutions in the towns, cities, and countries where they live.

The Integration and Inclusion of Immigrants

The integration and inclusion of immigrants has been a long-standing issue in countries of mass immigration. At the beginning of the 20th century in the United States, for example, perceived differences between immigrants (often from Southern and Eastern Europe) and the native born were viewed as enormous, and the scientific community, policy makers, and the public shared the view that the new immigrants were likely to dilute the racial and cultural purity of native-born Americans (Hernandez & Darke, 1999; U.S. Immigration Commission, 1911). Similarly, in Australia, the white Australia immigration policy, with roots in the middle of the 19th century, was formalized in the Immigration Restriction Act of 1901 and warmly applauded at the time by most sections of society (Department of Immigration and Citizenship, 2007).

In response to increased immigration in the United States around the beginning of the 21st century, when immigrant eligibility for public benefits was restricted by the federal government, new studies were initiated to assess the circumstances and policies with respect to the inclusion and integration of immigrants and their children (e.g., Fix, Papademetriou, & Cooper, 2005; Hernandez, 1999; Hernandez & Charney, 1998). In view of rising immigration across Europe, the European Union recently has begun to vigorously pursue issues of immigrant integration.

In 2003, the Council of the European Union argued that it is "necessary to elaborate a comprehensive, and multidimensional policy, on integration of legally residing third country nationals who ... should be granted rights and obligations comparable to those of EU citizens" (Presidency Conclusions, 2003). One year later, the council urged that "[S]tability and cohesion within our societies benefit from the successful integration of legally resident third-country nationals and their descendants," that is, their children. The council went on to say that "To achieve this objective, it is essential to develop effective policies, and to prevent the isolation of particular groups." Furthermore, "a comprehensive approach involving stakeholders at the local, regional, national, and European levels is therefore essential" (Presidency Conclusions, 2004).

In expanding on this position, in 2004 the European Union established a set of "Common Basic Principles for Immigrant Integration Policy in the European Union." The European Union also proposed in 2005 the creation of an integration fund, with an allocation of 1.8 billion euros for the period 2007–2013. In addition, the European Union has developed a *Handbook of Integration for Policy Makers and Practitioners* as a practical guide to fostering immigrant integration policies and programs in European Union member states (European Commission, 2007).

The common basic principles for immigrant inclusion and integration policy established by the Council of the European Union and the representatives of the governments of the member states include the following (emphasis added):

Employment is a key part of the integration process and is central to the participation of immigrants, to the contributions immigrants make to the host society, and to making such contributions visible.

Basic knowledge of the host society's *language*, history, and institutions is indispensable to integration; enabling immigrants to acquire this basic knowledge is essential to successful integration.

Efforts in *education* are critical to preparing immigrants, and particularly their descendants, to be more successful and more active participants in society.

Access for immigrants to institutions, as well as to *public and private goods and services*, on a basis equal to national citizens and in a non-discriminatory way is a critical foundation for better integration....

The *practice of diverse cultures and religions* is guaranteed under the Charter of Fundamental Rights and must be safeguarded, unless practices conflict with other inviolable European rights or with national law.

The *participation of immigrants in the democratic process* and in the formulation of integration policies and measures, especially at the local level, supports their integration.

Going further, the "Second Annual Report on Migration and Integration" of the European Commission urged that:

In order to successfully integrate and participate in all aspects of life, migrants must be provided with basic rights in terms of *access to education, housing, health-care, and social services.* (emphasis added)

It also noted that "as part of the action programme to combat social exclusion, the Commission has commissioned a study on access to decent housing for migrants and ethnic minorities" (European Commission, 2006).

Returning to this issue in 2007, "the Council [of the European Union] and the Representatives of the Governments of the Member States emphasize the need to continue to strengthen the integration policies of Member States with a view to managing diverse societies, counteracting all forms of discrimination and intolerance, maintaining social cohesion and ensuring that immigrants are able to reach their full potential and are able to participate to the fullest extent possible in the social, economic, cultural and civic life of the relevant Member State" (Council of the European Union, 2007).

These ideas clearly connect with issues of social inclusion and social exclusion. As defined in the Charter of the Fundamental Rights of the European Union, "Social inclusion is a process which ensures that those at risk of poverty and social exclusion gain the opportunities and resources necessary to participate fully in economic, social and cultural life and to enjoy a standard of living and well-being that is considered normal in the society in which they live. It ensures that they have greater participation in decision making which affects their lives and access to their fundamental rights" (Council of the European Union, 2004b).

These efforts provide a broad and comprehensive framework for discussing results in this chapter pertaining to the demographic circumstances of children in immigrant families and to various aspects of their integration, including language, civic participation, education, employment, and housing. While data presented here do not directly measure integration and inclusion, they do portray the lives of children in immigrant families compared with the lives of children in native-born families along social, economic, and civic dimensions relevant to the assessment of integration and inclusion, shedding light on the extent to which children in immigrant families in the eight settlement countries covered in this study have access to the resources necessary to participate fully in the societies of their adopted homelands.

Two-Parent Families

Before turning to statistical indicators reflecting immigrant integration, the extent to which children in immigrant families live with two parents merits attention, because parents living with children have the most immediate responsibility for providing the nurturing and other resources children need to survive and thrive. Research in the United Kingdom and in the United States indicates that children living with two parents tend, on average, to be somewhat advantaged in their educational success compared to children in one-parent families (Cherlin, 1999; Hernandez, Denton, & Macartney, 2008; McLanahan & Sandefur, 1994).

Overall, children in immigrant families with origins in low- and middle-income countries are about as likely or are more likely than children in native-born families to live with two parents in seven of the eight study countries, excluding only the Netherlands. The differences are in the range of 0%–10%. Perhaps surprising, results regarding the proportion of children in immigrant families with origins in high-income countries are similar to results for the low- and middle-income group, with differences of no more than 5% separating the two immigrant groups. In each of these seven countries at least 83% of children in immigrant families with low- and middle-income origins live with two parents.

Only in the Netherlands does the proportion living with two parents among children in native-born families (89%) exceed the level for children in immigrant families with origins in low- and middle-income countries (75%), although in the Netherlands the proportion also is comparatively low for children with origins in high-income countries (74%). Among the low- and middle-income group in the Netherlands, the difference compared to children in native-born families is accounted for mainly by children with origins in the Dominican Republic, Suriname, the Congo, Ethiopia, Ghana, Somalia, Angola, and Netherlands Antilles. Most of these countries are either Caribbean nations with long traditions of one-parent families or they are African countries where single parents, often the mothers, are fleeing with their children as refugees to escape severe economic disturbances or civil wars.

Overall, then, children in immigrant families in these eight affluent countries are generally more likely than children in native-born families to live in two-parent families, and the exceptions tend to prove the rule, because they often involve single mothers who have with enormous difficulty and in the face of great hardships left their country of birth to escape to the Netherlands.

Language

The language or languages spoken by children and their families are especially relevant to two of the European Union principles of immigrant integration (Council of the European Union, 2004a) (emphasis added). One principle is that "The *practice of diverse cultures and religions* is guaranteed under the Charter of Fundamental Rights (of the European Union) and must be safeguarded, unless practices conflict with other inviolable European rights or with national law." A second principle is that "Basic knowledge of the host society's *language* ... is indispensable to integration."

The capacity to speak the parents' language of origin can be critical to maintaining elements of origin culture and religion, because important aspects of origin culture are embedded in the heritage language (Alba & Nee, 2003). Although there is considerable diversity, among three of the eight affluent countries for which results are available, a majority of children in immigrant families speak the parents' heritage language at home: 56% in Australia, 73% in France, and 77% in the United States. Given the value of this aspect of immigrant culture, it is important that public policies support the use of the heritage language among children and parents.

At the same time, most children in immigrant families learn the language of the settlement country as they make friends, attend school, and pursue other activities. Research shows that in the United States, for example, most children prefer to speak the settlement country language rather than their parents' heritage language (Filhon, 2009; Portes & Rumbaut, 2001; Rumbaut, 1999; Simon, 1992). In addition, research indicates that in France 80% of immigrant parents speak at least some French with their children, and in the United States, 94% of children in immigrant families live with parents who speak at least some English at home.

Nonetheless, if – as is often the case – children learn the settlement society language more quickly than their parents, the children may be called upon to serve as linguistic intermediaries between parents and various institutions, such as schools, medical care providers, social service agencies, and the police and courts. This role may be essential in helping immigrant families negotiate and integrate into the unfamiliar terrain of the settlement society, but it can also lead to conflicts by undermining traditional parent–child roles and parental authority (Park, 2001, 2002; Portes & Rumbaut, 2001; Sung, 1987; Valenzuela, 1999; Zhou and Bankston, 1998). At the same time, children in immigrant families with dual language skills can become well-positioned as an important human resource for the economies of settlement societies by serving as linguistic bridges between settlement societies and the countries and cultures from which their parents immigrated.

These benefits can be fostered and the difficulties minimized through policies and programs that foster bilingual fluency and literacy among children, beginning at the earliest ages, as well as training for parents in the language of the settlement society. Dual language programs in schools and two-generation literacy programs provide two possible approaches to achieving these goals. At the same time, before and as immigrants begin to become fluent in the settlement society language, it is critical that education, health, and other organizations reach out and provide interpretive services in the heritage languages of children and their parents. Without these efforts, these organizations may be cutting themselves off from the rapidly growing client population of immigrant children and families (Hernandez et al., 2008).

As children and parents learn the language of their adopted homeland, they are making substantial investments and important tangible commitments to the settlement society. Results presented here suggest that most children in immigrant families, and their parents, are becoming linguistically integrated and are making a powerful commitment to the settlement society. Policies and programs tailored to the needs of these children and families could further benefit not only the immigrant groups but also the social integration and the economic vigor of the settlement societies.

Civic Participation

Turning to civic participation, the basic principles of immigrant integration established by the European Union (Council of the European Union, 2004a, emphasis added) note that "the *participation of immigrants in the democratic process* supports their integration." The European Union also has emphasized the importance of member states "ensuring that immigrants are … able to participate to the fullest extent possible in the … *civic life* of the relevant member state" (Council of the European Union, 2007, emphasis added). Three indicators relevant to civic participation pertain to the citizenship of parents and to the country of birth and citizenship of children.

Table 1.1. Parental Citizenship and Country of Birth among Children with Low- and Middle-Income Origins

Family Origin	Australia (%)	France (%)	Germany (%)	Italy (%)	Netherlands (%)	Switzerland (%)	United Kingdom (%)	USA (%)
Parent who is citizen of settlement country	13.6	–	–	18.0	26.4	54.9	–	28.7
Child was born in settlement country	21.7	87.4	1.0	63.1	86.7	66.7	83.0	76.7

Source: Prepared by Donald J. Hernandez from UNICEF-IRC project on children and immigrant families (Hernandez, Macartney, & Blanchard, 2009).

Parents who are citizens of the settlement country are full members of the political community. They have the legal right to participate in all aspects of civil life, including voting in elections. Among the five settlement countries with available data, often at least one in four children in immigrant families from low- and middle-income countries have at least one citizen parent with associated civic and political rights (Table 1.1). However, the proportions vary by country of origin. Without presenting specific estimates, we note that the proportions often are lower for children with origins in selected countries in the Middle East and North Africa, in sub-Saharan Africa, and in Eastern Europe (Hernandez et al., 2009). Thus children with these origins are sometimes less likely to have parents who have been fully incorporated into civic life through political citizenship in the settlement country.

Children in immigrant families who were born in the settlement country may be especially likely to participate in the civic life of that society because most of these children are likely to be lifelong residents of the settlement country. Only in Australia is the proportion as low as 22%. More than six in 10 children in immigrant families with origins in low- and middle-income countries living in the other seven study countries were born in the settlement country (Table 1.1). These second-generation children are likely to have a strong commitment to the country where their parents have settled, not only because they were born in the settlement country, but also because they are likely to be lifelong residents in the country, attending the schools and learning the language and customs as they grow older. In fact, most of these children may have little or no personal experience with their parents' country of birth.

Not only were many children in immigrant families born in the settlement country, but many are citizens of the settlement country, especially in countries that provide for birthright citizenship. In the four countries with available data, the proportion is one-third in Switzerland (32%), about one-half in Italy (49%), and more than four out of five in Australia (85%) and the United States (82%). These children clearly will play an important role in the long-term future of the countries where their parents have chosen to settle.

Parental Education

The principles of immigrant integration established by the European Union include the following. "Efforts in *education* are critical in preparing immigrants, and particularly their descendants, to be more successful and more active participants in society" (Council of the European Union, 2004a, emphasis added).

Any effort to foster increased educational attainments among immigrants must begin with an assessment of their current educational accomplishments. As a starting point, it is important to note that research in the United States has long shown that children whose parents have completed fewer years of school tend, on average, to complete fewer years of school themselves and to obtain lower paying jobs when they reach adulthood (Blau & Duncan, 1967; Featherman & Hauser, 1978; Sewell, Hauser, & Wolf, 1980).

Immigrant parents often have high educational aspirations for their children (Hernandez & Charney, 1998; Kao, 1999; Rumbaut, 1999), but they may know little about the educational system of their adopted homeland, particularly if they have completed comparatively few years of school. Parents with little schooling may, as a consequence, be less comfortable with the education system, less able to help their children with schoolwork, and less able to negotiate effectively with teachers and school administrators. Thus measuring the education attainments of children's parents is essential to assessing the educational needs of parents and children.

Results are presented here for fathers' education, but the patterns of results for mothers are generally similar to the patterns for fathers. Focusing first on higher educational attainments, the proportion of children in immigrant families with origins in low- and middle-income countries whose fathers have completed the first stage of tertiary education or higher ranges from about one in 10 in France and Italy to about two in 10 in Switzerland and the United States and to about three in 10 in Australia (Table 1.2).

Table 1.2. Father's Educational Attainment among Children in Immigrant Families by Income of Origin Country and in Native-Born Families

Family Origin	Australia	France	Germany	Italy	Netherlands	Switzerland	United Kingdom	USA
Percent of children with father's education								
First stage tertiary or higher								
Low-middle income origins	31.2	11.6	16.2	11.8	16.6	22.4	39.7	19.6
High-income origins	19.4	10.1	20.3	10.5	43.6	35.4	45.1	39.5
Native-born families	15.9	22.6	36.7	9.7	36.0	37.4	28.7	28.2
Percent of children with father's education								
Upper secondary								
Low-middle income origins	49.1	28.1	40.0	33.8	34.0	33.7	29.3	35.4
High-income origins	59.8	41.5	44.3	33.2	36.4	35.1	38.8	48.4
Native-born families	58.5	50.8	56.4	32.7	42.7	54.3	52.2	59.9
Percent of children with father's education								
less than upper secondary								
Low-middle income origins	19.6	60.3	43.9	54.4	27.6	43.9	31.0	45.1
High-income origins	20.8	48.4	35.9	56.3	20.0	29.6	16.1	12.1
Native-born families	25.6	26.6	7.4	57.6	21.3	8.3	19.2	11.9

Source: Prepared by Donald J. Hernandez from UNICEF-IRC project on children and immigrant families (Hernandez, Macartney, & Blanchard, 2009).

Compared to children in native-born families, children with origins in low- and middle-income countries are more likely by 8%–15% to have highly educated fathers in Australia and the United Kingdom (Table 1.2). There is little difference in Italy, but differences in the opposite direction range from 8%–15% in France, the Netherlands, the United States, and Switzerland to a 21% difference in Germany.

At the opposite end of the educational spectrum, children with origins in low- and middle-income countries are slightly less likely (4%–5%) than those in native-born families to have fathers who completed less than upper secondary school in Australia and Italy while differences in the opposite direction in the Netherlands and the United Kingdom are small compared to the corresponding disadvantage in fathers' education for the immigrant group of 33%–37% in France, Germany, Switzerland, and the United States.

Perhaps surprising, children in immigrant families with origins in high-income countries are more similar to children with origins in low- and middle-income countries than to children in native-born families regarding the proportion with fathers who have completed less than upper secondary education in Australia, France, Germany, and Switzerland (Table 1.2). Children with origins in high-income countries are less similar to those with origins in low- and middle-income countries, and more similar to children in native-born families regarding the proportion with fathers completing less than upper secondary school in two of the settlement countries studied here, the United Kingdom and the United States.

Without presenting specific statistics here, and with some exceptions, another important result is that immigration from low- and middle-income countries by persons with limited education is more likely to occur from nearby regions. On the other hand, immigration from low- and middle-income countries by persons with the highest education levels is more likely to occur from distant regions (Hernandez et al., 2009).

In other words, immigrants from Mexico to Europe are more likely to be highly educated than immigrants from Mexico to the United States, while immigrants from Africa to the United States are more likely to be highly educated than immigrants from Africa to Europe. The implication of this is that the educational levels and needs of persons from diverse origins differ depending on the settlement country.

Overall, there is considerable consistency across study countries for children in immigrant families with origins in low- and middle-income countries in the proportion with parents who have a specific level of educational attainments. Large proportions, ranging from 28% to 60%, have parents who have completed less than an upper secondary level of schooling, with the exception of Australia at 20%. This suggests migration to these settlement countries is often by persons with limited education seeking to improve their economic opportunities through immigration to an affluent country. Insofar as the Council of the European Union and the governments of the member states have established the principle (Council of the European Union, 2004a, emphasis added) that "Efforts in *education* are critical in preparing immigrants ... to be more successful and more active participants in society," these results suggest that many children of immigrants have parents who would benefit from such efforts by affluent countries.

In addition, it seems likely that parents provided with the opportunity to complete additional years of school in their adopted homeland will be in a better position to help their children with schoolwork. This may especially be the case for children with parents from low- and middle-income countries who have limited education. It is in the interest not only of these children and families, but also of the broader populations in these affluent countries, that these children have access to the opportunities and the resources that will allow them to succeed in school and later in the labor force.

Parental Employment

The basic principles of immigrant integration of the European Union with regard to employment indicate the following. "*Employment* is a key part of the integration process and is central to the participation of immigrants, to the contributions immigrants make to the host society, and to making such contributions visible" (Council of the European Union, 2004a, emphasis added).

In each of the eight study countries, at least three in five children with origins in low- and middle-income countries have fathers who are employed, and this rises to about nine in 10 in Italy, Switzerland, and the United States (Table 1.3). Differences in fathers' work are fairly small (2%–13%) when comparing children with origins in low- and middle-income countries to children in native-born families in Australia, Italy, Switzerland, the United Kingdom, and the United States. However, larger differences in France (24%), Germany (32%), and the Netherlands (26%) suggest that fathers of children with origins in low- and middle-income countries may have fewer opportunities to integrate into the labor force than is the case for the other countries in this study.

Table 1.3. Father's and Mother's Employment among Children in Immigrant Families by Income of Origin Country and in Native-Born Families

Family Origin	Australia	France	Germany	Italy	Netherlands	Switzerland	United Kingdom	USA
Percent of children with father employed								
Low-middle income origins	80.7	62.7	60.4	87.1	69.2	87.3	76.1	92.2
High-income origins	86.2	86.7	81.3	85.0	94.5	94.6	89.5	94.2
Native-born families	85.7	86.2	92.3	84.9	94.9	97.8	89.2	95.1
Percent of children with father employed full time								
Low-middle income origins	68.0	–	49.1	82.4	41.5	83.8	59.9	84.7
High-income origins	74.5	–	67.8	81.7	59.3	90.3	80.8	87.9
Native-born families	74.7	–	83.4	82.0	58.3	92.7	81.8	90.1
Percent of children with mother employed								
Low-middle income origins	49.3	34.8	30.6	37.8	37.9	52.1	42.3	61.0
High-income origins	57.8	70.7	46.1	41.5	63.9	63.2	60.2	59.1
Native-born families	56.2	72.1	67.7	46.9	73.1	61.4	64.8	75.8
Percent of children with mother employed full-time								
Low-middle income origins	26.4	–	9.7	25.3	5.5	25.0	18.1	44.2
High-income origins	22.1	–	12.8	28.1	8.3	20.3	21.3	42.9
Native-born families	19.3	–	18.8	33.9	4.7	11.1	19.0	49.4

Source: Prepared by Donald J. Hernandez from UNICEF-IRC project on children and immigrant families (Hernandez, Macartney, & Blanchard, 2009).

Half to a large majority of children with origins in low- and middle-income countries who have fathers in the home have fathers employed full time. Among three countries, the differences between children with origins in low- and middle-income countries and in native-born families are small, but they rise to a 9% difference in the Netherlands, a 22% difference in the United Kingdom, and a 34% difference in Germany.

Children are much less likely to have employed mothers than to have employed fathers. Still, about one-third or more children with origins in low- and middle-income countries have mothers who are employed, rising to 42% in the United Kingdom, 49% to 52% in Australia and Switzerland, and 61% in the United States. Patterns of differences between children with origins in low- and middle-income countries and in native-born families are generally similar for mothers and fathers. The gap is smallest in Australia, Italy, Switzerland, and the United States. But it is substantially larger in the United Kingdom, and especially in France, Germany, and the Netherlands.

The proportion of children with origins in low- and middle-income countries with mothers in the home who have mothers employed full time varies greatly from only one in 20 in the Netherlands to more than four in 10 in the United States. Perhaps surprising, the proportion of children from immigrant families originating in low- and middle-income countries whose mothers work full time are fairly similar to those for children in native-born families (Table 1.3).

Parental employment is important in part because it is a major source of economic resources for children. The importance of income and social transfers are reflected in this basic principle established by the European Union: "Access for immigrants to institutions, as well as to *public and private goods and services*, on an equal basis to citizens in a non-discriminatory way is a critical foundation for better integration" (Council of the European Union, 2007, emphasis added).

Access to public and private goods and services largely depends, of course, on the income available to children and their families from employment and on social transfers from national governments to families. Despite high rates of work by parents and of full-time work by fathers, some families have incomes too low to lift them out of poverty, in part because some jobs have lower hourly wages. Social transfers act to reduce poverty, but the programs in different countries vary in their effectiveness in reducing child poverty in both native-born and immigrant families.

The chapter in this volume by Smeeding et al. presents new results regarding poverty for these children. The results indicate that social transfers substantially reduce poverty among children in immigrant families in most countries included in that study, excluding in particular the United States, but that these children nevertheless experience higher poverty rates than children in native-born families.

Housing

In its second annual report on migration and integration, the European Commission asserted that "In order to successfully integrate and participate in all aspects of life, migrants must be provided with basic rights in terms of *access to ... housing*" (emphasis added). "As part of the action programme to combat social exclusion, the Commission has commissioned a study on *access to decent housing* for migrants" (European Commission, 2006, emphasis added).

One measure of access to decent housing for children is the extent to which they live in overcrowded housing, which can make it difficult for a child to find a place to do homework and which can have negative consequences for behavioral adjustment and psychological health (Evans, Saegert, & Harris, 2001; Saegert, 1982). Children are classified here as living in overcrowded housing if they live in a home with more than one person per room (U.S. Bureau of the Census, 1994).

Few children in Australia experience overcrowded housing. But overcrowding is much more common in the other four countries with available data among children with origins in low- and middle-income countries. In Australia, there is little difference between children with origins in low- and middle-income countries and children in native-born families (Table 1.4). But immigrant groups are 21% to 23% more likely than native-born groups to live in overcrowded housing in Italy and the United Kingdom, and this gap nearly doubles to 41% in France and the United States.

Homeownership does not necessarily reflect the quality of housing, but it does reflect access to housing. Homeownership also represents an investment in and commitment by the family to the neighborhood and community in which the family lives. In each of the five affluent countries reporting new results for homeownership rates, a substantial majority of children in native-born families live in homes owned by their family. Among children with origins in low- and middle-income countries, between one-half and two-thirds live in family-owned homes in Australia, the United Kingdom, and the United States, while the proportion is nearly four in 10 in Italy and one in four in France. The immigrant–native born gaps are small in Australia and the United Kingdom, but much larger at 19%–33% in France, Italy, and the United States.

Table 1.4. Overcrowding and Family Homeownership among Children in Immigrant Families by Income of Origin Country and in Native-Born Families

Family Origin	Australia	France	Germany	Italy	Netherlands	Switzerland	United Kingdom	USA
Percent of children in overcrowded housing								
Low-middle income origins	12.4	59.9	–	64.0	–	–	32.8	52.2
High-income origins	6.5	31.2	–	48.6	–	–	11.2	16.3
Native-born families	8.8	18.6	–	43.4	–	–	10.2	11.2
Percent of children in family-owned home								
Low-middle income origins	66.2	25.4	–	36.8	–	–	61.3	52.2
High-income origins	73.6	56.0	–	62.5	–	–	68.7	66.0
Native-born families	69.0	57.8	–	66.7	–	–	67.8	70.6

Source: Prepared by Donald J. Hernandez from UNICEF-IRC project on children and immigrant families (Hernandez, Macartney, & Blanchard, 2009).

These results regarding overcrowded housing suggest that many children in immigrant families from low- and middle-income countries who live in three of the four settlement societies with available data live in families who have limited access to housing units with the space needed for comfortable living. Still, many of these children live in families showing a strong commitment through the purchase of a home to their local neighborhoods, towns, cities, and adopted homeland.

School Enrollment among Adolescents

As noted earlier in this chapter, the European Commission has urged that "In order to successfully integrate and participate in all aspects of life, migrants must be provided with basic rights in terms of *access to education*" (emphasis added). Similarly, the Council of the European Union and representatives of the governments of the member states have established the principle that: "Efforts in *education* are critical to preparing immigrants, and particularly their descendants, to be more successful and more active participants in society" (European Commission, 2006, emphasis added).

This section focuses specifically on school enrollment of adolescents aged 15–17, distinguishing two groups (representing a shift in groups from previously described analyses): immigrant adolescents, including only the foreign-born, and native-born adolescents, including both the second-generation born in the settlement society (to one or two parents not born in the country) and the third or later generations (adolescents and their parents were born in the settlement country).

Immigrant adolescents with origins in low- and middle-income countries are more likely to be enrolled in school than are native-born adolescents in two settlement countries, Australia (95% vs. 85%) and the United Kingdom (92% vs. 85%). These also are the two countries where children in immigrant families from low- and middle-income countries are substantially more likely than those in native-born families to live with a father who has completed the first stage of tertiary education or higher.

Among the three other settlement countries with available results, the proportion enrolled in school also exceeds 90% only for the United States (93%) among immigrant adolescents with origins in low- and middle-income countries. This is, however, 4% less than the proportion of native-born adolescents in the United States (97%) enrolled in school. Immigrant adolescents are much less likely than native-born adolescents to be enrolled in school in Switzerland (80% vs. 91%) and Italy (71% vs. 86%). In these three countries, then, immigrant adolescents are substantially less likely than the native born to be enrolled in school. These countries might especially benefit from additional efforts to make educational opportunities available to immigrant adolescents.

Conclusions

This chapter presents results from the first study to develop internationally comparable estimates regarding the number of children living in immigrant families and their circumstances related to language, civic participation, education, employment, and housing. The focus is on eight affluent countries in the European Union and around the world coping with a global demographic transformation, and seeking, often for the first time, to integrate culturally and ethnically diverse immigrants and their children into civic, educational, and economic institutions while safeguarding the cultural heritage and religious freedom of immigrants. Results presented here identify important resources for children in immigrant families and major challenges confronting these children and families.

Still, results were not reported for each of the eight countries for all of the important topics presented here, because the necessary data were not collected in the census, registration system, or major surveys in some countries. We could not, for example, calculate results for language use at home in five countries, for child's citizenship in four countries, for parental citizenship in three countries, or for overcrowding and homeownership in three countries. A complete understanding of the situation of children in immigrant families will require, therefore, additional data collection in many of these countries.

In addition, it was not possible to include in this early study results for many of the other affluent countries also experiencing rapid immigration. In order to gain a more complete understanding of the lives of children in immigrant families, their potential contributions, and their needs as they seek to integrate into the countries where their parents have settled, the analyses of census, registration, and survey data presented here should be extended to encompass as many nations as possible. These analyses could be undertaken by the countries themselves or though an expanded collaborative effort similar to the UNICEF project that provided the foundation for the results in this chapter (Hernandez et al., 2009).

In the countries included in the present study, children of immigrants often live in two-parent families. They bring important bilingual skills to settlement countries for the global marketplace, they and their parents often are citizens of the settlement country, and they usually work to support themselves and are putting down deep roots by investing in homeowner-ship in their local neighborhoods and communities. At the same time, these children often live with parents who have limited educational attainments, which combined with low wages and substantial part-time work leads to high poverty and overcrowded housing conditions.

Children in immigrant families in these eight countries, and in many other countries, will during the coming decades become an important force in the economies and the political systems of these countries, and they will contribute substantially to the support of the rapidly aging nonimmigrant populations of these countries. These nations will be well-served by develop-ing policies that assure the integration and inclusion of the rapidly growing populations of children in immigrant families. They also will be well-served by expanded data collection and repeated studies of the kind presented here to assess changes in the lives of children in immigrant families. The need for repeated studies to regularly monitor the changing situation is reflected in the fact that the results presented here are mainly from around the year 2000 and do not, therefore, reflect the global financial crisis beginning in 2007. Without expanded and repeated studies, affluent nations with large immigrant populations will not have basic, up-to-date information neces-sary to develop effective policies to promote the integration and well-being of these children and ensure that they are in a position to effectively con-tribute to the society and broader economy of the countries where their parents have settled.

REFERENCES

Alba, R., & Nee, V. (2003). *Remaking the American mainstream: Assimilation and contemporary immigration.* Cambridge: Harvard University Press.
Blau, P. M., & Duncan, O. D. (1967). *The American occupational structure.* New York: Wiley.
Cherlin, A. J. (1999). Going to extremes: Family structure, children's well-being, and social sciences. *Demography, 36*(4), 421–8.
Coleman, D. (2006). Immigration and ethnic change in low-fertility countries: A third demographic transition. *Population and Development Review, 32*(3), 401–46.
Council of the European Union. (2004a). "Immigrant Integration Policy in the European Union – *Council conclusions*." Press Release, 2618th Council Meeting, Justice and Home Affairs, Brussels, 19 November 2004. Retrieved 5 July 2008 from http://ue.eu.int/ueDocs/cms_Data/docs/pressData/en/jha/82745.pdf.
    (2004b). Joint report by the Commission and the Council on social inclusion. 7101/04. Brussels, 5 March 2004. Council of the European Union. Retrieved 5 July 2008 from http://ec.europa.eu/employment_social/soc-prot/soc-incl/final_joint_inclusion_report_2003_en.pdf.

(2007). Press Release. 2807th Council meeting. Justice and Home Affairs. Luxembourg, 12–13 June 2007. Brussels, Council of the European Union. Retrieved 5 July 2008 from http://www.statewatch.org/news/2007/jun/jha-12-13-june-07-concl-day-one.pdf.

Department of Immigration and Citizenship. (2007). Fact Sheet 8 – Abolition of the 'White Australia' Policy. Canberra: Commonwealth of Australia. Retrieved 9 July 2008 from http://www.immi.gov.au/media/fact-sheets/08abolition.htm.

European Commission. (2006). Second Annual Report on Migration and Integration. Commission document SEC (2006) 892. 11526/06 Limite Migr 107. Soc 355. Brussels, 11 July 2006. The Council of the European Union.

(2007). *Handbook on integration for policy-makers and practitioners.* Second edition, May 2007. Written by Jan Niessen and Yongmi Schibel on behalf of the European Commission Directorate General for Justice, Freedom and Security. Retrieved 6 July 2008 from http://ec.europa.eu/justice_home/doc_centre/immigration/integration/doc/2007/handbook_2007_en.pdf.

Evans, W. G., Saegert, S., & Harris, R. (2001). Residential density and psychological health among children in low-income families. *Environment and Behavior, 33*(2), 165–80.

Featherman, D. L., & Hauser, R. M. (1978). *Opportunity and change.* New York: Academic Press.

Filhon, A. (2009). Transmettre l'arabe et le berbère en France, Les cahiers de l'Ined, n°163.

Fix, M., Papademetriou, D. G., & Cooper, B. (2005). Leaving too much to chance: A roundtable on immigrant integration policy. Washington, DC: Migration Policy Institute. Retrieved 9 July 2008 from http://www.migrationpolicy.org/pubs/LeavingTooMuch_Report.pdf.

Hernandez, D. J. (Ed.). (1999). *Children of immigrants: Health, adjustment, and public assistance.* Washington, DC: National Academy Press.

Hernandez, D. J., & Charney, E. (1998). *From generation to generation: The health and well-being of children in immigrant families.* Washington, DC: National Academy Press.

Hernandez, D. J., & Darke, K. (1999). Socioeconomic and demographic risk factors and resources among children in immigrant and native-born families: 1910, 1960, and 1990. In Donald J. Hernandez (Ed.), *Children of immigrants: Health, adjustment, and public assistance* (pp. 19–125). Washington, DC: National Academy Press.

Hernandez, D. J., Denton, N. A., & Macartney, S. E. (2008). Children in Immigrant Families: Looking to America's Future. *Social Policy Report,* Volume 22, Number 3, Ann Arbor, MI: Society for Research in Child Development. Retrieved 10 July 2008 from http://www.srcd.org/index.php?option=com_content&task=view&id=232&Itemid=1.

Hernandez, D. J., Macartney, S., & Blanchard, V. L. (2009). *Children in immigrant families in eight affluent countries: Their family, national, and international context.* Florence, Italy: UNICEF Innocenti Research Centre.

Kao, G. (1999). Psychological well-being and educational achievement among immigrant youth. In Donald J. Hernandez (Ed.), *Children of immigrants: Health, adjustment, and public assistance* (pp. 410–77). Washington, DC: National Academy Press.

McLanahan, S., & Sandefur, G. (1994). *Growing up with a single parent: What hurts, what helps.* Cambridge, MA: Harvard University Press.

Park, L. (2001). Between adulthood and childhood: The boundary work of immigrant entrepreneurial children. *Berkeley Journal of Sociology, 45,* 114–35.

(2002). Asian immigrant entrepreneurial children. In L. T. Vo & R. Bonus (Eds.), *Contemporary Asian American communities* (pp. 161–74). Philadelphia, NJ: Temple University Press.

Portes, A., & Rumbaut, R. G. (2001). *Legacies: The story of the immigrant second generation.* Berkeley and New York: University of California Press & Russell Sage Foundation.

Presidency Conclusions. (2003). Thessaloniki European Council 19 and 20 June 2003. Brussels, 1 October 2003: The Council of the European Union. 11638/03. Polgen 55. Retrieved 9 July 2008 from http://ue.eu.int/ueDocs/cms_Data/docs/pressdata/en/ec/76279.pdf.

(2004). Conclusions de la Presidence. Texte en, Conseil Europeen – Bruxelles. 04 & 0r Novembre 2004. Burxelles, le 05 Novembre 2004. D/04/5. Retrieved 9 July 2008 from   http://ec.europa.eu/justice_home/news/information_dossiers/2005-2009/docs/presidency_conclusions_en.pdf.

Rumbaut, R. G. (1999). Passages to adulthood: The adaptation of children of immigrants in Southern California. In D. J. Hernandez (Ed.), *Children of immigrants: Health, adjustment, and public assistance* (pp. 478–545). Washington, DC: National Academy Press.

Saegert, S. (1982). Environment and children's mental health: Residential density and low income children. In A. Baum & J. E. Singer (Eds.), *Handbook of psychology and health. Vol. II, Issues in child health and adolescent health* (pp. 247–71). Hillsdale, NJ: Lawrence Erlbaum Associates.

Sewell, W. H., Hauser, R. M, & Wolf, W. C. (1980). Sex, schooling, and occupational status. *American Journal of Sociology, 83*(3), 551–83.

Simon, P. (1992). Pratiques linguistiques et consommation médiatique. In M.Tribalat (coll. B. Riandey), De l'immigration à l'assimilation. Enquête sur les populations étrangères en France Paris, INED/La Découverte, 1996, 188–213.

Sung, B. L. (1987). *The adjustment experience of Chinese immigrant children in New York City.* New York: Center for Migration Studies.

Valenzuela, A. Jr. (1999). Gender role and settlement activities among children and their immigrant families. *American Behavioral Scientists, 42,* 720–42.

U.S. Bureau of the Census. (1994). *Housing of lower-income households* (Statistical Brief, SB/94/18). Retrieved 9 January 2006 from http://www.census.gov/aspd/www/statbrief/sb94_18.pdf.

U.S. Census Bureau. (2004). U.S. Interim Projections by Age, Sex, Race, and Hispanic Origin, <http://www.census.gov/ipc/www/usinterimproj/> Internet Release Date: March 18, 2004.

U.S. Immigration Commission. (1911). *Report of the immigration commission, Volume 4. Emigration conditions in Europe.* Washington, DC: U.S. Government Printing Office.

World Bank. (2007). *Atlas of global development: A visual guide to the world's greatest challenges.* Washington, DC: World Bank: New York: HarperCollins Publishers.

Zhou, M., & Bankston, C. L. (1998). *Growing up American: How Vietnamese children adapt to life in the United States.* New York, NY: Sage.

2 Better Fortunes?

Living Arrangements and School Enrollment
of Migrant Youth in Six Western Countries

Audrey N. Beck and Marta Tienda

Introduction

Between 1970 and 2005, the number of international migrants more than
doubled, rising from 82 million to 191 million (Freeman, 2006). Migrants
disproportionately hail from less developed nations and the vast majority of them are destined for developed countries. Recent UN data indicate
that nearly 10% of the population living in developed regions is foreign-
born, compared to less than 1.3% in developing regions (Zlotnik, 2006).
International migration flows also have involved growing numbers of
women and children. Despite growing research and policy interest in
population movements (GCIM, 2005; UN, 2006) and recognition of the
feminization of migration (Morokvasic, 1984; Sassen-Koob, 1984; Tienda
& Booth, 1991), the rising prevalence of children and youth in migrant
streams has received little systematic scrutiny (see Harttgen & Klasen,
2008; Rossi, 2008). Consequently, whether and how migration improves or
diminishes the well-being of youth with migration backgrounds remains
poorly understood.

One reason for the limited research about migration and child well-being
is that these lines of inquiry largely operate in non-overlapping spheres, but
paucity of data, particularly that suitable for cross-national comparisons, is
another reason. Release of standardized international public use microdata
census samples (Integrated Public Use Microdata Series; IPUMS) for several immigrant receiving nations offers a propitious opportunity to begin
filling this large research gap by characterizing the demographic scope of
youth migration and the proximate environments that shape their integration prospects.

Given the heightened risks that come with adjusting to new cultural and linguistic contexts, we focus on living arrangements that may amplify or ameliorate the challenges of integration prospects as reflected in their school enrollment patterns. Families not only represent the proximate contexts that shape integration prospects for young people, but the unit also experiences changes in membership through migration (Rossi, 2008). Educational attainment is a key indicator of assimilation that determines the likelihood of successful economic and social integration in adulthood (Portes & Rumbaut, 2006). Our substantive goal is to describe the living arrangements of migrant youth and to identify which arrangements and contexts of reception are most conducive to child well-being as measured by school enrollment. Specifically, we document cross-national variation in the living arrangements of youth with migration backgrounds in six Western countries – France, Greece, Portugal, Spain, Israel, and the United States. By examining variation in the prevalence of parent absence and extended living arrangements as well as size and composition of households, we identify countries where immigrant youth face the most optimistic integration prospects. Methodologically, we also illustrate the need for a child-centric perspective that does not assume migrant children and youth live with their parents or in family households.

The second section characterizes the six Western countries as contexts of reception based on social policies conducive to successful integration and productive youth development. In the third section, we first develop theoretical links between migrant status, living arrangements, and youth well-being and illustrate how particularly vulnerable youth, namely those who live without their parents, are excluded from conventional operational definitions of migrant youth. Subsequently we compare the living arrangements of children and youth according to migration status to consider whether and in what ways living arrangements are related to school enrollment. The final section summarizes key findings and identifies the social policy arrangements most conducive to successful developmental outcomes of youth with migration backgrounds.

Host Societies as Contexts of Reception

Policies of receiving governments, labor markets, and local community attributes define what Portes and Rumbaut (2001) dubbed "contexts of reception," namely the social climate and disposition of host nations to integrate newcomers. They distinguish between passive acceptance, in which reception is little more than benign neglect, and active encouragement, usually associated with extensive resettlement assistance and easy pathways to citizenship. As the proximal contexts of early socialization, families are often more important than these distal factors in shaping immigrant integration. Young people derive their economic sustenance and emotional support from families – including extended and nonresidential arrangements; however, the links between family structure and child well-being are seldom considered by migration researchers. This is surprising because migration often disrupts nuclear units, separating youth from one or more of their parents during critical developmental periods (Rossi, 2008).

Although migration has been increasing throughout Europe since the creation of the European Union, there is considerable cross-national variation in the timing, composition, and volume of flows. Our selection of countries was guided by both practical and theoretical considerations. Practically, we restricted our focus to nations that met our selection criteria and also participated in the international public use microdata samples (IPUMS) project (Minnesota Population Center, 2009). Theoretically, we sought to represent variation in contexts of reception among nations that qualify as immigrant receiving. Around the year 2000, the foreign-born population for the six nations ranged from 32% for Israel to roughly 5% for Portugal and Spain (see Table 2.1). These nations represent long-standing host countries, such as the United States and Israel, and formerly labor sending nations that reversed their status to immigrant receiving, such as Spain and Portugal. All four European nations have aging populations, with about 16% of their residents aged 65 and over.

The six nations differ in other ways likely related to the well-being of migrant children and youth, such as levels of income inequality (lowest for France and highest for Portugal); child poverty rates (also lowest for France among the countries with comparable data); and youth employment rates. Particularly striking are the levels of "idleness" during late adolescence, which approach one in four youth aged 15 to 19 in Israel. *Idleness* refers to youth who are neither employed nor enrolled in school, which signals a problematic transition to adulthood. Educational outcomes also vary considerably, as indicated by the uneven college graduation rates. In the United States and Israel approximately one in three persons at "typical graduation age" complete postsecondary education compared with less than 20% in Greece. Performance on the PISA science exam at age 15 likely reflects a confluence of factors including the structure of the school system, the effort made by the state to equalize educational outcomes across migration status, as well as the selectivity of the migrant groups. With this ambiguity in mind, the average scores reveal inequities between native youth and those with

Table 2.1. Contexts of Reception: Demographic, Economic, and Social Characteristics for Israel, the United States, Greece, France, Portugal, and Spain circa 2000

Country	ISR	US	GRC	FRN	POR	SPN
Demographic Context						
Total Population (in 1000s)	6084	282194	10918	59049	10226	40264
As a Percent of the Total Population						
Population 65 or Older	9.9	12.4	16.6	16.1	16.2	16.8
Foreign Born	32.3[a]	11.0	10.3[b]	7.4	5.1	4.9
Economic Context						
GDP Per Capita ($US)	23302	34574	18389	25232	17067	21295
Income Inequality: Gini Coefficient[d]	.392[e]	0.381	0.321	0.281	0.416	0.319
Child Poverty Rate (aged 0–17)	NA	20.6	13.2	7.6	16.6	17.3
Labor Force Context						
Youth Employment (aged 15–24)	28.2	59.7	26.9	23.2	42.0	36.3
Idle Males (aged 15–19)[c]	26.2	6.8	6.9	3.4	6.2	7.7
Idle Females (aged 15–19)[c]	24.9	7.3	11.2	3.2	9.2	8.2
Educational Context						
College Graduation Rates (at typical age of graduation)	32.2[c]	34.4	14.5	24.5	23.2	30.4
Performance on science scale (PISA), age 15[d]						
Foreign Born	467.7	441.7	428.2	437.7	411.6	427.9
Third + Generation	461.9	498.9	477.6	504.5	478.5	493.6
Second Generation	444.6	456.1	NA	456.3	NA	NA
Public Expenditures and Benefits						
Social as a % of GDP	11.9	14.5	19.2	27.9	19.6	20.3

Notes: Idle indicates neither employed nor in school.
Source: Unless noted, data from 2000 reports. [a]1995 Census, IPUMS-International. Authors' calculation. [b]2002 OECD. [c]2004 OECD. [d]2006 OECD. [e]2007–2008 Human Development Report.

migration backgrounds. In every nation except Israel, where the children of immigrants score higher than their host country counterparts, youth with migrant backgrounds fare worse than their host country natives. Of course, these national averages conceal considerable within-country heterogeneity that depends on the national origins and timing of arrival of the youth.

We also sought to represent variation in social benefits and policies toward immigrants, most sharply represented by citizenship laws. The last panel of Table 2.1 shows considerable variation in social expenditures as a percent of GDP, with France the most generous in providing publicly funded social benefits and Israel the least generous, with the United States not far ahead. Despite efforts by the architects of the Treaty of Lisbon to standardize immigration policy across member states, to date no comprehensive set of regulations exists with the notable exception of family reunification and admission of students and researchers (HWWI, 2009:4).[1] Cross-national differences in the terms of membership influence not only the integration prospects of young migrants, but their chances of successful family reunification.

Attempts to establish consistent integration policies also have failed, except for nonbinding consensus about the importance of language acquisition and the value of including immigrants in all social programs as a matter of principle rather than law (e.g., Council of Ministers, HWWI, 2009). The speed at which several nations, but especially Spain, transitioned from immigrant sending to host societies for migrants has left national governments ill prepared to accommodate a large influx of foreigners. This is particularly problematic for young people, who often require language transition programs and cultural adjustment.

Regulation of citizenship also differs across the six nations based on their reliance on birth or descent (or both); in the waiting times required for naturalization; and changes in requirements for citizenship (see Table 2.2). Theoretically, citizenship represents the highest stage of membership in a nation state (Tienda, 2002). According to the Citizenship Law Dataset compiled by Bertocchi and Strozzi (2008), the United States offers the most generous membership policies for second-generation youth because all persons born on U.S. soil automatically acquire citizenship, irrespective of their parents' citizenship or legal status. In 1948, Israel and Portugal also granted citizenship *jus soli* (by birthplace), but Spanish and Greek citizenship could only be acquired through descent (*jus sanguinis*). France allowed mixed pathways to citizenship then and does so currently.

Israel changed its citizenship requirements when it passed the Law of Return in 1950, which gives all persons of Jewish ancestry and their spouses the right to become citizens upon migrating and settling in the young nation. In addition, Israel allows residents to become citizens through naturalization or marriage and requires the shortest waiting time for naturalization – less than four years – of the countries compared. By 2001 Spain, Greece, and Portugal also had modified their citizenship laws, allowing mixtures of birth and ancestry to serve as avenues by which to become

---

[1] Several European nations have sought to align their family reunification principles to the European Convention on Human Rights. Principles and practices, however, do not always coincide.

Table 2.2. Regulation of Citizenship in Six Developed Nations, 1948–2001

Country	ISR	US	GRC	FRN	POR	SPN
Citizenship Laws						
1948	Jus soli	Jus soli	Jus sanguinis	mixed	Jus soli	Jus sanguinis
1975	Jus sanguinis	Jus soli	Jus sanguinis	mixed	Jus soli	Jus sanguinis
2001	Jus sanguinis	Jus soli	Jus sanguinis	mixed	mixed	mixed
Time to Naturalization (in Years)	4	3	–	3	2	2

Notes: "Jus sanguinis": countries subject to jus sanguinis (by descent) without any jus soli (by birthplace) element. "Mixed": countries that apply a mixed regime reflecting elements of both jus sanguinis and jus soli. "Jus soli": countries subject to full soli.
Source: The Citizenship Laws Dataset. Bertocchi and Strozzi, 2009.

full-fledged citizens. Waiting periods for naturalization differ appreciably, however, with Portugal, France, and Spain imposing the longest terms before immigrants can apply for citizenship. Immigrants to the United States must wait at least five years to apply for U.S. citizenship, but application rates differ appreciably by regional origin and the requirements to do so have been tightened (e.g., language and civics proficiency). Moreover, since 1996 the value of citizenship has increased in the United States because several federal laws differentiated access to social benefits for immigrants according to citizenship status (Tienda, 2002).[2]

Living Arrangements and Well-being of Migrant Youth

As the most proximate context for child development, family structure influences numerous outcomes for young people. An extensive literature shows that children and adolescents reared in single-parent households exhibit lower educational achievement than children living in two-parent households (McLanahan & Sandefur, 1994). Unstable living arrangements resulting from divorce or remarriage also are associated with poor cognitive and behavioral outcomes (Cavanagh & Huston, 2006; Cavanagh, Schiller, & Riegle-Crumb, 2006; Fomby & Cherlin, 2007; Osborne & McLanahan,

---

[2] The Personal Responsibility and Work Opportunity Reconciliation Act of 1996 and the Illegal Immigration Reform and Immigrant Responsibility Act of 1996 are the two most important, although immigration policy is included in other federal legislation, especially since 2001.

2007). Parent absence is particularly deleterious for the well-being of dependent youth because it often implies lower or unstable economic resources (Bianchi, Subaiya, & Kahn, 1997; Holden & Smock, 1991; McLanahan & Sandefur, 1994) and frequent relocation, which disrupts local friendship networks (McLanahan & Sandefur, 1994; South, Crowder, & Trent, 1998).

The resource implications of more complex arrangements, such as extended family or multiple subfamily households, for child well-being are less clear, however. On the one hand, coresidence with extended kin can supplement deficits in parental emotional support and economic resources (Cherlin & Furstenberg, 1994; Peréz, 1994; Tienda & Glass, 1985). Extended family structures may also provide in-kind resources, such as child care (Jendrek, 1993). On the other hand, extended family structures may reflect a compensatory strategy for economically precarious families afforded by "doubling up" through multifamily arrangements or the presence of extended kin or nonfamily boarders (Angel & Tienda, 1982). Likewise, depending on age and gender composition, the addition of more members to the household can intensify competition for resources. The significance of extended living arrangements for child well-being also depends on their transitory or permanent status and the family life cycle stage when doubling up occurs.

Although less research has focused on children living without any parent, research in the United States suggests that nonparental living arrangements are economically heterogeneous and often temporary (Hynes & Dunifon, 2007). In the United States these are largely fostering situations, with the majority of children living with a grandparent or aunt or uncle (Hynes & Dunifon, 2007; U.S. Census Bureau, 2004). The prevalence of parental absence and extended living arrangements provides a window into the well-being of youth with migration backgrounds in countries with distinct contexts of reception.

Children living in migrant households are more likely to have a shifting roster of residents or live in crowded households (Capps, 2001). Irrespective of the particular structure, family instability can also be detrimental to household functioning and, ultimately, child well-being. Research focusing on children living with their mothers claims that stresses associated with family change often spill over into the parent–child relationship, altering the quality, quantity, and consistency of mothers' parenting (Engfer, 1988). Family change often alters mothers' emotional resources, rendering the myriad aspects of parenting more difficult (Hetherington, 1989; Meadows, McLanahan, & Brooks-Gunn, 2008).

Migration, Family Arrangements, and Child Well-being

Because migration disrupts families and undermines social ties, part of its influence on child well-being operates via changes in living arrangements (Smith, Lalonde, & Johnson, 2004). Migration alters living arrangements when family members move separately, regardless of whether the motives are economic or the result of policy barriers that govern family reunification. Many families succeed in reconstituting themselves in their host society, but the process can span many years. As a consequence of legal barriers and sequential migration of family members, transnational families have been on the rise, with children separated from parents either because they are left behind (Rossi, 2008) or because they migrate in order to supplement family income or to study (Suárez-Orozco, Todorova, & Louie, 2002). Children who cross borders alone often find themselves in fostering arrangements, at times with relatives, but often with unrelated members of a sending country network (Mazzucato & Schans, 2008).

The disruptive effect of migration on the family is only one facet of the numerous challenges facing children and adolescents with migrant backgrounds. Many must also contend with host country language acquisition and learn to navigate new education and cultural systems as they master age-dependent developmental tasks. Children born to immigrant parents also share their parents' adjustment challenges, such as translating or explaining institutional arrangements (e.g., Fuligni, this volume). Living arrangements may amplify other challenges that migrant youth face and may account for some of the social and economic disadvantages that researchers attribute to migration status per se.

Research linking family arrangements and child well-being tends to be country-specific and largely U.S.-centric (for a recent review see Amato, 2005). Other literature that examines cross-national variation in family structure seldom focuses on child well-being. In some countries, the social safety net provides financial supports typically associated with the family, thereby ameliorating the impact of nontraditional structures (Pong et al., 2003; but see Björklund et al., 2007). With a few recent exceptions, however, research on comparative family arrangements largely ignores the significance of migration status for young people.

Studies that examine family arrangements by migration status usually focus on a single or small number of countries (e.g., Hernandez, Denton, & Macartney, 2008; Landale, Oropesa, & Bradatan, 2006; Van Hook & Glick, 2007; for an exception, see work by Hernandez and colleagues in this volume). Because of the interest in parental resources, most studies that examine the impact of family structure on migrant children and youth restrict their focus to those living with *at least one parent*. For youth with migrant backgrounds, this strategy excludes vulnerable young people and underestimates the more unstable living arrangements. The following analyses not only evaluate the significance of this exclusion restriction, but also illustrate the complexity of migrant youths' living arrangements in a cross-national perspective.

Data and Operational Definitions

The Integrated Public-Use Microdata Series-International (University of Minnesota, 2009) is a collection of census data files that has been harmonized over more than 44 countries to provide users with comparable measures. Owing to its representativeness and large sample sizes, census data is ideal both to document country-level patterns and to obtain estimates for subgroups that are too small to represent in survey data. For this study we use the samples provided to the Minnesota Population Center by Israel, France, Greece, Spain, Portugal, and the United States.[3] For each of these countries, the files contain the requisite information to link children and youth to household members.[4] To ensure the most comparable universe of youth and to isolate a consistent age span that precedes employment eligibility in these countries, we restrict our sample to persons under the age of 16.[5]

Because children are presumed to reside in family households, most analysts omit children living in nonparental units, thus defining their focus as a parent-centric rather than child-centric (for exceptions see work by Landale and colleagues, 2006). This approach to identifying migrant youth is reasonable given philosophical support for family reunification as a human rights principle (HWWI, 2009) and the tendency for children to be left behind when their parents migrate (Rossi, 2008). Practices often differ from principles, however. Because we suspect that conventional approaches exclude children with the weakest support system, rather than exclude migrant youth who do not live with a parent, we used nativity status of

---

[3] We would like to also acknowledge the Central Bureau of Statistics in Israel, the National Institute of Statistics and Economic Studies in France, the National Statistical Office in Greece, the National Institutes of Statistics in Portugal and Spain, and the Bureau of the Census in the United States. We use the following samples: Israel (1995), the United States (2000), Greece (2001), France (1999), Portugal (2001), and Spain (2001).

[4] Publically available microdata for Canada and the United Kingdom did not allow for linkages between household members and, consequently, could not be included despite their importance as prominent immigrant receiving nations.

[5] Israel census data is grouped into age ranges; to avoid including the late adolescent period, we had to restrict the tabulations to youth below the age of 15.

children to identify migrant youth and subsequently linked parent charac-teristics to youth records when available. This strategy allowed us to differ-entiate between children born to foreign versus native parents and also to approximate first and second migration generations.[6]

We use the IPUMS linkages provided by the Minnesota Population Center to determine household relationships; children are linked to par-ents in the household through a complex algorithm that utilizes pieces of information such as the link to the household head,[7] the person order of the census listing, the age, marital status, and childbearing information of the "potential parent." These links do not differentiate between biological and social parent relationships, such as stepfather or stepmother. Given the limited information available in most census data, even the best linking algorithms will incorrectly link children to adults that are not their actual parents (hence the term "potential parent"). Such misclassifications are likely more severe in more complex households, particularly those that include one or more subfamilies. We expect that this linking system may overestimate the existence of the child's parent in the home, which would render our estimates of parent-absent living arrangements conservative. Countries differ with respect to the quality of parent–child linkages; there-fore some of the differences in living arrangements of migrant youth across contexts likely reflect variation in precision of the links to parents. Given the consistency of our results across contexts, differences attributed to data limitations may be modest.

We also use census information on youths' age, gender, and year of arrival to describe the demographic profile of children living in different

---

[6] When children are not living with parents, it is not possible to differentiate between second and third generation. Thus, there is a number of second-generation youth in our category "third generation, not living with parents"; however, we see the benefits of including all youth as outweighing this measurement error.

[7] We use the MOMLOC (mother location) and POPLOC (father location) variables to link youth to parents; complete information on this issue is available through the IPUMS-I web-site. Parents that are listed adjacent to children are considered the strongest possible links. In combination with other pieces of information, potential parents are allowed to link to a child when they are 10 to 54 years older; the exact age range depends on the relationship to the household head and the type of union. France, Portugal, Spain, and the United States did not report childbearing information in the census files analyzed. Therefore in those cases this information cannot be used to improve the accuracy of the linkages. The linking algorithm in Spain utilizes additional information to link parents and children; although this information likely identifies additional nonparental arrangements that would have been otherwise misclassified, it may also be too restrictive, particularly in more complex households, and overestimate the degree to which children do not live with parents.

arrangements. Last, we use an indicator of whether the children were enrolled in school. Unfortunately, only four countries furnished school enrollment status over the age range of interest: France, Portugal, Spain, and the United States. The Israeli data also provides enrollment status, but only for persons aged 16 and older. Countries differ in the reference period for measuring enrollment status, which may impact the measured enrollment differentials. For the United States, youth had to have attended or been enrolled since February 1 of the census year, but in Portugal the school enrollment question sought to determine regular attendance at school. Both France and Spain inquired about enrollment at the time of the census enumeration. We measure enrollment for youth between ages 3 and 15 for two reasons. One is to minimize discrepancies that merely reflect differences in the age for which enrollment is ascertained. Age 3 is the youngest age at which all four countries report enrollment information. Early education, before the age of 6, may include programs such as prekindergarten; thus some portion of these enrollment tabulations may reflect opting out of optional educational training rather than nonenrollment during compulsory years (we have noted in the text the few instances where inequities differ by age/compulsory nature of enrollment). Yet these early educational experiences are associated with positive outcomes at school entry and thereafter for children, and in many countries maximizing enrollment in such programs is a goal. Although these tabulations are occasionally based on small sample sizes, early enrollment is pervasive in France and Spain (>75%), but much lower in the United States (50%–65%) and Portugal (45%–60%). Another reason we chose the age range 3–15 to analyze enrollment is to minimize differences in the structure of secondary education. Therefore, we chose 15 as an upper limit, an age in which children are of secondary school age in each country.

Living Arrangements of Migrant Youth

Table 2.3 illustrates how the criteria used to identify youth with migration backgrounds via the presence of a parent rather than from the child's perspective (regardless of parental presence), alters the population estimate. The advantage of including only children linked to parents is that it permits approximating three generational statuses for youth, namely the foreign-born, youth born to immigrant parents in the host country (second generation), and youth born in the target country to native-born parents (third and higher generation status). For youth who do not reside

Table 2.3. Percent of Youth Residing in Two-Parent Households by Migrant Generation, Ages 0–15

Country	ISR[a]	US	GRC	FRN	POR	SPN
Living in Parental Households						
Foreign Born	84.0	83.9	91.8	86.0	85.5	76.8
Second Generation[b]	94.7	86.8	95.7	89.9	92.6	86.6
Native Born to Native Parents (3 + Generation)	93.3	77.9	93.1	83.6	92.4	88.7
N	149,757	2,907,960	151,917	578,722	79,185	302,356
All Youth Foreign Born	77.1	78.1	85.1	79.1	79.4	62.6
Native Born (3 + Generation)	84.0	74.4	88.9	84.5	89.5	86.2
N	161,030	3,024,887	158,605	587,191	81,606	312,622

[a] Israel is through age 14.

[b] Second generation can only be ascertained when a parent is present; therefore, there are no differences by universe of youth.

Source: IPUMS-I, Minnesota Population Center

with at least one parent, it is only possible to distinguish between native- and foreign-born youth.[8]

A comparison of the sample sizes in the upper and lower panel reveals the consequences of using parents' presence to define the sample of children and youth with migration backgrounds. The number of migrant children and youth who do not live with at least one parent ranges from a high of 7% in Israel to less than 2% in France, with the other countries around the midpoint of these extremes (4% for the United States and Greece vs. 3% for Portugal and Spain). The estimates for Greece are conservative because the census does not identify individuals living in group quarters. In all countries, the vast majority of youth under age 16 reside with two parents, but there is noteworthy variation across countries. Among children living with parents (in the top panel), the United States and France stand out as the only countries where the share of third-generation youth living with two parents is lower than that of second- or first-generation youth. For the

---

[8] Because second-generation status can only be determined in the censuses we examine when children are living with parents, tabulations for second-generation youth do not vary when children living without parents are included in the sample. Landale and colleagues (2006), using other data, estimate that a smaller proportion of second-generation Mexican youth in the United States live in nonparental households compared to 3+ generation youth, but we are unaware of any prevalence measures for living arrangements in other countries.

United States, this largely reflects the high shares of mother-only black, Puerto Rican, and Mexican families (Landale et al., 2006).

Despite many countries' endorsements of family reunification as an important aspect of immigration policy, nontrivial shares of youth under 16 do not live with either parent, as revealed by the lower panel of Table 2.3. Identifying youth with migration backgrounds by imposing a coresidence requirement necessarily inflates the shares living with two parents, particularly those born outside of the target country. For example, in France the share of foreign-born youth who reside with two parents drops seven percentage points when migrant youth who do not reside with parents are included in the sample. As a consequence, and contrary to estimates based only on youth residing with parents, migrant youth in France are worse off relative to third-generation youth. For Spain the differentials are even more pronounced: Less than two in three foreign-born youth lived with two parents according to the most recent census, a difference of approximately 14 percentage points compared with estimates based on coresidence matched parents.[9] Even in Greece, the nation where two-parent households are most prevalent irrespective of generational status, the share of foreign-born youth who reside with two parents is seven percentage points lower when youth residing without their parents also are counted.

Table 2.4 provides further insight into the living arrangements of youth under 16 years of age by generational status and household composition. Complex living arrangements may include either one or both parents, but also other relatives, unrelated subfamilies, or nonfamily members such as boarders. Of particular interest are the shares of youth who live in complex families and those who reside with no parent. In all countries, foreign-born youth are more likely than their host country counterparts to live in complex family structures, although the levels differ appreciably, from single digits in France to between 30% and 40% in the United States and Spain, respectively. Second-generation youth living in the United States, Greece, and Spain also tend to live in doubled up households, which likely reflects the arrival of relatives from source countries or temporary housing support for host country relatives who relocate. Despite these country-specific differences, in all six countries foreign-born youth who live with parent(s) are

---

[9] Although cross-sectional data do not allow us to adjudicate between two mechanisms that undergird the number of youth residing without parents, the data are consistent with the arrival of child beachheads who are sent ahead of their parents to live with early network settlers as well as a pattern of independent youth settlement that might involve large numbers of undocumented migrant youth.

Table 2.4. Living Arrangements of Youth by Generation (%), Ages 0–15

	Israel[a]			United States			France		
	FB	2nd	3rd +	FB	2nd	3rd +	FB	2nd	3rd +
Both Parents	60.4	87.5	78.6	55.0	63.7	65.3	72.5	84.0	81.4
Single Parents	10.5	4.1	4.6	8.4	8.0	15.9	13.3	8.7	12.5
Complex Family	21.3	8.4	7.0	30.3	28.4	114.7	8.9	7.2	4.5
No Parent	7.7	–	9.8	6.4	–	4.1	5.3	–	1.7
N (in 1000s)	14.2	45.6	104.0	164.6	545.5	2,533.0	18.1	122.8	452.8
	Greece			Portugal			Spain		
	FB	2nd	3rd +	FB	2nd	3rd +	FB	2nd	3rd +
Both Parents	64.8	77.4	73.9	64.8	78.4	75.6	35.6	96.0	76.1
Single Parents	5.6	3.5	5.3	10.1	5.4	5.7	8.3	5.4	7.4
Complex Family	23.2	19.1	16.5	18.5	16.5	15.7	38.8	25.6	13.7
No Parent	6.4	–	4.3	6.6	–	2.9	17.3	–	2.8
N (in 1000s)	12.5	19.4	136.9	3.6	10.1	75.0	12.4	19.6	287.0

[a] Israel is through age 14.
[b] Second generation can only be ascertained when a parent is present.
Source: IPUMS-I, Minnesota Population Center

also more likely than their native-born counterparts in similar arrangements to experience more varied and complex living arrangements.

In general, foreign-born youth are more likely than their third-generation counterparts to reside with neither parent, which puts them at risk of poor developmental outcomes. Typically foreign-born youth are two to three percentage points more likely to live without their parents compared with youth born in the host country, with the notable exception of Spain, where over one in six foreign-born youth aged 0 to 15 do not live with either parent. Depending on the age at arrival, this arrangement places youth at high risk of poor academic and socioemotional outcomes, particularly during childhood and early adolescence (Landale et al., 2006). One possible reason that the apparently less favorable living arrangements faced by Spain's migrant youth may reflect greater measurement precision is because Spain's census has a specific pointer to biological parents. This pointer may reduce erroneous linkages to adults that are not the children's parents, particularly in more complex households. Rather than assert that migrant youth in Spain are more likely to live in nonparental households, it is conceivable that the lower prevalence of nonparental residence observed in other countries may reflect incorrect links to "probable parents."

Further analyses to discern the living arrangements of youth who do not live with parents revealed that the majority of these youth – both native- and foreign-born – reside within multigenerational or composite (a mix of family and nonfamily members) households.[10] Whether these family households include members of the youth's extended family (e.g., siblings, cousins, or "fictive" kin) surely influences the nature and quality of emotional and financial support available, but census data do not permit us to establish ties among all members. But presumably the most vulnerable youth are those living outside the structure of a family. Family structure, even if children's own parents are missing, offers routines, resources, and emotional support seldom comparably available in group quarters. Although the prevalence of nonfamily living arrangements is low, foreign-born youth are more likely than their native-born counterparts to live in these precarious arrangements. For example, in Spain, approximately 15% of foreign-born youth but only 6% of native-born youth living without parents resided in households without an identifiable family. In Israel and France, significant numbers of children reside in group quarters: These shares range from 17% to 56%, depending on generational status. In Israel, approximately 40% of foreign-born youth who do not live with parents reside in group quarters, compared to only 17% of native-born youth.

Length of Residence and School Enrollment

To consider how living arrangements are associated with migration background and youth outcomes, we examine length of residence and school enrollment status. The former indicates whether extended and nonfamily arrangements are likely to be transitory or enduring features influencing developmental trajectories of youth, and the latter is a key marker for a range of subsequent outcomes related to the transition to adulthood. Only four countries report arrival and enrollment outcomes for their foreign-born population, however.

Table 2.5 shows that in the United States and Greece, children living outside a parental household tended to be recent immigrants, which could indicate a temporary arrangement until the family was fully reconstituted. In the United States, 50% of youth under the age of 16 who did not live with either parent arrived less than two years before the census, compared to

---

[10] In Israel, 28% of foreign-born and 63% of native-born youth living without parents are living in households so complex as to be "unclassifiable"; in other countries children are rarely living in unclassifiable arrangements. Residence in group quarters is extremely rare in all countries, less than 2% of all youth below the age of 16 live in group quarters (less than 4% in Israel). Only Spain and the United States data allow for disaggregation by group quarter type and show that half of youth in group quarters are institutionalized and half in other nonspecified group quarters.

Table 2.5. Percent of Foreign-Born Youth Aged 0–15 with Specified Years Since Arrival by Living Arrangement

	Both Parents	Single Parents	Complex Family	No Parent
Israel				
<= 4 Years	43.7	48.0	46.7	42.1
5 to 6 Years	41.9	38.5	47.0	41.4
7 + Years	14.4	13.5	6.3	16.4
N	8,600	1,491	3,030	1,101
United States				
<= 2 years	30.0	23.4	37.5	49.5
3 to 5 years	27.1	25.1	25.7	21.6
6 + years	42.9	51.5	36.8	28.8
N	85,048	13,069	46,814	2,842
Greece				
<= 2 years	18.0	16.3	20.7	34.7
3 to 5 years	36.3	36.8	37.1	35.4
6 + years	45.7	46.9	42.2	30.0
N	6,022	435	2,022	557
Spain				
<= 2 years	46.3	37.5	57.1	44.6
3 to 5 years	20.7	25.9	17.7	21.0
6 + years	33.0	36.6	25.1	34.3
N	4,417	1,035	4,826	2,088

Note: Year of immigration not available in France and Portugal.
Source: IPUMS-I, Minnesota Population Center

30% of those living in two-parent nuclear families. Recently arrived youth who live with their parents also are highly likely to reside in complex household arrangements (38%) in the United States, consistent with temporary doubling up strategies as foreign-born residents become acclimated to their host society.

These findings are also in line with research (not limited to youth) by Van Hook and Glick (2007), which shows that recent U.S. immigrants are more likely to live in extended family households or non-kin households compared with earlier arrivals or native residents. Presumably earlier arrivals have had more time to reunite their families and find alternative housing. Similar patterns obtain for other countries as well. For example, in Spain, 57% of youth living in complex arrangements were recent arrivals, and in all countries compared proportionately more recently arrived youth live in complex arrangements than in two-parent nuclear families.

Age and gender distributions (not shown) revealed small differences by generation and living arrangements. For example, foreign-born youth

Table 2.6. Percent of School-Eligible Youth Enrolled in School by Living Arrangement and Generation

	Both Parents	Single Parents	Complex Family	No Parent
United States				
FB	93.6	95.4	88.8	78.3
2nd	88.6	92.0	85.0	–
3+	91.6	92.0	88.7	89.7
France				
FB	90.2	91.2	86.8	73.9
2nd	82.4	88.4	79.0	–
3+	81.1	88.0	75.9	80.1
Portugal				
FB	86.7	91.8	80.3	88.8
2nd	60.9	73.3	59.9	–
3+	71.7	81.2	66.5	81.7
Spain				
FB	94.5	95.9	94.4	91.6
2nd	96.6	95.8	94.1	–
3+	97.4	96.5	96.2	89.4

[a] Includes early education.
[b] Second generation can only be ascertained when a parent is present.
Note: School enrollment is only asked for youth aged 16 and older (Israel) and not asked in Greece.
Source: IPUMS-I, Minnesota Population Center

living without parents are slightly older than their counterparts residing in family arrangements, which is to be expected given the higher demands on parents from young children. Also, larger shares of boys reside in nonparental arrangements in France, Israel, and the United States, but only among foreign-born youth. Overall, gender differences in living arrangements are small and the age and sex distributions do not indicate systematic vulnerabilities along these lines.

Census data lack a rich set of youth outcomes to gauge well-being, but do include a key status that has lifelong consequences, namely school enrollment status. If living arrangements link migration status to child outcomes, we expect lower enrollment rates among foreign-born youth, but especially those who do not reside with parents. Table 2.6 reports school enrollment status by family arrangements, generation, and country. Children living in complex family arrangements and nonparental households fare worse with respect to school enrollment, irrespective of generational status. However, only in the United States are foreign-born children educationally disadvantaged if they do not reside with parents; about three-fourths of school-eligible youth are enrolled compared with 89% of similarly situated native-born youth. Auxiliary analyses (not shown) reveal that the U.S. foreign-born disadvantage is evident in both early educational enrollment (before the age of 6) and later enrollment (ages 13–15). In the other countries that report enrollment status, foreign-born youth are enrolled at similar or higher rates as third-generation youth.

Equally striking are the occasionally low rates of enrollment of second-generation youth; in most countries this pattern for second-generation youth is driven by lower enrollment in early education. For example, only 60% to 66% of second- and third-generation Portuguese youth living in complex families are enrolled in school, which is lower than the rates for youth living without parents. Among school-aged youth residing with two parents, Portuguese youth average the lowest enrollment rates among the countries compared. Why over one in four native-born Portuguese school-aged youth who reside with both parents are not enrolled in school warrants further disaggregation by place of residence and family economic circumstances. This level of nonenrollment surely represents formidable risks for the transition to adulthood, but appears to be more serious for the second generation, particularly those reared in complex families. Although second-generation youth residing in France and Spain do not appear to be educationally disadvantaged based on school enrollment status, the censuses available to us capture the cusp of a period of more rapid immigration, particularly for Spain. It will be of interest to determine at the next census whether enrollment disparities have increased during the last decade when many more second-generation children reached school age.

Conclusions

Migration is both a risk and an opportunity for child development. International movement represents a great opportunity for youth who can avail themselves of better education systems compared with their origin nations, but this presumes that there are no barriers to entry. Unfortunately, census data precludes comparisons with comparable nonimmigrant youth from the origin countries, which is necessary to draw causal inferences about improved or diminished educational outcomes. Source countries to the receiving nations differ appreciably, partly as a matter of history and geography, and partly due to immigration policies and reception contexts that determine eligibility for admission and access to social supports.

On the risk side of the ledger, family disruption, particularly when moves involve separation from parents at young ages, has deleterious consequences for child well-being (Amato, 2005; Rossi, 2008). Demands of cultural and structural assimilation further complicate the challenges of normative development, especially if youth must master a new language and adjust to different cultural expectations. Living arrangements function as proximate settings for socialization and integration; however, children's experiences within these households likely vary with age at migration which influences the pace and scope of adjustment and deserves further elaboration in future research. On this dimension youth with migration backgrounds differ from their native counterparts in ways that place them at greater risk of poor outcomes, but there is great variation among the countries compared.

Using coresidence as a marker of living arrangements most conducive to child well-being, youth with migration backgrounds fare best in Greece. Based on the share of migrant youth who do not live with both parents, the most precarious living arrangements occur in Spain, where over one-third of all foreign-born youth under 16 years of age do not reside with either parent. In all of the nations considered, however, anywhere from 15% (Greece) to 23% (Israel) of foreign-born youth reside with one parent or none. We argued that residence in some form of family arrangement is preferable to institutional group quarters, but differences in measurement precision across census files hampered our ability to draw firm inferences.

The unusually high share of foreign-born youth who do not live with either parent in Spain likely signals the more precise identification of actual parents compared with other nations where linking algorithms could only approximate "probable parents" based on the composition of family households, but also a degree of overestimation. Still, the pervasiveness of non-parent and sole-parent households with migrant youth does not bode well for their long-term welfare. Variation in school enrollment status by family living arrangements provides further evidence about the precarious well-being of youth with migration backgrounds, particularly in Portugal and Spain.

Despite their many strengths, census data cannot capture the degree of instability faced by children and youth. Recent research in the United States reveals that the cross-sectional "married or cohabiting parents" versus "single parent" dichotomy obscures complex variation in children's exposure to family instability that in turn influences well-being of youth (Cavanagh & Huston, 2006; Fomby & Cherlin, 2007; Osborne & McLanahan, 2007). Additionally, this underestimation may be particularly acute, and of a different nature, for migrant youth as the migration process may involve lengthy separations and a shifting roster of household members (Hatch, 2010; Van Hook & Glick, 2007). Other research suggests that cross-sectional data may also underestimate the extent to which children live in nonparental households before reaching adulthood (Hynes & Dunifon, 2007). Census data also do not allow us to determine the strength of the couple union; as research suggests a deleterious impact of parental conflict, relying only on parental presence to infer child well-being may obscure consequential distinctions between families (Fomby & Osborne, 2010).

Our key youth outcome does require further policy attention to prevent migration from generating social and economic divisions between native and foreign-born youth. Given that enrollment in primary and secondary school is not systematically associated with migration status in most contexts, it is conceivable that country-specific laws are responsible for upholding mandatory enrollment requirements. Further analyses are required to substantiate this possibility and to identify whether migration for the purpose of improving educational prospects is responsible for the higher enrollment rates among foreign-born youth in France, Portugal, and Spain. Improving educational prospects of native and foreign-born youth is both actionable and essential to promote successful transitions to adulthood and to ensure that young people acquire the necessary skills to replace the aging workers of their host countries and to contribute to economic productivity rather than become dependents of the state.

REFERENCES

Amato, P. R. (2005). The impact of family formation change on the cognitive, social and emotional well-being of the next generation. *Marriage and Child Well-being: The Future of Children, 15*, 75–96.

Angel, R., & Tienda, M. (1982). Determinants of extended household structure: Cultural pattern or economic need? *The American Journal of Sociology, 87*(6), 1360–83.

Bertocchi, G., & Strozzi, C. (2008). International migration and the role of institutions. *Public Choice, 137*, 81–102.

Bianchi, S. M., Subaiya, L., & Kahn, J. R. (1997). The gender gap in the economic well-being of nonresident fathers and custodial mothers. *Demography, 36*(2), 195–203.

Björklund, A., Ginther, D. K., & Sundström, M. (2007). Family structure and child outcomes in the USA and Sweden. *Journal of Population Economics, 20*, 183–201.

Capps, R. (2001). "Hardship among Children of Immigrants: Findings from the 1999 National Survey of America's Families" The Urban Institute, Series B, No. B-29.

Cavanagh, S. E., & Huston, A. (2006). Family instability and children's early problem behavior. *Social Forces, 85*, 551–81.

Cavanagh, S. E., Schiller, K. S., & Riegle-Crumb, C. (2006). Marital transitions, parenting, and schooling: Exploring the link between family-structure history and adolescents' academic status. *Sociology of Education, 79*(4), 329–54.

Cherlin, A. J., & Furstenberg, Jr., F. (1994). Stepfamilies in the United States: A reconsideration. *Annual Review of Sociology, 20*, 359–81.

Engfer, A. (1988). The interrelatedness of marriage and the mother-child relationship. In R. A. Hinde and J. Stevenson-Hinde (Eds.), *Relationships within families: Mutual influences* (pp. 105–18). Oxford, UK: Clarendon.

Fomby, P., & Cherlin, A. J. (2007). Family instability and child well-being. *American Sociological Review, 72*, 181–204.

Fomby, P., & Osborne, C. (2010). The influence of union instability and union quality on children's aggressive behavior. *Social Science Research, 39*(6), 912–24.

Freeman, R. B. (2006). People flows in globalization. *Journal of Economic Perspectives, 20*(2), 145–70.

Global Commission on International Migration (GCIM). (2005). *Migration in an interconnected world: New directions for action.* Report of the GCIM http://www.gcim. org/attachements/gcim-complete-report-2005.pdf.

Hamburgisches Welt Wirtschafts Institut (HWWI). (2009). Country Profile: European Union. *Migration Focus,* No. 17. Available online at (http://www.focus-migration. de/uploads/tx_wilpubdb/CP_17_EU_01.pdf).

Harttgen, K., & Klasen, S. (2008). Well-being of migrant children and migrant youth in Europe. Unpublished manuscript prepared for the Youth Migration Conference, 24–26 April, Bellagio, Italy.

Hatch, P. (2010). "U.S. Immigration Policy: Family Reunification." Washington DC: League of Women Voters. Available online at (www.lwv.org).

Hernandez, D. J., Denton, N. A., & Macartney, S. E. (2008). Children in immigrant families: Looking to America's future. *Social Policy Report, 22*(3).

Hetherington, E. M. (1989). Coping with family transitions: Winners, losers, and survivors. *Child Development, 60*, 1–14.

Holden, K. C., & Smock, P. J. (1991). The economic costs of marital dissolution: Why do women bear a disproportionate cost? *Annual Review of Sociology, 17*, 51–78.

Hynes, K., & Dunifon, R. (2007). Children in no-parent households: The continuity of arrangements and the composition of households. *Children and Youth Services Review, 29*, 912–32.

Jendrek, M. P. (1993). Grandparents who parent their grandchild: Effects on lifestyle. *Journal of Marriage and Family, 55*, 609–21.

Landale, N. S., Oropesa, R. S., & Bradatan, C. (2006). Hispanic families in the United States: Family structure and process in an era of family change. In M. Tienda and F. Mitchell (Eds.), *Hispanics and the future of America* (pp. 138–78). Washington DC: National Academies Press.

Mazzucato, V., & Schans, D. (2008). "Transnational families, children, and the migration-development nexus." Social Science Research Council Migration and Development Conference Paper No. 20.

McLanahan, S., & Sandefur, G. (1994). *Growing up with a single parent: What hurts, what helps.* Harvard University Press.

Meadows, S. O., McLanahan, S., & Brooks-Gunn, J. (2008). Family structure changes and maternal health trajectories. *American Sociological Review, 73*, 314–34.

Minnesota Population Center. *Integrated Public Use Microdata Series – International: Version 5.0.* Minneapolis: University of Minnesota, 2009.

Morokvasic, M. (1984). Birds of passage are also women.... *International Migration Review, 18*(4), 886–907.

Osborne, C., & McLanahan, S. (2007). Partnership instability and child well-being. *Journal of Marriage and Family, 69*, 1065–83.

Peréz, L. (1994). The household structure of second-generation children: An exploratory study of extended family arrangements. *International Migration Review, 28*(4), 736–47.

Pong, S., Dronkers, J., & Hampden-Thompson, G. (2003). Family policies and children's school achievement in single- versus two-parent families. *Journal of Marriage and the Family, 65*, 681–99.

Portes, A., & Rumbaut, R. G. (2001). *Legacies: The story of the immigrant second generation.* Berkeley & New York: California and Russell Sage Foundation.

(2006). *Immigrant America: A portrait.* Berkeley: University of California Press.

Rossi, A. (2008). "The impact of migration on children in developing countries." Unpublished manuscript prepared for the Migrant Youth and Children of Migrants in a Globalized World Conference, 24–26 April, Bellagio, Italy.

Sassen-Koob, S. (1984). Notes on the incorporation of third world women into wage-labor through immigration and off-shore production. *International Migration Review, 18*(4), 1144–67.

Smith, A., Lalonde, R. N., & Johnson, S. (2004). Serial migration and its implications for the parent-child relationship: A retrospective analysis of the experiences of the children of Caribbean immigrants. *Cultural Diversity & Ethnic Minority Psychology, 10*(2), 107–22.

South, S. J., Crowder, K. D., & Trent, K. (1998). Children's residential mobility and neighborhood environment following parental divorce and remarriage. *Social Forces, 77*(2), 667–93.

Suárez-Orozco, C., Todorova, I. L. G., & Louie, J. (2002). Making up for lost time: The experience of separation and reunification among immigrant families. *Family Process, 41*, 625–43.

Tienda, M. (2002). Demography and the social contract. *Demography, 39*(4), 587–616.

Tienda, M., & Booth, K. (1991). Gender, migration, and social change. *International Sociology, 6*, 51–72.

Tienda, M., & Glass, J. (1985). Household structure and labor force participation of black, Hispanic, and white mothers. *Demography, 22*(3), 381–94.

United Nations. (2006). International Migration Report 2006: A Global Assessment. Population Division: Department of Economic and Social Affairs.

U.S. Census Bureau. (2004). Children with grandparents by presence of parents, sex, race, and Hispanic origin for selected characteristics: 2004. Available at http://www.census.gov/population/socdemo/hh-fam/cps2004/tabC4-all.csv.

Van Hook, J., & Glick, J. E. (2007). Immigration and living arrangements: Moving beyond economic versus cultural needs. *Demography, 44*(2), 225–49.

Zlotnik, H. (2006). The dimensions of migration in Africa. In Tienda et al. (Eds.), *Africa on the Move: African migration and urbanisation in comparative perspective* (pp. 15–37). Johannesburg: Wits University Press.

3 Income Poverty and Income Support for Minority and Immigrant Households with Children in Rich Countries

Timothy M. Smeeding, Karen Robson, Coady Wing, and Jonathan Israel Gershuny

Introduction

The well-being of the children of immigrants (also termed *minorities* in many European nations) is a key concern in many rich countries. Much of the concern centers on how government policies alleviate poverty and inequality and provide opportunities to immigrant children. These health, education, and income support policies are at the center of debates about how to promote the integration of immigrants and their children into a host society and how the future generations in the host nation will fare. Rich nations have a large stake in the well-being of immigrants' children because these children stay in large numbers, with the potential to contribute to or to drain economic resources in the society where they grow up. Moreover, children from poor families do less well in terms of future education and income, among both immigrants and nonimmigrants. And the increasing prevalence of children of immigrant origin makes the cause for concern all the more urgent in rich nations (Huston, 1994; Huston, McLoyd, & Garcia, 2008; Lichter, 1997; Schnepf, 2007). We therefore begin with the premise that rich nations should reduce child poverty for their own sakes as well as for the sake of the children themselves. Some rich nations (e.g., the United States) do not seem concerned about the well-being of children in general, nor of poor children or immigrant children in particular (Massey, 2010; Rainwater & Smeeding, 2003).

Some analysts argue that the very availability of government redistribution discourages immigrant integration because it increases the number of low-skilled migrants entering immigrant cohorts and reduces incentives for immigrants to invest in host-country-specific human capital after they have arrived (Borjas, 2006). Some see a race to the bottom whereby countries systematically reduce benefits so as to avoid attracting hordes of immigrants who would become benefit dependent (Menz, 2006; Sapir, 2006; Sassen, 2008). A more nuanced and current view is that while immigrants are a net fiscal benefit to society, there is also evidence that in several European Union (EU) nations immigrants are more likely to consume social welfare services than nonimmigrants with similar socioeconomic characteristics. Several EU nations are considering restricting access to welfare services to reduce income transfer dependency (Boeri, 2009). Others argue that immigrants to the EU are quite unlikely to be welfare recipients (Kahanec & Zimmerman, 2008).

Still other analysts contend that immigrant poverty is itself a barrier to integration because it facilitates the exclusion of immigrants and their children from various social aspects of the host country and promotes a fragmented and intolerant society (Parsons & Smeeding, 2006). In either case, the extent to which the children of immigrants and natives receive differential benefits from government income redistribution policies is important to the study of immigration both across and within countries.

In this chapter, we examine poverty status and social transfer support for households with immigrant children in 14 countries. We use data from the Luxembourg Income Study (LIS) and the datasets underlying the European Statistics on Living Conditions (SILC) to construct relative measures of income poverty based on definitions of income that both exclude and include government redistribution. In particular, our estimates of cross-nationally equivalent measures of poverty and inequality provide an overall indicator of the effectiveness of the complex mix of policies employed in a set of rich countries. We are not able to study the children temporary immigrants leave behind in the sending country.

Our analysis reveals considerable cross-national variation in the degree of success and failure in alleviating poverty and inequality in the presence of shared pressures related to globalization, job instability, population aging, and migration. And while there is evidence of cross-national convergence in the design and evaluation of social policy, national social policies continue to differ substantially in ways that are important to the analysis of the social outcomes experienced by different groups (Banks et al., 2005).

Our results strongly suggest that country-specific policies can and do make a difference in the material living conditions faced by children in immigrant and native-born families. We find that countries with strong redistributive welfare states tend to have strong antipoverty effects that alleviate material deprivation for both immigrants and natives. Countries that have weak redistributive welfare states have smaller effects on both immigrant and native poverty rates.

Further, our data do not suggest that there is, as of the data collection period, a race to the bottom in confining benefits to native-born citizens or cutting benefits for immigrants. In an earlier paper with less appropriate European data, there was difficulty identifying immigrants and only those who were in Europe by 1990 could be studied (Smeeding, Wing, & Robson, 2009). With the new SILC data we have the capability to study a more recent and more clearly defined set of immigrants observed in 2006 in Europe and also the LIS data for 2000 to 2004.

The chapter begins by reviewing nation-specific concepts and measures of immigrant status and relative income poverty in different countries. We conclude with a discussion of the relationship between policy differences and outcome differences for children and their families among the several countries and consider the implications of our analysis for research and for antipoverty policy.

Cross-National Comparisons of Poverty: Methodology and Measurement

There is considerable consensus on the appropriate measurement of poverty in a cross-national context. Most of the available studies and papers on this topic share similarities that guide our methodological strategy. Differing national experiences in social transfer and antipoverty programs provide a rich source of information for evaluating the effectiveness of alternative social policies in fighting child poverty. Most rich nations share a concern over low incomes and poverty.[1] While there is not complete international consensus on guidelines for measuring poverty, international bodies such as the United Nations Children's Fund (UNICEF), the Organization for Economic Cooperation and Development (OECD), the European Statistical

---

[1] In fact, "official" measures of poverty (or measures of low-income status) exist in very few nations. Only the United States (U.S. Census Bureau, 2003) and the United Kingdom (UK Department for Work and Pensions, 2007) have regular "official" poverty series. In Canada there is a series of Low Income Cutoffs (LICOS), which are often debated but never formally introduced as national guidelines (Statistics Canada 2005). In northern Europe and the Nordic countries the debate centers instead on the level of income at which minimum benefits for social programs should be set and on "social exclusion" (Atkinson et al., 2002). Most recognize that their national social programs already ensure a low poverty rate under any reasonable set of measurement standards for natives at least. The case of immigrants is less well-known in all of these nations, though the same poverty lines are used for all residents of a country, immigrants or majority citizens.

Office (Eurostat), and the Luxembourg Income Study (LIS) have published several cross-national studies of the incidence of child poverty in recent years. A large subset of these studies is based on LIS data.[2]

For purposes of international comparisons, poverty is almost always a relative concept. A majority of cross-national studies define the poverty threshold as one-half of national median income. To maintain consistency with the cross-national poverty literature, in this study we use the 50% of median income standard to establish our national poverty lines. Immigrant children are therefore evaluated as members of the society within which their families live. Additional cross-national research shows that relative and absolute poverty outcomes are highly correlated (e.g., using the official U.S. absolute poverty lines in other rich nations; see Smeeding, 2006, table 3).

Measurement of Poverty and Immigrant Status

This chapter reports poverty rates among immigrant and native-born families in several different rich countries. The estimates come from surveys conducted in each country. In this section, we explain how we defined the poverty line in each country and how we classified survey respondents as belonging to immigrant or native-born families.

Construction of National Poverty Lines

- Comparisons of poverty across nations are based on many choices. Three important elements of a measurement of income poverty are (i) a poverty line that defines a minimum level of resources required to obtain an "acceptable" standard of living; (ii) a measure of resources such as income; and (iii) an equivalence scale that accounts for economies of scale in household size, which, for example, can allow two people living together to attain a given standard of living with fewer resources than twice the amount for one person living alone. After establishing these elements for each country, we estimate the poverty rate for households with children living in immigrant and nonimmigrant units. Next, we describe some of the details of our approach. Our poverty rates are based on disposable cash and near-cash income (DPI), which includes all types of money income, minus direct income and payroll taxes, *and also includes* all cash

---

[2] For UNICEF, see UNICEF Innocenti Research Centre (2000), Bradbury and Jäntti (2005), and Chen and Corak (2005); for the OECD, see Förster and Pellizzari (2005); for the European Union, see Atkinson et al. (2002); and, for LIS, see Gornick and Jäntti (2009), Smeeding (2005), and Rainwater and Smeeding (2003).

and near-cash transfers to individuals, families, or households, such as food stamps and cash housing allowances, and refundable tax credits, such as the Earned Income Tax Credit (EITC in the United States) and the Working Families Tax Credit (WFTC in the United Kingdom). These income aggregates constitute our resource measure. In order to determine the antipoverty effects of social transfers and tax policy, we also use a second and different measure, namely "before-tax-and-transfer" market income (MI), which includes only earnings, income from investments, private transfers, and occupational pensions, but which does not take into account reductions to available income associated with tax payment or additions to available income associated with cash transfers and near-cash transfers to individuals, families, or households.[3]

- In comparing poverty rates produced using an MI definition to the poverty rates produced using DPI, which is a more complete measure of (post-tax and transfer) resources, we learn about the combined effects of government programs on poverty levels. DPI includes resources that people receive through social insurance, cash universal benefits like child allowances, and social assistance (which includes all forms of income-tested benefits targeted at poor people, including refundable tax credits, and near-cash food and housing benefits) and it subtracts direct income and payroll taxes paid.

- For international comparisons of poverty and inequality, the "household" is the only comparable income sharing unit available for all nations studied here. Household income is assumed to be shared among individuals within a household. Poverty rates are sometimes calculated as the percentage of all persons in a specific category who are members of households of that specific category and who have incomes below the poverty line. But we focus here on the poverty rate of households with children (aged 17 and under), distinguishing them according to whether they live in a majority- or minority-immigrant household unit, where minority-immigrant household units include at least one immigrant or minority in each household. Equivalence scales are used in income poverty research to adjust household income for economies of scale in the use of resources. The basic idea is that groups of people living together can often achieve a minimum standard of living with fewer total resources than

---

[3] Market income includes earnings, income from investments, occupational (private and public sector) pensions, child support, and other private transfers. For the calculation of poverty rates, MI refers to gross income in all countries but Austria, Belgium, Greece, Ireland, Italy, and Spain, where MI is net of taxes and social contributions.

would be required if each person lived alone. The equivalence scale used for this purpose, as in many cross-national studies, is a single parameter scale with a square-root-of-household-size scale factor.[4]

- After adjusting household incomes with the equivalence scale to reflect differences in household size, we compare the resulting adjusted incomes to 50% of the national median adjusted income. The median adjusted income is our estimate of the national relative poverty line. Families with size-adjusted income less than this line live in poverty.

Researchers have shown that income and household structure affect children's life chances and thus, the real income level of children and their parents is of serious social concern (Duncan & Brooks-Gunn, 1997; McLoyd, 1998; Sigle-Rushton & McLanahan, 2004).

Definitions of Immigrants and Minorities
The analysis in this chapter relies on data from the LIS and the EU-SILC. These databases combine data from several country-specific surveys. These surveys contain different types of information that can be used to identify immigrant and native-born respondents. In this section, we describe our definitions of immigrant status for each country.

The definitions of *immigrant* that we find in the LIS project are not completely consistent across countries. These differences reflect historical, political, social, and economic judgments made by each nation. These LIS definitions are:

> Definition one: "born outside the survey country"; United States, Canada, Italy, France
> Definition two: "non-national"; Australia, Germany, Sweden
> Definition three: "multiple national"; Austria, Belgium, Portugal
> Definition four: "nonwhite or minority"; United Kingdom

By far, the least satisfying definition for studying immigrants is that used in the LIS UK data, where immigrant status is not identified, only minority

---

[4] Formally, adjusted disposable income (ADPI) is equal to unadjusted household income (DPI) divided by household size (S) raised to an exponential value (e), $ADPI = DPI/S^e$. We assume the value of e is 0.5. To determine whether a household is poor under the relative poverty measure, we compare its ADPI to 50% of the national median ADPI. National median ADPI is calculated by converting all incomes into ADPI and then taking the median of this "adjusted" income distribution. The equivalence scale that we employ is robust; especially when comparing families of different size and structure (e.g., elders and children). See Atkinson, Rainwater, and Smeeding (1995) for detailed and exhaustive documentation of these sensitivities.

status. Definition three is taken from the Eurostat's European Community Household Panel (ECHP) files used in LIS, which asks respondents about their current country compared to the one in which they were born. If they respond that the current country is different from the one where they were born they are considered immigrants, because they have declared that they are "multiple national" regardless of citizenship status in either country. In contrast, the 2004 to 2006 definition in the new EU Statistics of Income and Living Conditions surveys (SILC), which we use in this chapter, asks the following in each nation: (a) What was your country of birth (EU country of current residence, other EU, or other non-EU nation)? And then, if not same as country of survey, (b) Do you hold one or two (or more) citizenships? Use of the SILC effectively combines definitions two and three for all EU nations from 2004 forward. For several countries we use the new SILC. These include Austria, Belgium, Denmark, Ireland, the Netherlands, and the United Kingdom. The SILC data collection allows five possible combinations of immigrants to be distinguished:

(1) "came from EU country (other than host nation) and citizen (of host nation)"
(2) "came from non-EU country and citizen (of host nation)"
(3) "came from EU country (other than host nation) and not citizen (of host nation)"
(4) "came from non-EU country and not citizen (of host nation)"
(5) "came from non-EU country and citizenship is EU country (other than host nation)"

But the available sample sizes force us to combine the first five into one large immigrant group in order to have sufficient samples for analysis. Further, we decided to study only older (EU17) samples and not the "new" Eastern European countries in the SILC in order to restrict the countries examined to a more comparable group. It is important to note, however, that the main findings of our analysis are not sensitive to the choice of the LIS or SILC datasets for a given country, and that cross-national patterns we observe do not disappear when analyses are expanded to include the Eastern European countries.

Immigrants in the Study Sample

Differences in the prevalence of immigrant or nonimmigrant households are apparent in Table 3.1, where we present estimates of the weighted percentage of households who are immigrant (or minority) according to

Table 3.1. The Prevalence of Immigrants: Households[a] with an Immigrant Head

Country	Dataset	Year	Percent Immigrant
United States	LIS	2000	12.9
Italy	LIS	2000	2.3
United Kingdom	SILC	2006	12.8
Canada	SLID	2002[b]	20.8
Australia	LIS	2001	27.4
Ireland	SILC	2006	12.8
Germany	LIS	2000	8.3
Belgium	SILC	2006	12.6
Austria	SILC	2006	16.6
Netherlands	SILC	2006	6.7
France	LIS	2000	8.3
Denmark	SILC	2006	6.1
Sweden	LIS	2001	4.1
Finland	LIS	2000	5.6
Average			16.6%

[a] Households containing at least one immigrant. It was not possible to determine the immigrant-nonimmigrant composition of household members in all datasets, and so we report households with an immigrant.
[b] SLID is the Survey of Labor Income Dynamics in Canada; the same survey used by LIS.
Source: Authors' calculations from LIS and (EU) SILC.

the definitions just given. While on average 16.6% of the households studied have at least one immigrant, there is considerable variation in the percentage of households with minorities/immigrants in these national samples. Reasons for these measured differences across countries include not only actual differences across countries in the comparative size of immigrant populations but also differences across countries in sampling design, types of surveys, and how immigrants and minorities are counted in the surveys. The German Socio-Economic Panel added a "booster" sample of immigrants in the 1990s and that addition was also followed as part of their survey. This (unweighted) sample was the basis for the 2006 SILC German estimates. While this expanded sample is more representative of the current immigrant population in Germany, German survey takers suggest that their estimates are low, especially for more recent immigrants, because only German-speaking interviewers go to each address.

In the United States, the sampling frame is household addresses, and the data include legal and illegal immigrants, assuming that the latter respond as much as do the former. But if the language of interview is only the native one, we expect higher nonresponse from more recent immigrants than for long-standing ones. Indeed, the U.S. data have been used to estimate both legal and illegal immigrants, termed "undocumented aliens," based on the CPS samples that underlie the U.S. LIS data employed here (Passel, 2005). In countries with registration systems, sampling frames may include only registered immigrants or registered households.

We estimate that, in Australia, immigrants represent about 27% of the household population.[5] This compares to about 21% in Canada (where naturalized citizens are not counted as immigrants but non-naturalized are so counted), 8% in Germany, and 13% in Ireland, Belgium, and the United States. In the United States, when foreign-born but naturalized immigrants are also included in the definition of minority, we find 13% of all households with an immigrant (and we designate these naturalized immigrants by an asterisk in tables and figures that follow). Without the nationalized members, the U.S. percentage is 9%. The more inclusive definition corresponds most closely to Australia's definition. It also includes undocumented immigrants in the United States and perhaps also in Australia and Canada, though we are not certain of the extent of these phenomena at this time.[6] The percentage of immigrant or minority households therefore varies from the high 27% observed in Australia all the way down to 2.3% in the Italian 2000 LIS data. With regard to Sweden, we also observe that the 2000 LIS data show only 4% immigrant, but it should be noted that Swedish 2006 SILC data show 10% immigrant, suggesting recent rapid growth in immigrant populations in Sweden, which also seems likely in many other EU nations.

The Literature and the Data

There is a fairly large and recent literature on poverty and inequality in EU welfare state nations (e.g., Atkinson et al., 2002; Marlier, 2008; Micklewright & Stewart, 2001). And these have mentioned immigration since the release of the ECHP in the mid-1990s followed by the SILC in the mid-2000s. We do not attempt to measure "social exclusion" here (see Dennis & Guio, 2003) because such measures are not available outside of the EU. As far as the welfare state is concerned, there is some evidence that emergence of

---

[5] Remember that these "non-Australians" include both non-naturalized and naturalized citizens.

[6] Indeed, we worked with the Canadian survey takers to eliminate all incomplete records and those where the immigrant had so recently arrived as to have no Canadian income. Overall, 2.20% of the immigrant records and 2.15% of the immigrant population were dropped due to this filter.

safety nets for the elderly has helped the elder population enormously in all nations but has left the families and children we study here at risk (Marlier, 2008). Studies of the level and dynamics of poverty suggest that labor market issues, especially high and persistent unemployment and short-term job contracts, are as much a source of poverty as are low wages for natives (Amuedo-Dorantes & Serrano-Padial, 2005). But far less is known about immigrants and minorities and their access to welfare state transfers in cash or in kind (health and education).

There is a vast international literature on labor markets and work by legal and illegal immigrants and natives, and that literature shows that immigrants sometimes reduce wages and job opportunities of natives (e.g., see Borjas, 2006; Borjas, Grogger, & Hanson, 2007, for the United States). But in other nations, immigration is shown to have no effect on unemployment rates (see Islam, 2007, on Canada). The comparative literature is sparser but covers the United States and Canada, where Canadian immigration policy leads to higher educational and better job outcomes for at least the first two generations of immigrants (Aydemir & Sweetman, 2007). In fact, high rates of undocumented immigration can have profound effects on low-wage unregulated job markets such as those of the United States (Borjas et al., 2007). The European economics literature compares occupational outcomes (van Tubergen, 2006), earnings levels (Adsera & Chiswick, 2006), and other economic consequences (Brucker, Frick, & Wagner, 2006) across immigrant and nonimmigrant groups. Almost all such inquiries suggest that international migrants arrive primarily seeking work and not redistributive social benefits per se. Of course, excellent higher education systems in many nations attract high-quality foreign students, but many ultimately return to their native lands or go elsewhere for work (Crul & Vermeulen, 2006). In the end, the key question is to identify the net gains and losses to immigration, and at least for the United States, the National Academy of Sciences finds that immigration pays handsome long-run dividends to the immigrant receiving nation (Smith & Edmonston, 1998).

United States poverty rates of various sorts have been calculated for households with immigrant children from many countries of origin and for native-born families (Hernandez & Macartney, 2010; Hernandez, Denton, & Macartney 2007; Hernandez et al., 2009). But the literature on immigrant versus nonimmigrant poverty and social program support is still in its infancy outside the United States. Menz (2006) and others write on welfare retrenchment in Europe in reaction to immigration, but provide no evidence of its actual effects on individual outcomes or poverty status (as in Boeri, 2009). Capps and Fortuny (2006) suggest higher child and family poverty among U.S. immigrant children. A comparative EU–U.S. paper by

Morrissens (2006) looks at six rich nations and finds varying outcomes for employment and unemployment benefit generosity only. And Hernandez et al. (2009) have written a recent paper comparing child poverty using nonharmonized data for a small set of rich nations.

In this chapter, we examine a larger number of countries than in previous work using harmonized survey data. We also include a multiplicity of other tax and transfer benefits not examined by Morrissens (2006). Moreover, this chapter updates our recent work using the LIS and ECHP to study all populations and children as well (Smeeding et al., 2009). The use of the SILC data is an important contribution because the SILC data are based on more recent annual survey samples in Europe and therefore offer a more representative sample of households with immigrant children in Europe.

Data

The data we use for this analysis are mainly taken from the Luxembourg Income Study (LIS) database, which now contains over 160 household income data files for 35 nations covering the period from 1967 to 2004 (www.lisproject.org). For this chapter, we have focused our analysis on nations where we can identify migrants (as suggested previously). Therefore, we have decided to focus on 14 nations for the remainder of this chapter, each with an LIS database from 2000 or later. We also use the EU Survey of Income and Living Conditions (SILC) and add seven other nations outside of the LIS database, where the SILC files offer more recent samples, as well as nations where immigrants are not well covered in the LIS. The final set includes five English-speaking nations (Australia, the United States, Canada, Ireland, and the United Kingdom) and nine European nations (Austria, Belgium, France, Netherlands, Italy, and Germany), including three Nordic nations (Denmark, Finland, and Sweden). We incorporate all of Germany, including the eastern states of the former German Democratic Republic (GDR), in most of our analyses. Thanks to the cooperation of Brian Murphy at Statistics Canada, we also have access to a special version of the Canadian data that includes all minority and immigrant respondents and therefore allows us to go beyond the LIS data where immigrant status is suppressed in the Canadian data for privacy purposes.

Results: Poverty among Nations, Households with Immigrant and Native Children

Much of the concern over social and economic vulnerability of all populations, immigrants and nonimmigrants alike, is centered on social programs mainly used to support the qualified (social insurance) and the needy (income maintenance) in all nations. Here we examine poverty among households with children (under age 18) in native-born and immigrant groups and we examine the antipoverty effect of government policy for each of these subgroups. We conclude with a brief summary of what we have learned about how government support affects poverty and inequality for vulnerable children in immigrant and nonimmigrant households from a comparative perspective.

Overall – Global Relative Poverty Levels and Antipoverty Effects for Households with Children

Relative poverty rates using MI and DPI in the 14 nations we cover in this chapter are given in Figure 3.1 for all (immigrant and nonimmigrant) households with children. The overall DPI poverty rate for all households with children using the 50% poverty threshold varies from 3% in Finland to 22% in the United States, with an average rate of about 11% across the 14 countries included in Figure 3.1. Earlier work (Gornick & Jäntti, 2009; Munzi & Smeeding, 2008) suggests that using a lower relative poverty rate (such as the 40% of median rate) makes little difference in terms of overall poverty rate rankings.

Higher overall DPI poverty rates are found in English-speaking nations with a relatively high level of overall inequality (the United States, Canada, Australia, Ireland, and the United Kingdom) and in Mediterranean countries such as Italy. Canadian and British poverty rates among households with children currently stand at about 15% and are, therefore, below the U.S. levels. The lowest poverty rates are more common in smaller, well-developed, and high-spending welfare states (Sweden, Finland, and Denmark), where they are about 5%. Middle-level rates are found in major continental European countries where income support and unemployment compensation are more generous, where social policies provide more generous support to single mothers and working women (through paid family leave, for example), and where social assistance minimums are high. For instance, Austria, France, Belgium, the Netherlands, and Germany have poverty rates for households with children in the 7%–9% range.

The poverty rates for households with children are highest in countries with many single parents, low wages, and low levels of transfer support. Poverty rates computed using household MI for households with children do not differ among countries as much as do those calculated after-taxes-and-transfers DPI. Different levels and mixes of government spending have

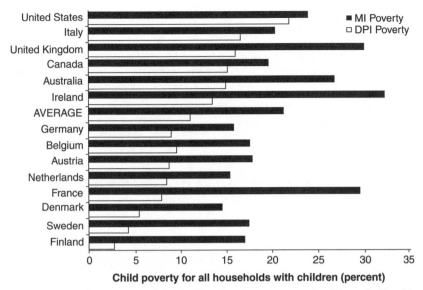

Figure 3.1. Market income and disposable income poverty rates for all households with children (aged 0–17).
Source: Authors' calculations from LIS and EU SILC.

sizable effects on national DPI poverty rates (Smeeding, 2006). We compute the difference in DPI and MI poverty for each country and then express this difference as a percentage of MI poverty as a summary measure of the reduction in poverty associated with government transfers. The percentage difference between MI and DPI poverty is the smallest in the United States at only 8%. The difference is largest in Sweden, the United Kingdom, France, and Scandinavia, where it ranges from 60% to 75%. On average, tax benefit programs reduce household child poverty by about one-half.

These results are not surprising given 20 years or more of LIS research and related cross-national research using other datasets. They fit well with Esping-Andersen's (1990, 1999) welfare state typologies and other recent results (Gornick & Jäntti, 2009). But now the question that needs to be answered is: How do these poverty rates and social policy impacts differ for immigrant child households as opposed to native-born child households?

Poverty in Immigrant (Minority) Households with Children

In all rich nations, and now especially in Europe, there is growing concern about the status of immigrants and other minority groups (Boeri, 2009; Parsons & Smeeding, 2006). We begin with Table 3.2, which summarizes

Table 3.2. Child Poverty Rates by Minority Status across Countries

	Market Income and Disposable Income Poverty for Households with Children			
	Majority (Nonimmigrant)		Minority (Immigrant)	
	MI Poverty	DPI Poverty	MI Poverty	DPI Poverty
United States (%)	21.9	19.9	41.4	40.3
United States*	21.9	19.8	33.7	33.0
Italy	20.4	16.6	15.5	14.7
United Kingdom	27.5	14.6	43.2	23.3
Canada	17.8	13.7	27.5	21.7
Australia	24.9	13.3	32.1	19.7
Ireland	30.9	13.0	39.7	16.7
Germany	14.7	8.0	21.9	14.5
Belgium	13.7	7.4	36.1	19.7
Austria	15.4	7.3	26.7	14.0
Netherlands	12.4	6.7	46.7	27.3
France	29.9	6.1	56.1	18.5
Denmark	12.0	4.4	40.5	17.2
Sweden	15.4	3.6	49.3	13.6
Finland	17.1	2.8	15.6	3.5
AVERAGE (%)	19.7	10.5	35.1	19.8

*Includes only naturalized citizens.
Source: Authors' calculations from LIS and EU SILC.

child MI and DPI poverty rates by nonimmigrant and immigrant status for each country in our sample. In all countries but one, the DPI poverty rate for households with children is higher in the minority population than in the majority population. For all 14 countries in the combined sample, migrant households with children have greater MI poverty rates and greater DPI poverty rates than do native-born households with children by a factor of about two to one. When including taxes and benefits, DPI poverty rates for immigrant households with children are about 20% on average, compared to 10.5% for comparable nonimmigrant native households with children. MI poverty rates for natives are much less scattered than are those for immigrants. MI rates for nonimmigrant units with children in Table 3.2 range from about 12% to 30%; for immigrant households with children the MI rates vary from 15% to 56%.

In France, Germany, Sweden, and other nations with low child poverty, the overall immigrant household DPI poverty rate is more than twice the native household poverty rate. In the United States and Belgium, the immigrant poverty rate is nearly twice the native poverty rate. When naturalized

foreign-born household heads are included in the U.S. immigrant definition, the immigrant DPI poverty rate is still more than 13 percentage points
higher than the native poverty rate.

This pattern of high overall immigrant poverty rates is reversed only in
Italy, where immigrant poverty rates are actually lower than native poverty
rates. Immigrant poverty rates in Canada and Australia differ by 8 to 10
percentage points from nonimmigrant rates, despite evidence that the skill-
biased immigration policies pursued in Canada and Australia are successful in selecting/admitting immigrants able to succeed economically after
arriving. Ireland, which has the same immigration strategy, has a smaller
difference in poverty across immigrant and nonimmigrant households with
children. Germany is another important destination country, but one where
the immigrant rate is far below the native rate, and one like the United
States, where skilled immigration is discouraged.

These differences are consistent with those recently published by
Eurostat (Marlier, 2008), where at the 60% of median poverty standard, the
poverty rates for immigrant households (heads or spouses born outside
the EU country of destination) were 40.6% compared to 17.6% for households with children whose parents were both born within the country of
residence. We now turn to the matter of the effect of antipoverty policy on
these results.

Antipoverty Effects for Households with Children
by Immigration Status

We also show MI and DPI poverty rates for majority and minority households (with children) in each of the countries in our sample in Figures 3.2
and 3.3, respectively. For nonimmigrant households in the United States
(Figure 3.2), the antipoverty effect is a 10% reduction (from about 22% to
20%); for immigrant households (Figure 3.3), it is only a 2% reduction (from
about 42% to 41%), with a similar small effect when naturalized immigrants
are included. On average, the reduction in overall poverty across all countries is from 20% to 10% for majority households with children, but from
35% to 20% for minority households with children (see Table 3.2). Effects
for both groups are larger in the high-spending welfare states (northern and
central Europe) and smaller in the English-speaking nations. For minorities, starting and ending poverty rates are higher, as we expected, but percentage reductions in poverty are also high for minorities, for instance, in
France, the United Kingdom, Ireland, Belgium, and Sweden, where minority effects are about the same as for majorities.

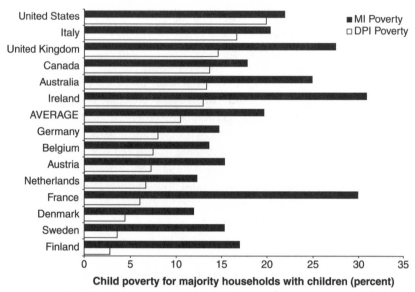

Figure 3.2. Market income and disposable income poverty for majority (nonimmigrant) households with children (aged 0–17).

Source: Authors' calculations from LIS and EU SILC.

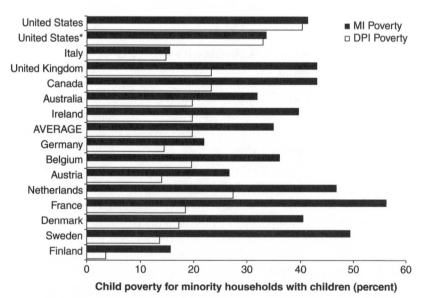

Figure 3.3. Market income and disposable income poverty for minority (immigrant) households with children (aged 0–17).

*Includes naturalized immigrants only.

Source: Authors' calculations from LIS and EU SILC.

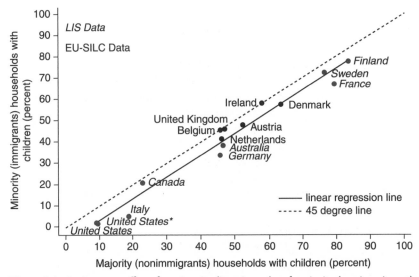

Figure 3.4. Antipoverty effects for minority (immigrant) and majority (nonimmigrant) households with children.

*Includes naturalized immigrants only.

Notes: Countries in italic print are from LIS, countries in regular print are from EU SILC.

Source: Authors' calculations based on LIS and EU SILC.

Figure 3.4 presents our key result, as it plots the percentage difference between the MI and DPI poverty rates for immigrant or minority households with children against the percentage difference in MI and DPI poverty for native or majority households with children. Antipoverty effects are measured as the difference between MI and DPI poverty, expressed as a percentage of MI poverty. The scatter plot highlights the distribution of government antipoverty effects with respect to immigrant or minority status in each country. First note that if antipoverty effects were evenly distributed among immigrants and nonimmigrants, each country's data point would fall along the dashed 45-degree line, based on the size of their antipoverty effect. Data points from countries that reduced poverty by a higher percentage for natives fall below the 45-degree line (dashed line). Figure 3.4 plots the simple regression line for the countries in our sample as well.

We denote LIS and SILC data according to italicized (LIS) and regular (SILC) print in Figure 3.4. In cases where we have two estimates, we put the LIS estimate in Figure 3.4. In Figure 3.5, we used all the SILC points we had (again in regular print), adding in only the LIS estimates in italics.

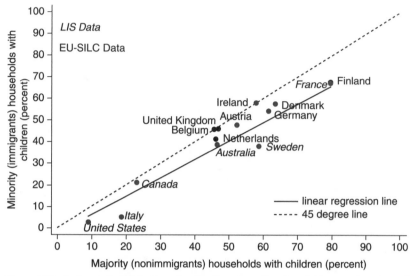

Figure 3.5. Antipoverty effects for minority (immigrant) and majority (nonimmigrant) households with children.

Notes: Countries in italic print are from LIS, countries in regular print are from EU SILC.

Source: Authors' calculations based on LIS and EU SILC.

The results are very much the same in both figures. The regression line in Figure 3.4 shows that in most countries overall antipoverty reductions are systematically related for households with immigrant or minority children and for those with native or majority children. The results fall very much along a line. The LIS Nordic Scandinavian nations are at the top end; the United States, Italy, and Canada at the bottom; with the rest of the European Union bunched in the middle. The United States stands out with a relatively small antipoverty effect, especially for immigrants (around one percentage point), but also for nonimmigrants (about two percentage points). Italy does even less for minority children (less than one percentage point in poverty reduction), while Belgium, Ireland, Canada, and the United Kingdom have almost identical percentage poverty reductions for immigrant and native population groups. The others are lower for minorities by a relatively fixed differential of six to seven percentage points, meaning that the rest provide slightly higher support to native than immigrant populations. But over-all these nations are similarly successful in reducing MI poverty for both groups. The results are only slightly different when estimates in Figure 3.5 rely on the SILC for the largest possible number of these same 14 nations.

We prefer the LIS emphasis in Figure 3.4 as we trust the data more and we have all of the non-EU estimates in the LIS only. However, the SILC gives similar results in Figure 3.5.

Discussion and Explanation

Comparative cross-national relative poverty rankings suggest that the 14 nations we analyze have several distinct groupings in terms of overall poverty, with the English-speaking and southern European countries belonging to the worst half of the ranking, and the north-continental European and Nordic countries to the better half. We find this pattern for both native and immigrant households with children. Indeed, in the end, the country of residence makes much more difference in poverty than does native or immigrant status.

As the figures have shown, the U.S. poverty rates are positioned at or near the top of the range for both population groups. We also know from previous work that a substantial fraction of the variance in nonelderly cross-national poverty rates is accounted for not by variation in work or in unemployment, but by the cross-national variation in the incidence of low pay. Because the United States has the highest proportion of workers in relatively poorly paid jobs, it also has the highest poverty rate, even among parents who work half time or more (Smeeding, 2006). Countries that have a significantly lower incidence of low-paid employment also have significantly lower poverty rates than the United States.

But the prevalence of low-pay workers is, in fact, not the only source of poverty or contributor to poverty rate differences across countries. While low pay is a good predictor of poverty rates, and while poorly educated workers (immigrant and nonimmigrant alike) do not do well at keeping their families from poverty based on earnings alone, other factors, such as the antipoverty efforts of the government, are also important predictors of the poverty rate. Social spending reduces poverty in the analyses presented here. And as a result of its low level of spending on social transfers to the nonaged with children, the United States has a very high overall poverty rate for all groups.

Households with immigrant children are more likely to be poor than households with native children and by a wide margin in most nations. However, for the most part, the effects of social tax benefit programs on poverty for immigrant households with children in Figures 3.3 and 3.4 vary much more extensively by country of destination than by immigrant versus nonimmigrant status. That is, high antipoverty effects are found for both groups in the majority of generous welfare state nations (e.g., Belgium, Sweden, France, Austria), and for somewhat less generous ones (e.g., Canada) as well. Small effects are found in the one nation not known for its generosity to any group (the United States). In the rest of these nations, children receive substantial support though immigrant children receive just a little less support. Thus we conclude that policy can and does make a difference in poverty for both immigrant and native children, but that the effects are stronger across countries than within countries

Conclusions

Other comparative research suggests that what seems most distinctive about the American poor is that the least skilled among them work more hours than do the resident parents of most other nations where we can observe work hours (Smeeding, 2006). More generally, the United States differs from most nations that achieve lower poverty rates because of its emphasis on work and self-reliance for working-aged adults, regardless of the wages workers must accept or the family situation of those workers – immigrants or natives. These immigrants also receive less (as do the natives) in transfer benefits than do their peers in other countries. And these results are also heavily influenced by low pay for low-skilled immigrants and natives (Smeeding, 2006). Thus, high immigrant child poverty is not driving the incredibly high child poverty rates in the United States – other features of the U.S. economic and social situation are responsible for this outcome for both native and immigrant households with children. A similar conclusion for the United States is reached in Raphael and Smolensky (2009).

More research needs to be undertaken in order to more firmly establish how different types of households are affected by *specific* social transfer programs and how they aid immigrant and native families in all of these nations, both in the short term and across the life course. The interaction between household structure and immigrant status is clearly an important element of poverty and inequality in industrialized countries, with immigrant households containing children at a higher risk of poverty in many cases. Hours worked, taxes paid, and benefits received can be studied for all groups in each nation. The hours-education-earnings compositions differ greatly among the countries studied, with Australia and Canada having a more skills-driven immigration policy than that found in the United States. New and better data from the SILC will allow for a much better and more recent picture of immigrant makeup and social policy effects in those nations when the 2005 and 2007 datasets, for the first time also including many immigrant active middle-income countries like Brazil, will become part of LIS in 2012. Further, we have not been able to determine how health and education policies affect immigrant and minority versus majority youth. But health care is largely need-based and immigrant-blind in most rich nations except in the United States, where insurance is often a prerequisite (Maquet-Engsted & Stewart, 2009). Education systems in all nations serve the youth who reside there, though differences in school quality and outcome between immigrant and native children can also be observed (Schnepf, 2007).

Policy Implications

With the United States at the bottom of the ranking of social transfers, it is in a good position to learn from European antipoverty and inequality policies for immigrants and nonimmigrants alike. As long as nations like the United States rely almost exclusively on low-skilled immigrants and on the job market to generate incomes for working-aged families, changes in the jobs and wage distributions that affect the earnings of less-skilled workers will inevitably have a big effect on poverty for the children of immigrant working-aged adults. One expects that such low-skilled workers are paid wages below those paid to even the lowest skilled U.S. native workers (for evidence, see Borjas, 2006; and Borjas et al., 2007). At the same time, welfare reform in the United States has pushed many native-born low-income women into the labor market and they have stayed there as Temporary Assistance for Needy Families (TANF) rolls continue to fall. It is unlikely that many immigrant mothers in the United States are receiving TANF benefits because of their declining importance as a source of income support and because of sanctions against foreign-born mothers in state TANF programs. Even with the $25.4 billion the United States spent on TANF in 2009, only $11.2 billion is in the form of cash assistance; the rest is in the form of child care and transportation assistance, training, and other services (Pear, 2003). While the switch from cash to services has undoubtedly helped account for higher earnings among low-income parents, it has not helped move many of them from poverty (Cancian & Danziger, 2009).

Of course, labor markets alone cannot reduce poverty because many jobs do not provide incomes at the level that allow the poor to earn their way out of poverty. In all nations, single parents with young children, disabled workers, and the unskilled will face significant challenges earning an adequate income, no matter how much they work and no matter their nationality.

The relationship between antipoverty spending and poverty rates is of course complicated, so the arguments discussed in this chapter are, at best, suggestive. But new results presented here indicate that national anti-poverty and anti-inequality policies can make a difference in the lives of children, regardless of their immigrant or native status. As the British have demonstrated in the United Kingdom, carefully crafted public policy certainly reduces poverty for all children (Bradshaw, 2002; Hills, 2003; Hills & Waldfogel, 2004; Smeeding & Waldfogel, 2010).

Of course, direct and indirect costs of antipoverty programs are now widely recognized (but frequently overstated) in public debate (see Garfinkel, Rainwater, & Smeeding, 2006; Lindert, 2004). The wisdom of expanding programs targeted at children and poor families, especially those of immigrant background, depends on one's values and subjective views about the economic, political, and moral tradeoffs of poverty alleviation. Among the critics of public spending on the poor, economic efficiency losses associated with a larger government budget and targeted social programs for minority and majority families are concerns. For others, who are in our estimation correct, investments in poor children will pay back these costs several times over in future income growth.

It is hard to argue that the United States and other rich nations cannot afford to do more to help the poor, particularly low-skilled workers. If the United States is to reduce child poverty, it will need to make antipoverty spending a higher priority, as did the British and as do most European nations. In particular, it will have to do a better job of combining work and benefits targeted to low-wage workers in low-income families. There is already evidence that such programs produce better outcomes for native children (Clark-Kauffman, Duncan, & Morris, 2003).

These programs could also work in the United States if redistributive tax policy were broadened to serve all workers, including the parents of immigrant children. Expansions in the EITC and refundable tax credits for larger families and for absent parents can also supplement wages and reduce poverty for low-income parents of all types (Berlin, 2007; Edelman et al., 2009), and availability of high-quality early childhood education and health insurance (Brown et al., 1999; Magnuson & Votruba-Drzal, 2009) could help all young children and their families, both immigrant and native.

Authors' Note

The authors would like to thank the Jacobs Foundation, the Russell Sage Foundation, and the Marie Curie Action Fund for support. We also thank

Brian Murphy for his help in preparing the Canadian data for this manuscript, and the University of Oxford for access to the EU-SILC data that underlie this publication. We thank David Chancellor, Deborah Johnson, Emma Caspar, and Dawn Duren for help with manuscript preparation. We thank Brian Nolan, Marta Tienda, Sara McLanahan, Ann S. Masten, Donald J. Hernandez, and seminar participants at the Princeton Seminar "Migrant Youth and Children of Migrants in a Globalized World" for helpful suggestions. Finally, the authors thank the Luxembourg Income Study member countries especially for their support. The conclusions reached are those of the authors alone and not of their sponsoring institutions.

REFERENCES

Adsera, A., & Chiswick, B. (2006). Divergent patterns in immigrant earnings across European destinations. In C. A. Parsons and T. M. Smeeding (Eds.), *Immigration and the transformation of Europe* (pp. 85–110). Cambridge, UK: Cambridge University Press.

Amuedo-Dorantes, C., & Serrano-Padial, R. (2005). Fixed-term employment and its poverty implications: Evidence from Spain. *Focus, 23*(3), 42–5.

Atkinson, A. B., Cantillon, B., Marlier, E., & Nolan, B. (2002). *Social indicators: The EU and social inclusion.* Oxford, UK: Oxford University Press.

Atkinson, A. B., Rainwater, L., & Smeeding, T. (1995). Income distribution in OECD countries: Evidence from the Luxembourg Income Study (LIS). Social Policy Studies No. 18. Paris: Organization for European Cooperation and Development.

Aydemir A., & Sweetman, A. (2007). First and second generation immigrant educational attainment and labor market outcomes: A comparison of the United States and Canada. In Chiswick (Ed.), *Research in labor economics, Vol. 27. Immigration – trends, consequences and prospects for the United States* (pp. 215–70). Amsterdam: Elsevier.

Banks, J., Disney, R. F., Duncan, A., & Van Reenen, J. (2005). The internationalization of public welfare. *The Economic Journal, 115*(502), C62–C81.

Berlin, G. (2007). Rewarding the work of individuals: A counterintuitive approach to reducing poverty and strengthening families. *The Future of Children, 17*(2, Fall), 17–42.

Boeri, T. (2009). Immigration to the land of redistribution. IZA Working Paper No. 4273, June. Bonn.

Borjas, G. (2006). Making it in America: Social mobility in the immigrant population. *The Future of Children, 16*(2), 55–71.

Borjas, G., Grogger, J., & Hanson, G. H. (2007). Immigration and African-American employment opportunities: The response of wages, employment, and incarceration to labor supply shocks. National Bureau of Economic Research Working Paper No. 12518, Cambridge, MA.

Bradbury, B., & Jäntti, M. (2005). Child poverty, labor markets, and public policies across industrialized countries. Social Policy Research Center, Sydney: University of New South Wales.

Bradshaw, J. (Ed.) (2002). *The well-being of children in the UK.* London: Save the Children.

Brown, E. R., Wyn, R., Yu, H., Valenzuela, A., & Dong, L. (1999). Access to health insurance and health care for children in immigrant families. In D. J. Hernandez (Ed.), *Children of immigrants: Health, adjustment, and public assistance* (pp. 126–86). Washington, DC: National Academy Press.

Brucker, H., Frick, J. R., & Wagner, G. G. (2006). Economic consequences of immigration in Europe. In C. A. Parsons and T. M. Smeeding (Eds.), *Immigration and the transformation of Europe* (pp. 111–46). Cambridge, UK: Cambridge University Press.

Cancian, M., & Danziger, S. (2009). Changing poverty and changing antipoverty policies. In M. Cancian and S. Danziger (Eds.), *Changing poverty, changing policies* (pp. 1–31). New York: Russell Sage Foundation.

Capps, R., & Fortuny, K. (2006). *Immigration and child and family policy.* The Urban Institute and Child Trends Roundtable on Children in Low-Income Families. Available at: http://www.urban.org/url.cfm?ID=311362.

Chen, W. H., & Corak, M. (2005). Child poverty and changes in child poverty in rich countries since 1990. Luxembourg Income Study Working Paper No. 405. Syracuse, New York: Center for Policy Research, Syracuse University.

Clark-Kauffman, E., Duncan, G. J., & Morris, P. (2003). How welfare policies affect child and adolescent achievement. *American Economic Review, 93,* 299–303.

Crul, M., & Vermeulen, H. (2006). Immigration, education and the Turkish second generation in five European nations: A comparative study. In C. A. Parsons and T. M. Smeeding (Eds.), *Immigration and the transformation of Europe* (pp. 235–50). Cambridge, UK: Cambridge University Press.

Dennis, I., & Guio, A.-C. (2003). Poverty and social exclusion in the EU after Laeken, part 1. *Statistics in Focus.* Brussels: Eurostat.

Duncan, G. J., & Brooks-Gunn, J. (Eds.). (1997). *Consequences of growing up poor.* New York: Russell Sage Foundation.

Edelman, P., Greenberg, M., Holt, S., & Holzer, H. (2009). Expanding the EITC to help more low-wage workers. Georgetown Center on Poverty, Inequality, and Public Policy, Georgetown University, Washington, DC, September.

Esping-Andersen, G. (1990). *The three worlds of welfare capitalism.* Cambridge, UK: Polity Press.

(1999). *The social foundations of postindustrial economies.* Oxford, UK: Oxford University Press.

Förster, M. F., & Pellizzari, M. (2005). Trends and driving factors in income distribution and poverty in the OECD area. Occasional Paper No. 42, Paris: Organization for Economic Cooperation and Development, Labour Market and Social Policy.

Garfinkel, I., Rainwater, L., & Smeeding, T. M. (2006). A reexamination of welfare states and inequality in rich nations: How in-kind transfers and indirect taxes change the story. *Journal of Policy Analysis and Management, 25,* 897–919.

Gornick, J. C., & Jäntti, M. (2009). Child poverty in upper-income countries: Lessons from the Luxembourg Income Study. In S. B. Kamerman, S. Phipps and A. Ben-Arieh (Eds.), *From child welfare to child wellbeing: An international perspective on knowledge in the service of making policy* (pp. 339–68). New York: Springer Publishing Company.

Hernandez, D. J., Denton, N. A., & Macartney, S. (2007). Child poverty in the U.S.: A new family budget approach with comparison to European countries. In H. Wintersberger, L. Alanen, T. Olk, and J. Qvortrup (Eds.), *Childhood, generational order and the welfare state: Exploring children's social and economic welfare, Vol.1 of*

COST A19: Children's welfare (pp. 109–40). Odense: University Press of Southern Denmark.

Hernandez, D. J., Denton, N. A., Macartney, S., & Blanchard, V. L. (2009). Poverty and human resources for children in the United States and selected rich countries. In J. Qvortrup (Ed.), *Structural, historical, and comparative perspectives: Sociological studies of children and youth, Vol. 12* (pp. 81–113). Bingley, UK: Emerald Group Publishing Limited.

Hernandez, D. J., & Macartney, S. E. (2010). Children of immigrants and the future of America. In E. L. Grigorenko and R. Takanishi (Eds.), *Immigration, diversity, and education* (pp. 7–25). New York and London: Routledge/Taylor and Francis Group.

Hills, J. (2003). The Blair government and child poverty: An extra one percent for children in the United Kingdom. In I. Sawhill, (Ed.), *One percent for the kids: New policies, brighter futures for America's children* (pp. 156–78). Washington, DC: Brookings Institution.

Hills, J., & Waldfogel, J. (2004). "A 'Third Way' in welfare reform: What are the lessons for the U.S.?" *Journal of Policy Analysis and Management, 23*, 765–88.

Huston, A. C. (Ed.). (1994). *Children in poverty: child development and public policy.* Cambridge, UK: Cambridge University Press.

Huston, A. C., McLoyd, V. C., & Garcia, C. (2008). Children and poverty: Issues in contemporary research. *Child Development, 65*(2 June), 275–82.

Islam, A. (2007). Immigration unemployment relationship: The evidence from Canada. *Australian Economic Papers, 46*(1, March): 52–66. Available at SSRN: http://papers. ssrn.com/sol3/papers.cfm?abstract_id=969086.

Kahanec, M., & Zimmerman, K. (2008). Migration in an enlarged EU: A challenging solution? DIW Discussion Paper No. 849, December. Berlin, Germany: DIW (German Institute of Economic Research).

Lichter, D. T. (1997). Poverty and inequality among children. *Annual Review of Sociology, 23*(August), 121–45.

Lindert, P. H. (2004). *Growing public, Vol. 1, The story: Social spending and economic growth since the eighteenth century.* New York: Cambridge University Press.

Magnuson, K., & Votruba-Drzal, E. (2009). Enduring influences of child poverty. In M. Cancian and S. Danziger (Eds.), *Changing poverty, changing policies* (pp. 153–79). New York: Russell Sage Foundation.

Maquet-Engsted, I., & Stewart, D. (2009, November 4). Income indicators for the EU's Social Inclusion Strategy. Presented to the Association for Public Policy Analysis and Management European Measures of Income, Poverty, and Social Exclusion: Recent Developments and Lessons for U.S. Poverty Measurement, Washington, DC. Available at http://www.umdcipe.org/conferences/AppamSpecialMeeting/ conf_agenda_papers.html.

Marlier, E. (2008, January). "Child poverty and well-being in the EU: Current status and way forward." Brussels, Belgium: EU Social Protection Committee.

Massey, D. (2010, May 2). The new Latino underclass: Immigration enforcement as a race-making institution. Paper presented to the Tobin Conference on Inequality. Available at http://whiteboard.tobinproject.org/sites/whiteboard.tobinproject.org/ files/announcement_files/Massey%20Abstract%20and%20Paper.pdf.

McLoyd, V. (1998). Socioeconomic disadvantage and child development. *American Psychologist, 53*(2), 185–204.

Menz, G. (2006). "Useful" *Gastarbeiter*, burdensome asylum seekers, and the second wave of welfare retrenchment: Exploring the nexus between migration and the welfare state. In C. A. Parsons and T. M. Smeeding (Eds.), *Immigration and the transformation of Europe* (pp. 393–418). Cambridge, UK: Cambridge University Press.

Micklewright, J., & Stewart, K. (2001). Child well-being in the EU – and enlargement to the east. In K. Vlaminck and T. M. Smeeding (Eds.), *Child well-being, child poverty and child poverty in modern nations: What do we know?* (pp. 99–127). Bristol, UK: Policy Press.

Morrissens, A. (2006). Immigrants, unemployment and Europe's varying welfare regimes. In C. A. Parsons and T. M. Smeeding (Eds.), *Immigration and the transformation of Europe*. Cambridge, UK: Cambridge University Press.

Munzi, T., & Smeeding, T. M. (2008). Conditions of social vulnerability, work and low income: Evidence for Spain in comparative perspective. In L. Costabile (Ed.), *Institutions for social well-being: Alternatives for Europe* (pp. 33–73). New York: Palgrave-Macmillan Publishers.

Parsons, C. A., & Smeeding, T. M. (Eds.). (2006). *Immigration and the transformation of Europe*. Cambridge, UK: Cambridge University Press.

Passel, J. S. (2005). Estimates of the size and characteristics of the undocumented population. Washington, DC: Pew Hispanic Center. Available at http://pewhispanic.org/reports/report.php?ReportID=44.

Pear, R. (2003, October 13). Welfare spending shows huge shift from checks to service. *The New York Times.*

Rainwater, L., & Smeeding, T. M. (2003). *Poor kids in a rich country: America's children in comparative perspective.* New York: Russell Sage Foundation.

Raphael, S., & Smolensky, E. (2009). Immigration and poverty in the United States. In M. Cancian and S. Danziger (Eds.), *Changing poverty, changing policy* (chapter 5, pp. 122–50). Russell Sage Press, NY.

Sapir, A. (2006). Globalisation and the reform of European social models. *Journal of Common Market Studies, 44,* 369–90.

Sassen, S. (2008). Fear and strange arithmetics: When powerful states confront powerless immigrants. *Open Democracy.* Available at http://www.opendemocracy.net/article/fear-and-strange-arithmetics-when-powerful-states-confront-powerless-immigrants.

Schnepf, S. (2007). Immigrants' educational disadvantage: An examination across ten countries and three surveys. *Journal of Population Economics, 20,* 933–1433.

Sigle-Rushton, W., & McLanahan, S. (2004). Father absences and child well-being: A critical review. In D. P. Moynihan, L. Rainwater, and T. M. Smeeding (Eds.), *The future of the family* (pp. 116–57). New York: Russell Sage Foundation.

Smeeding, T. M. (2005). Public policy and economic inequality: The United States in comparative perspective. *Social Science Quarterly, 86*(5), 1–50.

  (2006). Poor people in a rich nation: The United States in comparative perspective. *Journal of Economic Perspectives, 20,* 69–90.

Smeeding, T., & Waldfogel, J. (2010). Fighting poverty: Attentive policy can make a huge difference. *Journal of Policy Analysis and Management, 29*(2, Winter), 401–7.

Smeeding, T. M., Wing, C., & Robson, K. (2009). Differences in social transfer support and poverty for immigrant families with children: Lessons from the LIS. In E. Grigorenko and R. Takanishi (Eds.), *Immigration, diversity, and education* (pp. 26–47). Routledge, NY.

Smith, J. P., & Edmonston, B. (1998). *The immigration debate: Studies on the economic, demographic, and fiscal effects of immigration.* U.S. National Academies of Science. Washington, DC: National Academies Press.

Statistics Canada. (2005). *LICOS – Low Income Cutoffs for 2003.* Ottawa.

UNICEF Innocenti Research Centre. (2000). A league table of child poverty in rich nations. In *Innocenti Report Card No. 1.* Florence: UNICEF.

United Kingdom Department for Work and Pensions. (2007). Opportunity for all: Sixth annual report, 2004. London, UK: Department for Work and Pensions.

United States Census Bureau. (2003). Income in the United States: 2002. *Current Population Reports,* P60–221. Washington, DC: Government Printing Office.

van Tubergen, F. (2006). Occupational status of immigrants in cross-national perspective: A multilevel analysis of seventeen western societies. In C. A. Parsons and T. M. Smeeding (Eds.), *Immigration and the transformation of Europe* (pp. 147–71). Cambridge, UK: Cambridge University Press.

4 Age at Immigration and the Education Outcomes of Children

Miles Corak

Introduction

There is no simple or single answer to the question of how migration influences the well-being of children. The answer will very much depend upon the counterfactual state that represents the basis for any causal comparison. Would the children of immigrants have been better off: if the parents had decided not to migrate; the parents had migrated to a different country; if the parents had migrated at a different point in the children's life cycle; or if the children had been born in the new country? Each question presupposes a different counterfactual, all of them relevant to assessment of the children's well-being.

Even this series of questions does not exhaust the possible dimensions of the issue. But to keep the counterfactual explicitly in mind does help to structure analysis, keep its relevance in perspective, and ultimately to highlight the possible public policy mechanisms that can be both addressed and evaluated. The analysis in this chapter focuses on only one of these questions and on a particular measure of child well-being: How would the education outcomes of a child differ if he or she had migrated at a different point in the life cycle? Focusing on this question is one way of allowing the concerns of child migrants to be informed by the research on child development. This growing literature underscores the importance of the early years in determining adult social and economic success. The suggestion that the full development of a child's social and cognitive competencies passes through a series of stages in which competencies at one stage build the foundation for subsequent developments implies the need to give distinct attention to child migrants. Children, in a way different from adults, face important transitions in their lives, and migration may have long-lasting impacts on their capacities to become successful and self-reliant adults, impacts that may be much more costly and difficult to remedy at a later stage.

The next section briefly sketches this literature, particularly with reference to sensitive periods in second language acquisition. The objective of the analysis in the subsequent sections is to uncover the extent and nature of distinct periods during which there is a greater risk of not completing high school. Does the likelihood of high school graduation for migrant children change discretely after a particular age at arrival in the host country?

This is an exercise in description and there is a certain caution required in ascribing a causal interpretation to the findings. As such this research is the first step in answering the question of whether a particular child would have been better off if his or her parents had changed countries when he or she was younger or older. Causal inference is difficult to make because the same child is not observed in two different states and a randomized experiment cannot be relied upon. The analysis is based upon observational data potentially subject to selection problems that make a clear causal inference difficult without convincingly controlling for the unobserved influences that may vary with the child's age at arrival in the destination country. This said, the analysis of Canadian census data offers a very large and representative sample to document high school graduation by age at arrival, but also according to the country of origin and its linguistic distance from English and French, Canada's two official languages.

The findings suggest that there is in fact a distinct age beyond which child migrants experience a greater risk of not completing high school, that its presence is associated in a predictable way with the extent of the challenges faced in learning one of Canada's official languages, and that it is likely no older than the age of nine. This point in the child's life cycle is associated with the period when elementary school children make the transition from learning to read to reading to learn. It is not possible to distinguish the role of the social and learning environments of schools in determining this outcome from the role of maturational changes children go through during this period in their lives. As such the threshold uncovered could well reflect the structure of the education system and public policy choices as much as it reflects sensitive periods in a child's development.

Overview and Motivation

The importance of the early years on the development of the adult capacities of children is studied and acknowledged in a large growing literature from a number of different disciplines. Knudsen et al. (2006) offer a particularly clear and succinct summary of the major findings, but just as important, they sketch out the logic of an argument stressing the relevance for public policy. Their discussion begins with the observation that early experiences seem to have long-lasting consequences, influencing adult competencies as well as social and labor market success. How and why this occurs has important implications, in their view, for the future productivity of society and raises a need for public policy to invest in the development of young children from disadvantaged backgrounds. Their policy recommendations rest on the claim that the returns to social investments in children during the early years exceed those offered to school-aged children, which in turn are greater than remedial training offered to adults: "the most cost-effective strategy for strengthening the future of the American workforce," the authors state, "is to invest greater human and financial resources in the social and cognitive environments of children who are disadvantaged, beginning as early as possible. The greatest return derives from investing in disadvantaged children because their home environments are impoverished" (Knudsen et al., 10161).

Early experiences influence social, emotional, and cognitive capacities in a way that impacts adulthood because learning is hierarchical and because it progresses through a series of so-called sensitive periods. The early development of skills influences the ability to master related and other skills and ultimately determines competencies at later stages in life. "Skills beget skills," meaning that capabilities at a particular point in life are based upon foundations set at earlier points. Learning is subject to sensitive periods during which specific skills can be mastered with greatest ease and productivity. Knudsen et al. (2006) make a point of citing language acquisition as illustrating this hierarchical process subject to sensitive periods, in particular highlighting second language acquisition. "Learning a second language as an adult requires far greater effort than learning it as a child, and the result is never complete" (Knudsen et al. 2006, 10158). They make note of Johnson and Newport (1989), a study of 46 Chinese and Korean immigrants who came to the United States as children and whose English proficiency was tested in adulthood after at least 10 years since arrival. They claim that this study shows that proficiency does not vary with age at arrival up to the age of 7, and then deteriorates with each subsequent year. By late adolescence language proficiency is no better than for those who arrived as adults in their 20s and 30s.

This in part explains the interest of social scientists in the acquisition of a second language by immigrants, who in some sense experience a sharp depreciation in the value of competencies obtained with the language of their country of origin. The fact that their competencies may not be suited to the language in their country of destination, and that language acquisition must start anew at an older stage in life, offers a test of the relevance and importance of sensitive periods in the learning process. This is an aspect of why the study of child migrants deserves attention. Children are likely to experience migration differently than adults, with distinct opportunities and challenges because of how the learning process occurs. Further, if the logic of the public policy argument put forward by Knudsen et al. (2006) is accepted, they also represent a group for which public policy, for better or worse, can make a difference in long-term outcomes that have broad social implications.

Thomas and Johnson (2008), Birdsong (2006), and many of the essays in Birdsong (1999) offer an overview of the literature on language and second language acquisition. The theoretical research in this area often associates sensitive periods with puberty, though there does not appear to be a consensus on this. Some theoreticians consider 5 or 6 years of age to be an important turning point, others 12 to 15 years. Further, in some perspectives puberty is associated with the stage at which declines in second language competencies end, but in others with the stage at which it begins (Birdsong, 2006, 18–19).

The empirical literature is addressed to the exact timing of any discrete changes in the relationship between age at arrival and second language competence. In fact, Johnson and Newport (1989), who focus on a test of grammatical judgment, is only one of many empirical studies adopting this research design. Flege (1999) and Flege, Munro, and MacKay (1995) are of particular interest as they describe results from a sample of 240 Italians who came to Canada as children or young adults and had been in the country for an average of 32 years when studied. Their focus, like that of much of this literature, is on the degree to which the second language is spoken with a foreign accent. In this research the capacity to speak English with a native-like accent declines linearly with age, and no distinct thresholds are apparent in the data. Chiswick and Miller (2008) and Hakuta, Bialystok, and Wiley (2003) are also of interest in that the U.S. census is used to study the self-reported language abilities of a large sample of immigrants. Hakuta et al. (2003) study 2.3 million immigrants of Spanish and Chinese backgrounds who had been in the country at least 10 years. They find a linear decline in language ability and no evidence of discontinuities. Their analysis, however, does not focus specifically on children and is restricted to examining possible discontinuities at ages 15 and 20 years. Chiswick and

Miller (2008) offer a more comprehensive use of the data, but reach broadly similar conclusions. In fact, the reviews by Birdsong (2006, 1999) suggest that the evidence is not clear, in part reflecting methodological differences associated with different outcomes and disaggregation of the data across studies. These studies are often based on relatively small samples of specific groups, often with little control for possible other influences, Hakuta et al. (2003) and Chiswick and Miller (2008) being notable exceptions.

This is a somewhat more ambiguous picture than that painted by Knudsen et al. (2006) and other analysts and advocates of the importance of the early years for public policy, but it should be noted that the focus is on a limited set of outcomes which may be associated in varying degrees with social and economic success in adulthood depending upon the context.

Accordingly, the outcome focused on in this chapter is not on foreign accent or language skills, but one more directly tied to socioeconomic outcomes in adulthood – high school graduation – though perhaps less informative about the specific mechanisms at work. Educational attainment is directly related to future productivity, but in addition to being associated with maturational changes associated with language competencies it also highlights the role of public policy. The structure of the school environment, both as a learning and a social environment, is also likely associated with outcomes. Even if there are no sensitive periods in language acquisition they may be evident in eventual education attainment because the structure of the schooling system may accentuate, rather than alleviate, the challenges migration implies for children. In other words, it may well be that "skill begets skill," but this could reflect institutions that do not offer children more than one opportunity to master skills necessary for further advancement. Since some aspects of learning are progressive, math skills perhaps being the most obvious example, even a temporary event that prevents children from fully mastering the skill at a given age when it is first presented in the curriculum may have long-lasting consequences if the education system does not offer other opportunities to develop the missed foundational skills at a later stage. In particular, early and strongly enforced tracking could have consequences for long-term outcomes even if there are no sensitive periods in the development of cognitive and social competencies.

Data and Measurement

The analysis used the 2006 Canadian census. The census was administered to all households, but a random sample of 20% of the population was required to complete the so-called long form version of the questionnaire, offering detailed socioeconomic information on a very large number of respondents. This was the source of our analysis because it offers information on educational attainment and also on immigration background including country of origin and age at arrival. The potentially very large sample size makes this data one of the more important sources of information on immigrants to Canada, supporting a large number of studies but only a surprising few on child migrants.[1]

The file for analysis was based upon all adults between the ages of 35 and 55 in 2006, a sample of about 2.1 million representing a population of 10.2 million. A number of restrictions are used to ensure accuracy and consistency of the data, but principally to restrict the respondents to those who report they are immigrants arriving in the country before the age of 18. These restrictions lead to a sample size of 111,302.[2]

The analysis focused on age at arrival (AaA), calculated from information on the year the individual recalls arriving in Canada.[3] It should

---

[1] Aydemir, Chen, and Corak (2009a, 2009b) use the 2001 version of these data to study second-generation Canadians, while Ferrer and Riddell (2008) and Schaafsma and Sweetman (2001) use similar public use versions on earlier years to offer evidence of earnings and age at arrival. Ferrer, Green, and Riddell (2006) also examine issues associated with age at arrival from other surveys. See also Ornstein (2006a, 2006b) for the use of the full version of the long-file respondents, though he does not focus on age at arrival. Böhlmark (2009, 2008) and Gonzalez (2003) are examples of studies from other countries using large samples of representative data to study education and earnings outcomes. Both authors find that education outcomes deteriorate for children migrating after the age of 9. Böhlmark (2009, 2008) examines child migrants to Sweden with administrative data and finds that this is the case for GPA and final grades but not necessarily for level of education attainment, while Gonzalez, using U.S. Census data, finds that the negative impact of arrival after about the age of 9 to 12 is strongest for those coming from Mexico. Böhlmark (2009) is a notable reference since particular attention is paid to selection biases that may make causal inference difficult. The author uses sibling differences to identify a causal impact, and finds that the results are in fact similar to cross-sectional regressions controlling for country of origin and parental education.

[2] The details of this sample selection process are described in the discussion paper version available at www.iza.org/profile?key=83.

[3] Strictly speaking this is the age at landed immigrant status, but it is not apparent that respondents answer the question in this way. Further, it should be noted that individuals who recently entered the country as refugees are not included in the analysis. These individuals do not have a value for the year at arrival because they do not have landed immigrant status. This also implies that it is not possible to know whether a given immigrant initially came as a refugee and then subsequently received landed immigrant status or citizenship. For all immigrants who came as refugees, the age at arrival variable in our analysis will in a sense overstate the true age at arrival if the respondents do in fact report on the year landed immigrant status was obtained. This would not capture any time spent in the country prior to becoming a landed immigrant.

be distinguished from a number of concepts used in the second language acquisition literature, which are likely more conceptually relevant measures. The most studied measure, and the one considered the most strongly predictive of second language competencies, is age of acquisition (AoA). This refers to the age at which the individual is immersed in the new language context. AoA may not be the same thing as AaA if, for example, a child arrived in the country during the preschool years and was not exposed to English or French until starting school. Both of these measures are also distinct from age of first exposure (AoE), which indicates when the individual first became exposed to the second language. This could well be before AaA as a result of the language of instruction in formal schooling in the country of origin, visits to other countries, or contact with relatives or other speakers of the second language. AaA will often coincide with AoA but obviously this is not an experience that will characterize all migrants from the many different source countries to Canada, or even within the same source country.[4] Further, there will be a potential bias using the data to uncover a sensitive period to the extent that AaA differs from AoE.

The total sample size consisted of 55,016 men and 56,286 women. On average there are 3,056 observations at each age at arrival for men and 3,127 for women. The analysis was restricted to individuals who arrived before the age of 18 in part to focus on individuals considered children according to the UN Convention on the Rights of the Child, but also because there was a sharp rise in the number of individuals who arrive in the country between the ages of 18 and 20.[5] Though individuals under the age of 21 may be admitted to the country with their parents and considered as children, this increase suggests that this population likely also has a significant number of individuals who arrived as independent migrates.[6]

While roughly 3,000 individuals arrived in the country at each age between newborn and 17, it was also the case that (with the possible

---

[4] See Birdsong (2006, 11–12) for a more detailed discussion; he also offers length of residence (LoR) as another distinct measure.

[5] This is particularly the case at ages 18 and 19 when 4,005 and 4,392 men report arriving in the country, and 4,686 and 5,872 women do so. These numbers fall at age 20 to the range of earlier ages, about 3,000.

[6] This said, it should also be noted that younger children may arrive in the country independently. These individuals may be as young as 16 and 17 who come for short periods to study in Canadian high schools as part of student exchanges. To the extent that they stay in the country or emigrate as adults from their origin country at a later date they may also play a part in influencing the patterns in these data.

exception of the oldest category) the largest fraction of children arrived in the country between the ages of 1 and 5. This raises the possibility that some parents time their migration decision with the welfare of their children in mind. If parents consider possible age at arrival effects on their children's welfare when timing the emigration decision then it is possible that the distribution of unobserved parental characteristics may vary across the age at arrival distribution. Motivated or altruistic parents more inclined to invest effectively in their children may be overrepresented in the early age at arrival groups. Their children will perform better than a randomly selected group of children because of the enriched environment in which they were raised, making comparisons and causal inferences across age at arrival thresholds suspect. At the same time it should also be noted that generally parents do not have complete discretion as to when they will emigrate, the application being subject to administrative rules and delays, and therefore the scope for selection biases of this sort may be constrained.

The information respondents offered on their country of origin was used to classify each origin county into broad categories according to the linguistic distance of the dominant language spoken in the country from English, as well as adding a classification for English-speaking and French-speaking countries. In order to do this the linguistic distance measure developed by Chiswick and Miller (2005) was used, making some minor corrections and adaptations to the Canadian case.

The categorization focused on the dominant language in the country of origin, and it began by creating a correspondence between the language codes in Chiswick and Miller (2005) for the U.S. census to those in the Canadian census. Not all of the languages they used were found in the Canadian census but a correspondence was established by aggregating languages if necessary. This permitted a characterization of all the languages into three categories: low, medium, and high. The low category collected languages farthest from English, having a score lower than two in Chiswick and Miller's terms; the medium category languages stood at a medium distance from English, having a language score equal to two; and the high category referred to languages closest to English, having linguistic scores of more than two.[7]

---

[7] In the process of creating this language to language score mapping, some discrepancies were discovered in Chiswick and Miller's table. For example, Burmese appeared in two separate sections with a different language score assigned to it in each instance. Fortunately, Burmese was not a language that appeared in the Canadian census code set, so this turned out not to be problematic. However, in the case of Thai and Laotian, the discrepancy was

The next step in categorizing the over 100 countries of origin that appear in our data was done using the full sample of immigrants from the census data (not just the immigrant children and young adults, 35 to 55 years old in 2006). If over 75% of the people coming from a particular country spoke a language that fell into one of the five categories – low, medium, high, English, French – then the origin country was assigned that category. Not all individuals in the sample can be categorized with confidence because more than one language was spoken in their country of origin. This ambiguity affected about 10% of our sample, with the result that over 90% of the individuals in the analytical sample were assigned a language category. This led to a smaller sample of 101,884, made up of 50,253 men and 51,631 women, used when linguistic distance formed part of the analysis.

The sample was further subdivided into particular source countries to the extent permitted by sample size. On this basis the English-speaking source regions were the United Kingdom, the United States, and the rest of the world in which English is spoken. Those countries with official languages with a high linguistic similarity to English were also divided into three groups: Italy, Portugal, and the rest of the world. The groups with a low linguistic similarity were Hong Kong, India, and the rest of the world. Two remaining groups included those in which the language of the origin country was French and those speaking languages an intermediate distance from English, referred to as medium.[8]

A summary of the sample sizes and proportions by region of origin classified into these 11 groups is offered in Table 4.1. Immigrants from the United Kingdom represented just over one-fifth of the entire sample, and as a group those from English-speaking countries represented about 40%. Immigrants from countries with a high similarity to English were the next largest group, collectively representing about one-third of the sample. The smallest group were those from French-speaking regions, with just under 3% of the total sample.

---

important. In one instance, Laotian was listed as the primary language having a language score of 1.50, with Thai listed as being in the same group. And, in the second instance, the reverse is listed (Thai being primary and Laotian being in the same group) but with a language score of 2.00. With the language scores being so different, the language group assigned to these languages would change depending on which score is used. To handle this issue, the two languages were considered independent with the primary language having the "correct" score assigned to it. Laotian was given a score of 1.50, putting it in the low category, while Thai was given a score of 2.00, putting it in the medium category.

[8] A detailed listing of the countries that fall into these groups is offered in the appendix to the discussion paper version of the chapter.

Table 4.1. Sample Sizes and Proportions by Regions of Origin Classified According to Linguistic Distance from English and French: Men and Women

	Men		Women	
	Unweighted Sample Size	Percent	Unweighted Sample Size	Percent
English				
Rest of World	5,131	10.2	5,946	11.5
United Kingdom	10,693	21.3	10,916	21.1
United States	3,899	7.8	4,510	8.7
French	1,285	2.6	1,477	2.9
High Similarity to English				
Italy	5,687	11.3	5,518	10.7
Portugal	3,803	7.6	3,866	7.5
Rest of World	7,039	14.0	6,957	13.5
Low Similarity to English				
Hong Kong	1,786	3.6	1,774	3.4
India	2,004	4.0	1,973	3.8
Rest of World	4,841	9.6	4,510	8.7
Medium Similarity to English	4,085	8.1	4,184	8.1
Total	50,253	100	51,631	100

Overall Descriptive Results and Some Cautions

The weighted averages of individuals not having a high school diploma for each age at arrival were calculated using these data, and are offered in Figure 4.1 along with a local polynomial smooth of the data.[9] This is the major descriptive finding motivating more in-depth analysis. There is a clear and distinct variation in the chances of high school graduation. At the broadest level this is in accord with the hypothesis of a sensitive period: There are no changes in the proportion of high school dropouts during the earliest years, then a distinct change in the slope with the proportion increasing practically linearly with each additional year beyond age 7 or 8. At age 8 or younger, 14.7% of men on average did not obtain a high school diploma, but after that the number grew to 19.7%. For women these averages were 11.3% and 18.2% respectively. A linear least squares regression model fit to these data in a way that permits a break in the

[9] The smooth is meant only as a descriptive device to aid visualization of the patterns in the data. It is not the correct tool to identify a discrete change in these patterns and is used only to highlight a possible turning point worthy of more detailed analysis.

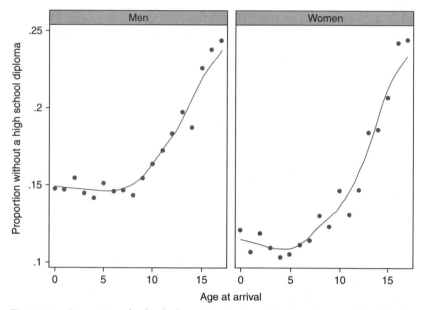

Figure 4.1. Proportion of individuals arriving in Canada before the age of 18 without a high school diploma in adulthood: By age at arrival and gender.

Note: Derivation by author from Statistics Canada, Census 2006 using analytical files described in the text. Each data point represents the proportion of individuals by age at arrival without a high school diploma who were 35 to 55 years of age in 2006. The continuous line is an estimated local polynomial smooth based upon weighted data calculated using a linear smooth and an epanechnikov kernel.

constant and slope of the relationship at the turning points of the local polynomial smooth in Figure 4.1 suggests that the chances of being a high school dropout rise by 1.2 percentage points for every year that a boy arrives in the country after age 8 and by 1.5 percentage points for every year a girl arrives after age 7.[10]

The results in Figure 4.1 also support the possibility of other breaks, particularly after age 14 for men. This is likely associated with the institutional structure of the Canadian education system, which at the time appropriate for the sample of individuals under study had a minimum school leaving age of 16. If a boy arrived in the country at the age of 15 or older he was much more likely to not obtain a high school diploma than if he had

---

[10] These weighted regressions explain 97% of the total variation in the data for men, and 95.1% for women. Using a turning point of age 8 for men also leads to the highest R-squared among all possible thresholds between ages 5 and 12. For women this happens at age 10.

arrived at age 13 or 14. A similar jump in the chances of being a high school dropout also occurred for girls of the same age, but in addition there was a distinct increase after age 12.

There are at least three cautionary issues that need to be addressed before these findings can be causally related to sensitive periods in language acquisition. The first is the issue of self-selection that has already been noted. If, in some sense, unobserved family characteristics vary across the age at arrival distribution in a way that implies children who arrive earlier are raised in a family environment more favorable to their long-term success, then the results in Figure 4.1 overstate the relative success rates during the early years compared to a randomly selected group of individuals. The sharp distinction at the age of 7 or 8 may not be as clear, and the overall level of dropping out not as low, depending upon how these unobserved influences vary over the age distribution during these earlier years. A similar reasoning but opposite in direction applies to the findings at older ages.

Second, there could very well be heterogeneity along other dimensions such as country of origin. Immigrants to Canada come from a wide range of countries, and therefore their previous exposure to English and French varies significantly. It could be that the similarity of the language in the country of origin to English or French – and hence the difficulties that must be overcome in learning the new home country's languages – also varies across the distribution of age at arrival. If those arriving at younger ages are disproportionately from English- or French-speaking countries, or countries with a language close to English or French so that it is easier to learn one of Canada's official languages, then a similar bias could result.

Finally, and related to both of these factors, prior exposure to one of the official languages, even if the source country is not an English- or French-speaking country, could vary. As mentioned, age at arrival should not necessarily be equated with age of acquisition or age of first exposure, which could depend on country of origin, formal schooling in the source country context, parental investment, or exposure to relatives or visits to English- or French-speaking countries. If those who arrive at a young age are more likely to have been exposed to one of the official languages before arriving to Canada then their outcomes would be more favorable than otherwise and bias the findings toward the type of nonlinear pattern displayed in Figure 4.1. This could very well be the case if some parents are preparing their children for migration to the country, or chose the country of destination according to where they expect their children will be more likely to succeed.

Results by Country and Language of Origin

These cautions are addressed by examining the patterns in high school graduation by language of origin and mother tongue. The sample frequencies by age at arrival for the 11 groups of origin countries according to their linguistic distance from English are displayed in Figure 4.2. This figure offers the information for men only, but there were no notable differences in the patterns for women. These raw sample sizes make clear, for example, that the patterns in the overall data – namely a greater tendency for children to arrive between the ages of 1 to 5 – are due in large measure to immigrants from just two regions: the United Kingdom and countries linguistically close to English (particularly countries other than Portugal and Italy). The suggestion is that the overall group of individuals who arrived in the country at a particularly young age is disproportionately from English-speaking countries and countries where the linguistic challenge in learning English is lowest. As such if they are less likely to drop out of high school because they have no or lower linguistic challenges in learning the dominant language, they will contribute to an overstatement of the educational attainment – relative to a randomly chosen child of the same age – for the group of children actually observed in the sample. This selection effect combined with an opposite tendency at the other end of the age at arrival distribution, namely an overrepresentation of children from countries with languages that are not similar to English, could produce the pattern depicted in Figure 4.1. Children arriving in the country at the oldest ages, however, were somewhat more representative of the entire population of children. It is the case that those from countries with languages least like English have an overall tendency to arrive at a later age, but this was also the case for children arriving from countries other than the United Kingdom or the United States in which the language spoken is English.

There are perhaps three messages to glean from this information. First, all other things being equal, we could expect any patterns in the likelihood of being a high school dropout across age at arrival to be muted for those from English-speaking countries of origin, and if present due to factors other than language or to more subtle language effects associated for example with accent.

Second, the causal role of language should be clearest for countries with populations speaking languages at the greatest distance from English, subject to some control being made for nonlanguage effects. It should also be clearest for individuals who came from Portugal (and possibly Italy) as the frequency distribution does not appear to vary by age at arrival and

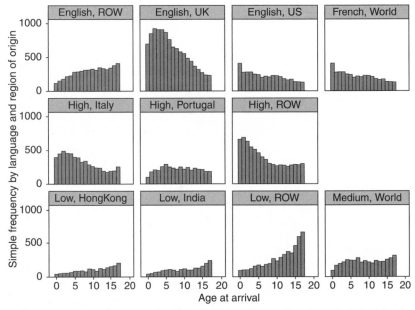

Figure 4.2. Sample frequency distribution by language and region of origin: Men by age at arrival.

Note: Derivation by author from Statistics Canada, Census 2006 using analytical files described in the text.

hence the selection problem is likely to be less of an issue. The best comparison group by which to judge the causal impact of age at arrival and to net out these other effects is most likely immigrants from English-speaking countries other than the United Kingdom or the United States. The reason for this is that the pattern in the frequency distribution by age at arrival is roughly similar for these countries as it is for countries that are least like English, those with a low linguistic distance score.

Third, the possible selection bias needs to be addressed by controlling for variations in the degree of parental investments in children across the age at arrival distribution. One way to do this with the available data is to attempt to measure age of first exposure. The Canadian census contains a number of indicators of language ability. The closest measure that can possibly speak to the age of first exposure is the so-called mother tongue. Question 16 of the census asks: "What is the language this person first learned at home in childhood and still understands?" The possible responses are: English, French, and Other. Figure 4.3 graphs for men and, for each of the 11 source regions, the proportion by age at arrival answering "Other." The fraction of

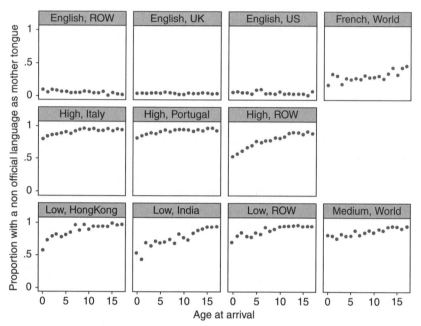

Figure 4.3. Proportion with a language other than English or French as a mother tongue: Men by age at arrival.

Note: Derivation by author from Statistics Canada, Census 2006 using analytical files described in the text.

individuals whose first language was not one of the two official languages is, as might be expected, low among those originally from English-speaking regions, and relatively high among non-English-speaking regions. But in some of these later cases it also varies systematically by age at arrival, and somewhat more so for men. In particular, 74.7% of men and 80.2% of women from countries (other than Italy and Portugal) with populations speaking languages with a high similarity to English have a language other than English or French as their mother tongue. But only 67.4% of men who arrived at the age of 8 or younger do so compared to 87.8% of those who arrived after 8 years of age. For women these proportions are 74.9% and 89.4%.

Just as important, the figures show a systematic rise in the proportion with a non-official language as a mother tongue for countries with populations whose main languages have the lowest similarity to English. This is particularly so for men. The proportion of those with a non-official mother tongue increases on average by more than one percentage point for each additional year for those from French-speaking countries, those with a high linguistic score (other than Italy and Portugal), Hong Kong, India, and for men from countries with low and medium linguistic scores. There is only a very shallow positive gradient for men and women from Italy and Portugal.[11]

These patterns suggest that the linguistic challenges that a cohort of young immigrants faces varies not just according to their region of origin, but also within region of origin. More important, it does so in a way that suggests those arriving at younger ages will likely find it easier to learn English because it was more likely to be the language they first learned.

At the same time it should be noted that to some degree these patterns may overstate the potential for this selection problem. The mother tongue question refers to the language first learned and still understood, not simply to the language first learned. So some fraction of individuals may have had a first exposure in a non-official language, subsequently lost the ability to understand, and answered the census question by responding accordingly. The outcomes for those from Italy and Portugal are in this sense likely to be among the groups least affected by a selection problem, as the gradient between age at arrival and mother tongue being a non-official language is the flattest, and will therefore likely be even flatter if the question truly captured first exposure. In other cases it will be important to control for mother tongue in the hope of capturing a more accurate estimate of the impact of age at arrival on schooling success.

Table 4.2 offers estimates from a series of least squares models that attempt to address these issues by controlling for mother tongue and region of origin. The results presented are for the choice of threshold maximizing the adjusted R-squared among all possible thresholds from age at arrival of 5 to 12. The preferred model is the last one presented for each gender, indicating that the best-fitting model uses a threshold of age 8. For men this is not a significant change from what visual inspection of Figure 4.1 would suggest. For women a threshold at age 10 maximizes the adjusted

---

[11] The weighted least squares estimates of the gradient between the proportion with a non-official language as mother tongue and age at arrival for each of the source regions are:

	English ROW	UK	US	French	Italy	Portugal	High ROW	Hong Kong	India	Low ROW	Medium
Men	−0.003	−0.000	−0.001	0.011	0.008	0.006	0.022	0.014	0.023	0.010	0.011
Women	−0.003	−0.000	−0.002	0.015	0.006	0.005	0.016	0.010	0.018	0.006	0.008

Boldface indicates statistical significance with a marginal significance level of at least 0.05, using robust estimates of the standard errors. The relatively sharp gradients for those from Hong Kong and India may reflect not only the English-related history of these regions, but also the emigration of ex-patriots, ethnicity not being controlled for in these regressions.

Table 4.2. Least Squares Regression Results for Most Likely Thresholds of Age at Arrival Impacts on Not Having Graduated from High School: Men and Women

	Men			Women		
	T = 7	T = 7	T = 8	T = 10	T = 10	T = 8
Age at arrival	0.000105	−0.00183	−0.000805	0.00223	0.00124	−0.000532
T	−0.0138	−0.00805	0.00250	−0.0123	−0.0100	−0.0107
T x Age at arrival	0.0112	0.0106	0.0127	0.0168	0.0152	0.0163
Mother tongue		0.112	0.143		0.112	0.220
Region of origin	none	none	eleven	none	none	eleven
Constant	0.150	0.0930	0.0592	0.131	0.0725	0.0218
R-squared adjusted	0.0980	0.284	0.790	0.168	0.358	0.733
F-test – p value	0.0010	0.000	0.000	0.000	0.000	0.000

Note: Derivation by author from Statistics Canada, Census 2006 using analytical files described in the text.

T refers to the threshold used in the estimation of a piecewise linear least squares model. Results presented are those for models with highest adjusted R-squared among all possible thresholds from 5 to 12 years. Sample size is 198 observations on weighted averages by age at arrival from 0 to 17 for each gender, representing 50,253 men and 51,631 women. All regressions use analytical weights. Standard errors are robust to heteroscedasticity, with shading indicating the marginal significance level: **less than or equal to 0.05**; greater than 0.05 and less than or equal to 0.10; greater than 0.10. Region of origin controls refer to indicator variables for the 11 regions categorized by linguistic distance from English and French as described in the text, with the omitted category for the sake of the regression analysis being the group of English-speaking countries other than the United Kingdom or the United States. P value for the F-test refers to the null hypothesis that all regressors except the constant equal zero.

R-squared when mother tongue is controlled for as well as when it is not. But the suggestion in the last column of the table, which also controls for region of origin, suggests this is due to compositional changes in the underlying sample.

These results continue to hold when a more detailed analysis is undertaken by region of origin. Selections of the descriptive results are presented in Figures 4.4 through 4.6 for men. And a summary of the regression results is offered in Table 4.3 for men and Table 4.4 for women. These tables report the coefficients of the threshold maximizing the R-squared after searching over all possible thresholds from 5 to 12 years of age. The regressions also control for mother tongue.

For men born in the United Kingdom, the United States, and other countries in which English is the language spoken, there is at best a weak relationship between age at arrival and educational attainment. For those from countries other than the United Kingdom or the United States, the break point occurs at age 11, with the chances of not obtaining a high school diploma increasing discretely by about four percentage points but not changing any further with each subsequent year. The model has

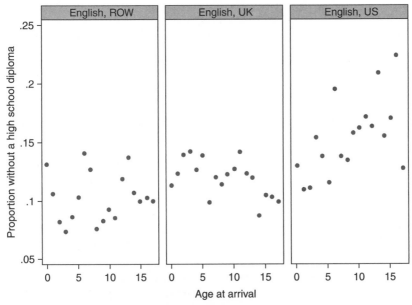

Figure 4.4. Proportion of individuals without a high school diploma in adulthood: Men from English-speaking countries, by age at arrival.

relatively low explanatory power. The preferred results for the United Kingdom have higher explanatory power, but suggest that the rate of not obtaining high school credentials is actually higher for those arriving at younger ages. For men from the United States, the preferred model does not involve a threshold, but rather a linear increase in the chances of dropping out. For women from the United States there is a break, but it occurs very early, at age 5. All this said, the overall chances of not having a high school diploma are relatively low, never over 15% (with the major exception being men who came to Canada from the United States after the age of 10).

This contrasts sharply with the results for those from countries with populations who do not speak English highlighted in the next panels of the tables and for men in the remaining figures. Considering regions with populations speaking languages with a high similarity to English suggests a break point at age 5 or 6, the exception being Italy where it is 9 for men and 11 for women. The least squares models fit the data very tightly, explaining up to 97% of the variation in the Italian and Portuguese data and more than 70% for the remaining countries. In large measure it is the data from this group of countries that drives the overall results depicted in Figure 4.1.

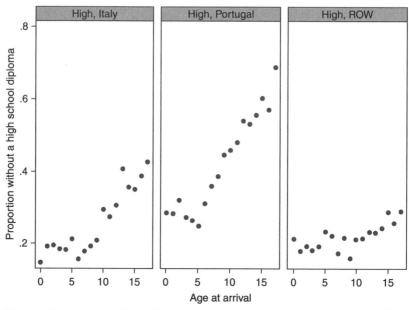

Figure 4.5. Proportion of individuals arriving in Canada before the age of 18 without a high school diploma in adulthood: Men from countries with populations speaking languages with a high resemblance to English, by age at arrival.

As Figure 4.5 illustrates, the high school dropout rates are particularly high for those from Portugal, reaching over 60% for those who arrived after the age of 15. This high overall level is well-known, as described by Nunes (2008), and studied in more detail in Ornstein (2006a, 2006b, 2006c). This is a community that began its migration to Canada in the 1950s and continued migrating to Canada into the 1990s. Nunes notes that these migrants were predominantly from poor, rural regions of Portugal with relatively very low levels of education. In this sense they are a self-selected group, and the very low overall rate of attaining high school relative to other immigrant groups is not a new finding. What is new and particularly relevant in the current context is that this pattern varies markedly according to age at arrival, being two to three times lower for those who arrived as preschoolers compared to those who arrived as adolescents. A roughly similar story can be told for those from Italy.

Even if the levels of high school graduation are lower, the pattern across age at arrival is similar for countries whose predominant languages have the least resemblance to English. With the single exception of women from

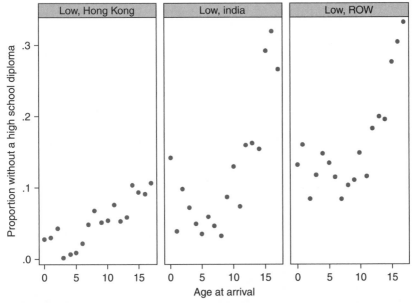

Figure 4.6. Proportion of individuals arriving in Canada before the age of 18 without a high school diploma in adulthood: Men from countries with populations speaking languages with a low resemblance to English or French, by age at arrival.

countries other than Hong Kong or India, the threshold that maximizes the R-squared occurs at ages 9 or younger, with values always higher than 0.75 and as high as 0.98.

Conclusion

This analysis of the education outcomes of a large sample of adults who came to Canada as child migrants suggests the following three conclusions. First, there is a distinct pattern in the chances of not obtaining a high school diploma that varies with age at arrival in a way consistent with a sensitive period in learning a second language. The chances of not being a high school graduate do not vary with age at arrival for those who came to the country before 9 years of age, but increase by over a percentage point for every year past this age. There are also discrete increases in this risk at around the age of 14 or 15 which likely reflect the fact that during the relevant period the legal school leaving age was 16 years old, but also a discrete increase for women at after 12 years of age. These results are robust to controls for the possibility that first exposure to English or French occurred before migration.

Table 4.3. Least Squares Regression Results for Most Likely Thresholds of Age at Arrival Effects on not Obtaining a High School Diploma: Men by Origin Region According to Linguistic Distance from English

	Turning point with maximum R-Squared (T)	Age at Arrival	T	T × Age at Arrival	R-squared	P value for F-test of all regressors equal to zero
English						
Rest of World	11	−0.00215	**0.0427**	−0.00546	0.279	0.0705
United Kingdom	5	0.00417	−0.0209	**−0.00539**	0.498	0.0389
United States	None	**0.00353**			0.401	0.0193
High Similarity to English						
Italy	9	**−0.0111**	**0.0799**	0.0302	0.951	0.000
Portugal	6	0.00280	**0.0644**	0.0256	0.969	0.000
Rest of World	6	0.0140	**−0.0522**	0.000116	0.743	0.0001
Low Similarity to English						
Hong Kong	5	**−0.00766**	0.0193	0.0136	0.868	0.000
India	7	−0.0160	−0.0121	0.0377	0.892	0.000
Rest of World	7	0.00826	−0.0490	0.0225	0.962	0.000
Medium Similarity to English	None	0.00466	**0.120**	−0.00782	0.532	0.0005
French	6	−0.00387			0.745	0.0003

Note: Derivation by author from Statistics Canada, Census 2006 using analytical files described in the text.

T refers to the threshold used in the estimation of a piecewise linear least squares model. Results presented are those for models with highest R-squared among all possible thresholds from 5 to 12 years. Sample size for each line is 18 observations on weighted average attainment by age at arrival from 0 to 17. All models include a constant term and a control for the proportion of each age group not having English or French as a mother tongue. All regressions use analytical weights. Standard errors are robust to heteroscedasticity, with shading indicating the marginal significance level: less than or equal to 0.05; greater than 0.05 and less than or equal to 0.10; greater than 0.10. P value for the F-test refers to the null hypothesis that all regressors except the constant equal zero.

Table 4.4. Least Squares Regression Results for Most Likely Thresholds of Age at Arrival Effects on not Obtaining a High School Diploma: Women by Origin Region According to Linguistic Distance from English

	Turning point with maximum R-Squared (T)	Age at Arrival	T	T×Age at Arrival	R-squared	P value for F-test of all regressors equal to zero
English						
Rest of World	11	0.000573	−0.0259	0.0107	0.396	0.0051
United Kingdom	8	**−0.00296**	0.0158	0.000655	0.760	0.000
United States	5	−0.00573	0.0120	**0.0135**	0.662	0.0001
High Similarity to English						
Italy	11	0.00672	0.0369	**0.0399**	0.976	0.000
Portugal	5	0.00317	−0.00469	**0.0309**	0.966	0.000
Rest of World	6	−0.00191	0.0482	0.00577	0.717	0.0001
Low Similarity to English						
Hong Kong	9	**−0.00744**	**−0.0502**	**0.0188**	0.752	0.000
India	8	−0.00292	−0.0224	**0.0371**	0.952	0.000
Rest of World	11	0.00146	**0.0349**	**0.0356**	0.987	0.000
Medium Similarity to English	5	**0.00401**	−0.0448	**0.00428**	0.878	0.000
French	12	−0.00150	0.0694	−0.0143	0.495	0.0147

Note: Derivation by author from Statistics Canada, Census 2006 using analytical files described in the text.
T refers to the threshold used in the estimation of a piecewise linear least squares model. Results presented are those for models with highest R-squared among all possible thresholds from 5 to 12 years. Sample size for each line is 18 observations on weighted average attainment by age at arrival from 0 to 17. All models include a constant term and a control for the proportion of each age group not having English or French as a mother tongue. All regressions use analytical weights. Standard errors are robust to heteroscedasticity, with shading indicating the marginal significance level: less than or equal to 0.05; greater than 0.05 and less than or equal to 0.10; greater than 0.10. P value for the F-test refers to the null hypothesis that all regressors except the constant equal zero.

Second, these patterns have something to do with the challenges children face in learning a second language as they vary in a predictable way according to the linguistic distance of the language in the country of origin from English. There is no discernable pattern between high school graduation and age at arrival for those who came to Canada from English- or French-speaking countries. Though the overall levels in high school graduation vary significantly across other origin countries, the nature of the pattern is the same: no change in the early years, followed by a distinct change in slope. The threshold for this change corresponds to the first years of primary school, being reasonably estimated to be as young as age 5 for some regions and likely no older than age 9 in all the others.

Third, the underlying reasons for these findings require further study. The research had the benefit of using a large and diverse sample of immigrants and controlled for some of the more important aspects of the underlying heterogeneity. The focus was on education outcomes because of the policy relevance of the issue, but the patterns uncovered are distinct and robust in a way that cannot be described of previous research that has focused specifically on language proficiency. More detailed analysis is necessary to discern the degree to which the findings are due to maturational changes in the cognitive capacities of children to learn a second language, sensitive periods in their social development, or to institutional features of the education system that are not sufficiently attuned to the needs and challenges of children in the senior primary or young adolescent age groups.

Future research, particularly in a comparative context, would be helpful to discern the relative roles of these factors, particularly that of institutional design. It may well be that education systems that track students into different streams at a very early age may reinforce or aggravate preexisting risks associated with cognitive and social integration. This would be a particularly relevant policy issue to focus on, and underscores the need to appreciate the distinct challenges confronting child migrants.

Author's Note

Earlier versions of this chapter were presented to a research seminar at Statistics Canada in October 2009, the Research Seminar on Child Migration in Comparative Perspective supported by the Princeton Institute for International and Regional Studies at Princeton University in August 2009, and the Jacobs Foundation Conference 2009 on Capitalizing on Migration, The Potential of Immigrant Youth held at Schloss Marbach,

Germany in April 2009. The comments and feedback of participants at these seminars, and also the detailed comments by Ann Masten, Karmela Liebkind, and Marta Tienda, are acknowledged with thanks, as is the support of the Jacobs Foundation. The research assistance of Ive Delahousse, who was responsible for the data development, is also acknowledged with appreciation. A more detailed version with a supplementary appendix is available as an IZA Discussion Paper at http://www.iza.org/profile?key=83. This chapter is adapted from an abridged working paper version published as Miles Corak (2011), "Age at Immigration and the Education Outcomes of Children." Statistics Canada, Analytical Studies Research Paper Series, Catalogue number 11F0019 Issue 20113, and used with permission.

REFERENCES

Aydemir, A., Chen, W., & Corak, M. (2009a). Intergenerational earnings mobility among the children of Canadian immigrants. *Review of Economics and Statistics*, *91*(2), 377–97.
    (2009b). Intergenerational education mobility among the children of Canadian immigrants. IZA Discussion Paper No. 3759.
Birdsong, D. (1999). Introduction: Whys and why nots of the critical period hypothesis for second language acquisition. In D. Birdsong (Ed.), *Second language acquisition and the critical period hypothesis* (pp. 1–22). Hillsdale NJ: Lawrence Erlbaum Associates.
    (2006). Age and second language acquisition and processing: A selective overview. *Language Learning*, *56*, 9–49.
Böhlmark, A. (2008). Age at immigration and school performance: A siblings analysis using Swedish register data. *Labour Economics*, *15*, 1366–87.
    (2009). Integration of childhood immigrants in the short and long run-Swedish evidence. *International Migration Review*, *43*(2), 387–409.
Chiswick, B. R., & Miller, P. W. (2005). Linguistic distance: A quantitative measure of the distance between English and other languages. *Journal of Multilingual and Multicultural Development*, *26*(1), 1–16.
    (2008). A test of the critical period hypothesis for language learning. *Journal of Multilingual and Multicultural Development*, *29*(1), 16–29.
Corak, M. (2011). Age at immigration and the education outcomes of children. *Statistics Canada*, Analytical Studies Research Paper Series, Catalogue number 11F0019, Issue 2011336.
Ferrer, A., Green, D. A., & Riddell, W. C. (2006). The effect of literacy on immigrant earnings. *Journal of Human Resources*, *41*(2), 380–410.
Ferrer, A., & Riddell, W. C. (2008). Education, credentials, and immigrant earnings. *Canadian Journal of Economics*, *41*(1), 186–216.
Flege, J. E. (1999). Age of learning and second language speech. In D. Birdsong (Ed.), *Second language acquisition and the critical period hypothesis* (pp. 101–32). Hillsdale NJ: Lawrence Erlbaum Associates.

Flege, J. E., Munro, M. J., & MacKay, I. R. A. (1995). Factors affecting the strength of perceived foreign accent in a second language. *Journal of the Acoustical Society of America, 97*(5), 3125–34.

Gonzalez, A. (2003). The education and wages of immigrant children: The impact of age at arrival. *Economics of Education Review, 22,* 203–12.

Hakuta, K., Bialystok, E., & Wiley, E. (2003). A test of the critical period hypothesis for second-language acquisition. *Psychological Science, 14*(1), 31–8.

Johnson, J. S., & Newport, E. L. (1989). Critical period effects in second language learning: The influence of maturational state on the acquisition of English as a second language. *Cognitive Psychology, 21,* 60–99.

Knudsen, E. I., Heckman, J. J., Cameron, J. L., & Shonkoff, J. P. (2006). Economic, neurobiological, and behavioural perspectives on building America's future workforce. *Proceedings of the National Academy of Sciences, 103*(27), 10155–62.

Nunes, F. (2008). Striking a balance in Canada's diversity dialogue: The case of the Portuguese-Canadian community. *Canadian Diversity, 6*(2), 121–6.

Ornstein, M. (2006a). *Ethno-racial groups in Montreal and Vancouver, 1971–2001: A demographic and socio-economic profile.* York University, Institute for Social Research.

(2006b). *Ethno-racial groups in Toronto, 1971–2001: A demographic and socio-economic profile.* York University, Institute for Social Research.

(2006c). Moving the watermill: Collectively addressing the needs of Luso-Canadian at-risk youth. Paper presented to a meeting with the Chief Justice of Ontario and the Portuguese-Canadian National Congress. University of Toronto.

Schaafsma, J., & Sweetman, A. (2001). Immigrant earnings: Age at immigration matters. *Canadian Journal of Economics, 34*(4), 1066–99.

Thomas, M. S. C., & Johnson, M. H. (2008). New advances in understanding sensitive periods in brain development. *Current Directions in Psychological Science, 17*(1), 1–5.

Part 2

WHO SUCCEEDS AND WHY?

Developmental, Social-Psychological,
and Sociocultural Perspectives

5 Positive Immigrant Youth Adaptation in Context

Developmental, Acculturation, and Social-Psychological Perspectives

Frosso Motti-Stefanidi, John Berry, Xenia Chryssochoou, David Lackland Sam, and Jean Phinney

Immigration is one of the defining issues of the 21st century. It is now an essential, inevitable and potentially beneficial component of the economic and social life of every country and region. The question is no longer whether to have migration, but rather how to manage immigration effectively so as to enhance its positive and reduce its negative impacts. Well-informed choices by migrants, governments, home and host communities, civil societies, and the private sector can help realize the positive potential of immigration in social, economic and political terms. (Brunson McKinley, Director General, International Organization for Migration, 2007)

Introduction

Staggering numbers of people from across the globe have left their home countries to settle in nations foreign to them. Many of these immigrants have a strong commitment to putting down roots in their new countries, as evidenced by the fact that they stay throughout their lives and over generations (see chapter by Hernandez, this volume). The presence of immigrants presents opportunities and challenges for receiving societies. To capitalize on migration, receiving societies must ensure the successful integration and full realization of the immigrants' potential (Berry, 2006). Thus, it is crucial that receiving societies invest in the adaptation and well-being of immigrant youth.

The quality of adaptation among immigrant youth can be judged on the basis of success in developmental and acculturative tasks. Like all children, immigrant children face normative developmental challenges (Masten, Burt, & Coatsworth, 2006), but they also face the acculturative challenges that stem from the need to adapt to the realities of at least two cultures

(Phinney et al., 2001). Successful adaptation with respect to both kinds of challenges can be a harbinger of future adaptation, indicating prospects for positive long-term outcomes of immigrant youth and their receiving societies. Concomitantly, failure to adapt may have negative, and possibly cascading, consequences for the future success of individuals and societies (Masten et al., 2005; Masten & Cicchetti, 2010).

To explain individual and group differences in the quality of adaptation among immigrant youth, it is important to acknowledge that immigrant children, like all children, are developing organisms (Sam, 2006) and that development always emerges from interactions of individuals with their contexts (Boyce et al., 1998). Cognitive, affective, and social developmental processes, as well as normative developmental contexts, such as family, school, and peer groups, all play a role in adaptation and development. In addition, however, immigrant youth face unique ecological circumstances not shared by nonimmigrant children. Immigrant status and culture, and related social variables such as discrimination, are of central importance in explaining individual differences in adaptation (Garcia Coll et al., 1996; see chapters by Liebkind, Jasinskaja-Lahti, & Mähönen, this volume; also Sirin & Gupta, this volume).

In psychology, the adaptation of immigrant youth has been examined from three distinct, though interrelated, perspectives within the subdisciplines of developmental psychology, acculturation psychology, and social psychology. Developmental researchers emphasize the role of the proximal environment (Bronfenbrenner & Morris, 2006), including the family, peer groups, and schools, in which children's lives are embedded. Acculturation researchers stress the influence of culture, particularly the context of the immigrants' home culture and the receiving society's culture (Berry et al., 2006). Social psychologists often focus on the social processes that characterize the new societal and intergroup context, including such contextual phenomena as discrimination (see chapter by Liebkind et al., this volume; Verkuyten, 2005, also this volume). Each subdiscipline offers a unique contribution to the study of immigrant youth adaptation. However, we believe that an integrative approach blending concepts, methods, and evidence from these three perspectives will yield a more informative understanding of who succeeds among immigrant youth and why.

The primary goal of this chapter is to propose such an integrative framework encompassing developmental, acculturation, and social-psychological approaches to the study of individual differences in immigrant youth adaptation. The chapter consists of three main sections. In the first section, we delineate the major principles and constructs pertinent to research on immigrant youth from these three perspectives. In the second section, we discuss the definition of successful adaptation in immigrant youth, as well as key individual and contextual factors and processes that promote or hinder adaptation. In the third section, we present the integrative model, which consists of three levels of analysis ranging from the individual to the societal, and discuss its implications.

In keeping with McLoyd's (2006) distinction between the conceptual and ideological perspectives on issues of race, ethnicity, and culture, we emphasize that the integrative model we propose reflects a conceptual (rather than ideological) approach to the issue. Nonetheless, the chapter also reflects three fundamental beliefs shared by the authors about adaptation in the context of immigration in general and with respect to immigrant youth adaptation in particular. First, we believe that the adaptation of immigrant children needs to be examined in its own right and not always in comparison to the mainstream standard, which often leads to the conclusion that immigrant youth suffer from either a genetic or cultural inferiority. Second, we believe that even though our emphasis is on immigrant youth adaptation, native youth also must adapt to the presence of immigrants in the country and to a multicultural reality. Intercultural contact changes immigrants and it also changes natives, although typically to a lesser degree, and brings about the pressing need for mutual accommodation (Berry, 2006). And finally, in keeping with the suggestions of the European Union's Commission of the European Communities (2003), we assume that in order to promote the adaptation of immigrants, it is important to acknowledge that all peoples living in a country should be allowed to maintain their heritage cultures and that any barriers to full economic, social, cultural, and political participation in society should be eliminated.

Core Principles of Three Perspectives on Immigrant Youth Adaptation

A Developmental Perspective
To explain individual differences in immigrant youth adaptation, it is important to use a developmental lens since immigrant children are developing organisms. In developmental psychology, development often is discussed in terms of systematic and successive changes in the structure, organization, and functioning of children's biological, emotional, cognitive, and behavioral systems, with increasing complexity, differentiation and integration within and across these systems generally moving the organism in the direction of increasing adaptability (Masten, 2006;

Sroufe et al., 2005). Development arises from many interactions within individuals (among genetic and hormonal systems, personality, and cognition) and among individuals and the contexts (e.g., family, school, neighborhood) in which their lives are embedded (Bronfenbrenner & Morris, 2006; Gotlieb, Wahlsten, & Lickliter, 2006; Lerner, 2006). Furthermore, it is argued that all levels of organization within the ecology of human development, ranging from genes and cells, to individual mental and behavioral functioning, to school and family contexts, and ultimately to society and culture, are interconnected, mutually influencing each other.

Developmental changes have a significant impact on the way children attribute meaning to reality (Magnusson & Stattin, 2006) and in the way they act on and interact with their environment (Bronfenbrenner & Morris, 2006). For example, around 6 years of age children acquire the basic cognitive skills that allow them to perceive discrimination within given situations, but not until adolescence, after having acquired more advanced cognitive skills, can they identify discrimination at the societal, institutional, and systemic levels (Brown & Bigler, 2005).

Changes are also observed in the developmental tasks and issues (e.g., school achievement, rule abiding behavior, getting along with peers, identity formation) characteristic of different periods in an individual's life (Masten et al., 2006; McCormick, Kuo, & Masten, 2011). Individuals are expected to engage and become competent in age-appropriate developmental tasks that reflect psychosocial milestones of development. Multiple stakeholders, including parents, teachers, other society members, and young people themselves, often consider the quality of adaptation with respect to these developmental tasks an index for how well development is proceeding and how it will proceed in the future. However, in the case of immigrant youth, family and teachers may have conflicting developmental expectations rendering adaptation a more challenging task for them.

Furthermore, developmental changes also occur in the contexts in which children spend their time and with whom and how they spend it. Such changes may present new opportunities and challenges for their adaptation. For example, in many societies, young children spend much of their time with families, whereas adolescents spend much more time with friends (Masten et al., 2006). Friends who support each other in fulfilling their academic obligations have a beneficiary effect on immigrant students' academic achievement (Fuligni, 1997), whereas spending unsupervised time with peers is associated with risky behavior and lower academic performance in Mexican adolescents (Updegraff et al., 2006).

The most influential description of human development nested in context is Bronfenbrenner's bioecological model of human development (Bronfenbrenner & Morris, 2006). According to this model, children's lives are embedded in hierarchically nested, multidimensional, continuously unfolding, and changing contexts. Bronfenbrenner and Morris (2006) described four hierarchically nested levels of environmental influence. The *microsystem* involves children's interaction with the persons, objects, and symbols in their immediate environment, such as the family and the school. The *mesosystem* involves the interactions between the different microsystems in children's lives. The *exosystem* refers to environmental influences that do not directly involve children, but may impact their development. The *macrosystem* refers to the broader and more distal social and historical context, involving societal, cultural, and institutional-level influences. The influence of the distal context on adaptation is considered to be indirect, filtering through the proximal environment (Boyce et al., 1998; Magnusson & Stattin, 2006).

Even though developmental theorists have increasingly called attention to the importance of the distal sociocultural environment, they place special emphasis in their studies on the interpersonal, relational dimension of the proximal contexts. Human development is seen as the result of interactions that must take place on a fairly regular basis and over an extended period of time between an active and evolving human organism and the persons in his or her immediate environment. These proximal processes are considered the "primary engines of development" (Bronfenbrenner & Morris, 2006).

Children are not passive receivers of experience and, therefore, contexts are not the sole influence on their adaptation. Instead, they exert their human agency and thus influence the course of their own development within the opportunities and constraints of historical and social circumstances (Bronfenbrenner & Morris, 2006). Human agency is first reflected in their self-initiated efforts at interpreting, evaluating, and making sense of their social environment and experience (Kuczynski & Navara, 2006). In that vein, a distinction has been drawn between the actual, objective environment and the perceived environment (Magnusson & Stattin, 2006). Children's subjective experience and unique perception of the world may actually shape their effective experience of the environment and are, therefore, most likely to affect the quality of their adaptation (Boyce et al., 1998). Furthermore, individual differences in children's personalities significantly contribute to shaping their social environment. For example, as their ability to self-regulate increases, their personalities shape their choices about the activities they become involved in and the people they associate with (Caspi & Shiner, 2006).

Finally, to understand intra-individual change in the patterns of immigrant youths' adaptation, it is important to take into account that the developmental system is characterized by the potential for change in response to experience, that is, by plasticity. The plasticity of the developmental system allows for the promotion of positive youth development through the alignment of strengths of individuals and contexts (Lerner, 2006; also see chapter by Lerner, this volume).

Immigrant youth are developing organisms, a fact that has significant implications when trying to explain individual differences in their adaptation. However, immigrant youth live with and between at least two cultural worlds. The same contexts that propel their development are also the arena where their acculturation takes place.

An Acculturation Perspective

Acculturation refers to the process of cultural and psychological change that takes place as a result of contact between cultural groups and their individual members (Redfield, Linton, & Herskovits, 1936). These changes continue after initial contact in culturally plural societies, where ethnocultural communities maintain features of their heritage cultures and where they interact with others in the larger society.

Acculturation takes place in various ways; it is a multidimensional process. The adaptations that groups and individuals make to living in culture contact settings take place over time. Occasionally this process is stressful, but often it results in some form of mutual accommodation, which refers to the changes that groups and individuals in both groups make in order to live together in relative harmony. Most recent acculturation research has focused on how immigrants (both voluntary and involuntary) have changed following their entry into and settlement in receiving societies (see Sam & Berry, 2006 for an overview of this literature). Today, there are many different kinds of peoples in contact. In addition to immigrants, refugees and sojourners (such as guest workers) constitute important groups that experience intercultural contacts as a result of social, political, and economic factors. Acculturating groups experience various outcomes from this process, such as discrimination and rejection. Furthermore, they often have to compete with dominant communities for recognition and equitable access to resources. However, acculturation also takes place by way of globalization, as cultural influences spread around the world to local populations.

Graves (1967) introduced the concept of *psychological acculturation,* which refers to changes in an individual who is a participant in a culture contact situation and influenced both by the external (usually dominant) culture and by the changing (usually nondominant) culture of which the individual is a member. There are two reasons for keeping the cultural and psychological levels distinct. The first is that most acculturation researchers view individual human behavior as interacting with the cultural context within which it occurs; hence separate conceptions and measurements are required at the two levels (Berry et al., 2011). The second reason is that not every individual enters into or participates in the dominant culture or changes in the same way during their acculturation; vast individual differences exist in psychological acculturation, even among individuals who have the same cultural origin and who live in the same acculturative arena.

Berry (2006) developed a framework that outlines and links cultural and psychological acculturation and identifies the two (or more) groups in contact (see also Sam & Berry, 2010). This framework portrays a number of features of the acculturation process at both the group and individual levels. At the group level are key features of the two original cultural groups prior to their major contact. Migrants and members of the receiving society bring cultural and psychological qualities with them to the contact setting. The compatibility (or incompatibility) in cultural features and personal attributes between the two cultural communities in contact needs to be examined as a basis for understanding the acculturation process set in motion following contact. Second, it is important to understand the nature of the contact relationship between the groups. It may be one of domination of one group over the other, of mutual hostility, or of respect. Third, we need to understand the resulting cultural changes that emerge during the process of acculturation in both groups. No cultural group remains unchanged following culture contact; acculturation is a two-way interaction resulting in actions and reactions to the contact situation (see chapter by Kağitçibaşi, this volume). In many cases, most change takes place in the nondominant communities; however, all societies of settlement (particularly metropolitan cities) have experienced massive transformations following periods of receiving migrants. These changes can be minor or substantial and range from easily accomplished to a source of major cultural disruption.

At the individual level, we need to consider the psychological changes that individuals in all groups undergo and the immigrants' eventual adaptation to their new situations. These changes can consist of rather easily accomplished behavioral shifts (e.g., in ways of speaking, dressing, and eating) or they can be more problematic (e.g., producing acculturative stress;

Berry & Sam, 1997), manifested by uncertainty, anxiety, and depression. Adaptations can be primarily psychological (e.g., sense of well-being or self-esteem) or sociocultural (Ward, Bochner, & Furnham, 2001), linking the individual to others in the new society as manifested, for example, in competence in the activities of daily intercultural living.

We see important individual and group differences in the way people seek to address the process of acculturation. These variations have become known as *acculturation strategies* (Berry, 1980). This concept signifies preferences regarding how to acculturate and includes attitudes (toward ways of acculturating), behaviors (such as language use and friendship choices), and cultural identities (both national and ethnic). Clearly these aspects of acculturation differ from one another (Liebkind, 2001; Liebkind et al., this volume): Some refer to attitudinal preferences; others refer to cultural practices, including retention and change; and yet others refer to feelings of belonging.

From the point of view of immigrant and ethnocultural groups, there are four acculturation strategies. When individuals do not wish to maintain their cultural heritage and seek daily participation with other cultures in the larger society, the assimilation strategy is defined. In contrast, when group members place a value on holding on to their original culture, and at the same time wish to avoid interaction with others, then the separation alternative is defined. When immigrants express an interest in both maintaining their original culture and interacting with other groups, integration is the strategy. Finally, when there is little possibility or interest in cultural maintenance (often for reasons of enforced cultural loss) and little interest in having relations with other groups (often for reasons of discrimination) then marginalization occurs.

From the point of view of the receiving society, other terms are employed. Assimilation, when sought by the dominant group, is termed the *melting pot*. When separation is forced by the dominant group, it is referred to as *segregation*. Marginalization, when imposed by the dominant group, is *exclusion*. Finally, for integration, when diversity is a widely accepted feature of the society as a whole and embraces various ethnocultural groups, it is called *multiculturalism*.

An important question is whether relationships develop between the acculturation strategies of members of nondominant groups and the acculturation expectations of the larger society. The two sets of strategies represent parallel approaches to acculturation. Research on this issue has been carried out since the 1970s (Berry, Kalin, & Taylor, 1977), and has been the focus of interactive acculturation models (Bourhis et al., 1997; Kağitçibaşi, this volume; Navas et al., 2007).

During the course of development, features of culture are transmitted from individual to individual. Berry et al. (2011) described three sources of cultural transmission, from parents, teachers, and peers to children, arguing that in all three cases the influence is in fact bidirectional. During the process of acculturation, an individual becomes enmeshed in a network of multiple interpersonal and intergroup relations. For immigrant youth, these multiple relationships are typically more complex than for nonimmigrant youth. Most people in nonimmigrant children's proximal environment represent one culture; these contribute to their enculturation (i.e., the transmission of their own culture). However, immigrant children interact with people who represent at least two different cultures. Parents, members of the family's ethnocultural group, and peers with the same ethnicity transmit the culture of the country of origin. Teachers and native peers transmit the culture of the receiving society. This interplay between cultural transmission from within a person's own ethnocultural group and transmission from the new culture constitutes the complex matrix of cultural influences during the course of development among acculturating youth.

Acculturation for immigrant children involves learning the characteristics of two cultures mainly through their interactions with people in their proximal environment. However, the contexts responsible for acculturation mirror the beliefs of the wider society regarding multiculturalism, which have a significant impact on immigrant children's adaptation.

A Social-Psychological Perspective

Despite their long interest in intergroup relations, identity, and prejudice, social psychologists only recently focused specifically on ethnicity and migration (see Chryssochoou, 2000, 2004; Deaux, 2006; Verkuyten, 2005). Immigration challenges the real and symbolic boundaries of nation states and as a consequence, changes the framework of representations, intergroup relations, and identity dynamics. It is within this new context that immigrant and nonimmigrant youth grow up.

Social psychologists have suggested that in order to understand the phenomenon of immigration and ethnic identity, we need to consider different levels of analysis (Deaux, 2006; Verkuyten, 2005). The following levels have been suggested (Doise, 1986): the individual, the inter-individual, the group (positions and intergroup relations), and the societal (ideologies, representations, institutional constraints). Although social psychology focuses on the processes involved at the societal and group levels, there is growing interest in inter-individual processes and interactions (Verkuyten, 2005) and in individual differences. In fact, according to Moscovici (1988), social psychology is characterized by the mediation of others (real or symbolic, individuals or groups) in the relation between an organism and the social context. Social psychology can contribute to the understanding of immigrant youth adaptation and development by investigating how, directly or through others (individuals, groups, media, or virtual communities if one thinks of social networks on the Internet), the social context becomes salient and influences choices and behaviors. To do so, it is important to analyze how individuals and groups perceive the social context and what the consequences of this perception are.

Several issues in immigrant research are of social-psychological interest. Social psychology focuses on how beliefs and representations are generated and what they do for the lives of individuals and groups. Another research interest is how identities are constructed, enacted, and mobilized, and with what consequences for intergroup relations and social cohesion (see also chapter by Verkuyten, this volume). Moreover, social psychology investigates how power dynamics and social positions influence social relations. These issues characterize the social context, as perceived by individuals and groups, mainly at two different levels of analysis: the societal level and the group level.

As discussed in the previous section, for immigrant youth the proximal contexts (family, school, peers, neighborhood in which they are socialized [Bronfenbrenner & Morris, 2006]) comprise both the cultures of origin and the culture of the receiving society (Berry, 1997). Moreover, their immigrant status gives them an additional social position beyond the one attached to their gender. Often this position coincides with a low socioeconomic status (see also chapter by Nolan, this volume), and it is unclear whether the way they are perceived and treated relates to their different cultural background, their social class, or both. Thus, immigrant youth need to understand this position, overcome any barriers that may impede their advancement, and use the resources they have in order to succeed.

What challenges do immigrant youth face? The societal level is characterized by the different belief systems and social representations that exist in the society at large as well as their culture of origin (Verkuyten & Yildiz, 2006). These representations include beliefs regarding the way the receiving society is representing itself (i.e., as a culturally homogeneous nation, as a multicultural nation, as an immigration nation) and its relation to the new members (i.e., former colonial subjects, new economic immigrants). Research has shown that beliefs about multiculturalism and essentialistic beliefs about the ingroup and the outgroup influence intergroup relations and the acceptance of the new immigrants by others (Verkuyten & Brug,

2004). Representations also affect beliefs about individual mobility and success. Beliefs about the legitimacy of the system, perceptions of acculturative expectations, and social mobility have been found to intervene in the choices of immigrants and their social insertion (Bourhis et al., 1997). All these beliefs are transmitted as part of the general process of cultural transmission by different agents of influence and "entrepreneurs of identity" (Reicher & Hopkins, 2001) to young people. They are communicated through politicians, media, and education and migration policies either directly or through youngsters' proximal environment (family, neighborhood, teachers, and peers) and influence both individual and collective choices. Research needs to investigate further which of these factors contribute to the well-being and successful development of immigrant youth and which obstruct them.

Immigrant youth occupy different positions: They are young, of immigrant origins, with particular cultural, national, and religious backgrounds; they often grow up in poor families and differ on gender ideologies. These identities are constructed within a framework of intergroup relations often characterized by power asymmetries and competition. Discrimination and negative stereotypes are the outcomes of these power asymmetries and have important consequences for the everyday life of young people (see also chapter by Liebkind et al., this volume). Discriminative behaviors and negative stereotyping from majority members communicate to young people the position they have in society and the level of success that they can obtain, and they undermine people's well-being (Jasinskaja-Lahti & Liebkind, 2007). Restricted social mobility and feelings of injustice might lead young people to become marginalized, to reject the receiving society, to consider themselves only as members of their ethnic group (Berry et al., 2006), or to fight collectively to redress these inequalities. The specific conditions that would lead to either choice are investigated with particular groups and social conditions.

Of particular interest is how young people of immigrant descent negotiate different memberships and combine social identities and how discrimination influences this process (see also chapter by Sirin & Gupta, this volume). Any social identity carries "the project" of the group it represents (Chryssochoou, 2003). Social psychology has established that people wish to belong to groups considered worthy in society. Thus, when the opportunity is open to belong to a more valued group, people would do so (Tajfel & Turner, 1986). However, this desire could cause immigrants to psychologically de-identify with their heritage culture, which could be difficult and painful. Although immigration often positions people in a low socioeconomic level, their cultural identity and their socioeconomic status should not be confused (Liebkind, 2001).

However, in the case of migration, the process becomes more complex. Receiving societies might not give members of low-status immigrant groups the opportunity to become full members of the national ingroup. In addition, discrimination might lead immigrants to reactive ethnicity (Branscombe, Schmitt, & Harvey, 1999; Rumbaut, 2008), feeding the receiving society's beliefs and fears about immigrants' divided loyalties. In turn, these beliefs undermine immigrants' perception of compatibility between ethnic and national identities with consequences for well-being and intergroup attitudes (Jasinskaja-Lahti, Liebkind, & Solheim, 2009; see also chapter by Liebkind et al., this volume). It is also possible that members of the receiving society sustain beliefs of incompatibility between identities in order to maintain their privileges (Chryssochoou & Lyons, 2011). This context frames young people's choices and actions.

Power asymmetries have consequences at the level of the individual and at the level of society at large. Discrimination and low status foster negative stereotypes that impact self-perception and reduce possibilities of advancement. In particular, studies found that when members of minority groups are aware of the negative stereotype existing in a particular domain against them, the fear of confirming the stereotype (stereotype threat) might have disrupting effects and might block them in such a way so they actually confirm the negative stereotype, effectively creating a situation of self-sabotage. (Crocker, Major, & Steele, 1998). Stereotype threat, fear of rejection, and situations in which devalued identity is made salient might lead young people of immigrant descent to disengage from particular domains, such as education, putting their future at risk and confirming predicted negative outcomes for their social group.

Identification with the receiving group is a marker of inclusion and positive intergroup attitudes. Moreover, the development of dual identity has been shown to be related to the politicization of immigrants and to their better social integration in society (Simon & Ruhs, 2008). As the climate developed in the receiving society and the perceptions and threats felt by all groups involved became important aspects of the context, social-psychological research focused particularly on the receiving society in order to understand the threats felt by majorities due to migration and in order to propose possible interventions (Green, 2007). However, the context is rapidly changing and it is important to study how minority groups and individuals react to these changes. For instance, in the aftermath of the attacks of September 11, 2001, the context became extremely negative for Muslims in the United States and research showed young people were obliged to quickly renegotiate their identities as Muslims and American (Sirin & Fine, 2008; see also chapter by Sirin & Gupta, this volume). Social-psychological research, aiming to unpack societal and group contexts and their consequences, needs to be included with studies of the development and adaptation of immigrant youth in the larger social framework that facilitates or obstructs adaptation.

Successful Adaptation of Immigrant Youth

In order to integrate these three distinct disciplinary perspectives to account for individual differences in immigrant youth adaptation, it is important to address the issues inherent in defining successful adaptation. Developmental and acculturation psychologies offer unique perspectives on how successful adaptation might be defined.

In developmental psychology, as noted earlier, developmental task theory offers a conceptual framework for judging positive adaptation in children. Success can be defined in terms of competence in age-salient developmental tasks (Masten et al., 2006). The quality of children's adaptation is assessed based on whether they meet the expectations and standards for behavior and achievement related to tasks that parents, teachers, and society set for them, expectations that they themselves usually come to share.

In this perspective, adaptive success is multidimensional and developmental in nature (Masten et al., 2006; McCormick et al., 2011). Success in a toddler or preschooler might be defined, for example, by achievements such as learning to walk and talk, early identity understanding (e.g., that one is a boy or girl), and early forms of behavioral self-control (beginning to comply with rules and commands when an adult is present). Success in the adolescent years might be defined, for example, by success in school, having close friends, knowing and obeying the laws of the society, more advanced self-control (e.g., complying with rules of the family when no one is monitoring), and establishing a cohesive, integrated, and multifaceted sense of identity.

Children do not pass or fail these tasks. However, the effectiveness with which they engage and master these developmental challenges has significant implications for their self-perception as well as for the way others perceive them and their future prospects. The quality of children's adaptation with respect to the tasks of one developmental period forecasts success or failure in future developmental tasks (Masten et al., 2006).

Developmental tasks can be organized into broad domains: individual development; relationships with parents, teachers, and peers; and functioning in the proximal environment and in the broader social world (Sroufe et al., 2005). For example, self-regulation and identity formation are developmental tasks pertinent to individual development. School adjustment and success, civic engagement, and political participation of youth characterize their functioning in the proximal and distal social environments. Furthermore, forming and maintaining positive relationships with parents, teachers, and peers are significant goals throughout development and are concurrently and over time related to success in other domains of adaptation.

There are commonalities and differences in developmental tasks across cultures. Developmental task theory places adaptation and development in cultural and historical context (Masten et al., 2006), but the complexities of adaptation in the context of multiple cultures with potentially conflicting developmental task expectations has not been elucidated very well to date (McCormick et al., 2011). Particularly problematic for understanding adaptation of immigrant youth is the assumption that they face only one set of developmental tasks, the one defined by the dominant culture. This monoculture assumption is called into question in the case of immigrant children, whose lives are embedded in proximal contexts representing at least two different cultures (Oppedal, 2006; Sam, 2006). For immigrants, parental ethnotheories – the values and beliefs parents consider adaptive for success in their culture (Harkness & Super, 1996) and which guide their cultural pathways (Weisner, 2002) and their child-rearing practices (Ogbu, 1991) – may be at odds with the criteria for success set by teachers. In a context in which youth face contradictory developmental goals, expectations, and socialization practices, adaptation with respect to developmental issues may be more challenging than it is for their nonimmigrant peers.

The success of immigrant children's adaptation is, therefore, not only judged by the way they deal with developmental challenges, but also by the way they deal with the challenges of simultaneously enculturating and acculturating and of living with and growing between two cultures. This point leads to consideration of the acculturative tasks that immigrant youth face. Based on evidence that the learning and maintenance of both cultures is conducive to better developmental outcomes and psychological well-being (Berry et al., 2006; Sam, 2006), immigrant children face the task of learning the language, values, beliefs, behaviors, and customs typical of the larger society as well as those of their home culture (Oppedal, 2006; Sam, 2006); of making sense of and bridging their different worlds (Cooper, 2003); and of developing positive ethnic and national identities (Phinney et al., 2001).

Developmental and acculturative tasks are intricately related. To succeed in certain developmental tasks such as doing well in school, immigrant children need to achieve a level of competence in the language and other facets of the receiving society's culture (Suárez-Orozco, Suárez-Orozco, & Todorova, 2006). It follows that positive school adjustment indicates that adaptation with respect to both developmental and acculturative tasks is proceeding well. Furthermore, maintaining positive relations with parents during adolescence presupposes that the immigrant child can strike a balance, through the processes of accommodation and negotiation with parents, between demands for autonomy and willingness to adhere to family values (Kuczynski & Navara, 2006; Kwak, 2003).

It should be noted here that the term *sociocultural adaptation*, as used by acculturation psychologists, refers primarily to doing well in school and other dominant culture environments. These indices of adaptation would fall under the broader rubric of developmental tasks in the developmental science concept.

The need to evaluate the success of immigrant youth adaptation raises questions related to the norms against which to compare their behavior and achievement. Current behavior and performance related to youths' future adaptation in the receiving society should be compared to that of their native peers. For example, doing adequately well in school, which presupposes receiving grades comparable to the normative performance of native students, and not dropping out early, are important markers of present adaptation and forerunners of future adaptation in society for both immigrant and native youth (Masten & Motti-Stefanidi, 2009).

A related issue concerns the values that should be used when evaluating adaptive outcomes, especially when private values, that is, values related to linguistic and cultural activities, to religious expression, and to the domestic and interpersonal domains of the family (Bourhis et al., 1997), and the values of the larger society are at odds with each other. Bourhis et al. (1997) noted that Western nation states, independent of their ideological orientation regarding the acculturation of immigrants, expect immigrants to adopt the public values of the host country. However, success could be judged not by whether immigrant youth have espoused either set of values, but by whether they have been able to select, interpret, resist, or manage the competing messages stemming from their family, school, peers, and the media, and to form their unique working models of culture (Kuczynski & Navara, 2006).

Another important marker of positive adaptation is good internal functioning (versus distress and misery) (Masten et al., 2006). The presence of self-esteem and life satisfaction and the absence of emotional symptoms are common markers of psychological well-being used by developmental and acculturative researchers (e.g., Berry et al., 2006; Masten et al., 2006). The evidence is contradictory regarding the psychological well-being of immigrant, compared to native, youth (e.g., Alegría et al., 2008; Berry et al., 2006; Motti-Stefanidi et al., 2008). Immigrant youths' psychological well-being seems related to several factors, including the immigration policies of the society of settlement and their acculturation orientations (Berry et al., 2006; Motti-Stefanidi et al., 2008). Psychological well-being and successful adaptation with respect to developmental and acculturative tasks are interrelated, influencing each other concurrently and across time.

A seminal study, the International Comparative Study of Ethnocultural Youth (ICSEY) project, conducted in 13 countries, examined 5,366 immigrant youth aged 13 to 18 years and studied their adaptation with respect to developmental and acculturative tasks and their psychological well-being (Berry et al., 2006). The group-level analyses comparing immigrant and national youth revealed that, on the whole, the groups were equally well adjusted. In some cases the immigrant youth were better adjusted with respect to developmental tasks such as school adjustment and lack of conduct problems than the national youth. The two groups did not differ with respect to their psychological well-being. Furthermore, it was found that immigrant youth who developed competencies in both their home culture and the culture of the new society did better with respect to the developmental tasks examined, but not with respect to psychological well-being. Immigrant youth with an ethnic orientation fared better with respect to developmental tasks and reported higher psychological well-being, although the effect was stronger for the latter.

The question of how well immigrant children adapt with respect to different developmental tasks compared to their native classmates remains an unresolved issue to date. In recent years, a number of mainly North American researchers have reported, for example, findings revealing that some immigrant students are doing better in school than their national peers, and in any case better than expected given the fact that they live with higher socioeconomic risk (e.g., Berry et al., 2006; Fuligni, 1997; Kao & Tienda, 1995). The presence of this phenomenon, which came to be known as the "immigrant paradox" (see also chapter by Garcia Coll et al., this volume), refers to the finding that first-generation immigrants show better adaptation than either their national peers or second-generation immigrants, and/or the finding that second-generation immigrants' adaptation appears on par or worse than that of their national peers (Sam et al., 2008). Sam et al. (2008) also pointed out that the immigrant paradox seems to hold for adaptation with respect to developmental tasks (such as school adjustment) but not with respect to psychological well-being. In contrast to these findings, other researchers have reported a significant achievement gap between immigrant and native youth (e.g., Cooper, 2003; Motti-Stefanidi et al., 2008).

In the rest of this section, positive adaptation of immigrant youth is discussed in terms of key developmental and acculturative tasks and contexts. The focus is on tasks of central interest in the developmental, acculturation, and social-psychological literatures.

School Adjustment

Schools are one of the most important developmental contexts for all children and adolescents in contemporary societies. They play an instrumental role in helping children acquire the knowledge and the thinking skills, as well as the behaviors and values, important for the welfare of youth and society. For immigrant children and adolescents, schools also serve as one of the main acculturative contexts, since they represent, and introduce the immigrants to, the culture of the receiving society (Suárez-Orozco & Suárez-Orozco, 2001; see also chapter by Horenzcyk & Tartar, this volume). A successful trajectory through school is an asset for the future employment opportunities and choices of most youth (Masten & Motti-Stefanidi, 2009), and is considered by many immigrant students as the avenue for upward social mobility and for a better life than their parents had (Fuligni, 1997).

Different individual characteristics, such as cognitive abilities (Masten et al., 2006), proficiency in the language of the receiving culture (Suárez-Orozco et al., 2006), and a strong motivation to succeed in school (Fuligni, 1997), are linked to academic achievement. Acculturation orientation has also been shown to be related to school achievement among immigrant youth. According to some studies a bicultural orientation (Berry et al., 2006; Phinney et al., 2001), and according to others, a national orientation, not an ethnic or a bicultural (e.g., Motti-Stefanidi et al., 2008) orientation, have been linked to better school adjustment. Finally, a number of school characteristics, such as nondifferential treatment by teachers (Roeser et al., 1998), family, and peer factors have been shown to contribute to a positive school outcome (Fuligni, 1997; see also chapter by Horenzcyk & Tartar, this volume).

Family Relations

Maintaining positive family relations is an important task throughout development. During adolescence this task requires letting go of complete dependence on parents and other family members for care and survival, taking on adult roles, and contributing to the care, well-being, and survival of others (Greenfield et al., 2003). For adolescents to achieve this task, parents have to resolve a challenging issue: allowing the increasingly maturing and competent adolescent to make decisions and be more responsible for his or her life vis-à-vis sustaining the close bond that has characterized their relationship with the child during the first decade of life (Kağitçibaşi, 2007).

Some developmental scientists regard this developmental task as the period of individuation and separation, characterized by increasing time with, influence from, and growing attachment to peers. The idea that this developmental task entails separation from parents has been questioned in recent years, particularly with respect to diverse cultures (e.g., Georgas et al., 2006; Kwak, 2003). Research suggests that the assumed separation process entails finding a balance between what has variously been referred to as "autonomy and relatedness" and "individuation and connectedness" (Kroger, 2007; Ryan & Lynch, 1989; see also chapter by Kağitçibaşi, this volume). Finding the correct balance is conducive to adolescent adjustment, as the balance provides children the opportunity to develop the ability to think and act independently within the context of supportive relationships with parents (e.g., Kuczynski & Navara, 2006).

Research further suggests that families and societies differ in the extent to which they emphasize the autonomy–relatedness balance, with Western, industrialized societies emphasizing more autonomy, and non-Western societies emphasizing more relatedness. According to the eco-cultural model of Berry et al. (2011), these differences in emphasis reflect the various eco-cultural challenges faced in different societies.

Through socialization and enculturation, in what has been referred to as *cultural transmission* (Schönpflug, 2008; Vedder et al., 2009), parents and societies inculcate in their children the culture of the society. During these processes, the prevailing norms, values, and beliefs of the society (which have arisen as an adaptation to the eco-cultural challenges) may be passed on. The autonomy–relatedness balance takes its root in the two fundamental types of cultural values: (1) assertiveness, independence, competitiveness, and autonomy, and (2) compliance, nurturing, and obedience, with both value sets transmitted during enculturation and socialization. The extent to which autonomy or relatedness is emphasized, expected, and granted during adolescence depends on the society (Rothbaum et al., 2000), the ethnic group (Phinney et al., 2005), and the socioeconomic conditions of the family (Kağitçibaşi, 2007).

In an immigration context, the development of autonomy and relatedness grow complicated because parents and adolescents are involved in an acculturation process. During this process, adolescents and parents have different experiences of cultures and different future expectations (Bornstein & Cote, 2006; Kwak, 2003), and this may result in conflicts within the family. For example, in the ICSEY study (Berry et al., 2006), the values held by youth and their parents with respect to youth obligations and youth rights differed in both the immigrant samples and in the larger society. However, this difference was greater in the immigrant samples. Moreover, the greater the generational difference in the obligations valued in the immigrant samples, the worse the psychological well-being and adaptation of immigrant youth with respect to developmental tasks. This is an example of one of the most common forms of conflict within immigrant families, variously known as the "assimilation gap," the "acculturation gap," the "intergenerational gap," and the "developmental gap" (Merz et al., 2009).

Peer Relations

Peer relations are important for children's development and acculturation. Developing and maintaining positive peer relations is an important developmental task that forecasts future adaptation (Masten et al., 2006). Youth who relate well to normative peers at school also perceive school more favorably and perform better in the classroom. On the other hand, peer rejection has been shown to predict, longitudinally, poor academic achievement and truancy. Furthermore, children and adolescents who get along with peers, have friends, and are accepted by classmates show higher self-esteem and fewer behavioral and emotional symptoms than their rejected peers, currently and over time (for review see Rubin, Bukowski, & Parker, 2006).

Peer relations are closely linked with the previously described developmental task of autonomy and relatedness. These two developmental tasks seem to go hand in hand: As adolescents enter into the autonomy phase, often spending less time with their parents, they spend increasing time with and develop closer friendships with peers.

Children and adolescents often choose friends who are similar to themselves in terms of socioeconomic status, ethnicity, and chronological age. Consistent with this phenomenon, termed *friendship homophily*, immigrant youth tend to choose friends from within their own ethnic group (Quillian & Campbell, 2003; Strohmeier & Spiel, 2003; Titzmann & Silbereisen, 2009;

see also chapter by Spiel et al., this volume). However, length of residence in the new country and ethnic composition of the neighborhood are related to immigrant youth choices regarding their friends. Longer residence in the society of settlement and living in more ethnically diverse neighborhoods are related to more contact with national peers than with peers from their own ethnic group (Phinney et al., 2006).

Friendships from one's own ethnic group and/or from the national society likely play fundamental roles in the process of acculturation. It could be argued that association with national peers introduces immigrant youth to the new culture, and association with ethnic peers supports immigrant parents' efforts at maintaining the home culture.

Civic Engagement and Political Participation

Civic engagement and political participation in the context of immigration includes involvement in the political sphere and involvement with others in the community (Jensen & Flanagan, 2008). It concerns forms of political and civic participation such as voting, protesting, volunteering, joining associations, and assuming leadership positions. Civic engagement is considered to "enhance development by giving people positive motivations, beneficial peer networks, feelings of worth and longer time horizons" (Levine, 2008). Youth who engage in civic and political activities are more likely to be successful in other domains. For young people, in general, being civically engaged is an indication of their interest in the society in which they live (see also chapter by Silbereisen et al., this volume). For immigrant youth, it is also an indicator of their inclusion in the society. Research (Lopez & Marcelo, 2008) has shown that the civic engagement rates of immigrant and nonimmigrant youth in the United States are similar.

Both contexts of immigrant youth (ethnic group and society of settlement) are possible environments for civic engagement. Immigrant youth have civic assets because of their biculturalism that enable them to contribute to both cultures (Jensen, 2008, see also chapter by Lerner et al., this volume), and civic activities are an indicator of how they negotiate the relationship between the two societies. They can be engaged in activities that promote the aims, values, and needs of their ethnic group and/or of the receiving society according to their understanding of how the "social contract" applies to people like them (Wray-Lake, Syvertsen, & Flanagan, 2008). The terms of this contract are filtered through lay theories and stereotypes of the dominant group about particular ethnic groups and multiculturalism (Sirin & Fine, 2008). Young people of immigrant descent learn what it means to be a citizen through everyday experiences and challenges such as discrimination. Their perception of the receiving society as just or not relates to these experiences.

People's engagement in civic activities might be an expression of a collective identity. When this identity concerns the ethnic group, the sense of "we" might include shared grievances, ethnic pride, common cultural and religious values, and a common fate. If the ethnic group has a low position within society, people might opt to abandon it and join the high-status group. This is why often, for immigrant youth, mobility has been erroneously conflated with assimilation (Waters, 2008). However, young people could act as group members to enhance the position of their ethnic group when the boundaries of the groups are not permeable and when they perceive the asymmetries between groups as illegitimate and changeable (Tajfel, 1974).

Identifying as a member of the ethnic group, however, is not enough for engaging in collective political activities. To do so it is important that a *politicized collective identity* is formed. Simon and Klandermans (2001) propose three antecedents for the formation of a politicized collective identity: a) awareness of shared grievances; b) adversarial attribution; and c) involvement of the wider society in the conflict. This theorization considers political participation as the outcome of processes of social influence (Mugny, 1982). Thus for participation three poles should be present: a minority group with a collective identity and awareness of shared grievances, a powerful adversary to blame for one's condition, and society at large that is supposed to take a position. If young immigrants acknowledge that their ethnic group suffers from injustice, attribute this condition to a particular group, institution, or authority, and seek to win the support of the larger society, they become collectively politicized and might engage in actions of protest and claiming. To do so they need to claim inclusion in the wider social group (Jensen, 2008).

In cross-sectional and longitudinal studies with Turks in Germany (Simon & Ruhs, 2008), the authors concluded that dual identification with the ethnic group and the receiving society is not a consequence of prior politicization, but rather is its antecedent. Moreover, identification with Germany reduced acceptance of political violence and was associated with weakened support for radical ingroups over time, especially for those with strong Turkish identification. It is possible that young people who follow an integration strategy and develop a dual identification are more prone to engage in political activities on behalf of their ethnic group within the wider context of the receiving society. Their political participation might also signal that they feel included in this society.

Identity Formation

The formation of a secure, coherent identity is one of the primary tasks of adolescence (Erikson, 1968). For immigrant youth, a secure identity is central to dealing with the differing demands of their multicultural context and becoming a productive member of society.

According to Erikson (1968), the process of achieving an identity is located "in the core of the individual and yet also in the core of his [sic] communal culture" (22). Individuals do not form an identity in isolation; the contexts in which adolescents grow up are as important as the individuals' actions and choices. Contexts of identity formation can both enhance and restrict the formation of adult identities, depending on the extent to which they provide options and obstacles (Ogbu, 1991). For all youth, the family, peer group, and community are key factors in determining whether young people achieve a coherent and stable identity (Kroger, 2007). For immigrant youth, these settings include differing, often conflicting, expectations and possibilities.

Identity formation is strongly influenced by parental expectations and goals. In many cases, families immigrate to a new country in order to provide educational and career opportunities for their children. However, immigrant parents often lack the background to understand the issues that children face. Parents may be too uninformed or too busy working multiple jobs to provide the guidance the youth need in developing an identity in a diverse society (Fuligni & Fuligni, 2007; Portes & Rumbaut, 2001).

Schools and classmates are also important influences on identity formation, as young people strive to find their place in the world. When peers, teachers, or the community do not provide positive role models and options, immigrant youth often find their identities in the underclass of gangs and antisocial activities (Portes & Rumbaut, 2001; Suárez-Orozco & Suárez-Orozco, 2001). A secure identity helps young people to deal more effectively with challenges in their communities and in the larger society and to integrate the differing demands of each (Kiang, Yip, & Fuligni, 2008).

Identity formation for adolescents involves making decisions across various domains important to their lives, such as occupation, religion, gender, and lifestyle. For immigrant youth, cultural identity, that is, a secure sense of oneself as a cultural being, is arguably the most important identity domain. To achieve a secure cultural identity, young people must explore and internalize feelings and attitudes regarding who they are in relation to the diverse and often conflicting values, attitudes, and practices in their multiple contexts (Sirin & Fine, 2008); they must develop a sense of belonging to one or more cultural groups. However, immigrants may have broad contacts with their new society and adopt its language and customs without necessarily self-identifying as part of the national group or giving up their ethnic identity (Snauwaert et al., 2003).

Across virtually all immigrant studies, the dominant and preferred pattern of identity in immigrant youth is a bicultural identity in which individuals have a strong sense of belonging to both their ethnic culture and the larger dominant or mainstream culture (Phinney & Devich-Navarro, 1997). Nevertheless, some youth retain a separated ethnic identity, often as a result of obstacles or rejections that prevent them from identifying with the larger society. Other youth may strive for an assimilated national identity. These differing identity patterns are formed as young people wrestle with the demands of the environment and make decisions across the diverse contexts of their lives, including family, peers, school, and community (see also Verkuyten, this volume).

Within the family, adolescents balance competing pressures as they try to resolve questions about adherence to ethnic or national cultural values. Immigrant adolescents must make daily decisions on how to deal with parents over cultural differences, such as parents' more restrictive attitudes on whom to date or on the choice of college major (Phinney et al., 2005). Parents may influence these decisions, for example, with the expectation that one child will maintain the ethnic traditions (Pyke, 2005). As a result, one sibling in a family may remain strongly ethnically identified while another becomes more identified with the larger society.

Immigrant adolescents face similar cultural identity negotiations among their peers. They may feel pressure from their same-ethnic peers to remain identified with their own group (Fordham & Ogbu, 1986). Conversely, recently arrived immigrant youth may be scorned by American-born peers for being too ethnic (Palmer, 2007). The process of constructing a cultural identity requires young people to explore these issues and decide where they stand.

The ethnic composition of schools also influences cultural identity processes. In many immigrant communities, schools are often made up of diverse immigrant groups so that cultural identity issues involve defining oneself in relation to other minority groups, rather than to the larger society (Way et al., 2008). The ethnic composition of their communities constrains the identity options of young immigrants. In communities that are almost entirely ethnic, a strong ethnic identity may be more common than a bicultural identity (Berry et al., 2006). In order to become bicultural, young people need opportunities to meet and interact with members of the larger society.

However, contact with the mainstream society can result in experiences of discrimination and rejection that constrain the development of a national identity. Although most immigrants arrive with a desire to become part of their new country, they often meet obstacles to doing so (Liebkind et al., this volume; Sirin & Fine, 2008). Immigrants who are discriminated against are less likely to identify with the larger society or become bicultural (Berry et al., 2006). Nevertheless, most immigrants are not passive in the face of discrimination; rather, they resist and challenge discrimination (Phinney, 2006; Sirin & Fine, 2008). The development of a secure ethnic identity can serve as a buffer against discrimination (Lee, 2005; Verkuyten, this volume). Encouraging cultural retention among immigrants leads to stronger ethnic communities that provide support for young people to develop positive cultural identities and resist the destructive effects of discrimination.

Cultural identity develops within the context of larger social and historical forces (Bhatia & Ram, 2001). It is easier for immigrants to feel accepted in societies with a strong history of immigration, such as the United States and Canada, than in those where immigration is a recent phenomenon (Berry et al., 2006). Furthermore, with longer residence in their country of settlement, more immigrant youth have bicultural identities and fewer show the confusion of a diffuse identity (Berry et al., 2006).

In summary, developing a secure cultural identity involves integrating multiple influences, both developmental and acculturative. In situations that provide opportunities for exploration, young people can match their own preferences, abilities, and goals with choices that allow for continued productive development. If their choices are restricted or lacking in positive options, they may turn to destructive means of self-validation. When societies provide basic supports to immigrants, such as educational and occupational choices, and promote positive and accepting attitudes toward them in the larger society, immigrant youth can achieve secure cultural identities that form the basis for becoming productive members of society.

Cultural Competence

Successful adaptation in the areas discussed earlier forms the basis of cultural competence. Culturally competent individuals have gained the knowledge and skills to live comfortably within their various cultural contexts (Clement & Noels, 1992; Oppedal, 2006). They are able to communicate effectively in the ethnic and national languages and to switch between them as necessary. They can socialize with friends from their own and other groups. They are aware of the differing practices and values of various groups and can choose among them as appropriate. To achieve such cultural competence, immigrant youth must successfully negotiate their multiple worlds of family, peers, school, and society by learning how to navigate across cultural borders (Liebkind, 2001).

In a study of students in diverse high schools in California, Phelan, Davidson, and Yu (1998) identified the many borders that these youth must negotiate, including psychological, sociocultural, socioeconomic, linguistic, and gender-related borders. They must learn to deal with structural borders, such as institutional factors that impede students from doing well in school due to lack of information, resources, or services.

Adolescents from immigrant families vary in the extent to which they are able to accomplish this negotiation process. Phelan and her colleagues found four different patterns of adaptation to the challenges of multiple worlds. For nonimmigrant youth, mainly those from European American backgrounds, the worlds of family, school, and peers were congruent so that there were minimal problems in making transitions among them. However, for students with differing or noncongruent cultural worlds, that is, most immigrant youth, the authors found three patterns that differed in how and how well the students fared. One group, the more culturally competent, managed border crossings and adapted to different settings by alternating between settings or blending aspects of different worlds. A second group found border crossings difficult, causing discomfort or friction due, for example, to values or practices that differed between home and school. These students were struggling to adjust, and they were more likely to do poorly in school. A third group perceived the borders as so incongruent that crossing them was resisted or seen as impossible. These students showed the poorest adaptation; they might reject school completely or immerse themselves in their peer culture. This research highlights the complex, interactive nature of the acculturation process. Immigrant youth may want to integrate into their multicultural communities, but if the barriers between their cultural worlds are difficult or impossible for them to cross, they will have little opportunity to develop as culturally competent members of society.

An Integrative Framework for Research on Immigrant Youth Adaptation

Immigrant youth adaptation, arising from multifaceted and multidetermined processes, cannot be accounted for by any one discipline, and certainly not from one subdiscipline of psychology. The full story of who among immigrant youth succeeds and why requires a multidisciplinary

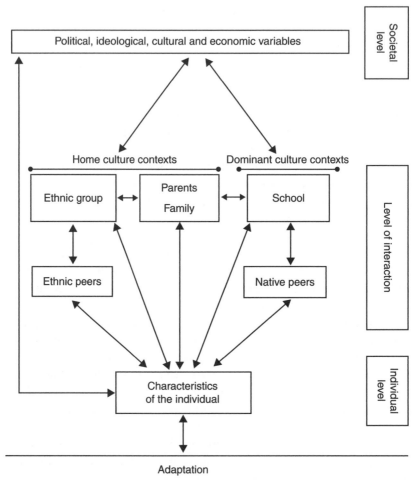

Figure 5.1. Immigrant youth adaptation in context: An integrative framework.

and integrative approach. Here, as a first step, we focus on integrating the developmental, acculturation, and social-psychological perspectives. These approaches to the study of the phenomenon of immigration in general and of immigrant youth adaptation in particular are based on different paradigms and intellectual traditions, have different emphases, focus on different research questions, and follow different methods in this area of investigation. However, to build a more comprehensive understanding of positive adaptation in immigrant youth, it is important to bring these perspectives together.

A model of our integrative framework is provided in Figure 5.1. The backbone of the model is conceived in three levels: the individual level, the level of interaction, and the societal level. These levels are interconnected and embedded within each other. No precedence is given in this model either to the individual as sole agent or to society as sole determinant of individual differences in immigrant youths' adaptation. Instead it is argued that both the individual and society, that is, sociocultural circumstances and structures and human agency, play a central role in the adaptive processes that lead to the success (or failure) of immigrant youth. The three-level approach was proposed by Verkuyten (2005), but closely follows a similar model proposed by Deaux (2006), whose purpose was to study issues of ethnicity and migration. Both models are comprehensive and heuristically useful for situating different perspectives to the issue under investigation and for explaining individual differences in immigrant youth adaptation from these perspectives.

The middle level of this model, the level of interaction, refers, according to Verkuyten (2005), to the dynamics of the everyday and concrete contacts in many different situations. All three approaches, developmental, acculturation, and social psychological, stress the importance of this middle space and of the role of social interactions for the outcomes they study, and consider the contexts in which such interactions take place as a privileged ground for investigating the phenomena of interest. Developmental and acculturation psychologies have provided a detailed account of the social networks that constitute the lived space of immigrant children as well as of the contextual factors and interpersonal processes related to their adaptation. The level of interaction in the proposed model is then elaborated to include the contexts of interaction considered by developmental (Bronfenbrenner & Morris, 2006) and acculturation psychologists (Berry et al., 2011) as central for the development and acculturation of immigrant youth (Figure 5.1).

Before proceeding with the more detailed presentation of the three levels, it is important to clarify the concept of levels, which is used by developmental and social psychologies, with each discipline denoting somewhat different ideas or phenomena. Developmental psychologists have used the term mostly to refer to levels of context (micro, meso, exo, and macrosystemic). Social psychologists use the idea of levels to refer mostly to levels of analysis (individual, interactive, societal levels of analysis) or of scientific explanation. The levels of analysis as conceived by social psychologists are considered interdependent, but each level is viewed as analytically different from the other two (Bronfenbrenner & Morris, 2006; Verkuyten, 2005). For example, individual differences in school adjustment, an important developmental task for all youth, can be explained by individual variables examined at the individual level of analysis, where variables are assigned to individuals, and/or by contextual variables, either at the interactive or at the societal level, where the independent variables are examined at the level of class, school, city, or country. To do justice to the different levels of analysis, multilevel statistical models, such as HLM models (Raudenbush & Bryk, 2002), are necessary. These methods allow investigators to examine hierarchical, or nested, data structures and to disentangle individual and group effects on the outcome of interest.

The definition of context, within and across these three subdisciplines of psychology, is also a possible source for confusion (Liebkind, 2006; Verkuyten, 2000). For example, context may refer to the social or physical context, to interactions that take place at a fairly regular basis and over an extended period of time, or, in contrast, to interactions that take place in a specific circumstance as presented in an experimental condition, or to immigration conditions. This variability in the definition of context renders the comparison and integration of findings from different studies a complex task.

The first level of the proposed model, the individual level, concerns intra-individual characteristics such as personality, temperament, motivation, self-regulation, and cognition. The second level, the level of interaction, includes the contexts in which the child is in continuous interaction with other people. These are the contexts that developmental psychologists call proximal. This term will be used in the rest of the chapter to refer to social contexts in the child's immediate environment. In the case of immigrant youth, these contexts serve the purposes of development and acculturation and are divided into those representing the home culture and into those representing the culture of the receiving society (Berry et al., 2011). However, this level could also include, even though they are not depicted in Figure 5.1, contexts in which the persons are not in direct contact and interaction with the immigrant child but are in regular interaction with people who are. These contexts form, in Bronfenbrenner's Bioecological Model, the exosystem (Bronfenbrenner & Morris, 2006). For example, native peers' parents and people in immigrant parents' workplace would be part of the exosystem. Finally, immigrants' home cultures are also represented at this level mainly through parents' working models of culture, that is, of the beliefs, attitudes, values, and practices formed in their culture of origin (Kuczynski & Navara, 2006) as well as by their ethnic group network and their ethnic peers.

The third level includes societal-level variables such as cultural beliefs, social representations, and ideologies shown to impact immigrants' adaptation (e.g., Jasinskaja-Lahti & Liebkind, 2007). Ideally, in a multicultural society that values diversity and equity among all ethnocultural groups, both immigrants' home culture and the culture of the receiving society would be represented at the societal level. Multicultural societies recognize different ethnocultural groups' uniqueness and specific needs, and this is reflected at the societal level by the fact that their institutions have adapted so as to accommodate for the presence of all groups (Berry, 2006). Currently, though, in most countries, only the culture of the receiving society is actually represented at this level, since their institutions follow uniform programs and standards based on the receiving society's cultural views. However, immigrants, due to developments in modern communication technology, are, not only exposed through the media to the norms, values, ideologies, and representations of the receiving society, but also to those of their home country (Deaux, 2006). In major cities around the world, which host large numbers of immigrants, foreign-language channels often broadcast exclusively in their language. However, immigrants can also watch, through cable television, programs directly from their home country. Finally, this level includes variables reflecting power positions within society, such as ethnicity and social class (Chryssochoou, 2004).

Taking a top-down approach, societal-level variables may have an impact on youth in two possible ways, either indirectly, by filtering through the contexts of the child's proximal environment (e.g., Boyce et al., 1998; Magnusson & Stattin, 2006; Verkuyten, 2005), or directly, for example, through media exposure.

The indirect path of influence results from the way societal-level variables contribute in shaping the contexts of children's everyday interactions (Garcia Coll et al., 1996). However, it should be noted here, for some immigrant groups actual local circumstances (characterized, for example, by high concentration of this immigrant group) may be different, and more important, than national policies and other societal-level variables. Even though these ethnic groups may be considered to have low status and lack of power on the level of society, they have a different experience, with regard to discrimination and prejudice, at the local level, where the majority–minority model is redefined (Liebkind, 2006).

In the case of immigrant youth, societal-level variables predominantly filter through contexts, such as the school, that represent the dominant culture. They actually become instantiated in the school context, the functioning of which is usually guided by the laws, values, and beliefs of the dominant, receiving culture. Schools teach knowledge and thinking skills to all students. Furthermore, they constitute one of the contexts for the enculturation of native youth, and the main acculturative context for immigrant youth (Vedder & Horenczyk, 2006). However, powerful social variables, such as ethnicity and social class, and their derivatives, such as discrimination, prejudice, and segregation, also become instantiated in this context and contribute in shaping the unique experiences of immigrant youth (Garcia Coll et al., 1996), having the potential to adversely affect their development and their acculturation (Ward et al., 2001; Wong et al., 2003).

The societal-level variables also filter through the peer group. For example, in a study of the classroom contextual effects of race on children's peer nominations, it was found that both white and black students, independent of the race composition of the classroom, rated white students more positively than black students. The authors argued that the dominant social position of white students, prevalent in the larger societal context, filtered through the peer context (Jackson et al., 2006).

The societal-level variables also affect immigrant children's adaptation through their influence on contexts representing their home culture, such as the family. Immigrant parents learn the characteristics of the new culture and become exposed to the influence of social variables, such as discrimination and prejudice, through their regular contact with native people at work, in the neighborhood, through their dealings with the health system, and other such institutions (Garcia Coll et al., 1996). Perceived discrimination reported by immigrants has been associated with stronger ethnic identity, weaker national identity, and lower commitment to the new culture (Berry et al., 2006; Ward et al., 2001; see also chapter by Liebkind et al., this volume). In this context, immigrant parents need not only to acculturate their children to their home culture, but must also support them in getting along in the culture of the receiving society and in succeeding in society at large, and, furthermore, to help them understand and teach them how to deal with, issues of discrimination and prejudice (Phinney & Chavira, 1995).

How do proximal contexts affect immigrant children's quality of adaptation? Children's regular interactions with people in their proximal environment have been viewed as the primary engines for their development (Bronfenbrenner & Morris, 2006) and acculturation (Oppedal, 2006; Sam, 2006). Proximal contexts need to provide immigrant children with normative experiences, such as supportive and caring relationships with teachers, as well as with experiences that address immigration-related issues, such as nondifferential treatment by ethnicity on the part of teachers (Roeser et al., 1998). The effect of proximal relational processes may be moderated by structural features of contexts such as the family's socioeconomic status or the availability of immigrants' own ethnocultural social network, which supports parents in their efforts to acculturate their children to the home culture (e.g., Halgunseth, Ispa, & Rudy, 2006).

Children are active agents in their development and acculturation (Bronfenbrenner & Morris, 2006; Kuczynski & Navara, 2006). Influences from societal- (e.g., media) and interaction-level variables are processed by them before they become translated into an adaptational outcome. The meaning they attribute to experience functions as a mediator between the actual context and their behavior and adaptation in that context (Magnusson & Stattin, 2006). They actively construct working models of culture, which need to accommodate for the often competing messages emanating from their parents, their peers, their teachers, and the broader social context. As their ability to self-regulate develops, immigrant children also become better able to position themselves with respect to the values and demands of the family and those of the larger society, to accept or reject them in their totality or in part, as well as to choose the environments in which they will spend their time and the people with whom they will become involved.

More than the attributes of any of the proximal contexts or of the individual, according to the person-environment fit theory, the congruence between the characteristics that the individual brings to the environment and the characteristics of the environment is the most important determinant of the quality of youth adaptation (Eccles et al., 1993). The match between the needs of developing and acculturating immigrant children and the opportunities afforded them by their proximal environments significantly predicts adaptation. For example, the schools that offer immigrant students the opportunity to experience their learning environment as relevant and meaningful promote better adaptation (Roeser et al., 1998). Along the same line, the quality of interactions between people in children's proximal contexts may also meet, or fail to meet, the latter's developmental and acculturative needs. For example, parents and teachers who support the missions of school and the family are likely to have a positive influence on children's adaptation (Coatsworth et al., 2000). Following this argument, the degree of congruence, or the cultural distance, between the social contexts of immigrant youth is also an important predictor of their adaptation. For example, for immigrant groups who value strong family embeddedness and delayed autonomy, migrating to an individualistic society may put a strain on parent–child relations, as adolescents demand autonomy sooner than parents are ready to grant it to them (Kwak, 2003).

The influences in the proposed integrative model are bidirectional, which implies that not only do factors related to the three levels have an impact on the quality of immigrant youth adaptation, but the latter in turn also feeds back and influences children's functioning, as well as the functioning of the proximal contexts and of society. Success or failure with respect to adaptational outcomes would be expected to have an impact on individual characteristics, such as self-efficacy, as well as on proximal processes, and as a result quality of adaptation at time 1 would indirectly influence quality of adaptation at time 2 (Bronfenbrenner & Morris, 2006). Furthermore, some adaptational outcomes, such as civic engagement and political participation, would be expected to have an impact on society through collective action (Silbereisen & Chen, 2010).

An important dimension not depicted in Figure 5.1 is the time dimension. Children's development and acculturation, of course, both involve change over time. However, as already mentioned, acculturation not only changes immigrants, but is also a mechanism of social change, since the characteristics of the receiving society are changed through the cultural contact between ethnocultural groups (Berry et al., 2011). Furthermore, children's proximal contexts are themselves undergoing changes as they adapt to the new reality. For example, parents' working models of culture, which were mainly formed based on the traditions of the culture of origin, are also undergoing change in light of immigration, teachings of "experts," and as a result of their present and future economic and social positions (Halgunseth et al., 2006). These parallel changes at all three levels would be expected to influence intra-individual change in immigrant youth adaptation (Szapocznik & Coatsworth, 1999).

Inter-individual differences in intra-individual change in the adaptation of immigrant youth have been examined in a number of longitudinal studies. Such studies may compare changes over time in immigrant groups compared with native peers. For example, in a three-wave, longitudinal study of adaptation among immigrant students and their native Greek peers, it was found that the former had at all times significantly lower school performance than the latter, and furthermore, that performance decreased in all three groups to a similar extent from age 12 to age 15 (Motti-Stefanidi, Asendorpf, & Masten, in press). The similar pattern in longitudinal change in adaptation suggests that it may be related to a developmental rather than an acculturative process.

Two time variables, age at migration (see chapter by Corak, this volume) and years spent in the new country (Berry et al., 2006), have an important influence on immigrant youths' adaptation. The first is a rough index of children's developmental stage at the time they migrated, and the second, of their degree of acculturation to the new culture. In what concerns time at migration, children who migrated before starting primary school seem to have a smoother adaptation over time than children who migrated later, and those who migrated in adolescence seem to have more difficulties in their adaptation than children who migrated earlier (Berry et al., 2006; Phinney, 2006). It should be noted here that immigrant children who were doing well before migrating, probably because they had adequate social and individual resources to support their development, and after an initial period of difficulties following migration, would be expected to do better than children who were not doing that well before migrating. Furthermore, with more years spent in the new country, an increase toward adopting the integrated and the national acculturation profiles and a move away from the diffuse profile have been reported, a change that may be due to acculturation (Berry et al., 2006).

This integrative framework allows an organized approach to addressing the question of what determines positive immigrant youth adaptation. The three levels of analysis proposed are viewed as interdependent but analytically distinct (Verkuyten, 2005). Each of the three levels of process is assumed to make an independent, unique contribution to understanding the adaptation of immigrant youth.

Immigration is a challenging phenomenon not only for the individuals migrating, but for their proximal contexts and receiving societies. Societies, schools, families, as well as individuals, both immigrants and natives, need to adapt to the new reality created by the coexistence of people from different cultures. Each level may present opportunities and/or challenges for immigrant youth adaptation. Immigrant children who live in societies that have developed a multicultural ideology would be expected to show better adaptation than children who live in societies that hold negative attitudes toward the presence of immigrants in the country (Berry et al., 2006). Furthermore, immigrant children whose lives are embedded in contexts that deal more effectively with the issues raised by immigration and with which they address their needs would be expected to be better adapted than their peers whose proximal contexts do not have these characteristics. Finally, immigrant children's personal resources, such as a good cognitive capacity, high self-efficacy, or an easygoing temperament may also promote their positive adaptation (Masten et al., 2006). One could conceive of immigrant children who live in societies that are not positive toward the presence of immigrants but who attend a well-functioning school and/or have a resilient family as being better adapted than children whose proximal environments do not have such positive qualities.

Conclusion

The purpose of this chapter was to integrate the developmental, acculturation, and social-psychological perspectives in order to account for individual differences in immigrant youth adaptation. Adaptation was examined
in a developmental and acculturative context, taking into account the influence of societal and individual level variables.

This integrative account underscores the complexity of defining and
explaining immigrant children's adaptation. Development and acculturation
processes are intricately related and, therefore, difficult, if not impossible, to
disentangle. First, behavior and performance with respect to developmental
and acculturative tasks, which are the basic criteria for judging the quality of
immigrant youth's adaptation, are intertwined, influencing each other currently and over time. Second, the contexts in which children interact with
other people on a regular basis and that propel developmental change support immigrant children's acculturation and enculturation. Third, society,
children's social contexts, and, of course, children themselves, are in a state
of continuous, interdependent change partly resulting from acculturation
and affecting their adaptation. Furthermore, development and acculturation take place in a larger societal context often replete with discrimination
and prejudice, with negative consequences for both.

Most immigrants move to a new country with the intention to stay and
make a better life for themselves and their children. It is in the interest of
receiving societies to ensure their positive adaptation. Policy and program
initiatives, which will promote a positive public attitude toward immigrants,
are needed. Politicians and the mass media have a major responsibility in
educating the public (Commission of the European Communities, 2003).
A positive attitude of native populations will be reflected in the functioning
of proximal environments, for example, through more positive attitudes of
teachers toward immigrant children, and should result in the allocation of
resources to children's proximal contexts, that will be used, for example, to
develop school programs and to offer educational support appropriate for
their needs. Support in the proximal contexts of immigrant children will serve
to promote positive development and effective adaptation in the new country,
for the good of the immigrants and for the benefit of society as a whole.

Authors' Note

The names after the first author appear in alphabetical order.

The authors wish to thank Lauren Pacelli for her editorial assistance.

REFERENCES

Alegría, M., Canino, G., Shrout, P. E., Woo, M., Duan, N., Vila, D., Torres, M., Chen, C., & Meng, X.-L. (2008). Prevalence of mental illness in immigrant and non-immigrant U.S. Latino groups. *American Journal of Psychiatry, 165*, 359–69.

Berry, J. W. (1980). Acculturation as varieties of adaptation. In A. Padilla (Ed.), *Acculturation: Theory, models and some new findings* (pp. 9–25). Boulder: Westview Press.

(1997). Immigration, acculturation and adaptation. *Applied Psychology: An International Review, 46*, 5–68.

(2006). Contexts of acculturation. In D. L. Sam and J. W. Berry (Eds.), *The Cambridge handbook of acculturation psychology* (pp. 97–112). Cambridge, UK: Cambridge University Press.

Berry, J. W., & Sam, D. L. (1997). Acculturation and adaptation. In J. W. Berry, M. H. Segall, & C. Kağitçibaşi (Eds.), *Handbook of cross-cultural psychology, Vol. III: Social behavior and applications* (2nd ed., pp. 291–326). Boston, MA: Allyn & Bacon.

Berry, J. W., Kalin, R., & Taylor, D. (1977). *Multiculturalism and ethnic attitudes in Canada.* Ottawa: Supply & Services.

Berry, J. W., Phinney, J. S., Sam, D. L., & Vedder, P. (Eds.). (2006). *Immigrant youth in cultural transition: Acculturation, identity and adaptation across national contexts.* Mahwah, NJ: Lawrence Erlbaum Associates.

Berry, J. W., Poortinga, Y. H., Breugelmans, S., Chasiotis, A., & Sam, D. L. (2011). *Cross-cultural psychology: Research and applications* (3rd ed.). Cambridge: Cambridge University Press.

Bhatia, S., & Ram, A. (2001). Rethinking "acculturation" in relation to diasporic cultures and postcolonial identities. *Human Development, 44*, 1–18.

Bornstein, M., & Cote, L. (Eds.). (2006). *Acculturation and parent-child relationships.* Mahwah, NJ: Lawrence Erlbaum Associates.

Bourhis, R. Y., Moïse, L. C., Perreault, S., & Senécal, S. (1997). Towards an interactive acculturation model: A social-psychological approach. *International Journal of Psychology, 32*(6), 369–86.

Boyce, W. T., Frank, E., Jensen, P. S., Kessler, R. C., Nelson, C. A., Steinberg, L. et al. (1998). Social context in developmental psychopathology: Recommendations for future research from the MacArthur Network on Psychopathology and Development. *Development and Psychopathology, 10*(2), 143–64.

Branscombe, N. R., Schmitt, M. T., & Harvey, R. D. (1999). Perceiving pervasive discrimination among African Americans: Implications for group identification and well-being. *Journal of Personality and Social Psychology, 77*(1), 135–49.

Bronfenbrenner, U., & Morris, P. A. (2006). The bioecological model of human development. In R. M. Lerner (Ed.), *Handbook of child psychology. Vol. 1: Theoretical models of human development* (6th ed., pp. 793–828). Hoboken, NJ: Wiley.

Brown, C. S., & Bigler, R. (2005). Children's perceptions of discrimination: A developmental model. *Child Development, 76*, 533–53.

Caspi, A., & Shiner, R. L. (2006). Personality development. In R. M. Lerner (Ed.), *Handbook of child psychology. Vol. 3: Social, emotional, and personality development* (6th ed., pp. 300–65). New York: Wiley.

Chryssochoou, X. (2000). Multicultural societies: Making sense of new environments and identities. *Journal of Community and Applied Social Psychology, 10*, 343–54.

(2003). Studying identity in social psychology. Some thoughts on the definition of identity and its relation to action. *Language and Politics, 22*, 225–42.

(2004). *Cultural diversity: Its social psychology*. Oxford: Blackwell.

Chryssochoou, X., & Lyons, E. (2011). Perceptions of (in)compatibility between identities and participation in the national polity of people belonging to ethnic minorities. In A. E. Azzi, X. Chryssochoou, B. Klandermans, and B. Simon (Eds.), *Identity and participation in culturally diverse societies: A multidisciplinary perspective* (pp. 69–88). Oxford: Wiley-Blackwell.

Clement, R., & Noels, K. (1992). Towards a situated approach to ethnolinguistic identity: The effects of status on individuals and groups. *Journal of Language and Social Psychology, 11*(4), 203–32.

Coatsworth, J. D., Pantin, H., McBride, C., Briones, E., Kurtines, W., & Szapocznik, J. (2000). Ecodevelopmental correlates of behavior problems in young Hispanic females. *Applied Developmental Science, 6*(3), 126–43.

Commission of the European Communities (2003). *Communication on immigration, integration and employment*, COM (2003)336, Brussels.

Cooper, C. R. (2003). Bridging multiple worlds: Immigrant youth identity and pathways to college. *International Journal of Behavioral Development, 27*(6, Suppl.), 1–4.

Crocker, J., Major, B., & Steele, C. (1998). Social stigma. In D. T. Gilbert, S. T. Fiske, and G. Lindzey (Eds.), *The handbook of social psychology* (pp. 504–53). Boston, MA: McGraw-Hill.

Deaux, K. (2006). *To be an immigrant*. New York: Russell Sage Foundation.

Doise, W. (1986). *Levels of explanation in social psychology*. Cambridge, UK: Cambridge University Press.

Eccles, J. S., Midgley, C., Wigfield, A., Miller-Buchanan, C., Reuman, D., Flanagan, C. et al. (1993). Development during adolescence: The impact of stage-environment fit on young adolescents' experiences in schools and in families. *American Psychologist, 48*(2), 90–101.

Erikson, E. (1968). *Identity: Youth and crisis*. New York: Norton.

Fordham, S., & Ogbu, J. (1986). Black students' school success: Coping with the burden of "acting White." *The Urban Review, 18*(3), 176–296.

Fuligni, A. J. (1997). The academic achievement of adolescents from immigrant families: The roles of family background, attitudes, and behavior. *Child Development, 68*, 261–73.

Fuligni, A., & Fuligni, A. (2007). Immigrant families and the educational development of their children. In J. Lansford, K. Deater-Deckard, and M. Bornstein (Eds.), *Immigrant families in contemporary society* (pp. 231–49). New York: Guildford Press.

Garcia Coll, C., Lamberty, G., Jenkins, R., McAdoo, H. P., Crnic, K., Wasik, B. H. et al. (1996). An integrative model for the study of developmental competencies in minority children. *Child Development, 67*, 1891–914.

Georgas, J., Berry, J. W., van der Vijver, F. J. R., Kağitçibaşi, C., & Poortinga, Y. H. (2006). *Families across cultures: A 30 nation psychological study*. Cambridge, UK: Cambridge University Press.

Gotlieb, G., Wahlsten, D., & Lickliter, R. (2006). The significance of biology for human development: A developmental psychobiological systems view. In R. M. Lerner (Ed.), *Handbook of child psychology. Vol. 1: Theoretical models of human development* (pp. 210–58). Hoboken, NJ: Wiley.

Graves, T. (1967). Psychological acculturation in a tri-ethnic community. *South-Western Journal of Anthropology, 23*, 337–50.

Green, E. G. T. (2007). Guarding the gates of Europe: A typological analysis of immigration attitudes across 21 countries. *International Journal of Psychology, 42*(6), 365–79.

Greenfield, P. M., Keller, H., Fuligni, A., & Maynard, A. (2003). Cultural pathways through universal development. *Annual Review of Psychology, 54*, 461–90.

Halgunseth, L. C., Ispa, J. M., & Rudy, D. (2006). Parental control in Latino families: An integrated review of the literature. *Child Development, 77*(5), 1282–97.

Harkness, S., & Super, C. M. (Eds.). (1996). *Parents' cultural belief systems: Their origins, expressions, and consequences.* New York: Guilford.

International Organization for Migration. http://www.iom.int.

Jackson, M. F., Barth, J. M., Powell, N., & Lochman, J. E. (2006). Classroom contextual effects of race on children's peer nominations. *Child Development, 77*(5), 1325–37.

Jasinskaja-Lahti, I., & Liebkind, K. (2007). A structural model of acculturation and well-being among immigrants from the former USSR in Finland. *European Psychologist, 12*(2), 80–92.

Jasinskaja-Lahti, I., Liebkind, K., & Solheim, E. (2009). To identify or not identify? National dis-identification as an alternative reaction to perceived ethnic discrimination. *Applied Psychology, 58*(1), 105–28.

Jensen, L. A. (2008). Immigrants' cultural identities as sources of civic engagement. *Applied Developmental Science, 12*(2), 74–83.

Jensen, L. A., & Flanagan, C. A. (2008). Immigrant civic engagement: New translations. *Applied Developmental Science, 12*(2), 55–6.

Kağitçibaşi, Ç. (2007). *Families, self and human development across cultures: Theory and applications.* Mahwah, NJ: Lawrence Erlbaum.

Kao, G., & Tienda, M. (1995). Educational aspirations of minority youth. *American Journal of Education, 106*(3), 349–84.

Kiang, L., Yip, T., & Fuligni, A. (2008). Multiple social identities and adjustment in young adults from ethnically diverse backgrounds. *Journal of Research on Adolescence, 18*, 643–70.

Kroger, J. (2007). *Identity development: Adolescence through adulthood* (2nd ed.). Thousand Oaks, CA: Sage Publications.

Kuczynski, L., & Navara, G. (2006). Sources of change in theories of socialization, internalization and acculturation. In M. Killen and J. Smetana (Eds.), *Handbook of moral development* (pp. 299–327). Mahwah, NJ: Erlbaum.

Kwak, K. (2003). Adolescents and their parents: A review of intergenerational family relations for immigrant and non-immigrant families. *Human Development, 46*, 115–36.

Lee, R. M. (2005). Resilience against discrimination: Ethnic identity and other-group orientation as protective factors for Korean Americans. *Journal of Counseling Psychology, 52*(1), 36–44.

Lerner, R. M. (2006). Developmental science, developmental systems, and contemporary theories. In R. M. Lerner (Ed.), *Handbook of child psychology. Vol. 1: Theoretical models of human development* (pp. 1–17). Hoboken, NJ: Wiley.

Levine, P. (2008). The civic engagement of young immigrants: Why does it matter? *Applied Developmental Science, 12*(2), 102–4.

Liebkind, K. (2001). Acculturation. In R. Brown and S. Gaertner (Eds.), *Blackwell hand-book of social psychology: Intergroup processes* (pp. 386–406). Oxford: Blackwell.

(2006). Ethnic identity and acculturation. In D. L. Sam and J. W. Berry (Eds.), *Cambridge handbook of acculturation psychology* (pp. 78–96). Cambridge, UK: Cambridge University Press.

Lopez, M. H., & Marcelo, K. B. (2008). The civic engagement of immigrant youth: New evidence from the 2006 Civic and Political Health of the Nation Survey. *Applied Developmental Science, 12*(2), 66–73.

Magnusson, D., & Stattin, H. (2006). The person in context: A holistic-interactionistic approach. In R. M. Lerner (Ed.), *Handbook of child psychology. Vol. 1: Theoretical models of human development* (pp. 400–64). New Jersey: Wiley.

Masten, A. S. (2006). Developmental psychopathology: Pathways to the future. *International Journal of Behavioral Development, 31*, 46–53.

Masten, A. S., Burt, K., & Coatsworth, J. D. (2006). Competence and psychopathology in development. In D. Cicchetti and D. Cohen (Eds.), *Developmental psychopathology. Vol. 3: Risk disorder and psychopathology* (2nd ed., pp. 696–738). New York: Wiley.

Masten, A. S., & Cicchetti, D. (2010). Editorial: Developmental cascades. *Development and Psychopathology, 22*, 491–5.

Masten, A. S., Long, J. D., Roisman, G. I., Burt, K. B., Obradović, J., Roberts, J. M., Boelcke, K., & Tellegen, A. (2005). Developmental cascades: Linking academic achievement, externalizing and internalizing symptoms over 20 years. *Developmental Psychology, 41*(5), 733–46.

Masten, A. S., & Motti-Stefanidi, F. (2009). Understanding and promoting resilience in children: Promotive and protective processes in schools. In T. Gutkin and C. Reynolds (Eds.), *The handbook of school psychology* (4th ed., pp. 721–38). Hoboken, NJ: Wiley.

McCormick, C. M., Kuo, S. I., & Masten, A. S. (2011). Developmental tasks across the lifespan. In K. L. Fingerman, C. Berg, J. Smith, and T. C. Antonucci (Eds.), *The handbook of lifespan development* (pp. 117–40). New York: Springer.

McLoyd, V. (2006). The legacy of *Child Development's* 1990 special issue on minority children: An editorial retrospective. *Child Development, 77*, 1142–8.

Merz, E-M., Özeke-Kocabas, E., Oort, F. J., & Schuengel, C. (2009). Intergenerational family solidarity: Value differences between immigrant groups and generations. *Journal of Family Psychology, 23*, 291–300.

Moscovici, S. (1988). Le domaine de la psychologie sociale. In S. Moscovici (Ed.), *Psychologie sociale* (pp. 5–22). Paris: Presses Universitaires de France.

Motti-Stefanidi, F., Asendorpf, J. B., & Masten, A. S. (in press). The adaptation and psychological well-being of adolescent immigrants in Greek schools: A multilevel, longitudinal study of risks and resources. *Development and psychopathology.*

Motti-Stefanidi, F., Pavlopoulos, V., Obradović, J., Dalla, M., Takis, N., Papathanasiou, A., & Masten, A. S. (2008). Immigration as a risk factor for adolescent adaptation in Greek urban schools. *European Journal of Developmental Psychology, 5*(2), 235–61.

Motti-Stefanidi, F., Pavlopoulos, V., Obradović, J., & Masten, A. (2008). Acculturation and adaptation of immigrant adolescents in Greek urban schools. *International Journal of Psychology, 43*(1), 45–58.

Mugny, G. (1982). *The power of minorities.* London: Academic Press.

Navas, M., Rojas, A. J., García, M., & Pumares, P. (2007). Acculturation strategies and attitudes according to the Relative Acculturation Extended Model (RAEM): The perspectives of natives versus immigrants. *International Journal of Intercultural Relations, 31,* 67–86.

Ogbu, J. (1991). Immigrant and involuntary minorities in comparative perspective. In M. Gibson and J. Ogbu (Eds.), *Minority status and schooling: A comparative study of immigrant and involuntary minorities* (pp. 3–33). New York: Garland.

Oppedal, B. (2006). Development and acculturation. In D. L. Sam and J. W. Berry (Eds.), *The Cambridge handbook of acculturation psychology* (pp. 97–112). Cambridge, UK: Cambridge University Press.

Palmer, J. (2007). Who is the authentic Korean American? Korean-born Korean American high school students' negotiation of ascribed and achieved identities. *Journal of Language, Identity and Education, 6,* 277–98.

Phelan, P., Davidson, A. L., & Yu, H. C. (1998). *Adolescents' worlds: Negotiating family, peers and school.* New York: Teachers College Press.

Phinney, J. (2006). Ethnic identity exploration in emerging adulthood. In J. Arnett and J. Tanner (Eds.), *Emerging adults in America* (pp. 117–34). Washington, DC: American Psychological Association.

Phinney, J., Berry, J. W., Vedder, P., & Liebkind, K. (2006). The acculturation experience: Attitudes, identities and behaviors of immigrant youth. In J. W. Berry, J. S. Phinney, D. L. Sam, and P. Vedder (Eds.), *Immigrant youth in cultural transition: Acculturation, identity and adaptation across national contexts* (pp. 71–116). Mahwah, NJ: Lawrence Erlbaum Associates.

Phinney, J. S., & Chavira, V. (1995). Parental ethnic socialization and adolescent coping with problems related to ethnicity. *Journal of Research on Adolescence, 5,* 31–53.

Phinney, J. S., & Devich-Navarro, M. (1997). Variations in bicultural identification among African American and Mexican American adolescents. *Journal of Research on Adolescence, 7,* 3–32.

Phinney, J. S., Horenczyk, G., Liebkind, K., & Vedder, P. (2001). Ethnic identity, immigration and well-being: An interactional perspective. *Journal of Social Issues, 57,* 493–510.

Phinney, J. S., Kim-Jo, T., Osorio, S., & Vilhjalmsdottir, P. (2005). Autonomy and relatedness in adolescent-parent disagreements: Ethnic and developmental factors. *Journal of Adolescent Research, 20,* 8–39.

Portes, A., & Rumbaut, R. (2001). *Legacies: The story of the immigrant second generation.* Berkeley, CA: University of California Press.

Pyke, K. (2005). "Generational deserters" and "black sheep": Acculturative differences among siblings in Asian immigrant families. *Journal of Family Issues, 26,* 491–517.

Quillian, L., & Campbell, M. E. (2003). Beyond Black and White: The present and future of multiracial friendship segregation. *American Sociological Review, 68,* 540–66.

Raudenbush, S. W., & Bryk, A. S. (2002). Hierarchical linear models: Applications and data analysis methods (2nd ed.). Newbury Park, CA: Sage.

Redfield, R., Linton, R., & Herskovits, M. J. (1936). Memorandum for the study of acculturation. *American Anthropologist, 38,* 149–52.

Reicher, S., & Hopkins, N. (2001). *Self and nation.* London: Sage.

Roeser, R. W., Eccles, J. S., & Sameroff, A. J. (1998). Academic and social functioning in early adolescence: Longitudinal relations, patterns, and prediction by experience in middle school. *Development and Psychopathology, 10*, 321–52.

Rothbaum, F., Pott, M., Azuma, H., Miyake, K., & Weisz, J. (2000). The development of close relationships in Japan and the United States: Paths of symbiotic harmony and generative tension. *Child Development, 71*, 1121–42.

Rubin, K. H., Bukowski, W., & Parker, J. (2006). Peer interactions, relationships and groups. In N. Eisenberg (Ed.), *Handbook of child psychology. Vol 3: Social, emotional, and personality development* (pp. 571–645). New York: Wiley.

Rumbaut, R. G. (2008). Reaping what you sow: Immigration, youth, and reactive ethnicity. *Applied Developmental Science, 12*(2) 108–11.

Ryan, R. M., & Lynch, J. H. (1989). Emotional autonomy versus detachment: Revisiting the vicissitudes of adolescence and young adulthood. *Child Development, 60*, 340–56.

Sam, D. L. (2006). Adaptation of children and adolescents with immigrant background: Acculturation or development. In M. Bornstein and L. R. Cote (Eds.), *Acculturation and parent-child relationships: Measurement and development* (pp. 97–112). Mahwah, NJ: Lawrence Erlbaum Associates.

Sam, D. L., & Berry, J. W. (Eds.). (2006). *Cambridge handbook of acculturation psychology.* Cambridge, UK: Cambridge University Press.

Sam, D. L., & Berry, J. W. (2010). Acculturation: When individuals and groups of different cultural backgrounds meet. *Perspectives on Psychological Science. 5*, 472–81.

Sam, D. L., Vedder, P., Liebkind, K., Neto, F., & Virta, E. (2008). Immigration, acculturation and the paradox of adaptation. *European Journal of Developmental Psychology, 5*, 138–58.

Schönpflug, U. (Ed.). (2008). *Cultural transmission: Psychological, developmental, social and methodological aspects.* Cambridge, UK: Cambridge University Press.

Silbereisen, R. K., & Chen, X. (2010). *Social change and human development: Concepts and results.* Sage: London.

Simon, B., & Klandermans, B. (2001). Politicized collective identity: A social psychological analysis. *American Psychologist, 56*, 319–31.

Simon, B., & Ruhs, D. (2008). Identity and politicization among Turkish migrants in Germany: The role of dual identification. *Journal of Personality and Social Psychology, 95*(6), 1354–66.

Sirin, S., & Fine, M. (2008). *Muslim American youth: Understanding hyphenated identities through multiple methods.* New York: New York University Press.

Snauwaert, B., Soenens, B., Vanbeselaere, N., & Boen, F. (2003). When integration does not necessarily imply integration. *Journal of Cross-Cultural Psychology, 34*, 231–9.

Sroufe, L. A., Egeland, B., Carlson, E. A., & Collins, W. A. (2005). *The development of the person: The Minnesota study of risk and adaptation from birth to adulthood.* New York: Guilford.

Strohmeier, D., & Spiel, C. (2003). Immigrant children in Austria. Aggressive behavior and friendship patterns in multicultural school classes. *Journal of Applied School Psychology, 19*, 99–116.

Suárez-Orozco, C., & Suárez-Orozco, M. (2001). *Children of immigration*. Cambridge, MA: Harvard University Press.

Suárez-Orozco, C., Suárez-Orozco, M., & Todorova, I. (2006). *Moving stories: Educational pathways of immigrant youth*. Cambridge, MA: Harvard University Press.

Szapocznik, J., & Coatsworth, J. D. (1999). An ecodevelopmental framework for organizing the influences on drug abuse: A developmental model of risk and protection. In M. Glantz & C. R. Hartel (Eds.), *Drug abuse: Origins and interventions* (pp. 331–66). Washington, DC: American Psychological Association.

Tajfel, H. (1974). Social identity and intergroup behaviour. *Social Science Information*, *13*, 65–93.

Tajfel, H., & Turner, J. (1986). The social identity theory of intergroup behavior. In S. Worchel & W. Austin (Eds.), *Psychology of intergroup relations* (pp. 7–24). Chicago, IL: Nelson-Hall.

Titzmann, P. F., & Silbereisen, R. K. (2009). Friendship homophily among ethnic German immigrants: A longitudinal comparison between recent and more experienced immigrant adolescents. *Journal of Family Psychology*, *23*, 301–10.

Updegraff, K. A., McHale, S. M., Whiteman, S. D., Thayer, S. M., & Crouter, A. C. (2006). The nature and correlates of Mexican-American adolescents' time with parents and peers. *Child Development*, *77*(5), 1470–86.

Vedder, P., Berry, J. W., Sabatier, C., & Sam, D. (2009). The intergenerational transmission of values in national and immigrant families: The role of zeitgeist. *Journal of Youth and Adolescence*, *38*, 642–53.

Vedder, P. H., & Horenczyk, G. (2006). Acculturation and the school. In D. L. Sam and J. W. Berry (Eds.), *The Cambridge handbook of acculturation psychology* (pp. 419–29). Cambridge, UK: Cambridge University Press.

Verkuyten, M. (2000). The benefits to social psychology of studying ethnic minorities. *European Bulletin of Social Psychology*, *12*(3), 5–21.

(2005). *The social psychology of ethnic identity*. New York: Psychology Press.

Verkuyten, M., & Brug, P. (2004). Multiculturalism and group status. The role of ethnic identification, group essentialism and protestant ethic. *European Journal of Social Psychology*, *34*(6), 647–61.

Verkuyten, M., & Yildiz, A. A. (2006). The endorsement of minority rights: The role of group position, national context, and ideological beliefs. *Political Psychology*, *27*(4), 527–48.

Ward, C., Bochner, S., & Furnham, A. (2001). *The psychology of culture shock*. London: Routledge.

Waters, M. C. (2008). The challenges of studying political and civic incorporation. *Applied Developmental Science*, *12*(2), 105–7.

Way, N., Santos, C., Niwa, E., & Kim-Gervey, C. (2008). To be or not to be: Exploration of ethnic identity development in context. In M. Azmitia, M. Syed, and K. Radmacher (Eds.), *The intersections of personal and social identities* (pp. 61–79). San Francisco, CA: Jossey-Bass.

Weisner, T. S. (2002). Ecocultural understanding of children's developmental pathways. *Human Development*, *45*, 275–81.

Wong, C. A., Eccles J. S., & Sameroff A. (2003). The influence of ethnic discrimination and ethnic identification on African American adolescents' school and socio-emotional adjustment. *Journal of Personality, 71*(6), 1197–232.

Wray-Lake, L., Syvertsen, A. K., & Flanagan, C. A. (2008). Contested citizenship and social exclusion: Adolescent Arab American immigrants' views of the social contract. *Applied Developmental Science, 12*(2), 84–92.

6 Understanding the Immigrant Paradox in Youth

Developmental and Contextual Considerations

Cynthia Garcia Coll, Flannery Patton, Amy Kerivan Marks,
Radosveta Dimitrova, Rui Yang, Gloria A. Suarez, and
Andrea Patrico

Introduction

The *immigrant paradox* refers to surprising data indicating that as immigrant generations go by, and as immigrant individuals acculturate to the host country, their developmental outcomes deteriorate (see Table 6.1 for a description of the variation in research designs and definitions used to demonstrate the immigrant paradox). In other words, members of the first generation, presumably the least acculturated and for the most part poorer and less educated, have better health, behavior, academic progress, and attitudes than native-born and more acculturated individuals. However, the robustness of these findings varies as a function of ethnic group, developmental outcome, host country, and age. In addition, much of the literature fails to provide insights into the processes underlying these findings, although this knowledge is crucial to formulating better policies and practices to support and enhance positive developmental outcomes for children of immigrants. The key questions remain: How can we prevent deterioration of outcomes as acculturation progresses? What can we learn from the groups or individuals who are succeeding in spite of all odds? Can this knowledge inform interventions for children and adolescents who are not doing well?

In this chapter, we attempt to provide some understanding of the immigrant paradox during childhood and adolescence, specifically in the areas of risk behaviors (e.g., illicit substance and alcohol use and abuse, sex risk behaviors including sex with multiple partners and lack of contraception, and delinquency) and academic performance (e.g., achievement, attitudes, and behaviors). We chose these two areas of behavior because of the

Table 6.1. Types of Group Comparisons Used to Document the Immigrant Paradox

Children of immigrants (first and second generations)		Third + generations
First generation (immigrant children and adolescents)	Shows a significantly better outcome than	Second and third + generations
Second generation	⟶	Third + generations
Less acculturated (e.g., less English use, less time spent in the United States, less American cultural orientation)		More acculturated

Note: See recommendations by Sam et al., 2008 for a conservative approach to documenting the paradox.

extensive research done in each domain in North America and Europe, and also because these two areas are highly predictive of successful pathways into adulthood (Masten, Burt, & Coatsworth, 2006). In other words, we contend that if children of immigrants succeed in school and do not engage in risk behaviors, they have a high probability of making a successful transition into adulthood as citizens of the new country.

We start with the theoretical considerations that guide our understanding of how youth adapt to and adopt new cultures, while at the same time retaining, modifying, or rejecting the original cultures of their parents. We present a brief review of available literature on academic performance and risk behaviors from North America and Europe, paying special attention to contextual and developmental considerations. We find evidence that supports the existence of the immigrant paradox in some countries, in some developmental stages, and in certain domains. This chapter aims not only to find convergence of evidence for the existence of the immigrant paradox, but also evidence of what might explain it.

This chapter highlights the importance of understanding why the immigrant advantage is lost over time and how we can learn from the success of individuals and groups to prevent deterioration. This information can then be used to support the formulation of policies that promote resilience in those lacking it and the creation of preventive interventions to support immigrant advantages over time. The need for a more balanced approach to the incorporation of immigrants into the host country is indicated – where the strengths of the first generation are identified and supported as the individuals acculturate. Finally, our review supports a bicultural model of adaptation for new immigrant youth over a straight assimilation model.

Historical and Theoretical Orientations

The second generation of immigrants generally comes into contact with the courts as delinquents more frequently than the first one ... not difficult to understand ... living in an isolated immigrant colony ... [the first-generation immigrant] is at least supported and controlled by Old world traditions ... personal morale and community control are maintained (Wirth, 1931).

As exemplified by the quote just cited, the observation of the first-generation immigrant advantage by social scientists may have originated around the time of the earliest waves of massive migrations into the United States. These observations were made unsystematically, without much evidence explaining the protective role of the traditional culture that is lost over time. Only during the last 40 years has a systematic body of research emerged that can speak to this phenomenon. Early work in the 1970s and 1980s primarily focused on documenting health outcomes, describing what was called the "epidemiological paradox."

The epidemiological paradox was first documented by Teller and Clyburn (1974) in their work on neonatal outcomes of Mexican immigrant mothers in Texas. This research showed that infants born to Mexican women – who were poorer, less formally educated, and in many cases had no prenatal care – had better birth outcomes (higher birth weight, lower perinatal complications) than infants born to Mexican Americans and the population at large. Fuller et al. (2009) have replicated these findings in a recent national representative sample, the Early Childhood Longitudinal Study – Birth Cohort (ECLS-B). Markides & Coreil (1986) also used the concept of the epidemiological paradox in a review of the literature on the health status of Latinos in the southwestern United States, extending the findings to a myriad of health outcomes. Since those early studies, other studies have found evidence for the epidemiological paradox across various ethnic groups (Latinos, Asians) and health outcomes: low birth weight, infant mortality, adult health outcomes, and adult mortality (Hummer et al., 2007; Landale et al., 1999; Singh & Siahpush, 2002). Evidence continues to mount suggesting that as generations go by and individual acculturation progresses, the health outcomes of U.S. immigrant populations deteriorate. Changes in lifestyle such as diet and increases in stress have been suggested as possible explanations (e.g., Kaplan et al., 2004; McDonald & Kennedy, 2005), but the evidence remains elusive in terms of pinpointing specific mechanisms responsible for this phenomenon.

Most of these early studies were conducted with adults in the United States, but slowly evidence has accrued to indicate similar processes for developmental outcomes at earlier ages. For example, the immigrant advantage has been found in several adolescent health outcomes, including obesity, asthma, and health problems causing them to miss school (Harris, 1999; Lara et al., 2005; Popkin & Udry, 1998). In contrast, the findings on mental health are less consistent. Research has indicated that first-generation immigrants have higher incidences of depression and feelings of alienation while other research has documented higher levels of well-being and fewer somatic complaints in first-generation groups (Harker, 2001; Kao, 1999; Steinhausen et al., 1997; Yu et al., 2003).

Beginning in the 1990s and especially since 2000, evidence on risky problem behaviors and academic performance has been added to data showing paradoxical patterns. Risk behaviors change in their expression according to the age of the child, but in general they may indicate maladaptation, the possibility of self-harm, or problems with the law. Academic performance not only refers to grades and test scores, but also to academic attitudes, behaviors, and level of engagement in school. Although these dimensions of academic performance are more intangible and difficult dimensions, they remain central components of successful academic trajectories.

Our current thinking on the immigrant paradox has been influenced by three major theoretical bodies of literature including models of resiliency, acculturation, and bioecological development. These frameworks guide our questions, analyses, and interpretations of the findings that follow in this chapter. First, how do we explain why some children and adolescents with immigrant backgrounds demonstrate resilience and others do not? The recent work by various investigators on the origins of resilience in children and adolescents has influenced our perspective (Luthar, 2006; Masten, 2007). They have contributed to a view of resilience – or unexpected optimal outcomes in spite of being exposed to a variety of high-risk conditions – as a complex function of the bidirectional interactions between individuals and their environments. In other words, both individuals and contexts can contribute to resilient outcomes. As such, measurement of subjects and their settings (family, school, peers, and neighborhood) are needed. Within this framework it is possible that in spite of being poor, uneducated, and unfamiliar with the host country culture, immigrant youth, their families, their neighbors, and their peers might share protective factors that support resilient youth outcomes.

A second theoretical framework that informs our conceptual approach to the immigrant paradox is contemporary work on acculturation processes based on research on differential outcomes of children of immigrants as children, adolescents, and adults. Various investigators (e.g., Portes, Fernández-Kelly, & Haller, 2005; Portes & Zhou, 1993) have developed and applied a framework based on the concept of segmented assimilation as the most accurate model of present day acculturation. In earlier views of acculturation, learning English and adopting the new host culture in its entirety was considered the ideal mode of incorporation (i.e., assimilation). But observations across many studies and samples have led to a very different view. As Portes, Fernández-Kelly, and Haller (2005) express this perspective: "The central question is not whether the second generation will assimilate to American society, (many fear that these individuals will not in spite of all the data against it) but to what segment of that society they will assimilate" (1000).

Racism, bifurcated labor markets, and exposure to poverty and crime are among the most challenging conditions confronted by today's second generation. Changes (political, economic, and cultural) in the context of reception and in the countries of origin contribute to cohort effects and ethnic group differences. Resources to confront the new challenges can come from their own families or the institutions and networks to which the youth and family are exposed.

Differential access and utilization contribute to individual and ethnic group-level differences observed in acculturation outcomes. These differences have been characterized by three patterns: upward mobility with full acculturation and economic integration, downward mobility with full acculturation and integration to the underclass, and integration with the middle class and preservation of original ethnic culture (Zhou, 1997). In particular, this framework leads to the question: Why do some individuals and not others, and some groups and not others, see dramatic downward assimilation as acculturation proceeds?

Finally, our theoretical lens is also informed by developmental systems theory, including the frameworks proposed by Bronfenbrenner (1979, 1995) and Garcia Coll et al. (1996, 2004). In these frameworks, developmental outcomes are seen as the product of many interacting forces among embedded and interacting systems, including youth, their families, neighborhoods, schools, peers, and sociocultural environments. Macrosystems such as the policy structures and societal attitudes of the receiving country influence the quality and climate of the microsystems (e.g., schools, families, and neighborhoods). One fundamental question is in what specific ways does the political and social climate (in relation to immigrants) influence and interact these microsystems that more directly shape developmental trajectories? How do youth, family, neighborhoods, schools, and peers contribute to downward assimilation? And, more interesting, what aspects of these contexts support positive outcomes for individuals and groups?

In the following sections, we discuss the extant data on risk behaviors and academic performance pertinent to the immigrant paradox, drawing on the most compelling findings from research in North America and Europe. While we attempt to make generalizations about generational trends based on the cumulative wisdom of the findings, information on the host country and country of origin variability is presented if available. The evidence is powerful in part due to the fact that for some ages and areas of development, there is strong evidence for the immigrant paradox in spite of the differences in host country, context of reception, and immigrant group.

Documenting the Paradox: A Review of Risk Behaviors in Immigrant Youth

Related to the study of the risk behavior paradox, research in the United States and Canada shows lower levels of emotional and behavioral problems in first-generation children compared to later generation peers (Beiser et al., 2002; Chang, Morrissey, & Koplewicz, 1995; Crosnoe, 2006a, 2006b; Jutte et al., 2003; Ma, 2002). While few in number, studies examining childhood also show the immigrant paradox directly in risk behaviors across pan-ethnic groups (e.g., Latino, Asian) and in many country-of-origin groups – even the most economically disadvantaged (e.g., Mexican Americans in the United States).

Regarding adolescence, the evidence is more robust and convincing. In the United States, first-generation and less acculturated adolescents have lower rates of externalizing behavior, delinquency, substance and cigarette use, and arrest or incarceration than later generation and more acculturated adolescents. These findings have also been documented across pan-ethnic groups and in a variety of country-of-origin groups (e.g., Mexican, Chinese and Filipino; Bui & Thongniramol, 2005; Willgerodt & Thompson, 2005). There are far fewer studies looking at these differences in Canadian adolescents but in what limited work does exist there is evidence of comparable trends (Georgiades et al., 2006; Ma, 2002; Wong, 1999).

One exception to this consistency of findings is sexual behaviors. While many studies document lower likelihood of having had a sexual experience as well as lower likelihood of having multiple sexual partners for first-generation adolescents, they also document less use of safe sexual practices and less knowledge about sexual risk among the first generation (Afable-Munsuz & Brindis, 2006; Guilamo-Ramos et al., 2005; Hahm, Lahiff, & Barreto, 2006; McDonald, Manlove, & Ikramullah, 2009).

European studies on behavioral patterns in adolescence have focused on antisocial behaviors, bullying, delinquency, and substance use. Accordingly, findings from several European studies further corroborate the risky–problem behavior paradox, showing that immigrant adolescents display lower levels of bullying and victimization (Strohmeier, Spiel, & Gradinger, 2008), antisocial behaviors (Sam et al., 2008), and overall drinking and alcohol use (Amundsen, Rossow, & Skurtveit, 2005). Such evidence shows a uniform pattern in various ethnic groups (e.g., former Yugoslavian, Turkish, Vietnamese, Pakistani, Iranian, Iraqi, and Central, Latin, and South American) and different receiving countries (e.g., Austria, the Netherlands, Finland, Portugal, Sweden, and Norway).

Risk behaviors could be viewed as resulting from struggles with sociocultural adaptations and reflecting individual ability to deal with daily problems, particularly in the areas of peer and school settings. Interesting, whether the outcome studied involves tobacco or alcohol use, smoking, or delinquency, data from the United States and numerous other countries (e.g., Sweden, the United Kingdom, and Spain) provide evidence that despite higher *risk* for behavioral problems, immigrant children and adolescents are successfully coping within the receiving country. These trends provide an excellent lens through which to examine the relationship between successful behavioral adaptations and the possible protective factors (in schools, families, neighborhoods, and peer groups) sustaining positive adjustment outcomes in immigrant populations.

Documenting the Paradox: A Review of Academic Performance in Immigrant Youth

Success in academic settings is commonly considered a primary developmental task for children and adolescents (Masten et al., 2006). For immigrant youth, being successful in school indicates a good sociocultural adaptation through the ability to adequately interact with and perform in the host society (Vedder & Horenczyk, 2006). Like the research in risk behaviors, we find that research on academic performance in immigrant youth is focused primarily on adolescence.

Although research with adolescents showed the largest paradox effect sizes we observed in the literature, there also was evidence of paradoxical patterns emerging earlier, in elementary school. In general, kindergarten-aged first- and second-generation Asian children are outperforming third-generation children in reading and math, whereas for Latinos the pattern is the opposite (Crosnoe, 2006a; Han, 2006). However, there is evidence that first- and second-generation Latino youth show the immigrant paradox in achievement growth, especially for reading, compared with their third-generation peers (Crosnoe, 2006a; Palacios, Guttmannova, & Chase-Lansdale, 2008). Within pan-ethnic groups (e.g., Latino), there is substantial variability between country-of-origin (e.g., Mexican, Cuban) groups in academic performance. For example, while Chinese, Indian, and Cuban first- and second-generation third graders outperform their third- and later generation peers in math, first- and second-generation Mexican, Puerto Rican, Filipino, Laotian, and Cambodian third graders perform below the levels of their peers. These groupings point to average level of parent education as a major influence on early test scores. There is evidence, however, that first-generation elementary school children, as a whole, outscore native-born children in both math and reading in the United States (Conger, Schwartz, & Stiefel, 2003) and that, in Canada, elementary school children from recent immigrant families have higher school performance than later generation peers (Georgiades, Boyle, & Duku, 2007).

In adolescence, first- and second-generation Asian immigrant youth outperform their later generation peers for grades (Fuligni, 1997; Pong & Hao, 2007) and Asian and Latino first-generation groups show more positive academic attitudes and behaviors than later generation peers (Glick & White, 2003; Portes & Rumbaut, 2001; Rosenbaum & Rochford, 2008; Suárez-Orozco & Suárez-Orozco, 1995). For example, first-generation youth are less likely to engage in negative school behaviors (e.g., cutting class), are more likely to spend more time on homework, and are more likely to report positive associations with their schools. There is evidence that for some country-of-origin groups who do not show the immigrant paradox in academics early on (e.g., Mexican Americans) they show evidence of first-generation advantage during adolescence (e.g., lower levels of course failure, higher math and science grades; Crosnoe, 2005).

Research on academic performance in Europe has primarily focused on school attainment with little work done on grades and test scores during elementary and high school. However, evidence shows that some immigrant groups experience the immigrant paradox in academic attitudes and behaviors. For example, Vietnamese adolescents show better school adjustment in terms of self-reported feelings toward schooling and perceived behavior problems within an academic setting than native Finns (Liebkind, Jasinskaja-Lahti, & Solheim, 2004), whereas Turkish and Moroccan students report higher levels of school motivation than their host Dutch peers (Vedder, Boekaerts, & Seegers, 2005).

Evidence of the immigrant paradox appears in the literature on risky/problem behaviors and academics, both in Europe and North America, and during childhood and adolescence. However, the evidence also indicates that the child's age, country of origin, and receiving country may moderate the immigrant paradox. In other words, the evidence for the immigrant paradox is stronger at some ages than others, in some immigrant groups than in others, and in some receiving communities compared to others.

Based on the extant literature on the immigrant paradox with respect to risk behaviors and academic performance, we conclude the following.

I. The immigrant paradox appears in birth outcomes – first-generation mothers have very low incidence of low birth weight babies.

II. This advantage might be expressed in the healthy socioemotional development seen in childhood and adolescents, as evidenced through low levels of risky and problems behaviors.

III. In academic performance, the immigrant paradox is more consistently found in attitudes and behavior than in grades and test scores. Increasingly, from middle childhood through adolescence, first-generation and less acculturated individuals have more positive attitudes and behaviors conceptualized as supportive of academic performance (i.e., time spent on homework). But grades and test scores show a very different pattern differing by age, country of origin, and destination. For example, among immigrants from Latin American countries in the United States, first-generation immigrants enter school less prepared than native youth but are in an accelerating mode where their rate of growth, in reading, for example, is faster than that of their native-born counterparts (Crosnoe, 2006a; Palacios, Guttmannova, & Chase-Lansdale, 2008). However, although positive attitudes and academic performance remain, Latino immigrants never catch up with their native-born counterparts. In contrast, first-generation Asians are equal to or above subsequent generations and their white counterparts in achievement, initially and over time.

IV. Country of origin appears to moderate the relationship between generation and developmental outcomes. Country of origin can be seen as a proxy for pre-immigration cohort characteristics such as language, education, reasons for migration, and receiving contexts in the host country (i.e., immigration policies and access to health, housing, and education resources). It is possible that countries that have more egalitarian public policies might not see the degree of deterioration over time seen in countries where policies are less accommodating (Berry, 1997; 2005).

Explaining the Paradox: Individual, Family, Community, and Peer-Level Resources

Developmental considerations refer to the many interacting systems that interact and transact in order to determine individual and cohort outcomes. In the language of Bronfenbrenner (1979), individual characteristics interact with micro-, meso-, exo-, macro-, and chronosystems to shape developmental pathways over time. But what are the mechanisms behind the immigrant paradox? How can these sources of influence operate to bring about what we consider paradoxical findings? The analysis of the acculturative process in immigrant children and adolescents provides several explanatory factors mediating the positive outcomes reflected in the paradox.

Individual Factors

Biculturalism
Connection to and competence in both cultures has been found to be protective for children of immigrants (Berry et al., 2006; Portes & Rumbaut, 2001; Suárez-Orozco & Suárez-Orozco, 1995). It is likely that recent immigrants or those who traveled at later ages would maintain stronger connections to their original culture even if they might be quickly acculturating. These connections could facilitate better outcomes through a better ability to integrate cultural frameworks.

Fluent Bilingualism
Concomitantly, bilingualism is associated with better outcomes among immigrants (Han, in press). Individuals that are fluently bilingual can move effectively between their home and host country cultures. Moreover, retaining fluency in one's home language allows enduring access to resources engrained within extended family and ethnic community contexts. This may be particularly important for youth as sharing a common language with parents guarantees that children are not completely alienated from their families of origin and that parental authority is maintained.

Family Obligations and Orientation
Studies have shown that high levels of perceived family obligations and orientation are related to better academic performance in adolescents from various immigration backgrounds (e.g., Fuligni, 2001). Perceived family

obligations and orientation appear to mediate the relationship between higher levels of motivation and first-generation immigrant status.

Psychological Attributes

Individual psychological-level variables accounting for the presence of the immigrant paradox include motivation, self-control, and self-esteem. Self-esteem had direct and significant effects on the school adjustment of immigrant adolescents – higher self-esteem was related to better adjustment at school (Liebkind et al., 2004).

Another individual-level variable mediating paradoxical outcomes among immigrant youth is self-control. Self-control and perceived sanctions (e.g., getting caught, shame, loss of respect) explained lower rates in delinquent behaviors for first-generation immigrants compared to their second- and later generation counterparts (Vazsonyi & Killias, 2001).

Microsystems: Family Factors

Parental Support

Evidence shows that strong parental support in the families of first-generation youth supports optimal outcomes at school. Parental support may promote immigrant youth school adjustments by alleviating the effects of perceived discrimination and by enhancing adolescents' ethnic identities (Liebkind et al., 2004).

Strong Educational Aspirations

Strong educational aspirations of immigrant parents also mediate and account for the more favorable school patterns of their children (Vallet & Caille, 1999). Higher parental academic expectations, especially when shared with children (e.g., Glick & White, 2003; Hao & Bonstead-Bruns, 1998; Kao, 2004), underlie individual and group successes observed in the academic performance of children of immigrants.

Parental Monitoring/Strictness

In a number of studies, immigrant parents are found to be more strict than native parents. During their children's adolescence, immigrant parents tend to monitor their children more closely and keep track of their whereabouts and their contacts with peers. This higher level of monitoring partially explains advantages in grade point average and lower levels of delinquency in first-generation adolescents (Bui, 2009; Pong, Hao, & Gardner, 2005).

Microsystems: Peer Factors

As children age, peer groups become a major influence on their developmental pathways. It appears that this is no less the case for immigrant youth. Research shows that first-generation adolescents have more first- and second-generation friends and more co-ethnic friends (Cavanagh, 2007; Harris, Harker, & Guo, 2003) than do later generations. First-generation youth report sharing positive academic and social values with their peers and getting academic support from their friends (Fuligni, 1997). Some research has demonstrated that belonging to a peer group that shares interest in academic performance partially explains first-generation advantage and fully explains second-generation advantage in grade point average (Harris et al., 2003). Although there is widespread acknowledgment from an ecological point of view that parent and peer contexts interact with one another, we are unaware of studies directly examining how these two contexts come together to explain the immigrant paradox. From a theoretical perspective, the degree to which adolescents acculturate within their peer networks (i.e., prefer to make friends with peers outside their ethnicity) is likely related in part to cultural practices in the home. Future studies should aim to directly examine the interactions between the family and peer contexts as they are linked with acculturation and developmental outcomes. It might be that as children and adolescents acculturate more quickly than their parents (Portes & Rumbaut, 1996), this widening gap in the cultural values and practices of the peer context and home context may partially explain some of the increased behavioral problems observed in more highly acculturated immigrant adolescents.

Microsystems: School Factors

The findings on the role of schools are mixed. In some studies, school characteristics have not explained first-generation advantage in academic performance as often children of immigrants (especially Latino immigrants) are more likely to attend low-quality schools with many negative processes than are native-born children (Han, 2006; Pong & Hao, 2007). It is more likely that first-generation advantage is seen in spite of the low performing characteristics of schools rather than because of them. However, school context (i.e., class and school size, average attendance, and rate of parent participation) and teacher characteristics (i.e., average level of teacher education and experience, percentage of new teachers at school, and teacher ethnicity) partially mediate first-generation advantage in academic aspirations

(Marks, 2009). In addition, first-generation adolescents who are succeeding may be clustered at certain types of schools (Crosnoe, 2005).

Microsystems: Neighborhood Factors

Similarly, the evidence is mixed for neighborhoods. Neighborhood structural characteristics (e.g., SES, average education level, and immigrant concentration) and intrageneration closure (e.g., how well parents report knowing other parents in the community) have not explained first-generation advantage (Han, 2006; Pong et al., 2005). However, ethnographic research supports the possibility that ethnic enclaves (e.g., Bankston & Zhou, 1997) support immigrant youth through increased social capital and community closure. Ethnic enclaves can facilitate the transfer of important information about which schools are high performing and the pathways that bring children successfully into higher education among community members. This is best seen in certain Asian immigrant communities in Europe, Canada, and the United States that have organized such efforts to promote the educational and financial success of newcomers.

Conclusions: Policies, Implications, and Remaining Questions

Integration policies and the presence of pluralistic attitudes toward immigrants influence the average level of adaptation of immigrant youth in the receiving country (Phinney et al., 2001). A favorable context of policy and sociocultural reception of immigrants plays an important role in their successful adaptation by moderating the negative attitudes of the members of the host society and by promoting the development of social networks for the immigrant community (Berry, 1997; Portes & Rumbaut, 2001). Therefore, there is reason to believe that policies that lead to language and cultural maintenance and to bilingualism and biculturalism in newcomers will lead to much better developmental outcomes. Moreover, it is in the best interests of immigrant youth, their families, and society to foster the success of immigrant youth. Supporting immigrant families and youth in operationalizing their high educational aspirations and expectations is clearly an important goal for receiving societies that have much to gain from immigrant success and much to lose from their risk behaviors or academic problems in terms of human capital. Supporting peer groups that help in maintaining traditional cultural capital at the same time they are attaining educational credentials might be effective. Supporting ethnic organizations that serve as brokers between newcomers and school systems is critical in building parent confidence and comfort with school involvement. The formulation and operationalization of public policies that support all these initiatives and the promotion of public attitudes that recognize the strengths immigrants bring and the importance of their collective success to the well-being of the country – given low birth rates and the aging of the native population – is critical for most First World countries (Hernandez, Macartney, & Blanchard, in this volume).

Important Questions for Future Research

Although we have made progress in documenting when and where this phenomenon is observed, many important questions remain.

1. *Why do we observe differences in the immigrant paradox by receiving country and within countries by nationalities?* As argued by various researchers, receiving and sending contexts differ in many respects. Characteristics of these contexts can contribute to the extent to which an individual or group is a match or mismatch with the host countries. There are various ways in which a mismatch may manifest; for example, there could be an economic mismatch (i.e., leaving a country as a professional, but taking a low-wage job in receiving country), a cultural mismatch (i.e., parents leaving a more collectivist society and having to manage an individualistic school system for their children), and/or a social stratification mismatch (i.e., acculturating into communities where families of color do not have the same social mobility opportunities). More research is needed that ascertains the attitudes, cultural practices, and public policies of various countries that lead to immigrant success not only in the first generation but beyond.

2. *Why is the immigrant paradox stronger in adolescence than in early and middle childhood?* In both academic performance and risk behaviors, the evidence for the immigrant paradox is stronger during the adolescent period than during childhood. This could be a function of there being a greater number of studies done on adolescence than on childhood. But perhaps there is a developmental explanation for these findings. We know that immigrant adolescents perceive more family obligations and their parents have higher expectations and monitor their whereabouts more closely than native parents. We propose that these processes may protect more recent immigrants from the normative processes of native adolescents – more specifically they protect these adolescents from the loss of strong parental influence, an increased peer orientation, and

involvement in high-risk behaviors. While native adolescents' school engagement may decrease and their involvement in risk behaviors may increase as they separate and rebel from their families, immigrant adolescents remain close to their families and in this way remain protected. During early and middle childhood, in contrast, children in both native and nonnative families are influenced by a family system that encourages the development of optimal outcomes in offspring.

3. *Does age of migration matter for risky and academic performance?* If the gradual process of acculturation and disengagement with the native culture explains in part the immigrant paradox, age at migration might be an important variable to examine within the first generation (See Corak, this volume). Rumbaut (2004) finds that the developmental period at which an individual arrived in the United States affects a variety of outcomes and acculturation patterns. Those who came during adolescence or young adulthood appear less acculturated in terms of language proficiency and ethnic identity (e.g., more likely to identify with their nation of origin) than individuals who arrived earlier. In addition, Rumbaut found that age at immigration significantly influenced educational attainment and behavioral outcomes, regardless of the country-of-origin group. For example, Rumbaut finds that the rates of arrest rise with increasing time in the United States; while 10.6% of immigrants who had immigrated when they were between the ages of 6 and 12 had been arrested, 15.6% of those who came during early childhood (0–5 years) had, and nearly 20% of those who were born in the United States (to immigrant parents) had. The work on the immigrant paradox suggests that immigrants should not be studied as a homogeneous group. Rather, future research has to not only take into account age of migration and generation, but also the context of migration and immigration. Moreover, the influence of age of migration, generation, and cohort will vary depending on developmental outcome studied. Also, is it possible that cultural ties to culture of origin are most beneficial for some domains, such as well-being or mental health, whereas ties to the receiving culture are helpful in others, such as academic performance and work success.

4. *How do aspects of the developmental contexts (i.e., families, neighborhoods, schools, peers) of immigrant youth combine to support positive outcomes?* Part of Bronfenbrenner's ecological framework refers to the relation between microsystems – family, school, neighborhood, peers. This layer of interactions is called the mesosystem. For children in immigrant families, there might be very different resources and demands in each of their microsystems. Do contexts need to align with one another

to promote positive outcomes? How do we create that alignment? On the other hand, how can youth negotiate opposing or contradicting messages between different aspects of the mesosystem?

5. *How can schools and communities better support each generation of immigrant heritage youth?* If we adopt a framework of bilingualism/ biculturalism as a key factor for youth in immigrant families, how can schools and neighborhoods support such developmental outcomes? Dual language programs (in which native and host country languages are used for academic instruction) have been successfully implemented in Canada and various parts of the United States (e.g., Collier & Thomas, 2004). Other modes of bilingual education and immersion lead to a quick loss of the native language, perhaps contributing to the deterioration of outcomes observed over time.

6. *Can we better understand how acculturation happens so we can work toward closing relationship gaps between parents and their adolescents?* We need to understand how some immigrant youth can effectively build strong bilingual/bicultural skills or how some can easily relate to the values and modes of being of various cultures. Why as some individuals acculturate do they lose their connection with their culture and family of origin while others do not? How can we better support families in which members have different levels of acculturation?

Current approaches to the study of developmental outcomes in immigrant populations primarily espouse theoretical frameworks that concentrate on the deficits that immigrant families and children bring and develop in this country. The findings behind the immigrant paradox – the fact that in some immigrant groups and for some development stages and outcomes more recent and less acculturated immigrants demonstrate surprisingly positive adaptations – challenge the notion that immigrant populations are lacking in strength or resilience.

As research on immigration matures, evidence on the intricacies of each immigrant group and receiving context suggests that general policies are not likely to work across all situations. Attention to developmental stage and age of migration is also crucial. In addition, moving from a focus on outcomes to a focus on the processes underlying the outcomes is essential. It is important to understand the ways in which family, peer, and neighborhood contexts influence each other and the ways in which they contribute to the outcomes of immigrant youth. Furthermore, at present there is a scarcity of literature reviews and particularly meta-analyses concerning outcomes of immigrant youth. More comprehensive and systematic reviews will be paramount in guiding future analyses and discussion on the immigrant paradox.

The findings examined in this chapter do not support the notion that we should cease aiming to support the successful adaptations of immigrants in new countries. On the other hand, they do support current efforts to maintain bicultural and bilingual adaptations and to support immigrant children's relationship with their families and their cultures of origin. Findings also indicate the importance of learning from successful immigrant youth to develop better support for those who are not as successful. As fertility rates drop and as populations age, the children of immigrants become the source of future economic growth and stability of nations. This reality justifies careful attention to the success of immigrant youth and their descendants and to the effective translation of findings into successful policies across the globe.

REFERENCES

Afable-Munsuz, A., & Brindis, C. D. (2006). Acculturation and the sexual and reproductive health of Latino youth in the Unites States: A literature review. *Perspectives on Sexual and Reproductive Health, 38*(4), 208–19.

Amundsen, E. J., Rossow, I., & Skurtveit, S. (2005). Drinking pattern among adolescents with immigrant and Norwegian backgrounds: A two-way influence? *Addiction, 100*(10), 1453–63.

Bankston, C. L., & Zhou, M. (1997). The social adjustment of Vietnamese American adolescents: Evidence for a segmented-assimilation approach. *Social Science Quarterly, 78*(2), 508–23.

Beiser, M., Hou, F., Hyman, I., & Tousignant, M. (2002). Poverty, family process, and the mental health of immigrant children in Canada. *American Journal of Public Health, 92*, 220–7.

Berry, J. W. (1997). Immigration, acculturation, and adaptation. *Applied Psychology: An International Review, 46*(1), 5–68.

   (2005). Acculturation: Living successfully in two cultures. *International Journal of Intercultural Relations, 29*(6), 697–712.

Berry, J. W., Phinney, J. S., Sam, D. L., & Vedder, P. (2006). Immigrant youth: Acculturation, identity and adaptation. *Applied Psychology: An International Review, 55*, 303–32.

Bronfenbrenner, U. (1979). *The ecology of human development: Experiments by nature and design.* Boston, MA: Harvard University Press.

   (1995). Developmental ecology through space and time: A future perspective. In P. Moen, G. H. Elder Jr., and K. Luscher (Eds.), *Examining lives in context: Perspectives on the ecology of human development* (pp. 619–47). Washington, DC: American Psychological Association.

Bui, H. N. (2009). Parent-child conflicts, school troubles, and delinquency among immigrants. *Crime & Delinquency, 55*, 412–41.

Bui, H. N., & Thongniramol, O. (2005). Immigration and self-reported delinquency: The interplay of immigration generations, gender, race, and ethnicity. *Journal of Crime and Justice, 28*, 71–99.

Cavanagh, S. E. (2007). The social construction of romantic relationships in adolescence: Examining the role of peer networks, gender, and race. *Sociological Inquiry, 77*, 552–80.

Chang, L., Morrissey, R. F., & Koplewicz, H. S. (1995). Prevalence of psychiatric symptoms and their relation to adjustment among Chinese American youth. *Journal of Academic Child and Adolescent Psychiatry, 34*, 91–9.

Collier, V. P., & Thomas, W. P. (2004). The astounding effectiveness of dual language education for all. *NABE Journal of Research and Practice, 2*(1), 1–20.

Conger, D., Schwartz, A. E., & Stiefel, L. (2003). *Who are our students? A statistical portrait of immigrant students in New York City elementary and middle schools.* New York: Taub Urban Research Center.

Crosnoe, R. (2005). The diverse experiences of Hispanic students in the American educational system. *Sociological Forum, 20*(4), 561–88.

(2006a). Health and the education of children from racial/ethnic minority and immigrant families. *Journal of Health and Social Behavior, 47*, 77–93.

(2006b). *Mexican Roots, American Schools Helping Mexican Immigrant Children Succeed.* Stanford University Press, Stanford, CA.

Fuligni, A. (1997). The academic achievement of adolescents from immigrant families: The roles of family background, attitudes, and behavior. *Child Development, 68*(2), 351–63.

Fuligni, A. J. (2001). A comparative longitudinal approach to acculturation among children from immigrant families. *Harvard Educational Review, 71*, 566–78.

Fuller, B., Bridges, M., Bein, E., Jang, H., Jung, S., Rabe-Hesketh, S., Halfon, N., & Kuo, A. (2009). The health and cognitive growth of Latino toddlers: At risk or immigrant paradox? *Maternal and Child Health Journal, 13*(6), 755–68.

Garcia Coll, C., Lamberty, G., Jenkins, R., McAdoo, H. P., Crnic, K., Wasik, B. H., & Vázquez García, H. (1996). An integrative model for the study of developmental competencies in minority children. *Child Development, 67*(5), 1891–914.

Garcia Coll, C., & Szalacha, L. A. (2004). The multiple contexts of middle childhood. *The Future of Children, 14*(20), 81–97.

Georgiades, K., Boyle M., & Duku, E. (2007). Contextual influences on children's mental health and school performance: The moderating effects of family immigrant status. *Child Development, 78*(5), 1572–91.

Georgiades, K., Boyle, M., Duku, E., & Racine, Y. (2006). Tobacco use among immigrant and nonimmigrant adolescents: Individual and family level influences. *Journal of Adolescent Health, 38*(4), 443.e1–443.e7.

Glick, J. E., & White, M. J. (2003). The academic trajectories of immigrant youths: Analysis within and across cohorts. *Demography, 40*(4), 759–83.

Guilamo-Ramos, V., Jaccard, J., Pena, J., & Goldberg, V. (2005). Acculturation-related variables, sexual initiation, and subsequent sexual behavior among Puerto Rican, Mexican, and Cuban youth. *Health Psychology, 24*(1), 88–95.

Hahm, H. C., Lahiff, M., & Barreto, R. M. (2006). Asian American adolescents' first sexual intercourse: Gender and Acculturation Differences. *Perspectives on Sexual and Reproductive Health, 38*(1), 28–36.

Han, W. J. (2006). Academic achievements of children of immigrant families. *Educational Research and Review, 1*(8), 286–318.

Han, W. J. (in press). Bilingualism and academic achievement: Does generation status make a difference? In C. Garcia Coll and A. Marks (Eds.), *Is becoming American a developmental risk?* American Psychological Association.

Hao, L., & Bonstead-Bruns, M. (1998). Parent–child differences in educational expectations and the academic achievement of immigrant and native students. *Sociology of Education, 71,* 175–98.

Harker, K. (2001). Immigrant generation, assimilation, and adolescent psychological well-being. *Social Forces, 79*(3), 969–1004.

Harris, K. M. (1999). The health status and risk behavior of adolescents in immigrant families. In D. J. Hernandez (Ed.), *Children of immigrants: Health, adjustment and public assistance* (pp. 286–347). Washington, DC: National Academy of Sciences Press.

Harris, K. M., Harker, K., & Guo, G. (2003, May). The role of peers in the adaptation processes of immigrant youth. Paper presented at the annual meetings of the Population Association of America, Minneapolis, MN.

Hummer, R. A., Powers, D. A., Pullum, S. G., Gossman, G. L., & Frisbie, W. P. (2007). Paradox found (again): Infant mortality among the Mexican-origin population in the United States. *Demography, 44*(3), 441–57.

Jutte, D. P., Burgos, A., Mendoza, F., Ford, C. B., & Huffman, L. C. (2003). Use of the Pediatric Symptom Checklist in a low-income, Mexican American population. *Archives of Pediatrics & Adolescent Medicine, 157,* 1169–76.

Kandula, N., Kersey, M., & Lurie, N. (2004). Assuring the health of immigrants: What the leading health indicators tell us. *Annual Review of Public Health, 25,* 357–76.

Kao, G. (1999). Psychological well-being and educational achievement among immigrant youth. In D. J. Hernandez (Ed.), *Children of immigrants: Health, adjustment, and public assistance* (pp. 410–77). Albany, NY: National Academy Press.

(2004). Parental influences on the educational outcomes of immigrant youth. *International Migration Review, 38,* 427–50.

Kaplan, M., Huguet, N., Newsom, J., & McFarland, B. (2004). The association between length of residence and obesity among Hispanic immigrants. *American Journal of Preventive Medicine, 27*(4), 323–6.

Landale, N. S., Oropesa, R. S., Llanes, D., & Gorman, B. K. (1999). Does Americanization have adverse effects on health?: Stress, health habits, and infant health outcomes among Puerto Ricans. *Social Forces, 78*(2), 613–41.

Lara, M., Gamboa, C., Kahramanian, M., Morales, L. S., & Hayes Bautista, D. H. (2005). Acculturation and Latino health in the United States: A review of the literature and its sociopolitical context. *Annual Review of Public Health, 26,* 367–97.

Liebkind, K., Jasinskaja-L, I., & Solheim, E. (2004). Cultural identity, perceived discrimination, and parental support as determinants of immigrants' school adjustments. *Journal of Adolescent Research, 19*(6), 635–56.

Luthar, S. S. (2006). Resilience in development: A synthesis of research across five decades. In D. Cicchetti and D. J. Cohen (Eds.), *Developmental psychopathology: Risk, disorder, and adaptation* (2nd ed. vol. 3.) (pp. 739–95). Hoboken, NJ: Wiley.

Ma, X. (2002). The first ten years in Canada: A multi-level assessment of behavioral and emotional problems of immigrant children. *Canadian Public Policy – Analyse de Politiques, 28*(3), 395–418.

Markides, K. S., & Coreil, J. (1986). The health of Hispanics in the Southwestern United States and epidemiological paradox. *Public Health Reports, 101*(3), 253–65.

Marks, A. K. (April, 2009). *Explaining the education immigrant paradox in adolescence: The mediating roles of school context and teacher characteristics.* The Jacobs Foundation Conference, "Capitalizing on Migration: The potential of immigrant youth." Marbach, Germany.

Masten, A. S. (2007). Resilience in developing systems: Progress and promise as the fourth wave rises. *Development and Psychopathology, 19*(3), 921–30.

Masten, A. S., Burt, K., & Coatsworth, J. D. (2006). Competence and psychopathology. In D. Cicchetti and D. Cohen (Eds.), *Developmental psychopathology, Vol 3, Risk, disorder and psychopathology* (2nd ed.) (pp. 696–738). New York: Wiley.

Masten, A. S., Garmezy, N., Tellegen, A., Pellegrini, D., Larkin, K., & Larsen, A. (2006). Competence and stress in school children: The moderating effects of individual and family qualities. *Journal of Child Psychology and Psychiatry, 29*(6), 745–64.

McDonald, J. A., Manlove, J., & Ikramullah, E. (2009). Immigration measures and reproductive health among Hispanic youth: Findings from the National Longitudinal Survey of Youth, 1997–2003. *Journal of Adolescent Health, 44*, 14–24.

McDonald, J. T., & Kennedy, S. (2005). Is migration to Canada associated with unhealthy weight gain? Overweight and obesity among Canada's immigrants. *Social Science & Medicine, 61*(12), 2469–81.

Palacios, N., Guttmannova, K., & Chase-Lansdale, P. L. (2008). Early reading achievement of children in immigrant families: Is there an immigrant paradox? *Developmental Psychology, 44*(5), 1381–95.

Phinney, J. S., Horenczyk, G., Liebkind, K., & Vedder, P. (2001). Ethnic identity, immigration, and well-being: An interactional perspective. *Journal of Social Issues, 57*(3), 493–510.

Pong, S., & Hao, L. (2007). Neighborhood and school factors in the school performance of immigrants' children. *International Migration Review, 41*(1), 206–41.

Pong, S., Hao, L., & Gardner, E. (2005). The roles of parenting styles and social capital in the school performance of immigrant Asian and Hispanic adolescents. *Social Science Quarterly 86*(4), 928–50.

Popkin, B., & Udry, J. (1998). Adolescent obesity increases significantly in second and third generation U.S. immigrants: The National Longitudinal Study of Adolescent Health. *The Journal of Nutrition, 128*(4), 701–6.

Portes, A., Fernández-Kelly, P., & Haller, W. (2005). Segmented assimilation on the ground: The new second generation in early adulthood. *Ethnic and Racial Studies*, http://www.informaworld.com/smpp/title%7Edb=all%7Econtent=t713685087%7Etab=issueslist%7Ebranches=28–v28 *28* (6) 1000–1040.

Portes, A., & Rumbaut, R. G. (1996). *Immigrant America: A portrait* (2nd ed.). Berkeley: University of California Press.

Portes, A., & Rumbaut, R. G. (2001). *Legacies: The story of the immigrant second generation.* Berkeley, CA: University of California Press.

Portes, A., & Zhou, M. (1993). The new second generation: Segmented assimilation and its variants. *Annals of the American Academy of Political and Social Sciences, 530,* 74–96.

Rosenbaum, E., & Rochford, J. A. (2008). Generational patterns in academic performance: The variable effects of attitudes and social capital. *Social Science Research, 37*(1), 350–72.

Rumbaut, R. G. (2004). Ages, life stages, and generational cohorts: Decomposing the immigrant first and second generations in the United States. *International Migration Review, 38(3),* 1160–205.

Sam, D. L., Vedder, P., Liebkind, K., Neto, F., & Virta, E. (2008). Immigration, acculturation and the paradox of adaptation in Europe. *European Journal of Developmental Psychology, 5*(2), 138–58.

Singh, G., & M. Siahpush (2002). Ethnic-immigrant differentials in health behaviors, morbidity, and cause-specific mortality in the United States: An analysis of two national databases. *Human Biology, 74*(1), 83–109.

Steinhausen, H., Winkler Metzke, C., Meier, M., & Kannenberg, R. (1997). Behavioral and emotional problems reported by parents for ages 6 to 17 in a Swiss epidemiological study *European Child & Adolescent Psychiatry, 6*(3), 136–41.

Strohmeier, D., Spiel, C., & Gradinger, P. (2008). Social relationships in multicultural schools: Bullying and victimization. *European Journal of Developmental Psychology, 5,* 262–85.

Suárez-Orozco, C., & Suárez-Orozco, M. (1995). *Transformations: Migration, family life, and achievement motivation among Latino adolescents.* Stanford, CA: Stanford University Press.

Teller, C. H., & Clyburn, S. (1974). Trends in infant mortality. *Texas Business Review, 29,* 97–108.

Vallet, L. A., & Caille, J-P. (1999). Migration and integration in France. Academic careers of immigrants' children in lower and upper secondary school. Paper prepared for the Conference European Societies or European Society? Migrations and Inter-Ethnic Relations in Europe, Obernai, September 23–28, 1999.

Vazsonyi, A. T., & Killias, M. (2001). Immigration and crime among youth in Switzerland. *Criminal Justice and Behavior, 28,* 329–66.

Vedder, P., Boekaerts, M., & Seegers, G. (2005). Perceived social support and well being in school: The role of students' ethnicity. *Journal of Youth and Adolescence, 34,* 269–78.

Vedder, P., & Horenczyk, G. (2006). Acculturation and the school. In D. L. Sam and J. W. Berry (Eds.), *The Cambridge handbook of acculturation psychology* (pp. 419–38). Cambridge, UK: Cambridge University Press.

Willgerodt, M. A., & Thompson, E. A. (2005). Generational status on parent and family relations among Chinese and Filipino adolescents. *Public Health Nursing, 22*(6), 460–71.

Wirth, L. (1931) Culture, conflict and delinquency. *Social Forces, 9*(4), 484–92.

Wong, S. K. (1999). Acculturation, peer relations and delinquent behavior of Chinese-Canadian youth. *Adolescence, 34* (133), 107–19.

Yu, S., Huang, Z., Schwalberg, R., Overpeck, M., & Kogan, M. (2003). Acculturation and the health and well-being of U.S. immigrant adolescents. *Journal of Adolescent Health, 33*(6), 479–88.

Zhou, M. (1997). Segmented assimilation: Issues, controversies, and recent research on the new second generation. *International Migration Review, 31*(4), 975–1008.

7 The Contributions of Youth to Immigrant Families

Andrew J. Fuligni and Eva H. Telzer

Introduction

The settlement of the foreign born to a new country often is a collective process that involves the participation of multiple family members. Children play an active role in the adaptation of many immigrant families because of cultural traditions and situational imperatives. Culturally, many immigrants to North America and Europe come from societies that emphasize the role of children in supporting and maintaining the household. For example, immigrants from Asian and Latin American countries may bring with them traditions in which children are expected to participate in sibling care, meal preparation, home cleaning, and financial support of other family members (Fuligni, 1998; Tseng, 2004). Sometimes referred to as "filial piety" or "familism," these expectations are common and defining features of what it means to be a good son or daughter in the native cultures of many immigrants.

At the same time, the act of settling in a new and different society creates imperatives for the active contribution of younger family members. Foreign-born parents often do not possess the skills, knowledge, and social capital to quickly integrate into the host society. They may lack sufficient facility with the dominant language and need to work long hours in unstable jobs with irregular work schedules (Zhou, 1997). Parents must interact with institutions such as schools and governmental agencies with little prior knowledge about the norms and expectations of such interactions. By default, children contribute to the management of the household by virtue of their availability, language ability, and relative comfort with engaging with social institutions in the new society.

Adolescents play a particularly significant role in the adaptation and adjustment of immigrant families. More so than younger children, they have developed the skills, abilities, and maturity to take on responsibilities in the home. Adolescents can assist with the care and support of younger children in the household. They have accumulated experience with the schools of the host society that enables them to advise on educational decisions for themselves and their younger siblings. Teenagers may be seen by official agencies as possessing enough maturity to broker interactions between agency personnel and foreign-born parents. Finally, older adolescents have reached the legal age at which they can work in most societies, thereby adding a potential additional source of needed income to immigrant families.

This chapter reviews the contributions made by youth to the adaptation and adjustment of immigrant families. We do so in order to achieve two goals. The first is to highlight these adolescents as valuable assets to their families and countries of settlement, the latter of which often struggle with finding ways to facilitate the societal integration of immigrants. The second goal is to draw attention to a significant and dominant feature of the lives of youth from immigrant families, a feature that tends to be overlooked in traditional models of child and adolescent development that pay little attention to the instrumental contributions of children to the household. Due to the historical shift in developed societies from viewing children as being useful to viewing them as precious, developmental research has traditionally focused on what parents and families do for children rather than on what children can do for their families (Fuligni, 2001a). Yet numerous examples abound of how children in different societies and social conditions engage in high levels of family assistance. Children and adolescents in regions such as Africa, Latin America, and Asia have long played significant roles in household maintenance and support (e.g., Weisner, 1982). Even in developed societies, families in certain regions (e.g., farm families in the American Midwest; Elder & Conger, 2000) and economic locations (e.g., poor rural families; Burton, 2007) rely upon their teenagers to support and assist the family. As described in these studies, playing such a significant role in the maintenance of the household can both promote and impede adolescents' development in complex ways, and this chapter attempts to identify the conditions under which family assistance can be positive or negative for the adjustment of teenagers from immigrant families.

We review findings from our own research and that of others as appropriate. Our findings are based upon two longitudinal studies of adolescents from Latin American, Asian, and European backgrounds. The Bay Area Study of Youth from Immigrant Families took place in a medium-sized school district in the San Francisco Bay area of California. Approximately 1,000 students from Asian, Latin American, and European backgrounds completed biennial surveys from the beginning of middle school through the end of high school. After high school, approximately 75% of them participated in two in-depth telephone interviews. The second study was a longitudinal study of approximately 750 high school students in the Los Angeles area entitled the UCLA Study of Adolescents' Daily Lives. Students from Asian, Latin American, and European backgrounds completed questionnaires each year of high school. After completing the questionnaires, the students were given a packet of 14 daily diary checklists in which they were to check off the occurrence of a specified set of activities and experiences each night before they went to bed. In each of these studies, official school record information was collected and a subset of participants took part in in-depth personal interviews.

The chapter is organized into two primary sections. The first describes the contributions made by youth to immigrant families and includes a discussion of variability in these contributions by adolescents' national origin, economic resources, and gender. The second section focuses on the effects that these different types of family contributions can have on the adolescents' educational adjustment and psychological well-being. Finally, the chapter concludes with a brief discussion of the implications of these findings for efforts to facilitate the adjustment and development of this unique population of youth.

Types of Family Contributions

Daily Household Management
Immigrant children play a central role in the daily lives of their families by actively contributing to household management. Due to economic and cultural challenges, these children often must rise to the forefront of household management. Aware of their parents' personal sacrifices and employment in low-status jobs with irregular work hours that often require them to be away from their family for long hours, children from immigrant families often spend significant time meeting their families' daily demands.

Youth from immigrant families assist their households in diverse ways including engaging in chores around the house, taking care of siblings, and running errands for the family. In Valenzuela's (1999) qualitative work with Mexican families, one main theme of assistance was youths' role as surrogate parents. Children contributed to the household by cooking, dressing, bathing, transporting, babysitting, caring for, and providing for younger siblings. Parents would often consult with their older children about disciplinary matters for younger siblings.

In our Daily Lives Study, we examined what children do to help their families by employing a daily diary method. Each evening for two weeks, adolescents indicated whether they had engaged in any of the following seven activities: helped clean the apartment or house, ran an errand for the family, helped to cook a meal for the family, took care of siblings, helped siblings with their schoolwork, helped parents with official business (for example, translating letters, completing government forms), and helped parents at their work. The first three activities represent assisting in the maintenance of the *household*, the next two represent assisting *siblings*, and the latter two represent assisting *parents*. We examined the proportion of days adolescents did each type of assistance behavior. Participants also indicated how much total time they assisted their families in any of the activities that day, and we examined the average amount of time youth assisted their families each day.

Virtually all ninth graders (98%) helped their families on at least one day of the study. Helping to clean, cook, and run errands for the family was the most common type of activity reported by adolescents, occurring on 58% of the study days. Helping siblings by taking care of them and assisting them with their homework was the next most frequent type of activity, occurring on 27% of the study days. Helping parents with official business and at their work occurred on only 8% of days. Overall, adolescents engaged in 1.43 types of assistance behaviors per day and spent nearly an hour on average helping their families each day (Telzer & Fuligni, 2009a).

We have found consistent ethnic and generational differences in youths' family assistance behaviors. Youth from Latin American backgrounds tend to assist their families more than do youth from Asian backgrounds, who in turn assist their families more than do youth from European backgrounds. For example, ninth graders from Mexican backgrounds spent 1.30 hours on average helping their families each day compared to 0.87 hours among youth from Chinese backgrounds and 0.64 hours among youth from European backgrounds (Telzer & Fuligni, 2009a). For youth from Mexican backgrounds, those from immigrant families usually report spending more days assisting their families than their third-generation peers who tend to fall between those from Mexican immigrant and European nonimmigrant families (Hardway & Fuligni, 2006). These ethnic differences remain across the high school years and are generally consistent even after controlling for socioeconomic differences and family structure, such as grandparents living in residence, residing in a two-parent household, and having more siblings (Hardway & Fuligni, 2006; Telzer & Fuligni, 2009b).

Family structure seems to only minimally affect youths' support of the household. Although 25% of adolescents lived in single-parent households, the youth did not differ from their peers living in dual-parent households in their family assistance behaviors. Having grandparents living in the household did not affect the amount of time youth assisted their families (Hardway & Fuligni, 2006; Telzer & Fuligni, 2009a). However, youth whose parents have less education tended to assist their families more (Hardway & Fuligni, 2006). Finally, there are no clear gender differences in youths' support of the household, with some studies reporting that females assist their families more (Fuligni, Yip, & Tseng, 2002; Telzer & Fuligni, 2009b; Valenzuela, 1999), whereas others do not find gender differences (Telzer & Fuligni, 2009a).

Language and Cultural Brokering
Language and cultural brokering refers to adolescents' role in translating for their parents and mediating cultural differences between the families and the host societies. Much of the research in this area has tended to be qualitative with smaller samples, providing rich descriptions of the complex nature of brokering, but not necessarily providing many statistical estimates of rates and frequencies. Children from many different cultures and linguistic backgrounds perform a variety of tasks and often act as mediators and decision makers for their families (McQuillan & Tse, 1995; Orellana, Dorner, & Pulido, 2003). Ethnographic studies have suggested that brokering occurs in schools, banks, stores, restaurants, and doctors' offices, and children translate for parents, siblings, peers, teachers, and administrators. Immigrant youth are not merely translating words; they are interpreting scenarios and taking action in order to accomplish goals for their families (Orellana et al., 2003). As Orellana et al. (2003) describe, "children do much more than move words and ideas between speakers" (517); they actively participate in conversations, often acting as mediators, asking and answering questions, and keeping their families' best interests in mind. These children intervene, mediate, or advocate on behalf of their parents, often acting as the primary decision maker for the family (Valenzuela, 1999). Even when translators are available, parents often use their children because they trust a family member more than an unknown translator (Valdes, Chavez, & Angelelli, 2003). Brokering often occurs within seven domains: educational, commercial, medical/health, cultural, legal/state, financial, and housing/residential.

The most common type of brokering occurs within the educational domain (Orellana et al., 2003; Tse, 1996). Immigrant youth often interpret report cards, notes from teachers, and calls from school staff; decide how to contact teachers regarding concerns; and translate at parent–teacher conferences (Orellana et al., 2003). In addition, immigrant children often become closely involved in their younger siblings' education. They accompany their families to check out schools for their siblings, call schools to report their siblings' absences, and play an important role in their siblings' school success (Valenzuela, 1999).

Within the commercial domain, immigrant youth shop for or with parents, fill out credit applications, register complaints about merchandise, and interpret receipts and ads. Everyday necessities are usually located outside of the home, and unlike other brokering, the commercial domain often involves sending children out on their own to make inquiries or to complete transactions independently. In fact, some parents have never completed an errand on their own due to language and cultural barriers (Orellana et al., 2003).

Youth from immigrant families help in the medical domain by filling out/ giving insurance information, translating at a doctor's appointment, and interpreting instructions for medications (Orellana et al., 2003). Immigrant youth do not just translate between parents and doctors; they help make health-related decisions by asking and answering questions (Orellana et al., 2003). In contrast to other types of brokering, immigrant youth sometimes find medical brokering to be more difficult (Valenzuela, 1999). For example, translating their parents' complicated medical ailments to doctors and then explaining the doctors' responses back to parents can be awkward and sometimes embarrassing for children (Valenzuela, 1999). Despite the difficulty with this type of brokering, it is quite common among immigrant families (Orellana et al., 2003), suggesting that it is seen as particularly important, perhaps because of the sensitivity involved.

In terms of cultural brokering, immigrant youth translate TV shows, movies, and the radio, read and translate letters or emails, and interpret song lyrics. These instances most often take place in the home (Orellana et al., 2003). In addition, children often act as teachers, introducing their families to American holidays, cultural traditions, and values. In this way, immigrant children take on the role as socializing agents by conveying important cultural information to their families.

Immigrant youth broker in the legal/state domain by helping their parents study for citizenship exams, filling out applications for welfare, and helping to renew parents' green cards. Often, brokering in the legal realm involves interactions that may have very important and negative consequences for the families. For example, youth may have to negotiate for citizenship and legal residence, welfare, Women, Infant, and Children (WIC), and social security benefits. Thus, brokering in the legal/state domain is characterized not only by children helping their parents to access information but also by withholding information and access from others. Such children assert their power to reduce authorities from scrutinizing their family by presenting their family in a positive light (Orellana et al., 2003; Valdes et al., 2003).

Immigrant children often play a central role in their families' finances. They open bank accounts, write checks, help to pay bills, decide which bills to pay and how money will be spent, review bank statements, and mediate transactions with the bank. Thus, immigrant children who broker in the financial domain are well aware of their families' finances (Orellana et al., 2003).

Finally, in the housing/residential domain, immigrant youth broker by translating between their parents and landlords, helping to settle rental disputes, and communicating with neighbors (Orellana et al., 2003). If something is broken and needs repairing, children often communicate with landlords in order to make arrangements for repairs. According to Valenzuela's qualitative work, a 16-year-old Mexican female took it upon herself to help her family refinance their home. She completed all the paperwork and made phone calls to different banks in order to help her family save money through a lower interest rate (Valenzuela, 1999).

The limited research on immigrant child brokering suggests that it is a common activity that occurs in everyday ways (Orellana et al., 2003). Several studies examining brokering among Mexican and Asian youth report that most brokering occurs at home (70%–86%), in stores (57%–80%), or in school (47%–80%) (Orellana et al., 2003; Tse, 1995, 1996). Over 60% of immigrant youth translate words for their parents, 53% translate and interpret letters, and 51% make and answer phone calls. Fewer children broker in more difficult situations such as translating legal documents (14%), bank statements (20%), report cards (29%), or parent–child conferences (30%) (Orellana et al., 2003). Although it is a difficult task, brokering within the medical domain appears to be common. Among Mexican youth, 40% reported brokering for their parents in regard to medical issues, and among 45 immigrant parents, nearly all reported that their children had assisted them in various ways related to health services (Orellana et al., 2003; Valenzuela, 1999).

Although no studies have directly compared cultural brokering across ethnic groups, research suggests that brokering is a common activity for youth from diverse ethnic backgrounds. Tse (1995) found that among U.S. and foreign-born Latin American youth, 100% reported brokering for their families regardless of their place of birth or age of arrival. Among Vietnamese youth, 97% reported engaging in brokering for their families. In addition, 90% of Chinese and Vietnamese high school students reported brokering for their families, and those who did not report personally brokering had an older sibling who did broker (Tse, 1996). Finally, in a qualitative study of immigrant adults from different cultural and linguistic backgrounds (Cambodian, Chinese, Korean, Vietnamese, and Mexican), all adults reported acting as the primary decision maker for their families when they were children by conveying important cultural information about school, governmental, and business procedures and acting as translators among teachers, neighbors, friends, parents, siblings, and other relatives (McQuillan & Tse, 1995).

In terms of generational differences, Orellana and colleagues (2003) and Tse (1995) found that all Mexican children, regardless of their generation, reported brokering for their families. In fact, even third- and fourth-generation children brokered (Orellana et al., 2003). Although youth from all generations broker, the longer families are in the United States, the less brokering their children do (Jones & Trickett, 2005; Trickett & Jones, 2007). For instance, 92% of second-generation youth reported brokering for their parents compared to 98% of first-generation youth (Trickett & Jones, 2007). Despite the lower frequency, it is apparent that even later generation youth broker at high rates.

Many studies have found that brokering is more frequent among females than males (Buriel et al., 1998; Valenzuela, 1999; Weisskirch, 2005), although some studies have not found gender differences (Love & Buriel, 2007; Weisskirch & Alva, 2002). In addition, brokering is more common among the eldest children, and there is a positive correlation between family size and brokering (Valdes et al., 2003; Weisskirch & Alva, 2002). Brokering often begins soon after arriving in the United States and often as early as 8 or 9 years of age (McQuillan & Tse, 1995; Tse, 1996). Youth from families with higher parental education tend to broker less (Buriel et al., 1998; Jones & Trickett, 2005).

Work and Financial Assistance

Children of immigrant parents play an important role in their families' financial stability. Rather than being solely dependents who require economic assistance from their parents, immigrant youth often actively participate in their families' economic well-being. Immigrant youth contribute to the financial well-being of their households in three ways: (1) as financial contributors, (2) working for the family business, or (3) assisting their parents with their employment.

Older children of immigrant families often gain employment to help their families financially. As teenagers, they often work one or two part-time jobs in order to provide financial assistance (Valenzuela, 1999). For instance, many Mexican youth reported giving their families half their paycheck, paying any outstanding bills, and buying groceries or other items that their families needed (Valenzuela, 1999). In many immigrant families, parents do not explicitly ask their children to contribute. Rather, out of a sense of family obligation, immigrant youth take it upon themselves to ensure that bills are paid on time and groceries and other necessities can be afforded (Song, 2001; Valenzuela, 1999). These adolescents have a deep sense of commitment to their families' financial well-being.

Family-run businesses are increasingly common among immigrant families in the United States (Park, 2002). Although the family plays a central role in immigrant entrepreneurial life, children have remained relatively invisible in research examining family businesses. Sociological work has begun to unpack immigrant children's roles in their families' businesses and has shown that unpaid family labor is essential to the survival of family businesses (Park, 2002). At a young age, many youth from immigrant families adopt a role of authority in the business and feel a deep sense of responsibility for the family business, often because it is a way to bring and hold the family together (Park, 2002). Children can begin working for family business as early as 7 years of age (Song, 2001). As young children, they watch and learn from older siblings and family members and gradually take on more responsibilities until they become integral workers in the business (Song, 2001). Children assist family businesses in diverse ways, such as organizing, supervising others, ringing up checks, managing employees and customers, taking orders, and acting as a cultural bridge between their parents and customers (Park, 2002). In addition to assisting with everyday things, immigrant children often act as the mediator or problem solver, particularly during difficult times (Park, 2002). They act as cultural interpreters, helping their parents do things that are in sync with the new society's values, making decisions on their own, and defining what is and is not a concern. Many youth feel that their parents are dependent on them for the well-being of the family business and that it is their obligation to assist (Park, 2002; Song, 2001).

In addition, immigrant children often help their families financially by helping their parents with employment issues. They fill out job applications, make phone calls about employment possibilities, accompany parents to work to act as an interpreter, and mediate complex financial situations such as filling out income taxes (Orellana et al., 2003; Valenzuela, 1999). Additionally, immigrant children play an important role in their parents' employment stability by informing their parents of workers' rights, taxes, benefits, and other issues related to their jobs (Valenzuela, 1999). By contributing financially to their families, working for family businesses, and assisting with their parents' employment, immigrant youth reduce frustration associated with integration, facilitate permanent settlement in their new culture, and help with the successful social and economic adaptation of their families (Song, 2001; Valenzuela, 1999).

Because so little research has examined children's roles as active financial contributors to their families, it is not clear how often or how much immigrant youth contribute to their families. Park's (2002) sociological work with Chinese and Korean families found that youth often worked for family businesses full time on the weekends and during the summer (Park, 2002). Their lives were often structured around the hours of the business (Song, 2001). Additionally, whenever there was an emergency or difficult situation, children were usually the first to be contacted to resolve the problem (Park, 2002). In our Daily Lives Study, we have found that assisting parents at their workplace is not a frequent type of assistance, occurring on only 8% of days (Telzer & Fuligni, 2009a). Despite its low frequency across individuals as a whole, Park's qualitative work with 43 Chinese and Korean American adolescents whose families owned small businesses found that within these families, nearly all youth reported helping their parents with their businesses (Park, 2002).

Additionally, little research has examined group differences in immigrant youths' financial contributions to their families. In our Bay Area Study, youth from immigrant families were more likely to contribute financially to their families than those from American-born families, and youth from Filipino and Latin American backgrounds contributed financially to their families more than youth from East Asian or European backgrounds. In addition, youth from families with lower incomes contributed more financially. Finally, we found that males were more likely than females to provide financial assistance (Fuligni & Witkow, 2004). In contrast, Valenzuela found that females contributed more financially to their families and acted as mediators on financial concerns more often than males (Valenzuela, 1999). These contrasting findings may be due to methodological differences. For example, Valenzuela's (1999) qualitative study included interviews with 44 Mexican immigrant families, whereas our work used quantitative methods with over 750 adolescents from diverse backgrounds (Fuligni & Witkow, 2004). As researchers become more aware of immigrant children's central role in their families' economic well-being, they will be able to better define and quantify what youth do to assist their families financially, which youth assist their families more (e.g., lower socioeconomic status, lower parental acculturation, gender, ethnic, and generational differences), and how this financial support affects their daily lives.

Implications for Adolescent Development

The contributions of youth play a central role in the process by which immigrant families adapt to a new and different society. Beyond the benefits accrued to the larger family, however, what impact does family assistance have upon the adolescents themselves? Youth presumably receive an indirect return on their assistance through the improved family well-being obtained by enabling parents to work, raising the overall level of family income, and facilitating interactions with schools and official agencies. Yet do the acts of family assistance themselves – sibling care, translating, working in the family business, contributing financially – have direct effects upon the adolescents' adjustment and development?

Two competing hypotheses can be offered. On the one hand, it is possible that such activities create a burden for teenagers who must take on additional responsibilities at a young age. Extensive household duties, the challenge of negotiating complex interactions with official agencies, and the responsibility of contributing to the family's income could become too much for teenagers to manage. It may be particularly difficult when such duties are not the norm for teenagers in the new society and adolescents must balance family responsibilities with other typical adolescent activities such as schoolwork, extracurricular activities, and socialization with peers. Indeed, an existing literature on what has been called "parentification" or "adultification" has suggested that children's well-being can suffer when they are asked to take on excessive responsibilities in the home (Burton, 2007; Jurkovic, 1997).

On the other hand, family assistance may not be so negative and could even be positive for adolescents because it is a productive and meaningful activity. The role of children in maintaining the household is a cultural norm for many immigrant families, and adolescents who provide such support likely feel that they are acting like good sons and daughters. This, in turn, will make them feel that they are valued members of the family. Similarly, helping the family provides youth with a way to be productive members of their community, an opportunity often seen as lacking in contemporary industrialized societies such as North America and Europe. The ability to be valued and productive should be particularly significant for adolescents from immigrant families who are attempting to develop a sense of purpose in a new and different society in which they frequently encounter experiences that suggest that they are devalued, different, and excluded. In this sense, family assistance can be a source of what has been called "eudaimonic well-being." *Eudaimonic well-being* refers to a larger sense of purpose, direction, and meaning that one obtains in one's life (Ryan & Deci, 2001). It has been argued that developing this sense of connection, purpose, and direction is a key developmental task (Ryff, 1989, 1995). Eudaimonic well-being can be stimulated by challenge and difficulty, which is why some have called it a particularly relevant aspect of adjustment and development among minority populations (Ryff, Keyes, & Hughes, 2003).

Research that has systematically examined the developmental implications of adolescents' contributions to immigrant families has emerged only recently and is limited. The available evidence suggests that both of these hypotheses may be correct – family assistance is both burdensome and meaningful for adolescents from immigrant families. The extent to which the negative effects on adolescents outweigh the positive effects likely depends upon the magnitude of the contributions adolescents are asked to make as well as the larger family context in which those contributions occur.

Educational Adjustment

The impact of family assistance on the educational adjustment of youth from immigrant families is complex, showing different patterns for the adolescents' sense of obligation to help their families as compared to the actual provision of assistance. Adolescents' sense of obligation to support and assist their families is generally associated with higher levels of academic motivation. In our own work, we have found that youth who believe in the importance of helping family also endorse the value and utility of education for their future and have higher aspirations to attend college (Fuligni, 2001b). Similar patterns have been observed in ethnographic studies of immigrant families from Vietnam (Caplan, Choy, & Whitmore, 1991; Zhou & Bankston, 1998), India (Gibson & Bhachu, 1991), and Latin America (Suárez-Orozco & Suárez-Orozco, 1995). Adolescents from immigrant families often recognize the sacrifices made by their parents to offer their children a better life and believe that trying hard and doing well in school is one of the best ways to repay and help their parents in the future. As a 14-year-old boy from a Mexican immigrant family who participated in one of our studies told us:

[T]hey did so much for us, especially my dad. They worked so hard just to get where we are and I really appreciate that. And, I mean … the way I can pay them back right now is to get good grades. And by doing what I'm supposed to. But, I want to give them more than that when I get older. Like their own house, or I don't know … a maid or something.

Unfortunately, the very real need to help their families on a daily basis can make it difficult for students from immigrant families to succeed and meet their educational aspirations. In the Daily Lives Study, we examined the association between family assistance and performance in school across the years of high school (Telzer & Fuligni, 2009b). Specifically, we estimated whether changes in family assistance within individual adolescents were associated with simultaneous changes in their academic achievement. Results suggested that the total amount of time students spent helping their families was not necessarily a problem for academic performance. Changes in the amount of time students spent helping their families was not associated with changes in their grade point average across high school. Instead, the manner in which students managed their familial duties made a difference. Increases in the number of days students spent helping their families each week was associated with declines in grade point average among students from Asian and Latin American backgrounds. That is, compared to those who spent the same amount of time helping their families, students who could not limit their family duties to only a couple of days per week were worse off academically than those who could do so.

Our findings highlight the importance of adolescents from immigrant families finding a way to manage their family assistance so that it does not interfere with their schoolwork. The challenge of doing so is exemplified by the following statement by a participant in one of our studies, a ninth grader from a Mexican immigrant family:

[S]ometimes I get irritated and frustrated about the fact that I have to sit late at night. Sometimes during the weekday, they [her parents] would go late at night to Wal-Mart or something, or to the market because they wouldn't have time during the day. So, she [her mother] leaves it up to me to watch my little brother or sister. Sometimes I have a lot of homework so I tell her I have homework and she says, "Oh, you have to watch your brother and sisters." I wind up staying up really late or sometimes I wind up finishing it in class.

It is important to note that this student is trying hard to complete her schoolwork despite the challenges and, according to her report, is getting the work done. But it is not hard to imagine that the repeated need to balance family demands with her schoolwork will take a toll on the student's performance in school over the long term.

Language and cultural brokering could be seen as having a similar effect on academic achievement because it can be as difficult and demanding as more general household assistance. For instance, Umaña-Taylor (2003) suggests that brokering places youth at risk for lower academic outcomes and limits their educational opportunities because they feel it is their responsibility to continue brokering. Yet some observers have suggested that it may have a salutatory effect because the activity itself develops cognitive and linguistic complexity that can enhance academic performance. Consistent with this prediction, Buriel et al. (1998) found that language brokering positively predicted academic achievement and Orellana et al. (2003) observed that children who acted as language brokers for their families scored higher on standardized tests of reading and mathematics. It is difficult, however, to draw strong conclusions about the direction of causality in these findings because other research has suggested that families select their most mature and competent children to act as language brokers in the first place (Valdes et al., 2003; Valenzuela, 1999). Furthermore, these studies do not use longitudinal methods, precluding the ability to infer causality. It also is unclear whether the academic improvements were due to better cognitive abilities as compared to other characteristics such as motivation and maturity. Nevertheless, the possibility that language and cultural brokering provides adolescents from immigrant families with opportunities to improve their cognitive and linguistic skills is intriguing and should be pursued in future research.

Finally, it is not surprising that the need to provide financial support can make it difficult for adolescents from immigrant families to pursue their education beyond the high school years. In the Bay Area study, we found that those who were providing such financial assistance to parents and siblings were less likely to enroll in postsecondary schools (Fuligni & Witkow, 2004). Among those who did enroll, financial support was linked to a lower likelihood of receiving a degree. Family assistance was difficult for all youth regardless of generational status and ethnic background, even though those from immigrant families did it more often than others. Financial assistance becomes a particular issue for youth from immigrant families after the high school years because of their greater employability and the need to help the family can arise at any point. For example, a sense of obligation to the family helped to fuel the motivation of one of our study participants from a Chinese immigrant family and helped him to attend and receive a degree from a prestigious four-year university (Fuligni, Rivera, & Leininger, 2007). But his desire to pursue graduate education was thwarted by his father suddenly becoming unemployed:

I'm finding myself in a position where I have to possibly just start paying my parents' mortgage, because my father's laid off.... I mean I had all these plans to, like go to grad school and study graphic design like abroad. It puts a hamper on things.

The situation faced by this youth highlights the fact that the need to assist and support the family is a lifelong obligation for many of those from immigrant families, and it can become an acute and pressing need at any point in their development if the family faces a sudden crisis. If such a crisis occurs at a key point of educational transition, it could potentially have a negative long-term impact upon eventual attainment.

Psychological Well-Being

We examined the association between daily family assistance and psychological well-being in the Daily Lives Study (Telzer & Fuligni, 2009a). Each day, adolescents completed a diary in which they reported the amount of time they spent helping their families in a variety of ways, including household chores, sibling care, and helping parents with official business. Participants also indicated the degree to which they felt burdened, happy, anxious, and depressed on a daily basis. Correlation analyses indicated that although those who spent more time helping the family felt a greater sense of burden ($r = .28$, $p < .001$), they did not indicate higher levels of psychological distress ($r = -.03$, ns). In fact, despite the sense of burden, adolescents who helped their families more reported significantly greater daily happiness ($r = .17$, $p < .001$). An important source of this happiness was the greater sense of role fulfillment these adolescents derived from helping. Specifically, adolescents who spent more time helping felt more like a good son, daughter, or sibling, and this in turn led to greater feelings of happiness. Role fulfillment accounted for 78.8% of the effect of family assistance on happiness. These associations were observed at the daily level as well. Using multilevel modeling (HLM; Bryk & Raudenbusch, 1992) designed to analyze nested data of the type collected for this study (i.e., daily-level data nested within individuals), we found that youth felt more role fulfillment and happiness on the days they spent more time helping their families. The finding that family assistance is associated with happiness at the individual level and the daily level suggests that assisting the family is associated with an immediate sense of happiness on days during which adolescents help their families as well as an overall sense of happiness over time as adolescents help their families more. These findings were observed for those from immigrant and nonimmigrant families alike, as well as for those from different ethnic backgrounds. Family assistance, therefore, appeared to have similar psychological correlates across generations despite being more common in immigrant families.

Systematic research on the implications of other forms of family assistance for psychological well-being is quite limited, making it difficult to draw strong conclusions (Morales & Hanson, 2005). But the few studies that have been done suggest similar themes of both burden and role fulfillment. Adolescents who engage in language and cultural brokering for their parents sometimes report the stress and pressure they feel when they need to assist their parents with serious issues, such as financial negotiations or interactions with health care agencies (Valenzuela, 1999). Given the complexity of such matters, language brokering rarely requires simple translation. It also can require adolescents to mediate and negotiate on behalf of their parents and families, putting them in the position of making decisions that have real impact upon the well-being of their families. Language and cultural brokering can also disrupt the power balance in the home, potentially creating frustration on the part of the parents because they cannot conduct official business on their own (Umaña-Taylor, 2003). Although little research has been done on this issue, it is possible that brokering could put strain on family relationships that eventually have a negative impact upon the psychological well-being of the adolescent. For instance, among families with two monolingual Spanish-speaking parents (i.e., parents do not speak English and depend on their English-speaking children), parents reported less parenting effectiveness and greater internalizing problems in their children (Martinez, McClure, & Eddy, 2008). Finally, the extent to which adolescents engage in language brokering can make a difference. Love & Buriel (2007) found that teenagers who brokered for many different people had higher levels of depressive feelings than those for whom their brokering was more limited.

At the same time, some youth report that the ability to help parents and families through cultural and language brokering makes them feel closer to their parents and helps establish more trusting relationships (Buriel et al., 1998; McQuillan & Tse, 1995). In addition, it can enhance feelings of mastery, efficacy, independence, and maturity (McQuillan & Tse, 1995; Tse, 1996; Wu & Kim, 2009). Many youth who broker for their families feel proud of doing so, enjoy brokering, and feel more connected to their culture of origin (Tse, 1995; Valdes et al., 2003). Similar to other forms of family assistance, therefore, language and cultural brokering makes adolescents from immigrant families feel needed and provides them with a meaningful way to contribute (Orellana et al., 2003).

Ethnographic studies of teenagers who work in the family business or make financial contributions suggest that youth have feelings of being burdened, different, and torn between their family obligations and the very different norms for teenagers in their settlement societies. For example, adolescents and young adults from entrepreneurial Asian immigrant families interviewed by Park (2002) often highlighted their frustrations at having to work for the family while their peers were socializing and participating in the extracurricular activities typical of American teenagers. Park also suggests that working in a family business can give rise to both premature adultification and prolonged childification. That is, adolescents take on mature responsibilities early in life, but those responsibilities never change and youth find it difficult to break into new roles that provide them with independence and adult status. Finally, the lack of boundaries between work and family life in an entrepreneurial immigrant household can create strain as the differences between a supervisor–employee relationship and a parent–child relationship become blurred.

Yet the youth interviewed by Park also discussed how their work experiences with their families brought them more insight into the occupational world of adult society and helped them in their own career decision making. Adolescents working for their families evidenced a sense of achievement that they were able to help their families succeed in American society. Working in the family business, therefore, likely has the same complex effect upon psychological well-being as other types of family contributions such as helping at home, translating, and serving as a cultural broker. It is a challenging and demanding activity that nevertheless has a great deal of meaning for youth and their families.

Conclusion

Youth from immigrant families play a central role in the adaptation of their families to a new society. Their contributions span the range from mundane household tasks to providing financial support to their parents and siblings. Systematic research into the actual prevalence and magnitude of these behaviors is only beginning to emerge, but existing studies suggest that family assistance is a fundamental aspect of the lives of these adolescents that has complex implications for their adjustment and development. In addition, the extent to which immigrant families rely upon their teenagers suggests that these youth not only help their families but also assist countries in their efforts to facilitate immigrant integration. Host societies often struggle with ways to enhance the economic progress and cultural assimilation of the foreign born, and adolescents from immigrant families work to achieve these goals on a daily basis. The contributions of youth, therefore, go beyond just their families and extend to the larger society in which they are working and developing to become productive members as adults.

Given the lack of a large body of research, it is too early to make specific practice or policy recommendations regarding adolescents' contributions to immigrant families. Nevertheless, we believe the findings reviewed in this chapter have three implications for researchers and those involved with the integration of immigrant families to consider. First, further study of the specific conditions under which family assistance can be either positive or negative for adolescent development is needed. Our own work and that of others suggests that family assistance can be a difficult but highly meaningful activity for those from immigrant families. We need to better understand when the difficulty outweighs the meaningfulness for different activities, individuals, and families. For example, it is not hard to imagine how helping to manage the household would look qualitatively different for adolescents with healthy and gainfully employed parents as compared to those whose parents cannot work because of significant physical or mental health difficulties. Existing research suggests that family assistance in and of itself is not automatically positive or negative for adolescents. The context in which that assistance occurs should make a big difference and research should focus on better understanding how the context shapes the developmental implications of contributing to the family.

Second, efforts to facilitate the adjustment of adolescents from immigrant families need to incorporate an understanding of the significance of family assistance in the lives of these youth. The obligation to care for siblings or prepare meals can make it difficult for adolescents to become involved in after-school programs or scheduled intervention activities. Designing of these programs and activities, therefore, needs to take into account the family demands on the time of these youth. Schools and colleges should be aware of how a family emergency can suddenly command the time and attention of students, especially those from immigrant and low-income families, resulting in absences or late assignments that are not due to a lack of effort or motivation. The difficulty in dealing with such matters, of course, would be to allow flexibility without lowering expectations and standards. At the same time, efforts to assist immigrant families in figuring out ways to best manage the demands placed upon their adolescents would be important. Many immigrant parents have limited educational experiences of their own and may not understand what is necessary for students to succeed in the new society. The key would be to focus on managing the daily family demands without working to undermine the larger sense of family obligation of these youth, given that a sense of duty to support and assist the family is a critical source of academic motivation in the first place.

Finally, youth from immigrant families represent an important asset for their host societies that should be recognized but not exploited. These adolescents make significant contributions to their families, serving to facilitate their long-term settlement and integration. It would be worthwhile to conduct rigorous economic studies that quantify the amount of that contribution at the societal level and to determine the savings these youth may provide to host societies because of a reduced need for social services and financial support for these families. At the same time, it would be important to examine whether the quality of the assistance provided by adolescents to immigrant families approximates the quality that could be offered by government-run services. For example, the state of California enacted legislation that mandated translation services in health care facilities largely over concerns that the reliance upon child translators resulted in a lower quality of care for immigrants. There was limited evidence that the quality of care actually was lower, but the statute was passed because of larger arguments regarding equality of access to health care for diverse populations. The situation highlights how the contributions of youth to immigrant families have implications at the individual, family, and societal levels. It is a critical feature of the lives of these immigrant youth and their families that merits further appreciation and understanding.

REFERENCES

Bryk, A. S., & Raudenbusch, S. W. (1992). *Hierarchical linear models: Applications and data analysis methods.* Newbury Park, CA: Sage.
Buriel, R., Perez, W., De Ment, T. L., Chavez, D. V., & Moran, V. R. (1998). The relationship of language brokering to academic performance, biculturalism, and self-efficacy among Latino adolescents. *Hispanic Journal of Behavioral Sciences, 20*(3), 283–97.
Burton, L. (2007). Childhood adultification in economically disadvantaged families: A conceptual model. *Family Relations, 56*(4), 329–45.
Caplan, N., Choy, M. H., & Whitmore, J. K. (1991). *Children of the boat people: A study of educational success.* Ann Arbor, MI: University of Michigan Press.

Elder, Jr., G. H., & Conger, R. D. (2000). *Children of the land: Adversity and success in rural America.* Chicago, IL: University of Chicago Press.

Fuligni, A. J. (1998). Adolescents from immigrant families. In V. McLoyd and L. Steinberg (Eds.), *Research on minority adolescents: Conceptual, theoretical, and methodological issues* (pp. 127–43). Mahwah, NJ: Lawrence Erlbaum Associates Publishers.

(2001a). *Family obligation and assistance during adolescence: Contextual variations and developmental implications.* San Francisco, CA: Jossey Bass.

(2001b). Family obligation and the academic motivation of adolescents from Asian, Latin American, and European backgrounds. In A. Fuligni (Ed.), *Family obligation and assistance during adolescence: Contextual variations and developmental implications, (New Directions in Child and Adolescent Development Monograph)* (pp. 61–76). San Francisco, CA: Jossey-Bass.

Fuligni, A. J., Rivera, G. J., & Leininger, A. (2007). Family identity and the educational progress of adolescents from Asian and Latin American backgrounds. In A. J. Fuligni (Ed.), *Contesting stereotypes and creating identities: Social categories, social identities, and educational participation* (pp. 239–64). New York, NY: Russell Sage Foundation Press.

Fuligni, A. J., & Witkow, M. (2004). The postsecondary educational progress of youth from immigrant families. *Journal of Research on Adolescence, 14*(2), 159–83.

Fuligni, A. J., Yip, T., & Tseng, V. (2002). The impact of family obligation on the daily behavior and psychological well being of Chinese American adolescents. *Child Development, 73,* 302–14.

Gibson, M. A., & Bhachu, P. K. (1991). The dynamics of educational decision making: A comparative study of Sikhs in Britain and the United States. In M. A. Gibson and J. U. Ogbu (Eds.), *Minority status and schooling: A comparative study of immigrant and involuntary minorities* (pp. 63–96). New York, NY: Garland.

Hardway, C., & Fuligni, A. J. (2006). Dimensions of family connectedness among adolescents with Mexican, Chinese, and European backgrounds. *Developmental Psychology, 42*(6), 1246–58.

Jones, C. J., & Trickett, E. J. (2005). The adolescent culture broker role: A study of adolescents and mothers from the former Soviet Union. *Journal of Social Psychology, 145,* 405–27.

Jurkovic, G. J. (1997). *Lost childhoods: The plight of the parentified child* (p. 252). Philadelphia, PA, US: Brunner/Mazel.

Love, J. A., & Buriel, R. (2007). Language brokering, autonomy, parent-child bonding, biculturalism, and depression: A study of Mexican American adolescents from immigrant families. *Hispanic Journal of Behavioral Sciences, 29*(4), 472–91.

Martinez, C. R., McClure, H. H., & Eddy, J. M. (2008). Language brokering contexts and behavioral and emotional adjustment among Latino parents and adolescents. *The Journal of Early Adolescence, 71,* 71–98.

McQuillan, J., & Tse, L. (1995). Child language brokering in linguistic minority communities: Effects on cultural interaction, cognition and literacy. *Language and Education, 9,* 195–215.

Morales, A., & Hanson, W. E. (2005). Language brokering: an integrative review of the literature. *Hispanic Journal of Behavioral Sciences, 27,* 471–503.

Orellana, M. F., Dorner, L., & Pulido, L. (2003). Accessing assets: Immigrant youth's work as family translators or "para-phrasers." *Social Problems, 50*(4), 505–24.

Park, L. S. (2002). Asian immigrant entrepreneurial children: Negotiating work, family, and community. In L. T. Vo & R. Bonus (Eds.), *Contemporary Asian American communities: Intersections and divergences* (pp. 161–77). Philadelphia: Temple University Press.

Ryan, R. M., & Deci, E. L. (2001). On happiness and human potentials: A review of research on hedonic and eudaimonic well-being. *Annual Review of Psychology, 52*, 141–66.

Ryff, C. D. (1989). Happiness is everything, or is it? Explorations on the meaning of psychological well-being. *Journal of Personality and Social Psychology, 57*(6), 1069–81.

(1995). Psychological well-being in adult life. *Current Directions in Psychological Science, 4*(4), 99–104.

Ryff, C. D., Keyes, C. L. M., & Hughes, D. L. (2003). Status inequalities, perceived discrimination, and eudaimonic well-being: Do the challenges of minority life hone purpose and growth? *Journal of Health and Social Behavior, 44*(3), 275–91.

Song, M. (2001). Chinese children's work roles in immigrant adaptation. In P. Mizen, C. Pole, and A. Boiton (Eds.), *Hidden hands: International perspectives on children's work and labor* (pp. 55–69). New York: RoutledgeFalmer.

Suárez-Orozco, C., & Suárez-Orozco, M. M. (1995). *Transformations: Immigration, family life, and achievement motivation among Latino adolescents.* Stanford, CA: Stanford University Press

Telzer, E. H., & Fuligni, A. J. (2009a). Daily family assistance and the psychological well being of adolescents from Latin American, Asian, and European backgrounds. *Developmental Psychology, 45*, 1177–89.

(2009b). A longitudinal daily diary study of family assistance and academic achievement among adolescents from Mexican, Chinese, and European backgrounds. *Journal of Youth and Adolescence, 38*, 560–71.

Trickett, E. J., & Jones, C. J. (2007). Adolescent cultural brokering and family functioning: A study of families from Vietnam. *Cultural Diversity and Ethnic Minority Psychology, 13*, 143–50.

Tse, L. (1995). Language brokering among Latino adolescents: Prevalence, attitudes, and school performance. *Hispanic Journal of Behavioral Sciences, 17*, 180–93.

(1996). Language brokering in linguistic minority communities: The case of Chinese and Vietnamese-American students. *Bilingual Research Journal, 20*, 485–98.

Tseng, V. (2004). Family interdependence and academic adjustment in college: Youth from immigrant and U.S.-born families. *Child Development, 75*(3), 966–83.

Umaña-Taylor, A. J. (2003). Language brokering as a stressor for immigrant children and their families. In M. Coleman and L. Ganong (Eds.), *Points and counterpoints: Controversial relationship and family issues in the 21st century: An anthology* (pp. 157–9). Los Angeles: Roxbury.

Valdes, G., Chavez, C., & Angelelli, C. (2003). A performance team: Young interpreters and their parents. In G. Valdes (Ed.), *Expanding definitions of giftedness: The case of young interpreters from immigrant countries* (pp. 63–97). Mahwah: Lawrence Erlbaum.

Valenzuela, A. (1999). Gender roles and settlement activities among children and their immigrant families. *American Behavioral Scientist, 42*, 720–42.

Weisner, T. S. (1982). Sibling interdependence and child caretaking: A cross-cultural view. In M. Lamb and B. Sutton-Smith (Eds.), *Sibling relationships: Their nature and significance across the lifespan* (pp. 305–27). Hillsdale, NJ: Erlbaum.

Weisskirch, R. S. (2005). The relationship of language brokering to ethnic identity for Latino adolescents. *Hispanic Journal of Behavioral Sciences, 27,* 286–99.

Weisskirch, R. S., & Alva, S. A. (2002). Language brokering and the acculturation of Latino children. *Hispanic Journal of Behavioral Sciences, 24,* 369–78.

Wu, N. H., & Kim, S. Y. (2009). Chinese American adolescents' perceptions of the language brokering experience as a sense of burden and sense of efficacy. *Journal of Youth and Adolescence, 38,* 703–18.

Zhou, M. (1997). Growing up American: The challenge confronting immigrant children and children of immigrants. *Annual Review of Sociology, 23,* 63–95.

Zhou, M., & Bankston, C. L. (1998). *Growing up American: How Vietnamese children adapt to life in the United States.* New York, NY: Russell Sage Foundation.

8 Specifying Social Psychological Adaptation of Immigrant Youth

Social Identity, Intergroup Attitudes, and Intergroup Interactions

Karmela Liebkind, Inga Jasinskaja-Lahti, and Tuuli Anna Mähönen

Introduction

Given that cultural diversity has the potential to put severe strains on the cohesion of communities, integration of immigrants can be regarded as a vitally important goal of multicultural societies. It is generally accepted that successful multiculturalism requires that all subgroups within a society develop a real sense of belonging to the mainstream society, expressed as a national identity (e.g., Brewer, 2000; Report of the Community Cohesion Panel, 2004). While the importance of a common identity for positive intergroup relations to emerge has been highlighted for decades in social psychological studies, we argue in this chapter that the social psychological aspects of immigrant integration has neither been properly defined nor sufficiently studied as an acculturation outcome of immigrant youth (Chryssochoou, 2004; Liebkind, 2001, 2006). In contrast to previous theorizations on attitudes and identities as cognitive acculturation outcomes (Arends-Tóth & Van de Vijver, 2006; Masgoret & Ward, 2006), we consider social psychological adaptation to encompass not only cognitive but also emotional, evaluative and, behavioral components of social identity and intergroup relations (Liebkind, 2001; Simon, 2004; Verkuyten, 2005). Moreover, we propose that the development of complex and flexible social identities (including national and ethnic components), positive intergroup attitudes, and positive intergroup interactions are the essence of social psychological adaptation and successful integration.

In adolescence, the task of developing positive intergroup attitudes and intergroup interactions coincides with the developmental stage in which immigrant youth have to negotiate and solidify their identity (Erikson,

1968). In addition, ethnic minority identities can in multicultural societies be considered to represent subordinate group identities within the national superordinate group. Immigrant youth can perceive these two cultural identities as mutually oppositional or even exclusive (Benet-Martinez & Haritatos, 2005). Verkuyten and Yildiz (2007) have noted that ethnic minority identities may, when perceived by their holders to be threatened in one way or another, become oppositional to the national identity. Ethnic minority identity derives from membership in an ethnic group. In this chapter, *ethnic group* refers to a group whose members believe that they share some common ancestry and cultural characteristics such as language, habits, and/or religion (e.g., the Finns, the Russians). It should be kept in mind that, at least in Europe, both majority and minority groups "have cultures" and "are ethnic" in this sense; ethnicity is not a feature of minority group members only.

However, the development of ethnic and national identities does not happen in a social vacuum. Instead, social identities, intergroup attitudes, and interactions influence each other *reciprocally* (Simon, 2004; Verkuyten, 2005). How we perceive self and other is related to processes of identity definition (Drury & Reicher, 2000; Reicher, 2004). For immigrant youth, therefore, ethnic and national identities play a crucial role, mediating between experiences and behavior: Identities both follow and precede interaction in the social world (Reicher, 2004; Simon, 2004). Research at the interface of social and acculturation psychology has, for example, focused on the effects of perceived discrimination that make it hard – or impossible – for ethnic minority members to identify with the superordinate national group (e.g., Jasinskaja-Lahti, Liebkind, & Solheim, 2009). Minority members' contacts with the majority group as well as their intergroup attitudes and identification options largely reflect their feelings of acceptance by and inclusion in the larger society (e.g., Branscombe, Schmitt, & Harvey, 1999), and feelings of rejection are found to harm intergroup relations between ethnic majority and minority groups (e.g., Barlow, Louis, & Terry, 2009; Shelton, Richeson, & Vorauer, 2006).

In this chapter we apply a social psychological approach to immigrant adaptation[1] focusing on the reciprocal and interactive nature of intergroup attitudes as consequences of and antecedents to ethnic and national identity among immigrant youth. More specifically, we take a threat perspective to the attitude formation and identification patterns of minority youth. The

---

[1] This approach is more specific than the social psychological approach to immigration research in general presented by Motti-Stefanidi et al. in Chapter 5 of this volume.

concept of threat has been defined in various ways, but in this chapter, the definition of each kind of threat has been derived from its specific implications for identity (Breakwell, 1986, 46). Two forms of identity threats are especially relevant for the purpose of the present chapter. First, threatening information or behavior can be intentionally directed at the ingroup by the outgroup and take the form of *discrimination* (Branscombe, Ellemers et al., 1999). Second, indirect identity threats exist related to the conflicting motivations and aspirations of majority and minority group members. The question of cultural maintenance – whether or not immigrants feel that their wish to maintain their heritage culture in the new society is approved by the majority – is crucial for immigrants' motivation to integrate (e.g., Berry, 1997; Bourhis et al., 1997).

Thus, *cultural discordance* – defined as disagreement between majority members and immigrants regarding the latter's degree of adherence to their heritage culture – can be considered to represent an indirect threat to the value of minority group members' identity. This threat influences the outgroup's attitudes and identification patterns (Mähönen, Jasinskaja-Lahti, & Liebkind, 2011; Rohmann, Florack, & Piontkowski, 2006). In this chapter we first present a literature review on the social psychological adaptation of immigrant youth and on the threats of perceived discrimination and cultural discordance. Next, we illustrate the reviewed research with some new empirical results on the effects of these threats on the identities and intergroup attitudes of immigrant youth. We then conclude with an overview of practical remedies for improving intergroup relations among youth.

Social Identities, Intergroup Attitudes, and Intergroup Relations

Intergroup Attitudes in Childhood and Youth

Social psychological adaptation is very much dependant on reciprocally positive intergroup attitudes. Intergroup attitudes emerge in early childhood and can have a profound impact on social relations for a lifetime (Gaertner et al., 2008). The extent and quality of social relations with both ingroup and outgroup members are especially important in adolescence for the development of intergroup attitudes as well as social identities. In addition to the normative identity exploration that all youth undergo, ethnic minority youth crystallize and formulate an identity related to their racial and ethnic group membership (Phinney et al., 2006).

However, research literature presents mixed evidence regarding the developmental sequence of intergroup attitudes among children and adolescents in that some studies indicate a development toward more positive intergroup attitudes while others indicate development toward more negative intergroup attitudes: The development of intergroup attitudes among children and adolescents depends on a combination of cognitive and social factors (Abrams & Rutland, 2008; Barrett, 2007). On the one hand, intergroup bias is found to decrease in adolescence due to the increasing capability of fairness judgments and to the greater adherence to social norms (Enesco et al., 2008). Age has been positively associated with social perspective taking ability, which, in turn, is associated with a better understanding of how groups operate and apply norms (Abrams & Rutland, 2008). On the other hand, stereotypic expectations also are found to increase with age. Moreover, not all children and adolescents respond according to accepted social values and expectations, and adolescents surrounded by a highly prejudiced environment will probably maintain prejudiced attitudes despite their newly developed cognitive capabilities (Enesco et al., 2008). Finally, implicit, ingroup serving biases likely develop early and largely remain invariant over time, even though the explicit attitudes change (Banaji et al., 2008).

In the literature on the development of intergroup attitudes and relationships among children and adolescents it can be noted that much more research has been conducted on the attitudes of majority or high-status group members relative to the attitudes of minority or low-status group members. It may not be surprising given the history of the former's perpetuating prejudice toward minority groups, but a full understanding of intergroup relations and the development of prejudice requires the study of all groups (Killen & Levy, 2008).

The Relationship between Social Identity and Intergroup Behavior

In multicultural contexts, intergroup attitudes guide intergroup behavior. Such behavior occurs when members of one group act toward members of another group in terms of their group memberships rather than for personal or idiosyncratic reasons. According to Social Identity Theory (SIT), social identity processes have implications for intergroup behavior (Tajfel, 1978; Tajfel & Turner, 1986). SIT proposes that people's group memberships are incorporated into their self-concepts, and when people's category memberships become salient in a social situation, intergroup differentiation and intragroup assimilation emerge; similarities between members of the ingroup and differences between ingroup and outgroup members are exaggerated. SIT maintains that groups seek *positive distinctiveness* from other groups and that this is usually achieved by favorable social comparison (Tajfel & Turner, 1986). Favorable comparison is not identical to outgroup discrimination, although it also can be manifested as discriminative behavior (Reicher, 2004).

Because of our presumed need for a positive self-concept, it follows that there will be a bias in social comparisons to look for ways in which one's own group can be distinguished favorably from other groups. *Intergroup bias* refers to the systematic tendency to evaluate the ingroup and its members more favorably than the outgroup and its members. This group-serving tendency can take the form of favoring the ingroup and/or derogating the outgroup (Hewstone, Rubin, & Willis, 2002). Children as young as 6 years of age display remarkably similar tendencies as adults to enhance the standing of their ingroup at the expense of outgroups and display prejudice and discrimination against selected outgroups (Nesdale, 2008). However, social and developmental psychologists have emphasized the need for making a distinction between ingroup and outgroup aspects of intergroup behavior; ingroup preference cannot be equated with outgroup evaluation (Verkuyten, 2008). Prejudice specifically connotes outgroup derogation, or negativity toward outgroups (Bohner, 2001; Pfeifer et al., 2007).

Besides ingroup favoritism or outgroup derogation, group members might use other strategies to enhance their group identity. These strategic options include: (1) leaving the negatively evaluated group, (2) changing the level of categorization, (3) social competition to change the status relations or the allocation of resources between groups, (4) changing the dimensions of evaluation, and (5) changing the reference group of evaluation (Tajfel & Turner, 1979, 1986). The search for positive group distinctiveness is one of the basic findings of social psychology, possibly because ingroup loyalty cannot be maintained without clear group boundaries (Brewer, 1991). Intergroup behavior tends to occur whenever one or more social identity is salient, and this is often the case when immigrant youth interact with the native population of a country.

Factors Influencing Intergroup Attitudes and Relations between Minority and Majority Youth

The Role of Ethnic and National Identities
Ethnic identity is generally seen as embracing various aspects, including self-identification, feelings of belongingness and commitment to a group, a sense of shared values, and attitudes toward one's own ethnic group (Liebkind, 2006). In a number of studies, ethnic identity is defined simply

as the ethnic component of social identity (Liebkind, 1992). Ethnic identity becomes especially central during adolescence. Ethnic minority adolescents must not only negotiate the identity formation process in terms of interpersonal relationships and occupation, but must also contend with their minority group status within the majority culture and define how this cultural aspect of their identity informs who they are and who they will become (Umaña-Taylor & Updegraff, 2007).

Within social psychology, the strength of identification with one's ingroup has often been assumed to correlate positively with ingroup favoritism or outgroup derogation, and some research, at least among adults, has supported this hypothesized relationship (e.g., Hodson, Dovidio, & Esses, 2003; Liebkind et al., 2004; Perreault & Bourhis, 1999). Also contradictory findings have been presented. For example, research looking especially at ethnic identity development in adolescents and young adults has suggested that strong ethnic identities constitute markers of maturity, consideration of intergroup differences, and are ultimately associated with *less* intergroup bias (Pfeifer et al., 2007; Phinney, Ferguson, & Tate, 1997; Phinney, Jacoby, & Silva, 2007; Wittig, 2008). Thus, a strong ethnic identification of minority members may in some contexts imply positive and in other negative attitudes toward the national outgroup (i.e., the majority/majorities of the country of settlement).

The mixed results may partly originate from the different aspects of ethnic identity measured, as few investigators have measured the pertinent social identities in any detailed manner. For example, when operationalizing ethnic identity as the centrality and personal evaluation of or personal affect toward membership in the ethnic group (instead of studying the strength of identification per se), Pfeifer et al. (2007) found children's strong ethnic identity to be related to higher ingroup favoritism. Moreover, minority children who reported a stronger national than ethnic identity demonstrated significantly less ingroup favoritism and outgroup derogation (Pfeifer et al., 2007).

Another reason for the mixed results may be that the relationship between social identity and intergroup attitudes is age related. Although social identity theory is not explicitly developmental, it implies, in contrast to cognitive developmental theory (Aboud, 1988), that children's intergroup attitudes are likely to become more biased with age as ethnic or other social identities become incorporated into the self-concept (Abrams & Rutland, 2008). According to Pfeifer and her colleagues (2007), however, both SIT and cognitive-developmental theory may be right: As children increasingly identify with relevant social groups, they more likely make social comparisons that positively differentiate their ingroup from relevant outgroups. Thus, intergroup bias may be expected to increase with ethnic identity strength in accordance with classic group identity effects at the earliest stages of ethnic identity development, but a more complex understanding of ethnic identity could possibly be achieved only after going through all the stages of identity development (Pfeifer et al., 2007).

As noted before, however, social identities and intergroup relations (attitudes, contact, and interaction) influence each other reciprocally (Drury & Reicher, 2000; Simon, 2004; Verkuyten, 2005). Social identities follow from as well as precede intergroup interaction (Reicher, 2004; Simon, 2004). Interactions are also pivotal for intergroup attitudes (Dovidio, Glick, & Rudman, 2005). Research on adult populations has addressed both causal directions: how intergroup interactions or contact influence intergroup attitudes (the Contact Hypothesis, e.g., Binder et al. 2009; Dovidio, Gaertner, & Kawakami, 2003) and how intergroup attitudes affect intergroup behavior (discrimination and contact; Pettigrew & Tropp, 2006). However, group size and group status influence the level of reciprocity between social identities and interactions; by virtue of their advantaged demographic, status, and institutional control position, the attitudes of majority members are likely to have a stronger impact on the identities and intergroup attitudes of minority members than vice versa (Bourhis et al., 1997).

Integrating Ethnic and National Identities

Among adolescents and adults alike, ethnic and national identities may, but do not necessarily, conflict with each other (e.g., Phinney et al., 2001; Phinney et al., 2006; Verkuyten, 2005, 2007). Immigrants and ethnic minorities differ in the extent to which they perceive their cultural identities as largely integrated and compatible or dissociated and difficult to integrate (Benet-Martinez & Haritatos, 2005). Empirically, the correlation between national and ethnic identity has varied from zero association to strong positive or negative association, regardless of the age of the respondents (e.g., Phinney et al., 2001; Verkuyten, 2005).

Individuals may integrate their multiple social identities in different ways: The content of minority identities may include varying proportions of minority/ethnic and majority/national components, and these two components may be parallel or hierarchical. Within acculturation research, integration has a distinct meaning as an acculturation orientation shown by individuals who want to retain their heritage culture and/or identity while also adopting the majority culture (e.g., Berry et al., 2006). However, the integration orientation varies considerably depending on whether the orientation toward the country of settlement is defined in terms of *identity* (Hutnik, 1991), *culture* (Bourhis et al., 1997), or *contact* (Berry, 1997; Berry et al., 2006). Immigrants may be far less inclined to identify with the dominant society or to adopt parts of its culture (while simultaneously retaining their heritage culture and/or identity) than to have regular contact and good relationships with the majority population and participate in the society (Snauwaert et al., 2003). In addition, the integration orientation can refer to any proportion of the mainstream culture (or identity) and the heritage culture (or identity) preferred or adopted (Simon & Ruhs, 2008), to shifting from one to the other depending on context, or to the creation of a new culture or identity (Arends-Tóth & van de Vijver, 2006; Liebkind, 2001; Verkuyten, 2005). As noted before, immigrants can also, to varying degrees, perceive the mainstream culture (or identity) and their heritage culture (or identity) as oppositional (Benet-Martinez et al., 2002).

Identity integration requires reduction of possible conflict between different identities through two alternative solutions: If the two identities (ethnic and national) are compatible rather than oppositional (Amiot et al., 2007; Benet-Martinez & Haritatos, 2005), they can be integrated into a new hybrid cultural identity. Provided that a superordinate identity allows for sufficient complexity and diversity in how it is construed (Hornsey & Hogg, 2000a, 2000b), a second solution is to consider the national identity as a superordinate category (Amiot et al., 2007): Immigrants may perceive their own ethnic group and the national outgroup as subgroups of a common, superordinate (national) ingroup. The degree of compatibility of different identities has been associated with positive intergroup attitudes and interactions (Benet-Martinez & Haritatos, 2005).

In order to prevent or overcome a conflictual relationship between superordinate/national and subgroup/ethnic identification, different theoretical models within the SIT framework have been formulated. While some research has assumed that total decategorization – playing down all group memberships – is the key to harmonious intergroup relations (e.g., Brewer, 1999), other research suggests that if members of two groups could recategorize themselves as belonging to a single superordinate category more favorable attitudes toward all the fellow members of new, larger ingroup should ensue (Gaertner et al., 2008). However, the fundamental limitation of both the decategorization model and the recategorization model is that they threaten to deprive individuals of valued social identities in smaller, less inclusive groups (Brewer, 1999; Crisp, Stone, & Hall, 2006). The prospect of a superordinate group identity may constitute a threat which actually increases bias; a common ingroup identity may be unrealistic in the face of powerful ethnic categorizations and many minorities are likely to resist assimilation into a superordinate category dominated by a majority outgroup (Brewer, 2000, Hornsey & Hogg, 2000a, 2000b).

The dual identity model (Dovidio, Gaertner, & Saguy, 2007; Gaertner et al., 2008) aims to remedy these problems. A dual identity encompassing national and ethnic identity refers to a context "in which subgroup identities are maintained within the context of a superordinate entity" (Gaertner et al., 2008, 145). This model acknowledges simultaneously the need to belong to a superordinate nation state (similarity at the superordinate level of identification) and the need to be different (distinctiveness at the subgroup level of identification), thereby supplying optimal distinctiveness (Brewer, 1991; Dovidio et al., 2007; Hornsey & Hogg, 2000a, Hornsey & Jetten, 2004). Nested or common ingroup identities can foster positive intergroup relations only if they represent sufficiently inclusive and complex superordinate national identities which transcend cultural boundaries and facilitate successful intergroup contacts (Gaertner et al., 2008; Hewstone et al., 2002; Hornsey & Hogg, 2000a, 2000b; Stone & Crisp, 2007; Waldzus, Mummendey, & Wenzel, 2005). Possessing a sufficiently inclusive superordinate group identity in addition to a subgroup identity (i.e., having a dual identity) can reduce biases at the subgroup level also among children and adolescents (Pfeifer et al., 2007). Some developmental research (Cameron & Rutland, 2008) suggests that the effectiveness of the dual identity approach may be age dependent: Older (at least 9 years) rather than younger children can simultaneously consider subordinate and superordinate categories. This suggests that the positive effects of dual identity may be limited to older children, as the cognitive capacity required for integrating multiple selves and resolving conflicting identities develops over time.

However, contrary to their developmental prediction, Cameron, Rutland, Brown, and Douch (2006) found in an extended contact intervention in a British elementary school that a dual identity and a common ingroup identity were equally effective among younger and older age groups. Cameron et al. (2006) devised an intervention that consisted of reading several stories to children that portrayed friendships between majority and refugee children. In some of these stories the category memberships of the protagonists were little emphasized and their individual identities were stressed (decategorization); in others the superordinate (school) category membership was a recurring theme (common ingroup identity); in still others, the subgroup identities of the protagonists as host majority members and refugees were salient while simultaneously underlining their common school identity (dual identity). There was also a control group of children who were exposed to no stories. The dual identity intervention was the most effective extended contact model. Although the intervention was more effective in changing children's intended outgroup behavior than it was for changing intergroup attitudes, this study shows that prejudice reduction tools designed on the basis of social psychological identity processes are effective in children as young as 5 years old (Cameron et al., 2006).

The results of social psychological studies on dual identity parallel findings in acculturation research, where clear benefits of dual or accumulative identification have been shown for immigrants' well-being and intergroup relations: Secure and positive dual identity is found to be associated with better well-being and more positive attitudes toward outgroups (e.g., Berry et al., 2006; Brewer & Pierce, 2002; Horenczyk & Ben-Shalom, 2001; Phinney & Alipuria, 1996). On a more general level, however, one major problem for the dual identity approach is that members of majority and minority groups may have different preferences for the content of the superordinate identity, that is, what that identity and the relations between the subgroups within it should look like. Although both majorities and minorities may prefer identity integration as a goal, majority members may mean a more assimilative identity and minority members may mean a more separate identity with the term (Jasinskaja-Lahti et al., 2003; Phinney et al., 2001). Overall, however, social and acculturation psychologists seem to agree that maintaining a positive subgroup identity within a common superordinate identity is the best option from the viewpoint of positive intergroup relations. It is possible, however, that a bicultural identity does not necessarily require a positive relationship between the two identities: Strong ethnic and strong national identities can coexist in an integrated identity even when the two identities are independent of each other (Mähönen et al., 2011).

It is important to note, however, that different factors may prevent immigrants from identifying with the superordinate national group. Even if cultural differences are not perceived to be insurmountable, negative intergroup interactions such as perceived discrimination or cultural discordance may effectively prevent the favorable development of national identification and positive outgroup attitudes. These detrimental effects will be addressed next by combining SIT-driven lines of theorization with research that takes more strongly into consideration the impact of the social context on identities and intergroup relations.

The Role of Negative Acculturation Experiences
Perceived Discrimination. The migration experiences most likely to influence social psychological and other dimensions of integration include

perceived discrimination (e.g., Bourhis et al., 1997). The bulk of research on the link between discrimination and adaptation has focused on the psychological aspects of immigrant adaptation. A consistent and robust finding among adult and adolescent immigrants alike is that perceived discrimination has direct and strong impact on the psychological well-being and health of immigrants: for example, on depression, low self-esteem, delinquency, and substance use (e.g., Jasinskaja-Lahti, Liebkind, & Perhoniemi, 2006; Rivas-Drake, Hughes, & Way, 2008; Seaton, Yip, & Sellers, 2009; Williams, Neighbors, & Jackson, 2003).

Perceived discrimination is also a serious obstacle for ethnic groups to achieve a sense of national identity and for harmonious intergroup relations. Ethnic minority group members' contacts with the majority group as well as their intergroup attitudes and identification options largely reflect their feelings of acceptance by and inclusion in the larger society (e.g., Branscombe et al., 1999; Jasinskaja-Lahti et al., 2009). Research suggests that perceived discrimination encourages hostility among minority members toward the national outgroup (e.g., Schmitt & Branscombe, 2002). Similarly, Nesdale (2008) has found that children as young as 7 to 10 years old react to peer group rejection by expressing prejudice toward the rejecting group.

Ethnic minority members sometimes cope with the experience of being discriminated against (1) by seeking to assimilate into the majority by increasing national identification (e.g., Rumbaut, 2008); (2) by developing a so-called reactive ethnicity (the Rejection-Identification Model, RIM; e.g., Branscombe et al., 1999), also referred to as a re-ethnicization process (Skrobanek, 2009, see also Rumbaut, 2008); or (3) by reducing national identification (the Rejection-Dis-Identification Model, RDIM; Jasinskaja-Lahti et al., 2009; Verkuyten, 2008). According to Rumbaut (2008), assimilation is the modal response of the children of European immigrants in the American experience characterized by ethnic identity shifts toward the thinning of their ethnic identities. This partly reflects the high degree of social mobility and intermarriage with the majority population among white European immigrants as well as a relatively positive reception and low degree of prejudice and discrimination toward this group in the core society. However, the reception of white European immigrants in the United States has not been totally unproblematic, especially during earlier waves of immigration they experienced considerable discrimination (Alba, 1996; Diner, 1996; Gold & Phillips, 1996).

In case of culturally more distant or socially disadvantaged groups, perceived discrimination against one's social ingroup has, in accordance with RIM, been found to increase ingroup identification (Outten et al., 2009;

Schmitt & Branscombe, 2002). This identity reaction may be an effort to maintain a positive self-image, as social identity is defined as the person's awareness of membership in, and the emotional value and significance attached to, a specific social group (Tajfel, 1978). Although RIM has received impressive empirical support, particularly among African Americans (for a review, see Schmitt & Branscombe, 2002), in some studies the relationship between perceived discrimination, ethnic identity, and well-being has not been found (i.e., Jasinskaja-Lahti et al., 2009). This was explained by a high degree of ingroup identification obtained among the immigrants studied (i.e., Russian speakers in Finland): Minor increases in ingroup identification probably do not significantly enhance psychological well-being, or, alternatively, it may not be a desirable option in cases where the ingroup is likely a consistent target of pervasive derogation.

Even if reactive ethnicity may buffer against the negative consequences of perceived discrimination, studies with ethnic minority samples in Europe and the United States indicate that, when talking about low-status groups, the positive effects may not be confined to well-being: A stronger sense of belonging to one's group may also be associated with more positive attitudes toward outgroups (e.g., Phinney et al., 2007; Verkuyten, 1992). Thus, it seems that minority members' negative attitudes toward the national majority may be related to the national and not the ethnic dimension of their social identity. However, the RIM largely ignores the coexistence of these two meaningful identity dimensions among immigrants and ethnic minorities. The role of each of these identities in the adaptation process of immigrant youth should be considered separately as they may interact or have different psychological consequences (Jasinskaja-Lahti et al., 2009).

People's willingness to act in favor of any group (e.g., the national society) to which they belong flows from the identity information they receive from that group (Simon & Stürmer, 2003; Tyler & Blader, 2003). With continuing negative identity information, the immigrants may resort to separatist identities (Simon & Ruhs, 2008; Verkuyten, 2007) or re-ethnicization (Skrobanek, 2009). If, then, the perception of ethnic discrimination stemming from the national society is experienced as unfair treatment, it can be assumed that these experiences will discourage immigrants from identifying with the superordinate national group and result in a tendency to disengage from it (i.e., national disidentification). This disidentification, in turn, may result in increased hostility toward the national majority (Jasinskaja-Lahti et al., 2009).

The RDIM (Jasinskaja-Lahti et al., 2009) suggests that perceived discrimination may in some contexts prevent minority members from developing a sense of belonging to a superordinate group. As a result, disidentification from and hostile attitudes toward the superordinate national group will occur (Jasinskaja-Lahti et al., 2009). The RDIM also suggests that decreased national identification may mediate the effect of perceived discrimination on attitudes toward the national majority. In a study of the relationship between perceived discrimination and national identification among immigrants from 13 countries (Berry et al., 2006), immigrant adolescents who felt that they were being discriminated against tended to reject a national identity by disidentifying from the national majority group. In contrast, those who did not feel discriminated against were likely to show national identity profiles. Thus, perceived discrimination was clearly associated with immigrants' tendency to distance themselves from the larger society. In addition, Verkuyten and Yildiz (2007) found increased ethnic identification to serve as a partial mediator of the negative effect of perceived rejection on national identification.

Cultural Discordance. The strength of ethnic and national identifications and subsequent outgroup attitudes of minority members depend not only on perceived discrimination, but also on more indirect threats posed by negative policies, discourses, and attitudinal climate in the society at large (Bourhis et al., 1997). The political climate, reflected in public discourse, has been shown to impact the intergroup attitudes of 18–26-year-old immigrants; Verkuyten and Zaremba (2005) found in their longitudinal study that after the public discourse in the Netherlands had turned radically against Muslim immigrants and multiculturalism in 2001 and 2002, identity concerns changed the subsequent attitudes of immigrants of Turkish descent toward the Dutch as well as toward other ethnic outgroups in a negative direction.

Cultural diversity in the society stimulates immigrants' integration only if there is a match between the diversity policy of the society and the expectations of immigrants (Bourhis et al., 1997). Problems usually arise when the society puts pressure on cultural minorities to adjust to dominant national identities that do not allow for inclusion of aspects of the heritage culture. This pressure usually results from lack of appreciation for the diversity represented by the minority groups. In recent studies, this kind of denigration of minority group membership has been approached though the concepts of low public regard (Seaton et al., 2009), identity undermining (Sindic & Reicher, 2009), and cultural discordance – a disagreement between majority members and immigrants regarding the latter's degree of adherence to their heritage culture (Rohmann et al., 2006). As a consequence of these identity threats, people are likely to reject membership in superordinate bodies, as any superordinate identity must be viewed "as a source of positive identity that does not conflict with or contradict cherished attributes of subgroup identity" (Hornsey & Hogg, 2000a, 143, see also Branscombe, Ellemers et al., 1999; Sindic & Reicher, 2009).

The concordance or discordance of the acculturation attitudes of majority and minority groups (i.e., whether the immigrant values the heritage culture and thus desires to maintain it in the new society, and whether the immigrant feels that this maintenance is allowed and approved by the majority) is crucial for the adaptation and integration of immigrants in the society (Ait Ouarasse & Van de Vijver, 2004; Berry, 1997; Berry et al., 2006; Horenczyk & Munayer, 2007; Pfafferott & Brown, 2006). The *concordance model of acculturation* (CMA) proposes that the greater the mismatch in acculturation attitudes, the more threatening and less enriching the intergroup situation will be perceived to be, and that high values of culture discordance indicate that immigrants prefer to maintain their culture to a higher degree than they think is accepted by the host community (Piontkowski, Rohmann, & Florack, 2002; Rohmann et al., 2006, 689). Immigrants often experience cultural discordance, that is, they perceive the majority group's expectations of immigrant assimilation as considerably stronger than their own willingness to assimilate (e.g., Horenczyk, 2000). However, far less is known about the reactions to and consequences of negative experiences of this kind than of the reactions to perceived discrimination.

The Joint Effects of Perceived Discrimination and Cultural Discordance

Even though perceived discrimination and cultural discordance both represent negative acculturation experiences, the identity consequences of the former have mainly implied changes in the *strength* of ethnic and national identification, whereas the latter can be assumed to have consequences also for the *relationship* between the two identity dimensions. In our recent study among Russian-speaking immigrant adolescents living in Finland (Mähönen et al., 2011), we showed that negative acculturation experiences such as perceived discrimination and cultural discordance had a crucial but distinct impact on the identification patterns. According to the results obtained, both perceived discrimination and cultural discordance had a negative effect on the national identification of ethnic minority youth. However, their ethnic and national identifications were negatively associated and appeared as oppositional only when there was a perceived discordance between their wish to maintain their heritage culture and the perceived attitude of the majority group toward immigrants' maintenance of their ethnic heritage. When no cultural discordance was experienced and, in fact, immigrant youth felt that their adherence to their heritage culture was supported, ethnic and national identification were independent of each other. In contrast, perceived discrimination had only a direct negative effect on the national identification of immigrant youth (cf., RDIM, Jasinskaja-Lahti et al., 2009) and perceived discrimination did not moderate the association between ethnic and national identification.

In light of these results, we suggest that immigrant youth react differently to direct and indirect identity threats (Mähönen et al., 2011). When immigrant youth are confronted with direct and intentional discrimination (Branscombe, Ellemers et al., 1999), they can react to it in a straightforward manner by acting upon just one of their two group identities – either by increasing their ethnic identification (Branscombe et al., 1999) or by decreasing their national identification (Jasinskaja-Lahti et al., 2009; see also Verkuyten & Yildiz, 2007). However, when cultural discordance is experienced as a result of the perceived conflict between the aspirations of the national majority and the immigrants, it represents a threat to the value (Breakwell, 1986) or distinctiveness (Branscombe et al., 1999) of the immigrants' ethnic identity. Thus, the identity reaction to this kind of threat requires the positioning of oneself in relation to both groups simultaneously, resulting in the polarization of the two identities. This could explain why, in the study by Mähönen et al. (2011), cultural discordance, but not perceived discrimination, moderated the relationship between ethnic and national identification, although both of these acculturation experiences had direct negative effects on the national identification of immigrant youth. The identity processes caused by direct and indirect identity threats have implications also for the intergroup attitudes of minority youth. An additional analysis of the same data revealed that both threats had a negative impact on outgroup attitudes, either directly (perceived discrimination) or indirectly through lowering the level of national identification (both threats, cf. Figure 8.1).

It thus looks as if negative acculturation experiences could lead to a vicious circle of social psychological maladaptation. Perceived discrimination and perceived cultural discordance seem to lead to increased hostility toward and separation from the national group. This, in turn, may predispose immigrant youth to even more perceived discrimination as it may make the majority – especially an insecure majority (Liebkind, 1992; Moscovici & Paicheler, 1978; Simon et al., 2001) – resort to even more discriminatory behavior (Jasinskaja-Lahti et al., 2009). Results from the longitudinal study by Seaton and colleagues (2009) showed that incidents

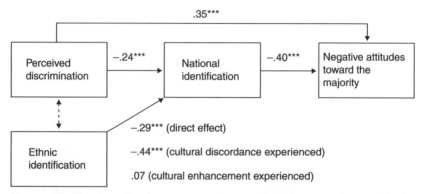

Figure 8.1. The interplay between negative acculturation experiences, identity processes, and outgroup attitudes among Russian-speaking youth living in Finland (N = 132). $\chi^2 = 656$; $df = 2$; $p = .720$.

Note: The model is controlled for age at arrival. Perceived discrimination, ethnic identification, and age at arrival were set to correlate in the model. All correlations were non-significant. In a hierarchical regression analysis cultural discordance was negatively and significantly related to national identification.

of ethnic discrimination reinforced adolescents' notion that general society has a negative perception of their ethnic ingroup, which further increased perceptions of ethnic discrimination. Thus, experiences seem to predict views, social identities, and intergroup attitudes, which seem to predict experiences (Seaton et al., 2009).

These results emphasize the need for an inclusive superordinate national identity and call for a shift in emphasis: If the national identity is perceived to be inclusive enough, identity negotiations between immigrant youth and majority members can change from those concerning the immigrants' ethnic identity to those concerning the common national identity. This does not mean that ethnic identities should not be negotiated, but that those negotiations must include the ethnic identity of the majority population: The latter must not coincide with national identity. A sufficiently inclusive superordinate national identity requires a balance between protecting people's needs for group distinctiveness and ensuring that this security does not evolve into ethnocentrism or an overly rigid policing of intergroup boundaries (Hornsey & Hogg, 2000a).

Conclusions – What Can Be Done?

Social psychological adaptation among immigrant youth in terms of positive intergroup attitudes and interactions and concomitant complex and flexible social identities has only recently become a focus of attention among politicians and researchers who recognize the potential dangers of intergroup tensions in the future. The research reviewed in this chapter clearly points to the detrimental influence of negative acculturation experiences such as perceived discrimination and cultural discordance on identity formation and intergroup attitudes of immigrants, particularly immigrant children and youth. If membership groups are valuable to self-conception, individuals want to maintain the perception of them as being (a) positive and (b) clearly distinguishable from other relevant comparison groups (Crisp & Beck, 2005). Perceived discrimination and cultural discordance threaten the achievement of these motivational goals among children and adults alike (Verkuyten, 2008).

Consequently, research emphasizes the importance of positive acculturation experiences for successful adaptation of immigrant youth. Particularly, research has tried to:

(1) identify buffering factors which increase the resilience of immigrant youth in the face of negative acculturation experiences (e.g., Rivas-Drake et al., 2008), and to

(2) find interventions to curb the occurrence of their negative acculturation experiences (e.g., Paluck & Green, 2009; Turner & Brown, 2008).

For example, some theorists (Branscombe et al., 1999; Schmitt & Branscombe, 2002) have suggested that having positive affect toward one's own ethnic group may buffer or protect minority youth from the negative outcomes attributed to discrimination. However, the results regarding the relationship between perceived discrimination and positive affect toward one's ethnic group among youth are mixed (Rivas-Drake et al., 2008; Seaton et al., 2009).

There is, however, another important factor that may protect youth from ethnic discrimination but which has been remarkably understudied, namely, perceptions of public regard – immigrant youths' perceptions of the majority members' views of their ingroup (Rivas-Drake et al., 2008). The buffering effects of high public regard should not be overlooked: Seaton and colleagues (2009) found that perceived discrimination influenced in a negative direction adolescents' beliefs of others' evaluations, that is, their perceptions of public regard. Rivas-Drake and colleagues (2008), in turn, found that more favorable public regard, but not positive affect toward their own group, functioned as a protective factor for Chinese American youth who perceived discrimination.

Perceptions of how majority members value one's ingroup derive from the environment which consists of interrelated and nested structures like family, peers, school, neighborhood, and society. On a societal level, immigrant policies still revolve primarily around demands that are made of immigrants and how they should adapt, ignoring the fact that successful integration of minority groups also requires the majority group to provide opportunities and remove obstacles. For example, European multiculturalism has always been targeted at immigrants and minorities rather than the majority group (Verkuyten, 2008).

Therefore, attempts to address the social psychological adaptation of immigrant children and youth from an intergroup perspective should include efforts to prevent or reduce negative acculturation experiences at their roots. As intergroup stereotypes and prejudices emerge in early childhood (Abrams & Rutland, 2008), childhood and adolescence are strategically the optimal periods to begin to assault the cognitive, motivational, and cultural forces that contribute to the development of prejudice (Gaertner et al., 2008) in majority and minority children alike. For the past 50 years, intergroup contact theory (Allport, 1954) has represented one of psychology's most effective strategies for improving intergroup relations. This theory poses that intergroup contact fosters intergroup harmony when the participants are of equal status in the contact situation, the interaction is cooperative rather than competitive, it has common goals and support from authorities, law, or custom, and sufficient friendship potential (Dovidio et al., 2008). Important mediators of the contact–attitude link include the reduction of intergroup anxiety (i.e., the arousal that occurs as a result of negative expectations of cross-group interaction, including fear of sanctions from ingroup members) and the increase of empathy for outgroup members (Pettigrew, 2008a; Vonofakou et al., 2008).

However, future research needs to focus more on the multilevel factors that curb contact's ability to reduce prejudice (e.g., identity threat), as these are now the most problematic both theoretically and practically yet the least understood (Pettigrew, 2008b). The fact is that everyday contact between ethnic groups in multicultural settings often bears little resemblance to the ideal contact conditions outlined by the contact hypothesis, with separatist identities, avoidance, or intergroup conflict as a result. An important challenge for societies and educational settings alike is to reduce the uncertainty and tensions that have evolved in interethnic relationships, to prevent racism and discrimination, and to foster healthy intercultural relationships (Vedder et al., 2006, cf. chapter by Horenczyk & Tatar, this volume).

Scholars seeking to understand and remedy the social problems related to prejudice have common interests with policy makers who in many countries spend considerable amounts of money on interventions aimed at prejudice reduction in schools, neighborhoods, and regions beset by intergroup conflict. Given these practical objectives, it is natural to ask what has been learned about the most effective ways to reduce prejudice. As the school environment constitutes such a salient and important world for children and youth, it is no surprise that Paluck and Green (2009) found in their review that a disproportionate percentage (88%) of field experiments aimed at evaluating prejudice reducing techniques are devoted to school-based interventions. While criticizing both the practical and the theoretical value of much prejudice reduction research, Paluck and Green (2009) nonetheless point to the apparent success of various techniques based on narrative and normative communication (e.g., Liebkind & McAlister, 1999; McAlister et al., 2000) and to their potential for reducing prejudice in the real world through narrative persuasion, the changing of social norms, the increase of cross-group empathy, and the use of extended contact.

The persuasive and positive influence of peers (indirectly via observation or directly via discussion) is an especially promising area of prejudice reduction, highlighting the communicative and normative nature of prejudice change (Mähönen et al., 2010; Paluck & Green, 2009). Research has shown that perceived social norms about cross-ethnic friendship relations partially mediate the association between direct cross-ethnic contact and positive outgroup evaluation (Feddes et al., 2009). However, as cross-ethnic friendships are relatively uncommon compared to same-ethnic friendships (cf. chapter by Spiel and Strohmeier, this volume), a more widespread reduction in prejudice can potentially occur from vicarious experiences of friendship, that is, knowledge of ingroup members being friends with outgroup members (Cameron et al., 2006; Vedder et al., 2006), provided that both of these are perceived as typical members of their groups (Cameron & Rutland, 2008). This Extended Contact Hypothesis (Wright et al., 1997; Wright, Aron & Brody, 2008) maintains, and empirical evidence supports (e.g., Cameron et al., 2006; Liebkind & McAlister, 1999), that observing an ingroup member having a close relationship with an outgroup member is sufficient for more positive intergroup attitudes to emerge.

However, the immediate and longitudinal effects of direct intergroup friendship are stronger than those of indirect friendship, and both effects are usually stronger for majority than for minority children (Binder et al., 2009; Feddes et al., 2009; Tropp & Prenovost, 2008). In the long run, therefore, the aim of interventions to improve social psychological acculturation outcomes of immigrant children and youth should aim at lowering the threshold for forming direct cross-group friendships where the subgroup identities of both are maintained and mutually valued within a sufficiently inclusive superordinate national identity.

The truth about entire genres of prejudice reduction interventions, including diversity training, educational programs, and sensitivity training in health and law enforcement professions, is that they have never been evaluated with experimental methods. Nonexperimental research in the field has yielded information about prejudice reduction program implementation, but has failed to answer the question of what works to reduce prejudice in these real-world settings (Paluck & Green, 2009). However, research evidence on patterns and processes of ethnic and national identification can help to design interventions to reduce intergroup bias; on the one hand, a too strong emphasis on common superordinate identities may actually increase bias in high ingroup identifiers (Crisp & Beck, 2005), while negative acculturation experiences or an exclusive emphasis on subgroup identities may result in disidentification from the superordinate group, segregationist identities, and hostile intergroup relations (Jasinskaja-Lahti et al., 2009). Thus, while providing immigrants with optimally distinct social identities (Brewer, 1991) and curbing the occurrence of negative acculturation experiences are far from easy tasks, these processes are nevertheless most likely to lead to the most successful adaptation outcomes.

REFERENCES

Aboud, F. E. (1988). *Children and prejudice*. Oxford, UK: Blackwell.
Abrams, D., & Rutland, A. (2008). The development of subjective group dynamics. In S. R. Levy and M. Killen (Eds.), *Intergroup attitudes and relations in childhood through adulthood* (pp. 47–65). Oxford, UK: Oxford University Press.
Ait Ouarasse, O. A., & Van de Vijver, F. J. R. (2004). Structure and function of the perceived acculturation context of young Moroccans in the Netherlands. *International Journal of Psychology, 39*, 190–204.
Alba, R. D. (1996). Italian Americans: A century of ethnic change. In S. Pedraza and R. Rumbaut, (Eds.), *Origins and destinies. Immigration, race and ethnicity in America* (pp. 172–81). Belmont, CA: Wadsworth Publishing Company.
Allport, G. W. (1954). *The nature of prejudice*. Reading: Addison-Wesley.
Amiot, C. E., de la Sablonnière, R., Terry, D. J., & Smith, J. R. (2007). Integration of social identities in the self: Toward a cognitive-developmental model. *Personality and Social Psychology Review, 11*, 364–88.
Arends-Tóth, J., & Van de Vijver, F. J. R. (2006). Issues in the conceptualization and assessment of acculturation. In M. H. Bornstein and L. R. Cote (Eds.), *Acculturation and parent child relationships: Measurement and development* (pp. 33–62). Mahwah, NJ: Erlbaum.
Banaji, M. R., Baron, A. S., Dunham, Y., & Olson, K. (2008). The development of intergroup social cognition: Early emergence, implicit nature, and sensitivity to group

status. In S. R. Levy and M. Killen (Eds.), *Intergroup attitudes and relations in childhood through adulthood* (pp. 87–102). Oxford: Oxford University Press.

Barlow, F. K., Louis, W. L., & Terry, D. J. (2009). Minority report: Social identity, cognitions of rejection and intergroup anxiety predicting prejudice from one racially marginalized group towards another. *European Journal of Social Psychology, 40*, 805–18.

Barrett, M. (2007). Theoretical accounts of how children's knowledge, beliefs and feelings about nations and states develop. In M. Barrett (Ed.), *Children's knowledge, beliefs and feelings about nations and national groups* (pp. 253–96). Hove: Psychology Press.

Benet-Martinez, V., & Haritatos, J. (2005). Bicultural Identity Integration (BII): Components and psychosocial antecedents. *Journal of Personality, 73*, 1015–50.

Benet-Martinez, V., Leu, J., Lee, F., & Morris, M. W. (2002). Negotiating biculturalism: Cultural frame switching in biculturals with oppositional versus compatible cultural identities. *Journal of Cross-Cultural Psychology, 33*, 492–515.

Berry, J. W. (1997). Immigration, acculturation, and adaptation. *Applied Psychology, 46*, 5–34.

Berry, J. W., Phinney, J. S., Sam, D. L., & Vedder, P. (2006). Immigrant youth: Acculturation, identity, and adaptation. *Applied Psychology, 55*, 303–32.

Binder, J., Zagefka, H., Brown, R., Funke, F., Kessler, T., & Mummendey, A. (2009). Does contact reduce prejudice or does prejudice reduce contact? A longitudinal test of the contact hypothesis among majority and minority groups in three European countries. *Journal of Personality and Social Psychology, 96*, 843–56.

Bohner, G. (2001). Attitudes. In M. Hewstone and W. Stroebe (Eds.), *Introduction to social psychology: A European perspective* (pp. 239–82). Oxford: Blackwell.

Bourhis, R. Y., Moïse, L. C., Perreault, S., & Senecal, S. (1997). Towards an Interactive Acculturation Model: A social psychological approach. *International Journal of Psychology, 32*, 369–86.

Branscombe, N. R., Ellemers, N., Spears, R., & Doosje, B. (1999). The context and content of social identity threat. In N. Ellemers, R. Spears, and B. Doosje (Eds.), *Social identity. Context, commitment, content* (pp. 35–58). Oxford: Blackwell Publishers.

Branscombe, N. R., Schmitt, M. T., & Harvey, R. D. (1999). Perceiving pervasive discrimination among African Americans: Implications for group identification and well-being. *Journal of Personality and Social Psychology, 77*, 135–49.

Breakwell, G. M. (1986). *Coping with threatened identities*. London: Methuen & Co. Ltd.

Brewer, M. B. (1991). The social self: On being the same and different at the same time. *Personality and Social Psychology Bulletin, 17*, 475–82.

(1999). The psychology of prejudice: Ingroup love or outgroup hate? *Journal of Social Issues, 55*, 429–44.

(2000). Superordinate goals versus superordinate identity as bases of intergroup cooperation. In D. Capozza and R. Brown (Eds). *Social identity processes: Trends in theory and research* (pp. 117–32). Thousand Oaks, CA: Sage.

Brewer, M. B., & Pierce, K. P. (2002). Social identity complexity and outgroup tolerance. *Personality and Social Psychology Bulletin, 31*, 428–37.

Cameron, L., & Rutland, A. (2008). An integrative approach to changing children's intergroup attitudes. In S. R. Levy and M. Killen (Eds.), *Intergroup attitudes and relations in childhood through adulthood* (pp. 191–203). Oxford: Oxford University Press.

Cameron, L., Rutland, A., Brown, R., & Douch, R. (2006). Changing children's inter-group attitudes toward refugees: Testing different models of extended contact. *Child Development*, *77*, 1208–19.

Chryssochoou, C. (2004). *Cultural diversity: Its social psychology.* Malden: Blackwell.

Crisp, R. J., & Beck, S. R. (2005). Reducing intergroup bias: The moderating role of ingroup identification. *Group Processes & Intergoup Relations*, *8*, 173–85.

Crisp, R. J., Stone, H. C., & Hall, N. R. (2006). Recategorization and subgroup identifi-cation: Predicting and preventing threats from common ingroups. *Personality and Social Psychology Bulletin*, *32*, 230–43.

Diner, H. (1996). Erin's children in America: Three centuries of Irish immigration to the United States. In S. Pedraza and R. Rumbaut, (Eds.), *Origins and destinies. Immigration, race and ethnicity in America* (pp. 161–71). Belmont, CA: Wadsworth Publishing Company.

Dovidio, J. F., Gaertner, S. L., & Kawakami, K. (2003). Intergroup contact: The past, pre-sent, and the future. *Group Processes & Intergroup Relations*, *6*, 5–21.

Dovidio, J. F., Gaertner, S. L., & Saguy, T. (2007). Another view of "we": Majority and minority group perspective on a common ingroup identity. In W. Stroebe and M. Hewstone (Eds.), *European review of social psychology, Volume 18* (pp. 296–330). Chichester: John Wiley & Sons.

Dovidio, J. F., Gaertner, S. L., Saguy, T., & Halabi, S. (2008). From when to why: Understanding how contact reduces bias. In U. Wagner, L. R. Tropp, G. Finchilescu, and C. Tredoux (Eds.), *Improving intergroup relations: Building of the legacy of Thomas F. Pettigrew* (pp. 75–90). Oxford, UK: Blackwell.

Dovidio, J. F., Glick, P. S., & Rudman, L. A. (Eds.) (2005). *On the nature of prejudice: Fifty years after Allport.* Oxford, UK: Blackwell.

Drury, J., & Reicher, S. (2000). Collective action and psychological change: The emer-gence of new social identities. *British Journal of Social Psychology*, *39*, 579–604.

Enesco, I., Guerrero, S., Callejas, C., & Solbes, I. (2008). Intergroup attitudes and rea-soning about social exclusion in majority and minority children in Spain. In S. R. Levy and M. Killen (Eds.), *Intergroup attitudes and relations in childhood through adulthood* (pp. 105–25). Oxford: Oxford University Press.

Erikson, E. H. (1968). *Identity, youth and crisis.* New York: W. W. Norton.

Feddes, A. R., Noack, P., & Rutland, A. (2009). Direct and extended friendship effects on minority and majority children's interethnic attitudes. A longitudinal study. *Child Development*, *80*, 377–90.

Gaertner, S. L., Dovidio, J. F, Guerra, R., Rebelo, M., Monteiro, M. B., Riek, B. M., et al. (2008). The common in-group model. Applications to children and adults. In S. R. Levy and M. Killen (Eds.), *Intergroup attitudes and relations in childhood through adulthood* (pp. 204–19). Oxford, UK: Oxford University Press.

Gold, S. J., & Phillips, B. (1996). Mobility and continuity among Eastern European Jews. In S. Pedraza and R. Rumbaut, (Eds.), *Origins and destinies. Immigration, race and ethnicity in America* (pp. 182–94). Belmont, CA: Wadsworth Publishing Company.

Hewstone, M., Rubin, M., & Willis, H. (2002). Intergroup bias. *Annual Review of Psychology*, *53*, 575–604.

Hodson, G., Dovidio, J. F., & Esses, V. M. (2003). Ingroup identification as a moderator of positive-negative asymmetry in social discrimination. *European Journal of Social Psychology*, *33*, 215–33.

Horenczyk, G. (2000). Conflicted identities: Acculturation attitudes and the immigrants' construction of their social worlds. In E. Olstein and G. Horenczyk (Eds.), *Language, identity, and immigration* (pp. 13–30). Jerusalem: Magnes Press.

Horenczyk, G., & Ben-Shalom, U. (2001). Multicultural identities and adaptation of young immigrants in Israel. In N. K. Shimahara, I. Holowinsky, and S. Tomlinson-Clarke (Eds.), *Ethnicity, race, and nationality in education: A global perspective* (pp. 57–80). Mahwah: Lawrence Erlbaum.

Horenczyk, G., & Munayer, S. J. (2007). Acculturation orientations toward two majority groups: The case of Palestinian Arab Christian adolescents in Israel. *Journal of Cross-Cultural Psychology, 38,* 76–86.

Hornsey, M. J., & Hogg, M. A. (2000a). Assimilation and diversity: An integrative model of subgroup relations. *Personality & Social Psychology Review, 4*(2), 143–56.

(2000b). Subgroup relations: A comparison of mutual intergroup differentiation and common ingroup identity models of prejudice reduction. *Personality and Social Psychology Bulletin, 26,* 242–56.

Hornsey, M. J., & Jetten, J. (2004). The individual within the group: Balancing the need to belong with the need to be different. *Personality and Social Psychology Review, 8,* 248–64.

Hutnik, N. (1991). *Ethnic minority identity: A social psychological perspective.* Oxford: Clarendon.

Jasinskaja-Lahti, I., Liebkind, K., Horenczyk, G., & Schmitz, P. (2003). The interactive nature of acculturation: Perceived discrimination, acculturation attitudes and stress among young ethnic repatriates in Finland, Israel and Germany. *International Journal of Intercultural Relations, 27,* 79–97.

Jasinskaja-Lahti, I., Liebkind, K., & Perhoniemi, R. (2006). Perceived discrimination and well-being: a victim study of different immigrant groups. *Journal of Community & Applied Social Psychology, 16,* 267–84.

Jasinskaja-Lahti, I., Liebkind, K., & Solheim, E. (2009). To identify or not to identify? National disidentification as an alternative reaction to perceived ethnic discrimination. *Applied Psychology: An International Review, 58,* 105–28.

Killen, M., & Levy, S. R. (2008). Intergroup attitudes and relations in childhood through adulthood: An introduction. In S. R. Levy and M. Killen (Eds.), *Intergroup attitudes and relations in childhood through adulthood* (pp. 3–15). Oxford, UK: Oxford University Press.

Liebkind, K. (1992). Ethnic identity – Challenging the boundaries of social psychology. In G. M. Breakwell (Ed.), *The social psychology of identity and the self concept* (pp. 147–85). London: Academic Press (Surrey University Press).

(2001). Acculturation. In R. Brown and S. Gaertner (Eds.), *Blackwell handbook of social psychology: Intergroup processes* (pp. 386–406). Oxford: Blackwell.

(2006). Ethnic identity in acculturation. In D. L. Sam and J. W. Berry (Eds.), *The Cambridge handbook of acculturation* (pp. 78–96). Cambridge: Cambridge University Press.

Liebkind, K., & McAlister, A. L. (1999). Extended contact through peer modelling to promote tolerance in Finland. *European Journal of Social Psychology, 29,* 765–80.

Liebkind, K., Nyström, S., Honkanummi, E., & Lange, A. (2004). Group size, group status and dimensions of contact as predictors of intergroup attitudes. *Group Processes & Intergroup Relations, 7,* 145–59.

Masgoret, A.-M., & Ward, C. (2006). Culture learning approach to acculturation. In J. W. Berry, J. S. Phinney, D. Sam, and P. Vedder (Eds.), *Immigrant youth in cultural transition: Acculturation, identity, and adaptation across national contexts* (pp. 58–77). Mahwah: Lawrence Erlbaum Associates.

McAlister, A. L., Ama, E., Barroso, C., Peters, R. J., & Kelder, S. (2000). Promoting tolerance and moral engagement through peer modelling. *Cultural Diversity and Ethnic Minority Psychology, 6*, 363–73.

Moscovici, S., & Paicheler, G. (1978). Social comparison and social recognition: Two complementary processes of identification. In H. Tajfel (Ed.), *Differentiations between social groups: The social psychology of intergroup relations* (pp. 251–66). European Monographs in Social Psychology no. 14. London: Academic Press.

Mähönen, T. A., Jasinskaja-Lahti, I., & Liebkind, K. (2011). Cultural discordance and the polarization of identities. *Group Processes & Intergroup Relations, 14*, 505–15.

Mähönen, T. A., Jasinskaja-Lahti, I., Liebkind, K., & Finell, E. (2010). Perceived normative pressure and majority adolescents' implicit and explicit attitudes towards immigrants. *International Journal of Psychology, 45*, 182–9.

Nesdale, D. (2008). Peer group rejection and children's intergroup attitudes. In S. R. Levy and M. Killen (Eds.), *Intergroup attitudes and relations in childhood through adulthood* (pp. 32–46). Oxford, UK: Oxford University Press.

Outten, H. R., Schmitt, M. T., Garcia, D. M., & Branscombe, N. R. (2009). Coping options: Missing links between minority group identification and psychological well-being. *Applied Psychology, 58*, 146–70.

Paluck, E. L., & Green, D. P. (2009). Prejudice reduction: What works? A review and assessment of research and practice. *Annual Review of Psychology, 60*, 339–67.

Perreault, S., & Bourhis, R. Y. (1999). Ethnocentrism, social identification and discrimination. *Personality and Social Psychology Bulletin, 25*, 92–103.

Pettigrew, T. F. (2008a). Reflections on core themes of intergroup research (pp. 283–303). In U. Wagner, L. R. Tropp, G. Finchilescu, and C. Tredoux (Eds.), *Improving intergroup relations. Building of the legacy of Thomas F. Pettigrew* (pp. 75–90). Oxford, UK: Blackwell.

(2008b). Future directions for intergroup contact theory and research. *International Journal of Intercultural Relations, 32*, 187–99.

Pettigrew, T. F., & Tropp, L. R. (2006). A meta-analytic test of intergroup contact theory. *Journal of Personality and Social Psychology, 90*, 751–83.

Pfafferott, I., & Brown, R. (2006). Acculturation preferences of majority and minority adolescents in Germany in the context of society and family. *International Journal of Intercultural Relations, 30*, 703–17.

Pfeifer, J. H., Rubble, D. N., Bachman, M. A., Alvarez, J. M., Cameron, J. A., & Fuligni, A. J. (2007). Social identities and intergroup bias in immigrant and nonimmigrant children. *Developmental Psychology, 43*, 496–507.

Phinney, J. S., & Alipuria, L. L. (1996). At the interface of culture: Multiethnic/multiracial high school and college students. *Journal of Social Psychology, 136*, 139–58.

Phinney, J. S., Berry, J. W., Vedder, P., & Liebkind, K. (2006). The acculturation experience: Attitudes, identities and behaviors of immigrant youth. In J. W. Berry, J. S. Phinney, D. Sam, and P. Vedder (Eds.), *Immigrant youth in cultural transition: Acculturation, identity, and adaptation across national contexts* (pp. 71–116). Mahwah, NJ: Lawrence Erlbaum Associates.

Phinney, J., Ferguson, D. L., & Tate, J. D. (1997). Intergroup attitudes among ethnic minority adolescents: A causal model. *Child Development, 68,* 955–69.

Phinney, J. S., Horenczyk, G., Liebkind, K., & Vedder, P. (2001). Ethnic minority identity: A social psychological perspective. *Journal of Social Issues, 57,* 493–510.

Phinney, J. S., Jacoby, B., & Silva, C. (2007). Positive intergroup attitudes: The role of ethnic identity. *International Journal of Behavioral Development, 31,* 5, 478–90.

Piontkowski, U., Rohmann, A., & Florack, A. (2002). Concordance of acculturation attitudes and perceived threat. *Group Processes & Intergroup Relations, 5,* 221–32.

Reicher, S. (2004). The context of social identity: Domination, resistance, and change. *Political Psychology, 25,* 6, 921–45.

Report of the Community Cohesion Panel. (2004). *The end of parallel lives?* London: Home Office.

Rivas-Drake, D., Hughes, D., & Way, N. (2008). A closer look at peer discrimination, ethnic identity, and psychological well-being among urban Chinese American sixth graders. *Journal of Youth and Adolescence, 37,* 12–21.

Rohmann, A., Florack, A., & Piontkowski, U. (2006). The role of discordant acculturation attitudes in perceived threat: An analysis of host and immigrant attitudes in Germany. *International Journal of Intercultural Relations, 30,* 683–702.

Rumbaut, R. G. (2008). Reaping what you sow: Immigration, youth, and reactive ethnicity. *Applied Developmental Science, 12,* 108–11.

Schmitt, M. T., & Branscombe, N. R. (2002). The meaning and consequences of perceived discrimination in disadvantaged and privileged social groups. In W. Stroebe and M. Hewstone (Eds.), *European review of social psychology, Volume 12* (pp. 167–99). Chichester: John Wiley & Sons.

Seaton, E. K., Yip, T., & Sellers, R. M. (2009). A longitudinal examination of racial identity and racial discrimination among African American adolescents. *Child Development, 80,* 406–17.

Shelton, J. N., Richeson, J. A., & Vorauer, J. D. (2006). Threatened identities and interethnic interactions. *European Review of Social Psychology, 17,* 321–58.

Simon, B. (2004). *Identity in modern society. A social psychological perspective.* Oxford: Blackwell.

Simon, B., Aufderheide, B., & Kampmeier, C. (2001). The social psychology of minority–majority relations. In R. Brown and S. L. Gaertner (Eds.), *Blackwell handbook of social psychology: Intergroup processes* (pp. 303–23). Oxford: Blackwell.

Simon, B., & Ruhs, D. (2008). Identity and politicization among Turkish migrants in Germany: The role of dual identification. *Journal of Personality and Social Psychology, 95,* 1354–66.

Simon, B., & Stürmer, S. (2003). Respect for group members: Intragroup determinants of collective identification and group-serving behaviour. *Personality and Social Psychology Bulletin, 29,* 183–93.

Sindic, D., & Reicher, D. S. (2009). "Our way of life is worth defending": Testing a model of attitudes towards superordinate group membership through a study of Scots' attitudes towards Britain. *European Journal of Social Psychology, 39,* 114–29.

Skrobanek, J. (2009). Perceived discrimination, ethnic identity and the (re-)ethnicisation of youth with a Turkish ethnic background in Germany. *Journal of Ethnic and Migration Studies, 35,* 535–54.

Snauwaert, B., Soenens, B., Vanbeselaere, N., & Boen, F. (2003). When integration does not necessarily imply integration. *Journal of Cross-Cultural Psychology, 34,* 231–9.

Stone, C. H., & Crisp, R. J. (2007). Superordinate and subgroup identification as predictors of intergroup evaluation in common ingroup contexts. *Group Processes & Intergroup relations, 10*, 493–513.

Tajfel, H. (1978). Social categorization, social identity and social comparison. In H. Tajfel (Ed.), *Differentiation between social groups; Studies in the social psychology of intergroup relations* (pp. 61–76). London: Academic Press.

Tajfel, H., & Turner, J. C. (1979). An integrative theory of intergroup conflict. In W. G. Austin and S. Worchel (Eds.), *The social psychology of intergroup relations* (pp. 33–47). Monterey: Brooks/Cole.

(1986). The social identity theory of intergroup behavior. In S. Worchel and W. G. Austin (Eds.), *Psychology of intergroup relations* (pp. 7–24). Chicago: Nelson Hall.

Tropp, L. R., & Prenovost, M. A. (2008). The role of intergroup contact in predicting children's interethnic attitudes. In S. R. Levy and M. Killen (Eds.), *Intergroup attitudes and relations in childhood through adulthood* (pp. 236–48). Oxford, UK: Oxford University Press.

Turner, R. N., & Brown, R. (2008). Improving children's attitudes toward refugees: An evaluation of a school-based multicultural curriculum and an anti-racist intervention. *Journal of Applied Social Psychology, 38*, 1295–328.

Tyler, T. R., & Blader, S. L. (2003). The group engagement model: Procedural justice, social identity, and cooperative behavior. *Personality and Social Psychology Review, 7*, 349–61.

Umaña-Taylor, A. J., & Updegraff, K. A. (2007). Latino adolescents' mental health: Exploring the interrelations among discrimination, ethnic identity, cultural orientation, self-esteem, and depressive symptoms. *Journal of Adolescence, 30*, 549–67.

Vedder, P., Horenczyk, G, Liebkind, K., &. Nickmans, G. (2006). Ethno-culturally diverse education settings: problems, challenges and solutions. *Educational Research Review I*, 157–68.

Verkuyten, M. (1992). Ethnic group preferences and the evaluation of ethnic identity among adolescents in the Netherlands. *Journal of Social Psychology, 132*(6), 741–51.

(2005). *The social psychology of ethnic identity*. London: Psychology Press.

(2007). Religious group identification and inter-religious relations: A study among Turkish-Dutch Muslims. *Group Processes & Intergroup Relations, 10*, 341–57.

(2008). Multiculturalism and group evaluations among minority and majority groups. In S. R. Levy and M. Killen (Eds.). *Intergroup attitudes and relations in childhood through adulthood* (pp. 157–72). Oxford, UK: Oxford University Press.

Verkuyten, M., & Yildiz, A. (2007). National (dis)identification, and ethnic and religious identity: A study among Turkish-Dutch Muslims. *Personality and Social Psychology Bulletin, 33*, 1448–62.

Verkuyten, M., & Zaremba, K. (2005). Inter-ethnic relations in a changing political context. *Social Psychology Quarterly, 68*, 375–86.

Vonofakou, C., Hewstone, M., Voci, A., Paolini, S., Turner, R. N., Tausch, N., Tam, T., Harwood, J., & Cairns, E. (2008). The impact of direct and extended cross-group friendships on improving intergroup relations (pp. 107–23). In U. Wagner, L. R. Tropp, G. Finchilescu, and C. Tredoux (Eds.), *Improving intergroup relations. Building of the legacy of Thomas F. Pettigrew* (pp. 75–90). Oxford, UK: Blackwell.

Waldzus, S., Mummendey, A., & Wenzel, M. (2005). When "different" means "worse": In-group prototypicality in changing intergroup contexts. *Journal of Experimental Social Psychology, 41*, 76–83.

Williams, D. R., Neighbors, H. W., & Jackson, J. S. (2003). Racial/ethnic discrimination and health: Findings from community studies. *American Journal of Public Health, 93*, 200–8.

Wittig, M. A. (2008). A mutual acculturation model for understanding and undermining prejudice among adolescents. In S. R. Levy and M. Killen (Eds.). *Intergroup attitudes and relations in childhood through adulthood* (pp. 220–33). Oxford, UK: Oxford University Press.

Wright, S. C., Aron, A., & Brody, S. M. (2008). Extended contact and including others in the self. Building on the Allport/Pettigrew legacy (pp. 143–59). In U. Wagner, L. R. Tropp, G. Finchilescu, and C. Tredoux (Eds.), *Improving intergroup relations. Building of the legacy of Thomas F. Pettigrew* (pp. 75–90). Oxford, UK: Blackwell.

Wright, S. C., Aron, A., McLaughlin-Volpe, T., & Ropp, S. A. (1997). The extended contact effect: Knowledge of cross-group friendships and prejudice. *Journal of Personality and Social Psychology, 73*, 73–90.

9 Understanding Ethnic Minority Identity

Maykel Verkuyten

Introduction

There is a large body of research in North America and, to a lesser extent, in Europe indicating that a positive and strong ethnic minority identity is associated with subjective well-being and forms of adjustment. Ethnic identity seems to play an important role in the lives of ethnic minority youth. A strong ethnic identity can function as a *buffer* or protective factor against discrimination and stigmatization (Pascoe & Smart Richman, 2009), and ethnic identity can be a valuable *resource* because a clear sense of who one is ethnically gives self-confidence and a sense of grounding (LaFromboise et al., 1993). Furthermore, ethnic identity functions as the *basis* for ethnic group behavior and coordinated action (Turner, 1999). So there are good reasons for supporting and strengthening the ethnic identity of children and adolescents from immigrant and minority groups, for example, by multicultural education and forms of multicultural recognition. But these initiatives would benefit from a clear understanding of ethnic identity and the different approaches for studying it. The aim of this chapter is to provide an overview of the different ways in which ethnic identity is studied in psychological research and to emphasize the importance of examining ethnic practices and social interactions. Thus, the focus of the chapter is theoretical and empirical rather than applied toward trying to give practical suggestions and recommendations for the ethnic identity development of immigrant and ethnic minority youth.

Ethnic identity in this chapter is taken to refer to a (multidimensional) sense of collective identity based on the perception that one shares a common ethnocultural heritage with a particular group. Psychological research on immigrants and ethnic groups has adopted at least three theoretical perspectives on the concept of ethnic minority identity (Phinney, 1990). One is related to the social identity approach developed by Tajfel and Turner (1979). Another focuses on identity formation and goes back to the work of Erik Erikson (1968). A third examines ethnic and cultural identity as part of the acculturation process (Liebkind, 2001). All three offer psychological explanations, but in different ways. The first one focuses on group commitments and the ways in which minority members deal with a negative social identity, the second one is concerned with the developmental process of construing and achieving an inner sense of stability and continuity, and the third examines how ethnic identity changes through cultural contacts and how it relates to being a (new) member of the host society. All three are similar, however, in their emphasis on psychological structures and processes. This emphasis is important because it provides, for example, an understanding of what it actually feels like to be treated as an outsider, or what happens subjectively when youngsters define themselves as member of an ethnic group, and of the gradual changes in ethnic self-understanding in the acculturation process. In addition, the ethnic self is important for understanding ethnic behavior, which in many studies is considered an outcome of a sense of ethnic identity but can also be seen as an integral part of that identity.

In this chapter I argue that ethnic identity is intimately bound up with ethnic practices enacted and negotiated in social interactions. These practices are framed explicitly or implicitly in ethnocultural terms and shape people's everyday experiences. In addition to the psychological level of analysis, I stress the need to pay close attention to the level of interactions and the ways that youth communicate their ethnicity. The social world of youth and the meanings that their ethnic identities take are expressed and co-constructed with peers, parents, and various others, and in all sorts of settings, including the new media. Thus, the formation of an ethnic identity is based on negotiations with coethnics and outsiders within a local, national, and global context that is often strongly politicized.

In this chapter, I first briefly discuss the usefulness of making a distinction between the psychological and social interaction levels of analysis. Next, I examine the psychological level and discuss the importance of distinguishing between different dimensions of a sense of ethnic identity. Subsequently, I will discuss the three different ways in which psychology has conceptualized and theorized a sense of ethnic identity, and the implications of this for the questions being addressed. Finally, I focus on ethnic practices and identity enactment in the context of the ways in which minority youth live their daily lives.

Social Identities and Levels of Analysis

Social identity refers to the question of *what* someone is taken to be socially, rather than *who* someone is as an identifiable unique individual or *how* someone is in terms of personal preferences and dispositions (Verkuyten, 2005a). Hence, what is at stake is not that which distinguishes a person as an individual from other individuals, but that which is shared with others. The social identity concept indicates what a person is, how she or he is socially defined. It is about categorical characteristics – like gender, age, race, and ethnic background – that position or locate people in social space. In talking about social identities, we are not interested primarily in how a particular individual is to be known, but in what there is to be known about social categories. These are different things. Socially defined and recognized distinctions and designations are at stake, rather than individual qualities and characteristics.

Social identities are formed and defined in the social world independently of the particular individual located by them. Since an externally established identity typically comes about regardless of the wishes, preferences, and needs of the person in question, the internal appreciation of it (i.e., the way the person thinks and feels about a particular social identity) is obviously something else. Identity as a social reality – who and what somebody is socially – should not be confused with the sense of identity or the way that identity is psychologically meaningful. The latter is basically a subjective phenomenon, although this does not mean, of course, that the psychological meaning is formed independently of the social world. On the contrary, identity as a social reality concerns the social constructions or the ways in which categorical distinctions are made meaningful, collectively and in interaction. However, a sense of identity implies individual interpretation to which personal wishes, desires, needs, and experiences are important. The fact that these personal features have been socially formed and attained and that they are socially shared and used does not alter that.

The analytical distinction between social reality and subjective experience allows us to examine the discrepancies between subjective interpretation of an individual's sense of identity and the social identity or "identity-type" itself (Berger & Luckmann, 1966). The subjective experiencing (who you think and feel you are) may or may not tally with the objective designation (what you are taken to be). In addition, it allows us to examine social change in terms of the dialectic between subjective understanding and social reality. The socially defined reality provides the constraints and opportunities for the identity positions and meanings that one can claim and take up in interactions. And it is the subjective, interiorized sense of identity that suggests scope for individual interpretation, agency, and control.

Ethnic identity issues concern both personal interpretations and sociocultural constructions and these issues cannot be reduced to one another. This dual aspect is quite often neglected, not only in approaches that emphasize subjective interpretations and individual choice, but also in approaches that stress the role of, for example, social representations, public images, and cultural models that define and impose particular ethnic identity types. These two aspects come together in social interactions (Berger & Luckmann, 1966; House, 1981). It is in interactions that identity types are reproduced and changed, actualized, or challenged. And it is in interactions that a sense of ethnic self is formed (see also the chapter by Motti-Stefanidi et al.).

Dimensions of the Ethnic Self

Most of the studies on ethnic identity indicate that minority youth have a relatively positive sense of their ethnic identity. Mean scores are typically toward the positive end of the measurement scales and tend to be higher than for majority group peers. An example is the International Comparative Study of Ethnocultural Youth (ICSEY) that examined almost 40 different minority groups in 13 countries (Phinney et al., 2006). The following findings in this study are remarkable: All minority groups score above the neutral midpoint of the scale, there were few differences between the various ethnic minority groups, and almost all of these groups had a higher score than the national comparison group. These are striking findings considering the different migration histories, the ethnic and cultural group differences, the different socioeconomic positions in the host countries, and the various national contexts that differ in their immigration and integration policies.

One explanation for these findings is the shared minority position that would lead to a relatively strong sense of ethnic identity. The "rejection-identification model" is based on the idea that perceived group threat leads individuals to identify more strongly with their own ethnic group (Schmitt & Branscombe, 2002). Minority group individuals can cope with group threats by adopting group-based strategies that increase ethnic identification. Some experimental evidence has shown that threats can indeed increase ingroup identification (see Schmitt & Branscombe, 2002). In addition, survey research among racial and ethnic minority groups shows that higher perceptions of discrimination predict higher ingroup identification (e.g., Verkuyten & Yildiz, 2007). Discrimination presents a threat to one's ethnic identity, making individuals increasingly turn toward the minority ingroup. Thus, the vulnerable position of ethnic minority groups in the different countries might explain the relatively high level of ethnic identity. A similar process leads to a similar outcome.

However, we should not draw conclusions too quickly because there may be many roads that lead to Rome: A similar outcome can also be the result of different processes. For example, in most countries there is an ethnic hierarchy with a differential evaluation of various immigrant and ethnic minority groups (Hagendoorn, 1995). The different groups enjoy varying degrees of social acceptance but they all tend to have a similar strong and positive sense of ethnic identity. In addition, such an identity is typically also found among minority group children (under the age of 12) but this outcome tends not to be related to perceptions of their minority position. Simons and colleagues (2002), for example, found no association between identity development and perceived discrimination among African American children. Similarly, in the Netherlands, we found in two studies no associations between perceived discrimination and ethnic identity among Turkish, Moroccan, and Surinamese children (Verkuyten, 2002).

In two other studies, we not only examine ethnic identity among ethnic minority and majority youth in the Netherlands but also among comparable groups living in the country of origin. In one of these studies we compared Turkish Dutch early adolescents (10–12 years) with Dutch peers and with early adolescents living in Turkey (Verkuyten, 2005b). It turned out that the Turkish Dutch in the Netherlands had a significantly higher score than the Dutch, but an equally positive ethnic identity as the youth in Turkey. Thus, the Turkish Dutch youth resembled the Turks in Turkey. This suggests that the minority position is not the critical issue; cultural values and early socialization play a central role. The Turkish Dutch, for example, have emigrated from a country with a rich history and culture and a strong nationalist tradition. These are important resources for feeling proud of being Turkish and for emphasizing one's Turkish identity: both for Turks living in Turkey and for Turks living in the Netherlands where the emphasis on Turkish identity is supported by transnational networks and the availability of Turkish media. In addition, Turkish parents in the Netherlands are concerned with transmitting their traditions, history, and cultural values to their children. The relationship between parents and children is strongly affected by what is considered appropriate cultural behavior within the Turkish community, as most parents do not want their children to "Dutchify."

Thus, one's position in the Netherlands can mean different things and plays itself out within a broader sociocultural tradition and context. A minority position can affect ethnic identity in various ways, for example, by adolescents' own perceptions and negative experiences of being an immigrant or minority group member. But there is also ethnic socialization and the internalization of ethnocultural attitudes, beliefs, and practices that parents and peers express in verbal and nonverbal ways. Further, there are material, social, and political living conditions that prevail during childhood and adolescence and affect children's lives in all kinds of ways. The resulting emphasis on ethnic identity is very similar for the different groups but the corresponding processes might differ considerably. In short, different processes might lead to a similar strong and positive sense of ethnic identity. In addition, it can be argued that such an outcome does not tell us much about the complexities of minority youths' sense of ethnic identity.

In the ICSEY study, ethnic identity was measured with items that predominantly assess private regard or the evaluation of ethnic identity (e.g., "pride in ethnic culture," "happy to be ethnic," and "feels happy about ethnic culture"). This is an important aspect of the ethnic self but by no means the only one. Recent studies and reviews have identified and validated several psychological components of group identity, such as "importance," "centrality," "evaluation," "esteem," and "behavioral involvement" (e.g., Ashmore et al., 2004; Sellers et al., 1998). There is little agreement regarding the number and nature of the dimensions and it is not always clear whether terms such as identity "dimensions," "elements," "components," and "aspects" refer to the same things.

Centrality, importance, and evaluation are dimensional (attitude-like) properties that are relatively easy to assess. The fact that they can be distinguished empirically means that they can provide a more detailed understanding of ethnic minority identity. For example, a positive evaluation of one's ethnic identity does not have to imply that it is a central aspect of how one sees oneself, and when it is considered of key importance it does not have to be evaluated positively, as indicated by the example of stigma identities (Goffman, 1963). Thus, a similar score for the evaluation of one's ethnic identity among Turkish Dutch adolescents and Turks in Turkey does not necessarily imply that these groups consider this identity equally important, are equally aware of it in their daily life, and that their behavior is equally affected by it.

In addition, there is much less attention paid to identity aspects that refer to content and meaning (see Ashmore et al., 2004). Sellers and colleagues (1998) propose a model that tries to represent a synthesis of what they label as the underground and the mainstream approach of ethnic and racial identity. The latter focuses on more general dimensional properties associated with these identities such as centrality and regard, whereas the former focuses on describing the particular meanings attached to ethnic and racial identities. Within the underground perspective different frameworks have been proposed to describe the unique cultural and structural experiences associated with, for example, the position of African Americans (e.g., Cross, 1991) and white Americans (Helms, 1995). Thus, a similar ethnic identity score of Turkish Dutch in the Netherlands and Turkish adolescents in Turkey does not have to imply a similar understanding of what it means to be Turkish. An equally positive or important social identity can mean very different things and it is the meaning that gives direction to one's thinking and behavior. A strong identity tells us something about the intensity and stability of one's ethnic self but does not tell us much about how to live and interact with one's social environment and which actions implicate or express one's ethnic group membership.

Thus, different dimensions of the sense of ethnic identity can yield different results and a similar score for one dimension does not necessarily mean that there are no differences for other identity dimensions or aspects. Furthermore, the same dimension might also yield different results for the same minority group. In a paper on racial identity, Erikson (1966) argued that a sense of identity has conscious as well as unconscious aspects. He pointed out that there are aspects that are accessible only at moments of special awareness or not at all. In line with psychoanalytical ideas, he discussed repression and resistance. He claimed that racial minorities would have more negative self-feelings on an unconscious level. In social psychology the distinction between conscious and unconscious, or explicit and implicit, has been conceptualized in terms of dual attitudes (Wilson et al., 2000). The central idea is that people can have different evaluations of the same attitude object: an implicit attitude and an explicit attitude toward, for example, the ethnic self.

The distinction is important because it is possible that stereotypes and discrimination negatively affect the implicit rather than the explicit ethnic self-evaluation of ethnic minorities (Pelham & Hetts, 1999). The distinction has also given a new impetus to long-standing theories about qualitatively different forms of high (ethnic) self-esteem (see Kernis & Paradise, 2002). It is argued that there are at least two distinct types of high self-esteem: one that is relatively secure and confidently held, and another that is relatively defensive and fragile. Jordan and colleagues (2003) propose that defensive self-views are characterized by two discrepant attitudes toward the self. People with defensive high self-esteem would, on an explicit level, have a positive attitude toward themselves, whereas at an implicit level they would feel relatively negative about themselves. The combination of positive explicit and implicit self-esteem would be more characteristic for secure high self-esteem.

In our study and by using the evaluation of pronouns ("we"; Perdue et al., 1990) and a variant of the initials preference task (Nuttin, 1987), it turned out that, compared to the Dutch and the Turks in Turkey, the Turkish Dutch early adolescents (10–12 years old) had significantly less positive implicit ethnic self-esteem (Verkuyten, 2005b). Furthermore, the percentage of participants with defensive ethnic self-esteem (high explicit/low implicit) was significantly greater among the Turkish Dutch (44.4%) than in the other two samples (< 15%). Thus, although the Turkish Dutch reported an equally positive (explicit) ethnic identity, they suffered from lower implicit ethnic self-esteem. This was related to their disadvantaged position in the Netherlands because perceived discrimination was negatively related to implicit ethnic self-esteem but not to the explicit ethnic identity measure.

Theoretical Perspectives

Psychological research has adopted three main theoretical perspectives on adolescents' sense of their ethnic minority identity. These perspectives focus on psychological structures and processes and the ways in which these develop and play out in social contexts such as families, peer groups, schools, and neighborhoods (see also the chapter by Motti-Stefanidi et al.). In addition, this research is typically concerned with psychological and behavioral adjustment outcomes associated with particular ethnic self-understandings and self-evaluations (Burrow et al., 2006).

Identity Development
Erik Erikson was one of the first social scientists to investigate the incisive significance of identity processes in social reality. His formulation of eight stages in the psychosocial development of human beings is an achievement of classic significance in developmental psychology. According to Erikson (1968), people try to achieve a sense of stability and continuity by integrating understandings of themselves and their place in society. The emphasis is on the evolving sense of self that changes with age and development. The

interest is in the gradual formation of a secure and confident inner sense of one's ethnic self. It is the individual who explores the meanings of his or her ethnic group memberships and makes a commitment to a specific way of relating to the ethnic group. The psychological processes of exploration and commitment are considered central to identity development and this development is about achieving security and a sense of continuity. Inner states of the individual are at the core of this conception. "What does it mean to me that I am a member of this ethnic group?" is the question asked. Active learning and investigation into the various identity options resulting in a committed decision gives a secure, confident ethnic self-understanding.

An example of this approach is provided by Phinney (1989), who argues for ethnic identity entailing general phenomena that are relevant and comparable across groups. She proposes a three-stage progression from an unexamined ethnic identity through a period of exploration to an achieved or committed ethnic identity and she has developed a measure for assessing ethnic identity achievement that can be applied across groups (Phinney, 1992). In their longitudinal study among African and Latino Americans, French and colleagues (2006) found that ethnic identity exploration was very low among early adolescents and rose only for the middle adolescent cohort. Further, in a large-scale study among different ethnic minority groups in the United States, it was found that adolescents who had an achieved ethnic identity had the highest self-esteem scores (Martinez & Dukes, 1997, see also Lorenzo-Hernandez & Ouellette, 1998; Umaña-Taylor, 2004). But the empirical research on ethnic identity development lags behind the theoretical writing. The number of studies testing Phinney's model is limited; longitudinal research examining developmental trajectories is especially lacking. Moreover, the existing studies are predominantly restricted to the United States (but see Jasinskaja-Lahti & Liebkind, 1999).

In these developmental models, the early stages of development are seen as typical for older children and early adolescents. Thus, for these age groups, these models, for example, expect no relationship between perceived discrimination and the importance attached to ethnic identity. However, studies among middle adolescents have also not found such a relationship and have shown that only a numerical minority of African Americans, Asian Americans, and Hispanic Americans, as well as of Surinamese Dutch, have an achieved ethnic identity (see also Phinney et al., 1998; Verkuyten & Brug, 2002). Thus, an achieved ethnic or racial identity, or the development of a committed and secure sense of being a member of one's ethnic or racial minority group, appears to be more typical for late adolescence and young adulthood rather than for early and middle adolescence.

These developmental models also assume that ethnic identity is a psychologically important construct predictive of particular adjustment outcomes in immigrants' and minority adolescents' lives. Research has, for example, documented that developmental stages or phases of ethnic minority identity are linked to a range of key psychological (e.g., well-being), academic (e.g., educational achievement), and social adjustment outcomes (e.g., anti- and prosocial behaviors). In general, the findings indicate that adaptive outcomes are associated with more achieved ethnic identities (see Burrow et al., 2006).

Acculturation Perspective

The sense of ethnic minority identity is also studied from the perspective of acculturation. Behaviors, attitudes, values, and identifications that change with contacts between cultures are key issues in understanding the development of immigrant youth. Ethnic identity becomes salient as part of the acculturation process. The concepts of ethnic identity and acculturation are often used interchangeably, but it seems better to consider the latter a broader construct that encompasses a wide range of changes (Liebkind, 2006). A changing sense of ethnic identity and a developing sense of host national identity can be considered central aspects of the acculturation process. Ethnic identification and identification as a member of the new society can be thought of as two dimensions that vary independently (Hutnik, 1991). For example, for many young Turks living in Germany it is often not a question of being Turkish or German but a question of the extent to which they feel Turkish as well as the degree to which they feel German.

Hutnik (1991) makes a distinction between four identity positions: separation, where the identification is predominantly with one's own ethnic group; assimilation, where identification with the majority group predominates; integration (or hyphenated identity), where there is identification both with one's ethnic minority group and with the majority group; and marginality or diffusion, where one identifies with neither the ingroup nor the majority group. In several studies we have examined ethnic self-definitions among minority members of different ethnic groups and different ages (see Verkuyten, 2005a). In these studies we asked youth how they see themselves and we used four response categories representing Hutnik's four identity positions. In general, about half of the members of each ethnic and age group identified only with their ethnic minority group (separation). In addition, around a third opted for a hyphenated identity. In all samples there were few adolescents that took only the national identity or marginal position. In short, different studies have shown that the four forms of identification do exist, but not all to the same extent (see Sam & Berry, 2006). Defining oneself in terms of one's own ethnic group or in terms of a hyphenated position is more frequent, whereas adopting an assimilative and/or marginal position are rather exceptional. The same has been found in other countries such as the United States (e.g., Sanchez & Fernandez, 1993), Britain (e.g., Hutnik, 1991), Australia (e.g., Nesdale & Mak, 2000), Belgium (e.g., Snauwaert et al., 2003), and in the ICSEY study (Phinney et al., 2006).

There are indications that, from an adjustment point of view, the least desirable positions are the marginal and the assimilative ones. Both positions imply a kind of denial of the complex reality of living with two or more cultures, whereas acceptance of this is considered a prerequisite for effective coping. A marginal orientation is traditionally associated with psychological and behavioral problems and stress, and assimilation seems to be related to psychological costs such as cultural alienation, depression, fear, and loneliness (e.g., Arroyo & Zigler, 1995). In contrast to marginalization and assimilation, the correlates of integration and segregation appear to be more positive but the evidence for this is not very consistent or strong (see Brown & Zagefka, 2011; Rudmin, 2003). This indicates that preserving a tie with their own ethnic group and culture can have a positive influence on the psychological and social adjustment of immigrant and minority youth, depending on various conditions such as family life and community support (see the meta-analysis of Nguyen & Benet-Martínez, 2010).

Social Identity Approach

Intergroup approaches do not focus on developmental issues but rather on the situational salience of ethnicity and the strength of ethnic group commitment. The social identity approach emphasizes that people are psychological group members who often think, feel, and behave in terms of shared social identities. When social identities are psychologically salient people will act in terms of how their group ("we") is understood rather than as individual persons ("I"). The approach includes social identity theory that has a motivational focus (SIT; Tajfel & Turner, 1979) and the related self-categorization theory that is more concerned with cognitive processes (SCT; Turner et al., 1987). The former argues that people try to achieve a positive social identity by seeking distinctiveness for their ingroup compared to outgroups. The latter focuses on the contextual ways in which groups transform the self-understandings of individuals and how this transformation enables different people to think, feel, and behave in similar ways.

SIT is explicitly concerned with how people manage their ethnic identity in the sociostructural context in which they live (see also the chapter by Liebkind et al.). The theory proposes that the operation of motivational processes depends on ideological and structural features of the social world. Thus, the focus is much more on how ethnic minority members position themselves in their social world rather than on the inner development of a secure ethnic self. Tajfel (1981) was particularly interested in stigmatized and disadvantaged groups such as ethnic minority groups. Membership in these groups confers a negative identity and instigates identity management strategies (Tajfel & Turner, 1979). Depending on the nature of the social structure, members of low-status groups adopt different strategies to achieve a more positive social identity. According to SIT, beliefs about the stability and legitimacy of the status system and the nature of the group boundaries affect people's responses and strategies for achieving a positive identity. *Stability* refers to the extent to which group positions are changeable, and *legitimacy* refers to the extent to which the status structure is accepted as legitimate. *Permeability* refers to the extent to which individual group members can leave one group and join another. Perceived stability, legitimacy, and permeability would, interactively, determine the cognitive, emotional, and behavioral responses to the intergroup context and the strategies chosen in pursuing positive distinctiveness.

According to SIT, actions for improving the status and position of one's ethnic group are not very likely when the intergroup structure is perceived as being secure (stable and legitimate). In such a situation, and depending on the degree to which the boundaries between the groups are seen as permeable, ethnic minority members are more likely to make individual choices and to distance themselves from their ethnic group. The results of one of our studies among Turkish Dutch adolescents clearly support these ideas (Verkuyten & Reijerse, 2008; see also Bettencourt et al., 2001). When the interethnic relations were considered as relatively secure, perceived permeability was associated with lower Turkish identification. Hence, in a stable and legitimate intergroup structure in which, however, a person's fate is not tied to his or her ethnic minority group membership, Turkish Dutch adolescents tended to distance themselves from the Turkish ingroup. Furthermore, there was not only evidence of distancing from the ethnic ingroup but also of increased association with the higher-status majority group. In a secure intergroup context, higher perceived permeability was related to higher Dutch identification (see also Guimond et al., 2002). When the Turkish Dutch adolescents saw opportunities to gain acceptance in the Dutch majority group, they tended to dissociate themselves from the Turkish ingroup and to associate themselves more with the Dutch.

Thus, group identifications of ethnic minority members are guided by ideas about the stability and legitimacy of intergroup relations and the nature of the group boundaries. The three characteristics indicate that an understanding of ethnic identity among minority youth needs to take the broader sociocultural context into account. Group identification is dependent on the perceptions of the intergroup structure and the ideological context in which youngsters find themselves. The role of these factors is increasingly important during adolescence due to their growing understanding of society (Barrett & Buchanan-Barrow, 2005), but they may also play a role for older children and early adolescents, for example, through the internalization of parental attitudes and beliefs and in situations of proacted conflicts (Bar-Tal & Teichman, 2005).

Ethnic Identity Practices and Enactment

Self-categorization theory is concerned with what happens when in a particular situation people define and see themselves in terms of their shared social identities (Turner et al., 1987). When individuals perceive themselves as a member of an ethnic group they tend to act in terms of attributes (goals, norms, values, and beliefs) shared with other group members. Thus, an adolescent acts as an ethnic minority member only to the extent that she defines herself less as a unique individual and more as someone who is similar to other minority members and whose behavior is regulated by the meanings associated with her ethnic group. For self-categorization theory, ethnic practices and behaviors are not separate adjustment outcomes but rather part of what it means to be a member of an ethnic group. The ethnic behavior is associated with a psychologically salient sense of ethnic identity that actually allows ethnic behavior to take place. When people understand themselves in a particular way they tend to act in ways that correspond to the behavioral norms associated with that particular identity. Further, self-categorization theory considers coordinated group behavior possible because different people define themselves in terms of the same social category.

However, for understanding ethnic practices we should not only pay attention to internal processes but also to external opportunities and constraints and the ways in which people seek to deal with these. Ethnic identity is not only about self-understanding but also, for example, about Moroccan French youth being told that their behavior is "too national" (e.g., French) or "too ethnic" (e.g., Moroccan). Social identities are not like private beliefs or convictions that, in principle, can be sustained without expression and social recognition. These identities depend crucially on acknowledgment and acceptance by others which is precisely why different authors emphasize the crucial role of identity negotiations between subjective and objective definitions of ethnic identity (e.g., Burke & Stets, 2009; Liebkind, 2006; Verkuyten, 2005a; see also the chapter by Sirin and Gupta in this volume). Anthropologists, for example, have shown how people use particular behaviors to form and negotiate their ethnic identity in everyday interactions, and discourse analysts have shown how social identities are accomplished in the ongoing exchange of talk (Benwell & Stokoe, 2006). The ability to enact identity-related norms, values, and beliefs is important for a particular identity. Ethnic identities are sustainable to the extent that they are expressed and affirmed in acceptable practices, linguistic or otherwise. In contrast, the practical inability to live by or act on the basis of one's ethnicity is identity undermining (Mähönen, Jasinskaja-Lahti, & Liebkind, 2011; Sindic & Reicher, 2009). A Turkish German identity, in any real sense, implies, for example, that one is able to claim desired images, positions, and self-understandings in a variety of contexts and especially in public spaces. The wearing, or not wearing, of a headscarf communicates what kind of German Muslim you consider yourself to be and how you want to be seen and recognized by ingroup and outgroup members. And a ban on the headscarf is identity undermining for those who want to express their Muslim identity in that way.

Furthermore, the enactment of ethnicity can also shape the sense of ethnic identity. The proposition that social identities are maintained by others' acknowledgment implies that the reactions from others to one's identity expressions can fuel changes in self-understandings. Ethnic identities are communicated and negotiated and the outcomes of this can affect the way people see themselves. Identity performance elicits reactions from others and claims on, for example, membership authenticity can be questioned and identity meanings can be challenged. For example, in the United States after the 9/11 terrorists attacks and because of the wearing of symbols that display Sikh identity, the "Americanness" of Sikh men was increasingly challenged. They "moved from a comfortable sense of belonging to an uneasy state of being an outsider and a threatening one at that" (Bhatia & Ram, 2009, 146). It is not easy to feel like one belongs and to be a member of the national community when (suddenly) being confronted with one's nonwhite otherness. Similarly, when their "Americanness" is questioned, Asian Americans react with behaviors that assert and reinforce American practices, like advertising an American lifestyle (Cheryan & Monin, 2005).

"Doing ethnicity" confirms one's ethnic identity by expressing and confirming the value of the group symbolically (e.g., Verkuyten & de Wolf, 2002). Ethnic behaviors communicate one's distinctive ethnic identity; they tell others who you are, to which group you belong, and what this group membership means to you. Youngsters are engaged in actions that mark and implicate their ethnic identity. They perform behaviors relevant to the characteristics and norms conventionally associated with a particular ethnic identity and this identity performance can differ in relation to coethnics and to outgroup members (Klein et al., 2007).

Coethnics

People have a basic need to feel like they belong (Baumeister & Leary, 1995) and tend to act to secure acceptance as ingroup members. Being accepted as a full member of one's ethnic group implies demonstrations of authentic membership. Depending on the criteria that define group membership this is less or more difficult. Clay (2003) shows how African American youth use hip-hop culture, particularly rap music, to form and negotiate their black identity in everyday interactions with other African Americans. Ingroup acceptance as authentically black depends on one's ability to master the tools of hip-hop performance, that is the right language, clothes, posture, attitude, and bodily gestures.

Speaking and reading a particular language is often an important criterion for successful identity claims. Several studies have shown that a lack of ethnic language proficiency makes it difficult to feel fully accepted by coethnics. Chinese Canadian and Chinese Dutch youth, for example, emphasize the lack of Chinese literacy as an important shortcoming, from not being able to carry on a conversation, to not being able to understand the news as the "real" Chinese would (Belanger & Verkuyten, 2010). They argue that they are and feel Chinese, but at the same time are not Chinese "enough," or not "really" Chinese because they lack critical attributes of Chinese culture and therefore are not fully able to "do" Chinese. Similarly, among South Moluccan youngsters living in the Netherlands, the ability to speak the Malay language is used to authenticate a Moluccan identity ("If you can't speak Malay, you're not a real Moluccan") (Verkuyten, 2005a).

Outgroup Members

Identity enactment is not only about youth who want to express and authenticate their membership in relation to coethnics but also in relation to members of other ethnic groups and the wider society. In general, it is difficult to maintain an ethnic identity without acknowledgment by relevant outgroups and the intergroup sensitivity effect implies that people are more sensitive to outgroup than ingroup critics (Hornsey & Imani, 2004). In identity politics not only equal treatment and rights are at stake, but also the social recognition and public affirmation of the value of a particular ethnic history, culture, or lifestyle. After 9/11, Sikh males, because of their beards and turbans, were frequently confused with Muslim Arabs and experienced hostility in public places. To educate the public about how Sikhism is different from Islam, many Sikh groups in New York and around the United States waged a public relations campaign (Bhatia & Ram, 2009).

Disputes over group status find expression in issues such as the use of languages, symbols, the wearing of particular clothes, and specific behaviors. The public relations campaign of the Sikhs also focused on the significance of the turban in Sikhism. And Muslim immigrant girls who together with a headscarf have a Western dress style, cosmetics, and speech style communicate to the broader society that Muslim women can also be modern. Another example is the sociolinguistic phenomenon of language shifts (Giles, 1977). When ethnic identity is important for individuals they can adopt various strategies of so called "psycholinguistic distinctiveness" like accentuating their speech styles, switching to their ingroup language, and using specific dialects. Language maintenance and speech divergence are useful strategies for expressing one's identity in a distinctive and positive way.

A confirmation of ethnic identity can also be construed in contrast or opposition to the dominant group. On the individual level and following Goffman (1959), anthropologists talk about group memberships being *over-communication*. This means that ethnic or racial identity is shown off and indicated or claimed in almost all situations. A more positive example is the African American concept of "race man" or "race woman" which expresses that one's racial identity is the centerpiece of one's self-understanding and that one is devoted to the advancement of black people. There are also various examples of the communication of reactive or oppositional minority identities. This is the situation in which youngsters emphasize their ethnic or racial identity and stress characteristics and actions as being self-defining that differ from those typically valued by the majority group (e.g., Kosmitzki, 1996; Ogbu, 2008). For example, when the importance of schooling and educational achievement is emphasized, one's behavior and attitude can communicate that educational success is useless in a white supremacist society. And, in the media, when Moroccan Dutch male adolescents are portrayed as being aggressive, violent, and criminal, then it is exactly these antinormative characteristics that they increasingly might express in their gestures, spoken language, clothing, and public behavior (De Koning, 2008).

Conclusion

Ethnic identity is socially defined and negotiated but also provides a horizon for self-understanding, a source for positive and negative self-feelings, and an interior structure with which youngsters engage the world. It gives a sense of meaning, direction, and belonging, and it can be a source of confidence, pride, and productive behavior. So there is every reason to develop initiatives that support the ethnic identity of minority group children and adolescents. Initiatives will benefit, however, from a better understanding of the different processes involved, the different aspects and dimensions of ethnic identity, and the different ways of studying it.

Research typically focuses on a single aspect of the sense of ethnic identity, such as ethnic self-evaluation or the importance attached to one's ethnic group membership. But there are different aspects that can be distinguished empirically and therefore provide a more detailed understanding of ethnic minority identity. For example, explicit and implicit ethnic self-evaluation can differ resulting in a defensive ethnic self-esteem or they can correspond and characterize a secure ethnic self. Additionally, there are identity aspects that refer to content and meaning. A similar ethnic identity score does not have to imply a similar understanding of what it means to be an ethnic group member. An equally positive or important sense of ethnic identity can imply different values, norms, and beliefs and these meanings give direction to one's thinking and behavior. A strong or positive identity indicates the intensity and stability of one's ethnic self but does not provide guidelines about which actions implicate or express one's ethnic group membership and how one should live and interact with one's social environment.

Theoretically, ethnic identity is studied from various psychological perspectives that lead to different research questions and offer different views on how to support minority youth. Social identity theory, for example, focuses on group commitments and the situational salience of social identities. The emphasis is on the ways that people define a positive and distinctive ethnic identity in the sociostructural context in which they live. Developmental theories focus more on the gradual process of construing and achieving an inner sense of stability and continuity during adolescence. The development of such an inner sense depends, for example, on the cognitive capabilities for conceptualizing the self, on peer relations and family socialization practices (see Hughes et al., 2006). Acculturative psychologists are interested in ethnic identity changes through cultural contacts. They examine these changes in different contexts (e.g., public and private) and within the expectations and opportunities of the ethnic minority community and the wider society.

Each of these perspectives raises interesting and important questions and offers valuable starting points for examining the sense of ethnic identity of minority youth. Ethnic identities, however, are not only about subjective self-understandings that develop over time, shift contextually, or form part of the psychological acculturation process. Social identity refers to the question of what someone is taken to be socially. It is about socially defined and recognized distinctions and designations. Psychological researchers often forget or ignore this because they focus on people's (developing) sense of identity that is conceptualized and measured along attitude-like dimensions, by identity statuses such as diffusion and achievement, or by acculturation positions. But youth express their sense of ethnic identity and authenticate their ethnic group membership in identity-relevant behaviors (e.g., Clay, 2003; Verkuyten & De Wolf, 2002). Furthermore, youngsters can reject and resist categorization by means of behaviors that, sometimes, are antinormative and that offer an alternative model of how the world should be organized (e.g., Ogbu, 2008).

The study of ethnic identity needs to take the interactive nature of social identities into account. The implication is that in studying ethnic identity, not only should we consider psychological processes and structures, but we should also investigate social interactions and the ways in which ethnicity is negotiated and plays out in everyday life. It is important to examine exactly how these identities actually are taken up in interactions and the ways that identity choices are socially managed and negotiated. This improves our understanding about how ethnicity structures young people's lives and the ways in which youngsters are (not) able to assert and negotiate their desired ethnic identities.

These assertions and negotiations are informed by psychological structures and processes and are enabled or constrained by the ways that ethnic minorities groups are defined and treated in the broader society. It is at the level of actual interactions that the psychological and societal come together (House, 1981), and it is at the level of daily interactions that conditions should be established that help children and adolescents to develop a secure and positive sense of their ethnic group membership. In practice this can take many different forms, including multicultural education and the recognition of ethnic identities more generally. Multiculturalism and multicultural education can be important conditions for enacting and thereby socially affirming one's ethnic background. However, the diversity of multicultural ideas, initiatives, and programs is substantial and it is not clear when, why, and how multiculturalism has positive effects for ethnic minority youth (Banks & Banks, 1995). Thus, it is centrally important to consider the way in which ethnic and cultural diversity is actually defined, understood, and practiced, not only by parents, teachers, and authorities but also by youth themselves.

REFERENCES

Arroyo, C. G., & Zigler, E. (1995). Racial identity, academic achievement, and the psychological well-being of economically disadvantaged adolescents. *Journal of Personality and Social Psychology, 69,* 903–14.

Ashmore, R. D., Deaux, K., & McLaughlin-Volpe, T. (2004). An organizing framework for collective identity: Articulation and significance of multidimensionality. *Psychological Bulletin, 130,* 80–114.

Banks, J. A., & Banks, C. M. (Eds.) (1995). *Handbook of research on multicultural education.* New York: MacMillan.

Barrett, M., & Buchanan-Barrow, E (Eds.) (2005). *Children's understanding of society.* Hove, UK: Psychology Press.

Bar-Tal, D., & Teichman, Y. (2005). *Stereotypes and prejudice in conflict: Representations of Arabs in Israeli Jewish society.* Cambridge: Cambridge University Press.

Baumeister, R. F., & Leary, M. R. (1995). The need to belong: Desire for interpersonal attachments as a fundamental human motivation. *Psychological Bulletin, 117,* 497–529.

Belanger, E., & Verkuyten, M. (2010). Hyphenated identities and acculturation: Second generation Chinese of Canada and the Netherlands. *Identity: An international journal of theory and research, 10,* 141–63.

Benwell, B., & Stokoe, E. (2006). *Discourse and identity.* Edinburgh: Edinburgh University Press.

Berger, P., & Luckmann, T. (1966). *The social construction of reality.* Harmondsworth: Penguin Books.

Bettencourt, B. A., Dorr, N., Charlton, K., & Hume, D.L. (2001). Status differences in in-group bias: A meta-analytical examination of the effects of status stability, status legitimacy, and group permeability. *Psychological Bulletin, 127,* 520–42.

Bhatia, S., & Ram, A. (2009). Theorizing identity in transnational and diaspora cultures: A critical approach to acculturation. *International Journal of Intercultural Relations, 33,* 140–9.

Brown, R., & Zagefka, H. (2011). The dynamics of acculturation: An intergroup perspective. *Advances in Experimental Social Psychology, 44,* 129–84.

Burke, P. J., & Stets, J. E. (2009). *Identity theory.* Oxford: Oxford University Press.

Burrow, A. L., Tubman, J. G., & Montgomery, M. J. (2006). Racial identity: Toward an integrated developmental psychological perspective. *Identity: An International Journal of Theory and Research, 6,* 317–39.

Cheryan, S. & Monin, B. (2005). Where are you really from? Asian Americans and identity denial. *Journal of Personality and Social Psychology, 89,* 717–30.

Clay, A. (2003). Keepin' it real: Black youth, hip hop culture, and Black identity. *American Behavioral Scientist, 46,* 1346–58.

Cross, W. E. (1991). *Shades of Black: Diversity in African-American identity.* Philadelphia: Temple University Press.

De Koning, M. (2008). *Zoeken naar een 'zuivere' islam: Geloofsbeleving en identiteitsvorming van jonge Marokkaans-Nederlandse moslims.* Amsterdam: Bert Bakker.

Erikson, E. H. (1966). The concept of identity in race relations: Notes and queries. *Daedalus, 95,* 145–77.

(1968). *Identity: Youth and crisis.* New York: Norton & Company, Inc.

French, S. E. Seidman, E., Allen, L., & Aber, J. L. (2006). The development of ethnic identity during adolescence. *Developmental Psychology, 42,* 1–10.

Giles, H. (Ed.) (1977). *Language, ethnicity and intergroup relations.* London: Academic Press.

Goffman, E. (1959). *The presentation of self in everyday life.* New York: Doubleday.

(1963). *Stigma.* Englewood Cliffs, NJ: Prentice-Hall.

Guimond, S., Dif, S., & Aupy, A. (2002). Social identity, relative group status and intergroup attitudes: When favorable outcomes change intergroup relations ... for the worse. *European Journal of Social Psychology, 32,* 739–60.

Hagendoorn, L. (1995). Intergroup bias in multiple group systems: The perception of ethnic hierarchies. In W. Stroebe and M. Hewstone (Eds.), *European review of social psychology* (vol. 6, pp. 199–228). London: Wiley.

Helms, J. E. (1995). An update of Helm's White and People of Color racial identity models. In J. Ponterotto, J. M. Casas, L. A. Suzuki, and C. M. Alexander (Eds.), *Handbook of multicultural counseling* (pp. 181–98). Thousand Oaks, CA: Sage.

Hornsey, M. J., & Imani, A. (2004). Criticizing groups from the inside and the outside: An identity perspective on the intergroup sensitivity effect. *Personality and Social Psychology Bulletin, 30,* 365–83.

House, J. S. (1981). Social structure and personality. In M. Rosenberg and R. H. Turner (Eds.), *Social psychology: Sociological perspectives* (pp. 525–61). New York: Basic Books.

Hughes, D., Rodriguez, J., Smith, E. P., Johnson, D. J., Stevenson, H. C., & Spicer, P. (2006). Parents' ethnic-racial socialization practices: A review of research and directions for future study. *Developmental Psychology, 42,* 747–70.

Hutnik, N. (1991). *Ethnic minority identity: A social psychological perspective.* Oxford: Clarendon.

Jasinskaja-Lahti, I., & Liebkind, K. (1999). Exploration of the ethnic identity among Russian-speaking immigrant adolescents in Finland. *Journal of Cross-Cultural Psychology, 30,* 527–39.

Jordan, C. H., Spencer, S. J., Zanna, M. P., Hoshino-Browne, E., & Correll, J. (2003). Secure and defensive high self-esteem. *Journal of Personality and Social Psychology, 85,* 969–78.

Kernis, M. H., & Paradise, A. W. (2002). Distinguishing between secure and fragile forms of high self-esteem. In E. L. Deci and R. M. Ryan (Eds.), *Handbook of self-determination research* (pp. 339–60). Rochester, NY: University of Rochester Press.

Klein, O., Spears, R., & Reicher, S. (2007). Social identity performance: Extending the strategic side of SIDE. *Personality and Social Psychology Review, 11*, 28–45.

Kosmitzki, C. (1996). The reaffirmation of cultural identity in cross-cultural encounters. *Personality and Social Psychology Bulletin, 22*, 238–47.

LaFromboise, T., Coleman, H., & Gerton, J. (1993). Psychological impact of biculturalism: Evidence and theory. *Psychological Bulletin, 114*, 395–412.

Liebkind, K. (2001). Acculturation. In R. Brown and S. Gaertner (Eds.), *Blackwell handbook of social psychology: Intergroup processes* (pp. 386–406). Oxford: Blackwell.

   (2006). Ethnic identity and acculturation. In D. Sam and J. W. Berry (Eds.), *The Cambridge handbook of acculturation psychology* (pp. 78–96). Cambridge: Cambridge University Press.

Lorenzo-Hernandez, J., & Ouellette, S. C. (1998). Ethnic identity, self-esteem, and values in Dominicans, Puerto Ricans, and African Americans. *Journal of Applied Social Psychology, 28*, 2007–24.

Martinez, R. O., & Dukes, R. L. (1997). The effects of ethnic identity, ethnicity, and gender on adolescent well-being. *Journal of Youth and Adolescence, 26*, 503–16.

Mähönen, T. A., Jasinskaja-Lahti, I., & Liebkind, K. (2011). Cultural discordance and the polarization of identities. *Group Processes and Intergroup Relations*. DOI:10.1177/1368430210379006.

Nesdale, D., & Mak, A. S. (2000). Immigrant acculturation attitudes and host country identification. *Journal of Community and Applied Social Psychology, 10*, 483–95.

Nguyen, A., & Benet-Martínez, V. (2010). Biculturalism is linked to adjustment: A meta-analysis. (Submitted manuscript).

Nuttin, J. M. (1987). Affective consequences of mere ownership: The name letter effect in twelve European languages. *European Journal of Social Psychology, 17*, 381–402.

Ogbu, J. U. (2008). *Minority status, oppositional culture, and schooling.* New York: Routledge.

Pascoe, E. A., & Smart Richman, L. (2009). Perceived discrimination and health: A meta-analytic review. *Psychological Bulletin, 135*, 531–54.

Pelham, B. W., & Hetts, J. J. (1999). Implicit and explicit personal and social identity: Toward a more complete understanding of the social self. In T. R. Tyler, R. M. Kramer, and O. P. John (Eds.), *The psychology of the social self* (pp. 115–43). Mahwah, NY: Erlbaum.

Phinney, J. S. (1989). Stages of ethnic identity in minority group adolescents. *Journal of Early Adolescence, 9*, 34–49.

   (1990). Ethnic identity in adolescents and adults: A review of research. *Psychological Bulletin, 108*, 499–514.

   (1992). The Multigroup Ethnic Identity Measure: A new scale for use with diverse groups. *Journal of Adolescent Research, 7*, 156–72.

Phinney, J. S., Berry, J. W., Vedder, P., & Liebkind, K. (2006). The acculturation experience: Attitudes, identities, and behaviors of immigrant youth. In J. W. Berry, J. S. Phinney, D. L. Sam, and P. Vedder (Eds.), *Immigrant youth in cultural transition: Acculturation, identity, and adaptation across national contexts* (pp. 71–116). Mahwah, NJ: Lawrence Erlbaum.

Phinney, J. S., Madden, T., & Santos, L. J. (1998). Psychological variables as predictors of perceived ethnic discrimination among minority and immigrant adolescents. *Journal of Applied Social Psychology*, 28, 937–53.

Perdue, C., Dovidio, J., Gurtman, M., & Tyler, R. (1990). Us and them: Social categorization and the process of intergroup bias. *Journal of Personality and Social Psychology*, 59, 475–86.

Rudmin, F. (2003). Critical history of the acculturation psychology of assimilation, separation, integration, and marginalization. *Review of General Psychology*, 7, 3–37.

Sam, D. & Berry, J. W. (Eds.) (2006). *The Cambridge handbook of acculturation psychology*. Cambridge: Cambridge University Press.

Sanchez, J. I., & Fernandez, D. M. (1993). Acculturative stress among Hispanics : A bidimensional model of ethnic identification. *Journal of Applied Social Psychology*, 23, 654–68.

Schmitt, M. T., & Branscombe, N. R. (2002). Meaning and consequences of perceived discrimination in advantaged and privileged social groups. In W. Stroebe and M. Hewstone (Eds.), *European review of social psychology* (vol. 12, pp. 167–99). London: Wiley.

Sellers, R. M., Smith, M. A., Shelton, J. N., Rowley, S. A. J., & Chavous, T. M. (1998). Multidimensional model of racial identity: A re-conceptualization of African American racial identity. *Personality and Social Psychology Review*, 2, 18–39.

Simons, R. L., Murry, V., McLoyd, V., Lin, K-H., Cutrona, C., & Conger, R. D. (2002). Discrimination, crime, ethnic identity, and parenting as correlates of depressive symptoms among African American children: A multilevel analysis. *Development and Psychopathology*, 14, 371–93.

Sindic, D., & Reicher, S. (2009). "Our way of life is worth defending": Testing a model of attitudes toward superordinate group membership through a study of Scots' attitudes toward Britain. *European Journal of Social Psychology*, 39, 114–29.

Snauwaert, B., Soenens, B., Vanbeselaere, N., & Boen, F. (2003). When integration does not necessarily imply integration: Different conceptualizations of acculturation orientations lead to different classifications. *Journal of Cross-Cultural Psychology*, 34, 231–9.

Tajfel, H. (1981). *Human groups and social categories*. Cambridge: Cambridge University Press.

Tajfel, H., & Turner, J. C. (1979). An integrative theory of intergroup conflict. In W. G. Austin and S. Worchel (Eds.), *The social psychology of intergroup relations* (pp. 33–47). Monterey, CA: Brooks/Cole.

Turner, J. C. (1999). Some current issues in research on social identity and self-categorization theories. In N. Ellemers, R. Spears, and B. Doosje (Eds.), *Social identity: Context, commitment, content* (pp. 6–34). Oxford, UK: Blackwell.

Turner, J. C., Hogg, M. A., Oakes, P. J., Reicher, S. D., & Wetherell, M. (1987). *Rediscovering the social group: A self-categorization theory*. Oxford: Blackwell.

Umaña-Taylor, A. J. (2004). Ethnic identity and self-esteem: Examining the role of social context. *Journal of Adolescence*, 27, 139–46.

Verkuyten, M. (2002). Perceptions of ethnic discrimination by minority and majority early adolescents in the Netherlands. *International Journal of Psychology*, 37, 321–32.

(2005a). *The social psychology of ethnic identity.* Hove: Psychology Press.

(2005b). The puzzle of high self-esteem among ethnic minorities: Comparing explicit and implicit self-esteem. *Self and Identity, 4,* 177–92.

Verkuyten, M., & Brug, P. (2002). Ethnic identity achievement, self-esteem, and discrimination among Surinamese adolescents in the Netherlands. *Journal of Black Psychology, 28,* 122–41.

Verkuyten, M., & De Wolf, A. (2002). "Being, feeling and doing": Discourses and ethnic self-definitions among minority group members. *Culture and Psychology, 8,* 371–99.

Verkuyten, M., & Reijerse, A. (2008). Intergroup structure and identity management among ethnic minority and majority groups: The interactive effects of perceived stability, legitimacy, and permeability. *European Journal of Social Psychology, 38,* 106–27.

Verkuyten, M., & Yildiz, A. A. (2007). National (dis)identification, and ethnic and religious identity: A study among Turkish-Dutch Muslims. *Personality and Social Psychology Bulletin, 33,* 1448–62.

Wilson, T. D., Lindsey, S., & Schooler, T. Y. (2000). A model of dual attitudes. *Psychological Review, 107,* 101–26.

10 Muslim, American, and Immigrant

Integration Despite Challenges

Selcuk R. Sirin and Taveeshi Gupta

Introduction

The emergence of a Muslim American identity during the past decade presents a unique example of identity as a socially constructed phenomenon. The popular media, government agencies, and, more important, Muslims themselves have increasingly adopted the label "Muslim American" to refer to Americans of this specific religious origin despite the vast ethnic, racial, linguistic, theological, and historical differences among Muslims. Growing public interest in Muslims in general and Muslim Americans in particular has led to many public debates in the popular media, but it has not yet led to adequate empirical work to better understand the unique experiences of Muslims in the United States (see Sirin & Balsano, 2007).

In order to better understand how immigrant youth of Muslim backgrounds negotiate their identities in politically difficult times, specifically in the aftermath of the 9/11 attacks, we conducted three independent studies with elementary school students who come from immigrant-origin Muslim families (Sirin, Ryce, & Mir, 2009), adolescents (Sirin & Fine, 2007), and young adults (Sirin et al., 2008). Through surveys, interviews, identity maps, and focus groups, immigrant-origin Muslim American youth vividly portrayed the many challenges of being Muslim in the post-9/11 United States context. At the same time, and contrary to our expectations, they also found the strength and courage to claim both their Muslim and American identities by putting these aspects of their identity together in their "*hyphenated selves*" (see Sirin & Fine, 2007, 2008 for a more detailed discussion). Our findings show how a group of young people, caught in an historical struggle, traveled the distance between their Muslim and American identities. In this chapter we will briefly outline our findings in an effort to provide an empirical base to better understand the needs and strengths of this group of youth. Given the lack of demographic information about the population, the first section of the chapter is devoted to a brief introduction to Muslims and Muslim Americans.

Muslims and Muslim Americans

Muslim is the word used to identify those who belong to *Islam*, which means "one who submits to God" in Arabic. Muslims, like followers of the other two Abrahamic religions, Christianity and Judaism, believe in a single god, Allah, but they recognize Muhammad as the last prophet. Muslim Americans are part of a larger global community. According to the World Almanac (2001) there are now about 1.4 billion Muslims in the world. Despite the misconception in the West that most Muslims are Arab, the majority, about 80%, of Muslims are not Arab and live mostly in south Asia, sub-Saharan Africa, and central Asia. In addition to the predominantly Muslim countries, the numbers of Muslims are also growing in non-Muslim majority countries, mostly in Europe, North America, and Australia. For example, about 10% of the French population is Muslim, representing the largest group of Muslims in the Western world. Although not as high, the number of Muslims in the United Kingdom, Germany, and other European countries also represent a major minority group in each country (Rath & Buijs, 2006).

Not only are Muslims diverse in terms of ethnicity, they are also diverse in terms of religious practice. The vast majority of Muslims belong to one of four Sunni sects (Maliki, Shafi'i, Hanafi, or Hanbali) while a much smaller group (about 17%) belongs to Shi'a sects (Jaffari, Ismailliyah, or Alawite). The relations between members of Sunni Islam and Shi'a Islam (or Shi'ite Islam, Shi'ism) sects have been hostile since the post-Muhammad era, when various Muslim groups fought for power, ending in the bloody murder of Muhammad's two grandchildren. Unlike the Sunnis, who are considered more traditionalist in terms of following the word of the Qur'an, Shi'as give more weight to the role of imams, or religious scholars, who can interpret the Qur'an for everyday events and everyday problems. As immigrants, Sunnis and Shi'as are not engaged in open hostility, but often in their countries of origin, the hostility between the groups can lead to violence, as seen in Iraq. These differences and the historical roots of animosity among Muslim sects are difficult to understand in the West, partly because Muslim immigrants are viewed as all sharing the same religion and variations among sects are not visible – even the distinctions between Sikhs and Muslims was lost by many commentators as there was a spike in discriminatory attacks against Sikhs during the post-9/11 era (Goodstein, 2001).

As holds true for most other Americans, the history of Muslim Americans is also a history of immigration that can be traced back to the very early days of European expedition and the African slave trade, which included Muslim tribes from sub-Saharan Africa. While there were individual migrants and some converts since, the large-scale migration of Muslims did not begin until the late 19th century and took place in two waves. The first wave spanned the late 19th century and the early 20th century, and the second wave began during the mid-1960s and continued through the 1990s. These waves brought approximately two-thirds of today's Muslim American population to the United States. Perhaps the most striking difference between the two waves of immigrants was that, compared to earlier Muslim immigrants, most of the recent migrants of the second wave either had a college degree or came to the United States to pursue one. This change likely reflects shifts in U.S. immigration policy. Given these differences, both immigration status and generations spent in the United States are critical factors to consider when it comes to understanding Muslim American identity formation (Leonard, 2003; Pew Research Center, 2007).

In addition to these Muslim immigrants, there is a growing indigenous Muslim population in the United States, which has grown out of those who converted to Islam from other religions. The majority of this group is African American. Although Muslim groups in America have included African Americans since the arrival of slaves, the presence of Islam among this population became more prominent with the movements headed by Muslims during the last century. Specifically, the followers of the Nation of Islam, once led by Elijah Muhammad and popularized in the1960s by the charismatic leadership of Malcolm X, became a major force within the African American community (Leonard, 2003).

There is no official number of Muslims in the United States partly because the U.S. Census Bureau by law does not gather information about religious affiliation and also because, unlike other religious groups, mosques do not have membership rolls that can be used as a proxy for population size. Furthermore, even if there were such data, many Muslims do not attend mosques. In fact in most traditions of Islam, women are discouraged from going to mosques and services at mosques are not generally seen as central to Islamic practices. What makes estimating the number of Muslims in the United States even more challenging is the fact that even large-scale surveys fail to fully count the number of new immigrant and refugee groups that represent a large number of Muslims in the United States. Hence, because of these difficulties, the number of Muslims in the United States has been estimated to be anywhere between 2 million and 8 million (Leonard, 2003; Pew Research Center, 2007; Zogby, 2004).

Within both immigrant and indigenous groups, Muslim Americans are diverse in terms of race, ethnicity, religious practice, immigration status, and historical roots in the United States. While the exact number of Muslims in this country is a question with no clear answer, demographic characteristics of the known Muslim community in the United States is examined in greater detail with several nationwide surveys, including the recent surveys conducted by the Pew Research Center (2007) and Zogby (2004). Using these surveys, the CIA Factbook that also documents detailed information about this population, and several other secondary data sources (see Leonard, 2003 for a review), we can provide several important parameters about the Muslim population in the United States. The three major ethnic groups of Muslim communities in the United States are of south Asian, African American, and Arab origin. South Asians represent about 30% of the Muslim American population, with the majority coming from Pakistan, Bangladesh, and India. African American Muslims are mostly converts to the religion and they represent the largest indigenous Muslim group in the United States, representing around 25% of the entire Muslim American population. Arabs, coming from various countries such as Egypt, Palestine, and Saudi Arabia, represent an additional 25% of the Muslim population in the United States (the majority of Arabs in the United States, 75%, are Christian). The remaining 20% of Muslim Americans includes Iranians and smaller immigrant groups from Malaysia, Indonesia, Turkey, Afghanistan, sub-Saharan Africa, and central and Eastern Europe, as well as white and Latino converts.

We can glean a number of demographic characteristics from the three nationwide surveys conducted with Muslim Americans, including the Hartford Seminary survey titled Faith Communities Today (FACT, 2006) which surveyed all religious groups in the United States, the Zogby International survey (Zogby, 2004), and the Pew Research Center survey (2007). First, Muslims in the United States are one of the fastest growing segments of the population with some surveys showing more than a 108% increase in a single decade (Kosmin, Mayer, & Keysar, 2001). The 2000 FACT survey also shows that the number of mosques is growing faster than any other type of religious center in the United States. Second, similar to several other immigrant groups in the United States, Muslim immigrants, on average, are a much younger group than mainstream U.S. society. In fact, some surveys show that the proportion of young Muslim adults (aged 18–29) is at least twice as large as the general U.S. average. Only less than 10% of Muslims in the United States are 65 or older compared to 27% of the general population.

Third, Muslims in the United States are a highly educated group. With the 1965 immigration reforms, the influx of international students and professionals who came to the United States may have resulted in this outcome (Zogby, 2004). In fact, the percentage of Muslims with professional degrees is much higher than the U.S. average (Pew Research Center, 2007). According to the Zogby survey, close to two-thirds of Muslim Americans have at least a college degree, compared to the U.S. average of 28%. Higher educational attainment also shapes parental expectations. In our survey of young immigrants aged 12–18, 94% of their parents believed college is important and there were no differences in terms of gender, indicating that these parents have high expectations for their daughters and sons equally. Despite the high numbers of professional degrees and the low numbers of college dropouts among Muslims, they are on par with the national average when it comes to having no high school degree, around 5%, indicating a segment of immigrants arrived with no formal education.

Fourth, Muslim Americans are more affluent than any other religiously identifiable group in the United States. According to the Zogby survey, more than half of Muslim Americans earn more than $50,000 a year and a third have incomes of $75,000 or more, compared to the U.S. median income of $42,158 (Zogby, 2004). The Pew survey (2007), however, shows that this slight advantage is due mainly to the large number of immigrant-origin Muslims. The occupational statuses of Muslim Americans also reflect that the majority are middle class. About 23% of Muslim American adults work in professional/technical jobs, with an additional 10% working in managerial positions and 9% in medical fields. Furthermore, a majority of Muslim Americans own stock, either personally or through 401(k) or retirement plans, and own their own home. These general trends, however, mask another reality that emerges from an analysis of 2000 census data by Hernandez and colleagues (Hernandez, Denton, & Macartney, 2009). The poverty rate among children of immigrants who come from the predominantly Muslim countries of Afghanistan, Iraq, and Bangladesh is above 20%, compared to 8% of white children in poverty in the United States. These children in poverty, however, were also among the most likely to live in two-family households and to live with an employed father, compared to other immigrant groups in the United States (Hernandez et al., 2009).

Fifth, Muslim Americans are well integrated into mainstream U.S. society as evidenced by high citizenship rates and English proficiency. As a result of steady immigration by international students and professionals after the 1965 immigration act, today about 90% of Muslims living in the United States are U.S. citizens (Zogby, 2004). The use of English at home is also very common for immigrant-origin Muslims. According to the 2000 census data analysis by Hernandez et al. (2009), among the 14 largest immigrant groups in the United States, families from Pakistan, Bangladesh, Iraq, and Afghanistan were the most likely to be bilingual, around 80%, compared to all the other groups with the exception of immigrants from Africa.

Finally, it is important to identify some differences between European and American Muslim immigrants in terms of integration into mainstream society due to selective migration, different policies of integration, and varying levels of discrimination. As noted, on average, American Muslims are better educated, wealthier, and as a result, are equipped with more social and cultural capital affording them greater opportunity to become integral to mainstream U.S. society, which is not the case for most of the Muslim immigrants in Europe (Rath & Buijs, 2006). For example, while south Asian immigrants in the United States are one of the most employed groups in the United States, they are considered the underclass in the United Kingdom with an unemployment rate several times higher than the UK average (Sirin & Fahy, 2006). Also, while Muslim immigrants enjoy very high citizenship rates in the United States, most Muslims in Europe still struggle to gain citizenship rights. For example, Turkish immigrants settled in Germany as early as the 1960s as legal workers and yet none of the first, second, or third generation among this group of immigrants have been granted full citizenship rights.

Some of the differences between experiences of Muslims in the United States and in European countries arise from the nation state ideology that defines European nations like Germany and France and which makes it difficult to claim a "hyphenated identity," which, as we will see in the next section, is the main path for Muslims to integrate into the United States. While Muslims in the United States can claim their Muslim and American identities without compromising either, it is not easy for Muslim immigrants to claim French or German identities when such identities have for centuries been strictly defined by ethnic boundaries (for instance, see Huntington, 1992). It is also relevant to note that while Muslims in the United States represent the most diverse community of Muslims in the world, representing racial, ethnic, and religious groups from more than

100 countries where Muslims reside, European Muslims are typically more likely to come from the same country and culture and live in geographically concentrated settings once they arrive in Europe, as is the case with south Asian Muslims in the United Kingdom, African Muslims in France, and Turkish Muslims in Germany.

Muslim and American: Challenges in the Post-9/11 Context

Negative stereotypes about Muslims have been part of mainstream culture in the United States (see Brown, 2000 for a review of the pre-9/11 landscape). However, the terrorist attacks of September 11, 2001 made life more unbearable for many Muslims in the United States. Before 9/11 and despite the negative stereotypes, partly due to their cultural capital accumulated through education and income, immigrants from Muslim countries were on a similar path as other immigrant groups that came before them (Leonard, 2003). However, after 9/11, Muslims in America suddenly found themselves under surveillance, viewed with suspicion, and at the edge of moral exclusion from mainstream society (Opotow, 2005). Like the rest of the nation, Muslims in the country were also under attack on that day of terror, but unlike most others they were also the suspects, viewed as a potential threat to the safety of the nation. An environment of fear erupted with the attacks and very quickly turned into an unprecedented surge of Islamophobia, a claim that Islam supports violence and is in constant clash with Western values (Halliday, 2002).

As a result of the changed political and cultural climate for Muslims in the United States, hate crimes against Muslims increased by 17-fold in only one year (FBI, 2002) and unfortunately, they have not dissipated since then (Ahmad, 2004). To the contrary, annual surveys show that due to the wars in Iraq and Afghanistan as well as the ongoing War on Terror, anti-Muslim sentiments are as high or higher today as they were in the immediate aftermath of the attacks (Bryan, 2005; Cainkar, 2004, 2005; The Chicago Council on Global Affairs, 2007). In fact, according to *Washington Post*-ABC surveys, nearly half of Americans – 46% in 2006 – said they held unfavorable attitudes toward Islam, compared with 24% in January 2002 (for polling trends please see http://www.washingtonpost.com/wp-srv/politics/polls/postpoll_033109.html). The same polling data showed an annual increase in overall negative feelings about Islam from a 24% unfavorable rating in 2002 to 48% in 2009. Similar trends are also observed in other polls, including one conducted by Gallup (Deane & Fears, 2006). In the Gallup poll, about 25% of the participants admitted feeling prejudice toward Muslims.

A similar negative shift can also be observed in attitudes toward racial profiling. While a full 80% of Americans thought racial profiling was wrong before 9/11, nearly 60% favored it after the attacks " as long as it was directed at Arabs and Muslims" (Maira, 2004). Worse, in a 2006 *USA Today*/Gallup Poll, about 40% of the participants favored requiring Muslims, including U.S. citizens, to carry a special ID in order to protect the United States from a terrorist attack (Elias, 2006). These data show a rather hostile environment for Muslims living in the United States, and, not surprising, a new nationwide survey found that nearly 60% of adults believe that "Muslims are subject to a lot of discrimination" which makes this group the most vulnerable religious minority in the country (see Pew Research Center, 2009 for a broad review of survey data about levels of discrimination experienced by various religious groups including Muslims).

How young Muslim Americans experienced this period of fear and surveillance and how they negotiated their identities in this difficult time was the focus of our research. To address these main questions we studied a younger (Sirin & Fine, 2007) and an older cohort of youth (Sirin et al., 2008). The younger cohort included 70 adolescents (aged 11–19) in the New York metropolitan area. The older cohort included 137 young adults (aged 18–25)[1] who come from a wider geographic background throughout the United States, but at the time of the study most were living in the New York metropolitan area. All participants were children of immigrants who migrated from a wide range of countries including a large number of southeast Asian and Arab counties. In each study we used mixed methods of focus groups, interviews, surveys, and a novel technique called "identity maps" in our research with adolescents and young adults.

One of the most disturbing findings from our studies was the degree to which discriminatory acts have been woven intimately into the lives of the participants. Literature on racial and ethnic discrimination suggests that groups such as African Americans, Asians, and Hispanics have long experienced discrimination (Brody et al., 2006; Rosenbloom & Way, 2004; Takeuchi, 1998). Fisher, Wallace, and Fenton (2000) found that adolescents from various racial backgrounds experience distress in the face of discrimination in different ways. These authors found that African American and Hispanic adolescents report the highest levels of institutional discrimination while Asian youth report the highest levels of peer discrimination. Thus,

---

[1] For more details on study methods and sample characteristics, please see our book Sirin & Fine (2008) in which we present all the survey materials, protocols for the focus groups, and individual interviews, as well as instructions for identity maps.

to better understand the nature of discrimination faced by young Muslim men and women, we used surveys, focus groups, and maps and learned about the burdens of being Muslim, young, and American. Both younger and older cohort study participants completed Krieger and Sidney's (1996) checklist on discrimination that asked for the frequency of discrimination experienced at school, while shopping, on the street, and in a public setting because they are Muslim. Similar to other groups experiencing discrimination, a large proportion of Muslim youth, more than 80% of the participants in either of our studies, reported that they experienced discrimination at least one or more times during the previous 12 months. Perhaps even more unsettling was the finding that 11% of the younger cohort and 13% of the older cohort indicated that they experienced at least one act of discrimination on a daily basis. Not surprising, in both studies, school was the modal setting where Muslims had to deal with discrimination most. In an effort to put these statistics into perspective, Sirin (2005) conducted a comparative study at a suburban Northeast college campus with 145 undergraduate students, 71 of whom were of Muslim background and 75 of whom were of European American/Christian background. We asked the participants to rate their stress levels and the various ways in which they address stressful incidences on campus. The results confirmed other findings that Muslim students experience significantly higher levels of cultural stress on campus compared to the other group.

Perhaps surprising, we found no significant gender difference in terms of discrimination or acculturative stress as measured by a modified version of the *Societal, Attitudinal, Familial, and Environmental-Revised-Short Form* (SAFE-Short; Mena, Padilla, & Maldonado, 1987). However, young Muslim women who cover their hair (i.e., wear *hijāb*), compared to those who do not cover their hair, experience more discrimination. These findings confirmed our expectations that Muslim girls who are veiled and therefore more visibly Muslim have a more difficult path than relatively invisible Muslim boys (Sirin & Katsiaficas, 2012).

While these alarming statistics reveal the frequency of discrimination, through focus groups and interviews we heard a more complete and nuanced story. Young people, regardless of their age or gender, shared the weight of the heightened surveillance that they endure in their everyday lives. A young woman, Zahra, told us that she often feels misunderstood and judged because she is a Muslim. "We do live in a society that does, you know, not understand us. They do judge us. And it's very difficult to, you know, try to break away from that" (Sirin & Fine, 2008, 88). They offered stories of the surveillance and intense scrutiny they experienced in the national and local media, from federal agencies, and from police, as well as in their daily encounters with staring eyes.

As one young woman noted, being a U.S. citizen and having lived all of her life in the United States did not seem to provide her with any protection: "We have all these amendments and everything that are protecting us, but there's always a loophole. There's always ... some way that something can happen that shouldn't have happened but did happen" (Sirin & Fine, 2008, 91). Another woman in the focus group asked a question: "Why is [this country] treating me like an outsider? I don't feel as an outsider, and I shouldn't be treated like one, and neither should any other Muslim who resides here. They shouldn't be treated like outsiders." Fatima makes a similar point: "I think all *we* ask for is respect and acceptance, because *we, as Americans here*, haven't done anything directly to hurt any other Americans, so why are we being treated like this?" One young woman was concerned that even her name is a marker for scrutiny: "[M]y last name is Hussein. That's another problem. They look upon me like, 'Oh, my God. She might be related to Sadam Hussein' ... there is a lot of discrimination." And yet another participant spoke about traveling with a married sister who now has a Muslim-sounding name:

(They) ... think her last name is more Muslim than my last name ... they're probably, like, equal.... We were traveling and had to take, like, a few planes to get to wherever we needed to get to, and every time, there was always a security check on all her bags. Every single time ... they claim it was random, but I mean, we always feel like there is a side to it that's not random. You know, as they say "random selection," we always feel like we're picked for that random thing [laughs] and it's just like how random is it really when I'm always the one being searched? (Sirin & Fine, 2008, 92)

When dealing with peers, particularly for the young men, the scrutiny was relentless. As one young man told us his stories of being picked on because he is Muslim, others in the focus group nodded in active agreement (Sirin & Fine, 2007). Abid, a sophomore at a public high school, told us, "My history teacher got mad when I challenged him about the (Iraq) war.... I think his son is fighting there." Ahab, at age 11, the youngest and smallest in our male-only focus group, joined our conversation with a whisper, "I don't like it either when people think me, or my father, is going to throw a bomb" (Sirin & Fine, 2007, 155).

Despite higher incidences of discrimination, most youth indicated in their surveys that they did not accept discrimination as a fact of life. Close to 70% of the participants reported that they tried to do something about such unfair treatment. When we explored the differences between those who accepted discrimination and those who chose to do something about it, using the Youth Behavior Checklist's anxiety-depression subscale (Achenbach, 1991), we found that young people who fell in the latter category appeared significantly less worried in general compared to their counterparts who accepted discrimination as a fact of life, $M = 6.35$, $SD = 3.07$ vs. $M = 4.10$, $SD = 1.81$, $t = 3.1$, $p < .01$ (Sirin & Fine, 2008, 94). In other words, young Muslims who accepted discriminatory treatment as a fact of life reported more discrimination and more anxiety than their peers who resisted.

For many of our participants, faith in an all-knowing provided a larger spiritual context that helped some to deal with discrimination. This is evident from one of the quotes of a young boy:

Basically, my opinion on the whole thing is that wherever you are and wherever you go, you're always going to face racism. So, basically, the only thing you have with you is your faith and you have to have a strong faith in God, and you have to have humility and humbleness among other people, and then God will help you and you'll start gaining respect from other people for it. (Sirin & Fine, 2008 106–7)

How do we understand the ways in which these resilient, young adolescents deal with discrimination? The last two decades has seen an influx of research directed at understanding the mechanisms underlying perceived discrimination. In order to better interpret the antecedents and consequences of perceived discrimination faced by the young Muslim men and women in our studies, we turn to the theoretical framework of *attribution processes* concerned with individuals' responses to social disadvantage (Allport, 1979). Specifically, Major and Sawyer (2009) identified the difference between *attributions to discrimination* and *perceptions of discrimination*. This distinction is necessary to understand as it pertains to unpacking the dynamics underlying the strength shown by young Muslim men and women in the face of discrimination in our studies. Attributions to discrimination involve the explanations made by an individual that are *attributed* to the discriminatory event that will shape the coping process. On the other hand, perceptions of discrimination have been defined as the *frequency* of discriminatory events. Within the attribution framework, two main viewpoints have emerged that take into account the explanations that individuals attribute to the event, namely *minimization* and *vigilance* (Major, 1994). It has been noted that socially disadvantaged groups tend to underestimate their experiences of discrimination or minimize the extent to which they are discriminated against in order to not be termed as the victim (Carvello & Pelham, 2006; Crosby, 1982). On the other hand, some researchers have found that individuals who are frequent targets of discrimination become more vigilant in their perceptions of discrimination. As a consequence, they more often attribute negative events to discrimination than others (Baron, Burgess, & Kao, 1991). That was the case for our participants, as overwhelming majorities in our two studies not only reported an incident of discrimination but also their willingness to do something about it. We were, however, unable to disentangle whether youths' coping style changes the perception of discrimination, or whether the experience of discrimination shapes their coping style. It is plausible that youth who tend to feel helpless ("it is a fact of life") are more sensitive to discrimination or *more vigilant* than youth who deal with it by taking control of their experiences. It is also plausible to argue that young people who experience more discrimination are more likely to adopt the belief that it is a fact of life, and youth who experience less discrimination are in fact *minimizing* or underestimating their experience.

When we further explored how young people deal with discrimination we discovered that only rarely do they turn to their parents for support (Sirin & Fine, 2008, 103). In fact, in many cases we found that not only were they not sharing their more stressful experiences of religious discrimination but many were also attempting to protect the parents by helping their parents to better deal with discrimination in their own lives. As one young man noted, "I don't really tell my parents. They have enough to contend with." Salma told us about a specific conversation she had with her father, who works at a major hotel. When her father, who fled Macedonia years before, was asked by the hotel chef to taste a new chicken dish dipped in wine, he politely told the chef he was "allergic to chicken" instead of telling the truth, that he is a devout Muslim who does not drink alcohol. Salma could not believe that her father would hide his religion and told him, "'Dad, this is America. You can say you are Muslim and you don't drink wine.' My parents hide everything but we're free here." Thus, it seems that protecting parents from knowledge of persistent discrimination and "parenting parents" about the U.S. way of life appear to be two of the related labors of adolescents' "hyphenated selves" (Sirin & Fine, 2008, 103–4).

Negotiating the Muslim American Hyphen

Due to the limited research on Muslim youth identity formation processes, we relied on immigrant minority research in general in order to better understand how young Muslims negotiate their multiple immigrant identities. Many scholars in the field have highlighted two common patterns for immigrant identity negotiation process: the degree to which one identifies with the home country or majority culture and the degree to which one identifies with the host country or culture (see Berry, 1990, 1997; Berry et al., 2006; Phinney, Cantu, & Kurtz, 1997). Identities resulting from these pathways are varied in nature and have been termed bicultural or transcultural identity (Suárez-Orozco & Suárez-Orozco, 2001), fusion (Chuang, 1999), blendedness (Phinney & Devich-Navarro, 1997), cultural hybridity (Oyserman, Sakamoto, & Lauffer, 1998), alternating biculturalism (LaFromboise et al., 1993; Phinney & Devich-Navarro, 1997) or within-category and between-category multiplicity (Deaux, 2006). All these forms of identity negotiation patterns across cultures are somewhat distinct from the concept of hyphenated identities, which comes out of the notion that "social identities do not neatly partition themselves, but instead create points of intersection at which, for example, both gender and ethnicity define the experience" (Deaux, 2006, 119). Based on these theoretical foundations and with input from our participants through focus groups and interviews we discovered that there is a large group of young people who happily reside "on the hyphen" in the words of one of our participants without necessarily feeling the pull and push of two or more cultural traditions (Sirin & Fine, 2008, 85). By "hyphen" we refer to the identities that are at once joined and separated by history, the present sociopolitical climate, geography, biography, longings, and loss. The notion of living hyphenated selves is therefore similar to the notions of fusion or transcultural identity with one important distinction: With some evidence we argue that young people in particular have a capacity to create a *space between* contentious political and cultural contexts. That is, even when political or social conditions render these very different political and cultural contexts in tension or incompatible, young people somehow create a stable identity on the intersection, in between, at the hyphen. In other words, hyphenated selves are produced in the negotiation and acceptance of self and other, the imaginary "us" and "them" when the agency is neither with "us" nor with "them" but in the space between.

Following our theoretical insistence on understanding the notion of the hyphenated selves, we wanted to move beyond bicultural identification models that measure identification as a dichotomous variable (e.g., "Muslim first" vs. "American first" forced choice questions in the Pew surveys) or as a single bicultural continuum that moves between home and host cultures (e.g., Multicultural Ethnic Identification Measure). We are drawing on the debate in the acculturation literature between unidimensional and bidimensional models of acculturation (Berry, 1997; Ryder, Alden, & Paulhus, 2000). The unidimensional model of acculturation is different from the bidimensional model of acculturation in the way it treats the relations between the culture of home and the mainstream culture. According to Ryder et al. (2000), "uni-dimensional models are based on the implicit assumption that change in cultural identity takes place along a single continuum over the course of time" (49). In other words, this perspective believes that one must relinquish one type of identity (most often the identity of the heritage country) in order to acculturate to the mainstream culture (Gordon, 1964; Tweed, Conway, & Ryder, 1999). On the other hand, the bidimensional perspective suggests that acculturation can be more completely understood when researchers understand that multiple cultural identities can exist (Sayegh & Lasry, 1993). Ryder et al.'s review (2000) shows that, compared to the uni-dimensional approach, the bidimensional approach "is a more valid operationalization of acculturation" (49).

Through the use of multiple measures, including separate versions of the Collective Self-Esteem Scale for Muslim and American Selves, as well as identity maps, we were able to capture young peoples' identification with multiple groups without presuming a priori the assumption about identifying with one group at the expense of or in relation to the other group. In this measurement approach, we were most interested in how young people experience their hyphenated, bidimensional identity – in our case their Muslim and American identities. Our measurement approach, therefore, is rooted in the bidimensional measurement approach. Moving away from the unidimensional perspective allows us to study how immigrants balance multiple components of their lives as they are constantly situated in the context of multiple cultures (Cabassa, 2003).

The "Clash" Hypothesis: Can Youth Claim Muslim and American Identities?

Many public intellectuals in the West and Muslim fundamentalists disagree on many things but they agree on one hypothesis: that one cannot reconcile the differences in Islamic and Western cultures. As famously argued by Huntington (1992), there is a "clash of civilizations," irreconcilable, ontological differences between the Muslim and Western civilizations and no individual effort to bring these cultures into coexistence would work. While Huntington originally made this claim about international affairs in general terms, he later narrowed his claims to Muslim immigrants in the West (he also made similar claims about Latinos in the United States). After the 9/11 attacks, the tenor of public discourse shifted significantly in favor of the clash hypothesis as a source of justification for why there is conflict between Islam and the West in general and for why some Muslim immigrants fail to integrate into Western societies, particularly immigrant Muslims in Europe. As a result, Huntington (2004) revisited his original model in his 2004 book aptly titled *Who Are We? The Challenges to America's National Identity*. In his book, Huntington referred to Muslims as "the indigestible minority" claiming Muslims cannot be "digested" in the United States due to the incompatibility of being Muslim and being American (188). These views were shared by many fundamentalist Muslim scholars who argued that Muslims in the United States are either "victims" treated as second-class citizens or "sell outs" who hide their religion from others to be accepted in their host country. Soon, many commentators in the media made similar claims about Muslim immigrants in the West, both in the United States and in Europe, commenting about how "we" cannot accommodate "them," referring to Muslim immigrants. In our research (Sirin & Fine, 2008), we directly tested the validity of these claims using multiple methods to understand how young Muslims in the United States experience and negotiate the clash between these two cultures and whether they struggle to reconcile differences between Muslim and American values. We believe that Muslim Americans present an ideal case to explore the validity of the notion of hyphenated selves as a way to understand whether young people can find a space between two contentious cultural contexts. Specifically, in surveys we asked two sets of questions to the older cohort, aged 18–25 (Sirin & Fine, 2008). First, we asked the students about the degree to which they feel part of, identified with, and perceived by others as members of the "Muslim community" and "the mainstream American society." Second, we moved beyond identity and focused specifically on acculturation practices using a scale that explored young people's preferences for social and cultural activities involving their native/home and mainstream American cultures. In our measurement strategy for identity we deliberately avoided the forced choice dilemma in which participants are asked to pick one of two identities (Shih & Sanchez, 2005). Hence, our measurement model differed from other studies with Muslims in the United States and Europe, including the Pew surveys (2007) that forced people to pick either a Muslim or a nation-based identity (i.e., American in the United States, British in the United Kingdom). Using Muslim and American versions of the Collective Self Esteem scale (CSE; Luhtanen & Crocker, 1992), we were able to assess independently the degree to which young people identify with "Muslim communities" and with mainstream U.S. culture (Sirin & Fine, 2008). The results showed no significant *negative* correlation between how Muslim American youth view their Muslim and mainstream U.S. identifications, as one would expect following the clash hypothesis. An even more interesting finding was that when we looked at the associations in more detail across domains of identifications (i.e., CSE subscales) we found a significant *positive* relation between how youth view their membership in American mainstream society and their membership in the Muslim community at large, $r = .38$, $p<.005$ (Sirin & Fine, 2007, 126). The more the young people identify themselves as a member of the Muslim community, the more likely they were to also identify themselves as a member of mainstream U.S. society. Identification with one group either was unrelated to their identification with the other, or, perhaps more interesting in terms of young people's sense of membership, being a member of one group seems to strengthen their sense of membership in the other group.

If youths' identification with Muslim communities and with mainstream U.S. society are two relatively unrelated constructs, then what drives one's affiliation to each? In order to answer this question, we examined research on other immigrant, minority youth and hypothesized that discrimination-related stress (Branscombe et al., 1999), acculturative activities (Berry et al., 2006), and religiosity as specific variables for our population would all play a role in shaping how young people identify with their Muslim and/ or American identities (Sirin & Fine, 2007, 127–8). The results showed that the best predictor of Muslim identity was religiosity as measured by participation in Islamic religious practices and spiritual coping (e.g., "I seek Allah's help...when I am under a lot of stress"). For the mainstream American identification model, discrimination related-stress and preference for ingroup (i.e., Muslim) social and cultural practices weakened young people's identification with mainstream U.S. society. However, preference for American social and cultural practices alone strengthened the participants'/youths'/ Muslim youths' American identification. In other words, discrimination does not seem to independently strengthen immigrant youths' identification to the Muslim community, but it weakened their ties to mainstream U.S. society (see Jasinskaja-Lahti et al., 2009).

It is important to relate our findings to the work conducted by the Pew Research Center (2007) among Muslims living in the United States and Europe as well as among Christian Americans, which asked participants the following question: "Do you think of yourself first as an American or first as a Muslim?" In these surveys, a forced choice format gave the participants the option of selecting "American first," "Muslim first," "Both," or "Neither." For Christian Americans as well as for Muslims in Britain, France,

Germany, and Spain, the item was modified to reflect the correct identity category for each group. This line of questioning is problematic because the choices assume a dichotomy: There can only be one "first," wrongly suggesting that identifying as Muslim or American are mutually exclusive. In reality, while the former signifies one's religious affiliation the latter signifies one's national identity. The Pew survey's strength was its comparative nature as similar questions were asked to Christian and Muslim Americans, which provided some illuminating results. First, the surveys revealed that while 47% of all Muslim Americans identified as Muslim first, about 28% identified themselves as American first. For Christian Americans, the participants were almost equally split between Christian first (42%) and American first (48%). A comparison among devout Christians and devout Muslims (i.e., those who attend mosque once or twice a month) the rates of "American first" were 30% and 27% respectively (Pew Research Center, 2007).

The difference in the degree of affiliation as American first between Muslims and Christians must be interpreted in light of two important distinctions between these two groups. First, Muslims in the United States are a minority group, and like all other minority groups, it is plausible for those who are perceived negatively by others to more strongly identify with their own group (see Branscombe, Schmitt, & Harvey, 1999; Jetten et al., 2001). Second, while many of the Muslims are either the first or second generation of their families in the United States, the same cannot be said for the overwhelming majority of Christians. It would be more illuminating to compare immigrant-origin Muslims' experiences to those of other immigrant groups. However, despite comparisons between Muslim immigrants and other minority group immigrants, group comparison in terms of their preference for an American first option reveals an interesting phenomenon. Among all groups, including Christians in the United States and Muslims in Europe, support for the American first option was highest among Muslim Americans. About 20% of the participants indicated that they considered themselves equally Muslim and American.

The Pew surveys also provide further information about the differences between the American and European contexts for Muslim immigrants. For example, among Muslims in Europe, only French Muslims come close to American Muslims in terms of the rate of support for the Muslim first category. More important, compared to 48% of Muslims in the United States who claimed the America first category, only 3% of Spanish Muslims, 7% of British Muslims, and 13% of German Muslims claimed their national identities first (Pew Research Center, 2007). These findings highlight the unique identity patterns for Muslim Americans. Compared to Muslims in

Europe, Muslims in the United States were less likely to claim their religious identity first, more likely to claim their national identity first, and also more likely to claim both identities equally. These findings once again highlight the unique characteristics of American Muslims compared to European Muslims and also provide some evidence for their willingness to consider both of their identities equally even when the question is posed in a dualistic, forced choice format along a single continuum. Further results also show that about 25% of Muslim Americans claim their American identity first, even at a time when many in the United States have a negative view of Muslims, as evidenced in/by many public polls conducted at the same time as the Pew survey. Perhaps the negative views of Muslims are driving these young, Muslim Americans to assert their American identities more fervently. As they perceive themselves increasingly excluded from American culture, Muslim Americans become more cognizant and assertive of how strongly they value and identify with the United States.

Social and Cultural Preferences

In addition to young people's affiliation with Muslim and American collective identities, we also examined their social and cultural preferences to get a better sense of acculturation practices of Muslim youth. For this part of the study we used the Acculturation, Habits, and Interests Multicultural Scale for Adolescents (AHIMSA) by Unger et al. (2002). The scale is designed to measure bicultural or immigrant youths' preference to do social and cultural activities with people from the United States (assimilation), "the country my family is from" (separation), "both" (integration), or "neither" (marginalization). Because there was no significant age variation between younger and older youth in our two studies (Sirin & Fine, 2007, 2008) we present the results together in Table 10.1.

The results of the social and cultural preference analyses show that the modal path for all but two domains is one of integration, highlighting a strong commitment to engage in social and cultural activities across home and mainstream U.S. cultures. The other two domains in which integration was not the modal path were preferences for holidays and TV shows. The only home country orientation rated above the other options, an indication of isolation, is the preference to celebrate religious/cultural holidays, but even when considering this item a similar number of youth chose integration, preferring to celebrate both the U.S. and ethnic/religious holidays. At the same time, and perhaps predictably, the youth also had a strong preference for U.S. TV shows. Together these social and cultural preferences

Table 10.1. Social and Cultural Preferences of Muslim American Adolescents and Young Adults (Total scores)

	Mainstream U.S. *Assimilation*	The country my family from *Isolation*	Both *Integration*	Neither *Marginalization*
I am most comfortable being with people from…	12	14	71	3
My best friends are from…	27	16	51	7
The people I fit in with best are from…	18	23	53	5
My favorite music is from…	38	12	42	8
My favorite TV shows are from…	67	6	21	5
The holidays I celebrate are from…	4	46	43	6
The food I eat at home is from…	2	24	62	1
The way I do things and the way I think about things are from…	14	14	69	3

constitute the practices within which young people form their cultural values. Though much of psychological literature suggests that these two concepts, acculturative practices and social identity, are distinct (Erikson, 1965; Joas, 2000), there has been a recent attempt to create a link between cultural practices and identification to one's cultural values (Gecas, 2000; Hitlin, 2003). Drawing on the belief that when individuals pick values to identify with, they in turn add to their social and cultural practices, our results therefore indicate that immigrant Muslims in the United States do not seem to isolate or marginalize themselves from mainstream society in terms of their preferences for social and cultural practices. To the contrary, they are highly integrated into the social and cultural fabric of mainstream U.S. culture without necessarily giving up their strong ties to their home cultures. Thus, contrary to the claims of the clash hypothesis which would result in a more polarized, compartmentalized social and cultural life, youth who come from Muslim immigrant families are not reluctant to join the mainstream society socially nor culturally. In fact, for the most part, they chose social and cultural options that would lead to more integration with the mainstream culture.

Drawing on the Hyphen: Results from the Identity Maps

In order to further explore how young people negotiated the Muslim American hyphen, we utilized a novel technique called "identity maps." In both of our studies we reminded young people that we all have many identities and in this exercise we asked them to depict their "many" identities as Muslim and American teens or young adults (Sirin & Fine, 2007, 2008). We provided a blank paper and coloring pencils included with the survey materials. The results revealed rich data on how young people were creative in claiming their identities, not as a fixed category, but as a fluid and innovative process. Using previous work on immigrant and minority youth identity (Benet-Martinez et al., 2002; Phinney & Devich-Navarro, 1997), and based on our examination of the maps, we identified three meta categories in the maps: hybrid, parallel, and conflictual. Specifically, the maps were coded a) hybrid if the Muslim and American entities were fully blended in an integrated, nonconflicting way, b) parallel identities if both aspects of identity were depicted as if they were two separate worlds, or c) conflictual if the maps represented tension, conflicting elements, hostility, or the irreconcilability of the identities. With this scoring framework, we were able to differentiate between parallel and conflictual paths by highlighting the important distinction between comfortably commuting across multiple cultural frameworks (parallel worlds) and struggling to find a way to belong to any (conflictual).

Using this coding system, a majority of the participants, about 61%, constructed maps that reflect a hybrid Muslim American identity. These maps illustrated hyphenated selves as a form of integration by creatively combining several different aspects of personhood and claiming one's ethnic (e.g., Arab, Palestinian), religious (i.e., Muslim), and national (i.e., American) roots. This is how one participant described her path: "You're like a new culture. It's like those new restaurants that mix … you're like a fusion … a new fusion. And it's just interesting to be you, you know, because you're fusing two cultures in one" (Sirin & Fine, 2008, 137). Such notions of hybrid identities (Bhabha, 1994) are evident in identity maps that depict a flag half colored as the U.S. flag and half colored as the Pakistani flag. In yet another identity map indicative of such a fused identity is the image of a girl wearing a *hijāb* which has a green color to represent her Pakistani identity and a red, white, and blue color to represent her American identity.

About 29% of the participants constructed maps that reflected parallel lives or a separation between their Muslim and American identities. These maps presented a more dualistic lifestyle in which young people seemed to commute between two worlds with little or no effort and in this way smoothly navigated between different aspects of their lives. This type of an identity is suggestive of the alternation model of acculturation that was suggested by LaFromboise, Coleman, and Gerton (1993). LaFromboise et al. (1993) suggest that such an acquisition involves the individual knowing and understanding two different cultures. When we examined further, the surveys revealed that those who live parallel lives were significantly more involved in social and cultural activities of their home culture than those experiencing conflict or integration, in line with earlier researchers positing that an alternation model is suggestive of identities and individuals that have better psychological health (Liebkind, 2001). With identities rooted in two worlds, these young people engage substantially in the social (i.e., hanging out with people from their home culture) and cultural activities of their home countries (i.e., eating food, listening to music, and watching TV originating from one's home culture) while at the same time enjoying more mainstream American activities (Sirin & Fine, 2007).

Through our analysis of the maps, we found that only 11% of the participants constructed maps that indicated a conflictual identity process (Sirin & Fine, 2008, 129). In other words, only a small percentage seems to experience difficulty in reconciling these two cultural frameworks. Through the words of one participant we can hear the challenges of negotiating the hyphen: "There has always been this struggle of sort of conflating or managing all these identities within me. You know the main conflict comes from Islam and America ... there is always this constant struggle between defining my values as a Muslim or an American" (Sirin & Fine, 2008, 146).

In our work, (Sirin & Fine, 2008), we did not hear much about the so-called incompatibility of Muslim and American ways of life. Many see the current conflict as a political issue rather than a religious or cultural one and dismiss any suggestion that this would create problems for their own identity negotiation process. As one participant shared: "First I used to view it like, okay this is an Islamic/West conflict but now I realize that this is a power struggle ... this is nothing new." Many participants provided statements like "It's beautiful to be so multicultural.... I'm Syrian, Circassian, AND I'm American" or "it would be boring ... to be just Pakistani." A 15-year-old Egyptian girl noted while discussing the many advantages of belonging to both Muslim and American traditions: "Islam gives me meaning and the U.S. holds the promise of freedom to wear hijāb, practice religion like my brothers, to be educated and to educate others." Her perception that

American freedoms enhance her ability to practice Islam is a wonderful example of how many Muslim American youth synthesize these aspects of themselves in order to build strong, integrated identities. Most of the young people in our studies located the tension hypothesized in the clash of civilization argument as political and they did not feel these cultural or personal conflicts within themselves.

Conclusions

Historically and politically, it is a challenging time to be young and Muslim in the United States. A majority of the American public still perceives Muslims with suspicion and, not surprising, an even a larger majority of Muslims indicate that they experience discrimination and surveillance. Therefore, it has been suggested that the difficulty of reconciling and claiming the American and Islamic values that form their identities in the United States at this moment in history is real and has important ramifications for a lot of young people (Leonard, 2003; Opotow, 2005). Despite the popular imagination and scholarly claims about the incompatibility assumption, however, our research shows that only a small number of young people struggle with the notion that being Muslim is in direct conflict with mainstream American values and traditions. The evidence from surveys, maps, and focus groups indicates that young Muslim immigrants in the United States have a deep sense of themselves as both Muslim and American and refute a clash of civilizations perspective. These young men and women are engaged in an exciting identity negotiation process to create a hybrid identity that we call "hyphenated selves." Muslim immigrant youth in our study demonstrated that in multiple ways, even at a difficult historical period when one's multiple identities are pitted against each other in the public sphere, there is hope for a way out of fixed binaries at the individual level.

Acknowledgment

The work presented in this chapter is funded by a grant from the Foundation for Child Development to the first author.

REFERENCES

Achenbach, T. (1991). *Manual for the Youth Self-Report & 1991 Profile*. Burlington: University of Vermont, Department of Psychiatry.
Ahmad, M. I. (2004). A rage shared by law: Post-September 11 racial violence as crimes of passion. *California Law Review, 92(5)*, 1259–128.

Allport, G. W. (1979). *The nature of prejudice*. Reading, MA: Addison-Wesley.

Baron, R. S., Burgess, M. L., & Kao, C. F. (1991). Detecting and labeling prejudice: Do female perpetrators go undetected? *Personality and Social Psychology Bulletin, 17*, 115–23.

Benet-Martinez, V., Leu, J., Lee, F., & Morris, M. (2002). Negotiating biculturalism: Cultural priming in blended and alternating Chinese-Americans. *Journal of Cross Cultural Psychology, 33*(5), 492–516.

Berry, J. W. (1990). Psychology of acculturation: Understanding individuals moving between cultures. In R. W. Brislin (Ed.), *Applied cross-cultural psychology* (pp. 232–53). Newbury Park, CA: Sage.

(1997). Immigration, acculturation, and adaptation. *Applied Psychology: An International Review, 46*(1), 5–34.

Berry, J. W., Phinney, J. S., Sam, D. L., & Vedder, P. (Eds.) (2006). *Immigrant youth in cultural transition: Acculturation, identity, and adaptation across national contexts*. Mahwah, NJ: Lawrence Erlbaum.

Bhabha, H. K. (1994). *The location of culture*. London: Routledge.

Branscombe, N. R., Schmitt, M. T., & Harvey, R. D. (1999). Perceiving pervasive discrimination among African-Americans: Implications for group identification and well-being. *Journal of Personality and Social Psychology, 77*, 135–49.

Brody, G. H., Chen, Y., Murry, V. M., Ge, X., Simons, R. L., & Gibbons, F. X., et al. (2006). Perceived discrimination and the adjustment of African American youths: A five-year longitudinal analysis with contextual moderation effects. *Child Development, 77*(5), 1170–89.

Brown, M. D. (2000). Conceptualizing racism and Islamophobia. In J. ter Wal and M. Verkuyten, (Eds.), *Comparative perspectives on racism* (pp. 73–90). Aldershot: Ashgate Publishing Ltd.

Bryan, J. (2005). Constructing "the true Islam" in hostile times: The impact of 9/11 on Arab Muslims in Jersey City. In N. Foner (Ed.), *Wounded city: The social impact of 9/11.* (pp. 133–62). New York: Russell Sage Foundation.

Cabassa, L. J. (2003). Measuring acculturation: Where we are and where we need to go. *Hispanic Journal of Behavioral Sciences, 25*, 127–46.

Cainkar, L. (2004). The impact of the September 11 attacks and their aftermath on Arab and Muslim communities in the United States. *Global Security Quarterly, 13*. Retrieved on May 13, 2007 from http://www.ssrc.org/programs/gsc/publications/quarterly13/cainkar.pdf.

(2005). Space and place in the Metropolis: Arabs and Muslims seeking safety. *City and Society, 17*(2), 181–209.

Carvello, M., & Pelham, B. W. (2006). When friends become friends: The need to belong and perceptions of personal and group discrimination. *Journal of Personality & Social Psychology, 90*, 94–108.

Chuang, Y. (1999). Fusion: The primary model of bicultural competence and bicultural identity development in a Taiwanese-American family lineage. Unpublished doctoral dissertation.

Crosby, F. (1982). *Relative depression and working women*. New York: Oxford University Press.

Deane C., & Fears, D. (2006, March 9). Negative perception of Islam increasing. *Washington Post* A 01. Retrieved on April 23, 2007 from http://www.washington-post.com/wp-dyn/content/article/2006/03/08/AR2006030802221.html.

Deaux, K. (2006). To be an immigrant: Psychological design and social fabric. NY: Russell Sage.

Elias, M. (2006, August 10). USA's Muslims under clout. *USA Today.* Retrieved on September 12, 2009 from http://www.usatoday.com/news/nation/2006-08-09-muslim-american-cover_x.htm.

Erikson, E. H. (1965). *Identity, youth, and crisis.* 1st ed. New York: Norton.

Faith Communities Today. (2006). *FACT Survey.* Retrieved on September 2, 2009 from http://fact.hartsem.edu/Press/mediaadvsry5.htm.

Federal Bureau of Investigation. (2002).*2001 Hate Crime Report.* Washington, DC: The Author. Retrieved on September 23, 2006, http://www.fbi.gov/ucr/01hate.pdf.

Fisher, C. B., Wallace, S. A, & Fenton, R. E. (2000). Discrimination distress during adolescence. *Journal of Youth and Adolescence, 29*(6), 679–95.

Gecas, V. (2000). Values, identities, self-motives and social movements. In S. Stryker, T. J. Owens, and R. W. White (Eds.), *Self, identity and social movements* (pp. 93–109). Minneapolis: University of Minnesota Press.

Goodstein, L. (2001, November 10). American Sikhs contend they have become a focus of profiling at airports: A nation challenged. *The New York Times.* Retrieved April 10, 2010 from http://www.nytimes.com/2001/11/10/us/nation-challenged-civil-rights-american-sikhs-contend-they-have-become-focus.html?pagewanted=1.

Gordon, M. M. (1964). *Assimilation in American life.* New York: Oxford University Press.

Halliday, F. (2002). West encountering Islam – Islamophobia reconsidered. In A. Mohammadi (Ed.), *Islam encountering globalization* (pp. 14–35). London: Taylor & Francis.

Hernandez, D. J., Denton, N. A., & Macartney, S. (2009). School-age children in immigrant families: Challenges and opportunities for America's schools. *Teachers College Record, 111,* 616–58.

Hitlin, S. (2003). Values as the core of personal identity: Drawing links between two theories of self. *Social Psychology Quarterly, 66,* 118–37.

Huntington, S. P. (1992). The clash of civilizations? *Foreign Affairs, 72*(3), 22–49.

    (2004). *Who are we: The challenges to America's national identity.* New York: Simon & Schuster.

Jasinskaja-Lahti, I., Liebkind, K., & Solheim, E. (2009).To identify or not to identify? National disidentification as an alternative reaction to perceived ethnic discrimination. *Applied Psychology, 58,* 105–28.

Jetten, J., Branscombe, N. R., Schmitt, M. T., & Spears, R. (2001). Rebels with a cause: Group identification as a response to perceived discrimination from the mainstream. *Personality and Social Psychology Bulletin, 27,* 1204–13.

Joas, H. (2000). *The genesis of values.* Cambridge, UK: Polity Press.

Kosmin, B. A., Mayer, E., & Keysar, A. (2001). American religious identification survey. New York: City University of New York.

Krieger, N., & Sidney, S. (1996). Racial discrimination and blood pressure: The CARDIA Study of young black and white adults. *American Journal of Public Health, 86,* 1370.

LaFromboise, T., Coleman, H., & Gerton, J. (1993). Psychological impact of biculturalism: Evidence and theory. *Psychological Bulletin, 114,* 395–412.

Leonard, K. I. (2003). *Muslims in the United States: The state of the research.* New York, NY: Russell Sage.

Liebkind, K. (2001). Acculturation. In R. Brown and S. Gaertner (Eds.), *Blackwell handbook of social psychology: Intergroup processes* (pp. 386–406). Oxford, UK: Blackwell.

Luhtanen, R., & Crocker, J. (1992). A collective self-esteem scale: Self evaluation of one's social identity. *Personality and Social Psychology Bulletin, 18*, 302–18.

Maira, S. (2004). Youth culture, citizenship, and globalization: South Asian Muslim youth in the United States after September 11th. *Comparative Studies of South Asia, Africa, and the Middle East, 24*(1), 219–31.

Major, B. (1994). From social inequality to personal entitlement: The role of social comparisons, legitimacy appraisals, and group membership. In M. P. Zanna (Ed.), *Advances in experimental social psychology* (Vol. 26, pp. 293–348). San Diego, CA: Academic Press.

Major, B., & Sawyer, P. J. (2009). Attributions to discrimination: Antecedents and consequences. In T. Nelson (Ed.), *Handbook of prejudice, stereotyping and discrimination* (pp. 89–110). New York: Psychology Press.

Mena, F. J., Padilla, A. M., & Maldonado, M. (1987). Acculturative stress and specific coping strategies among immigrant and later generation college students. *Hispanic Journal of Behavioral Sciences, 9*(2), 207–25.

Opotow, S. (2005). Hate, conflict, and moral exclusion.In R. J. Sternberg (Ed). *The psychology of hate*. Washington, DC: American Psychological Association.

Oyserman, D., Sakamoto, I., & Lauffer, A. (1998). Cultural accommodation: Hybridity and the framing of social obligation. *Journal of Personality and Social Psychology, 74*, 1606–18.

Pew Research Center. (2007). Muslim Americans: Middle class and mostly mainstream. Retrieved on September 12, 2009 from http://www.Pewresearch.org/pubs/483/muslim-americans.

(2009). *Views of religious similarities and differences: Muslims widely seen as facing discrimination*. Retrieved on September 12, 2009 from http://Pewforum.org/newassets/images/reports/summer09/survey0909.pdf.

Phinney, J. S., Cantu, C., & Kurtz, D. A. (1997). Ethnic and American identity as predictors of self-esteem among African-American, Latino, and White adolescents. *Journal of Youth and Adolescence, 26*(2), 165–85.

Phinney, J. S., & Devich-Navarro, M. (1997). Variations in bicultural identification among African American and Mexican American adolescents. *Journal of Research on Adolescence, 7*(1), 3–32.

Rath, J., & F. Buijs. (2006). *Muslims in Europe: The state of research. IMISCOE Working Paper*.Retrieved on September 2, 2009 from http://www.imiscoe.org/publications/workingpapers/.

Rosenbloom, S. R., & Way, N. (2004). Experiences of discrimination among African American, Asian American, and Latino adolescents in an urban high school. *Youth & Society, 35*(4), 420–51.

Ryder, A. G., Alden, L. E., & Paulhus, D. M. (2000). Is acculturation unidimensional or bidimensional? A head-to-head comparison in the prediction of personality, self-identity, and adjustment. *Journal of Personality & Social Psychology, 79*, 49–65.

Sayegh, L., & Lasry, J. C. (1993). Immigrants' adaptation to Canada: Assimilation, acculturation and orthogonal cultural identification. *Canadian Psychology, 34*, 98–109.

Shih, M. J., & Sanchez, D. T. (2005). Perspectives and research on the positive and negative implications of having multiple racial identities. *Psychological Bulletin, 131,* 569–91.

Sirin, S. R. (2005). *Muslim adolescents on U.S. college campuses: Exploring ethnic identity.* Paper presented at the 2005 annual convention of the American Psychological Association (APA), Washington, DC.

Sirin, S. R., & Balsano, A. (2007). Pathways to identity and positive development for Muslim youth in the West. *Applied Developmental Science, 11,* 109–11.

Sirin, S. R., Bikmen, N., Mir, M., Zaal, M., Fine, M., & Katsiaficas, D. (2008). Exploring dual identification among Muslim-American emerging adults: A mixed methods study. *Journal of Adolescence, 31*(2), 259–79.

Sirin, S. R., & Fahy, S. (2006). What do Muslims want? A voice from Britain. *Analyses of Social Issues and Public Policy, 6*(1), 285–8.

Sirin, S. R., & Fine, M. (2007). Hyphenated selves: Muslim-American youth negotiating their identities across the fault lines of global conflict. *Applied Developmental Science, 11*(3), 151–63.

(2008). *Muslim American Youth: Understanding hyphenated identities through multiple methods.* New York: NYU Press.

Sirin S. R., & Katsiaficas, D. (2012). Religiosity, discrimination, and community engagement: Gendered pathways of Muslim American emerging adults. *Youth and Society, 43*(4), 1528–46.

Sirin, S. R., Ryce, P., & Mir, M. (2009). How teachers' values affect their evaluation of children of immigrants. *Early Childhood Research Quarterly, 24*(4), 463–73.

Suárez-Orozco, C., & Suárez-Orozco, M. (2001). *Children of immigration.* Cambridge, MA: Harvard University Press.

Takeuchi, D. T. (1998). Race, discrimination, and Asian Americans. Working Memorandum, Working Conference on "Social Science Knowledge on Race, Racism, and Race Relations," American Sociological Association, McLean, Virginia, April 26–7.

The Chicago Council on Global Affairs. (2007). *Final report on strengthening America: The civic and political integration of Muslim Americans.* Retrieved on September 12, 2009 from http://www.thechicagocouncil.org/taskforce_details.php?taskforce_id=8.

Tweed, R. G., Conway, L. G., & Ryder, A. G. (1999). The target is straw or the arrow is crooked. *American Psychologist, 54,* 837–8.

Unger, J. B., Gallaher, P., Shakib, S., Ritt-Olson, A., Palmer, P. H., & Johnson, C. A. (2002). The AHIMSA acculturation scale: A new measure of acculturation for adolescents in a multicultural society. *Journal of Early Adolescence, 22*(3), 225–51.

World Almanac and Book of Facts (2001). Mahwah, NJ: World Almanac Books.

Zogby, J. (2004). Muslims in the American public square: Shifting political winds and fallout from 9/11, Afghanistan, and Iraq. Retrieved on September 12, 2009 from http://www.zogby.com/news/ReadNews.cfm?ID=1303.

Part 3

WHAT WORKS TO PROMOTE THE POTENTIAL
OF IMMIGRANT YOUTH?

11 Autonomous-Related Self and Competence

The Potential of Immigrant Youth

Ciğdem Kağitçibaşi

Introduction

As a global phenomenon of great human significance, migration has been studied extensively from several disciplinary perspectives, including sociological, economic, demographic, and historical ones. Psychologists have been latecomers to this endeavor which is rather curious given that it is people, individuals, who migrate. Clearly, significant psychological processes are at work in the process of acculturation arising from migration, and they need to be understood in order to grasp the whole phenomenon (Kağitçibaşi, 2006, 2007, ch. 10). This chapter endeavors to show the key importance and relevance of psychological conceptualizations, particularly that of the self and of competence, for theory and applications regarding migration. The focus is on youth, given the general theme of the volume, and the approach used here will necessarily be selective.

Especially in the last two decades, the study of acculturation has benefited from psychological analysis. Though there are notable exceptions (e.g., Bourhis et al., 1997; Bourhis & Dayan, 2004), a great deal of research on acculturation has focused on "acculturating ethnic minorities" without a balanced look at the host societies. This problem has been noted and acknowledged by some researchers (see Liebkind, 2001; Sam & Berry, 2006; Schalk-Soekar & van de Vijver, 2004), nevertheless psychologists' involvement in research and thinking on the subject has led to an emphasis on *psychological acculturation* (e.g., Berry, 1997; Ward, 2001) without equal attention given to other forms of acculturation, such as economic or political. Yet acculturation of the migrant is also necessarily and profoundly influenced by the dominant culture and the lifestyle of the host society in which it takes place. This inherent bilateral dynamic is the key to understanding migration, especially its sociopsychological aspects, but it also renders the topic of study highly complex. In approaching the phenomena involved, different perspectives can be used considering the migrant family, migrant youth, generational dynamics, host society norms and conventions, objective conditions of living (schooling, work, housing, etc.), and a myriad of other issues. Any call for intervention or applications could stress any of these themes.

Two important issues relevant for "capitalizing on immigrant youth" emerge here. One of these is the need for concerted efforts on the part of immigrants and the host society to bridge the cultural gap standing in the way of full integration of the former. The other is the need to recognize the value of reciprocity in the acculturative changes taking place in this process. The latter issue, that of the possible beneficial changes in the host society, together with changes in the immigrants, is hardly touched upon in research, but is a significant aspect of the dynamics of immigration (see also Liebkind et al., this volume). It will be examined in this chapter mainly in terms of the "autonomous-related self." This is also a key concept in addressing the adaptive self-development of migrant youth with a family "culture of relatedness" (or collectivism) in the individualistic host society with a "culture of separateness" (Kağitçibaşi, 1985). Such adaptive self-development is considered an important potential of migrant youth. The competence of migrant youth also holds significant potential, as sociocultural adaptation (Ward, 2001) is based on the development of competence.

Although the concepts of self and competence are widely used, it may be in order to define them with regard to how they are understood here. I define *self* as the person, or "I," as it develops in social interaction, thus it is socially constructed. This is in the tradition of early symbolic interactionism (Cooley, 1922; Mead, 1934), which stressed the self-other dynamics. More recently, the "other" has been expanded to "culture." The mutual influence between the person (the mind) and society (culture) has been expressed dramatically by Shweder as "psyche and culture make each other up" (1991, 73) and later in terms of self as "cultural mode of being"(Kitayama, Duffy, & Uchida, 2007; Markus & Kitayama, 2004). As for *competence*, it is understood here in the general sense of development toward agency, (cognitive) capability, and adaptive behavior. In the context of immigration, it refers mainly to the proficiency for "socio-cultural adjustment," that is, success in school, work, and social integration in general (Ward, 2001).

Thus, I will use a contextual as well as a psychological perspective to understand the self-development and competence development of immigrant youth in divergent family and sociocultural contexts, informed by universalistic and interactionist/contextual views. While these two orientations are often taken to be opposites, I believe they are complementary and mutually informative (Kağıtçıbaşi, 2000). Self-development will be examined first; then the development of competence will be considered.

Individualistic/Collectivistic Contexts and the Family

Individualism is deep-seated in Western culture. Much has been written about it, tracing the roots of individualism in the history of ideas, in political and economic history, in religious history, and in the psychosocial history of Europe and the United States (see Kağıtçıbaşi, 1997 and Kağıtçıbaşi, 2007, chapter 4 for reviews). In the social sciences the seminal distinction made by Tönnies between *gesellschaft* and *gemeinschaft* (1957) has paved the way toward later similar conceptualizations (e.g., Kitayama et al., 2007; Markus & Kitayama, 1991, 2004; Triandis, 1990, 1995). Beyond scholarly work, individualism is evident in popular psychology, media, fiction, and so forth – indeed, in all walks of life. It has also influenced laws, conventions, and policies as well as educational philosophy and practice in Western societies. When taken to an extreme, such as in existential thought, it has meant the rejection of human relatedness, as dramatized in the closing words of Sartre's play *No Exit*, "Hell is other people!"

The migrant youth encounters and has to cope with this individualistic context. Most international migrants originate from the majority world[1] with its collectivistic "cultures of relatedness" (Kağıtçıbaşi, 1985). In this type of family and society, human relatedness is of utmost importance for interpersonal relations and for the construal of the self. Much has been written about cultures of relatedness over the years, particularly in describing interpersonal relations in Asian cultures, by anthropologists (e.g., Doi, 1973; Geertz, 1975), psychoanalysts (Kakar, 1978; Roland, 1988), and other observers (Rothbaum & Trommsdorff, 2007; see Kağıtçıbaşi, 2007 for a review). An important point is the degree and the extent of this relatedness. In cultures of relatedness with collectivistic outlooks, the boundaries of the self tend to overlap with those of close others, thus self-other dynamics also define the self. However, in individualistic "cultures of separateness," the clearly bounded self is more clearly separated from others.

---

[1] *Majority World* refers to what used to be called developing countries or the Third World. It points to countries outside of the individualistic West where the majority of the world's population resides.

Obviously, in all societies, stronger bonds exist with close others than with distant others, reflecting the ingroup–outgroup distinction. However, there tends to be a difference between traditional, collectivistic societies and modern individualistic ones in how marked a boundary they draw between their ingroups and outgroups; this distinction is more marked among the former. Accordingly, the behavior toward others within the ingroup is quite different than the behavior toward others outside of the ingroup in more traditional societies. In individualistic societies this distinction is much less marked, and the same behavior can extend even to distant others not known by the individual. There are important implications of this situation for trusting others and for the willingness to engage in organizations with others who are not familiar (Rothbaum & Trommsdorff, 2007; Yamagishi, 2002).

The family plays the key role here. I have proposed a theory of family change (Kağitçibaşi, 1990, 2007) where three prototypical family patterns are distinguished. The first, the family model of interdependence, is more common in less developed, rural, agrarian contexts with closely knit communities, that is "cultures of relatedness" or collectivism. This model is characterized by intergenerational interdependencies in the psychological/ emotional and material realms. The second, contrasting pattern of "independence" is the prototypical Western (middle class) model upholding individual uniqueness and independence in an individualistic culture of separateness. The third pattern, the psychological/emotional interdependence model, is a synthesis of the first two patterns and is posited to characterize especially the urban and more developed socioeconomic contexts within the Majority World culture of relatedness.

Recent evidence suggests that a global trend in the Majority World is a shift from the family model of interdependence toward the family model of psychological/emotional interdependence (e.g., Jose, Huntsinger, Huntsinger, & Liaw, 2000; Koutrelakos, 2004; Trommsdorff & Nauck, 2005; for a review see Kağitçibaşi, 2007, especially chapter 5). This does not imply a shift toward the Western family pattern of separation and independence as predicted by a general modernization perspective which posits a convergence toward the Western pattern with economic development. Instead, a different pattern of family relations emerges that combines intergenerational interdependence in the emotional (psychological) realm with independence in the material realm. This pattern differs from the traditional (rural/low SES) family pattern given the former's decreased intergenerational material interdependence. It also differs from the prototypical Western (middle class) family pattern in containing intergenerational psychological/emotional interdependence (Deković, Pels, & Model, 2006; Jose et al., 2000; Kağitçibaşi, 1982, 1990, 2007; Kim et al., 2005; Koutrelakos, 2004; Phalet & Schonpflug, 2001; Stewart et al., 1999).

It is understandable that material/economic interdependence would decrease with increased affluence, urbanization, and economic development. With these lifestyle changes, organized social support systems such as old age pensions, social security benefits, and life/health insurance become more readily available to the elderly so that they don't have to depend on their adult offspring for their livelihood. However, there is no reason why emotional/psychological connectedness or interdependencies should decrease with socioeconomic development, particularly in collectivistic cultures where relatedness values are cherished. Relatedness is not incompatible with socioeconomic development and urban lifestyles (Kağitçibaşi, 1990, 2005, 2007).

These transformations tend to accompany socioeconomic development and migration from less developed regions to more developed regions, both internal (rural to urban) and international (Bornstein & Cote, 2006; Kağitçibaşi, 2006, 2007 chapters 5 and 10). There are important implications of this family change for childrearing. In the traditional (rural/low SES) family pattern of interdependence, parents depend on their adult children for material benefits and old age security. Autonomy of the child is not desired because an autonomous child may develop into a separate, independent adult who attends to his/her own needs rather than those of the family of origin. With urbanization and socioeconomic development, however, material dependence on the offspring decreases, as having children starts to entail economic costs rather than assets and as parents acquire alternative sources of old age security. Thus, autonomy of the child is no longer a threat to the family well-being. Autonomy is also adaptive in urban lifestyles, particularly for success in school and in specialized employment. Therefore, there is more room for autonomy in childrearing. Nevertheless, there is also continuing parental control because close relations are desired rather than individualistic separation (i.e., relatedness is still highly valued). The resultant self is the "autonomous-related self" which is different from both the autonomous, separate self, prototypical of the Western middle class individualistic family pattern, and the heteronomous, related self, prototypical of the traditional collectivistic (low SES/rural) family (Kağitçibaşi, 1990, 2005, 2007). Again there are parallels between socioeconomic development and migration (rural to urban or international).

Autonomy, Relatedness, and the Self

Migration involving culture contact constitutes fertile ground for understanding self-development and in particular the development of the autonomous-related self. Such culture contact also presents a challenge to some
of the common assumptions in Western psychology, particularly those concerning adolescent adaptation and optimal development. Autonomy and
relatedness with others are key constructs here.

Autonomy and relatedness have long been viewed as basic needs;
nevertheless, they have also been construed as conflicting, such that
although the need for relatedness is recognized, separation is emphasized
as necessary for autonomy. This construal was the main thesis of "conflict
theories of personality" (Angyal, 1951; Bakan, 1966; Rank, 1945) and has
been an important perspective in psychoanalytically informed personality theory and clinical psychology. In particular, in infancy and again in
adolescence, autonomy-relatedness dynamics are considered a key developmental process in the sense that separation from mother (parents), as the
opposite of relatedness, is necessary for autonomy development. Thus, the
separation-individuation process hypothesized by Mahler and colleagues
(Mahler, 1972; Mahler, Pine, & Bergman, 1975) refers to "the psychological
birth of the infant," which is reiterated later during adolescence, the so-
called second separation-individuation period (Blos, 1979; A. Freud, 1958;
Hoffman, 1984; Kroger, 1998). In this line, Steinberg and Silverberg (1986)
proposed the influential concept of emotional autonomy from parents as
key for adolescent individuation.

This view is quite prevalent in Western psychology, both academic and
popular, and informs theoretical orientations and practice. Though some
criticism of this view has emerged recently, as discussed later in this chapter, the prevalence of this perspective remains mostly unchanged. It is also
shared by sociological accounts of "individualization theory" (Crockett &
Silbereisen, 2000; Neubauer & Hurrelmann, 1995). Thus, autonomy has
been prioritized in the Western world and in psychology, as reflected in an
emphasis on individual independence, agency, self-sufficiency, privacy, and
so forth, often at the expense of relatedness. What is the reason for this?
It does not appear to have an evolutionary basis which rather emphasizes
the survival value of relatedness and cooperation with others (Euler, Hoier,
& Rohde, 2001). Instead, this priority appears to be cultural (Kağitçibaşi,
2005, 2007). Western individualism may underlie the conflicting construal
of autonomy and relatedness as well as the emphasis put on autonomy
(independence, privacy, agency, and self-sufficiency of the individual).

From such an individualistic perspective, autonomy is often seen to combine two distinct meanings. One of these is an agentic disposition, to be able to act willfully. The other is being separate from others, being unique. The two meanings are often combined, and the emerging portrait is the independent self that is autonomous *and* separate – the prototypical individualistic self. Thus, autonomy and separateness are seen as intertwined. This intertwining can also be seen in measures of the *independent self* which include items that point to both autonomy and separateness (e.g., Gudykunst et al., 1996; Kitayama et al., 1991; Singelis, 1994; see Kağitçibaşi, 2005, 2007 for reviews). This outlook is in line with the long-standing individualistic stance in psychology and in the Western mind.

However, a closer look reveals that underneath these two meanings of being an agent and being separate from others lie two distinct dimensions, which I have called *agency* and *interpersonal distance* (Kağitçibaşi, 1996, 2005, 2007). It is neither logically nor psychologically necessary for autonomy to mean separateness if we recognize the existence of these two distinct dimensions. Agency extends from autonomy to heteronomy, and interpersonal distance extends from relatedness to separateness. The former has to do with the capacity for willful action while the latter concerns self-other relations. These underlying dimensions are in line with the two basic needs for autonomy and relatedness discussed before.

Given that these are distinct dimensions, it must be possible for each pole of each dimension to coexist with either pole of the other. Thus, a person's standing on the interpersonal distance dimension does not imply his or her standing on agency dimension. Clearly, the assumption of separation as a requisite for autonomy is not warranted. Considering a person's standing on these two dimensions as self-attributes, their distinctiveness allows for the four possible combinations: autonomous-separate self, autonomous-related self, heteronomous-separate self, and heteronomous-related self (Kağitçibaşi, 1996, 2005, 2007). These self configurations appear to emerge in the different family models (contexts) described earlier, in line with their different manners of child socialization.

Implications for Immigration and Immigrant Youth

These theoretical perspectives on family change and the self (Kağitçibaşi, 2005, 2007) have significant implications for immigration and particularly for immigrant youth. Most international migration emerges from countries with a "culture of relatedness" or collectivistic societies where close-knit human ties and the "family model of interdependence" are prevalent. As mentioned before, in this type of family, obedience-oriented childrearing is normative, which does not grant autonomy to the growing child. Combined with the emphasis on relatedness, this type of child socialization leads to the development of the "heteronomous-related self." Given the two basic needs for relatedness and autonomy, this type of self is not optimal; neither is it adaptive in immigration contexts where autonomy is an asset. In contrast, the receiving societies are characterized by the individualistic "culture of separateness" where the development of the "autonomous-separate self" is prevalent in the "family model of independence." Again this model leaves something to be desired, since it does not satisfy the need for relatedness.

An integrative synthesis of these two models is the "autonomous-related self" that emerges in the family model of "psychological/emotional interdependence" (Kağitçibaşi, 2005, 2007). This model is more optimal, since it satisfies both of the basic needs. Research provides support to the greater adaptive value of this self configuration (Blatt & Blass, 1996; Celenk, 2007; Chirkov et al., 2003; Chou, 2000; Jose et al., 2000; Weisner, 2002). This is particularly important in the migration context where both sociocultural and psychological adaptation are important (Ward & Kennedy, 1992). Sociocultural adaptation is manifested in fitting in and functioning successfully in the host society, and psychological adaptation is reflected in less acculturative stress and better psychological state (Phalet & Swyngedouw, 2004).

On the one hand, family relatedness, a characteristic of the culture of origin, provides the close human ties that are adaptive for "psychological adaptation." On the other hand, granting autonomy to the developing child provides both the satisfaction of a basic need and also equips the growing person with the competence required by urban industrial lifestyles, leading to "socio-cultural adaptation" (Ward, 2001). Thus, this more optimal model of self promises to contribute to the realization of the potential of immigrant youth.

The fourth possible combination, the heteronomous-separate self, may develop in family contexts which nourish neither autonomy nor relatedness, as in neglecting and hierarchical families. Since neither of the two basic needs is satisfied in this model, it appears to be problematic and will not be pursued here further.

Given that autonomy is beneficial for sociocultural adaptation in the destination contexts to which most youth immigrate, and relatedness is conducive to psychological adaptation in nearly all contexts, their combination would be conducive to what has been described as the "integration" acculturation strategy. Integration involves the maintenance of the heritage culture and identity and the acceptance of the host culture and language and building positive relations with it (Arends-Tóth & van de Vijver, 2006; Berry, 1990, 1997). It is considered a more optimal acculturation strategy than the "assimilation" and the "segregation" strategies. Extensive research evidence supports the adaptive value of the integration strategy (see Berry, 1997, 2006 for reviews). If autonomous-related self-development is vitally important for realizing the potential of migrant youth, it needs to be recognized as such and nurtured by the migrant family as well as by the host society, its institutions, and health/social service professionals. Capitalizing on this potential would support migrant youths' psychological and sociocultural adaptation.

Impediments and Supports in the Path toward Autonomous-Related Self

While the autonomous-related self appears appealing and favorable for promoting the potential of migrant youth, it may not be easily achieved. One impediment is "culture lag," or the persistence of the traditional family culture of total interdependence among migrants. The growing child's autonomy is no longer a threat to family livelihood over the family life cycle in the developed urban, industrial society where there are other sources of support in old age. Furthermore, autonomy is highly adaptive in the immigration context for success in school and specialized employment. Nevertheless, often migrant parents are reluctant to grant autonomy to the growing child (Deković, Pels, & Model, 2006; Leyendecker, Schöelmerich, & Citlak, 2006). The reasons for this may involve the force of habit, as well as adherence to customs, conventions, and norms regarding parent–child relations and discipline. Specifically, autonomous behavior on the part of the child may be interpreted as headstrong, even disrespectful. Parents may also be concerned about an autonomous child later becoming an independent youth who may separate from the family to take care of his or her own needs. Finally, immigrant parents may not understand the value of autonomous behavior for success in the host society. Indeed, research points to mismatches between parents' views of what is required for success at school and school expectations. For example, Nunes (1993) showed that Mexican parents in the United States believe, erroneously, that if their children are quiet, obedient, and listen to the teacher, they will succeed in school. Similarly, Deković and colleagues (2006) found that immigrant parents in the Netherlands have high educational aspirations for their children, but they often don't know how success is to be achieved and how to support their children in the process.

Immigrant parents should be helped to understand and appreciate the value of autonomy for the advancement of their growing children and also the possibility of the autonomous-related self, where autonomy does not imply separation from the family. In this way, autonomy may gain more support in childrearing. Parents can better appreciate autonomy if it is combined with relatedness.

Just as the value of autonomy needs to be appreciated by migrant parents, the value of relatedness needs to be recognized by the host society. Relatedness is an issue particularly for host society professionals who hold individualistic worldviews. As discussed at some length in the beginning of this chapter, there is a common assumption among the host society social workers, psychologists, and the general public that separation is necessary for the development of autonomy. Often the connectedness of migrant families is seen as a sign of being backward, as authoritarian constraint on the children, or even as pathological.

A rather amusing case reported by a clinical psychologist makes the point (Fisek, personal communication, 2011). In Germany, a Turkish child was referred by his school to counseling services. At the appointed time the child was brought in by his mother, accompanied by his younger sister, his uncle, his grandmother, and his grandfather. The social worker immediately jotted down "enmeshed family." As it turned out, there was a good reason for everyone to be there at that time. The uncle was the only one who could drive; there was no one to take care of the younger child; and the grandparents had never been to that part of the city and wanted to have an outing there!

The social worker's assumption of pathology without adequate evidence or understanding is typical of prejudiced and stereotypic attitudes. Beyond these kinds of bias, however, is reflected a particular worldview that does not construe autonomy and relatedness as compatible. It provides a cultural context that is not conducive to the development of the autonomous-related self for migrant or host youth. The overemphasis put on separation from parents does not promote well-being in adolescence (Aydin & Oztutuncu, 2001; Baumeister & Leary, 1995; Chou, 2000; Ryan, Deci, & Grolnick, 1995). As I discussed earlier, this bipolar, unidimensional conceptualization construes autonomy and relatedness as conflicting, assuming that as one increases, the other decreases.

The idea that separation-individuation is necessary for the development of autonomy is an abiding perspective despite a growing literature pointing to the importance of both autonomy and relatedness and to the value of their coexistence (e.g., Baumeister & Leary, 1995; Blatt & Blass, 1996; Cross & Madson, 1997; Guisinger & Blatt, 1994; Kağitçibaşi, 1996, 2007; Raeff, 1997). This issue is particularly salient in adolescence research. Since the 1980s the debate has centered on whether distancing (detachment) from parents is required for healthy autonomy development (e.g., Kroger, 1998; Steinberg & Silverberg, 1986) or whether a close, positive relationship with parents promotes adolescent autonomy (e.g., Grotevant & Cooper, 1986; Ryan & Lynch, 1989). Recent research has provided greater support to the latter view. Indeed, several studies have found that relatedness is associated with autonomy in both collectivistic and individualistic societies (Beyers & Goossens, 1999; Hodgins, Koeatner, & Duncan, 1996; Kim, Butzel, & Ryan, 1998; Meeus, Oosterweegel, & Vollebergh, 2002; Ryan & Deci, 2000; Ryan, Deci, & Grolnick, 1995; see Kağitçibaşi, 2007 for an extensive review).

There is also the issue of parental control. Ethnic minority parents tend to be labeled as authoritarian because of strong parental discipline, which can appear very controlling (Gonzales, Cauce, & Mason, 1996). But this may be a wrong attribution because there is often also relatedness and warmth in the family model of psychological/emotional interdependence. Indeed, ethnic minority research in Europe and the United States points to closely related family relations and parental control (Chao, 2000; Jose et al., 2000; Kwak, 2003; Lansford et al., 2003; Rudy & Grusec, 2001; Smetana & Gaines, 1999). For example, Deković, Pels, and Model (2006) in their work with six ethnic groups in the Netherlands, found that parents who use strong discipline are often also warm and supportive. They called this "an unlikely combination," however, because of the assumption that parental control means parental rejection and suppression of autonomy. This is based on the individualistic view that permissive independence-oriented parenting that allows for separation of the child from the parents is necessary for the development of autonomy. However, parental control, especially an "order setting" one (Lau et al., 1990), seems compatible with parental warmth and is not perceived by children as rejection (Baumrind, 1989; Kağitçibaşi, 2005, 2006, 2007; Rohner & Pettengill, 1985; Silk et al., 2003); it can even have a positive impact on developmental outcomes (Carlson & Harwood, 2003; Trommsdorff, 1985). Also, autonomy granting need not mean lack of parental control. Thus, Lin and Fu (1990) comparing Chinese, immigrant Chinese, and Anglo-American parents, found the Chinese groups to be higher on both parental control and encouragement of independence than the Anglo group. More research is needed to delineate the distinguishing features of positive and negative parental control in different contexts.

Given these considerations, we can say that some aspects of the immigrants' family culture could be seen as positive influences, even as valuable potential which could be capitalized upon for beneficial outcomes. Immigration involves culture contact that creates the potential for mutual influence and learning. Immigrants, particularly those with low levels of education, have a lot to learn from and need to acculturate to the host societies. However, from a cross-cultural psychological perspective, they have a lot to offer, also. Nevertheless, for the immigrant family culture to be a source of potential growth, it needs to shift from the family model of interdependence to that of psychological/emotional interdependence (Kağıtçıbaşı, 2007). While the former model involves relatedness but not autonomy, the latter model integrates relatedness with autonomy in childrearing. In fact, immigrants modeling the psychological/emotional interdependence family model and the autonomous-related self would make a real contribution to the host society.

Thus, a convergence toward the psychological/emotional interdependence model and the autonomous-related self could be achieved if these were encouraged among both the host society and the immigrants. These developments do not occur automatically; they need to be nurtured. The parenting components contributing toward such convergent development would be autonomy granting, warmth/relatedness, and order keeping control. These are considered to be positive orientations in child rearing, as supported by research (Deković et al., 2006; Jose et al., 2000; Kwak, 2003; Lau et al., 1990; Lin & Fu, 1990; Rudy & Grusec, 2001; Silk et al., 2003; see Kağıtçıbaşı, 2007, chapters 5 and 6 for a review). However, more empirical work is needed to examine the different components of parenting in changing sociocultural contexts. Bringing autonomy into the immigrant family culture and childrearing and bringing relatedness into the host society family culture and childrearing would be an important example of positive culture learning.

Development of Competence and the Importance of Early Enrichment

Beyond healthy self-development, adequate competence development is also highly important for the sociocultural adaptation of immigrant youth. The new environmental demands faced by youth who migrate to more technologically advanced urban societies were discussed earlier. In particular, academic knowledge and cognitive competence are required for advancement in education and in specialized jobs. This is rather different than the type of competence valued in traditional rural society where social intelligence (sensitivity and responsibility toward others) and practical/manual skills are important (Dasen, 1984).

Teaching and learning styles that were adaptive in the rural context often are not adaptive in the urban context. Obedience-orientation in childrearing rather than autonomy granting, mentioned before, as well as learning through imitation rather than through explanation and exploration, are the contextual attributes of the rural/traditional teaching and learning styles (Greenfield, 1999; Kağıtçıbaşi, 2007). In particular, learning based on imitation or rote memorization is limited in terms of conceptualization, transfer to new situations, and creative problem solving (Greenfield et al., 2003; Segall et al., 1999, 186).

A profound contextual shift is occurring across the world from rural subsistence economies where there is less specialized work and low/no schooling to urban economies with more specialized work and more schooling; from apprenticeship and demonstration/modeling to verbal explanation and school-like learning styles; and from competence involving social intelligence and practical/manual skills to school-like skills and cognitive competence (Greenfield, et al., 2003; Kağıtçıbaşi, 2007). Given the globally increasing similarities in urban technological life styles of knowledge-based societies, some common standards of competence are emerging which are needed for sociocultural adaptation to the postindustrial society. The expansion of public education is of particular importance here.

In the face of such global changes, less powerful sectors of society including immigrants, ethnic minorities, and poverty populations face difficult challenges. Schooling becomes the key resource and social mobilizer here; therefore, timely access to school and school readiness at the start play an important role for the development of competence. Concerted efforts have been expended in many countries to provide socioeconomically deprived children with early enrichment that would prepare them for school and would enhance their ability to benefit from formal schooling (see Kağıtçıbaşi, 2007 chapter 8 for a review). Such efforts are valuable in fighting school failure and drop out. One example is the Turkish Early Enrichment Project (TEEP) and its resultant program applications, which will be described next as a case in point.

TEEP as a Case in Point

TEEP was designed to promote overall human development in the context of rural to urban migration in Istanbul, Turkey (Kağıtçıbaşi, 2007 chapter 9; Kağitçibaşi, Sunar, & Bekman, 2001; Kağitçibaşi et al., 2009). The families participating in the study were mainly former villagers. Most of the mothers had only an elementary education; about two-thirds worked as unskilled factory workers. The original research was a four-year longitudinal intervention study (1982–6) conducted in low-income districts of Istanbul, Turkey, with mothers and their young children (3–5 years of age). Two follow-up studies were conducted in 1992 and in 2004. In the first year mothers and their children were studied for baselines. In the second and third years of the original study, a randomly selected sample of the mothers was given a mother-child training program. It focused on the cognitive development of children, which the mothers applied with their children at home, and on supporting and empowering mothers in their childrearing roles. In particular, mothers were provided with storybooks, materials, and communication techniques to help their children's school preparation. They also participated in group discussions designed to support their well-being, communication skills, self-concepts, and to enhance their knowledge and awareness of their children's needs and their own needs as women. This was done by reinforcing the existing close mother-child relationship on the one hand and by capitalizing on the existing communal support systems on the other. The latter were utilized in the group meetings of the mothers in the community. A second source of early enrichment was the educational childcare centers some of the children attended. Children were in one of three alternative care environments: an educational daycare center, a custodial daycare center, or home care.

The impact of intervention on both the mothers and the children was found to be notable in the fourth year of the study when reassessments were carried out with both mothers and children. The children from educational nursery schools showed better performance compared to those from custodial daycare centers and those cared for at home. At the same time, the mother-trained group of children was superior to the control group on school adjustment and self-concept. Mother training also positively influenced mothers' orientation to their children (Kağitçibaşi et al., 2001).

Longer term effects were studied through a follow-up study seven years later, and the gains from the intervention were found to be sustained. The adolescents (13–15 years of age) whose mothers participated in the mother training program surpassed the control group in cognitive performance and school achievement. They also showed greater autonomy, more positive self-concept, and better family and social adjustment. Eighty-six percent of the adolescents whose mothers had undergone training remained in school, but only 67% of the control group was still in school. Mother training also positively affected school grades throughout the years of compulsory education. As schooling is the main route for social mobility in urban low-income contexts, the social implications of these finding are very important. Both the mother-trained and educational daycare group of adolescents achieved higher scores than the other groups on a standardized vocabulary test (Kağitçibaşi et al., 2001).

A second follow-up study conducted 12 years after the first follow-up (19 years after the intervention) aimed to explore the continuing effects of early intervention on the participants' educational attainment, socioeconomic success, family relationships, and social participation and adjustment. The children were young adults at the time of the second follow-up with a mean age of 25 years. The results showed that compared to their peers who had received no early intervention, young adults who experienced early enrichment, in the form of attending an educational daycare center or having mother training, or both, did better in terms of several indicators of sociocultural adaptation and social integration in modern urban life. In particular, the training group had longer school attainment and higher university attendance. In line with this higher schooling, this group started gainful employment at a later age. This is important, since later entry into full-time employment involves more specialized work requiring more education and bringing in higher lifetime earnings. Accordingly, the experimental group had higher occupational status. They also obtained higher scores on a vocabulary test and owned more personal computers and credit cards. Clearly, these young people were more active participants in the knowledge society and modern economy (Kağitçibaşi et al., 2009).

Implications for Immigrant Children and Youth

Development of competence is a key aspect of immigrant youths' potential. Studies and observations show that there is much variability in competence and school success among different migrant groups. A common finding is that there may be mismatches between parental values and expectations and school requirements (Deković, et al., 2006; Nunes, 1993; Okagaki & Sternberg, 1993). I discussed this earlier with regard to autonomy; the same problem is seen regarding competence. Immigrant parents tend to have high educational expectations for their children, but are often not knowledgeable about what it takes to accomplish this. For example studies in Europe on ethnic minority children's cognitive development and school performance point to serious problems (Bornstein & Cote, 2006; Deković, Pels, & Model,

2006; Kaya, 2001). These issues could possibly be addressed by integrative and culturally sensitive support programs similar to TEEP. Thus the implications of TEEP are far reaching, particularly for groups who have experienced comparable rural-urban or international migration. They encounter similar challenges in the face of changing environmental demands.

TEEP has led to policy and program developments in Turkey (Kağitçibaşi et al., 2001, 2009). A Mother-Child Education Foundation (ACEV), established in 1993, has substantially revised the mother-child education program and increased its reach widely (to some 650,000 mothers and children). It has been endorsed as a nonformal, home-based early childhood education program by the Turkish Ministry of Education, beyond formal institutional preschool education, thus creating an educational policy change. It has been adapted to television. It is being implemented all over the country and beyond, with ethnic minorities in some European countries, and in Arabic translation in some Arab countries. It has the potential for more adaptations and wider usage.

Regarding the cognitive competence and school performance of immigrant children and youth, school preparation in early childhood is of particular importance. Research in Europe with immigrant groups points to inadequate adult verbal interaction with young children and correspondingly low levels of vocabulary and concept formation skills in children as young as three years of age (Leseman, 1993). Since the 1990s, similar findings abound in research with lower SES groups and ethnic minorities in several countries (Applegate, Burleson, & Dalia, 1992; Eccles & Harold, 1993; Korenman, Miller, & Sjaastad, 1995; Lee & Croninger, 1994; Peralta de Mendoza & Irice, 1995; Savasir, Sezgin, & Erol, 1992; see Kağitçibaşi, 2007 for a review). In particular, the extent and quality of maternal (or caretaker) speech appears to be a key factor here (van Tuijl & Leseman, 2004). Recent work further corroborates the significant impact of "home literacy environment" for the early development of linguistic and cognitive competence of children and youth (Aksu-Koc, 2005; Bornstein & Bradley, 2003; Duncan & Magnuson, 2003; Hart & Risley, 2003; Hoff, 2003; Senecal & Le Fevre, 2002). Home literacy environment includes verbal interaction and stimulation, familiarity with printed media, world knowledge, vocabulary, and the like.

Such research points to the significance for the immigrant child of competence in the host country language from early on. In most cases, immigrant children start school with lower levels of mastery of the host country language than the host country children (Crijnen, 2003). This constitutes the main disadvantage of the migrant child. Language and schooling in the mother tongue or the dominant language are long debated issues with strong political overtones.

Without going into the political aspects, certain principles and policy recommendations could be put forward, based on the previously cited research results (Kağitçibaşi, 2006, 2007 chapter 10). For the immigrant children to have a fair start in educational and life opportunities, their proficiency in the host country dominant language must be promoted. Since the migrant home most often lacks the capacity to do this, it is imperative that immigrant children benefit from preschool education at least from the age of 4 on (see also García, this volume). Depending on the circumstances, preschool may need to start earlier and may need to be compulsory. This type of educational investment is very important to improve the potential of immigrant children and youth, yet it has been lacking to a large extent. Especially in Europe, the result has been detrimental for immigrants, with a disproportionately large proportion of immigrant youth ending up in lower track schooling (such as Gesamptschule or Sonderschule in Germany) and/ or dropping out of education too early (Hagelund, 2008; Kaya, 2001).

A related problem in the schooling of immigrant children has been the negative impact of the low expectations of teachers. Many teachers assume immigrant children with inadequate language skills have lower cognitive capacity and therefore expect a lower level of academic performance from them. This has detrimental effects on the children, as research has demonstrated for a long time (Rosenthal & Jacobson, 1968). Thus, the children's inadequate language skills and the negative environmental factors work together in a vicious cycle to their disadvantage.

A problematic route pursued by some immigrant groups in Europe and supported by the host society governments is the establishment of separate ethnic and religious schools for immigrant children. This is to some extent in response to the negative experiences children have in regular schools. However, these schools only exacerbate the problem by separating immigrant children from the children of the dominant society and providing them with the type of education that will not contribute to their success and upward social mobility in the host society (Kağitçibaşi, 1997a; Kaya, 2001). Though there may be exceptions, "separate but equal" is difficult to achieve, as research and historical accounts on interracial relations in the United States have demonstrated since the human rights movements of the 1950s. Separate often implies "inferior," and it always means "different."

Furthermore, what is different tends not to be liked; this is especially the case in intergroup relations. Reinforcing religious or ethnic differences is not advisable because difference is problematic. Ever since Bogardus's Social

Distance Scale (1925), studies in intergroup relations have shown that the more different a group is viewed, the more it is rejected. What is different is not easily trusted and a (social) distance is put between self and the different "other." For example, an early study by Malewska-Peyre (1980) showed that there was more prejudice in France toward North African immigrants than toward Portuguese immigrants even though the former spoke French but the latter didn't. This was due to the fact that the French perceived the North Africans to be more different from themselves (in terms of religion and race) than they perceived the Portuguese to be. More recent work from Europe, Canada, and Israel has corroborated this finding (Arends-Tóth & Van de Vijver, 2006; Berry et al., 2002; Bourhis & Dayan, 2004; Montreuil & Bourhis, 2001).

Obviously differences exist and will continue to exist; full assimilation is not the answer. The issues involved appear to revolve around two main points. While on the one hand cultural diversity should be seen as rich and appreciated, on the other hand, the human commonality should be emphasized, bringing out something of a balance in intergroup/interethnic relations. I believe that not maximizing the differences would be a part of this balance, leading to integration.

What is needed is early support for school preparation and integration of immigrant children and youth in mixed schools rather than separating them from host society in ethnic/religious schools (Kağitçibaşi, 1997a, 2006; Kaya, 2001; Leyendecker, et al., 2006). The more immigrant youth become an integral part of the host society, the more of a potential they constitute for that society. This is globally relevant but is especially the case in European societies with aging populations. A better educated immigrant youth is a great economic and human asset. Much can be accomplished through policies and practices involving early childhood enrichment programs, especially including language learning and enhancing preliteracy and prenumeracy skills. Also needed are parent training and support programs, leading to greater involvement, participation, and empowerment of women in particular. Thus more concerted efforts are called for to help immigrant children, youth, and families to become integral parts of the host society, not separate from it.

Conclusion

In conclusion, promoting optimal human development to realize the potential of immigrant youth involves the integrative synthesis of competence and autonomous-related self. In the beginning of this chapter, I said that I would use a contextual as well as a psychological perspective in examining the issues involved in the development of self and competence. It may be claimed that I have been using mainly basic psychological theoretical perspectives in reaching this conclusion. Though it is true that the integrative synthesis of competence and autonomous-related self has possibly universal validity, I have tried to show that it is especially adaptive in the context of immigration. Thus the approach utilized here has been informed by a universalistic and an interactionist/contextual perspective.

Promoting competence that is conducive to sociocultural adaptation and autonomous-related self that is conducive to both sociocultural and psychological adaptation is an important two-pronged strategy for capitalizing on the potential of immigrant youth. If competence and autonomous-related self are promoted and both types of adaptations are achieved, the outcome is more optimal than if one or the other is lacking. Immigrant youth promises to constitute a significant benefit for the host society. However, their potential needs to be recognized and nurtured for this benefit to materialize. Recognition and nurturance on the part of the host society, as well as on the part of the migrant family, involves advancement toward optimal development.

Research on immigration and acculturation has for too long stressed problems faced by immigrants and host societies. A constructive approach to deal with these problems is to emphasize positive youth development (Lerner, this volume) and to make the effort to create extensive and sustainable programs, policies, and practices toward this goal. Social scientists and in particular psychologists can play a key role in this process of growth and in the realization of youths' potential and well-being.

REFERENCES

Aksu-Koc, A. (2005). Role of the home-context in the relations between narrative abilities and literacy practices. In D. Ravid and H. Bat-Zeev Shyldkrot (Eds.), *Perspectives on language and language development* (pp. 257–74). Dordrecht: Kluwer.

Angyal, A. (1951). A theoretical model for personality studies. *Journal of Personality*, 20, 131–42.

Applegate, J. L., Burleson, B. R., & Dalia, J. G. (1992). Reflection enhancing parenting as an antecedent to children's social-cognitive and communicative development. In I. E. Sigel, A. V. McGillicuddy DeLisi, and J. J. Goodnow (Eds.), *Parental belief systems* (pp. 3–40). Hillsdale, NJ: Lawrence Erlbaum Associates.

Arends-Tóth, J., & Van de Vijver, F. J. R. (2006). Issues in conceptualization and assessment of acculturation. In M. H. Bornstein and L. R. Cote, (Eds.), *Acculturation and parent-child relationships: Measurement and development* (pp. 33–62). Mahwah, NJ: Erlbaum.

Aydin, B. & Oztutuncu, F. (2001). Examination of adolescents' negative thoughts, depressive mood, and family environment. *Adolescence, 36,* 77–83.

Bakan, D. (1966). *The duality of human existence.* Chicago: Rand McNally.

Baumeister, R., & Leary, M. R. (1995). The need to belong: Desire for interpersonal attachments as a fundamental human motivation. *Psychological Bulletin, 117,* 497–529.

Baumrind, D. (1989). Rearing competent children, In W. Damon (Ed.), *Child development today and tomorrow* (pp. 349–78). San Francisco: Jossey Bass.

Berry, J. W. (1990). Psychology of acculturation, In J. Berman (Ed.), *Cross-cultural perspectives: Nebraska Symposium on motivation* (Vol. 37, pp. 201–34), Lincoln, NE: University of Nebraska Press.

(1997). Immigration, acculturation and adaptation. *Applied Psychology: An International Review, 46,* 5–68.

(2006). Acculturation: A conceptual overview. In M. H. Bornstein and L. R. Cote (Eds.), *Acculturation and parent-child relationships: Measurement and development.* Mahwah, NJ: Erlbaum.

Berry, J. W., Poortinga, Y. H., Segall, M. H., & Dasen, P. R. (2002). *Cross-cultural psychology. research and applications* (2nd Ed.). Cambridge UK: Cambridge University Press.

Beyers, W. & Goossens, L. (1999). Emotional autonomy, psychological adjustment, and parenting: Interactions, moderating, and mediating effects. *Journal of Research on Adolescence, 22,* 753–69.

Blatt, S., & Blass, R. B. (1996). Relatedness and self-definition: A dialectic model of personality development. In G. G. Noam and K. W. Fischer (Eds.), *Development and vulnerability in close relationship* (pp. 309–38). Mahvah, NJ: Lawrence Erlbaum Associates.

Blos, P. (1979). *The adolescent passage.* New York: International Universities Press.

Bogardus, E. S. (1925). Measuring social distance. *Journal of Applied Sociology, 2,* 299–308.

Bornstein, M. H., & Bradley, R.H. (2003). *Socioeconomic status, parenting, and child development.* Mahwah, NJ: Erlbaum.

Bornstein, M. H., & Cote, L. R. (2006) Parenting cognitions and practices in the acculturative process. In M. H. Bornstein and L. R. Cote, (Eds.), *Acculturation and parent-child relationships: Measurement and development* (pp. 173–96). Mahwah, NJ: Erlbaum.

Bourhis, R. Y., & Dayan, J. (2004). Acculturation orientations towards Israeli Arabs and Jewish immigrants. *International Journal of Psychology, 39,* 118–31.

Bourhis, R. Y., Moïse, L. C., Perreault, S., & Senécal, S. (1997). Towards an interactive acculturation model: A social psychological approach. *International Journal of Psychology, 32,* 369–86.

Carlson, V. J., & Harwood, R. L. (2003). Attachment, culture, and the caregiving system: The cultural patterning of everyday experiences among Anglo and Puerto Rican mother–infant pairs. *Infant Mental Health Journal, 24,* 53–73.

Celenk, O. (2007). Adult attachment styles, autonomous-relational self and gender roles as mediators between culture and relationship satisfaction for British and Turkish people. Master's Thesis. Brunel University.

Chao, R. K. (2000). Cultural explanations for the role of parenting in the school success of Asian-American children. In R. Taylor and M. Wang (Eds.), *Resilience across contexts: Family, work, culture, and community* (pp. 333–63). Mahwah, NJ: Erlbaum.

Chirkov, V., Kim, Y., Ryan, R., & Kaplan, U. (2003). Differentiating autonomy from individualism and independence: A self-determination theory perspective on internalization of cultural orientations and well being, *Journal of Personality and Social Psychology, 84*, 97–110.

Chou, K-L. (2000). Emotional autonomy and depression among Chinese adolescents. *Journal of Genetic Psychology, 161*, 161–9.

Cooley, C. H. (1922). *Human nature and the social order*. New York: Scribner's.

Crijnen, A. (2003). Emotional and behavioral problems of Turkish immigrant children, Adolescents and their parents living in the Netherlands – An overview. *ISSBD Newsletter, 2*(44), 7–9.

Crockett, L. J., & Silbereisen, R. K. (Eds.) (2000). *Negotiating adolescence in times of social change*. Cambridge UK: Cambridge University Press.

Cross, S. E., & Madson, L. (1997). Models of the self: Self-construals and gender. *Psychological Bulletin, 122*, 5–37.

Dasen, P. R. (1984). The cross-cultural study of intelligence: Piaget and the Baoule. *International Journal of Psychology, 19*, 407–34.

Deković, M., Pels, T., & Model, S. (Eds.) (2006). *Unity and diversity in child rearing: Family life in a multicultural society*. Lewiston, US: The Edwin Mellen Press.

Doi, T. (1973). *Anatomy of dependence*. Tokyo: Kodansha International.

Duncan, G. J., & Magnuson, K. A. (2003). Off with Hollingshead: Socioeconomic resources, parenting, and child development. In M. H. Bornstein and R. H. Bradley (Eds.), *Socioeconomic status, parenting, and child development.* (pp. 83–107). Mahwah: Erlbaum.

Eccles, J. S., & Harold, R. D. (1993). Parent-school involvement during the early adolescent years. *Teachers College Record, 94*(3), 568–87.

Euler, H. A., Hoier, S., and Rohde, P. A. (2001). "Relationship-specific closeness of intergenerational family ties: Findings from evolutionary psychology and implications for models of cultural transmission." *Journal of Cross-Cultural Psychology, 32*, 147–58.

Fisek, G. (2011) Personal communication.

Freud, A. (1958). *Adolescence: Psychoanalytic Study of the Child*, 13, 255–78.

Geertz, C. (1975). On the nature of anthropological understanding. *American Scientist, 63*, 47–53.

Gonzales, N. A., Cauce, A. M., & Mason, C. A. (1996). Interobserver agreement in the assessment of parental behavior and parent-adolescent conflict: African American mothers, daughters, and independent observers. *Child Development, 67*, 1483–98.

Greenfield, P. M. (1999). Cultural change and human development. *New Directions for Child and Adolescent Development, 83*, 37–59.

Greenfield, M., Keller, H., Fuligni A., & Maynard, A. (2003). Cultural pathways through universal development, *Annual Review of Psychology, 54*, 461–90.

Grotevant, H. D., and Cooper, C. R. (1986). Individuation in family relationships. *Human Development, 29*, 82–100.

Gudykunst, W. B., Matsumoto, Y., Ting-Toomey, S., & Nishida, T. (1996). The influence of cultural individualism-collectivism, self-construals and individual values on communication styles across cultures. *Human Communication Research, 22,* 510–43.

Guisinger, S., & Blatt, S. J. (1994). Individuality and relatedness; Evolution of a fundamental dialectic. *American Psychologist, 49,* 104–11.

Hagelund, A. (2008). "For women and children!" The family and immigration politics in Scandinavia. In R. Grillo (Ed.), *The family in question: Immigrant and ethnic minorities in multicultural Europe* (pp. 71–88). Amsterdam University Press.

Hart, B., & Risley, T. R. (2003). The early catastrophe. The 30 million word gap by age 3. *American Educator.* Retrieved March 02, 2005 from http://www.aft.org.

Hodgins, H., Koeatner, R., & Duncan, N. (1996). On the compatibility of autonomy and relatedness. *Personality and Social Psychology Bulletin, 22,* 227–37.

Hoff, E. (2003). The specificity of environmental influence: Socioeconomic status affects early vocabulary development via maternal speech. *Child Development, 74,* 1368–78.

Hoffman, J. A. (1984). Psychological separation of late adolescents from their parents. *Journal of Counseling Psychology, 31,* 170–8.

Jose, P. E., Huntsinger, C. S., Huntsinger, P. R., & Liaw, F-R. (2000). Parental values and practices relevant to young children's social development in Taiwan and the United States. *Journal of Cross-Cultural Psychology, 31,* 677–702.

Kağitçibaşi, C. (1982). Old-age security value of children: Cross-national socio-economic evidence. *Journal of Cross-Cultural Psychology, 13,* 29–42.

    (1985). Culture of separateness-culture of relatedness. *1984 Vision and Reality: Papers in Comparative Studies, 4,* 91–9.

    (1990). Family and socialization in cross cultural perspective: A model of change. In J. Berman (Ed.), *Cross-cultural perspectives: Nebraska Symposium on Motivation, 1989* (pp. 135–200). Lincoln: University of Nebraska Press.

    (1996). The autonomous-relational self: A new synthesis. *European Psychologist, 1,* 180–6.

    (1997). Individualism and collectivism. In J. W. Berry, M. H. Segall, and C. Kağitçibaşi (Eds.), *Handbook of cross-cultural psychology* (2nd ed., Vol. 3, pp. 1–50). Boston: Allyn and Bacon.

    (1997a). Whither multiculturalism? *Applied Psychology: An International Review, 44,* 44–9.

    (2000). Cultural contextualism without complete relativism in the study of human development, In A. L. Comunian and U. Gielen (Eds.), *International perspectives on human development* (pp. 97–115). Rome: Pabst.

    (2005). Autonomy and relatedness in cultural context. Implications for self and family. *Journal of Cross-Cultural Psychology, 36,* 403–22.

    (2006). An overview of acculturation and parent-child relationships. In M. H. Bornstein and L. R. Cote (Eds.), *Acculturation and parent-child relationships: Measurement and development* (pp. 319–22). Mahwah, NJ: Lawrence Erlbaum Associates.

    (2007). *Family, self, and human development across cultures: Theory and applications.* Mahwah, NJ: Lawrence Erlbaum Associates.

Kağitçibaşi, C., Sunar, D., & Bekman, S. (2001). Long-term effects of early intervention: Turkish low-income mothers and children. *Journal of Applied Development Psychology, 22,* 333–61.

Kağitçibaşi, C., Sunar, D., Bekman, S., Baydar, N., & Cemalcilar, Z. (2009). Continuing effects of early intervention in adult life: The Turkish Early Enrichment Project 22 years later. *Journal of Applied Developmental Psychology*. doi:10.1016/j. appdev.2009.05.003

Kakar, S. (1978). *The inner world: A psychoanalytic study of childhood and society in India*. Oxford: Oxford University Press.

Kaya, A. (2001). *"Zicher in Kreuzberg" Constructing diasporas: Turkish hip-hop youth in Berlin*. London: Transaction.

Kim, U., Park, Y-S., Kwon, Y-E., & Koo, J. (2005). Values of children, parent-child relationship, and social change in Korea : Indigenous, cultural, and psychological analysis. *Applied Psychology: An International Review, 54*, 338–55.

Kim, Y., Butzel, J. S., & Ryan, R. M. (1998). Interdependence and well-being: A function of culture and relatedness needs. Paper presented at The International Society for the Study of Personal Relationships, Saratoga Spring, NY.

Kitayama, S., Duffy, S., & Uchida, Y. (2007). Self as cultural mode of being. In S. Kitayama and D. Cohen (Eds.), *Handbook of cultural psychology* (pp. 136–74). New York: Guilford Press.

Kitayama, S., Markus, H. R., Kurokawa, M., Tummala, P., & Kato, K. (1991). Self-other similarity judgments depend on culture. University of Oregon, Institute of Cognitive Decision Sciences, Technical Report, No. 91–17.

Korenman, S., Miller, J., & Sjaastad, J. (1995). Long-term poverty and child development in the United States: Results from the NLSY. *Children and Youth Services Review, 17*, 127–155.

Koutrelakos, J. (2004). Acculturation of Greek Americans: Change and continuity in cognitive schemas guiding intimate relationships. *International Journal of Psychology, 39*, 95–105.

Kroger, J. (1998). Adolescence as a second separation-individuation process: Critical review of an object relations approach. In E. E. A. Skoe and A. L.von der Lippe (Eds.), *Personality development in adolescence: A cross-national and life span perspective. Adolescence and society* (pp. 172–92). New York: Routledge.

Kwak, K. (2003). Adolescents and their parents: A review of intergenerational family relations for immigrant and non-immigrant families. *Human Development, 46*, 15–36.

Lansford, J. E., Deater-Deckard, K., Dodge, K. A., Bates, J. E., & Pettit, G. S. (2003). Ethnic differences in the link between physical discipline and later adolescent externalizing behaviors. *Journal of Child Psychology and Psychiatry, 44*, 1–13.

Lau, S., Lew, W. J. F., Hau, K. T., Cheung, P. C., & Berndt, T. J. (1990). Relations among perceived parental control, warmth, indulgence, and family harmony of Chinese in Mainland China. *Developmental Psychology, 26*, 674–7.

Lee, V., & Croninger, R. (1994). The relative importance of home and school in the development of literacy skills for middle-grade students. *American Journal of Education, 102*, 286–329.

Leseman, P. (1993). How parents provide young children with access to literacy. In L. Eldering and P. Leseman (Eds.), *Early intervention and culture* (pp. 149–72). The Hague: UNESCO.

Leyendecker, B., Schöelmerich, A., & Citlak, B. (2006). Similarities and differences between first- and second-generation Turkish migrant mothers in Germany: The acculturation gap. M. H. Bornstein and L. R. Cote (Eds.), *Acculturation and parent-child relationships: Measurement and development* (kitabında) (pp. 297–315). Mahwah, NJ: Lawrence Erlbaum.

Liebkind, K. (2001). Acculturation. In R. Brown and S. Gaertner (Eds.) *Blackwell handbook of social psychology: Intergroup Processes* (pp. 386–406). Oxford: Blackwell.

Lin, C-Y. C. & Fu, V. R. (1990). A comparison of child-rearing practices among Chinese, immigrant Chinese, and Caucasian-American parents. *Child Development, 61,* 429–33.

Mahler, M. (1972). On the first three phases of the separation-individuation process. *International Journal of Psychoanalysis, 53,* 333–8.

Mahler, M., Pine, F., & Bergman, A. (1975). *The psychological birth of the human infant.* New York: Basic Books.

Malewska-Peyre, H. (1980). *Conflictual cultural identity of second generation immigrants.* Paper presented at the Workshop on Cultural Identity and Structural Marginalization of Migrant Workers, European Science Foundation.

Markus, H. R., & Kitayama, S. (1991). Culture and the self: Implications for cognition, emotion, and motivation. *Psychological Review, 98,* 224–53.

    (2004). Models of agency: Sociocultural diversity in the construction of action. In V. Murphy-Berman and J. J. Berman (Eds.), *Cross-cultural differences in perspectives on the shelf* (Vol. 49, pp. 1–57). Lincoln University of Nebraska Press.

Mead, G. H. (1934). *Mind, Self and Society.* Chicago: University of Chicago Press.

Meeus, W., Oosterweegel, A., & Vollebergh, W. (2002). Parental and peer attachment and identity development in adolescence. *Journal of Adolescence, 25,* 93–106.

Montreuil, A., & Bourhis, R. Y. (2001). Majority acculturation orientations toward "valued" and "devalued" immigrants. *Journal of Cross-Cultural Psychology, 32,* 698–719.

Neubauer, G., & Hurrelmann, K. (1995). Introduction: Comments on the individualization theorem. In G. Neubauer and K. Hurrelmann (Eds.), *Individualization in childhood and adolescence* (pp. 1–12). Berlin: Walter de Groyter.

Nunes, T. (1993). Psychology in Latin America: The case of Brazil. *Psychology and Developing Societies, 5,* 123–34.

Okagaki, L., & Sternberg, R. J. (1993). Parental beliefs and children's school performance. *Child Development, 64,* 36–56.

Peralta de Mendoza, O. A., & Irice, R. A. (1995). Developmental changes and socioeconomic differences in mother-infant picture book reading. *European Journal of Psychology of Education, 10,* 261–72.

Phalet, K. & Schonpflug, U. (2001). Intergenerational transmission of collectivism and achievement values in two acculturation contexts: The case of Turkish families in Germany and Turkish and Moroccan families in the Netherlands. *Journal of Cross-Cultural Psychology, 32,* 186–201.

Phalet, K. & Swyngedouw, M. (2004). A cross-cultural analysis of immigrant and host acculturation and value orientations. In H. Vinken, G. Soeters, and P. Ester (Eds.), *Comparing cultures* (pp. 183–212). Leiden: Brill.

Raeff, C. (1997). Individuals in relationships: Cultural values, children's social interactions, and the development of an American individualistic self. *Developmental Review, 17,* 205–38.

Rank, O. (1945). *Will therapy and Truth and reality.* New York: Knopf.

Rohner, R. P. & Pettengill, S. M. (1985). Perceived parental acceptance-rejection and parental control among Korean adolescents. *Child Development*, *56*, 524–8.

Roland, A. (1988). *In search of self in India and Japan*. Princeton: Princeton University Press.

Rosenthal, R., & Jacobson, L. (1968). *Pygmalion in the classroom: Teacher expectation and pupils' intellectual development*. New York, US: Holt, Rinehart & Winston, Inc.

Rothbaum, F., & Trommsdorff, G. (2007). Do roots and wings complement or oppose one another? The socialization of relatedness and autonomy in cultural context. In J. Grusec and P. Hastings (Eds.), *The handbook of socialization: Theory and research* (pp. 461–89). New York: Guilford Press.

Rudy, D., & Grusec, J. E. (2001). Correlates of authoritarian parenting in individualist and collectivist cultures and implications for understanding the transmission of values. *Journal of cross-cultural psychology*, *32*, 202–12.

Ryan, R. M., & Deci, E. L. (2000). Self-determination theory and the facilitation of intrinsic motivation, social development, and well-being. *American Psychologist*, *55*, 68–78.

Ryan, R. M., Deci, E. L., & Grolnick, W. S. (1995). Autonomy, relatedness, and the Self: Their relation to development and psychopathology. In D. Cicchetti & D. J. Cohen (Eds.), *Developmental psychopathology* (pp. 618–55). NY: Wiley.

Ryan, R. M., & Lynch, J. H. (1989). Emotional autonomy versus detachment: Revisiting the vicissitudes of adolescence and young adulthood. *Child Development*, *60*, 340–56.

Sam, D., & Berry, J. W. (Eds.) (2006). *Cambridge handbook of acculturation psychology*. Cambridge: Cambridge University Press.

Savasir, I., Sezgin, N., & Erol, N. (1992). 0–6 Yas Cocuklari icin gelisim tarama envanteri gelistirilmesi. (devising a developmental screening inventory for 0–6 year children). *Türk Psikiyatri Dergisi (Turkish Psychiatry Journal)*, *3*, 33–8.

Schalk-Soekar, R. G. S., & van de Vijver, F. J. R. (2004). Attitudes toward multiculturalism of immigrants and majority members in the Netherlands. *International Journal of Intercultural Relations*, *28*, 533–50.

Segall, M. H., Dasen, P. R., Berry, J. W., & Poortinga, Y. H. (1999). *Human behavior in global perspective. An introduction to cross-cultural psychology*. 2nd ed. Boston: Allyn and Bacon.

Senecal, M., & Le Fevre, J. A. (2002). Parental involvement in the development of children's reading skill: A five-year longitudinal study. *Child Development*, *73*, 445–60.

Shweder, R. A. (1991). *Thinking through cultures: Expeditions in cultural psychology*. Cambridge, MA: Harvard University Press.

Silk, J. S., Morris, A. S., Kanaya, T., & Steinberg, L. (2003). Psychological control and autonomy granting: Opposite ends of a continuum or distinct constructs? *Journal of Research on Adolescence*, *13*, 113–28.

Singelis, T. M. (1994). The measurement of independent and interdependent self-construals. *Personality and Social Psychology Bulletin*, *20*, 580–91.

Smetana, J., & Gaines, C. (1999). Adolescent-parent conflict in middle class African American families, *Child Development*, *70*, 1447–63.

Steinberg, L., & Silverberg, S. B. (1986). The vicissitudes of autonomy in early adolescence. *Child Development*, *57*, 841–51.

Stewart, S. M., Bond, M. H., Deeds, O. & Chung, S. F. (1999). Intergenerational patterns of values and autonomy expectations in cultures of relatedness and separateness. *Journal of Cross-Cultural Psychology, 30,* 575–93.

Triandis, H. C. (1990). Cross-cultural studies of individualism and collectivism. In J. J. Berman (Ed.). *Cross-cultural perspectives: Nebraska Symposium on Motivation* (pp. 41–134). Lincoln: University of Nebraska Press.

(1995). *Individualism and Collectivism.* Boulder, CO: Westview Press.

Trommsdorff, G. (1985). Some comparative aspects of socialization in Japan and Germany. I. R. Lagunes and Y. H. Poortinga (Ed.), *From a different perspective: Studies of behavior across cultures* (pp. 231–40). Lisse, Netherlands: Swets and Zeitlinger.

Trommsdorff, G. & Nauck, B. (Eds.) 2005. *The value of children in cross-cultural perspective: case studies from eight societies.* Berlin: Pabst.

Tönnies, F. (1957). *Community and society.* (C. P. Loomis, translator) East Lansing: Michigan State Press.

Van Tuijl, C., & Leseman, P. P. M. (2004). Improving mother-child interaction in low-income Turkish-Dutch families: A study of mechanisms mediating improvements resulting from participating in a home-based preschool intervention program. *Infant and Child Development, 13,* 323–40.

Ward, C. (2001). The A, B, Cs of Acculturation. In D. Matsumoto (Ed.), *The handbook of culture and psychology* (pp. 411–46). Oxford: Oxford University Press.

Ward, C., & Kennedy, A. (1992). Locus of control, mood disturbance and social difficulty during cross-cultural transitions. *International Journal of Intercultural Relations, 16,* 175–94.

Weisner, T. S. (2002). Ecocultural pathways, family values, and parenting. *Parenting: Science and practice, 2,* 325–34.

Yamagishi, T. (2002). The structure of trust: An evolutionary game of mind and society. *Hokkaido Behavioral Science Report, SP-13,* 1–157.

12 Thriving Among Immigrant Youth

Theoretical and Empirical Bases of Positive Development

Richard M. Lerner, Jacqueline V. Lerner, Edmond P. Bowers, and Selva Lewin-Bizan

Introduction

The positive or productive development of youth is a key focus of the contemporary study of adolescence (J. Lerner et al., 2009; Steinberg & Lerner, 2004). Based on the assumption that all young people have strengths, the "positive youth development" (PYD) perspective seeks to identify the individual attributes of youth that, when coupled with resources for healthy growth present in their social ecologies (e.g., their families, schools, faith institutions, or community-based youth programs), lead to thriving (i.e., to well-being and health) across the adolescent decade (e.g., Lerner, 2009). PYD is often operationalized by "Five Cs,": competence, confidence, connection, character, and caring (e.g., Eccles & Gootman, 2002; R. Lerner et al., 2005; Roth & Brooks-Gunn, 2003). The PYD perspective also includes the idea that the development of these Five Cs leads to the emergence of a "Sixth C," that is, youth contributions to their family, community, and society (Lerner, 2004; Zaff et al., 2010a). For instance, a positive developing young person may productively contribute to his or her context through enhancing the economic welfare of his or her family or community or by engaging positively with civil society or democratic institutions (Zaff et al., 2010a).

The PYD perspective is framed by a relational developmental systems model of human development (e.g., Overton, 2006, 2010); such models emphasize that mutually-influential relations between an individual and his or her contexts (represented as individual ←→ relations) constitute the fundamental process of human development across the life span. Methodologically, the perspective emphasizes that longitudinal research that involves change-sensitive measures and data analysis techniques is necessary to study this relational change process (Lerner, Schwartz, & Phelps, 2009).

Although the study of immigrant youth has not been a central focus of past scholarship pertinent to formulating or testing the PYD perspective (Forman et al., 2009; J. Lerner et al., 2009), extant theory and research about the development of immigrant youth is in fact consistent with many of the ideas associated with the PYD perspective. Indeed, we believe that more purposeful attention to immigrant youth by scholars using a PYD perspective could significantly extend the usefulness of the PYD approach to youth development and could enhance the understanding of the strengths and productivity of adolescent immigrants.

Accordingly, one goal of this chapter is to discuss the existing, but perhaps not often recognized, intersection that already exists between PYD-related scholarship and the literature on immigrant youth. Baltes (1997; Baltes, Lindenberger, & Staudinger, 2006) noted that many models used to study development (e.g., the life-span perspective) are not new viewpoints, in the sense of introducing ideas that cannot be found individually within other models of development. However, he noted that what might make a model useful is that the set of ideas it uses are uniquely integrated within it. The presence of such an integration within a given model can offer new interpretations, hypotheses, or research agendas.

The situation described by Baltes exists for the PYD perspective. Any of the ideas within it can be traced to different facets of the human behavior and development literature (e.g., see Lerner, 2002, 2004). However, the PYD perspective may be useful in that it offers an integration of these ideas not found in other approaches. Indeed, because, as we hope to illustrate, many of the ideas within the PYD perspective find voice within the literature about immigrant youth, it may be that a research agenda that explicitly capitalizes on these points of intersection could be of value in advancing both literatures. Accordingly, a second goal of this chapter is to suggest some components of a research agenda that could have these benefits.

To attain these goals we will discuss first the scholarship about immigrant youth that speaks to their strengths and to features of their positive development. This discussion will illustrate the already substantial points of intersection between the study of immigrant youth and the ideas found within the PYD perspective, at least as instantiated by extant longitudinal research framed by relational developmental systems theory and by the study of the Cs of PYD (e.g., Lerner, 2007; Lerner et al., 2005). We will then discuss some ideas for future research that would make the study of immigrant youth an explicit part of the agenda of the longitudinal research of PYD scholars.

Our hope is that we will propose ideas useful for new research directed to enriching empirical knowledge of how immigrant youth may thrive across their adolescent years.

The Strengths and Productive Development of Immigrant Youth

In a sense, the fundamental developmental task of an immigrant youth is to manifest positive development in his or her new national context. For both their own health and positive adaptation and for the welfare of their new country, immigrants to any nation have the need to understand how to build a positive future for themselves in their new country (Strohmeier & Schmitt-Rodermund, 2008; see too Fuligni & Telzer, this volume; Hernandez, this volume). Arguably, these challenges may be especially complicated in adolescence, when adjustments also have to be made to changing physiological, cognitive, emotional, and social relational characteristics.

Suárez-Orozco, Todorova, and Qin (2006) suggest that relatively little explicit empirical attention has been paid to the psychological well-being of immigrant youth. To the extent that this lacuna in the literature exists, it provides a rationale for making the study of immigrant youth an explicit focus within scholarship about PYD. In addition, the appropriateness of studying immigrant youth through use of a PYD perspective is underscored by what we believe is the considerable literature already available about the strengths of immigrant youth, and the consistency between this work with many of the ideas in the literature that discuss the nature of positive development among children and adolescents (e.g., Forman et al., 2009; Larson, 2000; Lerner, 2009; Masten et al., 2009).

For instance, scholarship about the acculturation of immigrant youth (e.g., Berry, 1997; Berry & Sam, 1997; Jensen, 2010a; Kağıtçıbaşı, 2007; Liebkind, 2006, 2009; Liebkind, Jasinskaja-Lahti, & Solheim, 2004; Sam, 2006; Ward, 2001) suggests that these young people have marked strengths and that they manifest characteristics that are indictors of PYD, as, for example, defined by Eccles and Gootman (2002), Lerner et al. (2005), and Roth and Brooks-Gunn (2003). For instance, Kağıtçıbaşı (2007, this volume) notes that nurturing the development of an autonomous but socially related sense of self among immigrant youth would promote well-being and psychological adaptation – two indicators of what many contemporary scholars studying adolescent development regard as reflective of positive development or thriving (e.g., J. Lerner et al., 2009). Similarly, Liebkind (2006, 2009; Liebkind et al., 2004; see too Liebkind, Jasinskaja-Lahti, & Mähönen, this volume; Verkuyten, this volume) provides empirical evidence for the value of a transcultural or bicultural and integrated identity for the acculturation and adjustment of immigrant youth.

Longitudinal, cross-national research (that employs, as we will suggest later, measures that have equivalence across age levels and a broad array of demographic marker variables, for example, religion, sex, ethnicity, and race) is needed to elucidate the processes through which these features of identity among immigrant youth emerge. Nevertheless, it is possible to conclude that such integrated identities among immigrant youth covary with positive psychological and social functioning and constitute strengths that afford resilience in the face of the quite evident adjustment challenges faced by these youth (e.g., Fuligni, 1998; Greenman & Xie, 2008; Liebkind, 2009; Masten, 2006, 2009; Masten et al., 2009; Mirsky & Peretz, 2006; Sirin & Fine, 2008; Strohmeier & Schmitt-Rodermund, 2008; Vazsonyi, Trejos-Castillo, & Huang, 2006; Yu et al., 2003).

Research about the "immigrant advantage" also underscores the potential strengths of immigrant youth and points to indicators of their positive development that align with the constructs (i.e., with several of the Cs) studied within the PYD perspective. For instance, in regard to the "C" of competence, Fuligni, Hughes, and Way (2009) reviewed research that shows that first- and second-generation youth achieve academically either at a level comparable to or, in some cases, better than, peers of third-generation immigrant status (e.g., Fuligni, 1997; Kao & Tienda, 1995; see too García-Coll et al., this volume).

In turn, however, Fuligni et al. (2009) noted that immigrant groups vary in regard to the presence of an immigrant advantage among youth. For instance, Asian immigrants may be more likely to manifest this advantage in academic achievement than is the case for immigrant Latino youth (e.g., Fuligni, 1997; Kao & Tienda, 1995). In fact, within the United States, there are few generational differences in drop out rates among immigrant Latino youth (e.g., Perreira, Harris, & Lee, 2006). Nevertheless, Fuligni et al. (2009) noted that there is also within-group variation. For instance, Latino immigrant youth from South America or Cuba will likely score more highly on indicators of the "C" of (academic) competence (academic achievement, enrollment in college) than Latino immigrant youth from Mexico or Central America (e.g., Portes & Rumbaut, 2001). Similarly, Fuligni et al. (2009) noted that the academic achievement of immigrant Chinese or Korean youth exceeds that of Hmong or Lao immigrant youth.

The variation discussed by Fuligni et al. (2009) allows us to point to one way in which scholarship about the PYD perspective might be interrelated usefully with the study of immigrant youth. Much of the longitudinal research involved in testing or refining ideas associated with the PYD perspective (e.g., Bowers et al., 2010; Lerner et al., 2005; Phelps et al., 2007; Phelps et al., 2009), focuses on interindividual differences in intraindividual change. The prototypic question here has been "What biopsychosocial features of what groups of individuals, and what features of their ecological settings, are associated with what trajectories of PYD?" As such, the variations across and within racial and ethnic groups in the immigrant advantage reviewed by Fuligni et al. (2009) could be elucidated by PYD-oriented longitudinal research that asked a comparable multipart question such as "What features of the immigrant experience, of what immigrant groups, from what countries of origin and in what new national settings, result in what levels of what indicators of achievement at what points in generational and ontogenetic time?"

There are other possible points of intersection between the literatures on immigrant youth and the PYD literature that are suggested by this within- and between-group variation in indicators of immigrant youth academic competence. Within this literature are findings that underscore that both individual and contextual variables provide bases of their successful functioning, not only in regard to the "C" of competence but in respect to other facets of PYD. For instance, and consistent with the work of Liebkind (2006, 2009; see too Liebkind et al., this volume) and Kağıtçıbaşı (2007, this volume) in regard to the facilitative role of transcultural or bicultural integrative identities for the successful development of immigrant youth, individual differences among immigrant youth in personological variables such as positive ethnic identity (Fuligni, Witkow, & Garcia, 2005; Yip, 2005; Yip & Fuligni, 2002) and comfort with both the culture of origin and with the new cultural/national setting (Berry et al., 2006) are linked to school engagement and to indicators of positive psychological and social functioning (i.e., with indicators of the Cs of confidence and connection). In turn, contextual variables related to socioeconomic status are related to more positive behavior and development among immigrant youth.

Another example of the potential use of integrating the study of immigrant youth with research about PYD derives from the burgeoning interest in the civic engagement and civic participation of immigrant youth (e.g., Abo-Zena, 2010; Jensen, 2010a; Jensen, 2010b; Jensen & Flanagan, 2008). As we have noted, a key hypothesis within the PYD perspective is that as a result of developing the "Five Cs" of competence, confidence, character, connection, and caring, adolescents will develop a sixth C of contribution, which may be manifested by behaviors directed to enhancing families, schools, and communities. Civic engagement and positive civic activities have been seen as important indicators of community contribution (Bobek et al., 2009: Zaff et al., 2010a; Zaff et al., 2010b). Although some scholars studying immigrant youth have hypothesized that a question exists about the commitment of immigrant youth to act to support civil society in their new national context (e.g., see Abo-Zena, 2010; Jensen, 2010b, for reviews), research summarized by Jensen (2010a) indicates that in late adolescence both immigrant and native-born youth have high levels of civic involvement and that few differences exist in regard to indicators of civic or political engagement (Stepick, Stepick, & Labissiere, 2008). Similarly, Lopez and Marcelo (2008) found that few differences existed among first- or second-generation immigrants and native-born youth (aged 15 to 25 years) in civic or political activity.

Moreover, and consistent with the work of Jasinskaja-Lahti, Liebkind, & Perhoniemi (2007), the civic contributions of immigrant youth are underlain by the fact that their bilingual and bicultural skills constitute an important resource for their new communities (Stepick et al., 2008). In addition, and consistent with the links between a transcultural or bicultural and integrated identity and thriving among immigrant youth (Liebkind, 2006, 2009; Liebkind et al., 2004; Kağıtçıbaşı, 2007), Jensen (2010a) suggests that possession of what she terms a cultural identity (of the sort described by Liebkind and colleagues and by Kağıtçıbaşı, this volume) is a pathway to positive civic and political engagement and is not an encumbrance to positive civic engagement. Indeed, Jensen (2010a) notes that such an integrative personal orientation is associated empirically with immigrant youth being substantially more likely to be engaged civically. In fact, this integrated identity is a source of resilience among immigrant youth who have experienced discrimination. For instance, Junn and Masuoka (2008) reported that such identities are sources not only of positive self- and group-regard but of actions that push back against the experience of discrimination.

In sum, from a PYD perspective, the literature on the nature of civic engagement and civic contribution of immigrant youth points to both the presence of the "C" of contribution and to the possession by immigrant youth of the Cs of confidence and character (e.g., see Jensen, 2010b; Jensen & Flanagan, 2008). Indeed, research about immigrant youth by Abo-Zena (2010) and by Forman et al. (2009), studies that explicitly used the PYD perspective as a frame for studying these young people, found that immigrant youth were thriving and, as well, contributing to their communities at levels commensurate with nonimmigrant youth. Furthermore, both the civic engagement facet of the literature on immigrant youth, as well as the other portions of this literature that we have briefly noted, suggest that the PYD perspective can do more than just use a new vocabulary (e.g., the Cs of PYD) to discuss the strengths of immigrant youth. We believe that our examples also suggest that embedding more prominently the study of immigrant youth within scholarship about PYD may enhance understanding of the bases of thriving among such youth. To explore this suggestion, we now turn to a discussion of how the ideas about the process of development found within the PYD perspective might be used to further the study of immigrant youth.

The Positive Youth Development Perspective and the Study of Immigrant Youth: Features of a Possible Research Agenda

A first, key contribution that may be made by the PYD perspective in regard to the study of thriving among immigrant youth involves the methodological implications derived from the emphasis on not just change but, more specifically, on individual ←→ context, relational change within the PYD perspective (Lerner, 2004, 2009). This contribution rests on the necessary inclusion in research of designs sensitive to the study of such change (i.e., researchers need to use one or another type of a longitudinal design; Collins, 2006; Lerner et al., 2009) and, as well, on the use within these designs of change-sensitive measures and data analysis techniques. If the goal of research about immigrant youth is to understand how they may thrive in the face of the national and cultural transitions they and their families may make, then such studies must be change-sensitive in all of these respects.

Moreover, from the standpoint of measurement, the measures used to study immigrant youth must provide psychometrically equivalent information (i.e., "measurement equivalence") across the points in ontogeny that are studied. Furthermore, such measures must show sensitivity to, for instance, the cultural, racial, ethnic, gender, sex, and religious characteristics of the samples of immigrant youth being studied. As we have already noted, the PYD perspective emphasizes the importance and substantive meaningfulness of diversity – of both intraindividual variation in development across sampled points in ontogeny and of between-person differences in such intraindividual change – a significance that arises as a consequence of young people's specific history of individual ←→ context relations within the development system (Lerner, 2009).

Accordingly, and perhaps especially when the study of immigrant youth involves comparisons among groups (e.g., see Fuligni et al., 2009), researchers must establish that there is measurement equivalence across all instances of diversity (age, plus some or all of the other demographic characteristics) involved in studying the groups of immigrant youth. From our perspective, much of the research on immigrant youth has not included these features of longitudinal study with measures that possess demonstrated sensitivity to change and that have proven psychometric equivalence across groups. As such, integrating the methodological approaches of researchers studying immigrant youth and researchers studying PYD more generally may be of benefit to enhancing the precision of the data about the development of these young people.

To illustrate this potential usefulness we may note that establishing point-in-time equivalence among measures is a formidable task. Establishing that there is measurement equivalence across trajectories of change (derived from scores from the repeated administration of measures) is a much more complicated task. Nevertheless, it is a task central to researchers studying the thriving process among immigrant youth. It is a task for which there are not abundant examples within the literature about immigrant youth. However, researchers studying PYD have generated several data sets successfully demonstrating measurement equivalence (e.g., Bowers et al., 2010; Gestsdóttir et al., 2009; Phelps, et al., 2009; Zaff et al., 2010b). Collaboration between researchers from the fields studying PYD and immigrant youth might, therefore, be useful in addressing these measurement challenges.

In addition, a second area of useful collaboration between scholars from these two fields of research would be greater elucidation of the details of the relational developmental process. As implied earlier in regard to the multipart question we suggested as useful for the longitudinal study of immigrant youth, the relational developmental systems model of youth development framing the PYD perspective would suggest that several features of individuals and of their context should be related within and, critically, across time in order to provide greater understanding of the process of development. That is, the PYD perspective uses a model of development that involves emphasis on the study of *relations* between individuals and setting, and not on the components of these relations per se (Overton, 2006, 2010). The stage-environment fit concept of Eccles (2004) is a case in point of such a relational approach. In addition, the model anticipates that nonrecursive relations will characterize change, as variables from individual and contextual settings interrelate across time and encounter normative and non-normative life and historical events that alter the trajectory of the life course (Baltes et al., 2006; Elder, 1998; Elder & Shanahan, 2006). Third, the model anticipates that relations across time will involve developmental cascades, wherein qualitatively different variables, existing within and across levels of organization within the development system, will interrelate to shape the pathways and outcomes of development (e.g., Masten et al., 2005; Masten & Cicchetti, 2010a, 2010b, 2010c).

Of course, as already implied by our acknowledgment that none of the ideas within the PYD perspective are unique to it, the study of immigrant youth has information about all three of these facets of the change process used to understand development within the PYD perspective (e.g., Jensen, 2010b; Jasinskaja-Lahti & Liebkind, 2007; see too, Liebkind et al., this volume). However, we believe that fruitful new work could be produced by designing and implementing new, longitudinal studies of immigrant youth that gathered psychometrically appropriate data (in the sense explained earlier) intended to elucidate all three of these facets of developmental process: relational change, nonrecursive change, and cascading change.[1]

Third, the PYD perspective could suggest some of the substantive instantiations of the variables included in change-oriented studies aimed at elucidating the individual ←→ context relations that provide the bases for and shape the course of thriving among immigrant youth. In addition, based on extant research about PYD (e.g., J. Lerner et al., 2009), the variables suggested for inclusion may be coupled with hypotheses about their role in the thriving process among immigrant youth.

For instance, Benson et al. (2006) have noted that it is possible to identify in every context within which youth exist (e.g., families, schools, and communities) specific resources – which are termed "developmental assets" – that, when linked to the strengths of youth, foster their positive development. Examples are mentors, out-of-school time programs, and access to high-quality classroom environments (Theokas & Lerner, 2006; see too Horenczyk & Tatar, this volume). However, Theokas and Lerner (2006) found that in every setting within which youth spent their time, the key developmental assets (the assets accounting for the most variance in scores for PYD) were other people – that is, adults who spend high quantities of high-quality time with youth (for instance, mentors in after-school programs, leaders of faith institutions, coaches of sports teams, classroom teachers, and of course parents). Given these findings, we could hypothesize that the presence of mentors in the pre- and post-country transitions of

---

[1] Together, these three facets of developmental change operationalize (from a measurement standpoint) emergent (or probabilistic epigenetic) change, which is a fundamental feature of development within relational developmental systems theories (e.g., Gottlieb, 1997, 1998; Lerner, 2002; Overton, 2006, 2010).

immigrant youth can be a significant moderator of the form and outcome of their trajectories of thriving.

To illustrate, one could hypothesize that the presence of mentors who express positive regard for bicultural integration could be a key developmental asset promoting thriving across the natural ecological settings of youth. In addition, such mentorship could be a key predictor of positive civic engagement and civil contribution (Oman, Flinders, & Thoresen, 2008). Research testing these hypotheses would involve longitudinal assessment of the presence and impact on youth ←→ mentor relations prior to and after the transition to the new national setting by the young person, that is, longitudinal research should include the preimmigration stage.

In addition, research pertinent to the PYD perspective points to variables that usefully operationalize the strengths of youth in that they identify a set of actions that locate and secure access to the developmental assets needed for thriving. For instance, Urban, Lewin-Bizan, and Lerner (2010) studied several characteristics of intentional self-regulation, attributes measured by youth abilities to select meaningful, positive goals; to possess executive functions (e.g., planning skills) or resource recruitment strategies to optimize the chances of attaining these goals; and to have the ability to compensate effectively when goals are blocked or when initial strategies fails (Freund & Baltes, 2002; Gestsdóttir et al., 2009). Urban et al. (2010) found that, when these indicators of intentional self-regulation were linked to developmental assets, youth thriving occurred. Given the empirical link between these self-regulation skills and PYD, studies of immigrant youth could ascertain whether the development of these skills (e.g., as operationalized by scores for selection, optimization, and compensation), when manifested in the presence of high levels of availability of developmental assets (e.g., sustained access to high-quality mentors), was beneficial (in comparison of the expression of self-regulation in the presence of low levels of key developmental assets) in the fostering of thriving across adolescence.

Accordingly, researchers studying PYD and immigrant youth could collaborate in longitudinal, relational studies of the impact for thriving of constancy or change in the links between self-regulation skills and developmental assets across the country of origin and the new national setting. Moreover, such research could use as indicators of thriving psychometrically equivalent measures of thriving and of its consequences (i.e., of the Five Cs and of youth contribution or civic engagement, respectively) that would afford the ability to relate the findings of such research to existing literature about PYD, some of which already includes data about the Five Cs and contribution among immigrant youth (e.g., Abo-Zena, 2010; Forman, et al., 2009).

Finally, another way we believe that scholars studying immigrant youth and PYD may collaborate is in regard to developing evidence-based arguments for positive, strength-based, and inclusive national and international policies regarding immigrant youth (see too Garcia Coll, this volume; Nolan, this volume). Capitalizing on the existing and, we hope, soon to be developed intersections in the two areas of research, scholars studying PYD and immigrant youth could collaboratively advocate on the basis of sound developmental evidence that policy makers, when proposing actions regarding the education, welfare, and opportunities afforded to immigrant youth, should take into account their strengths and potentials for positive developmental trajectories.

These scholars can now point to research that underscores the strengths of immigrant youth, their potential for positive development, and the ways in which their arguably singular characteristics – for instance, their bilingualism, their biculturalism, and their integrated identities – have been assets for their communities and bases of their positive contributions to civil society. If collaborative research along the lines we have suggested is in fact conducted, we believe that an even more compelling evidentiary basis will be created for policies that are more socially just and potentially more likely to promote thriving for the diversity of immigrant young people around the world.

Conclusions

The current research literature about immigrant youth points to their impressive psychological, behavioral, and social strengths. In turn, although the study of immigrant youth has not been a central feature of research testing the positive youth development perspective, the few studies in this latter literature that have explicitly assessed the nature of PYD among immigrant adolescents (e.g., Abo-Zena, 2010; Forman et al., 2009) underscore the presence of important strengths among these young people. One goal of this chapter has been to point to the intersection of evidence about the strengths of immigrant youth that may be derived from these two literatures. A second goal has been to suggest how even greater understanding of the bases for thriving among immigrant youth can be ascertained by new research about the process of individual ↔ context relations that constitutes the pathways of development for these young people.

Greater understanding of the developmental process involved in the thriving of diverse young people is of course research that is of value beyond the halls of academe. The twenty-first century is a period of increasing immigration for virtually all nations. Accordingly, enhancing the knowledge base about the ways in which thriving occurs can also result in better ideas about how we can intervene to enhance the relations between immigrant youth and their community and national settings. Simply stated, the results of the relational developmental research agenda we have suggested could be readily applied in both policies and programs aimed at enhancing the life chances and civic contributions of immigrant youth. As such, the benefits of the sorts of collaborations we have pointed to may be important for the health and welfare of not only these youth but, perhaps as well, the nations within which they live.

Acknowledgments

The writing of this chapter was supported in part by grants from the National 4-H Council and the Thrive Foundation for Youth.

REFERENCES

Abo-Zena, M. (2010). *Another Form of Unpacking: Understanding the Role of Religion in the Well-Being and Contribution of Immigrant-Origin Versus Non-Immigrant Youth.* Unpublished dissertation. Medford, MA: Tufts University.

Baltes, P. B. (1997). On the incomplete architecture of human ontogeny: Selection, optimization, and compensation as foundations of developmental theory. *American Psychologist, 52,* 366–80.

Baltes, P. B., Lindenberger, U., & Staudinger, U. M. (2006). Lifespan theory in developmental psychology. In R. M. Lerner (Ed.), *Handbook of child psychology: Vol. 1. Theoretical models of human development* (6th ed., pp. 569–664). Editors-in-chief: W. Damon and R. M. Lerner. Hoboken, NJ: Wiley.

Benson, P. L., Scales, P. C., Hamilton, S. F., & Sesma, A., Jr. (2006). Positive youth development: Theory, research, and applications. In R. M. Lerner (Ed.), *Handbook of child psychology: Vol. 1. Theoretical models of human development* (6th ed., pp. 894–941). Editors-in-chief: W. Damon and R. M. Lerner. Hoboken, NJ: Wiley.

Berry, J. W. (1997). Immigration, acculturation and adaptation. *Applied Psychology: An International Review, 46,* 5–68.

Berry, J. W., Phinney, J. S., Sam, D. L, & Vedder, P. (2006). Immigrant youth: Acculturation, identity, and adaptation. *Applied Psychology: An International Review, 55,* 303–32.

Berry, J. W., & Sam, D. L. (1997). Acculturation and adaptation. In J. W. Berry, M. H. Segall, and Ç. Kağıtçıbaşı (Eds.), *Handbook of cross-cultural psychology* (pp. 291–326). London: Allyn & Bacon.

Bobek, D. L., Zaff, J., Li, Y., & Lerner, R. M. (2009). Cognitive, emotional, and behavioral components of civic action: Towards an integrated measure of civic engagement. *Journal of Applied Developmental Psychology, 30*(5), 615–27.

Bowers, E. P., Li, Y., Kiely, M. K., Brittian, A., Lerner, J. V., & Lerner, R. M. (2010). The Five Cs Model of Positive Youth Development: A longitudinal analysis of confirmatory factor structure and measurement invariance. *Journal of Youth and Adolescence*, *39*(7), 720–35.

Collins, L. M. (2006). Analysis of longitudinal data: The integration of theoretical model, temporal design, and statistical model. *Annual Review of Psychology, 57*, 505–28.

Eccles, J. S. (2004). Schools, academic motivation, and stage-environment fit. In R. M. Lerner and L. Steinberg (Eds.), *Handbook of Adolescent Psychology* (2nd ed., pp. 125–53). Hoboken NJ: John Wiley & Sons.

Eccles, J. S., & Gootman, J. A. (Eds.). (2002). *Community Programs to Promote Youth Development/Committee on Community-Level Programs for Youth*. Washington DC: National Academy Press.

Elder, G. H., Jr. (1998). The life course and human development. In W. Damon (Series Ed.) and R. M. Lerner (Vol. Ed.), *Handbook of child psychology: Vol. 1. Theoretical models of human development* (5th ed., pp. 939–91). New York: Wiley.

Elder, G. H., Jr. & Shanahan, M. J. (2006). The life course and human development. In R. M. Lerner (Ed.). *Theoretical models of human development. Vol. 1. Handbook of Child Psychology* (6th ed., pp. 665–715). Editors-in-chief: W. Damon and R. M. Lerner. Hoboken, NJ: Wiley.

Forman, Y., Kiely, M., Du, D., Carrano, J., & Lerner, R. M. (2009). We're here, we're hopeful, and we can do well: Conceptions and attributes of positive youth development among immigrant youth. *Journal of Youth Development, 4*(1). Doi: 090401FA001.

Freund, A. M., & Baltes, P. B. (2002). Life-management strategies of selection, optimization and compensation: Measurement by self-report and construct validity. *Journal of Personality and Social Psychology, 82*, 642–62.

Fuligni, A. J. (1997). The academic achievement of adolescents from immigrant families: The roles of family background, attitudes, and behavior. *Child Development, 68*, 261–73.

   (1998). The adjustment of children from immigrant families. *Current Directions in Psychological Science, 7*(4), 99–103.

Fuligni, A. J., Hughes, D. L., & Way, N. (2009). Ethnicity and immigration. In R. M. Lerner and L. Steinberg (Eds.), *Handbook of adolescent psychology* (3rd ed., pp. 527–69). Hoboken, NJ: Wiley.

Fuligni, A. J., Witkow, M., & Garcia, C. (2005). Ethnic identity and the academic adjustment of adolescents from Mexican, Chinese, and European backgrounds. *Developmental Psychology, 41*, 799–811.

Gestsdóttir, S., Lewin-Bizan, S., von Eye, A., Lerner, J. V., & Lerner, R. M. (2009). The structure and function of selection, optimization, and compensation in middle adolescence: Theoretical and applied implications. *Journal of Applied Developmental Psychology, 30*(5), 585–600.

Gottlieb, G. (1997). *Synthesizing nature-nurture: Prenatal roots of instinctive behavior*. Mahwah, NJ: Lawrence Erlbaum.

   (1998). Normally occurring environmental and behavioral influences on gene activity: From central dogma to probabilistic epigenesis. *Psychological Review, 105*, 792–802.

Greenman, E., & Xie, Y. (2008). Is assimilation theory dead? The effect of assimilation on adolescent well-being. *Social Science Research, 37*, 109–37.

Jasinskaja-Lahti, I., & Liebkind, K. (2007). Structural model of acculturation and well-being among immigrants from the former USSR in Finland. *European Psychologist, 12*(2), 80–92.

Jasinskaja-Lahti, I., Liebkind, K., & Perhoniemi, R. (2007). Perceived ethnic discrimination at work and well-being immigrants in Finland: The moderating role of employment status and work-specific group-level control beliefs. *International Journal of Intercultural Relations, 31*(2), 223–42.

Jensen, L. A. (2010a). Immigrant youth in the United States. Coming of age among diverse cultures. In L. R. Sherrod, J. Torney-Purta, and C. A. Flanagan (Eds.). *Handbook of research and policy on civic engagement in youth.* Hoboken, NJ: Wiley.

      (2010b). *Bridging cultural and developmental approaches to psychology: New syntheses in theory, research, and policy.* New York, NY: Oxford University Press.

Jensen, L. A., & Flanagan, C. A. (2008). Immigrant civic engagement: New translations. *Applied Developmental Science, 12*(2), 55–6.

Junn, J., & Masuoka, N. (2008). Identities in context: Politicized racial group consciousness among Asian American and Latino youth. *Applied Developmental Science, 12*(2), 93–101.

Kağıtçıbaşı, Ç. (Ed.). (2007). *Family, self, and human development across cultures: Theory and applications.* Mahwah, NJ: Lawrence Erlbaum Associates.

Kao, G., & Tienda, M. (1995). Optimism and achievement: The educational performance of immigrant youth. *Social Science Quarterly, 76,* 1–19.

Larson, R. (2000). Towards a psychology of positive youth development. *American Psychologist, 55,* 170–83.

Lerner, J. V., Phelps, E., Forman, Y. E., & Bowers, E. (2009). Positive youth development. In. R. M. Lerner and L. Steinberg (Eds.), *Handbook of adolescent psychology,* 3rd ed. (pp. 524–58). Hoboken, NJ: Wiley.

Lerner, R. M. (2002). *Concepts and theories of human development* (3rd ed.). Mahwah, NJ: Lawrence Erlbaum Associates.

      (2004). *Liberty: Thriving and civic engagement among American youth.* Thousand Oaks, CA: Sage.

      (2007). *The good teen: Rescuing adolescents from the myths of the storm and stress years.* New York, NY: The Crown Publishing Group.

      (2009). The positive youth development perspective: Theoretical and empirical bases of a strength-based approach to adolescent development. In C. R. Snyder and S. J. Lopez (Eds.), *Oxford handbook of positive psychology* (2nd ed., pp. 149–63). Oxford, England: Oxford University Press.

Lerner, R. M., Lerner, J. V., Almerigi, J., Theokas, C., Phelps, E., Gestsdóttir, S., Naudeau, S., Jeličić, H., Alberts, A. E., Ma, L., Smith, L. M., Bobek, D. L., Richman-Raphael, D. Simpson, I., Christiansen, E. D., `& von Eye, A. (2005). Positive youth development, participation in community youth development programs, and community contributions of fifth grade adolescents: Findings from the first wave of the 4-H Study of Positive Youth Development. *Journal of Early Adolescence, 25*(1), 17–71.

Lerner, R. M., Schwartz, S. J., & Phelps, E. (2009). Problematics of time and timing in the longitudinal study of human development: Theoretical and methodological issues. *Human Development, 52,* 44–68.

Liebkind, K. (2006). Ethnic identity and acculturation. In D. L. Sam and J. W. Berry (Eds.), *The Cambridge handbook of acculturation psychology* (pp. 78–96). Boston: Cambridge University Press.

(2009). Ethnic identity and acculturation. In I. Jasinskaja-Lahti and T. A. Mähönen (Eds.), *Identities, intergroup relations and acculturation: the cornerstones of intercultural encounters* (pp. 13–38). Helsinki: Gaudeamus Helsinki University Press.

Liebkind, K., Jasinskaja-Lahti, I., & Solheim, E. (2004). Cultural identity, perceived discrimination, and parental support as determinants of immigrants school adjustments: Vietnamese youth in Finland. *Journal of Adolescent Research, 19(6)*, 635–56.

Lopez, M. H., & Marcelo, K. B. (2008). The civic engagement of immigrant youth: New evidence from the 2006 Civic and Political Health of the Nation Survey. *Applied Developmental Science, 12(2)*, 66–73.

Masten, A. S. (2006). Developmental psychopathology: Pathways to the future. *International Journal of Behavioral Development, 31*, 47–54.

(2009). Ordinary Magic: Lessons from research on resilience in human development. *Education Canada, 49(3)*, 28–32.

Masten, A. S., & Cicchetti, D. (Eds.) (2010a). Developmental cascades [Special Issue, Part 1], *Development and Psychopathology, 22(3)*, 491–715.

Masten, A. S., & Cicchetti, D. (Eds.) (2010b). Developmental cascades [Special Issue, Part 2], *Development and Psychopathology, 22(4)*, 717–983.

Masten, A. S., & Cicchetti, D. (2010c). Editorial: Developmental cascades. Developmental cascades [Special Issue, Part 1], *Development and Psychopathology, 22(3)*, 491–5.

Masten, A. S., Cutuli, J. J., Herbers, J. E., & Gabrielle-Reed, M. J. (2009). Resilience in development. In C. R. Snyder & S. J. Lopez, (Eds.), *The Handbook of Positive Psychology (2nd ed.)* (pp. 117–31). New York: Oxford University Press.

Masten, A. S., Roisman, G. I., Long, J. D., Burt, K. B., Obradović, J., Riley, J. R., Boelcke-Stennes, K., & Tellegen, A. (2005). Developmental cascades: Linking academic achievement and externalizing and internalizing symptoms over 20 years. *Developmental Psychology, 41*, 733–46.

Mirsky, J., & Peretz, Y. (2006). Maturational opportunities in migration: Separation individuation perspective. *International Journal of Applied Psychoanalytic Studies, 3(1)*, 51–64.

Oman, D., Flinders, T., & Thoresen, C. E. (2008). Integrating spiritual modeling into education: A college course for stress management and spiritual growth. *International Journal for the Psychology of Religion, 18(2)*, 79–107.

Overton, W. F. (2006). Developmental psychology: Philosophy, concepts, methodology. In R. M. Lerner (Ed.). *Theoretical models of human development. Volume 1 of handbook of child psychology* (6th ed., pp. 18–88). Editors-in-chief: W. Damon and R. M. Lerner. Hoboken, NJ: Wiley.

(2010). Life-span development: Concepts and issues. In R. M. Lerner (Ed-in-chief) and W. F. Overton (Vol. Ed.), *The handbook of life-span development: Vol. 1. cognition, biology, and methods* (pp. 1–29). Hoboken, NJ: Wiley.

Perreira, K., Harris, K. M., & Lee, D. (2006). Making it in America: High school completion among immigrant youth. *Demography, 43*, 511–36.

Phelps, E., Balsano, A. B., Fay, K., Peltz, J. S., Zimmerman, S. M., Lerner, R. M., & Lerner, J. V. (2007). Nuances in early adolescent developmental trajectories of positive and problematic/risk behaviors: findings from the 4-H study of positive youth development. In N. Carrey, M. Ungar, and Martin, A. (Eds.), *Child and Adolescent Psychiatric Clinics of North America, 16(2)*, 473–96.

Phelps, E., Zimmerman, S., Warren, A. E. A., Jeličić, H., von Eye, A., & Lerner, R. M. (2009). The structure and developmental course of Positive Youth Development (PYD) in early adolescence: Implications for theory and practice. *Journal of Applied Developmental Psychology, 30*(5), 571–84.

Portes, A., & Rumbaut, R. G. (2001). *Legacies: The story of the second generation.* Berkeley: University of California Press.

Roth, J. L., & Brooks-Gunn, J. (2003). What exactly is a youth development program? Answers from research and practice. *Applied Developmental Science, 7,* 94–111.

Sam, D. L. (2006). Adaptation of children and adolescents with immigrant background: Acculturation of development? In M. H. Bornstein and L. R. Cote (Eds.), *Acculturation and parent-child relationships: Measurement and development* (pp. 97–111). Mahwah, NJ: Lawrence Erlbaum Associates.

Sirin, S., & Fine, M. (2008). *Muslim American youth: Understanding hyphenated identities through multiple methods.* New York: New York University Press.

Steinberg, L., & Lerner, R. M. (2004). The scientific study of adolescence: A brief history. *Journal of Early Adolescence, 24(1),* 45–54.

Stepick, A., Stepick, C. D., & Labissiere, Y. (2008). South Florida's immigrant youth and civic engagement: Major engagement: Minor differences. *Applied Developmental Science, 12*(2), 57–65.

Strohmeier, D., & Schmitt-Rodermund, E. (Eds.). (2008). Immigrant youth in European countries: The manifold challenges of adaptation. *European Journal of Developmental Psychology, 5*(2), 129–37.

Suárez-Orozco, C., Todorova, I. L. G., & Qin, D. B. (2006). The well-being of immigrant adolescents: A longitudinal perspective on risk and protective factors. In F. A. Villarruel, and T. Luster (Eds.), *The crisis in youth mental health: Critical issues and effective programs, Vol. 2: Disorders in adolescence* (pp. 53–83). Westport, CT: Praeger Publishers/Greenwood Publishing Group.

Theokas, C., & Lerner, R.M. (2006). Observed ecological assets in families, schools, and neighborhoods: Conceptualization, measurement and relations with positive and negative developmental outcomes. *Applied Developmental Science, 10*(2), 61–74.

Urban, J. B., Lewin-Bizan, S., & Lerner, R. M. (2010). The role of intentional self regulation, lower neighborhood ecological assets, and activity involvement in youth developmental outcomes. *Journal of Youth and Adolescence, 39*(7), 783–800.

Vazsonyi, A. T., Trejos-Castillo, E., Huang, L. (2006). Are developmental processes affected by immigration? Family processes, internalizing behaviors, and externalizing behaviors. *Journal of Youth and Adolescence, 35*(5), 799–813.

Ward, C. (2001). The A, B, Cs of acculturation. In D. Matsumoto (Ed.), *The handbook of culture and psychology* (pp. 411–46). Oxford, England: Oxford University Press.

Yip, T. (2005). Sources of situational variation in ethnic identity and psychological well-being: A palm pilot study of Chinese American students. *Personality and Social Psychology Bulletin, 31(12),* 1603–16.

Yip, T., & Fuligni, A. J. (2002). Daily variation in ethnic identity, ethnic behaviors, and psychological well-being among American adolescents of Chinese descent. *Child Development, 77,* 1504–72.

Yu, S. M., Huang, Z. J., Schwalbger, R. H., Overpeck, M., Kogan, M. D. (2003). Acculturation and the health and well-being of U.S. immigrant adolescents. *Journal of Adolescent Health, 33*(6), 479–48.

Zaff, J. F., Hart, D., Flanagan, C. A., Youniss, J., & Levine, P. (2010a). Developing civic engagement within a civic context. In M. E. Lamb and A. M. Freund (Eds.), *Social and emotional development: Vol. 2, Handbook of life-span development* (pp. 590–630). Editor in chief: R. M. Lerner. Hoboken, NJ: Wiley.

Zaff, J., Boyd, M., Li, Y., Lerner, J. V., & Lerner R. M. (2010b). Active and engaged citizenship: Multi-group and longitudinal factorial analysis of an integrated construct of civic engagement. *Journal of Youth and Adolescence, 39*(7), 736–50.

13 The Role of Developmental Transitions in Psychosocial Competence

A Comparison of Native and Immigrant Young People in Germany

Rainer K. Silbereisen, Peter F. Titzmann, Andrea Michel,
Abraham (Avi) Sagi-Schwartz, and Yoav Lavee

Introduction

Germany is a country of immigration, as evidenced by the fact that the nation hosts the third largest number of immigrants worldwide (for a comparative overview see Hernandez, this volume). About 18% of the population comes from a migration background (Statistisches Bundesamt [Federal Statistical Office], 2008). Among the immigrant population, three groups can be distinguished: economic migrants; diaspora or repatriate migrants of often distant German ethnicity (*Aussiedler*); and refugees. Due to the substantial and diverse migrant population of Germany, integration and educational success are issues of growing public concern. Social and cultural exclusion of population subgroups endangers societal cohesion (Woellert et al., 2009). There also are concerns about the impact of lower achievement of migrant youth in the educational system, higher representation of young migrants among delinquents, and a growing separation from the majority German population on religious grounds (Mueller, 2006). One of the underlying issues for developmental outcomes of migrant youth may be related to how immigrant groups deal with developmental transitions. For example, the lower attendance rate of immigrant children and the delayed transition from family care to kindergarten can be viewed as a missed opportunity for nonnative children to become familiar with their German peers, the German language, and native customs (B. Becker, 2010).

The aim of this chapter is to present the results of our research investigating the effects of positive developmental transitions on psychosocial developmental outcomes among immigrants compared to native-born young people. We focused on the five aspects of positive development known as the Five Cs – competence, confidence, connection, character, and caring (Lerner et al., 2005). More specifically, we examined whether the effects of developmental transitions are similar across ethnic groups or vary, for instance as a function of differences in family resources or culture. Beyond the institutionally formalized transitions to kindergarten and school, our research investigated more informal, personal transitions, such as to romantic involvement in adolescence and partnership in young adulthood.

The chapter is organized into four parts. First, after an introduction to the history of the ethnic groups studied, we provide the theoretical framework of the study, clarifying our perspective on the role of transitions for psychosocial development, providing details about the Five Cs, and summarizing the conceptual model and hypotheses that we tested. Second, we describe the methods. Third, we present a summary of results. Finally, we discuss our results in regard to their implications for positive development among natives and immigrants in Germany, and draw first conclusions for social policy.

Immigrant Groups in Germany
The largest group of immigrants in Germany are repatriate immigrants (*Aussiedler*) numbering about 4 million out of a population of 80 million (Woellert et al., 2009). Among this group, 2.5 million have settled since 1990, mostly from successor countries of the former Soviet Union. Despite having German ancestors and, under certain conditions, receiving German citizenship upon arrival, this group is primarily Russian-speaking and its members typically perceived as Russian by the general German public. The second largest group of immigrants, with about 3 million people, are those of Turkish origin whose families came as temporary migrant workers in the 1970s, but of whom half are now German-born (Woellert et al., 2009). Despite having resided in Germany for generations, most of the Turkish population is viewed as foreign by the public because of their non-Western religious and cultural background. In addition, there are immigrants with refugee status in Germany who come from several countries across the world. From this group, we focus on a rather small cluster of less than 250,000 Russian Jewish refugees from the former Soviet Union. Like the German repatriates, they enjoy privileges related to immigration, although to a lesser extent, but are not awarded automatic citizenship and are, like the Turkish group, considered foreign (Dietz, 2000).

Beyond the historical particularities mentioned, ethnic German, Turkish, and Russian Jewish immigrants vary notably in terms of acculturation and educational success, despite often extended periods of German residency (Nauck, 2001; Woellert et al., 2009). These differences have been the basis of discussion especially during the scientific and public debate following the mediocre performance of Germany in the 2003 Program for International Student Assessment (PISA), and in studies examining the academic success of immigrant groups (Woellert et al., 2009). For some immigrant groups, such as the Turks, the transition from primary to secondary school is particularly problematic. Their difficulty is attributed to the unique German secondary school model, which is known to result in an early differentiation (around age 10 or 11) of ultimate school success by economic and social background (Alba, Handl, & Müller, 1998; Baumert & Maaz, 2008). Interesting, among the relatively few admitted to the academic branch of secondary school, social background seems to play no further role in educational success (Baumert & Maaz, 2008).

Against this backdrop, the research consortium on "Migration and Societal Integration," which mainly comprises researchers from sociology and psychology, was established and funded by the German Federal Ministry of Education and Research (for more details see www.migration.uni-jena. de). The aim was to investigate the adaptation of various immigrant groups during times of developmental transitions in Germany and Israel. These two countries were chosen because the comparison was expected to help in exploring the role of the larger political context of immigration relative to the effects of the transitions. In this chapter we address selected results from the German part of the study.

Developmental Transitions: Opportunities for Positive Development

Within the research consortium, our work focused on the role of developmental transitions for age-typical psychosocial outcomes across various ethnic groups. Across the life span, individuals face various more or less normative developmental transitions (George, 1993), defined as the movement into and exit from various institutional roles (Pearlin, 2009), and which usually expose individuals to new ecological settings and experiences. As such, transitions can alter the way individuals are treated and how they think, feel, or behave (Bronfenbrenner, 2005). Because of the substantial changes in opportunities that take place during periods of transitions, life-span psychology and life-course sociology have been interested in whether transitions can instigate new adaptation and the longer-term development of psychosocial functions (e.g., Walsemann, Gee, & Geronimus, 2009).

During development, periods of continuity are often followed by a time of rapid change, and transitions may trigger such change. The experiences rooted in transitions can be disruptive or empowering, but at the very least they challenge routines and thus help individuals find ways of adapting to the developmental issues of a particular life period. The aim of our research was to assess the effect of these developmental transitions relative to other socialization factors known to be relevant for the psychosocial outcomes in question, such as level of various family resources and regulation strategies. In the past, the transition from primary to secondary school has attracted substantial research. We included four other transitions in our study. The transitions from home to kindergarten and from home or kindergarten to school were studied as instances of institutionally formalized transitions in childhood. The transitions into romantic involvement in adolescence and into living together in adulthood were included as instances of less formalized, more private transitions.

Theoretically, we conceive these transitions as opportunities for individuals to gain new experiences that ultimately support developmental progression. In the following section, we highlight what is known about such experiences, although it was not feasible to assess them at the individual level in the study.

The *transition to kindergarten* complements and possibly compensates for socialization within the family context, which may be particularly relevant for the immigrant groups (Magnuson, Lahaie, & Waldfogel, 2006; Spiess, Büchel, & Wagner, 2003). Longitudinal studies indicate that children from families with lower socioeconomic status benefit from attending kindergarten, particularly with respect to the promotion of linguistic and cognitive capabilities (Kratzmann & Schneider, 2008). A recent study comparing native German and Turkish children found that language skills improved during the first year of kindergarten, but only for the immigrant group (B. Becker, 2010). In contrast to the family environment with its dominance of dyadic parent–child relations, the transition to kindergarten offers new opportunities for the development of peer relations. Sustained improvements in social skills have been found, probably rooted in peer interactions and the resolution of conflicts (Ahnert, 2007). The evidence suggests that kindergarten likely helps in overcoming potential limitations in cognitive and social skills (Sammons et al., 2004).

The *transition to primary school*, whether from kindergarten or home, can be especially critical for those not raised in the middle-class mainstream. According to Entwistle and Alexander (1989), the beginning of schooling marks the beginning of literacy and numeracy, is characterized by the first confrontation with the evaluation of academic performance, and, most important, marks the entrance to a new social world. The conventions of school, with its focus on self-monitored pursuit of academic tasks and occasional frustrations, can be mismatched, sometimes dramatically, with the expectations and habits children know from home, and this may be especially true for those with a migration background (Okagaki & Sternberg, 1993, see also Motti-Stefanidi et al., this volume). Although all children need to develop the skills required for managing school demands, this may be more difficult for children from migrant families who are not familiar with German mainstream culture and thus are less able to prepare their children for this normative transition (Penn, 1996). More specifically, parental aspirations and knowledge of how to pursue academic goals may play a crucial role in the early years of school attendance, with long-lasting programming effects influencing enrollment into either vocational/technical or (less often) academic branches of secondary schooling, with far-reaching consequences for future occupational success (Maaz et al., 2006). Research in German samples has shown that about one-third of children seem at least temporarily overwhelmed by the challenges of the transition to school; the main risk factors for children with difficulties in this transition are minority status and low socioeconomic standing (Hasselhorn & Lohaus, 2007). Against this backdrop, our research question was whether the transition to school results in similar gains or differences in competence development among migrants and natives.

The *transition to romantic involvement* in adolescence is a major developmental task for young people. It is defined here as a mutually acknowledged dyadic relationship in contrast to other relationships with peers that typically involve several adolescents. Romantic involvement is always characterized by a high level of intensity in mutual affection, but can vary in the degree of physical intimacy between the two individuals (Collins, 2003). Through adolescence, romantic relations become gradually more important than the two individuals' attachment to their respective peers (Connolly & McIsaak, 2009). Involvement in romantic relationships can vary in the degree of intimate activities, from holding hands, through various stages of physical contact, to intercourse (Smith & Udry, 1985). The question of the "right time" and appropriate level of sexual interaction among young people is a core element of cultural belief systems (Coates, 1999; Feldman & Gowen, 1998). Native German adolescents are involved rather early in intimate romantic relationships compared to other ethnic groups. In this context, the question of timing and the nature of romantic activities is particularly relevant for Turkish girls in Germany because their cultural traditions impose strict limits on any intimate relationship with boys (Boos-Nünning & Karakaşoğlu, 2007). Rather conservative expectations are also known for the families of

German repatriates (Schmitt-Rodermund & Silbereisen, 2009). In comparing ethnic groups, we were interested in whether there would be similar effects of romantic relationships on psychosocial development, even in the presence of varying levels of physical intimacy across groups.

The *transition to living together* in a household shared with a partner also involves many new challenges. For example, closer everyday encounters increase the likelihood of conflict (Chen et al., 2006), particularly concerning the assignment of daily duties (Batalova & Cohen, 2002). It also involves changes in social networks and can carry expectations concerning an increase in the commitment to and a change in the quality of the partnership (Grau, Mikula, & Engel, 2001). This transition can be expected to vary among ethnic groups, particularly when the groups differ in stereotypes concerning gender roles and views on the importance of marriage for living together. Turks often have a more traditional gender orientation in which the male partner has greater authority and marriage is preferred before cohabitation (Diehl, König, & Ruckdeschel, 2009; Sakalli, 2001). A rather traditional gender role orientation also is typical among immigrants coming from the former Soviet Union (Remennick, 2005). In contrast, as in other Western countries, German natives often do not view marriage as necessary for cohabitation (Smock, 2000). Many people in individualistically oriented societies begin a committed relationship with cohabitation without being married, whereas in collectivist societies a shared household comes only subsequent to marriage (Diener et al., 2000). These views are illustrated by countrywide census data for Germany (Statistisches Bundesamt [Federal Statistical Office], 2008) according to which about 15% of the native population, but only 6% of Turks, live together without being married. Among the younger cohorts (18–25 years of age), about 85% of native Germans who live with their partner are not married, whereas among immigrants this figure is only 40%.

The Five Cs of Positive Development
Each of the transitions considered in our study could have very different potential effects on dimensions of psychosocial functioning. Therefore, it was impossible to assess their effects on the same dimensions. Instead we focused on the concept of positive development as a framework. The theoretical assumptions of positive (youth) development were derived from developmental systems theory and focus on mutually influential interactions between the developing individual and the multilevel context (Lerner et al., 2005; see also Lerner et al., this volume). A core assumption in this framework is that the absence of deficits in adaptation is not sufficient for

Table 13.1. Outcome Variables Based on the Concept of the Five Cs

'C'	Kindergarten	School	Adolescence	Early adulthood
Competence	language competence	language competence[a]	dating competence[a]	self-efficacy[a]
Confidence	support seeking[a] & avoidance	support seeking[a] & avoidance	self-efficacy, self-esteem	
Connection			economic & traditional[b] partnership preferences	economic & traditional partnership preferences
Character	self-control	self-control[a]	delinquent beliefs	delinquent beliefs
Caring			civic engagement[a]	civic engagement

[a] These variables had significantly higher scores in the posttransition group than the pretransition group; [b] posttransition groups showed significantly lower scores than the pretransition group.
Source: According to Lerner et al. (2005).

being a healthy and successful person. More specifically, research on positive youth development has defined a number of framing constructs indicating positive development among individuals, the so-called Five Cs (Lerner et al., 2005; see also Lerner et al., this volume): *Competence* is a positive view of one's actions in domain-specific areas (e.g., interpersonal competence); *confidence* represents an internal sense of overall positive self-worth and self-efficacy; *connection* relates to positive bonds with people and institutions, such as peers or family; *character* involves respect for societal and cultural rules as well as the possession of standards for normative behavior; and *caring* represents a sense of sympathy for and empathy with others. Taken together, achievements in these domains are deemed the prerequisite for thriving, that is, for functioning at a level whereby individuals realize their potentials in terms of achievements and well-being (Lerner et al., 2005). A more comprehensive and separate assessment of all the Five Cs for each transition would have posed too great a burden on research participants, and thus we had to confine ourselves to the aspects of psychosocial functioning shown in Table 13.1. Nevertheless, in spite of the limitations, this framework justified comparisons across all transitions as far as the general Five Cs are concerned, and within formal and informal transitions with regard to the specific measures applied in this study. We describe each of the constructs more specifically later in this chapter.

Conceptual Model and Guiding Hypotheses

Given the conceptual model guiding our research, we presumed that the psychosocial outcomes of interest would be positively influenced by the experiences associated with the respective transition. We expected that the magnitude of effects attributable to the transitions might vary across the ethnic groups compared. These potentially differential effects on psychosocial outcomes were also thought to be influenced by other variables relevant for understanding the promotional effect of transitions, namely, age, gender, and family resources. Family resources were differentiated as economic, social, and cultural capital, which refer to financial situation, social network ties, and education (Bourdieu, 1986). Family resources were of interest because, in the German debate on differences in achievements between natives and immigrants, an issue often raised is whether these differences are basically rooted in social status differentials confounded with the groups, or whether such differences reflect true cultural orientations. Status differentials indeed seem to play a role in school achievement (Mandara et al., 2009), but it may also apply to a broader range of psychosocial outcomes.

Above and beyond the effects of age, gender, ethnic group, resources, and transition, we were interested in how people handled prototypic everyday hassles related to the transition experience and whether this had an effect on psychosocial outcomes. Our concept of strategies for dealing with such hassles was inspired by the model of Heckhausen (Heckhausen & Schulz, 1993), which defines different strategies for achieving goals when confronted with difficulties. We used this model to define two broad strategies of dealing with transition-specific everyday hassles. Engagement refers to resolving a hassle by tenaciously pursuing activities, including the mobilization of motivation and finding alternatives that compensate for failed initial attempts. In contrast, disengagement takes over when obstacles to overcoming a hassle seem too high and when one needs to detract from it in order to save resources or avoid getting the blame for failure.

Finally, concerning the members of the immigrant groups, we had to bear in mind that they may vary in their degree of acculturation to Germany. This led to the question of whether, for example, differences in orientation to the host culture in Germany would be relevant in explaining any differential effect of transitions on the psychosocial outcomes of the groups studied. For immigrant children and adolescents, the transitions studied do not only include developmental tasks, but also confront them with differences in cultural norms and routines between their own and the host society (see also Motti-Stefanidi et al., this volume). Possible differences in acculturation thus might facilitate or hinder the effects of the transitions studied.

In a nutshell, the assumptions guiding our study were as follows. First, in line with the literature on the role of transitions, we expected to find an overall positive effect on the selected aspects of the Five Cs. Second, we were interested in determining whether effects of transitions would vary between natives and immigrants. We expected to find either no difference or an extra positive effect because of the experiences from two cultures come into contact. Especially concerning the formal transitions in childhood, institutional programs may result in a diminishing of possibly existing differences (see also García, this volume). We ruled out a negative effect reminiscent of the "ethnic penalty" observed for school achievement because the Five Cs refer to aspects of psychosocial functioning that are unlikely to be hampered by the new experiences after the transition. Although mean differences in the levels of Five Cs between the ethnic groups are not central for the purpose pursued in this chapter, we will discuss such differences when our data do not match relevant past research.

Format of the German Study on Transitions

In this section we describe the methodological background of the study and detail the sampling procedures and the assessment instruments used for this research. We also discuss briefly how the psychometric challenges were tackled when studying multiple ethnic groups.

Sampling Procedure

The sample was organized by a matrix comprising transitions studied, target persons assessed, and ethnic groups compared. With regard to the transition to kindergarten and school, mothers reported about their child; concerning romantic involvement, both the mother and adolescent were respondents. Concerning the latter transition, the adolescents reported about the outcome variables and whether or not they had already made the transition to romantic involvement, whereas their mothers reported on background variables, such as economic, cultural, and social capital. On the transition to living together, all information was gathered from the young adults themselves. The 16 cells (four transitions in four ethnic groups) of the matrix were each planned to hold 120 respondents. Utilizing random selection from data supplied by the registry offices in two large cities in different federal states in the west of Germany, and with the help of specially trained interviewers, we recruited a total sample of 2,110 participants. In

Table 13.2. Sample Sizes by Ethnic Group and Transition

	Kindergarten		School		Adolescence			Early adulthood	
	Before	After	Before	After	Before	After	Mothers	Before	After
Native Germans	40 (28%)	101 (72%)	99 (69%)	45 (31%)	33 (24%)	102 (76%)	135 (100%)	75 (62%)	46 (38%)
Ethnic German repatriates	40 (31%)	87 (69%)	51 (72%)	20 (28%)	20 (24%)	62 (76%)	82 (100%)	53 (75%)	18 (25%)
Russian Jewish immigrants	41 (35%)	75 (65%)	30 (48%)	32 (52%)	26 (35%)	47 (64%)	73 (100%)	98 (78%)	27 (22%)
Turkish immigrants	53 (45%)	64 (55%)	72 (64%)	41 (36%)	36 (30%)	85 (70%)	121 (100%)	66 (82%)	14 (18%)
Total	174 (35%)	327 (65%)	252 (65%)	138 (36%)	115 (28%)	296 (72%)	411 (100%)	292 (74%)	105 (26%)
	501		390		822			397	
	2,110								

Note: Percentages in brackets refer to the share of respondents in an ethnic group who have not yet made ("Before") versus already made the transition ("After")

the case of the Russian Jewish sample, however, snowball sampling was the only way to collect data within this community. Data collection took place from autumn 2007 to spring 2008. The particular cities chosen were selected because of their large populations of immigrants from all the groups studied. Note that the new federal states of the former GDR (East Germany) typically have very low densities of immigrants, so we confined data collection to the former West Germany.

The study was designed to include longitudinal data, covering the period of about a year around the transitions in question. However, we also planned for the possibilities of cross-sectional comparisons based on Wave 1, which is the data presented in this chapter. To gather the data according to this plan, we targeted individuals before and after each transition, which was accomplished by aiming at particular age brackets for the samples: 2 to 5 years for kindergarten, 5 to 7 years for school, 15 to 18 years for romantic involvement, and 20 to 30 years for living together as a couple. Overall there were enough respondents at Wave 1 who had or had not yet made each transition, and many of those who had not are expected to provide us with intraindividual change data at the second Wave (about 12 months apart). A breakdown of the samples is given in Table 13.2.

Definition of Transitions

For kindergarten and school, children were regarded as having made the transition if they had been at least six months in the new institution, as we assumed that the effects of transition needed some time to unfold. The transition to romantic involvement was coded as accomplished if the adolescent reported that he or she ever had a romantic partner. Living together as a couple was regarded as accomplished if the young adults indicated that they currently lived with their partner in a shared household. As shown in Table 13.2, the percentage of those having accomplished a transition varied between the type of transition and groups. For instance, a higher share of the Turkish group was not yet enrolled in kindergarten compared to the others, whereas a higher share of Russian Jewish immigrants had already made the transition to school. Except for a somewhat lower share among the Russian Jewish group, there were almost no significant differences concerning the prevalence of romantic involvement in adolescence. Concerning living together in young adulthood, about one-third of the native German adults reported cohabiting, whereas figures were much lower for the other groups, with the Turks again revealing the lowest level, with about one-fifth reporting living together with their partner.

As the comparability of the groups before and after the respective transition is crucial for interpreting the effects of the transitions on psychosocial outcomes in our cross-sectional data, we tested whether participants before and after the respective transitions were comparable in a number of sociodemographic aspects (age, degree of religiosity, number of children, employment status, and partnership status), family resources (educational level, financial assets, social capital), and acculturation-related variables among the immigrants (length of residence, use of the host language, citizenship, identification with host culture). A series of ANOVAs showed only few small age differences. Older participants were slightly more likely to have made the transition, and consequently we included age as control in regression analyses assessing the transition effects.

Measures of Background Variables and Positive Developmental Outcomes

Data were gathered by standardized interviews conducted by specially trained bilingual (female) interviewers fluent in German and the language of the respective immigrant group. In addition to the main variables of interest for this chapter, we assessed various other characteristics concerning immigration status and participants' experiences that help in interpreting the results.

Concerning family resources, cultural capital for the childhood and adolescence transitions was determined by mothers' educational level, and for the transition in young adulthood, the young adults' own educational level. Economic capital was indexed by a five-point self-assessment of the financial situation, ranging from "not at all sufficient to make ends meet" to "I can afford almost everything." This assessment revealed its validity by significant correlations with other information, such as the number of social transfer payments a family received, and was successfully applied in previous studies on the situation of immigrants in Germany (Mammey & Sattig, 2002). Social capital addressed respondents' so-called weak ties (Granovetter, 1973). To assess weak ties, a list of occupations ordered by increasing prestige was provided (from unskilled worker to physician), and participants were asked to check whether they knew people of these occupations well enough to ask them informally for advice. Following a procedure suggested by van der Gaag, Snijders, and Flap (2008), the score of social capital was calculated as the mean of the prestige of all occupations in which the respondent knew someone. The prestige rating of occupations was assessed by an established international measure, the International Socio-Economic Index of Occupational Status (Ganzeboom, De Graaf, & Treiman, 1992).

Following Heckhausen's model of developmental regulation (Heckhausen, Wrosch, & Schulz, 2010), regulation strategies were conceived as involving an individual's engagement or disengagement in dealing with transition-typical hassles. Based on the measure by Tomasik and Pinquart (2008) we let participants read two vignettes that characterized problematic transition-typical situations requiring a reaction. For example, the vignette concerning the transition to school refers to a teacher's reinforcement style that does not match the respondent's desired way of handling praise and punishment. Respondents were asked to imagine them being in the respective situations, and to indicate on a six-point scale between one (disagree) and six (agree) the degree to which they would show reactions of engagement and disengagement. Engagement referred either to attempts at changing the mismatch, to encouraging oneself to try harder, or to seeking help from others in order to succeed. These behaviors are typically shown when the obstacle to success seems controllable. Disengagement, in contrast, is chosen when perceived controllability is low. Here the statements referred to disengaging from the particular goal pursuit to avoid self-blame or to stop thinking about the situation and thereby find relief. The vignettes were formulated with the help of experts familiar with the particular transitions and situations (for details see http://www.migration.uni-jena.de/project1/regulation/).

As to earlier research, the two strategies do not represent opposite poles, but rather indicate two relatively independent dimensions of dealing with the hassles.

As already mentioned, the selection of psychosocial outcomes was guided by the principle of the Five Cs (Lerner et al., 2005), however, we were not always able to find reliable, meaningful, cross-culturally comparable, and short enough measures of positive development. Thus, some of our measures instead assessed a lack of positive development, such as delinquent beliefs in adolescence and young adulthood. In order to assess competence (positive view on one's actions) at the level of kindergarten and school, age-appropriate language competence was reported by the mother, using items from the NICHD study of early child care and youth development. This measure indicated whether the child could understand and communicate effectively in everyday situations, such as family interaction, play, and instruction, irrespective of which language was actually used (rated on a six-point scale; see https://secc.rti.org/). Confidence (sense of overall positive self-worth and self-efficacy) and connection (positive bonds with people and institutions) were assessed with items taken from an instrument for coping with age-typical problems developed by Eisenberg et al. (1993). We distinguished between seeking support from family or friends (e.g., "The child asks an adult or another child to help solve the problem") and problem avoidance, distancing oneself from difficulties (e.g., "The child leaves or avoids the problem situation"). These behaviors belong to the most common adaptive and maladaptive ways of coping during childhood, respectively (Zimmer-Gembeck & Skinner, 2011), and were also rated on a six-point scale between one (never) and six (very often). Concerning character (respect for societal and cultural rules for correct behavior) and caring (sense of sympathy and empathy for others), we used a measure taken from Gresham and Elliott (1990) that addressed whether children can control their temper when in conflict with others. Mothers rated how often their child behaves in a competent way, such as "Your child ends disagreements with you calmly" on a six-point scale between one (never) to six (always). As is evident here and elsewhere, in some instances we used the same variables as indicators for two Cs, due to time constraints in the assessments (see Table 13.1).

In the transition to romantic involvement in adolescence, competence was assessed as mature behavior in relation to dating using three items taken from Levenson and Gottman (1978). Using a scale from one (never) to six (very often) these items addressed how often adolescents felt able to maintain a romantic relationship based on mutual understanding and whether they were able to sense how their partner feels about them. Competence for the young adult group was assessed together with confidence in terms of general self-efficacy. This was measured following Jerusalem and Schwarzer (1992) with four items, such as "I can solve most problems if I invest the necessary effort." Assessment of all other Cs was accomplished in the same way for both age groups. Connection was assessed by asking for partnership preferences that could be traditional (based on parental agreement and the match of religion or ethnicity) or economic (status, finances, and education were prominent). We had no prejudice as to what kind of preference could indicate good connection. This measure based on Hetsroni (2000) required respondents to rate the importance of these characteristics on a scale from one (not important) to six (very important). Character was assessed via a scale of delinquent beliefs (i.e., participants responded on a six-point scale to items such as "Taking things from stores doesn't hurt anyone") taken from Finckenauer (1995). Caring was measured by level of civic engagement. This measure was inspired by the 2006 Shell Youth Study (Hurrelmann & Albert, 2006) and presented a list of seven items regarding the welfare of others (e.g., "I have been actively involved with supporting good relations between people of different cultures"). The sum of activities in which the adolescent was involved was used as the score.

Finally, we gathered additional information on the immigrant groups concerning their acculturation orientations toward their ethnic group and toward the host culture (Ryder, Alden, & Paulhus, 2000), their ethnic and host language proficiency (understanding, reading, or speaking their own language and German), their level of ethnic language use at home, and discrimination experienced at different locations and institutions because of their ethnic group membership (Strobl & Kühnel, 2000). We included these variables for the comparison among the immigrants because it was possible that differences in psychosocial outcomes that appear to be rooted in economic differences could upon closer examination be the result of differences in acculturation to life in Germany.

Challenges of Assessments in Culturally Diverse Populations

Comparative research on migration and immigration involving various ethnic groups of different origin, different cultural norms, different religious beliefs, and different migration histories presents a number of challenges. The first was the selection of instruments for assessing our outcomes. Although we could not rely on systematic studies investigating the cross-cultural applicability of all instruments used in our research for the specific groups studied, we aimed at using instruments that have already been applied successfully to various ethnic groups and also did some pilot testing. Since a detailed discussion of the cross-cultural validity of all instruments is beyond the scope of this chapter, we describe our procedure through the following example. A particularly sensitive issue for more traditional or religious ethnic groups was our addressing sexual behavior, which served the purpose of learning more about the nature of the transition to romantic involvement in adolescence, independent of whether or not the transition already occurred. This additional measure was based on empirical evidence supporting a similar sequence of sexual behaviors across various cultural groups (Brook et al., 1994), beginning with holding hands, then kissing, French kissing, petting, and finally sexual intercourse. We decided to place these questions later in the questionnaire, because participants were found to be more open and more confident with the interview situation over time. In addition, interviewers were advised to stop asking about further experiences after adolescents first stated, "No, I haven't had this experience yet." This reduced the confrontation of inexperienced adolescents with explicit sexual questions. Furthermore, although the absolute majority of the interviews were conducted in privacy, in about one-third of the interviews with Russian Jewish and Turkish participants we had to accept that another person was in the vicinity (but without interfering with the interview). Related to this, it is important to note that respondents could point to their response on a sheet of paper providing all possible answer formats rather than responding verbally.

The second challenging issue was to ensure the scales used in the project were psychometrically equivalent across the ethnic groups studied. Concerning all variables, the equivalence of measurement across native and immigrant groups and across other variables of interest, such as gender and age groups, was analyzed. Confirmatory factor analyses revealed the expected factorial structure across all groups, and according to the results this structure applied equally well for all comparisons, including equal factor loadings.

Analytic Strategy

Starting with some descriptive analyses for the variables included in our study, results for our main research questions concerning the role of the transitions in promoting the psychosocial outcomes were accomplished by separate regression analyses per transition and outcome. A number of hierarchical steps were pursued. First, age and gender were included, followed in a second step by ethnic group, which were dummy coded so that each respective immigrant group was compared separately with the native

German group. In a third step, the indicators of family resources (social, economic, and cultural capital) were added, followed by a fourth step adding whether the transition had already occurred (yes/no) and, in a fifth step, by the regulation strategies of engagement and disengagement. The sixth and final step concerned a set of interaction terms between groups and transition and between groups and regulation. Results of this last step tell us whether the role of transition and regulation for the outcome in question differs by group. Of course, more interaction terms, such as interactions of gender and age with transitions, could be theoretically derived and included in our analyses, but due to the limited sample size we had to confine ourselves to those interactions directly related to our research questions. As we could not address the question of whether the acculturation-related variables were of relevance in explaining differences in psychosocial functioning when including the natives as a reference group, we performed another set of regression analyses including only the immigrant groups. In these analyses the Turkish group was used as reference group.

Findings on the Effects of Transitions on Psychosocial Outcomes

We begin with information on the descriptive results, referring to ethnic group differences in family resources and regulation strategies applied by individuals when dealing with transition-related challenges. This is followed by results on transitions. As the nature of the transitions studied may vary between ethnic groups, we added information about typical experiences related to the respective transitions. For example, although the share of adolescents who reported having had a romantic partner was quite similar between ethnic groups, actual experiences gathered in first romantic relationships may differ. We finish with the role of acculturation among the immigrants.

Ethnic Group Differences in Resources and Regulation Strategies
Concerning cultural capital, the Russian Jewish group and the native Germans reported the highest educational level across all transitions, followed by the German repatriates, with the Turkish group coming last by some distance. Native Germans had more economic capital than the other groups, where little intergroup difference was found. This reflects the fact that in 2006 the earned income of the Turkish population and of the German repatriates was lower by about 10% and 20%, respectively, than that of native Germans ("Datenreport 2008. Ein Sozialbericht für die Bundesrepublik Deutschland [Data report 2008. Social report for the Federal Republic of Germany],"

2008). Finally, there was almost a cleavage in the results for social capital. Native Germans were closely followed by the Russian Jewish group, with the repatriates and especially the Turks reporting very low levels of weak ties to people outside the family who, by their occupations, signify the accessibility to networks of knowledge and social influence. This requires qualification, though, because Turkish and German repatriate groups are known to heavily rely on family networks not addressed here (Nauck & Kohlmann, 1998) which, however, are less relevant when it comes to the exploration of opportunities in settings outside the kinship realm. The differences in the various forms of capital were less pronounced among the young adults, but the general picture could also be applied here.

When dealing with the transition-typical hassles described in vignettes, the participants more strongly endorsed engagement strategies in solving the hypothetical situation than disengagement strategies, reflecting the principle controllability of the hassles expressed in the vignettes. If a situation can be controlled, then engagement is the better strategy because it maintains an individual's future control capacity (Heckhausen & Schulz, 1993). As far as differences between the groups are concerned, in almost all transitions, irrespective of engagement or disengagement, the Turkish group endorsed the regulation strategies more highly than all other groups. On average, native Germans ranked second after the Turkish group, followed by the other two immigrant groups, who differed little between themselves. Again, these between-group differences were less pronounced among the young adults. An explanation for the group differences may be that Turkish mothers endorsed engagement and disengagement more strongly than mothers of the other groups because they have less knowledge about the institutions and compensate for this disadvantage by greater efforts in resolving the situation. We also assessed whether or not participants experienced the transition-typical hassles described in the vignettes. The frequency of having experienced such situations did, however, not differ among the ethnic groups.

Transitions in Childhood
In order to illustrate our analytic procedure and results, we use the transition to kindergarten as an example and focus on the outcome of seeking social support when confronted with a frustrating situation (as an instance of confidence or connection, and seen as a constructive means of handling difficulties), including all groups studied and comparing groups cross-sectionally before and after the transitions. As can be seen in Table 13.3, the small range of age differences observed did not play a role, whereas

Table 13.3. Regression Results for Kindergarten Children of All Groups Predicting Social Support Seeking When in Trouble (Standardized Coefficients)

	Step 1	Step 2	Step 3	Step 4	Step 5	Step 6
Age of the child	.02	.02	.02	−.06	−.05	−.05
Sex (1 = male; 2 = female)	.08+	.10*	.11*	.11*	.10*	.10*
Turkish (Dummy = 1)		.33***	.36***	.38***	.34***	.28***
Repatriate (Dummy = 1)		.36***	.40***	.39***	.42***	.40***
Russian Jewish (Dummy = 1)		.24***	.26***	.26***	.31***	.33***
Social capital			.04	.03	.00	.00
Economic capital			.06	.06	.04	.04
Cultural capital			.00	−.01	.02	.00
Transition (0 = no vs. 1 = yes)				.13*	.13*	.12*
Engagement					.21***	.23***
Disengagement					−.09*	−.09+
Turk x transition						.03
Repatriate x transition						.01
Russian Jew x transition						.05
Turk x engagement						.05
Repatriate x engagement						−.14*
Russian Jew x engagement						−.03
Turk x disengagement						.07
Repatriate x disengagement						.07
Russian Jew x disengagement						.01
Change in R^2		.11***	.00	.01*	.04***	.02
R^2	.01	.12***	.12***	.13***	.17***	.19***

Note: + p < .10; * p < .05; ** p < .01; *** p < .001.

girls tended to seek more support than boys. Next, compared to native Germans, all immigrant groups had a higher leaning toward seeking help from families or peers when confronted with a problem. None of the family resources played a role. Furthermore, differences in the levels of family resources did not neutralize the effects of immigrant status. The transition itself, however, was of relevance, as children already in kindergarten tended more toward seeking help from others as expected. Mothers who reported a higher tendency to take an active approach in regulation of transition-related hassles also reported higher levels of support seeking for their children; disengagement, on the other hand, was of no relevance. Only one of the interactions was significant, and this referred to lower support seeking among German repatriates combined with high engagement by their mothers. Most important, however, there was no interaction involving the experience of the transition. In sum, the transition to kindergarten seemed to result in more social support seeking, although at different levels across the groups. The differences between groups apparently remained unchanged over the transition. Finally, it would seem that the group differences in support seeking are cultural, in the sense that they could not be explained by differences in family resources, that is, by social network ties (social capital), financial resources (economic capital), and maternal education (cultural capital). The differences may be the result of cultural differences in parenting between immigrants and native families (Uslucan, 2009).

Avoidance as a reaction to problematic situations, the less constructive counterpart to support seeking, revealed basically the negative mirror image of the results on support seeking in the transition to kindergarten. The transition itself was not relevant, however, neither were family resources, and both German repatriates and Turkish children ranked lower in avoidance. Understandably, mothers' disengagement in dealing with problems seemingly promoted children's avoidance. Finally, none of the interactions was significant.

By and large, results concerning the transition to school and social support seeking versus avoidance looked similar. Having made the transition seemed to promote support seeking, whereas it was irrelevant for avoidance; immigrant groups ranked higher in support seeking and lower in avoidance. Family resources were also irrelevant and, although mothers' engagement in resolving school hassles helped support seeking, it was not related to avoidance. None of the interactions with group was significant.

For the sake of brevity, we do not report further analyses in detail. The other outcomes studied concerning kindergarten and school, that is, language competence (representing competence of the Five Cs) and self-control (representing character and caring), showed similar results. The immigrant groups differed from the native Germans; especially Turkish children according to their mothers showed higher self-control and lower language competencies in the transition to school. Family resources were of little relevance overall, and mothers' engagement was positively related to language competence and self-control. In contrast to the results on support seeking and avoidance, whether the child already attended kindergarten or not did not play a role, and neither did the interactions. Interesting, language competence was positively associated with the transition to school, as was self-control.

Equivalence of Transitions

Thus far we have treated the transitions and the implied associated experiences as alike between the ethnic groups studied. On closer examination, we did find some group differences in the quality of the transitions. Concerning kindergarten, there was a difference in the length of the experience in the new setting. The children who had accomplished this transition had spent on average between 18 months (immigrant groups) and 22 months (native Germans) in kindergarten at the time of assessment. Thus, when comparing before and after the transition, we actually assess the effect of more than one year in kindergarten. This was not originally planned, but resulted from delays in data gathering due to difficulties with the recruitment of bilingual interviewers. Further, German repatriates and Turks almost exclusively attended public city-run facilities, whereas about one-quarter or more of the other groups attended privately operated kindergartens. Finally, in Germany a lower share of children with a migration background attend preschool care facilities outside the family (R. Becker & Tremel, 2006), although this may not apply to the large cities we studied, which typically have a higher density and range of child care facilities (Statistisches Bundesamt [Federal Statistical Office], 2009). Concerning school, at the time of the interviews, children had spent on average between 8 months and 12 months (Turks and ethnic German repatriates respectively) in the new institution, with the other groups falling somewhere in between. The time these children had spent in kindergarten before school also varied little, between 38 months and 40 months on average. In sum, these ethnic group differences were minor and seem irrelevant for our results on the role of transitions.

Although the kindergarten experience of the children we assessed was actually almost twice as long as the children's experience of being in school, the results on psychosocial outcomes of the transition were about the same for both kindergarten and school, and where we did find any difference, it was even more pronounced concerning the transition to school. This seems to suggest that the difference in length of exposure is of no particular relevance concerning outcomes. However, given the fact that the content and structure of a day in school is more organized around particular educational goals than is common in kindergarten, this result perhaps should not come as a surprise.

Summary

Concerning our guiding question of the role of childhood transitions for the psychosocial functions studied in the four ethnic groups, results can be summarized as follows. The transitions to kindergarten and to school were relevant in the expected direction of higher levels of the Five Cs studied in four out of eight instances (see Table 13.1), but particularly concerning the transition to school. As there was virtually no interaction between transition and ethnic group, but quite striking differences between the immigrants and the native Germans in the psychosocial outcomes studied, the differences that existed before the transition seemingly remained unchanged, at least when comparing pretransition and posttransition. Moreover, differences in outcomes between native Germans and immigrants, and among the immigrant groups themselves, cannot be explained away by differences in family resources. The explained variance (R-Square) ranged between about 10% and 20%.

Transitions in Adolescence and Adulthood

The transitions in adolescence and young adulthood are less formalized and more private, but given our general concept and study design we were nevertheless able to ask similar questions to those posed with regard to the younger groups. The investigation here utilized the same six-step hierarchical regression analyses for each psychosocial outcome, as given in the example for support seeking in kindergarten (see Table 13.3).

Traditional partnership preferences and economic partnership preferences (both examples of connection in the language of the Five Cs) were much higher in the immigrant groups, but particularly for the Turks. The high endorsement of both preferences among immigrants is not surprising as characteristics such as affection and love were left out, which may have received higher endorsement by natives (Nauck, 2007). This effect was not reduced by differences in family resources, neither in adolescence nor in young adulthood, and females always scored more highly. Transitions played a role in the sense that traditional, but not economic partnership preferences were reduced in adolescence, thus indicating that the relevance of parental consent and matching religious and ethnic background was valued less among adolescents after the transition to first romantic involvement. Note that adolescents' dating competence (an instance of competence among the Five Cs) in the sense of higher interpersonal sensitivity toward their partner was also higher among those who had accomplished this transition (see Table 13.1).

Self-efficacy and self-esteem (representing confidence among the Five Cs for the adolescence group) were not related to the transition to romantic relations in adolescence, but the transition to cohabitation in young adulthood predicted higher levels of self-efficacy (representing competence and confidence for the young adults). With regard to delinquent beliefs (character), the transition to first romantic relationships showed no effect, and group differences were rather small with a higher leaning toward such beliefs among Turkish adolescents. Basically, the same applied for the young adults. Russian-Jewish young adults were also higher than the natives in delinquent beliefs.

Finally, civic engagement, which represented caring among the Five Cs for both the adolescent and young adult groups, appeared to be promoted by the debut of romantic relationship in adolescence. This seems plausible when keeping in mind that the accomplishment of important developmental tasks, such as establishing meaningful relationships, predicts later civic engagement (Obradović & Masten, 2007). Higher cultural capital also played a role in civic engagement. It would seem, therefore, as if romantic involvement creates a new awareness and provides opportunities for activities typical of young people. Among the young adults, however, the transition was not relevant, although social capital was a significant predictor of civic engagement.

A remarkable finding for the effects of the transition to romantic involvement and living together as couple was that, as for the transitions in childhood, we found no interaction effect between ethnic group and transition. Thus, again, existing differentials between the groups of native Germans and immigrants did not seem to change during the transition. This was the case for all outcomes studied.

Equivalence of Transitions
As with the transitions in childhood, the analyses reported thus far disregarded possible qualitative differences between the ethnic groups in the circumstances of the transitions. Given the more informal and private nature of these adolescent and young adult transitions, larger ethnic differences are particularly likely. Concerning the transition to romantic involvement in adolescence, unfortunately we do not have information about the length of time since a first romantic relation was formed or at which age. However, we do know that between 22% (German repatriates) and 26% (native Germans) were in a romantic relationship at the time of assessment, with the other groups falling in between. In about two-thirds of these cases, the current friendship was not the first such relationship. Thus, in contrast to the childhood transitions, the exposure to the new experiences in all likelihood was longer on average, but basically similar across the groups.

A core qualitative aspect for romantic relationships in adolescence is the level of sexual involvement, which we assessed following Smith and Udry (1985) with items ranging from holding hands to kissing, French kissing, petting, and finally to intercourse. Not surprising, we found quite remarkable differences between the ethnic groups studied. Although holding hands and kissing was ubiquitous at around 90% and higher, from French kissing onward the percentage of the native German group reporting having experienced a particular stage fell gradually to 44% having had sexual intercourse. The share of adolescents having had a particular experience in the other groups, particularly the Turks, fell to around half or less than that of the native Germans. For example, only 19% of Turks who had ever had a romantic partner indicated that they had experienced intercourse. Having a romantic relationship with a boyfriend/girlfriend for the Turks was associated with less progression in sexual intimacy as compared to native Germans of the same age.

Concerning the adult transition to living together, there were also remarkable but not unexpected differences in qualitative characteristics of the transitions among the ethnic groups. The share of those who lived with their partner (including those who were married and those who were not and, in accordance with our sampling strategy, had no children) varied between 53% (Turks) and 64% (German repatriates) with the other groups in between. The length of the current partnership was about three years on average and did not differ across groups. The clearest difference appeared concerning whether a respondent was married when living with a partner (of those cohabiting, 87% of the Turks, but only 15% of the native Germans were married) or whether there was an intention to marry. Here about 50% of the native Germans did not yet know when or if they would marry or ruled out marriage in general, whereas the German repatriates and the Russian Jewish immigrants were much more pro-marriage. Unfortunately, breaking down the analyses further to distinguish between living together and being married versus unmarried was not possible due to small cell sizes. In sum, the main difference between the ethnic groups concerning the transition to cohabitation with their partner is that among native Germans it is likely that the partnership is not related to marriage, whereas for the Turks this kind of living arrangement is almost exclusively reserved for married couples. For the German repatriates and the Russian Jewish sample, cohabitation appears much more like a waiting arrangement before the ultimate act of marriage.

Seen against the qualitative differences in the nominally equivalent transitions, the commonalities in the effects on psychosocial outcomes are again impressive. Although the sexual involvement among Turkish adolescents was much less progressed compared to the other groups, the degree of traditional partnership preferences was generally reduced through the transition, as in the other groups. Further, in spite of the fact that living together in adulthood meant marriage among Turks and ambivalence concerning such a commitment among the native Germans, these differences were never reflected in a differential effect on the psychosocial outcomes depending on the ethnic group. Obviously the reason for living together differs among young adults of different ethnicities, but the effects in terms of the Five Cs as assessed are alike.

Summary
Results for the two partnership transitions in adolescence and adulthood can be summarized as follows. Although the transitions played a role in the expected direction in four out of 12 instances (see Table 13.1), this effect was never moderated by group membership, that is, immigrants compared to native Germans. Neither were differences between immigrants and native Germans explained by family resources, which in any case had no great overall effect. Engagement played a role in promoting the Five Cs in adolescence and adulthood, but the effects were more scattered than those observed in childhood. The variance explained in the various analyses (R-Square) ranged from about 10% to 40%.

Immigration-Specific Predictors of Psychosocial Outcomes
All the results presented thus far referred to the entire sample. However, we also wanted to address the question of whether acculturation-related variables played a role in explaining psychosocial functions or in differences found between ethnic groups. For this reason, a second set of regression analyses was performed in which we looked at immigrant groups only (excluding the interaction terms as no effects were revealed in the previous analyses). We added predictors regarding differences among the immigrants in acculturation and intercultural relationships as a sixth regression step. The variables included were ethnic orientation, host orientation, ethnic language proficiency, host language proficiency, child's ethnic language use (adolescents' and young adults' ethnic language use for the two informal transitions), and perceived discrimination. In these analyses the Turkish group was used as reference group.

Our results showed that adding acculturation-related variables in the prediction of the psychosocial outcomes in terms of the Five Cs did not change the general pattern of results substantially for any of the groups. However, acculturation-related variables, especially ethnic and host orientation, added to the explanation of interindividual differences in psychosocial outcomes, but these effects did not reduce the size of any of the other effects. More specifically, mothers' ethnic orientation (which we conceived as the desire for same-ethnic social contacts, maintenance of cultural practice, and a belief in cultural values) predicted higher levels of support seeking in their children of kindergarten and school age. In the adolescent group, ethnic orientation was related to higher levels of self-efficacy, higher self-esteem, more traditional partner preferences, and higher levels of delinquent beliefs. In the young adult group, higher levels of ethnic orientation were also related to more traditional partner preferences. Mothers' orientations directed toward members of the host society predicted higher levels of language competence in the two childhood transitions and also predicted lower levels of avoidance in kindergarten-aged children and higher levels of self-control in those of school age. In the two informal transitions in adolescence and young adulthood, host orientation was only related to lower levels of delinquent beliefs among adolescents and higher levels of civic engagement among adults. The other acculturation-related variables studied were less relevant for the Five Cs. Host language proficiency predicted lower levels of economic partner preferences in adolescence, and perceived discrimination was associated with higher levels of civic engagement among adolescents and young adults. Taken together, these results indicate that cultural orientation can have an impact on psychosocial outcomes, which may be a key to the cultural origin of differences between natives and immigrants in the level of psychosocial functioning rather than differences in the level of resources available.

Conclusion and Outlook

The main question of our study was whether age-typical transitions in childhood, adolescence, and young adulthood have a positive effect on select psychosocial outcomes that are of relevance for the realization of an individual's potential for achievement and well-being. Furthermore, we wanted to know whether the effect of age-typical transitions varies as a function of the particular group studied in Germany, that is, natives and German repatriates, Russian Jewish immigrants, and members of the Turkish minority. To be precise, the presumed origin of any differences was not the transitions as such, but the particular experiences they provide, including new social roles and settings. The transition to kindergarten, for instance, brings a child into intense contact with a new social context comprising children from many different backgrounds. The new context provides learning opportunities, but also requires skills with which to handle the new interpersonal challenges (Ahnert, 2007). The transition to school means that a child is exposed to more structured learning than before, requires more attention and endurance, and needs to learn the skills required for managing complex tasks (Entwistle & Alexander, 1989). The transition to romantic involvement in adolescence is a major step toward new intimacy and mutual understanding, provides opportunities for the exploration of commitments, and requires discipline in handling new freedoms (Miller & Benson, 1999). Finally, the transition to living together as a couple brings two lives into alignment and interdependency over a large range of duties and pleasures, possibly with the added task of developing a perspective for procreation (Hsueh, Morrison, & Doss, 2009). In spite of these general characteristics, the actual experiences of immigrants can vary as evidenced by the large differences in qualitative aspects of the transition to romantic involvement in adolescence and living together in adulthood. Such differences were understandably smaller in the more institutionalized and standardized transitions to kindergarten and school.

Obviously, each of these developmental transitions could be the subject of a specialized paper, and the same applies to the various aspects of the psychosocial outcomes we have studied in this research. Our outcomes addressed the Five Cs representing positive youth development (Lerner et al., 2005; see also Lerner, this volume), but due to space and time limits of the survey we could not assess the various dimensions comprehensively (see Table 13.1). Likewise, we could not rely on a fuller set of antecedents to these outcomes, but had to confine ourselves to three forms of family resources and to engaged and disengaged regulation vis-à-vis transition-typical hassles.

Given our modest aim of a bird's eye view on the role of transition experiences for the psychosocial outcomes across the four transitions studied, these constraints posed little disadvantage. The findings showed that these transitions did indeed have an effect, as expected. This did not always apply, but did in most cases where there was a plausible relationship between the experiences likely to be gained during the time period studied and the target outcome variable under scrutiny. For instance, the transition to kindergarten was associated with a more mature style of seeking support from others. For the group of children who had made the transition to school, language competence was better than in the group who had not yet made this transition, in that posttransition children were more able to contribute to discussions at home, to understand how a story evolves, and to communicate the reasons behind their opinion. In the case of the transition in adolescence, dating competence was higher among those who had already experienced a romantic relationship. They knew better than pretransition youth how to read a potential partner's feelings and how to adapt their behavior accordingly. The transition to cohabitation in adulthood was related to self-efficacy. Those who had made the transition judged their capability to overcome problems by their own efforts higher than did the others. It should be underscored that we did not find a single instance of an overall negative association of transition experiences to psychosocial competence for all outcomes studied.

The most important result of the study, however, is that differences in psychosocial competence related to transition status were not moderated by ethnic/immigrant group membership. Thus, if there was an upward trend for a particular outcome between those approaching and those having achieved the transition, then this was similar across groups. There were ethnic/immigrant group differences, but these appeared quite stable across transitions. This was somewhat surprising, given the literature on the transition to school, which suggests additional strains that may put immigrants at a disadvantage (Hasselhorn & Lohaus, 2007). One may wonder, as well, why we did not replicate the positive effect of kindergarten attendance on the language skills of Turkish children (B. Becker, 2010). Note, however, there was no overall positive effect of this transition in Becker's study, and the skills measured referred to German vocabulary in identifying objects, whereas we were interested in whether the children are able to communicate effectively in everyday situations in the language spoken at home.

As in the case of transition to kindergarten, our results may be influenced by differential recruitment into the transition experience. Despite the fact that we investigated two German cities, which are much better equipped with childcare facilities than many other areas of Germany (Statistisches Bundesamt [Federal Statistical Office] 2009) and thus offer an easy access to those facilities, in the age range studied there were about 20% more of the native children in kindergarten than Turkish children. The share of Turkish children who did not (yet) attend a kindergarten in this age is of concern given the known benefits for migrant integration through better educational success among those with kindergarten experience (Magnuson et al., 2006; Spiess et al., 2003). As the transition to childhood institutions was related to positive developmental outcomes overall, achieving equal access and use of these facilities among all ethnic groups seems desirable.

Furthermore, the additional analyses showed that the effects on psychosocial outcomes were the same across ethnic groups despite the fact that the actual experiences related to the transition were rather different. The transition in adolescence is a case in point. The levels of sexual involvement in adolescence varied substantially between ethnic groups, and yet the same advancement in terms of the Five Cs was achieved. This result may be an instance of the principle of equifinality in development, that is, the same end state may be reached from a variety of different initial conditions (Cicchetti

& Rogosch, 1996). As a matter of fact we have additional evidence that adolescents of all ethnic groups on average revealed about the same level of satisfaction with their relationships.

Whatever the specific processes behind this equifinality in transition effects, they are probably related to the interplay between setting and culture, and according to our data, the cultural influence cannot be substituted by any of the three family resources examined, that is, by economic, social, and cultural capital. The levels of these resources varied remarkably across the groups studied, with the Turkish immigrants being especially low in educational attainment and social capital, which we understood as social ties to people of high occupational status outside family and kin. Although these differences were of relevance for some of the psychosocial outcomes studied, they did not eliminate the additional effect of the ethnic group membership. This is very interesting as it counteracts the view that ethnic differences in psychosocial outcomes are mainly related to social inequalities between natives and immigrants. This was shown for achievement in secondary school (Mandara et al., 2009; Walter, 2008) but obviously should not be generalized to other psychosocial outcomes and other transitions.

In hindsight, we may ask whether it was feasible at all to presume that the limited experience of transitions could potentially change the course of psychosocial development in a comprehensive way. For instance, as our results on adolescents have shown, their partnership preferences seemingly became less traditional with the experience provided by the transition, but whether this effect will last we cannot know based on the current data. Nevertheless, we presume the experience of negotiating a relationship helps to distance an individual from those aspects of a tradition that do not fit to their broader life circumstances.

As kindergarten and school follow a coherent pedagogical model of care and instruction and pursue specific goals of social and academic achievement, the persistence of the difference between ethnic groups in psychosocial outcomes across the transitions may indicate a missed opportunity for improvement. Of course we have no measure to know whether the lower levels achieved by some of the groups compared to the native Germans are nevertheless satisfactory concerning successful psychosocial development. Nevertheless, even when one takes into account that testing statistical interactions in regression analyses is a very conservative procedure that may overlook more subtle effects, the lack of differential effects on psychosocial outcomes across the groups studied came as a surprise. Whereas the fact that the regulation strategies mostly worked alike in all groups can be taken as demonstrating their robustness as a socialization experience, the homogeneity of the effects of the transition experiences is less satisfying from a social policy point of view. Future research may show whether more time after the transition is needed in order for differential effects to become apparent, whether institutions miss opportunities to deal adequately with cultural differences in children and therefore cannot diminish differences between ethnic groups, or whether the differences found are cultural in the sense that they cannot (and perhaps should not) be changed by the kind of experiences involved in these developmental transitions. Certainly more can be done in educational institutions, especially in Germany, to better integrate immigrants and to exploit the full potential these children have (see García this volume; Horenczyk & Tatar this volume).

Our study has many limitations, starting with the cross-sectional design employed thus far that compares different rather than the same individuals before and after the transitions. Prospective longitudinal data are more suitable to trace how psychosocial development changes within individuals after having accomplished a transition. Therefore, although we did not find any substantial difference in a number of potential confounds between the cross-sectional groups before and after the transitions, we will have to wait for longitudinal data to confirm the findings. Another limitation is that the sample was rather small when broken down to ethnic groups and accomplishment of transitions. Moreover, the data were confined to two large cities in Germany that have a high density of the nonnative groups we studied, and thus generalizability is an issue. Also the array of psychosocial outcomes gathered was limited by the nature of a survey that had to entail short assessment instruments. We tried to use only measures deemed equivalent across the ethnic groups, but more time for the interviews would have ensured we were on safer ground in this regard. Certainly, the nature of the transition experiences differed somewhat across transitions and groups, but we could identify what that meant for the psychosocial outcomes.

Beyond these caveats, the study has obvious strengths, such as the possibility of assessing whether ethnic differences in the psychosocial outcomes investigated can be explained by differences in family resources, referring to education, financial resources, and social ties. Likewise, we were able to find out whether the net effects of the transition experience (having controlled for sociodemographics and family resources) themselves can be explained by the kind of regulating responses toward transition-typical hassles. As neither the resources nor the regulation strategies could remove the effects of transitions, our conclusions concerning the solid transition effects we found are even more important.

As mentioned at the outset, our work is sited within a larger German-Israeli research consortium. This will allow us to test the generalizability of the results on the effects of transitions with a sample comprised of native Israelis, recent Jewish immigrants from Russia to Israel, and Israeli Arabs. The question is whether the transitions work alike concerning the psychosocial functions studied, in spite of different experiences with the absorption and integration of immigrants (Titzmann et al., 2011), and a stronger ethnic separation at least during childhood. However, this is beyond the scope of this chapter.

To sum up, the transitions addressed seem to promote psychosocial functioning in domains affected by transition-related experiences, and this applies to natives and immigrants alike. However, the quite remarkable ethnic differences we observed in the level of functioning among the individuals representing the conditions before the transitions occurred again to the almost identical degree when we looked at the individuals representing the posttransition conditions. If these differences include levels of psychosocial competence that are inadequate for success in Germany, this becomes a political and policy issue. Scientists, policy makers, and citizens all share a stake in understanding how transition experiences can be changed to promote greater success in immigrant groups and reduce differences in psychosocial outcomes between native Germans and immigrant youth living in Germany.

Authors' Note

The project "Regulation of Developmental Transitions in Second Generation Immigrants in Germany and Israel" (Principal Investigators: Yoav Lavee, Bernhard Nauck, Avi Sagi-Schwartz, Rainer K. Silbereisen, Anja Steinbach) was funded by the German Federal Ministry of Education and Research (BMBF; reference number 01GWS068, 01GWS069) as part of the interdisciplinary research consortium on "Migration and Societal Integration" (Director: Rainer K. Silbereisen). Special thanks go to our collaborators who were involved in the design and field work: Susanne Clauß, Falk Gruner, (Chemnitz University of Technology), Andrea Michel, Mohini Lokhande, Katharina Stößel, Peter F. Titzmann (University of Jena), and David Mehlhausen-Hassoen (University of Haifa). Last, but not least, we want to express our gratitude to all study participants.

REFERENCES

Ahnert, L. (2007). Entwicklung in kombinierter familiärer und außerfamiliärer Kleinkind- und Vorschulbetreuung [Development in combined familial and institutional kindergarten and preschool care settings]. In M. Hasselhorn and

R. K. Silbereisen (Eds.), *Enzyklopädie Psychologie, Serie V (Entwicklung), Band 4: Psychologie des Säuglings- und Kindesalters* (pp. 373–408). Göttingen: Hogrefe.

Alba, R. D., Handl, J., & Müller, W. (1998). Ethnic inequalities in the German school system. In P. H. Schuck and R. Münz (Eds.), *Paths to inclusion. The integration of migrants in the United States and Germany* (pp. 115–54). New York/Oxford: Berghahn Books.

Batalova, J. A., & Cohen, P. N. (2002). Premarital cohabitation and housework: Couples in cross-national perspective. *Journal of Marriage and Family, 64,* 743–55.

Baumert, J., & Maaz, K. (2008). Früh fördern statt spät reparieren [Early encouragement instead of late repairment]. *Max Planck Forschung, 4/2008,* 15–18.

Becker, B. (2010). Wer profitiert mehr vom Kindergarten? Die Wirkung der Kindergartenbesuchsdauer und Ausstattungsqualität auf die Entwicklung des deutschen Wortschatzes bei deutschen und türkischen Kindern [Who profits more from preschool attendance? The impact of time in preschool and quality of preschool environment on the development of German and Turkish children's German vocabulary]. *Kölner Zeitschrift für Soziologie und Sozialpsychologie, 62*(1), 139–63.

Becker, R., & Tremel, P. (2006). Auswirkungen vorschulischer Kinderbetreuung auf die Bildungschancen von Migrantenkindern [Effects of preschool education on the educational opportunities of immigrant children]. *Soziale Welt, 57,* 397–418.

Boos-Nünning, U., & Karakaşoğlu, Y. (2007). Sexuelle Normen und Erfahrungen mit sexueller Aufklärung von jungen Frauen mit Migrationshintergrund [Sexual norms and experiences with sex education of young women with migration background]. *BzGA FORUM, 3–2007,* 28–33.

Bourdieu, P. (1986). The forms of capital. In J. Richardson (Ed.), *Handbook of theory and research for the sociology of education* (Vol. 241–58). New York: Greenwood.

Bronfenbrenner, U. (2005). A future perspective (1979). In U. Bronfenbrenner (Ed.), *Making human beings human: Bioecological perspectives on human development* (pp. 50–59). Thousand Oaks, CA: Sage Publications Ltd.

Brook, J. S., Balka, E. B., Abernathy, T., & Hamburg, B. A. (1994). Sequence of sexual behavior and its relationship to other problem behaviors in African American and Puerto Rican adolescents. *The Journal of Genetic Psychology, 155,* 107–14.

Chen, H., Cohen, P., Kasen, S., Johnson, J. G., Ehrensaft, M., & Gordon, K. (2006). Predicting conflict within romantic relationships during the transition to adulthood. *Personal Relationships, 13,* 411–27.

Cicchetti, D., & Rogosch, F. A. (1996). Equifinality and multifinality in developmental psychopathology. *Development and Psychopathology, 8*(4), 597–600.

Coates, D. L. (1999). The cultured and culturing aspects of romantic experience in adolescence. In W. Furman, B. B. Brown, and C. Feiring (Eds.), *The development of romantic relationships in adolescence* (pp. 330–63). New York, NY: Cambridge University Press.

Collins, W. A. (2003). More than myth: The developmental significance of romantic relationships during adolescence. *Journal of Research on Adolescence, 13*(1), 1–24.

Connolly, J. A., & McIsaak, C. (2009). Romantic relationships in adolescence. In R. M. Lerner and L. Steinberg (Eds.), *Handbook of adolescent psychology. Vol.2: Contextual influences on adolescent development* (pp. 104–51). Hoboken: Wiley.

Datenreport 2008. Ein Sozialbericht für die Bundesrepublik Deutschland [Data report 2008. Social report for the Federal Republic of Germany] Bonn: Bundeszentrale für politische Bildung.

Diehl, C., König, M., & Ruckdeschel, K. (2009). Religiosity and gender equality: Comparing natives and Muslim migrants in Germany. *Ethnic and Racial Studies, 32,* 278–301.

Diener, E., Gohm, C. L., Suh, E., & Oishi, S. (2000). Similarity of the relations between marital status and subjective well-being across cultures. *Journal of Cross-Cultural Psychology, 31,* 419–36.

Dietz, B. (2000). German and Jewish migration from the former Soviet Union to Germany: Background, trends and implications. *Journal of Ethnic and Migration Studies, 26,* 635–52.

Eisenberg, N., Fabes, R., Bernzweig, J., Karbon, M., Poulin, R., & Hanish, L. (1993). The relations of emotionality and regulation to preschoolers' social skills and sociometric status. *Child Development, 64,* 1418–38.

Entwistle, D. R., & Alexander, K. L. (1989). Early schooling as a "critical period" phenomenon. *Research in Sociology of Education and Socialization, 8,* 27–55.

Feldman, S. S., & Gowen, L. K. (1998). Conflict negotiation tactics in romantic relationships in high school students. *Journal of Youth and Adolescence, 27,* 691–717.

Finckenauer, O. J. (1995). *Russian youth: Law, deviance, and the pursuit of freedom.* New Brunswick, NJ: Transaction Press.

Ganzeboom, H. B. G., De Graaf, P. M., & Treiman, D. J. (1992). A standard international socioeconomic index of occupational status. *Social Science Research, 21,* 1–56.

George, L. K. (1993). Sociological perspectives on life transitions. *Annual Review of Sociology, 19,* 353–73.

Granovetter, M. S. (1973). The strength of weak ties. *The American Journal of Sociology, 78,* 1360–80.

Grau, I., Mikula, G., & Engel, S. (2001). Skalen zum Investitionsmodell von Rusbult [Scales for assessing the model of investments by Rusbult]. *Zeitschrift für Sozialpsychologie, 32,* 29–44.

Gresham, F. M., & Elliott, S. N. (1990). *Social Skills Rating System Manual.* Circle Pines: American Guidance Service.

Hasselhorn, M., & Lohaus, A. (2007). Schuleintritt [School entry]. In M. Hasselhorn and W. Schneider (Eds.), *Handbuch der Entwicklungspsychologie* (pp. 489–500). Göttingen: Hogrefe.

Heckhausen, J., & Schulz, R. (1993). Optimisation by selection and compensation: Balancing primary and secondary control in life-span development. *International Journal of Behavior Development, 16,* 287–303.

Heckhausen, J., Wrosch, C., & Schulz, R. (2010). A motivational theory of lifespan development. *Psychological Review, 117,* 32–60.

Hetsroni, A. (2000). Choosing a mate in television dating games: The influence of setting, culture, and gender. *Sex Roles, 42,* 83–106.

Hsueh, A. C., Morrison, K. R., & Doss, B. D. (2009). Qualitative reports of problems in cohabiting relationships: Comparisons to married and dating relationships. *Journal of Family Psychology, 23,* 236–46.

Hurrelmann, K., & Albert, M. (2006). *Jugend 2006. 15. Shell Jugendstudie: Eine pragmatische Generation unter Druck [Youth 2006. 15th Shell Youth Study: A pragmatic generation under pressure].* Frankfurt: Fischer.

Jerusalem, M., & Schwarzer, R. (1992). Self-efficacy as a resource factor in stress appraisal processes. In R. Schwarzer (Ed.), *Self-efficacy: Thought control of action* (pp. 195–213). Washington, DC: Hemisphere.

Kratzmann, J., & Schneider, T. (2008). Verbessert der Besuch des Kindergartens die Startchancen von Kindern aus sozial schwachen Familien im Schulsystem? Eine Untersuchung auf Basis des SOEP [Does kindergarten attendance enhance starting chances in the school system for children from socially disadvantaged families? An examination based on the GSOEP.]. In J. Ramseger and M. Wagener (Eds.), *Chancenungleichheit in der Grundschule. Ursachen und Wege aus der Krise* (pp. 295–8). Wiesbaden: VS Verlag für Sozialwissenschaften.

Lerner, R. M., Lerner, J. V., Almerigi, J. B., Theokas, C., Phelps, E., Gestsdottir, S., et al. (2005). Positive youth development, participation in community youth development programs, and community contributions of fifth-grade adolescents: Findings from the first wave of the 4-H study of positive youth development. *Journal of Early Adolescence, 25*, 17–71.

Levenson, R. W., & Gottman, J. M. (1978). Toward the assessment of social competence. *Journal of Consulting and Clinical Psychology, 46*, 453–62.

Maaz, K., Hausen, C., McElvany, N., & Baumert, J. (2006). Stichwort: Übergänge im Bildungssystem. Theoretische Konzepte und ihre Anwendung in der empirischen Forschung beim Übergang in die Sekundarstufe [Transitions in the educational system. Theoretical concepts and their application in empirical research on the transition to secondary school]. *Zeitschrift für Erziehungswissenschaft, 9*, 299–327.

Magnuson, K., Lahaie, C., & Waldfogel, J. (2006). Preschool and school readiness of children of immigrants. *Social Science Quarterly, 87*, 1241–62.

Mammey, U., & Sattig, J. (2002). *Determinanten und Indikatoren der Integration der ausländischen Bevölkerung (Integrationssurvey). Projekt- und Materialdokumentation. [Determinant and indicators for integration of foreign populations (integration survey). Project and material documantation].* Wiesbaden: Bundesinstitut für Bevölkerungsforschung.

Mandara, J., Varner, F., Greene, N., & Richman, S. (2009). Intergenerational family predictors of the Black-White achievement gap. *Journal of Educational Psychology, 101*(4), 867–78.

Miller, B. C., & Benson, B. (1999). Romantic and sexual relationship development during adolescence. In W. Furman, B. B. Brown, and C. Feiring (Eds.), *The development of romantic relationships in adolescence* (pp. 99–121). Cambridge: Cambridge University Press.

Mueller, C. (2006). Integrating Turkish communities: a German dilemma. *Population Research and Policy Review, 25*(5–6), 419–41.

Nauck, B. (2001). Social capital, intergenerational transmission and intercultural contact in immigrant families. *Journal of Comparative Family Studies, 32*, 465–88.

— (2007). Bi-kulturelle Ehen, Familien und Partnerschaften [Bi-cultural marriages, families, and relationships]. In J. Straub, A. Weidemann and D. Weidemann (Eds.), *Handbuch interkulturelle Kommunikation und Kompetenz. Grundbegriffe – Theorien – Anwendungsfelder* (pp. 729–37). Stuttgart: Metzler.

Nauck, B., & Kohlmann, A. (1998). Verwandtschaft als soziales Kapital – Netzwerkbeziehungen in türkischen Migrantenfamilien [Kinship as social capital – network relations in Turkish migrant families]. In M. Wagner and Y. Schütze (Eds.), *Verwandtschaft. Sozialwissenschaftliche Beiträge zu einem vernachlässigten Thema* (pp. 203–35). Stuttgart: Enke Verlag.

Obradović, J., & Masten, A. S. (2007). Developmental antecedents of young adult civic engagement. *Applied Developmental Science, 11*(1), 2–19.

Okagaki, L., & Sternberg, R. J. (1993). Parental beliefs and children's school performance. *Child Development, 64*(1), 36–56.

Pearlin, L. I. (2009). The Life Course and the Stress Process: Some Conceptual Comparisons (Publication no. 10.1093/geronb/gbp106). Retrieved December 18, 2009: http://psychsocgerontology.oxfordjournals.org/cgi/content/abstract/gbp106v1.

Penn, H. (1996). Who influences policy in early childhood services? *International Journal of Early Years Education, 4*(3), 5–17.

Remennick, L. (2005). Cross-cultural dating patterns on an Israeli campus: Why are Russian immigrant women more popular than men? *Journal of Social and Personal Relationships, 22*, 435–54.

Ryder, A. G., Alden, L. E., & Paulhus, D. L. (2000). Is acculturation unidimensional or bidimensional? A head-to-head comparison in the prediction of personality, self-identity, and adjustment. *Journal of Personality and Social Psychology, 79*, 49–65.

Sakallı, N. (2001). Beliefs about wife beating among Turkish college students: The effects of patriarchy, sexism, and sex differences. *Sex Roles, 44*, 599–610.

Sammons, P., Elliot, K., Sylva, K., Melhuish, E., Siraj-Blatchford, I., & Taggart, B. (2004). The impact of pre-school on young children's cognitive attainments at entry to reception. *British Educational Research Journal, 30*(5), 691–712.

Schmitt-Rodermund, E., & Silbereisen, R. K. (2009). Immigrant parents' age expectations for the development of their adolescent offspring: Transmission effects and changes after immigration. In U. Schönpflug (Ed.), *Cultural transmission. Psychological, developmental, social, and methodological aspects* (pp. 297–313). New York: Cambridge University Press.

Smith, E. A., & Udry, J. R. (1985). Coital and noncoital sexual behaviors of White and Black adolescents. *American Journal of Public Health, 75*, 1200–3.

Smock, P. J. (2000). Cohabitation in the United States: An appraisal of research themes, findings, and implications. *Annual Review of Sociology, 26*, 1–20.

Spiess, C. K., Büchel, F., & Wagner, G. G. (2003). Children's school placement in Germany: Does Kindergarten attendance matter? *Early Childhood Research Quarterly, 18*, 255–70.

Statistisches Bundesamt [Federal Statistical Office]. (2008). *Statistisches Jahrbuch 2008 für die Bundesrepublik Deutschland [Statistical Yearbook 2008 for the federal republic of Germany]*. Retrieved on April 9, 2009 from http://www.destatis.de.

Office]. (2009). *Kindertagesbetreuung regional 2008 – Ein Vergleich aller 429 Kreise in Deutschland [Regional childcare 2008 – A comparison of all 429 administrative districts in Germany]*. Retrieved on October 18, 2009 from http://www.destatis.de.

Strobl, R., & Kühnel, W. (2000). *Dazugehörig und ausgegrenzt. Integrationschancen junger Aussiedler [Accepted and excluded: Chances of integration of young ethnic German immigrants]*. Weinheim: Juventa.

Titzmann, P. F., Silbereisen, R. K., Mesch, G., & Schmitt-Rodermund, E. (2011). Migration-specific hassles among adolescent immigrants from the former Soviet Union in Germany and Israel. *Journal of Cross-Cultural Psychology, 42*(5), 777–94.

Tomasik, M. J., & Pinquart, M. (2008). Adaptiver Umgang mit Anforderungen des sozialen Wandels [Adaptive regulation of demand related to social change]. In R. K. Silbereisen and M. Pinquart (Eds.), *Individuum und sozialer Wandel: Eine Studie zu Anforderungen, psychosozialen Ressourcen und individueller Bewältigung* (pp. 99–125). Weinheim: Juventa.

Uslucan, H.-H. (2009). Erziehung in Migrantenfamilien: Entwicklungs- und erziehungspsychologische Perspektiven [Raising children in migrant families: Developmental and educational psychological perspectives]. In K. Schneewind (Ed.), *Familien in Deutschland. Beiträge aus familienpsychologischer Sicht* (pp. 30–5). Berlin: Berufsverband Deutscher Psychologinnen und Psychologen.

van der Gaag, M., Snijders, T. A. B., & Flap, H. (2008). Position generator measures and their relationship to other social capital measures. In N. Lin and B. H. Erickson (Eds.), *Social capital. An international research program* (pp. 27–48). New York: Oxford University Press.

Walsemann, K. M., Gee, G. C., & Geronimus, A. T. (2009). Ethnic differences in trajectories of depressive symptoms: Disadvantage in family background, high school experiences, and adult characteristics. *Journal of Health and Social Behavior, 50*(1), 82–98.

Walter, O. (2008). Herkunftsassoziierte Disparitäten im Lesen, der Mathematik und den Naturwissenschaften: ein Vergleich zwischen PISA 2000, PISA 2003 und PISA 2006 [Ethnic disparities in reading, mathematic, and scientific achievement: a comparison of PISA 200, PISA 2003 and PISA 2006]. *Zeitschrift für Erziehungswissenschaft, 11 (Sonderheft 10)*, 149–68.

Woellert, F., Kröhnert, S., Sippel, L., & Klingholz, R. (2009). *Ungenutzte Potentiale. Zur Lage der Integration in Deutschland [Idle potentials. On the integration of migrants in Germany]*. Berlin: Berlin-Institut für Bevölkerung und Entwicklung.

Zimmer-Gembeck, M. J., & Skinner, E. A. (2011). The development of coping across childhood and adolescence: An integrative review and critique of research. *International Journal of Behavioral Development* (35), 1–17.

14 Conceptualizing the School Acculturative Context

School, Classroom, and the Immigrant Student

Gabriel Horenczyk and Moshe Tatar

Introduction

Schools are central for the development, enculturation, and adaptation of immigrants throughout the world. There are a variety of reasons that schools play such a key role: The school is a major arena for intergroup contact and acculturation; school adjustment is a primary task, and a highly important outcome, of the cultural transition process; schools tend to represent and introduce the new culture to immigrant children (Trickett & Birman, 2005), and many newcomers see schools as welcome avenues to participation and mobility (Vedder & Horenczyk, 2006). Thus, schools are highly important contexts, affecting in significant – sometimes crucial – ways the acculturation and adaptation of immigrant youth.

Research on acculturation and adaptation of immigrants is increasingly recognizing the important, even essential, role of context for understanding the processes and outcomes involved in cultural transitions. According to Phinney et al. (2001), "ethnic and national identities and their role in adaptation can best be understood in terms of an interaction between the attitudes and characteristics of immigrants and the responses of the receiving society, moderated by the particular circumstances of the immigrant group within the new society" (494). With immigration patterns becoming more diversified and plural societies facing new challenges for the successful integration of immigrant youth, careful attention and analysis of these intergroup factors are needed in order to account for the richness and complexity of most acculturating contexts (Horenczyk, 2009).

Contexts are often rich and complex. Ouarasse and van de Vijver (2004) differentiate between the majority (or mainstream) and minority contexts as perceived by immigrants. They report that the mainstream context seems crucial for work adaptation of immigrant adolescents and young adults in the Netherlands, whereas the minority context appears important for school success and good mental health. Verkuyten (2005) also emphasizes the role of context in social psychology in general, and in the study of ethnic identity among immigrants in particular, and calls for a context-sensitive approach to theory and research in the area. He argues for the multifaceted nature of the context impinging on the identity and adaptation of immigrants and makes the important distinction among the ideological context, the comparative group context, the cultural context, and the rhetorical/discursive context. As to schools in immigrant-receiving societies, they often include all the types of context proposed by Verkuyten (2005), thus exposing the newcomer to a variety of acculturation-related messages, not always clear or congruent (see chapter by Motti-Stefanidi et al., this volume).

This chapter focuses on the school acculturative context and its roles in the acculturation and adaptation of immigrant youth, informed primarily by social and cross-cultural psychology. We propose a conceptual and analytical framework for organizing and guiding research and practice on immigrants in schools. The framework is multilevel: It takes into account both school- and classroom-level factors. It also follows a multiperspective approach, as it examines the attitudes, perceptions, and behaviors not only of immigrants but also of the members of the majority society (primarily, but not solely, as perceived by the immigrant student). We first present an overview of the model and background literature that informed this conceptual approach. Next, we delineate this approach at two levels: the school level and the classroom level. We discuss multiple perspectives, examining how immigrants and nationals perceive the acculturative school context, and explore possible discrepancies between these attitudes and perceptions. We conclude with comments on the potential of research on immigrant education, and particularly the study of the school acculturative context, to inform efforts to promote the adaptation of immigrant youth.

Overview and Background of the Model

Our model extends earlier work on school context by distinguishing two levels of context and multiple players at each level. In regard to *levels*, we distinguish primarily between the school and the classroom levels. The acculturative context at the school level is reflected in what we term the School Multicultural Organizational Climate (SMOC), with its various components – concrete aspects, norms, values, and structural variables. At the classroom level, we delineate two major players: teachers and classmates (mostly nationals but sometimes also immigrants). This conceptual framework not only captures the richness and complexity of school acculturative contexts, but also allows for the examination of discrepancies within levels and perspectives, as well as between them. We will return to this central aspect of our model later.

Various studies document the importance of the school context for the academic, social, and psychological adaptation of immigrant students, alongside other contextual spheres (on the importance of the school context, see chapter by Spiel and Strohmeier, this volume). Recently, Gonzalez (2009) described the ways in which the school context affects ethnic identity and social integration among Mexican American adolescents in the United States. Grounded in an ecological systems approach, Han (2008) examined contextual factors related to the academic trajectories of immigrant and nonimmigrant students, with particular attention to the effects of school environments. Findings revealed that all the three aspects of the context assessed – family background, parental involvement, and school/neighborhood environments – were important to adolescents' risk for academic failure and social relationship problems. Along similar lines, Sabatier (2008) analyzed variables at multiple layers of contexts. Relationships with parents emerged as the main predictor of identity (ethnic and national) affirmation and exploration, and school context contributed – although modestly – to the prediction of identity patterns. Trickett and Birman (2005) also see the school as potential locus of cultural conflict and acculturative stress, which is hypothesized to be linked to maladaptive behaviors. In one of their studies (Birman, Trickett, & Buchanan, 2005), they examined acculturation and adaptation of immigrant students in two markedly different community contexts. Their findings revealed differential effects of the distinct contexts on the adaptation of the immigrant students. They conclude that schools may exert not only an assimilative "press" (which we will discuss in detail later), but also sometimes a "multiculturalist" press on the newcomers, rewarding different acculturative styles.

Although the importance of context in general, and school context in particular, for the understanding of the acculturation and adaptation of immigrants is widely accepted, there is little conceptual and empirical work on the different components of the school acculturative context and on their differential effects on psychological and school adaptation. A first conceptualization of school-level variables related to – and probably affecting – the integration of immigrant students in Israeli schools was offered by Tatar et al. (1994). They identified four basic school parameters: (1) the basic attitude of the school toward the integration of immigrants – assimilation to pluralism; (2) the priority given by the school to immigrant integration – high to low; (3) the school's perception of the change it is undergoing – a first-order (borrowing from Watzlawick et al.'s [1974] terminology) additive change or a second-order metamorphic change; and (4) the school's methods of coping – habitual (more of the same) or creative and entrepreneurial.

An example of a policy reflecting a habitual assimilative approach is a norm highly prevalent in culturally diverse schools: Immigrant students are encouraged – and even required – to use only the national language in school and to refrain from communicating in their ethnic language in class and during recess. The norm is often delivered and enforced by all members of the school's staff. On the other hand, a principal's call for the allocation of appropriate resources that will allow homeroom teachers and school counselors to work with mixed (immigrant and nonimmigrant) groups of parents about their relationships with their children and providing them with culturally sensitive techniques for strengthening parent-child relationships will be classified as a pluralistic, high prioritized, second-order, and even creative approach.

The four parameters proposed by Tatar et al. (1994) are largely interrelated, allowing two "pure" types of schools to be portrayed. In schools with an assimilationist orientation, the task of integrating immigrants is usually seen as marginal, no major structural or pedagogical changes are considered necessary, and routine coping strategies are maintained. At the other extreme, schools that adopt a multiculturalist philosophy assign a central place to the education of their immigrant students and tend to perceive the new composition of their student body as a turning point calling for qualitative change and the development and implementation of new coping strategies.

The model presented in this chapter extends this initial mapping, proposing a multilevel and multiperspective conceptualization of the school acculturative context. In our model, we examine contextual factors at multiple levels because a look at the complexity and the multifaceted nature of acculturative contexts would show us numerous concentric, and at times partially overlapping, levels affecting – directly or indirectly – immigrants' educational adaptation. A multiple-levels analysis, for example, might include the following: at the national level, language policies of the ministry of education and/or societal values regarding the importance of higher education, and, at the family level, the expectations of close relatives in regard to the immigrant's performance in school. Our analysis in this chapter will focus primarily on two central levels of the school acculturative context: the school and classroom levels. As to the multiperspective nature of our model, we will account mainly for the immigrants' and nationals' views of the school acculturative context and the possible discrepancies between them.

The School Level

At the school level, the school acculturative context can be conceptualized and mapped in terms of the School Multicultural Organizational Climate (Horenczyk & Tatar, 2002). The SMOC is one particular aspect of the school's organizational culture – namely, its approach to cultural diversity. The concept of organizational culture has gained popularity in the counseling and in the organizational literatures, focusing on the culture of single organizational units. An organizational culture is the characteristic spirit and belief of an organization, expressed in the norms and values that are held about how people should treat one another and the nature of the working relationships that ought to be developed. It is commonly assumed that a consolidated organizational culture leads to the attainment of the institution's goals (Mitchell & Willower, 1992). The organizational culture of an institution provides an identity for its members, generates commitment to the organization's mission, and contributes to the clarification and reinforcement of particular standards of behavior (Greenberg & Baron, 2000). From a practical point of view, the organizational culture provides informal norms that guide action and behavior (Burrello & Reitzug, 1993). Different levels of an organizational culture can be delineated: its artifacts, the organizational perspectives and values, and its tacit assumptions, beliefs, and attitudes (Schein, 1985). First, the artifacts are the tangible aspects of culture shared by members of the organization, that is, the verbal, behavioral, and physical manifestations of the organizational culture. Second, the perspectives and values are the socially shared rules and norms applicable to the given context. These rules and norms provide the evaluative standards by which members judge situations and people in the organization. Finally, the tacit beliefs are the basic assumptions that members hold about themselves and others, about their relationships to other persons, and about the nature of the organization in which they work (for a summary see Tatar & Bekerman, 2002).

The concept of organizational culture can assist us in the mapping of the school context in general and of the school acculturative context in particular. In our model (Horenczyk & Tatar, 2002), we propose as an initial classification the following major components of the SMOC:

1. Concrete aspects (in the school public space), such as curriculum contents, displays on the school walls, and ceremonies; the extent to which curricula and course contents are monocultural (by deriving its nature

from the dominant majority culture) – a factor that may create or reinforce feelings of exclusion through the marginalization of immigrants
(as recently indicated by Nusche, 2009).

2. Norms – behaviors rewarded/reinforced or punished by the school;
these norms may be conveyed via assessment tools and criteria that may
be culturally biased or culturally sensitive.

3. Values – importance of immigration-related values within the school
organizational culture, for example, recognition of immigrant students
as a unique group, retention of immigrants' cultures, and turning immigrant students into nationals.

4. Basic assumptions – the tacit beliefs that the various players in the
school context hold about immigrant and national students, about the
relationships among them, and about the multicultural nature of their
organization.

In an initial study using the SMOC classification components, we examined the relationship between perceived school climate and teachers' attitudes toward multiculturalism (Horenczyk & Tatar, 2002). Three out of the
four components of the SMOC were assessed: concrete aspects (measured
in terms of school scenarios), school norms related to policies vis-à-vis
immigrant students, and school multiculturalist values. Results of multiple
regression analyses showed that all three aspects of the school organizational culture contributed to the prediction of teachers' assimilationist and
pluralistic attitudes within the educational context.

As a next step, we propose to broaden the scope of the school acculturative context – at the school level – by adding to the SMOC an additional
component, namely, structural variables related to the school, particularly
to the immigration-related diversity in the institution. These variables, such
as the percentage of immigrant students and the proportion of immigrant
teachers, are highly relevant for the analysis of the school acculturative
climate and its role in immigrants' academic and social adaptation.

The Classroom Level

Different social agents play different roles in the school acculturative context at the classroom level: teachers (mostly nationals, but also immigrant
teachers) and classmates (national and immigrant peers). Attitudes, expectations, and behaviors of these various players are likely to affect the acculturation and adaptation of immigrant students.

Teachers

Teachers have been shown to be major players in the school acculturative context, exerting strong influences on the psychological and sociocultural adaptation of immigrant students. Teachers' behaviors and attitudes tend to epitomize the expectations held by the new culture with regard to the proper role of students (children and adolescents), and are also perceived as reflecting the criteria for success in their society (Luchtenberg, 2004; Tatar & Horenczyk, 1996). Recently, Suárez-Orozco, Pimentel, and Martin (2009) summarized research showing that positive and meaningful connections between immigrant students and their teachers – as well as with other non-parental adults in the school setting – can smooth their cultural transition into the new country. These kinds of protective relationships can provide immigrant students with compensatory attachments through the building of safe contexts (due to the frequent weakening of family ties in times of transition). Vedder, Boekaerts, and Seegers (2005) showed that whereas national Dutch youngsters reported more instructional support from their parents than from their teachers, immigrant adolescents reported more instructional support from their teachers.

Teachers' attitudes and behaviors vis-à-vis their immigrant students are crucial for understanding immigrants' adaptation to the new culture. Horenczyk and Tatar (2002) found that Israeli teachers endorsed pluralistic attitudes when referring to the integration of former Soviet Union (FSU) immigrants into the general society, but assimilationist attitudes were more predominant when related to the approach toward immigrants in educational contexts. The teachers seem to view education as the primary means for transforming the immigrant into an "Israeli," and they see the school as the most appropriate setting for attaining this goal. Similarly, in a study conducted among Israeli educational counselors, Tatar (1998) classified the views held by almost three-quarters of his respondents as reflecting at least to some degree an assimilationist approach and only the remaining one-quarter exhibiting a cultural pluralist outlook. Eisikovits (2008) documented the clash between the national building orientation of the Israeli teachers and the largely transnational attitude of the immigrant students.

The assimilationist attitudes of teachers do not characterize solely Israeli school acculturative contexts. Motti-Stefanidi and her colleagues (2008) also found that Greek teachers tend to promote the assimilation of immigrant groups. Based on theory and research suggesting that teacher beliefs and expectations often shape their behavior toward students, thus affecting students' learning and well-being, they examined acculturation patterns, psychological well-being, and school adjustment of two immigrant groups into Greek society: newcomers from the former Soviet Union and from Albania. Results showed that teachers reported higher academic performance and adaptation among immigrant students who reported higher involvement with Greek culture.

Teacher expectations have been proposed as a significant contributor to the lower performance of some ethnic and immigrant students. Why? Teachers may provide higher quality instruction to students from whom they expect more; students may perceive cues about what teachers expect, internalize these expectations, and become motivated and achieve according to the perceived expectations; those who face lower teacher expectations become concerned about being judged on the basis of stereotypes, increasing susceptibility to negative expectancy effects. Many studies in the United States suggest that teacher expectancy effects may be stronger for immigrant and minority-member groups than for European American students. In a series of studies, McKown and Weinstein (2008) examined the role of classroom context in moderating the relationship between child ethnicity and teacher expectations. Their main findings showed that the higher the classroom diversity and the higher the perceived differential teacher treatment, the more biased the teacher expectations. Moreover, in mixed classes, teachers expect more of specific cultural groups (e.g., European American and Asian American) than from other groups (e.g., African American and Latinos). Recently, Nusche (2009) summarized research evidence and policy on immigrant education in OECD countries and argued that educational outcomes are mediated, along with curricula and materials, by the "hidden curricula" reflected in teachers' expectations. She also suggested that lower expectations might have a detrimental effect on student motivation and achievement. According to Nusche (2009), this potential negative effect on immigrant students may be reduced by promoting awareness regarding discriminating teacher behaviors.

It is noteworthy that working with culturally diverse student populations is often considered a stressor and added burden to teachers' already heavy workload. According to Eisikovits (2008), many teachers have difficulties coping with multicultural classes: Some are unable able to move away from their own assimilationist stance and teaching habits; others do not know how to deal with immigrant students showing some degree of seclusionism. But is an assimilative orientation an asset for the teacher working with culturally diverse students, particularly within an assimilative acculturative context? In their study of teachers coping with stressors involved in working with immigrant students, Tatar and Horenczyk (2003) introduced the concept of diversity-related burnout, which reflects the extent to which teachers' personal and professional well-being is negatively affected by the daily coping with a culturally heterogeneous student body. The highest levels of diversity-related burnout were found among teachers categorized as assimilationists and who worked in schools perceived by them also to be assimilationist. Although the assimilationist perspective appears to entail a more uniform approach toward culturally diverse students, a strategy that can be seen as less effort- and time-consuming as well as one lacking the ambiguity and equivocality of a more pluralistic orientation, it would seem that the challenges posed by cultural diversity are so visible and concrete that they cannot be put aside. The efforts devoted to denying diversity and its educational demands are more detrimental to teachers' well-being as compared to the serious effort required to cope with cultural heterogeneity in the classroom (Tatar & Horenczyk, 2003).

A recent study conducted among immigrant teachers in Israel (Tatar, Ben-Uri, & Horenczyk, 2011) provides additional evidence for the detrimental effects of the teachers' assimilationist approach. The higher the assimilationist attitudes held by the immigrant teachers, the lower their sense of "immigration-related self-efficacy" – their sense of self-efficacy vis-à-vis teaching their immigrant students. In this context, it is important to note that relatively few immigrants are employed as teachers, even in immigrant-receiving countries. Sever (1994) attributed this underutilization of immigrant teachers to the belief that the rapid integration of immigrant students is a task more appropriate for nonimmigrant teachers. Thus, the immigrant teachers' more valuable asset (the knowledge and expertise in working with their former conational – now immigrant – students[1]) does not seem to constitute an advantage if the educational system emphasizes the transmission of the dominant culture to the immigrants as its main message to immigrant populations (Inglis & Philps, 1995; Michael, 2006).

National Peers

Peer relationships serve as a source of social and emotional support and as a context for learning and practicing social, cognitive, and language skills (Vedder & Horenczyk, 2006). Ample evidence has shown that support from peers is one of the factors contributing to the sociocultural and psychological adaptation of immigrant students (Berry, 2006; Liebkind, 2006). Usually social support is conceptualized and measured in terms of contacts and

---

[1] During the last two decades, immigrant students and teachers are mostly former conationals from the former Soviet Union.

assistance from co-immigrants (Mirsky, Baron-Draiman, & Kedem, 2002; Vedder et al., 2005; Yeh et al., 2008). However, as stated by Searle and Ward (1990), "the literature has been somewhat ambiguous about the source of social support, with some researchers emphasizing the need for good interpersonal relations with nationals and others highlighting the quality of relationships with co-nationals" (458).

Within our framework of the school acculturative context, we would like to emphasize – at the classroom level – the important role played by the national classmate. Following Rubin (1980), who claimed that the meaning of friendship reflects "the style of social interaction that characterizes and is valued by one given culture or subculture" (133), we have suggested that, through close contact with their national peers, immigrants become acquainted with – and eventually learn – the social and cultural messages concerning the behavioral norms and social roles expected from them, according to sex, age, and so forth (Horenczyk & Tatar, 1998). Relationships with national peers may function as an entree to the absorbing society, thus facilitating the immigrants' partial or full integration into their new society and culture. Quite often, national classmates can provide immigrant adolescents with the information as well as the social and institutional contacts that may help to alleviate their sense of estrangement and cultural shock and improve their personal, social, and academic adjustment (Horenczyk & Tatar, 1998).

Horenczyk and Tatar (1998) explored differences between immigrant and nonimmigrant students in friendship expectations (help and assistance, status, similarity, and avoidance of harm). Findings showed that immigrants assign greater importance than their national counterparts to all aspects of friendship expectations. Immigrants' friendship expectations were found to be positively correlated with social distress, especially among early adolescent girls.

National peers can be a valuable source of support for the immigrant adolescent during all phases of the cultural transition process. But, alternatively, nonimmigrant peers might be perceived by the newcomer as a source of prejudice and discrimination. As clearly summarized by Liebkind, Jasinskaja-Lahti, and Solheim (2004), perceived discrimination has turned out to have a strong negative effect on various aspects of the well-being of young immigrants. In a study conducted among immigrant adolescents in Israel, for example, perceived discrimination was negatively correlated with immigrants' adaptation (Horenczyk, 2008). The relationship was stronger for sociocultural as compared to psychological adaptation. Liebkind and her colleagues (2004) found that perceived discrimination had a significant negative effect on the school adjustments of immigrant adolescents. Perceived discrimination affected school adjustments indirectly through its detrimental effect on the adolescents' self-esteem and stress symptoms. Jasinskaja-Lahti and Liebkind (2001) concluded that perceived discrimination is one of the major psychological stressors that reduces the psychological adjustment of immigrants.

Perceived discrimination might reflect actual discrimination, but research evidence shows that this may not always be the case (Dion & Kawakami, 1996). Moreover, minority group members may not feel personal discrimination but still consider that their group is being treated unfairly. Moghaddam (1998) referred to this phenomenon as a "personal-group discrimination discrepancy" – the tendency for minority group members to perceive a higher level of discrimination directed at their group as a whole than at themselves as individual members of that group.

Within the school acculturative context, discrimination can be experienced from different players and at various levels. At the school level, for example, norms – such as those related to the use of native language – might be interpreted by the immigrant student or by immigrant parents as discriminatory. At the classroom level, discriminatory behavior might be attributed to national teachers or peers. Unfortunately, most studies on perceived discrimination do not differentiate in their instruments or in their analyses between teachers and peers as possible sources of discrimination. Although some questionnaires include items on each of them, total scores of perceived discrimination are often computed. A comprehensive conceptualization and investigation of the school acculturative context will have to make a clear distinction between levels and among levels in attributed discrimination.

Multiple Perspectives

School acculturative contexts are complex and dynamic networks, where immigrants negotiate their cultural identities and learn about the values, norms, and behaviors expected of them by the various agents of the majority society – inside and outside school. This process entails intricate communicational transactions, which allow newcomers to calibrate their identities and their behaviors with those of the receiving society (Horenczyk, 1996). Although the school acculturative context has its concrete expressions (in formal norms and documents, in visual features of the school space, etc.), much of its discourse is vague and open to different perceptions and interpretations. A comprehensive mapping of the school acculturative context needs to take into account these multiple perspectives: Newcomers and nationals may disagree on the nature of the school multicultural climate and its components (for instance, the extent to which the curricula grants expression to cultural diversity), on the pervasiveness and strength of assimilative pressures, and on what is expected of immigrant students in the various areas of school life.

Resnik et al. (2001), for example, conducted an ethnographic study of two elementary schools in Israel. They reported discrepancies between nationals and immigrants on the prevailing school ideology: Nonimmigrant teachers view their school as following an integrationist (pluralistic) approach, whereas the immigrant students – and the researchers' observations – revealed a clear assimilationist educational environment.

A multiperspective analysis of the school acculturative context will encourage us to explore various types of national-immigrant discrepancies at the classroom level and at the school level – for example, between the (national) teacher and immigrant students, between immigrant students and their national peers, between national and immigrant teachers. Grounded in similar assumptions, the Interactive Acculturation Model proposed by Bourhis and his colleagues (Bourhis et al., 1997) suggests that acculturation strategies of minority members are interrelated with the acculturation orientations of members of the majority society. Along similar lines, Piontkowski, Rohmann, and Florack (2002; see also Rohmann, Piontkowski, & van Randenborgh, 2008) put forward a concordance model of acculturation (CMA): The comparison of the attitudes of a dominant and a nondominant group gives rise to four levels of concordance that represent different possibilities of (mis)matched attitudes: consensual, culture-problematic, contact-problematic, and conflictual. In a *consensual* pattern, the attitudes of the receiving community match the attitudes of the immigrants. A *culture-problematic* discordance exists in the case of mismatched attitudes on cultural maintenance, whereas a *contact-problematic* discordance exists in the case of mismatched attitudes on the contact issue (e.g., if the national community adopts a segregation strategy while the immigrants want to integrate). Last, a *conflictual* pattern occurs in the case of mismatched attitudes on both acculturation issues, or if the dominant group prefers exclusion (see chapter by Liebkind, Jasinskaja-Lahti, and Mähönen, this volume).

In a series of studies, Horenczyk (1996, 2000) examined the acculturation attitudes of Israeli immigrants together with their "perceived acculturation expectations" – the expectations they attribute to members of the receiving society with regard to newcomers' social and cultural integration. The findings show a clear and consistent pattern of results (Horenczyk, 1996, 2000;

Horenczyk & Sankevich, 2006): Immigrants not only prefer the acculturation attitude of integration/biculturalism, but they also tend to perceive it as the primary acculturation ideology of their nonimmigrant peers. In one of these studies (Horenczyk, 1996), Israeli national-immigrant peers were also asked about the acculturation attitudes they expect from their immigrant peers. It was found that the most preferred expected acculturation attitude was also the bicultural one. This would suggest that in the collective discourse about acculturation, the rhetoric of multiculturalism has been widely adopted by both nationals and immigrants. Yet, a closer comparative examination of the immigrants' own acculturation attitudes and the perceived acculturation expectations revealed a more complex and less idyllic picture. Immigrants tend to perceive the majority society's expectations of immigrant *assimilation* as considerably stronger than their own willingness to assimilate (Horenczyk, 1996, 2000; Roccas, Horenczyk, & Schwartz, 2000). It would seem that the generally accepted rhetoric of multiculturalism does not have the same meaning for immigrants and for their national counterparts. From the point of view of the immigrant adolescent, the experience is one of pressure to assimilate more – and/or faster – than his or her own willingness to do so. The resulting internal conflict might have detrimental effects on immigrants' adaptation, as "assimilation discrepancies" were found to be negatively correlated with immigrants' well-being (Roccas et al., 2000).

Conclusion

In closing, we would like to argue for a multiperspective approach in the conceptualization, operationalization, and study of school acculturative contexts – on their various levels and components. We are particularly interested in possible discrepancies between and within levels and in their relation to acculturation and school adjustment of the immigrant student. Further elaboration and refinement of the present model will allow us to relate it to other multilevel models such as Bronfenbrenner's ecological framework (1979, 1989, 1995).

In this chapter, we have proposed initial guidelines for a comprehensive conceptualization and mapping of the school acculturative context, proposing a multilevel and multiperspective approach. The suggested model could guide further research aimed at identifying additional contextual variables – at different levels and from various perspectives – that would help refine the framework sketched in this chapter. Based on the premise about the centrality of schools in the lives of immigrant youngsters, and grounded in a contextual perspective on acculturation and adaptation, we suggest that the discipline of immigrant education in general, and the study of the school acculturative context in particular, should help us identify risk and resilience factors and conditions in order to promote the psychological and sociocultural adaptation and potential of immigrant youth.

Authors' Note

This chapter was written while Gabriel Horenczyk was a visiting fellow at the Helsinki Collegium for Advanced Studies.

REFERENCES

Berry, J. W. (2006). Stress perspective on acculturation. In D. L. Sam and J. W. Berry (Eds.), *The Cambridge handbook of acculturation psychology* (pp. 43–57). Cambridge: CUP.

Birman, D., Trickett, E., & Buchanan, R. (2005). A tale of two cities: replication of a study on the acculturation and adaptation of immigrant adolescents from the former Soviet Union in a different community context. *American Journal of Community Psychology, 35*, 87–101.

Bourhis, R. Y., Moise, L. C., Perreault, S., & Senecal, S. (1997). Towards an Interactive Acculturation Model: A social psychological approach. *International Journal of Psychology, 32*, 369–86.

Bronfenbrenner, U. (1979). *The ecology of human development: Experiments by nature and design*. Cambridge, MA: Harvard University Press.

(1989). Ecological systems theory. In R. Vasta (Ed.), *Annals of child development: Vol. 6. Six theories of child development: Revised formulations and current issues* (pp. 187–249). Greenwich, CT: JAI Press.

(1995). Developmental ecology through space and time: A future perspective. In P. Moen, G. H. Elder, and K. Luscher (Eds.), *Examining lives in context: Perspectives on human development* (pp. 619–47).Washington, DC: American Psychological Association.

Burrello, L. C., & Reitzug, U. C. (1993). Transforming context and developing culture in schools. *Journal of Counselling and Development, 71*, 669–77.

Dion, K. L., & Kawakami, K. (1996). Ethnicity and perceived discrimination in Toronto: Another look at the personal/group discrimination discrepancy, *Canadian Journal of Behavioural Science, 28*, 203–13.

Eisikovits, R. A. (2008). Coping with high-achieving transnationalist immigrant students: The experience of Israeli teachers. *Teaching and Teacher Education, 24*, 277–89.

Gonzalez, R. (2009). Beyond affirmation: How the school context facilitates racial/ethnic identity among Mexican American adolescents. *Hispanic Journal of Behavioral Sciences, 31*, 5–31.

Greenberg, J., & Baron, R. A. (2000). *Behavior in organizations*. New Jersey: Prentice-Hall.

Han, W. J. (2008). The academic trajectories of children of immigrants and their school environments. *Developmental Psychology, 44*, 1572–90.

Horenczyk, G. (1996). Migrant identities in conflict: Acculturation attitudes and perceived acculturation ideologies. In G. Breakwell and E. Lyons (Eds.), *Changing European Identities* (pp. 241–50). Oxford: Butterworth-Heinemann.

(2000). Conflicted identities: Acculturation attitudes and the immigrants' construction of their social worlds. In E. Olshtain and G. Horenczyk (Eds.), *Language, identity, and immigration* (pp. 13–30). Jerusalem: Magnes Press.

(2008). Cultural identities, perceived discrimination, and adaptation: Immigrant adolescents in Israel. In A. Stavans and I. Kupferberg (Eds.), *Studies in language and language education: Essays in honor of Elite Olshtain*. Jerusalem: Magnes Press.

(2009). Multiple reference groups: Towards the mapping of immigrants' complex social worlds. In I. Jasinskaja-Lahti and T. A. Mähönen (Eds.), *Identities, intergroup relations and acculturation: The cornerstones of intercultural encounters* (pp. 67–80). Helsinki: Gaudeamus Helsinki University Press.

Horenczyk, G., & Sankevich, V. I. (2006, July). Acculturation attitudes, perceived ingroup and outgroup expectations, and adaptation among immigrant adolescents. Paper presented at the 18th International Congress of the International Association for Cross-Cultural Psychology, Spetses, Greece.

Horenczyk, G., & Tatar, M. (1998). Friendship expectations among immigrant adolescents and their host peers. *Journal of Adolescence, 21*, 69–82.

(2002). Teachers' attitudes toward multiculturalism and their perceptions of the school organizational culture. *Teaching and Teacher Education, 18*, 435–45.

Inglis, C., & Philps, R. (1995). *Teachers in the sun – The impact of immigrant teachers on the labor force*. Canberra: Australian Government Publishing Services.

Jasinskaja-Lahti, I., & Liebkind, K. (2001). Perceived discrimination and psychological adjustment among Russian-speaking immigrant adolescents in Finland. *International Journal of Psychology, 36*, 174–85.

Liebkind, K. (2006). Ethnic identity and acculturation. In D. L. Sam and J. W. Berry (Eds.), *The Cambridge handbook of acculturation psychology* (pp. 78–96). Cambridge: CUP.

Liebkind, K., Jasinskaja-Lahti, I., & Solheim, E. (2004). Cultural identity, perceived discrimination, and parental support as determinants of immigrants' school adjustments: Vietnamese youth in Finland. *Journal of Adolescent Research, 19*, 635–56.

Luchtenberg, S. (2004). (New forms of) migration: challenges for education. In S. Luchtenberg (Ed.), *Migration, education and change* (pp. 40–63). Abingdon und New York: Routledge.

McKown, C., & Weinstein, R. S. (2008). Teacher expectations, classroom context, and the achievement gap. *Journal of School Psychology, 46*, 235–61.

Michael, O. (2006). Multiculturalism in schools: The professional absorption of immigrant teachers from the former USSR into the education system in Israel. *Teaching and Teacher Education, 22*, 164–78.

Mirsky, J., Baron-Draiman, Y., & Kedem, P. (2002). Social support and psychological distress among young immigrants from the former Soviet Union in Israel. *International Social Work, 45*, 83–97.

Mitchell, J. T., & Willower, D. J. (1992). Organizational culture in a good high school. *Journal of Educational Administration, 30*, 6–16.

Moghaddam, F. (1998). *Social psychology: Exploring universals across cultures.* New York: Freeman.

Motti-Stefanidi, F., Pavlopoulos, V., Obradovic´, J., Dalla, M., Takis, N., Papathanassiou, A., et al. (2008). Immigration as a risk factor for adolescent adaptation in Greek urban schools. *European Journal of Developmental Psychology, 5,* 235–61.

Nusche, D. (2009). *What works in migrant education? A review of evidence and policy options.* OECD Education Working Papers, No. 22, OECD Publishing, Paris.

Ouarasse, O. A., & van de Vijver, F. J. R. (2004). Structure and function of the perceived acculturation context of young Moroccans in the Netherlands. *International Journal of Psychology, 39,* 190–204.

Phinney, J. S., Horenczyk, G., Liebkind, K., & Vedder, P. (2001). Ethnic identity, immigration, and well-being: An interactional perspective. *Journal of Social Issues, 57,* 493–510.

Piontkowski, U., Rohmann, A., & Florack, A. (2002). Concordance of acculturation attitudes and perceived threat. *Group Processes & Intergroup Relations, 5,* 221–32.

Resnik, J., Sabar, N., Shapira, R., & Shoham, E. (2001). Absorption of CIS immigrants into Israeli schools: A semipermeable enclave model. *Anthropology & Education Quarterly, 32,* 424–46.

Roccas, S., Horenczyk, G., & Schwartz, S. H. (2000). Acculturation discrepancies and well-being: The moderating role of conformity. *European Journal of Social Psychology, 30,* 323–34.

Rohmann, A., Piontkowski, U., & van Randenborgh, A. (2008). When attitudes do not fit: Discordance of acculturation attitudes as an antecedent of intergroup threat. *Personality and Social Psychology Bulletin, 34,* 337–52.

Rubin, Z. (1980). *Children's friendships.* Cambridge, MA: Harvard University Press.

Sabatier, C. (2008). Ethnic and national identity among second-generation immigrant adolescents in France: The role of social context and family. *Journal of Adolescence, 31,* 185–205.

Schein, E. H. (1985). *Organizational culture and leadership.* San Francisco: Jossey-Bass.

Searle, W., & Ward, C. (1990). The prediction of psychological and sociocultural adjustment during cross-cultural transition. *International Journal of Intercultural Relations, 14,* 449–64.

Sever, R., (1994). *Immigrant absorption in education: Position paper.* Jerusalem: The Center for the Study of Social Policy in Israel. (In Hebrew).

Suárez-Orozco, C., Pimentel, A., Martin, M. (2009). The significance of relationships: Academic engagement and achievement among newcomer immigrant youth. *Teachers College Record, 111,* 712–49.

Tatar, M. (1998). Counselling immigrants: School contexts and emerging strategies. *British Journal of Guidance & Counselling, 26,* 337–52.

Tatar, M., & Bekerman, Z. (2002). The concept of culture in the contexts and practices of professional counselling: A constructivist perspective. *Counselling Psychology Quarterly, 15,* 375–84.

Tatar, M., Ben-Uri, I., & Horenczyk, G. (2011). Assimilation attitudes predict lower immigration-related self-efficacy among Israeli immigrant teachers. *European Journal of Psychology of Education, 26,* 247–55.

Tatar, M., & Horenczyk, G. (1996). Immigrant and host pupils' expectations of teachers. *British Journal of Educational Psychology, 66,* 289–99.

(2003). Diversity-related burnout among teachers. *Teaching and Teacher Education*, *19*, 397–408.

Tatar, M., Kfir, D., Sever, R., Adler, C., & Regev, H. (1994). *Integration of immigrant students into Israeli elementary and secondary schools: A pilot study.* Jerusalem: The NCJW Institute for Innovation in Education, School of Education, The Hebrew University (in Hebrew).

Trickett, E. J., & Birman, D. (2005). Acculturation, school context, and school outcomes: Adaptation of refugee adolescents from the Former Soviet Union. *Psychology in the Schools, 42*, 27–38.

Vedder, P., Boekaerts, M., & Seegers, G. (2005). Perceived social support and well being in school; The role of students' ethnicity. *Journal of Youth and Adolescence, 34*, 269–78.

Vedder, P., & Horenczyk, G. (2006). Acculturation and the school. In D. L. Sam and J. W. Berry (Eds.), *The Cambridge handbook of acculturation psychology* (pp. 419–38). Cambridge, UK: Cambridge University Press.

Verkuyten, M. (2005). *The social psychology of ethnic identity.* Hove: Psychology Press.

Watzlawick, P., Weakland, J. H., & Fisch, R. (1974). *Change: Principles of problem formation and problem resolution*: Oxford, England: W. W. Norton.

Yeh, C. J., Okubo, Y., Ma, P.-W. W., Shea, M., Ou, D., & Pituc, S. T. (2008). Chinese immigrant high school students' cultural interactions, acculturation, family obligations, language use, and social support. *Family Therapy, 35*, 161–76.

15 Peer Relations in Multicultural Schools

Christiane Spiel and Dagmar Strohmeier

Introduction

Peer relations in the school context play important roles in development and socialization, yet there has been surprisingly little research on the significance of peers for the acculturation of immigrant youth. Empirical studies on immigrants and host communities have primarily investigated acculturation orientations in terms of attitudes (Berry, 1997; Bourhis et al., 1997). Research that extends the acculturation model to actual behavior in peer relations is comparably rare (Graham, Taylor, & Ho, 2009), although relationships with peers play a major role in the development of cognitions, emotions, and behaviors in children and youth (Hawker & Boulton, 2000; Salmivalli & Isaacs, 2005).

For immigrants, school provides an opportunity to socialize. School is a place where native and immigrant children and youth spend a substantial part of the day. School provides prolonged firsthand contact with people from different cultures, ethnic backgrounds, and races, and is therefore an important context for forming peer relations. As a result, school can afford positive opportunities like friendships, learning about other cultures, understanding other ethnic groups; as well as negative experiences such as prejudice and racism, rejection and social exclusion, bullying and victimization (Schofield, 1995).

Friendships commonly contribute to self-esteem and socioemotional support (Hartup, 1996). Although the formation of interethnic friendships cannot be taken for granted in contact situations (Schofield, 1995), the interethnic friendships that embody the personalized and equal-status contact described by contact theorists such as Allport (1979) or Pettigrew (1998) do have many positive effects. Interethnic friendships were shown to be keystones in the reduction of prejudice and racial segregation (e.g., Schofield, 1995). Furthermore, having cross-racial friends was shown to have positive effects on psychological and sociocultural adaptation. Elementary school-aged children from the majority racial group in their classroom (either black or white) with a mutual interracial friend were reported to be more self-confident, more popular, and better leaders than majority racial group members without an interracial friend (Lease & Blake, 2005). Consequently, knowledge on how to support positive peer relationships and prevent negative ones can significantly contribute to the successful integration of immigrants in school, and lays the cornerstone to becoming an accepted and fully participating citizen in the host country.

This chapter is written from the perspective of educational and developmental psychology. It summarizes research on positive and negative peer relations in adolescents and preadolescents enrolled in multicultural schools in the United States and in Europe. It focuses on peer relations in general, including as a subgroup the peer relations between immigrant and native children and youth. Selected examples are used to illustrate the significance of research on cross-ethnic and cross-racial peer relations. Policy implications for promoting successful integration in multicultural schools are discussed.

For the purposes of this chapter, the terms *race*, *ethnicity*, and *immigrant* will be used as follows. *Race* refers to "a group of persons with shared genetic, biological, and physical features," while *ethnicity* refers to "a category that either ascribed or voluntary reflects a group's common history, nationality, geography, language, and culture" (Graham et al., 2009, 395). In the growing body of research conducted in Europe that is focused on immigrants, the most common variables used for classifications are country of birth of the child or youth, country of birth of both parents, and cultural group of the child or youth (e.g., mother tongue, ethnicity, race). Based on these variables, children and youth are usually distinguished based on their cultural group membership (e.g., Motti-Stefanidi et al., 2008; Strohmeier & Spiel, 2003) and/or their generational status (Titzmann & Silbereisen, 2009). In this chapter, we use the term *cultural group* when referring to an immigrant youth's language or ethnicity (e.g., Albanians, Turks, etc.). The term *generational status* is used when referring to an immigrant youth's history of immigration. *First generation* refers to youth who themselves immigrated to another country while *second generation* refers to youth born in the country of settlement but whose parents were born in another country. Finally, we use *cross-cultural* or *multicultural* as umbrella terms.

The handbook of peer interactions, relationships, and groups edited by Rubin, Bukowski, and Laursen (2009) provides a comprehensive overview of the corresponding research in the United States. However, as observed by Graham, Taylor, and Ho (2009), only 7% of the large body of research on peer relations published between 1986 and 2006 addressed race and ethnicity. Although many of the studies were conducted in urban school contexts that represent multiple ethnic groups, ethnic variables were rarely investigated systematically. Cross-ethnic and cross-racial peer relations are not the focus of many studies in North America. However, even fewer European studies have focused on peer relations between native and immigrant children and youth.

The goal of this chapter is to review the findings on two specific aspects of peer relations across race, ethnicity, and cultural groups. We focus on friendships as an example of positive peer relations and on bully-victim behavior as an example of negative peer relations. For both domains, we present an example from our own research to illustrate the specific insights research on peer relations can provide to the understanding of acculturation processes and adaptation in immigrant youth. Last but not least we explicitly include European studies. While U.S. studies primarily analyze peer relations among white, black, and Hispanic children and adolescents, European countries have a different focus due to different national histories concerning immigration, for example those stemming from guest worker policies. Furthermore, rapid changes are occurring in the numbers and compositions of immigrants across European countries that are raising the concerns of governments and societies with regard to immigration and acculturation policies and practices.

Positive Peer Relations

Research on positive peer relations in immigrant and minority youth has mainly focused on friendships. An additional focus is on friendship quality. To date, studies have been, for the most part, descriptive and poorly integrated. Students belonging to different ethnic, racial, cultural, or immigrant groups are studied and different methods for data collection have been used, ranging from peer nomination or questionnaires to observations.

Nonetheless, there is robust evidence that one of the major determinants of friendship selection is *homophily*, or the degree of similarity in age, gender, interests, attitudes, behavior, and so forth between potential friends (Berscheid, 1985; McPherson, Smith-Lovin, & Cook, 2001). Homophily is defined by a preference principle referring to the tendency for friendships to occur at higher rates between similar people than between dissimilar ones (Zeng & Xie, 2008). However, the pattern of having friends from the same cultural group is not only a result of personal preference but also of social structure (e.g., the cultural makeup of a classroom). Same ethnicity is one aspect of similarity on which friendship choices are based. In some studies, friendship homophily is defined as "the percentage of intra-ethnic friends out of all friends" (Titzmann & Silbereisen, 2009, 303). There is consistent evidence that children and adolescents show a preference for same-race or same-ethnicity friendships both in studies in the United States (Aboud, Mendelson, & Purdy, 2003; Graham et al., 2009; Quillian & Campbell, 2003; Shrum, Cheek, & Hunter, 1988); and in Europe (Baerveldt et al., 2004; Reinders, Greb, & Grimm, 2006; Reinders & Mangold, 2005; Strohmeier, Nestler, & Spiel, 2006; Strohmeier & Spiel, 2003; Titzmann & Silbereisen, 2009; Titzmann, Silbereisen, & Schmitt-Rodermund, 2007). These findings are independent of the methods applied for data collection which include, for example, sociometric nominations and observational techniques (Graham et al., 2009).

Results on gender and age effects with regard to intercultural friendships are mixed. While data concerning gender differences have been inconsistent (Graham et al., 2009), for age findings suggest an interaction with ethnic homophily, with cross-ethnic friendships declining as children grow older (Aboud et al., 2003; Titzmann & Silbereisen, 2009). However, findings are not fully consistent. Shrum et al. (1988) observed a curvilinear relationship between ethnic homophily and grade in a cross-sectional study of grades 3 through 12. Furthermore, it was shown that the length of stay in the host country is related to ethnic homophily (Titzmann & Silbereisen, 2009). Silbereisen and Titzmann (2007), who studied ethnic German immigrants from the former Soviet Union, found friendships to be almost 100% intra-ethnic shortly after arrival in the host country. Among newcomer immigrants, ethnic homophily decreases as a function of time spent in the new country (Titzmann & Silbereisen, 2009). Titzmann and Silbereisen (2009) observed a strong (negative) relationship between homophily in friendship choices and new language use in this group of immigrants. In their longitudinal study, new language use was the most important predictor in explaining individual differences in ethnic friendship homophily. As proficiency improves in the new language, homophily bias decreases (Titzmann & Silbereisen, 2009). This finding was independent from length of stay in the host country and opportunity structures.

Friendship homophily also appears to be influenced by the ethnic composition of schools and classrooms. According to the "opportunity hypothesis" (Hallinan & Teixeira, 1987), the likelihood of successful inter-ethnic exchange and subsequent friendships should be higher when the percentage of same-ethnicity or same-race peers is lower. This prediction has been supported for black and white students (Hallinan & Teixeira, 1987; for an overview see Graham et al., 2009) as well as for ethnic German immigrants from the former Soviet Union (Silbereisen & Titzmann, 2007; Titzmann & Silbereisen, 2009). Furthermore, the willingness to form cross-racial and cross-ethnic friendships may also be influenced by the organization of schools. In U.S. studies, academic tracking was shown to have negative effects on cross-ethnic friendships (e.g., Damico & Sparks, 1986; Kubitschek & Hallinan, 1998), most likely due to the resegregation of students by ethnicity. African American and Latino students are more likely to be placed in lower ability tracks in comparison to white and Asian students. According to Hallinan and Teixeira (1987), academic tracking appears to particularly inhibit the willingness of white students to form friendships with African American students. In general, there is a tendency for majority group members to be more segregated in comparison with immigrant minority groups and to show higher homophily bias than immigrants and minority group members in their friendship choices (Aboud et al., 2003; Hallinan & Teixeira, 1987; Howes & Wu, 1990; Spiel, 2009; Strohmeier et al., 2006; Strohmeier & Spiel, 2003).

Some studies have addressed the nature and quality of cross-ethnic or cross-racial friendships in comparison to same-ethnic/racial friendships. Aspects of friendship quality that have been studied include the following: stability, companionship, social support, intimacy, emotional security, self-validation, and leisure activities (e.g., Aboud et al., 2003; Bukowski, Hoza, & Boivin, 1994). While cross-race friendships were shown to be less stable than same-race ones (e.g., Aboud et al., 2003), little or no differences were found in the quality of cross-race or cross-ethnicity friendships compared to same-race or same-ethnicity friendships (Aboud et al., 2003; Eisikovits, 2000; Reinders & Mangold, 2005; Strohmeier et al., 2006). Only slight differences were observed for intimacy (Aboud et al., 2003) and leisure time activities (Strohmeier et al., 2006). Children belonging to the same ethnic group share more intimacy (Aboud et al., 2003) and interact with each other at home more often than they do with children from different ethnic groups (Strohmeier et al., 2006).

Developmental and educational research has also investigated peer processes and group dynamics in classrooms (for an overview, see Graham et al., 2009). Some U.S. studies have investigated racial differences in the meaning of popularity. Differences were found in the relationship between social acceptance and having a reputation for being aggressive (see Graham et al., 2009). Among African American youth, a positive relationship between aggression status and popularity was observed (e.g., Meisinger et al., 2007; Rodkin et al., 2000). It was found that African American boys were more likely to be in a popular and aggressive subgroup than white boys (Rodkin et al., 2000). Furthermore, peer norms supporting aggression seemed to be influenced by the number of African American students in a classroom, as popularity is only predicted by aggression in African American majority classrooms (Meisinger et al., 2007). However, studies focusing on within-racial group peer preferences found heterogeneity among African Americans (see Graham et al., 2009). To date, few studies on such topics have been conducted in Europe.

One positive focus of studies on group dynamics has been on companions and peer networks (Aboud et al., 2003). Companions not only include friends, but friends of friends. Therefore, the selection criteria for companions is not expected to show the strong homophily bias found for friendships and may closely reflect the number of available ingroup (same ethnicity) and outgroup classmates (Aboud et al., 2003). Results only partly support this assumption. Controlling for availability, both white and black students had more same-race than cross-race companions, independent of grade; while only older students (grades 5–6), and not younger ones (grades 1–3), had more same-race than cross-race friends who nominated each other mutually (Aboud et al., 2003). To date, European studies have not specifically focused on companions. However, in a study conducted by Titzmann and Silbereisen (2009), participants reported a rather large number of friendships, indicating that the friendships mentioned included an extended peer network.

Another positive focus of research on cross-ethnic and cross-racial peer relations examines the sense of belonging, which refers to feelings of being included, accepted, supported, and respected by teachers and peers (Juvonen, 2006). Belonging has been shown to relate to positive attitudes about school, motivation, and school achievement. Ethnic minority students reported a lower sense of belonging than white students. The lowest scores were observed for African American students (Faircloth & Hamm, 2005). Such findings point out the importance multicultural schools may have in fostering positive development. In the following section we present a study from our own research, which further illustrates the relevance of school in promoting cross-ethnic peer relations.

Example: Friendship Patterns Inside and Outside
School in Different Cultural Groups

In a study of primary school students in Vienna, we investigated whether there were differences in the friendship patterns of students from different cultural backgrounds inside versus outside of school (Spiel, 2009; Strohmeier, 2007; Strohmeier et al., 2006). Participants included 204 (114 girls, 90 boys) children aged 10 to 11 years old. In Viennese compulsory schools, around 50% of the students speak a mother tongue other than German. According to their cultural background, the students were categorized as native Austrian (n = 77), former Yugoslavian (n = 49), Turkish (n = 46), or gathered in a multicultural group (n = 37). The latter group comprised students stemming a diverse range of other cultural backgrounds. In order to gather information on their friendship patterns, the students were asked to write down the name, gender, first language, and classmate status (yes/no) for each of their friends. The students were free to choose their number of friends.

Results showed substantial differences in friendship patterns inside and outside school (see also Spiel, 2009). At school, native Austrian children showed much higher homophily bias when compared with the other three groups. Outside school, however, children of all groups showed a strong homophily bias in their friendship choices. Eighty-six percent of native Austrian, 77% of Turkish, 64% of former Yugoslavian, and 50% of children gathered in the multicultural group nominated friends from the same cultural group (see Figures 15.1 and 15.2).

The results support previous findings concerning homophily bias in cross-ethnic and cross-racial friendship choices (see Graham et al., 2009) and high segregation among host society members (see, e.g., Aboud et al., 2003; Hallinan & Teixeira, 1987). In addition, the results illustrate the importance of the school in providing opportunity structures for establishing friendships across cultures.

Negative Peer Relations

Research on negative peer relations in immigrant and minority youth has focused primarily on bullying and aggressive behavior and their underlying mechanisms, as well as on victimization and risk factors. Bullying is usually considered a complex relationship problem (e.g., Pepler, 2006) that is classified as a subset of aggressive behavior involving (1) intentional harm, (2) the repetition of negative acts, and (3) an imbalance of power (e.g., Olweus,

Friends at school

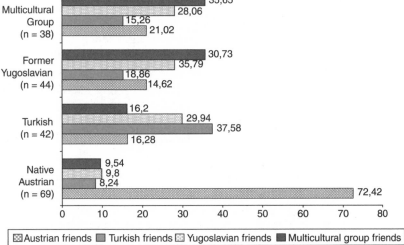

Figure 15.1. Friendship patterns at school depending on cultural group.

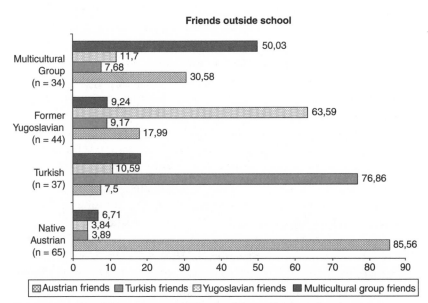

Friends outside school

Figure 15.2. Friendship patterns outside school depending on cultural group.

1991; Roland, 1989). The targets of bullying behavior are often labeled "victims" while the perpetrators of bullying are labeled "bullies" (Olweus, 1991). Bullying includes a variety of negative acts which can be realized face to face or indirectly. Physical aggression or verbal insults are the most visible and are therefore categorized as direct bullying. Hidden behavior such as social exclusion, spreading rumors, or manipulating relationships is considered indirect or relational bullying. In multicultural contexts, some studies also considered racially, culturally, or ethnically motivated bullying and victimization (Monks, Ortega-Ruiz, & Rodriguez-Hidalgo, 2008; Stefanek et al., 2011; Strohmeier, Atria, & Spiel, 2005; Verkuyten & Thijs, 2002). Racist, cultural, or ethnic bullying and victimization have been operationalized by formulating questions that pertain to racist remarks or racist exclusion (e.g., Jasinskaja-Lahti & Liebkind, 2001; Liebkind & Jasinskaja-Lahti, 2000; Verkuyten & Thijs, 2002) or by assessing victims' attributions regarding the causes of victimization (e.g., Strohmeier, Atria, & Spiel, 2005).

Until now, very few studies have compared the prevalence rates of general bullying and aggressive behavior between students belonging to different ethnic, cultural, or immigrant groups. Most of these studies have found no differences between natives and immigrants (Boulton, 1995; Eslea & Mukhtar, 2000; McKenney et al., 2006; Moran et al., 1993; Verkuyten & Thijs, 2002, 2006). Some studies found natives to be at higher risk for bullying others (Graham & Juvonen, 2002; Strohmeier & Spiel, 2003), while others found immigrants to be at higher risk for bullying others (Fandrem et al., 2010; Fandrem, Strohmeier, & Roland, 2009).

Also rare is research on peer victimization among students belonging to different ethnic, cultural, or immigrant groups. The majority of these studies have measured peer victimization in general, while some of the studies have focused on racist victimization. Most general victimization studies found no differences between natives and immigrants (Boulton, 1995; Eslea & Mukhtar, 2000; Fandrem et al., 2009; McKenney et al., 2006; Monks et al., 2008; Moran et al., 1993). Some studies found natives to be at higher risk for being victimized (Hanish & Guerra, 2000; Strohmeier & Spiel, 2003; Strohmeier, Spiel, & Gradinger, 2008; Verkuyten & Thijs, 2006), while one study found minority group immigrants to be at higher risk for victimization (Graham & Juvonen, 2002). Thus, based on these comparative analyses, there is little empirical evidence that immigrant or minority status, in and of itself, is a risk factor for general peer victimization (see also, e.g., Graham et al., 2009). In contrast, studies focused on racist victimization, a subtype of victimization in which the victim attributes the negative acts to her or his ethnicity, race, country of origin, or cultural group, have consistently found that ethnic minority or immigrant youth score higher on racist victimization scales in comparison to native youth (Jasinskaja-Lahti & Liebkind, 2001; Liebkind & Jasinskaja-Lahti, 2000; McKenney et al., 2006; Monks et al., 2008; Verkuyten, 2002; Verkuyten & Thijs, 2002). Thus, being an immigrant or a minority youth is associated with higher levels of perceived racist victimization.

A study conducted in Finland investigated whether interpersonal (e.g., rejection and friendlessness) or intrapersonal risk factors (e.g., anxiety, self-worth, depressive symptoms) mediate the association between immigrant status and general victimization (Strohmeier, Kärna, & Salmivalli, 2011). This study showed that interpersonal rather than intrapersonal risk factors were responsible for peer victimization among immigrant children living in Finland. In first-generation immigrants, victimization was fully mediated by rejection. In second-generation immigrants, both rejection and friendlessness mediated victimization. The total indirect effect for second-generation immigrants was smaller than that found for first-generation immigrants. Therefore, it appears to be important to consider and address general peer rejection in immigrant youth in order to understand and prevent peer victimization.

Some studies focused on the underlying mechanisms of bullying and aggressive behavior in immigrant youth. The underlying functions of aggressive behavior refer to the motive systems that predict such behavior. On a broad conceptual level, two motive systems are described as underlying functions for aggressive behavior: reactive and instrumental aggression (Card & Little, 2006; Dodge, 1991; Dodge & Coie, 1987; Vitaro & Brendgen, 2005; Vitaro, Brendgen, & Barker, 2006). Reactive aggression is seen as a reaction to a (perceived) provocation, threat, or frustration and is usually accompanied by strong feelings of anger. In contrast, instrumental aggression is a premeditated, calculated behavior used as an instrument to reach particular goals. The dominant emotions involved with this type of aggression are pleasure and stimulation. To gain power over another person is the goal most often investigated in aggression research (Card & Little, 2006), and was also found to be an important underlying goal for bullying others in general (Sijtsema et al., 2009; Veenstra et al., 2007).

Roland and Idsøe (2001) introduced another goal that perpetrators may intend to achieve through aggressive means, namely affiliation. Affiliation-related instrumental aggression is carried out in order to feel affiliated with other aggressors by establishing a common target. While power-related instrumental aggression was found to be more important for boys, affiliation-related instrumental aggression was more important for girls in the prediction of bullying behavior (Roland & Idsøe, 2001).

A large-scale study in Norway found that the underlying functions for general bullying behavior in immigrant versus native adolescent boys and girls were different (Fandrem et al., 2009). Immigrant boys (most of them first generation) bullied others because they wanted to feel affiliated with other peers, while native boys bullied others because they wanted to feel dominant and powerful. These findings are supported by another study conducted in Norway (Fandrem et al., 2010) which showed that immigrant boys, more than native Norwegian boys, bully in groups. Neither study analyzed the ethnic, cultural, or immigrant groups among the targets. A study from our own research in Austria reinvestigated and extended the Norwegian findings in a different national context (Strohmeier, Fandrem, Stefanek, & Spiel, 2012). The main results are summarized in the next section.

Example: Affiliation as an Underlying Motive for Aggressive Behavior in Immigrant Youth

In a study of Austrian secondary school students aged 14 to 19, we investigated the predictive power of the goal to be accepted by friends as an underlying function of aggressive behavior in comparison with reactive aggression (Strohmeier, Fandrem, Stefanek, & Spiel, 2012). We hypothesized that the goal of acceptance by friends, as an underlying motive for aggressive behavior, might be more important for first-generation immigrants than for natives or second-generation immigrants. First-generation immigrants who migrated and experienced resettlement firsthand were expected to have a higher need for affiliation than natives and second-generation immigrants. All three constructs, reactive aggression, acceptance as goal, and aggressive behavior were measured with six items parceled into three manifest variables (see Figure 15.3).

The sample included 339 native Austrians (51.6% girls), 126 first-generation immigrants (48.4% girls), and 175 second-generation immigrants (54.3% girls) with an average age of 15.61. Data were collected via self-assessments.

As shown in Figure 15.3, multiple group latent means and covariance structures (MACS) models revealed that the goal of being accepted by friends was a stronger predictor than reactive aggression for aggressive behavior in first-generation immigrants when compared with second-generation immigrants and natives. For both natives and second-generation immigrants, reactive aggression was a stronger predictor for aggressive behavior than acceptance by friends. Furthermore, gender moderated these associations. The goal to be accepted by friends was a very strong predictor

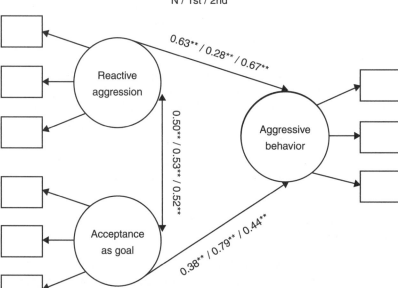

Figure 15.3. Multiple group comparisons of latent means structures.

of aggressive behavior in first-generation immigrant boys, but not in first-generation immigrant girls. This result is very much in line with the previous studies conducted in Norway which also found that immigrant boys bully others because they want to be affiliated with certain peers (Fandrem et al., 2009). Our findings are remarkably consistent with the findings from Norway, given the striking differences between the two countries in immigrant samples and context variables.

Shortcomings of Current Research and Directions for the Future

There are a number of shortcomings in existing research on peer relations in multicultural schools. To date, the number of studies focusing on peer relations in immigrant and minority youth is limited. Moreover, consistent findings for studies of positive and negative peer relations are remarkably lacking. These inconsistencies are likely due to multiple different, but partly interacting, shortcomings. Usually, systematic approaches are not used to address the following issues (an exception here is the ICSEY study proposed by Berry et al., 2006). Shortcomings include the following.

- The definition of target groups: The terms *immigrant status*, *ethnicity*, and *cultural background* are not consistently used across studies. Different variables are used for classification.
- The methods of data collection: Application of different assessment methods (e.g., peer nomination and self-assessment to define bullies and victims) has resulted in only partially comparable findings (e.g., Strohmeier et al., 2008).
- Although context variables at the national level vary, they are rarely investigated systematically; examples here include immigrant policy, history of immigration, numbers, and composition of immigrants.
- In addition, there is a lack of longitudinal studies with a developmental perspective.

To improve the quality of empirical evidence, we strongly recommend more systematic multinational collaborative research programs that combine empirical findings from peer relation research with theories on acculturation. Such research programs would include common definitions of target groups (agreed on by consensus) and a theoretically based selection of methods for data collection (ideally multi-informant approaches). These methods would be applied in different countries selected with regard to such context variables and target groups as, for example, history of immigration. To determine whether influences of context, migration, and individual factors can be isolated, the same immigrant or minority groups should be investigated in different host countries and in their countries of origin, assessing persons with and without migration experience. Moreover, longitudinal studies are essential for advancing the theoretical framework for this research and understanding the processes of development and change.

Promotion of Positive Peer Relations in Multicultural Schools

Despite the limitations in existing research, the findings reviewed in this chapter suggest strategies for the promotion of positive peer relations in multicultural schools. There are many possibilities to implement interventions to avoid ethnic homophily, bullying, and victimization and to foster positive peer relations in multicultural schools. Strategies which can be applied by individual teachers include the following:

- cooperative learning groups in which immigrant or minority students work together with natives to achieve a common goal or create a product as a group (Slavin, 1990, 1995; Slavin & Cooper, 1999);
- befriending strategies that emphasize similarities rather than differences between immigrant or minority students and native ones (Pettigrew & Tropp, 2000);
- multicultural approaches to education that systematically integrate learning about other cultures, races, and ethnicities into everyday teaching (e.g., Bigler, 1999; Grant & Sleeter, 2003; Sleeter & Grant, 2003).

We think that in order to capitalize on the potential of immigrant youth, comprehensive approaches that target not only immigrants or minority children but all students enrolled in multicultural schools are needed. This perspective is in line with interactive models of acculturation (Berry, 1997; Bourhis et al., 1997) and with peer relation research in general. The goal of sustainable changes in school culture, however, may require intervention programs that target the entire school staff as well as individual teachers. Two examples of evidence informed programs that target the whole school are the TALK (Schober et al., 2007) and the ViSC (Atria & Spiel, 2007; Spiel & Strohmeier, 2011) programs.

The TALK program is a training program to foster teacher competences to encourage lifelong learning (Schober et al., 2007). TALK provides teachers with the competences to systematically implement the enhancement of lifelong learning into their regular educational responsibilities and to design their instructional process in ways that encourage students to develop the skills and competences associated with lifelong learning. Moreover, TALK initiates school development to effectively implement the concept of lifelong learning and to intensify cooperation among teachers. In addition to promoting motivation and self-regulated learning, TALK explicitly fosters social skills with a specific focus on dealing with diversity. The social skills studied in TALK comprise communication skills, assertiveness, and behavioral control (see Weidner, 2003), as well as group and conflict management. The formation of heterogeneous groups and variations in grouping students is one measure of the TALK program. Teachers and students are trained in how to handle diversity (with respect to gender, nationality, ability, etc.) constructively and in how to perceive diversity as a resource. Consequently, potential conflicts and strategies for dealing with them are addressed in addition to methods of generating cooperative learning in a narrower sense (Schober et al., 2007).

The ViSC program provides another example of a program targeting the school as a whole, encompassing classes, teachers, and individual students. ViSC is a primary prevention program which aims to foster social competencies and reduce bullying and victimization among students (Atria & Spiel, 2007; Spiel & Strohmeier, 2011). ViSC provides measures that operate at schoolwide, classroom, and individual levels. Teachers are systematically trained to implement the components of the ViSC program and they are supervised during its implementation. Similar to the TALK program, the ViSC program has a specific focus on school development. So far, ViSC measures have been implemented and evaluated on the class level (Atria & Spiel, 2007; Gollwitzer, 2005; Gollwitzer et al., 2007; Gollwitzer et al., 2006; Spiel & Strohmeier, 2011). Overall, evaluations have delivered promising training effects, not only concerning bullying but also with respect to the perceived level of democracy in the classroom (Atria & Spiel, 2007; Spiel & Strohmeier, 2011).

Still, there is a need for intervention research that explicitly analyses program effects on different cultural groups. Such intervention studies should be conducted according to standards of evidence (see, e.g., Flay et al., 2005) to assist practitioners, policy makers, and administrators in determining which interventions are efficacious, which are effective, and which are ready for dissemination (Flay et al., 2005).

Conclusion

To summarize, promoting positive peer relations is an important strategy to capitalize on migration and to promote positive development in youth with and without immigration experience. Because schools are places where children and adolescents spend a substantial part of the day, they are one of the most important venues for promoting positive peer relations. However, capitalizing on migration necessitates comprehensive evidence-based approaches that include all students.

In research programs, same immigrant groups should to be studied in (a) different host countries, (b) in their country of origin (without migration), and (c) as migrants in their country of origin. Furthermore, to take the ecological perspective on development seriously (Bronfenbrenner, 1979), contextual factors should be systematically included in studies. Risks and protective factors should be analyzed in a longitudinal approach, and data analyses should systematically combine variable and person-oriented approaches (see, e.g., Bergman & Magnusson, 1997; von Eye & Spiel, 2010).

REFERENCES

Aboud, F., Mendelson, M., & Purdy, K. (2003). Cross-race peer relations and friendship quality. *International Journal of Behavioral Development, 27*(2), 165–73.

Allport, G. W. (1979). *The nature of prejudice. Unabridged. 25th anniversary edition.* Cambridge, MA: Perseus Books.

Atria, M., & Spiel, C. (2007). The Viennese Social Competence (ViSC) training for students: Program and evaluation. In J. E. Zins, M. J. Elias, and C. A. Maher (Eds.), *Bullying, victimization and peer harassment: A handbook of prevention and intervention* (pp. 179–98). New York: The Haworth Press.

Baerveldt, C., Van Duijn, M. A. J., Vermeij, L., & Van Hemert, D. A. (2004). Ethnic boundaries and personal choice. Assessing the influence of individual inclination to choose intra-ethnic relationships on pupils' networks. *Social Networks, 26*(1), 55–74.

Bergman, L. R., & Magnusson, D. (1997). A person-oriented approach in research on developmental psychopathology. *Development & Psychopathology, 9,* 291–319.

Berry, J. W. (1997). Immigration, acculturation and adaptation. *Applied Psychology: An International Review, 46*(1), 5–68.

Berry, J. W., Phinney, J. S., Sam, D. L., & Vedder, P. (2006). *Immigrant youth in cultural transition.* Mahwah, NJ: Lawrence Erlbaum.

Berscheid, E. (1985). Interpersonal attraction. In L. Gardner and E. Aronson (Eds.), *Handbook of social psychology* (pp. 413–84). New York: Random House.

Bigler, R. S. (1999). The use of multicultural curricula and materials to counter racism in children. *Journal of Social Issues, 44*(4), 687–705.

Boulton, M. J. (1995). Patterns of bully/victim problems in mixed race groups of children. *Social Development, 4*(3), 277–93.

Bourhis, R. Y., Moise, L. C., Perreault, S., & Senecal, S. (1997). Towards an interactive acculturation model: A social psychological approach. *International Journal of Psychology, 32*(6), 369–86.

Bronfenbrenner, U. (1979). *The ecology of human development: Experiments by nature and design.* Cambridge, MA: Harvard University Press.

Bukowski, W. M., Hoza, B., & Boivin, M. (1994). Measuring friendship quality during pre- and early adolescence: The development and psychometric properties of the friendship qualities scale. *Journal of Social and Personal Relationships, 11,* 471–84.

Card, N. A., & Little, T. D. (2006). Proactive and reactive aggression in childhood and adolescence: A meta-analysis of differential relations with psychosocial adjustment. *International Journal of Behavioral Development, 30*(5), 466–80.

Damico, S., & Sparks, C. (1986). Cross-group contact opportunities: Impact on interpersonal relationships in desegregated middle schools. *Sociology of Education, 59,* 113–23.

Dodge, K. A. (1991). The structure and function of reactive and proactive aggression. In D. Pepler and K. Rubin (Eds.), *The development and treatment of childhood aggression* (pp. 201–18). Hillsdale, NJ: Erlbaum.

Dodge, K. A., & Coie, J. D. (1987). Social information processing factors in reactive and proactive aggression in children's playgroups. *Journal of Personality and Social Psychology, 53,* 1146–58.

Eisikovits, R. A. (2000). Gender differences in cross-cultural adaptation styles of immigrant youths from the former USSR in Israel. *Youth and Society, 31*(3), 310–31.

Eslea, M., & Mukhtar, K. (2000). Bullying and racism among Asian schoolchildren in Britain. *Educational Research, 42*(2), 207–17.

Faircloth, B., & Hamm, J. (2005). Sense of belonging among high school students representing four ethnic groups. *Journal of Youth and Adolescence, 34*, 293–309.

Fandrem, H., Ertesvåg, S., Strohmeier, D., & Roland, E. (2010). Bullying and affiliation: A study of peer groups in native Norwegian and immigrant adolescents in Norway. *European Journal of Developmental Psychology, 7*(4), 401–18.

Fandrem, H., Strohmeier, D., & Roland, E. (2009). Bullying and victimization among Norwegian and immigrant adolescents in Norway: The role of proactive and reactive aggressiveness. *Journal of Early Adolescence, 29*(6), 898–923.

Flay, B. R., Biglan, A., Boruch, R. F., Gonzalez Castro, F., Gottfredson, D., Kellam, S., et al. (2005). Standards of evidence: Criteria for efficacy, effectiveness and dissemination. *Prevention Science, 6*(3), 151–75.

Gollwitzer, M. (2005). Könnten Anti-Aggressions-Trainings in der Schule wirksamer sein, wenn sie weniger standardisiert wären? In A. Ittel and M. v. Salisch (Eds.), *Lästern, Lügen, Leiden lassen: Aggressives Verhalten von Kindern und Jugendlichen* (pp. 276–312). Stuttgart: Kohlhammer.

Gollwitzer, M., Banse, R., Eisenbach, K., & Naumann, E. (2007). Effectiveness of the Vienna social competence training on implicit and explicit aggression. Evidence from an aggressiveness IAT. *European Journal of Psychological Assessment, 23*(3), 150–6.

Gollwitzer, M., Eisenbach, K., Atria, M., Strohmeier, D., & Banse, R. (2006). Evaluation of aggression-reducing effects of the "Viennese Social Competence Training." *Swiss Journal of Psychology, 65*(2), 125–35.

Graham, S., & Juvonen, J. (2002). Ethnicity, peer harassment, and adjustment in middle school: An exploratory study. *Journal of Early Adolescence, 22*(2), 173–99.

Graham, S., Taylor, A., & Ho, A. (2009). Race and ethnicity in peer relations research. In K. Rubin, W. M. Bukowski, and B. Laursen (Eds.), *Handbook of peer interactions, relationships, and groups* (pp. 394–413). New York: The Guilford Press.

Grant, C. A., & Sleeter, C. E. (2003). *Turning on learning. Five approaches for multicultural teaching plans for race, class, gender, and disability.* New York, NY: John Wiley & Sons.

Hallinan, M. T., & Teixeira, R. A. (1987). Opportunities and constraints: Black-White differences in the formation of interracial friendships. *Child Development, 58*(5), 1358–71.

Hanish, L. D., & Guerra, N. G. (2000). The roles of ethnicity and school context in predicting children's victimization by peers. *American Journal of Community Psychology, 28*(2), 201–23.

Hartup, W. W. (1996). The company they keep: Friendships and their developmental significance. *Child Development, 67*, 1–13.

Hawker, D., & Boulton, M. (2000). Twenty years' research on peer victimization and psychosocial maladjustment: A meta-analytic review of cross-sectional studies. *Journal of Child Psychology and Psychiatry and Allied Disciplines, 41*, 441–55.

Howes, C., & Wu, F. (1990). Peer interactions and friendships in an ethnically diverse school setting. *Child Development, 61*(2), 537–41.

Jasinskaja-Lahti, I., & Liebkind, K. (2001). Perceived discrimination and psychological adjustment among Russian-speaking immigrant adolescents in Finland. *International Journal of Psychology, 36*(3), 174–85.

Juvonen, J. (2006). Sense of belonging, social bonds, and school functioning. In P. Alexander and P. Winne (Eds.), *Handbook of educational psychology* (pp. 655–74). Mahwah, NJ: Erlbaum.

Kubitschek, W., & Hallinan, M. T. (1998). Tracking and students' friendships. *Social Psychology Quarterly, 62*, 1–15.

Lease, A., & Blake, J. (2005). A comparison of majority-race children with and without a minority-race friend. *Social Development, 14*(1), 20–41.

Liebkind, K., & Jasinskaja-Lahti, I. (2000). Acculturation and psychological wellbeing of immigrant adolescents in Finland. A comparative study of adolescents from different cultural backgrounds. *Journal of Adolescent Research, 15*, 446–69.

McKenney, K. S., Pepler, D., Craig, W. M., & Connolly, J. (2006). Peer victimization and psychosocial adjustment: The experiences of Canadian immigrant youth. *Electronic Journal of Research in Educational Psychology, 9*, 230–64.

McPherson, M., Smith-Lovin, L., & Cook, J. M. (2001). Births of a feather: Homophily in social networks. *Annual Review of Sociology, 27*(1), 415–44.

Meisinger, E., Blake, J., Lease, A., Palaedy, G., & Olejnik, S. (2007). Variant and invariant predictors of perceived popularity across majority-black and majority-white classrooms. *Journal of School Psychology, 45*, 21–44.

Monks, C., Ortega-Ruiz, R., & Rodriguez-Hidalgo, A. J. (2008). Peer victimization in multicultural schools in Spain and England. *European Journal of Developmental Psychology, 5*(4), 507–35.

Moran, S., Smith, P. K., Thompson, D., & Whitney, I. (1993). Ethnic differences in experiences of bullying: Asian and White children. *British Journal of Educational Psychology, 63*(3), 431–40.

Motti-Stefanidi, F., Pavlopoulos, V., Obradovic, J., Dalla, M., Takis, N., Papathanassiou, A., et al. (2008). Immigration as a risk factor for adolescent adaptation in Greek urban schools. *European Journal of Developmental Psychology, 5*(2), 235–61.

Olweus, D. (1991). Bully / victim problems among schoolchildren: Basic facts and effects of a school based intervention program. In D. J. Pepler and K. H. Rubin (Eds.), *The development and treatment of childhood aggression* (pp. 411–48). Hillsdale: Erlbaum.

Pepler, D. (2006). Bullying Interventions: A binocular perspective. *Journal of the Canadian Academy of Child and Adolescent Psychiatry, 15*(1), 16–20.

Pettigrew, T. F. (1998). Intergroup contact theory. *Annual Review of Psychology, 49*, 65–85.

Pettigrew, T. F., & Tropp, L. R. (2000). Does intergroup contact reduce prejudice? Recent meta-analytic findings. In S. Oskamp (Ed.), *Reducing prejudice and discrimination* (pp. 93–114). Mahwah, NJ: Lawrence Erlbaum.

Quillian, L., & Campbell, M. (2003). Beyond black and white: The present and future of multiracial friendship segregation. *American Sociological Review, 68*(4), 540–66.

Reinders, H., Greb, K., & Grimm, C. (2006). Entstehung, Gestalt und Auswirkungen interethnischer Freundschaften im Jugendalter. Eine Längsschnittstudie. *Diskurs Kindheits- und Jugendforschung, 1*, 39–57.

Reinders, H., & Mangold, T. (2005). Die Qualität intra- und interethnischer Freundschaften bei Mädchen und Jungen deutscher, türkischer und italienischer Herkunft. *Zeitschrift für Entwicklungspsychologie und Pädagogische Psychologie, 37*(3), 144–55.

Rodkin, P., Farmer, T., Pearl, R., & Van Acker, R. (2000). Heterogeneity of popular boys: Antisocial and prosocial configurations. *Developmental Psychology, 36,* 14–24.

Roland, E. (1989). A system oriented strategy against bullying. In E. Roland and E. Munthe (Eds.), *Bullying: An international perspective* (pp. 143–51). London: David Fulton.

Roland, E., & Idsøe, T. (2001). Aggression and bullying. *Aggressive Behavior, 27*(6), 446–62.

Rubin, K., Bukowski, W. M., & Laursen, B. (2009). *Handbook of peer interactions, relationships, and groups.* New York: The Guilford Press.

Salmivalli, C., & Isaacs, J. (2005). Prospective relations among victimization, rejection, friendlessness, and children's self- and peer-perceptions. *Child Development, 76*(6), 1161–71.

Schober, B., Finsterwald, M., Wagner, P., Lüftenegger, M., Aysner, M., & Spiel, C. (2007). TALK – A training program to encourage lifelong learning in school. *Journal of Psychology, 215*(3), 183–93.

Schofield, J. W. (1995). Improving intergroup relations among students. In J. A. Banks (Ed.), *Handbook of research on multicultural education* (pp. 635–46). New York, NY: Macmillan.

Shrum, W., Cheek, N., & Hunter, S. (1988). Friendship in school: Gender and racial homophily. *Sociology of Education, 61,* 227–39.

Sijtsema, J. J., Veenstra, R., Lindenberg, S., & Salmivalli, C. (2009). Empirical test of bullies' status goals: Assessing direct goals, aggression, and prestige. *Aggressive Behavior, 35*(1), 57–67.

Silbereisen, R. K., & Titzmann, P. (2007). Peers among immigrants – Some comments on "Have we missed something." In R. C. M. E. Engels, M. Kerr, and H. Stattin (Eds.), *Friends, lovers and groups. Key relationships in adolescence* (pp. 155–66). West Sussex, England: Wiley.

Slavin, R. E. (1990). Comprehensive cooperative learning models: Embedding cooperative learning in the curriculum and school. In S. Sharan (Ed.), *Cooperative learning: Theory and research* (pp. 261–83). New York: Praeger.

(1995). Cooperative learning and intergroup relations. In J. A. Banks (Ed.), *Handbook of research on multicultural education* (pp. 628–34). New York, NY: Macmillan.

Slavin, R. E., & Cooper, R. (1999). Improving intergroup relations: Lessons learned from cooperative learning programs. *Journal of Social Issues, 55*(4), 647–63.

Sleeter, C. E., & Grant, C. A. (2003). *Making choices for multicultural education: Five approaches to race, class, and gender.* New York, NY: John Wiley & Sons.

Spiel, C. (2009). Evidence-based practice: A challenge for European developmental psychology. *European Journal of Developmental Psychology, 6*(1), 11–33.

Spiel, C., & Strohmeier, D. (2011). National strategy for violence prevention in the Austrian public school system: Development and implementation. *International Journal of Behavioral Development, 35*(5), 412–18.

Stefanek, E., Strohmeier, D., Van de Schoot, R., & Spiel, C. (2011). Bullying and victimization in ethnically diverse schools: Risk and protective factors on the individual and class level. *International Journal of Developmental Science*, 5, 1–12.

Strohmeier, D. (2007). Soziale Beziehungen in multikulturellen Schulklassen: Wo liegen die Chancen, wo die Risiken? *Erziehung und Unterricht*, 157(9–10), 796–809.

Strohmeier, D., Atria, M., & Spiel, C. (2005). Bullying und Viktimisierung in multikulturellen Schulklassen. Wer ist betroffen? Wie begründen Opfer ihre Erfahrungen? In A. Ittel & M. v. Salisch (Eds.), *Lästern, Lügen, Leiden: Aggression bei Kindern und Jugendlichen* (pp. 204–19). Stuttgart: Kohlhammer.

Strohmeier, D., Fandrem, H., Stefanek, E., & Spiel, C. (2012). Acceptance by friends as underlying function of aggressive behaviour in immigrant adolescents. *Scandinavian Journal of Psychology, 53,* 80–88. *DOI: 10.1111/j.1467-9450.2011.00910.x.*

Strohmeier, D., Kärna, A., & Salmivalli, C. (2011). Intrapersonal and interpersonal risk factors for peer victimization in immigrant youth in Finland. *Developmental Psychology, 47*(1), 248–58.

Strohmeier, D., Nestler, D., & Spiel, C. (2006). Freundschaftsmuster, Freundschaftsqualität und aggressives Verhalten von Immigrantenkindern in der Grundschule. *Diskurs Kindheits- und Jugendforschung, 1,* 21–37.

Strohmeier, D., & Spiel, C. (2003). Immigrant children in Austria: Aggressive behavior and friendship patterns in multicultural school classes. *Journal of Applied School Psychology, 19*(2), 99–116.

Strohmeier, D., Spiel, C., & Gradinger, P. (2008). Social relationships in multicultural schools: Bullying and victimization. *European Journal of Developmental Psychology,* 5(2), 262–85.

Titzmann, P., & Silbereisen, R. K. (2009). Friendship homophily among ethnic German immigrants: A longitudinal comparison between recent and more experienced immigrant adolescents. *Journal of Family Psychology, 23*(3), 301–10.

Titzmann, P., Silbereisen, R. K., & Schmitt-Rodermund, E. (2007). Friendship homophily among diaspora migrant adolescents in Germany and Israel. *European Psychologist,* 12(3), 181–95.

Veenstra, R., Lindenberg, S., Zijlstra, B. J. H., De Winter, A. F., Verhulst, F. C., & Ormel, J. (2007). The dyadic nature of bullying and victimization: Testing a dual-perspective theory. *Child Development, 78*(6), 1843–54.

Verkuyten, M. (2002). Ethnic attitudes among minority and majority children: The role of ethnic identification, peer group victimization and parents. *Social Development,* 11(4), 558–70.

Verkuyten, M., & Thijs, J. (2002). Racist victimization among children in The Netherlands: The effect of ethnic group and school. *Ethnic and Racial Studies,* 25(2), 310–31.

(2006). Ethnic discrimination and global self-worth in early adolescents: The mediating role of ethnic self esteem. *International Journal of Behavioral Development,* 30(2), 107–16.

Vitaro, F., & Brendgen, M. (2005). Proactive and reactive aggression: A developmental perspective. In R. E. Tremblay, W. W. Hartup, and J. Archer (Eds.), *Developmental origins of aggression* (pp. 178–201). New York: The Guilford Press.

Vitaro, F., Brendgen, M., & Barker, E. D. (2006). Subtypes of aggressive behaviors: A developmental perspective. *International Journal of Behavioral Development, 30*(1), 12–19.

von Eye, A., & Spiel, C. (2010). Conducting person-oriented research. *Zeitschrift für Psychologie / Journal of Psychology, 218*(3), 151–4.

Weidner, M. (2003). *Kooperatives Lernen im Unterricht*. Seelze / Velber: Kallmeyer Verlag.

Zeng, Z., & Xie, Y. (2008). A preference-opportunity-choice framework with applications to intergroup friendship. *American Journal of Sociology, 114*(3), 615–48.

16 Latino Education in the United States

Immigration, Language, and Achievement

Eugene E. García

Introduction

Young Latino children aged 0–8 are currently the largest and fastest growing racial/ethnic minority subpopulation in the United States. In 2002, there were nearly 13 million Latino children and youths in the United States comprising about 18% of the nation's population under 18 years of age (Ramirez & de la Cruz, 2003). Latinos formed an even larger share of the very young that year. Of the 4 million babies born in the United States in 2002, nearly 877,000 were Latino, about 22% of the total – up from 16% a decade earlier (García & Gonzáles, 2006). The under-18 Latino population is anticipated to grow to over 17 million by 2020 (U.S. Census Bureau, 2003).

Despite extensive efforts over the past few decades to raise academic achievement among educationally and economically disadvantaged elementary and secondary school students, including low socioeconomic status (SES) Latinos, progress has been slow (Braswell et al., 2001; Grigg et al., 2003). It has been especially difficult to raise achievement levels in high schools, a problem of increasing concern to policy makers (Olson, 2005).

A promising and growing body of evidence shows that high-quality universal prekindergarten programs (UPK; for 3- and 4-year-olds) can have a positive impact on the school careers of many children, particularly those from low SES families and particularly Latino children in the United States (Bowman et al., 2001; Gormley, Gayer, & Dawson, 2004; Gormley & Phillips, 2003; Heckman & Masterov, 2004; Reynolds, 2003). As a result, there is reason to believe that the period from birth through age 8 constitutes the best window of opportunity for making improvements in the educational trajectories of disadvantaged Latino children in the United States.

Parties who advocate for voluntary UPK should be precise regarding its capacity to produce developmental and academic achievement gains. Such gains are optimized when the progress of structural, curricular, and instructional approaches are informed by sound theory and rigorous research. Clearly, the quality of the pre-K efforts relies on the training and expertise of personnel, instructional organizations, and attention to the development aspects of the children and families served (Kagan & Kauerz, 2006). For Latino children, research suggests that the most effective UPK programs directly address language and culture, providing sound instruction in both Spanish and English. In this chapter, I discuss several demographic attributes of young Latino children, their current early education profile in terms of access and achievement, and how increased access to high-quality UPK programs constitutes a promising approach to improving their educational opportunities. I end by offering a number of recommendations from the research literature to ensure the high quality of UPK programs for young Latinos.

Demographic Attributes

Children of Latino heritage in the United States are not a homogenous group but embody diverse social, cultural, and linguistic backgrounds (Montemayor & Mendoza, 2004; Ramirez & de la Cruz, 2003). Latino children come from long-term native-born populations as well as immigrant groups recently arrived and having various and unique combinations of histories, cultural practices, perspectives, and traditions. Recent growth in the young Latino population in the United States has been driven to a high degree by immigration patterns from Latin America (Ramirez & de la Cruz, 2003). In 2000, one in five children aged 0–8 in the United States was Latino (Hernandez, 2006). Of these children, over 64% were born into immigrant families in which at least one parent was born outside the United States. A large majority of young Latino children are of Mexican origin (65%), but substantial proportions have origins in Puerto Rico (9%), Central America (7%), South America (6%), Cuba (2%), and the Dominican Republic (3%) (Hernandez, 2006). Two-thirds of Mexican-origin and Cuban-origin children live in immigrant families, and this rises to about nine in 10 for those with origins in the Dominican Republic and Central or South America. Especially important is that the vast majority of young Latino children are, themselves, U.S. citizens: 85% of those with South American origins, 88% of those with Mexican origins, and 91% to 92% of those with origins in the

Dominican Republic and Central or South America (Capps et al., 2004; Hernandez, 2006).

Compared to whites and other racial/ethnic groups, Latino children and families demonstrate a number of favorable demographic attributes to overall well-being. In an analysis of census data, Hernandez (2006) found that a large proportion of Latino children live in two-parent households. Indeed, 77% of young Latino children aged 0–8 lived with two parents in 2000. The proportion rises to 81% to 86% for young children in immigrant families from Mexico, Central and South America, and Cuba. These proportions decrease, however, in native families from these regions as well as those from the Dominican Republic and Puerto Rico.

Latino children, on average, live in families with a strong work ethic and desire to succeed (Hernandez, 2006). Ninety-three percent of fathers living with these children worked during the year prior to the 2000 census survey. The proportion is the same in native-born and immigrant families. Moreover, Latino children are approximately three times more likely to have three or more adults (in addition to their fathers and mothers) living in the home who are also in the workforce.

Despite low socioeconomic circumstances, Latino families demonstrate various positive physical health outcomes. Studies have consistently found that Latinos, on average, have lower infant mortality rates, healthier birth outcomes, healthier diets, and lower rates of obesity compared to whites (Escarce, Morales, & Rumbaut, 2006). Variations in these domains have been found, however, between national-origin groups and by immigrant generation status. Latinos of Puerto Rican descent, for example, tend to have worse health status indicators than other national-origin groups while Latinos of Mexican and Central American origin often exhibit the most favorable health outcomes despite high poverty rates (Hernandez, 2006).

Survey data also have highlighted that Latino parents demonstrate a positive attitude toward education and the schooling of their children. Although parents of young Latinos, on average, do not have high levels of formal education attainment, they tend to have high educational aspirations for their children (Nuñez, Cuccaro-Alamin, & Carroll 1998). Parents express interest in enrolling their children in early education programs and supporting them through postsecondary schooling. A survey conducted by the Tomás Rivera Policy Institute found that over 90% of Latino parents felt that it is very important or somewhat important for children to attend preschool (Perez & Zarate, 2006).

Latino children live in a variety of home language environments. In general, Spanish dominates such environments with access to English as a second language. Because early language development is strongly associated with cognitive development and academic success (Risley & Hart, 2006), it is important to understand the intersection of Spanish and English for these children and how the native language can be leveraged to increase overall school success. Some young Latinos acquire English as their first language and maintain only monolingual proficiency throughout their life. Others speak Spanish as their first language and learn English as they enter public school. The proportional size of this particular subpopulation has grown rapidly over the past few decades. Indeed, the percentage of the overall child population in the United States who spoke a non-English native language rose from 6% in 1979 to 14% in 1999. The National Clearinghouse for English Language Acquisition reported that from the 1993–4 school year to the 2003–4 school year, K–12 enrollment of English language learners (ELL) grew over 65% while the total K–12 population grew less than 7%. The majority of this growth is attributable to increases in populations from Latin America. In 2000, Spanish accounted for 76% of all ELL students in preschool to fifth grade (NCELA, 2006).

Using data from a national sample of children born between December 2001 and January 2002, López, Barrueco, and Miles (2006) described the home language environments of Latino infants. The largest group (34%) of Latino infants lived in homes in which Spanish was the primary language, with some English. Twenty-two percent lived in a home in which English was primarily spoken, with some Spanish; 21% in English-only homes; and 19% in Spanish-only homes. In sum, it was found that approximately three in four Latino infants were exposed to some level of Spanish in the home.

The positive attributes which Latino children and families demonstrate – two-parent households, strong work ethic, physical health, positive attitude toward school/education – tend to decrease the negative effects of poverty and low parent education (Shields & Behrman, 2004). However, these attributes are not generally sufficient to sustain Latino students on a trajectory of educational success over time. Robust early interventions are necessary and have proven successful in increasing school readiness and decreasing pervasive achievement gaps.

Early Education

Currently, Latinos lag behind their white and Asian American peers at all proficiency levels of reading and mathematics (at least a half of a standard deviation) at the beginning and throughout K–12 schooling (Braswell, Daane, & Grigg, 2003; García et al., 2005; NCES, 2003; Reardon & Galindo, 2006). Educational achievement gaps of virtually all racial/ethnic groups are established during the early years of school and change little thereafter (García et al., 2005). Although some of the differences between racial/ethnic groups is accounted for by socioeconomic differences between groups (on average Latinos have lower SES than whites and Asian Americans), much of it is not (Reardon & Galindo, 2006). Using data from the Early Childhood Longitudinal Study, Kindergarten Cohort (ECLS-K; NCES, 2001), Reardon and Galindo (2006) found that Latino children scored .3 to .5 of a standard deviation lower in mathematics and reading than their white peers within all five SES quintiles (SES in ECLS-K is a composite of household income and parents' levels of education and occupation) from kindergarten through fifth grade. Hence, race/ethnicity had a substantial effect on early achievement over and above SES. In a separate analysis of ECLS-K data, Reardon (2003) noted that achievement differences by SES and race/ethnicity from kindergarten through first grade were existent and associated with various factors. That is, practices in the home and school influence racial/ethnic and SES achievement gaps in early education (García, Jensen, & Cuéllar, 2006).

Because academic achievement during the early elementary grades is strongly associated with sustained success throughout secondary and post-secondary schooling (Gilliam & Zigler, 2004; Magnuson & Waldfogel, 2005), Latino children are especially positioned to benefit from involvement in high-quality UPK programs. While no extensive study exists regarding the longitudinal impacts of Latino participation in prekindergarten across the country, current evidence suggests that Latinos – and children in general – who attend prekindergarten programs learn language, social skills, and practical skills related to enhanced achievement in the future. Indeed, an evaluation of the UPK program in Tulsa, Oklahoma revealed several benefits for young Latinos. In this study authors estimated the impact of prekindergarten on achievement – letter-word identification, spelling, and applied problems. The sample consisted of 1,567 children enrolled in prekindergarten and 1,461 kindergarten children who had just completed prekindergarten. As shown in Figure 16.1, gains for Latino students in this program were especially impressive. Latinos experienced a 79% gain in letter-word identification, a 39% gain in spelling, and a 54% gain in applied problem solving. This progress outpaces gains which naturally would have occurred during one year of a child's development.

While Latinos as a whole benefited from the Tulsa prekindergarten program, those primarily speaking Spanish at home benefited more. Latino

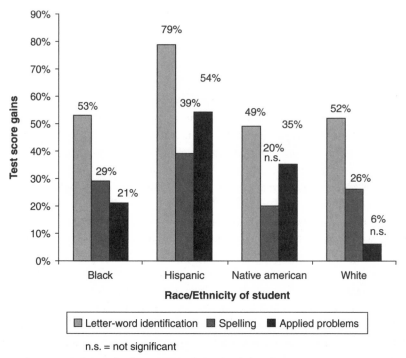

Figure 16.1. Effects of Tulsa pre-K program by race/ethnicity of student. Students of diverse races and ethnicities benefit from the Tulsa pre-K program.

students speaking English at home realized positive but statistically insignificant cognitive gains, while those speaking Spanish at home realized gains of 12 months in prereading, 4 months in prewriting, and 10 months in premath. In this work, students whose parents speak Spanish at home outnumber those whose parents speak English at home by nearly three to one, making it more difficult to detect statistically significant results in the latter group. The difference in effects for Spanish-speaking and English-speaking homes is not significant for prereading, marginally significant for prespelling, and significant for premath.

Similar to the general results, Latino students with parents born in Mexico benefited more from the Tulsa prekindergarten program. While Latino students with parents born in the United States realized significant prewriting gains of five months, those with parents born in Mexico realized significant gains in all three subtests: 13 months in prereading, four months in prewriting, and 10 months in premath. The difference in effects for children with parents born in Mexico and children with parents born in the United States is significant for premath but not for prereading or prewriting.

Latino students who took the Woodcock-Johnson Test (in English) and the Woodcock-Muñoz Batería (in Spanish) realized gains as measured by both testing instruments. This indicates that Latino students' gains are attributable to more than simply the acquisition of English language skills. However, the gains are higher for the Woodcock-Johnson Test than for the Woodcock-Muñoz Batería. The most obvious difference in effects is in the Letter-Word Identification Test; the Woodcock-Johnson score gains are dramatic (11 months), while the Woodcock-Muñoz score gains are statistically insignificant. In short, Latino students improved their cognitive skills (as evidenced by Woodcock-Muñoz score gains), but they also are improving their language skills (as evidenced by larger gains for the Woodcock-Johnson Test).

Momentum is currently building in the United States at all levels of government to make substantial investments and commitments to UPK programs. The provision of high-quality educational access for young children in the country is motivated not only by research in child development but also in economics. In terms of child development, neuropsychological research shows that the brains of very young children are extremely malleable during the early years of life (Ramey & Ramey, 1998; Shonkoff & Phillips, 2000). Indeed, a key characteristic of early childhood (0–3 years old) is the remarkably rapid brain development that occurs during this period. In many ways, these early years provide the foundation for the brain's lifelong capacity for growth and change. A strong neurological groundwork is established in early childhood through rich experiences that allow the brain to develop to the point of being able to process, encode, and interact with the environment (Kagan & Kauerz, 2006). High-quality early education programs can provide the necessary scaffolding and facilitate this development.

With regards to the financial investment in early education programs, economists Heckman and Masterov (2004) found that "enriched prekindergarten programs available to disadvantaged children on a voluntary basis ... have [a] strong track record of promoting achievement for disadvantaged children, improving their labor market outcomes and reducing involvement in crime." Moreover, educational policies that stress financial investment in early educational development cost less than those that seek to remedy early educational deficits at the middle school and high school levels. Simply stated, the later in life attempts are made to repair early deficits, the costlier remediation becomes (Ramey & Ramey, 1998; Reynolds, 2003; Reynolds & Temple, 2005).

Given the size, rapid growth, and comparatively low achievement levels of young Latino children in the United States, these children are particularly well situated to benefit from high-quality prekindergarten programs (García & Gonzáles, 2006). However, although enrollments among Latinos are on the rise, these children are less likely than their white, Asian, and African American peers to attend any sort of prekindergarten program (García et al., 2005). Currently, only 40% of 3-to-5-year-old Latinos attend a prekindergarten program compared to 60% of whites and African Americans (NCES, 2002). The low enrollment of Latino children in these programs is often misinterpreted as a function of the reluctance of Latino families to place their children in a center-based program. However, availability of high-quality and publicly funded programs is frequently limited in Latino communities which reduces access and, therefore, enrollment (Fuller, Bridges, & Livas, 2006).

Addressing UPK Quality

When they do enroll in prekindergarten, Latino children are more likely than their peers to attend low-quality programs: those with less prepared teachers, fewer resources, higher teacher to student ratios, and larger class sizes. Moreover, even when high-quality programs exist within communities, many parents are unaware that services are available due to a lack of community outreach. Language can also be a barrier to enrollment. Parents need to be able to communicate with the center, understand the enrollment paperwork, and engage meaningfully with the teacher (Hernandez, Mccartney, & Denton, 2010).

Targeted preschool programs such as Head Start and some prekindergarten programs are often associated with low-quality and do not always reach eligible children. Head Start, for example, reaches only about 35% of eligible children (Currie, 2001). Arizona, California, and Texas offer targeted prekindergarten programs, but these only meet four of the 10 quality benchmarks identified by the National Institute of Early Education Research (Barnett et al., 2005). Thus, because Latino children from all socioeconomic levels have shown to benefit cognitively from enrollment in high-quality preschool, the best evidence suggests that providing state-funded UPK programs constitutes a viable approach to early education delivery.

Research evidence also suggests that the success of UPK programs for Latinos depends on the extent to which language and culture are incorporated into the center, classroom, and instruction. Because approximately three out of four young Latinos are exposed to Spanish in the home (López, Barrueco, & Miles, 2006), the integration of Spanish and culturally relevant content is essential. A trademark of high-quality prekindergarten programs for Latino children is the provision of dual-language (English and Spanish) content and instruction by school staff who are bilingual and culturally competent (Barnett et al., 2006; Borman et al., 2006). This approach validates the child's cognitive and linguistic abilities while bridging home-school cultural differences – establishing an environment in which parents feel comfortable and are able to express themselves to teachers. This same research suggests that Latino children come to early learning venues lacking opportunities to develop rich language backgrounds in either Spanish or English (Reardon & Galindo, 2006). The absence of U.S.-educated adults in the home – the absence of U.S.-specific educational capital – places these students in particular circumstances that may lead to early achievement gaps (Risley & Hart, 2006).

In their study, Barnett et al. compared the effects of a dual-language program to a monolingual English program within the same school district. Children in the study were from Spanish and English backgrounds. Programs were compared on measures of children's growth in language, emergent literacy, and mathematics. Among the native Spanish speakers, those enrolled in the dual-language program demonstrated greater gains in phonological awareness in both English and Spanish and in Spanish vocabulary than children in the English-only program. Authors of this study concluded, therefore, that programs built around valuing and teaching relevant culture and traditions and addressing language differences and needs directly are among the most effective. This is consistent with research by Borman et al. (2006), who conducted a meta-analysis of the research on the achievement effects of the nationally disseminated school improvement programs known as "comprehensive" school reforms implemented in predominantly Latino elementary-school contexts.

Conclusion and Recommendations

The following recommendations are offered to improve educational opportunities for young Latinos in the United States. They emphasize the need for policy and practice in early education to directly address language and for curriculum and instruction to reflect relevant culture and traditions. Findings from the available research literature on schooling, language, and policy highlight the need for expanded UPK access and for these programs to have rich language environments, dual-language programs, and high-quality teachers and staff. These recommendations are based on the empirical research reviewed here and related development theory. The recommendations are primarily directed to parties who influence early education policy and practice at the federal, state, and local levels, including governments, private foundations, nonprofit organizations, and parents.

Universal Prekindergarten

Young Latino children aged 3 and 4 years old should have access to free, state-funded preschool whose enrollment is done on a volunteer basis – universal prekindergarten. Evidence suggests that high-quality UPK programs improve school readiness for young Latino children and decrease achievement differences between racial/ethnic groups at kindergarten entry. These programs should have bilingual and culturally competent staff to effectively engage students and to develop sustainable relationships with family members.

Moreover, federal and state efforts would be wise to adopt prekindergarten curricula in both Spanish and English. Because the majority of funding for preschool is provided by state and local governmental agencies, states and local communities (cities, counties, and local school districts) should work together to offer high-quality educational experiences with a variety of schedule options. In states where access to state-funded prekindergarten is not yet universal – available to all children – policy makers and program administrators should expand definitions of eligibility to include children with limited English proficiency. This should be an intermediate step, intended to increase Latino enrollment and serve more at-risk children until the larger goal of universal access is attained.

Rich Language Environments

UPK environments that include Latino children should be rich in language. Richness is defined through frequency and quality. In terms of frequency, research on cognitive development, language, and early experiences shows that the amount of talk and conversational exchange between adults and young children is strongly associated with school readiness and academic success in formal schooling. Teachers, aides, and other school personnel should engage young Latino students in casual talk as much as possible and, where feasible, encourage parents to do the same. Quality refers to language systems and culture. Young Latinos should be exposed to English and Spanish in the classroom and be provided with many opportunities to speak and express themselves in either language – allowing for linguistic exploration and mixtures. For young children managing more than one language, academic skills are much more likely to develop and, therefore, transfer between languages when environments allow access to knowledge through all language systems in culturally relevant ways (August & Shanahan, 2006). Otherwise, cognitive development is stifled.

Rich language environments that integrate Spanish and English on an ongoing basis will also facilitate important parent-school associations. Spanish-speaking parents are more likely to involve themselves in schools and classrooms in which Spanish is used on a regular basis (García & Frede, 2010).

Dual-Language Programs

Young Latino children should have access to high-quality dual language programs (i.e., two-way immersion) that teach English and Spanish language skills through content. Integrating native English and Spanish speakers in the same classroom, thereby fostering linguistic and ethnic equity among students, dual-language programs have been shown to support literacy development in English for Latino students without compromising Spanish skills. Moreover, research shows that academic achievement levels of young Spanish-speaking Latinos as well as their native English-speaking peers enrolled in dual-language programs are equivalent or, in many cases, superior to outcomes of students in mainstream classrooms.

Dual-language programs should be strategically structured to promote and sustain the development of students enrolled. Researchers at the Center for Applied Linguistics (CAL, 2005) have provided a set of principles to help school personnel establish and maintain high-quality programs. These suggest that the program create and maintain an infrastructure that supports an accountability process; use curriculum that promotes and maintains the development of bilingual, biliterate, and multicultural competencies for all students; use student-centered instructional strategies derived from research-based principles of dual-language education; recruit and retain high-quality dual-language staff; have knowledgeable leadership who promotes equity among groups and supports the goals of additive bilingualism, biliteracy, and cross-cultural competence; have a responsive infrastructure for positive, ongoing relations with students' families and the community; and that the program be adequately funded and supported by school staff, families, and the community (García and Frede, 2010).

High-Quality Teachers

The provision of rich language environments and high-quality UPK programs necessitates high-quality teachers. This means teachers are bilingual, proficient in both English and Spanish, and knowledgeable regarding the cultural and linguistic circumstances of Latino families, particularly the educational strengths and needs of their children. Indeed, research shows that the transfer of academic skills between languages is heightened and early achievement outcomes increased for young bilingual and emergent bilingual students when teachers use Spanish (in addition to English) in classroom instruction. The most successful teachers are fluent in both languages, understand learning patterns associated with second language acquisition, have a mastery of appropriate instructional strategies (i.e., cooperative learning, sheltered instruction, differentiated instruction, and strategic teaching), and have strong organizational and communication skills. With these skills, teachers will be able to interact with Latino parents appropriately, encouraging them to engage in literacy activities with their children at home; find out as much detail as possible about the linguistic backgrounds of their students; and develop creative and accurate assessments of the students' linguistic ability and development (García, 2005).

The optimal situation is for lead teachers and school staff in general to be proficient in both languages and familiar with students' cultures. However, when this is not possible, it is recommended that a language specialist be provided. Language specialists are bilingual professionals who serve as consultants to teachers and aides in the classroom to help Latino ELL (English Language Learners) students learn and achieve, recognizing and leveraging existent strengths. Having a language specialist in the classroom will also help monolingual teachers make essential links with Spanish-speaking parents.

Many of these specific reform initiatives have been aimed at linguistically and culturally diverse students for several decades. These have generated some movement at the policy, practice, and achievement levels. However, reform as it has been implemented to date has not produced the necessary robust changes in early educational performance. These reforms have ignored what counts for the academic success of young Latino students. New educational practices that have the following characteristics are beginning to demonstrate significant promise for young Latino students:

- Strategies that begin with the linguistic and cultural attributes of the students and build from there – they respect and engage previous knowledge bases regarding the student and cultural conceptualizations of academic content areas.

- Strategies that are directly responsive to the utilization of the linguistic background of the student that bridges to high levels of vocabulary, concept, and repertoires in English.
- Strategies that assess in various ways the development and learning and are utilized for changes in instructional architectures and delivery.
- Strategies that utilize multiple resources – human, fiscal, physical, temporal, and technological – to address instruction.
- Strategies that invest in early development of linguistic and cognitive development, building on the child's existing competencies.

Thinking differently about these students involves viewing them and our education system in new ways that may contradict conventional notions. This change in thinking allows us to come to a new set of realizations about the value and importance of schooling experiences and is leading us in the direction of innovation in education versus reform.

REFERENCES

August, D., & Shanahan. T. (Eds.) (2006). *Report of the national literacy panel on language minority youth and children*. Mahwah, NJ: Lawrence Erlbaum Associates.

Barnett W. S., et al. (2005). *The state of preschool: 2005 state preschool yearbook*. Rutgers: National Institute of Early Education Research.

Barnett, W. S., Yarosz, D. J., Thomas, J., & Blanco, D. (2006). *Two-way and monolingual English immersion in preschool education: An experimental comparison*. New Brunswick, NJ: National Institute for Early Education.

Borman, G. D., Hewes, G. H., Reilly, M., & Alvarado, S. (2006). *Comprehensive school reform for Latino elementary-school students: A meta-analysis*. Commissioned by the National Task Force on Early Childhood Education for Latinos. University of Wisconsin-Madison.

Bowman, B. T., Donovan, M. S., & Burns, M. S. (2001). *Eager to learn: Educating our preschools*. Washington, DC: National Academy Press.

Braswell, J., et al. (2001). *The nation's report card: Mathematics 2000*. Washington, DC: U.S. Department of Education, National Center for Educational Statistics (ED 453 086).

Braswell, J., Daane, M., & Grigg, W. (2003). *The nation's report card: Mathematics Highlights 2003*. Washington, DC: U.S. Department of Education, National Center for Education Statistics (NCES 2004451).

Capps, R., Fix, M., Ost, J., Reardon-Anderson, J., & Passel, J. (2004). *The health and well-being of young children of immigrants*. The Urban Institute.

Center for Applied Linguistics (CAL). (2005). *Guiding principles for dual language education*. Washington, DC: CAL.

Currie, J. (2001). *A fresh start for Head Start?* Washington, DC: Brookings Institution.

Escarce, J. J., Morales, L. S., & Rumbaut, R. G. (2006). The health status and health behaviors of Hispanics. In M. Tienda and F. Mitchell (Eds.), *Hispanics and the Future of America* (pp. 362–409). Washington, DC: The National Academies Press.

Fuller, B., Bridges, M., & Livas, A. (2006). *The supply of child care centers across Latino communities.* Paper presented on April 11 at the Annual AERA Conference in San Francisco, CA.

García, E. E. (2005). *Teaching and learning in two languages: Bilingualism and schooling in the United States.* New York: Teachers College Press.

García, E. E., & Frede, E. C. (Eds.). (2010). *Young English language learners: Current research and emerging directions for practice and policy.* New York: Teachers College Press.

García, E. E., & Gonzáles, D. M. (2006). *Pre-K and Latinos: The foundation for America's future.* Washington, DC: Pre-K Now.

García, E. E., Jensen, B. T., & Cuéllar, D. (2006). Early academic achievement of Hispanics in the United States: Implications for teacher preparation. *The New Educator, 2,* 123–47.

García, E. E., Jensen, B. T., Miller, L. S., & Huerta, T. (2005). *Early childhood education of Hispanics in the United States.* Tempe, AZ: The National Task Force on Early Childhood Education for Hispanics. Available online at http://www.ecehispanic. org/work/white_paper_Oct2005.pdf.

Gilliam, W., & Zigler, E. (2004). *State efforts to evaluate the effects of prekindergarten: 1977 to 2003.* New Haven: Yale University Child Study Center.

Gormley, W., Gayer, T., & Dawson, B. (2004). *The effects of universal pre-k on cognitive development.* Washington, DC: Public Policy Institute, Georgetown University.

Gormley, W., & Phillips, D. (2003). *The effects of universal pre-K in Oklahoma: Research highlights and policy implications.* Washington, DC: Georgetown Public Policy Institute, October 2003.

Grigg, W. S., Duaane, M. C., Jin, Y., & Campbell, J. R. (2003). *The Nation's Report Card: Reading 2002.* Washington, DC: U.S. Department of Education, National Center for Educational Statistics (ED 471–794).

Heckman, J., & Masterov, D. (2004). *The productivity argument for investing in young children.* Chicago, IL: Committee for Economic Development.

Hernandez, D. (2006). *Young Hispanic children in the U.S.: A demographic portrait based on Census 2000.* University at Albany, State University, NY: A report to the National Task Force on Early Childhood Education for Hispanics.

Hernandez, D., Maccartney, S., & Denton, N. A. (2010). A demographic portrait of young English language learners. In García,, E. E. and Frede, E. C., (Eds.), *Young English language learners* (pp. 10–41). New York, NY: Teachers College Press.

Kagan, S., & Kauerz, K. (2006). Preschool programs: Effective curricula. In R. E. Tremblay, R. G. Barr., and R. Peters (Eds.), *Encyclopedia on Early Childhood Development* [online]. Montreal, Quebec: Centre of Excellence for Early Childhood Development.

López, M., Barrueco, S., & Miles, J. (2006). *Latino infants and families: A national perspective of protective and risk factors for development.* A report to the

National Task Force on Early Childhood Education for Hispanics. Arizona State University.

Magnuson, K., & Waldfogel, J. (2005). Early childhood care and education: Effects of ethnic and racial gaps in school readiness. *The Future of Children, 15*(1), 169–96.

Montemayor, R., & Mendoza, H. (2004). *Right before our eyes: Latinos past, present, and future.* Tempe, AZ: Scholarly Publishing.

National Center for Education Statistics. (2001). *User's manual for the ECLS-K base year public-use data files and electronic codebook.* Washington, DC: NCES 2001–029 (revised).

———. (2002). *The condition of education 2002* (NCES 2002–025), Table 1–1. Washington, DC: U.S. Government Printing Office.

———. (2003). *Status and Trends in the Education of Hispanics.* (NCES 2003–007). Washington DC: U.S. Government Printing Office.

National Clearinghouse for English Language Acquisition. (2006). *The growing numbers of limited English proficient students: 1993–94–2003/04.* Office of English Language Acquisition (OELA): U.S. Department of Education.

Nuñez, A., Cuccaro-Alamin, S., & Carroll, C. D. (1998). *First-generation students: Undergraduates whose parents never enrolled in postsecondary education.* Washington, DC: U.S. Department of Education, Office of Education Research and Improvement.

Olson, L. (2005, January 26). Calls for revamping high schools intensify. *Education Week, 1,* 18–19.

Perez, P., & Zarate, M. E. (2006). *Latino public opinion survey of pre-kindergarten programs: Knowledge, preferences, and public support.* Los Angeles, CA: Tomas Rivera Policy Institute.

Ramey, C., & Ramey, S. (1998). Early intervention and early experience. *American Psychologist, 53*(2), 109–20.

Ramirez, R. R., & de la Cruz, P. G. (2003). *The Hispanic population in the United States: March 2002.* U.S. Census Bureau, U.S. Department of Commerce, Economic and Statistics Administration. Washington, DC.

Reardon, S. (2003). *Sources of educational inequality: The growth of racial/ethnic and socioeconomic test score gaps in kindergarten and first grade.* Population Research Institute. Pennsylvania State University.

Reardon, S., & Galindo, C. (2006). *K-3 academic achievement patterns and trajectories of Hispanics and other racial/ethnic groups.* Paper presented on April 11 at the Annual AERA Conference in San Francisco, CA.

Reynolds, A. (2003). The added value of continuing early intervention into the primary grades. In A. Reynolds, M. Wang, and H. Walberg (Eds.), *Early childhood programs for a new century* (pp. 163–96). Washington, DC: CWLA Press.

Reynolds, A., & Temple, J. (2005). Priorities for a new century of early childhood programs. *Infants & Young Children, 18*(2), 104–18.

Risley, T. R., & Hart, B. (2006). Promoting early language development. In N. F. Watt et al. (Eds.), *The crisis in young mental health: Early intervention programs and policies* (pp. 83–8). Westport, CT: Praeger.

Shields, M., & Behrman, R. (2004). Children of immigrant families: Analysis and recommendations. In R. Behrman (Ed.), *The Future of Children, 14*(2), 4–15.

Shonkoff, J. P., & Phillips, D. A. (2000). *From neurons to neighborhoods: The science of early childhood development*. National Research Council and Institute of Medicine (2000). Washington, DC: National Academy Press.

U.S. Census Bureau. (2003). *The Hispanic population in the United States: March 2002 Detailed Tables* (PPL-165). U.S. Dept. of Commerce, Economics and Statistics Administration, Bureau of the Census.

17 Promoting the Well-Being of Immigrant Youth

A Framework for Comparing Outcomes and Policies

Brian Nolan

Introduction

The well-being of immigrant youth – of the first or second generation – is intimately tied to their socioeconomic status and success, and these are important for social cohesion in society. Institutional settings and policies vary greatly from one country to the next, so studying key outcomes for immigrant youth in a comparative perspective illuminates which are most effective in promoting their well-being. In this chapter, a framework is presented for that exercise, highlighting recent literature on multidimensional well-being, social inclusion/exclusion, and child well-being. Then key findings from research on immigration and youth are examined within that framework in order to delineate the potential and the challenges associated with this approach to teasing out what works for immigrant youth.

Capturing Well-being

To assess the well-being of immigrant youth, one needs a clear conceptual perspective. There is now a substantial body of research focused on monitoring well-being, including across countries, from which much can be learned about the key dimensions of well-being and how they are measured for the general population and for children and young people. This can provide a general framework within which to set assessment of the situation of immigrant youth, supplemented by specific features of particular relevance for them (for a review see Fahey, Nolan & Whelan, 2003).

The focus on well-being is seen as moving beyond narrow or one-dimensional views of the human person or socioeconomic circumstances toward a more encompassing view that identifies a number of dimensions key to a rounded human life. (Such concepts of human well-being are culturally relative and essentially normative in character.) A central element is the extent to which people are enabled to attain their own ends. For example, Swedish welfare research focuses on "level of living" (Erikson & Aberg, 1987), defined in terms of access to resources in the form of money, possessions, knowledge, mental and physical energy, and social relationships, through which an individual can direct his or her living conditions. It is not simply *outcomes* that matter – because these can be affected by the choices people make – but rather the capacity to affect those outcomes in a purposive way. Similarly Sen (1993) defines *functionings* as the various things a person manages to do or be – such as being adequately nourished and in good health, having self-respect and being socially integrated – while *capability* reflects the alternative combination of functionings an individual can achieve.

If our paramount interest is in the lives that people can lead – then it cannot but be a mistake to concentrate exclusively only on one or other of the *means* to such freedom. We must look at impoverished lives and not just depleted wallets. (Sen, 2000, 3)

While empirically, the concept of capabilities has proved elusive, Sen's emphasis on the processes linking resources and outcomes, on empowerment, freedom, and expansion of choice, and on the fact that lives are intertwined with others in the household, community, and beyond, has been influential.

Well-being reflects not only living conditions and control over resources across the full spectrum of life domains, but also the ways in which people respond and feel about their life in those domains. Research on "quality of life" (developing from the 1960s principally in the United States, see for example Campbell et al., 1976) has concentrated very much on subjective well-being as the focus of interest, relying for the most part on responses to questions asking people to evaluate their own conditions. This research draws heavily on psychology and social psychology, and distinguishes for example between happiness and life satisfaction, the former being seen as more of an affective state whereas the latter represents more of a cognitive state (see for example McKennell & Andrews, 1980). More broadly, though, both objective and subjective aspects and indicators are generally incorporated into efforts to monitor well-being. In that sense, well-being can encompass but go beyond socioeconomic status and success, and also the notion of welfare as generally used in Nordic welfare state discourse (which highlights objective measures of resources), to include subjective or psychological well-being. It thus has close affinities with the concept of integration as it is generally used in migration research, and adaptation as that concept is understood within acculturation psychology.

While various categorizations of domains of well-being are in use (Fahey, Nolan & Whelan, 2003), the dimensions commonly employed include:

- Employment and working conditions
- Economic resources
- Knowledge, education, and training
- Health and health care
- Families and households
- Community life and social participation
- Housing
- Local environment and amenities
- Transport
- Public safety and crime
- Recreation and leisure activities
- Culture and identity, political resources, and human rights

The most relevant domains, and expectations for what constitutes well-being and defines success, will clearly vary from conception to old age, as emphasized in sociology's focus on the life course and in the developmental perspective of psychology. Core dimensions employed in monitoring focused on the well-being of children and youth are of particular relevance here (Ben-Arieh & Frones, 2009). The study by Bradshaw and colleagues for UNICEF (2007) for 21 developed countries employed six core dimensions:

- material deprivation,
- health and safety,
- education,
- family and peer relationships,
- behavior/lifestyles and risks, and
- subjective well-being.

The U.S. Federal Interagency Forum on Child and Family Statistics (building on Hauser, Brown, & Prosser, 1997) annual report organizes its indicators into a similar set of domains, while Hair et al. (2001) distinguish educational achievement and cognitive attainment, health and safety, social and emotional development, and self-sufficiency. Indicators tend to focus more on negative outcomes and problems rather than positive development and outcomes (see for example Moore, Lippman, & Brown, 2004), and the social and emotional domain is often underrepresented in practice.

Learning from Diversity

Institutional settings and policies, in relation to immigrants and to welfare state structures more broadly, vary greatly from one developed country to the next, and comparative analysis is a standard approach to learning about what works for groups regarded as vulnerable – children, older people, those with disabilities, and so forth. This is a challenging enterprise, especially when applied to immigrants. Looking at how similar immigrants fare in different countries ideally requires standardized analyses using nationally representative samples, standardized coding of variables, and standardized statistical models (Heath & Cheung, 2007). Identifying migrants is often problematic, with differences in information gathered across countries – and unwillingness in some (notably France) to distinguish second-generation migrants in standard statistical instruments. The outcome variables of interest must also be measured in a consistent fashion, which can be problematic when making comparisons across different education systems, for example, or with inadequate information on income, occupation, or indicators of broader well-being. Finally and crucially, the heterogeneity of the immigrant population itself needs to be taken into account: a wealth of reliable and comparable information about them and their background is needed if we are to measure how immigrants do compared to natives with the same characteristics and how similar immigrants fare in different countries. Capturing social background in order to filter out its effects is a challenge in dealing with any population, but is particularly problematic for both first- and second-generation immigrants.

Teasing out the role of institutions and policies in producing observed differences is also far from straightforward. Even focusing on one country, it is difficult to disentangle the impact of a specific institutional structure or policy innovation from broader economic and social trends and to be sure that changes in the composition of the immigrant population are not what is driving observed changes in outcomes. Randomized controlled trials are becoming fashionable in the social sciences and may play a useful role, but are generally informative about specific interventions rather than broader social structures. Even if a particular policy measure or intervention has worked in improving outcomes for immigrant youth in a particular setting, it can be hazardous to generalize to different institutional contexts and immigrant groups.

Alternative perspectives on what one means by doing well are also important. A common approach is to compare the situation of immigrants or ethnic minorities with that of others in terms of education, employment, living standards, health, and so forth, to identify any "immigrant/ethnic penalty." The question of whether immigrants do better in country A versus country B could also be considered in relation to a common standard: In which country do immigrants attain higher levels of education, income, or health? This might be an important factor in a potential migrant's assessment of options (both the average standard of living available and the probability of reaching or exceeding it should influence the choice of destination). For the second generation, by contrast, it may be the host country rather than the country of origin or potential alternative destinations that provides the main frame of reference in evaluating their own well-being.

The next section focuses on some of the key dimensions of well-being for migrant youth, beginning with education and proceeding to discuss the labor market, economic resources/poverty, health, housing, and social integration and cohesion.

Education

Educational attainment is a key determinant of subsequent earnings and occupational attainment, and differences in educational outcomes across social classes and income groups have been intensively investigated by social scientists for many years (e.g., Breen & Jonsson, 2005; Shavit & Blossfeld, 1993; Shavit & Müller, 1998). Explanations for the major differences observed (in all Western societies) generally focus on the different costs and benefits in progressing through the education system facing families at different points in the income distribution or class hierarchy, and cultural factors such as familiarity with the system and what it demands of students. This is also an area where a substantial body of research has been done on the position of migrants, both the first generation and the second generation (e.g., Crul & Vermeulen, 2003; Heath & Birnbaum, 2007; Schnepf, 2007). This brings out the importance of the traditional explanations for relatively poor outcomes when applied to migrants and the need to go beyond them. Among those who migrate and enter the education system of the host country, a high proportion may face structural and cultural deficits. The occupation and family income of their parents may be low, their parents will be unfamiliar with the education system and probably the broader cultural setting, and the children/youth themselves may have to learn the language. For the second generation, born in the host country of immigrant parents, those parents are on average still disadvantaged in the labor market and thus in income and class terms, and while language acquisition may be much less of an issue, parents' lack of exposure to the educational system, and perhaps broader cultural dissonance, may still represent significant handicaps.

Recent coordinated country studies of the children of migrants who came to Europe and North America in the second half of the 20th century provide important insights into the educational attainment of the second generation, taking social background into account (Heath & Birnbaum, 2007). They find large overall differences between ethnic groups before taking account of socioeconomic background, with a number having substantially lower educational attainment than the majority groups in the country, others doing less badly but still lagging behind, and only a few doing better. When the socioeconomic position of the parental generation (in terms of occupation, income, and/or education) is taken into account, this is sufficient to explain educational outcomes for those of European ancestry. Among those from developing countries, educational disadvantage sometimes exceeds that predicted by parental socioeconomic position, but the results differ from country to country and group to group – for example, social background explains all the Turkish disadvantage on completing second level in Germany and the North African disadvantage in test scores in France, whereas it explains only half the Mexican disadvantage in high school graduation in the United States and little of the disadvantage of boys of Caribbean origin in Britain. So traditional explanations emphasizing social background work rather well in explaining ethnic minority disadvantage and in stratifying ethnic groups in much the same way as majority groups, but several additional factors specific to migrants may also be at work. For example, Van de Werfhorst and van Tubergen (2007) from the Netherlands show that parental usage of the Dutch language and knowledge of the educational system are positively associated with children's test scores. Migrant children's drive and ambition may also be promoted by their parents, with migrants positively selected in those terms.

Another recent cross-national collaborative study focuses on Turkish second-generation immigrants in six European countries (Crul & Vermeulen, 2003). Their socioeconomic background is extremely low compared with the native populations of these countries, and combined with a traditional Muslim background means that Turkish immigrants are widely considered one of the toughest groups to integrate. The education level of the first-generation immigrants is particularly low, reflecting their rural subsistence farming background. For the second generation, major differences across countries in educational trajectories were found. A much higher proportion of the children of Turkish immigrants are channeled into a vocational track at lower secondary level in Germany and Austria than France, Belgium, and the Netherlands, and far more entered the preparatory track for higher education in France and Belgium. However, the dropout rate is also highest in France, with a much higher proportion leaving secondary school with no diploma at all, so there is a price to be paid for the high proportion getting to university. Those channeled into the German and Austrian apprenticeship system also benefit when it comes to transition into the labor market. The results do not point to any clear effect of integration policies aimed at migrants, but generic national institutional arrangements do matter.

Compensatory education programs aimed at migrants may potentially play an important role in educational outcomes. Fase (1994) brings out the differences across countries in such programs, in terms for example of whether they are integrated into the school curricula versus separate classes for migrants. Interesting, though, such differences seem to have few consequences for the educational status of immigrant children in the various countries. Esser (2004) provides evidence that language difficulties play a significant role in Turkish disadvantage in German schools, while Kristen (2008) explores why Turkish children are more likely than Germans to enter a school with a relatively large proportion of foreign nationals, contributing to an increasing ethnic separation. Rather than originating from ethnic differences in evaluation or school access, parents' perception are seen as of primary importance – unfamiliarity with the system means Turkish families frequently pay attention to only the school that accommodates more foreign nationals.

The critical role of parental socioeconomic background clearly means that institutions and policies that promote labor market success for the first generation can be expected to have direct effects in reducing educational disadvantage for their offspring. The structure of the educational system also matters. The general understanding from studies of social class inequalities in educational attainment is that early selection is associated with greater inequalities (e.g., Breen & Jonsson, 2005). Some countries which have early selection and tracking (such as the Netherlands and Germany) do appear to have relatively high minority disadvantage at age 15. The availability of second chance entry routes make it easier for minorities to progress (while also benefiting disadvantaged majority youth). In predominantly comprehensive systems with delayed selection (such as in Britain and the United States), however, particular problems may arise for comprehensive schools in neighborhoods with high concentrations of migrants and socioeconomic disadvantage, which may reduce ethnic minority opportunities. Programs directing additional resources to such schools, such as the French Zones d'Education Prioritaire, may have some impact although evaluation results are mixed (Bénabou, Kramarz, & Prost, 2005). Countries such as Germany with relatively small tertiary sectors with strong linkage between school performance and entry have lower ethnic minority participation than the U.S. system of mass higher education with its relatively loose linkage to school performance, although ethnic minorities are overrepresented in lower prestige institutions there. Similarly the case of France suggests that educational systems that allow many majority children into higher education are more accessible to ethnic minority groups as well – though of course a third-level qualification may then be less valuable in the labor market.

National educational systems also differ in school duration, face-to-face contact hours with teachers, selectivity, and supplementary help available to children and youth inside and outside school. The age education begins varies widely, and second-generation immigrant children have much greater opportunities to learn the majority language where it starts early. Limited contact hours and more emphasis on homework also disadvantage migrant children for whom help at home may be scant. Countries also differ in the extent of special assistance and support provided to youth with learning problems, and to migrant children in particular, notably language training. The language problems of the "1.5" generation clearly need to be addressed, but this is not a panacea and will not solve the problems of the second generation. There is considerable debate about structure language programs, for example transitional bilingual programs versus intensive instruction in the host country language, and integration into mainstream school programs versus outside school (see, e.g., Westin, 2003).

Finally, policies aimed at improving school standards generally by increasing parental information and choices may increase ethnic (and other) inequalities, since minority parents are likely to be less knowledgeable about the available choices. The fact that minorities may do particularly poorly early on but the gap tends to close as educational careers progress provides some ground for optimism, as well as illustrating the resilience and potential of such groups. This has a less benign interpretation, however, in that prospects in the labor market may also play a role: Discrimination on entry into the labor market may work to reduce the opportunity cost for migrant youth of continuing in education. In the current economic environment where unemployment is rising dramatically, the labor market prospects for immigrant youth may be particularly poor, and it is to employment and earnings that we now turn.

Employment and Earnings

There are many reasons why first-generation immigrants might fare poorly in the labor market: Their foreign qualifications may not be recognized, their lack of language fluency may be a hindrance, and their lack of experience in the destination labor market may prevent them from getting the kind of work they are qualified for. These issues will not apply with the same force to the second generation, but despite this a range of studies finds that ethnic minorities are disadvantaged in the labor market with respect to employment and occupational attainment, reflecting but going beyond what would be predicted on the basis of their educational attainment.

There have been many informative national studies of the employment experiences of migrants and their earnings vis-à-vis natives. These include Borjas (1999) on the United States; Dustmann et al. (2003) on the United Kingdom; Fertig and Schurer (2007) on Germany; Gross (1999) on France; Sanromá, Ramos, and Simón (2009) on Spain; and the individual country chapters in Zimmermann (2005). However, here our main focus is once again on learning from cross-country studies. Heath and Cheung (2007) report on a collaborative study covering the Western countries that have seen large numbers of immigrants in the second half of the 20th century. A clear pattern of ethnic stratification is found that continues, although often with reduced magnitude, in the second generation. The hierarchy is broadly similar, with groups of northwest European origins at the top, followed by those from other European countries and those with non-European origins toward the bottom. Most groups of non-European ancestry experience substantial ethnic penalties in terms of unemployment and occupational attainment (having controlled for their education levels), even in the second and later generations. In a few countries, notably Australia and Canada, the second generation of European ancestry does not experience any ethnic penalties while groups of non-European ancestry experience moderate ethnic penalties but only for employment. Those fortunate enough to be in work get jobs commensurate with their qualifications. This is also true in the case of Britain, Sweden, and the United States. In contrast, in many western European countries such as Austria, Belgium, France, Germany, and the Netherlands, ethnic penalties are quite substantial for non-European minorities both with respect to securing employment as well as in gaining access to salaried jobs. Ethnic minorities in Belgium and France are particularly disadvantaged.

There are a number of possible explanations for greater ethnic penalties being experienced in Western Europe than in North America or Australia.

First of all, the level of unemployment and the flexibility of the local labor market may be responsible. Second, prejudice against ethnic minorities and exclusionary or xenophobic attitudes may also in part explain these cross-national differences. Finally inclusivity, such as the ease of obtaining citizenship, and selectivity, such as immigration legislation that restricts entry to highly qualified migrations, may also contribute. The largest ethnic penalties, found in Austria, Belgium, and Germany, seem to be a legacy of guest worker programs in these countries that attracted mostly immigrants from a rural peasant background. However, the German and Austrian apprenticeship system may be effective in ensuring a relatively smooth transition to work for immigrant youth who follow that track, with lower unemployment among second-generation Turks in those countries than in France, Belgium, or the Netherlands, although a substantial group of second-generation Turks reach white-collar or professional positions in the latter.

The wide range of studies of migrants in individual countries (see examples in Zimmermann, 2005 and Kahanec & Zimmermann, 2009) support the conclusion from comparative studies that while it is essential to distinguish among different migrant groups and education plays a central role in labor market outcomes for migrants as for others, some migrant groups experience substantial and sustained disadvantage in the labor market. It is unlikely that the disadvantages of migrants in the labor market will disappear of their own accord, but what government action will help? Clearly, improving the educational performance of migrant youth should translate into better labor market outcomes, so the structural and compensatory issues discussed previously in relation to education are highly relevant. It is also important to note that some labor market structures have much wider divergence in outcomes between the more skilled versus the less skilled or educated. As in other domains, institutions and policies that effectively incorporate the disadvantaged, broadly defined, may be at least as important as those directed specifically to migrants.

Going beyond that, though, several other areas appear likely to be potentially important in narrowing gaps between (some) migrant groups and others in labor market outcomes. One is the way posteducation training is structured and the extent to which it seeks to meet the particular needs of immigrants and ethnic minorities. Major advances have been made in the way the impact of training and reintegration programs are evaluated, with increasingly sophisticated statistical methods and randomized trials being used. This research provides a basis for designing more effective intervention, which is all the more important in the current economic crisis. The same may be said of programs aimed at regenerating deprived urban areas, in which disadvantaged ethnic minorities are often concentrated.

The other area is perhaps the most obvious: discrimination and how to tackle it. Field studies in various countries have amply demonstrated the existence of substantial discrimination in hiring that disadvantages visible ethnic minorities (see for example Bendick, 1996; Carlsson & Rooth, 2007; McGinnity et al., 2009; Riach & Rich, 2002). Many countries have implemented stringent antidiscrimination legislation and education programs aimed at changing attitudes (among both employers and employees); vigorous implementation on both fronts seems essential if labor market outcomes for migrants in particular minority groups are to improve (Bassanini & Saint-Martin, 2008; OECD, 2008). A particularly contentious issue, of course, is whether it is desirable to go further and introduce affirmative action for minority groups: The conditions under which that does more good than harm for ethnic minorities are not obvious.

Economic Resources and Poverty

Disadvantage in the labor market for immigrants translates directly into lower household income and a heightened risk of poverty. For some, this is compounded by other risk factors – notably family size and a higher probability of falling through gaps in the social safety net, not least due to limited entitlements. Thus a wide variety of national and comparative studies have found immigrants to have above average poverty rates and, often, poverty rates that are higher than those of otherwise similar individuals and households (see for example Hoynes, Page, & Stevens, 2006; Parsons & Smeeding, 2006). As in other domains, though, immigrants cannot be sensibly seen as a homogenous group; immigrants reveal a great deal of variation in income and poverty outcomes not only across different countries of origin but also within ethnic groups. Immigrants in the United States are much more likely to be below the official poverty line than native U.S. citizens, with recent immigrants having a particularly high poverty rate. However, there is wide variation among immigrants from different countries, with those from, for example, Mexico or the Dominican Republic having much higher poverty rates than those from Poland or the Philippines. In Canada, immigrants are consistently overrepresented among the poor; their poverty rates are particularly high in larger cities with larger concentrations of immigrants and poverty rates are particularly high for visible minorities, who are mostly recent immigrants (Fleury, 2007; Kazemipur & Halli, 2001). In Europe, above average poverty risk for immigrants has been frequently noted across a wide range of countries. The comparative study by Lelkes (2007) shows migrants almost always have higher poverty rates than others, but the gap varies a great deal from one country to another, and between migrants from other EU countries versus those from outside the EU, who generally face much higher poverty rates.

Excess poverty for immigrants clearly reflects a number of distinct but interrelated factors, most important lower education and disadvantage in the labor market as already discussed, as well as family size and structure. When education and labor force status (as well as age and gender) are taken into account, Lelkes (2007) still finds that migrants have a poverty risk that is 6% to 15% higher than others with similar characteristics. As well as lower earnings and higher unemployment/inactivity rates, the higher poverty rate for immigrants may reflect inadequacies and gaps in social security structures, both in general and specific to immigrants. Migrants may be particularly likely to find themselves relying on safety net schemes, while differential access/rights in relation to income support may leave some without support or with lower levels than a native in the same circumstances would receive.

What can be done to address the high poverty rates, and limited economic resources more broadly, that face significant groups of immigrants? The key areas for policy certainly include promoting economic success via education and labor market policies along the lines discussed previously. These are the classic responses of liberal market economies to disadvantage: improve earnings capacity so that people can become self-sufficient. However, it is also clear from extensive comparative research on poverty that welfare state structures, and the social protection system in particular, also play a central role. Thus financial and other supports for families, in addition to employment and earnings, have been key components of what works for child poverty generally (see Whiteford & Adema, 2007; European Commission, 2008; UNICEF, 2007). Such supportive frameworks would be particularly important for immigrant families, but some further measures targeted specifically at them also have a role. This could include, for example, seeking to ensure that immigrants have the information required to take advantage of their entitlements and that factors underlying failure to take up benefits are addressed. The position of immigrants with limited entitlements – because they are illegally present or because entitlements are limited for noncitizens or in other ways that affect legal immigrants – also needs to be addressed, but there are often political obstacles to more generous treatment by the social welfare system.

Health

The health and health services utilization and needs of first- and second-generation immigrants has been the topic of a very substantial research literature, though much of that literature is focused on very specific migrant groups, conditions, and locations from which it is difficult to draw general conclusions. Much of the literature relates to the United States and Canada, and takes as point of departure the observation that the foreign-born population there has much lower rates of chronic conditions than the native-born, across a wide range of different conditions, but with a tendency to converge over time from immigration (see for example Jasso et al., 2004; McDonald & Kennedy, 2004; Singh & Miller, 2004). The gap in some other immigrant-receiving countries is in the other direction, though, for example in the Netherlands. There is clearly substantial variation in health across different immigrant groups within and across countries, and as in other areas it is not appropriate to treat immigrants as a homogenous group. Health selectivity of migrants – the "healthy migrant" effect – clearly plays an important role in producing the North American pattern, and this has been a very important theme in the research literature (Jasso et al., 2004). Another important theme is the role of culture, and in particular whether some immigrant groups benefit from cultural norms (for example in relation to diet and risky behaviors) that serve as a protective factor for health, with this buffering generally reducing from one generation to the next. Finally, the act of immigration may itself directly affect health, since it may be stressful with negative psychosocial impacts, potentially impacting, for example, heart disease. In exploring these topics, rigorous comparative studies are rare, however, with much of the literature focused on specific conditions and settings, often with small samples or relying on administrative data and without being able to control adequately for the composition of the populations involved or other factors.

Focusing on children and youth, U.S. research (e.g., Hernandez, 1999) also suggests that those in immigrant families have fewer specific acute and chronic health problems, as well as lower prevalence of accidents and injuries. Rates of low birth weight and infant mortality are also lower among children born to immigrant women than to U.S.-born women, despite their lower socioeconomic status. Among adolescents, overall immigrants are less likely than U.S.-born youth to consider themselves in poor health or have school absences due to health or emotional problems. First-generation immigrant adolescents are also less likely to report engaging in risky behaviors. However, this is less true of the second generation and by the third and later generations risky behaviors approach or exceed U.S.-born white adolescents (See for example Abraído-Lanza, Chao, & Florez, 2005). Adolescents in immigrant families appear to experience overall levels of psychological well-being and self-esteem that are similar to, if not better than, adolescents in U.S.-born families, but do report feeling less control over their own lives (Hernandez & Charney, 1998). The issue of acculturation and its potential impact on health has been much discussed and investigated, but the way in which key variables are measured varies so much from one study to another that it is very difficult to draw broad conclusions (Salant & Lauderdale, 2003).

Immigrants and their children may also be distinctive in terms of access to and utilization of health services. In the United States, recent immigrants seem much less likely to receive timely health care than others, although this diminishes with time since arrival, while in Canada there seems to be relatively little difference between the health services utilization patterns of immigrants and native-born, with any differences for recently arrived migrants disappearing quite quickly (see, for example, Laroche, 2000, McDonald & Kennedy, 2004). In the Netherlands, the health care system contains few financial barriers but due to cultural and communications barriers migrants benefit less from such services than others (Venema, Garretsen, & van der Maas, 1995). Specific patterns of health care use may be observed among recent immigrants in particular, with greater reliance on walk-in services such as accident and emergency departments rather than regular primary care providers (see for example Leduc & Proulx, 2004). Immigrants may not have the same entitlement to health services as others, and may be less likely to have health insurance where that plays an important role. Limited language proficiency may be a barrier in accessing services, as may lack of knowledge about what is available and appropriate and of the social support networks. Discrimination on the part of service providers could also be at work.

Undocumented immigrants clearly face particular health challenges. They are often distinctive in health status and needs, for example in terms of prevalence of communicable disease and immunizations on arrival and the conditions in which they live and work. Limited access to health services and unwillingness to use them can then exacerbate the problem, with obvious risks not just to the immigrants themselves but in public health terms to the broader community. Refugees and asylum seekers and youth migrating without their families may also have specific problems and needs. The situations from which they have come may have traumatic effects on psychological well-being, while migration itself and the conditions in which they are often forced to live in the receiving country while their legal situation is clarified are often additional stressors. Therapeutic interventions may well be required to meet immediate mental health needs, and in the longer term specially designed mental health services may also be required (see, for example, Pumariega et al., 2005).

Bollini and Siem (1995) argue for the importance of differences in entitlement and distinguish two broad groups of countries in terms of attitude to health care provision for migrants:

• Those displaying a passive attitude, in which migrants are expected to make use of the existing health system without any major modification; and
• Those with an active attitude, in which the special health needs of immigrant communities are acknowledged and steps are taken to minimize linguistic and cultural barriers, via specific services for different ethnic groups and changes within mainstream services to accommodate ethnic diversity.

In terms of what makes a difference in the domain of health for migrants and migrant youth in particular, then, key considerations are:

1) The structure of health care and its accessibility for the general population, especially the poor and disadvantaged;
2) The entitlements of different types of immigrant, including the undocumented in particular;
3) The extent to which special provision is made, within and alongside mainstream services, for the special needs of particular immigrant communities, either nested within broader programs targeting disadvantage (poor urban areas, for example), or aimed at health conditions particularly prevalent in specific migrant groups (such as infectious diseases).
4) The extent to which the needs of specific types of immigrants such as refugees and asylum seekers are met by the provision of specially designed and culturally and therapeutically appropriate services.

Housing and Physical Environment

There is a large amount of research demonstrating that the housing experiences (in terms of housing choice, quality, affordability, and location) of recent immigrants are generally, though not uniformly, worse that those of the native population, and for certain ethnic groups this can persist over several generations. For example, Carter (2005) reports that in Canada immigrants are likely to be in housing need, and Harrison (2005) reports that in the United Kingdom ethnic minorities live in significantly more overcrowded housing than the rest of the population. Finding a suitable place to live is the first step toward successful integration, but immigrants face specific disadvantages in accessing adequate housing, in addition to those associated with socioeconomic status. Apart from their often limited financial resources, finding appropriate housing may be made more difficult for the first generation by lack of knowledge, high housing costs in the urban areas where migrants often concentrate, shortage of suitable housing (especially for rental), and discriminatory practices by landlords and sellers. Immigrants frequently report serious problems in accessing housing, and may have to devote a high proportion of their incomes to meeting housing costs. At the extreme, immigrants (and especially refugees) may be particularly vulnerable to homelessness. Harvey (1994) for example estimated that 10% to 20% of homeless persons in the EU were migrants or refugees (see also Carter, 2005; Edgar et al., 2004; and Harrison, 2005).

For the second generation, rather than access per se the more salient issues are the quality of housing and the neighborhood. While many immigrant families do manage to move up the housing ladder, spatial concentration is common – reflecting reliance on ethnic ties for information and other advantages of colocation, as well as discrimination in the housing market. Spatial polarization along ethnic lines has been a major preoccupation in the United States, and also in the United Kingdom, and to a lesser extent in the Netherlands and Sweden, for example (Harrison, 2005; Musterd & Ostendorf, 1998). While it is not always the case that these neighborhoods are relatively deprived, that is also common, adding another potential layer of neighborhood effects to those associated with ethnic concentration. Housing and housing policy are thus potentially critical for the environment in which the second generation of immigrant youth grow up.

It is important not to overstate the extent of such immigrant polarization (for example, Musterd and Deurloo, 2002 stress that ethnic concentrations in the Netherlands are relatively small especially when compared to the United States) or its impact. The negative socioeconomic effects (unemployment, income, and poverty) often assumed to flow from living in a disadvantaged neighborhood are often difficult to pin down statistically. A substantial U.S. research literature does link living in segregated areas with poorer employment and earnings prospects for blacks (see for example Cutler & Glaeser, 1997), reflecting *inter alia* the migration of jobs from the inner city to outer suburbs (the spatial mismatch hypothesis). However, living in an enclave may also have advantages in accessing jobs: A Swedish study taking advantage of a shift in government policy to distribute refugee immigrants across areas concluded that living in enclaves actually improved labor market outcomes (Edin et al., 2000). This finding may not be generalizable to other immigrant groups and contexts, but serves as a cautionary note.

Housing market structures and policies vary widely across countries, most obviously in the extent of owner occupation but also in the way the state intervenes to assist low-income households in particular. Studies such as Musterd and Ostendorf (1998) conclude that in countries like Sweden and the Netherlands, where government spending on housing and social security is high, minority ethnic populations are likely to be less excluded than in the United Kingdom, where levels of public investment in housing and social security are lower (and the extent of spatial segregation may be less). Thus, improving social housing provision and other measures to meet the housing needs of low-income households generally are of central importance for immigrants. Similarly, broadly focused neighborhood renewal policies may be very important for immigrant youth. Going beyond that, the evidence suggests an important role for measures targeted specifically at immigrants and ethnic minorities to include:

- Improving access of recent immigrants in particular to rental or social housing;
- Addressing the restricted access to rights which is an important factor in the poorer housing conditions of some migrants (Edgar et al., 2004);
- Encouraging the development of mixed tenure estates;
- Implementing antidiscrimination legislation and procedures in rented and social housing; and
- Policy with respect to spatial settlement of immigrants is linked to broader debates about social mixing between the social classes and about how the goals of social policy in terms of integration or assimilation are framed, to which we return.

Family and Peer Relationships, Social Integration and Cohesion

While widely recognized as central to the well-being of youth, it is commonly the case that quantitative indicators of family and peer relationships, social participation and integration are much sparser than for the other domains discussed. For migrant youth this may be particularly important, since they face challenges over and above those of other young people, but for the most part the available studies relate to specific countries, and often specific migrant or ethnic groups – or even types of immigrants with very particular problems such as refugees and asylum seekers or unaccompanied minors. It is clear that exposure to traumatic conditions prior to migration, coupled with difficulties in acculturation in a new environment, can lead to severe psychological and behavioral problems (see for example Hyman, Vu, & Belser, 2000). More generally, though, migration itself is often a stressor, and the different pace of acculturation of first-generation migrants and their children in the destination country can put a strain on family relationships (Suárez-Orozco and Qin, 2006).

Immigration can lead to a change in power relationships and the role of women outside the household, which may conflict with patriarchal expectations on the part of men. Lack of language proficiency among parents may mean children and youth take on responsibilities for dealing with the outside world, and the division of work within the household may also be a source of strain (impacting differently on young men vs. women). Parental efforts to exercise discipline over their children, particularly where the host society is seen as a threat to their native culture, may be a source of conflict. This may center on risky or problem behaviors in the case of boys, but on patterns of socializing for girls. "Dissonant acculturation" between parents and children can lead to serious problems within the family. However, problem cases may be more visible to researchers and those providing social and health services support, giving rise to a tendency to overestimate the scale of such difficulties among immigrants relative to others. A comparison of Mexican immigrant and white Americans by Suárez-Orozco and Suárez-Orozco (1995), for example, found that immigrant and second-generation youth displayed *less* family conflict than their white counterparts (Levitt & Waters, 2002; Portes & Rumbaut, 2001).

Immigrant youth may find forming a coherent identity during adolescence particularly challenging if they have to inhabit different worlds at home and in school, with potential cultural dissonance, and this may be exacerbated by discrimination and negative images of their ethnic group in the dominant culture. A variety of sources in the host society, including school, media, and police, may convey messages about such negative stereotypes, affecting the individual's sense of self-worth – with important differences between young men and women, and across different ethnic groups. Conflicting messages from home and school may also pose problems in identity formation, particularly for girls. It appears that the ability to move easily across cultural contexts – rather than rapidly leaving behind their culture of origin – is the most adaptive for immigrant youths' development (see, for example, Portes & Zhou, 1993).

Despite the particular challenges that they face, research on migrant adaptation suggests that children and young people from immigrant backgrounds generally show satisfactory levels of psychological and social adjustment; indeed, some studies have shown them to be less involved in negative behaviors than their national peers and having at least as high levels of psychological well-being – an aspect of the "immigrant paradox." There have been many studies by psychologists and sociologists focused on the development of immigrant youth from different backgrounds and in different countries and settings, and it is clear that institutions and attitudes in the host country matter: Patterns of identity, language, and value retention, for example, are influenced by the social and political context, including perceived discrimination and fear of assimilation (Ward, 2008). However, more rigorous cross-country studies with standardized approaches and measures are needed to clarify the causal processes and key influences at work. The International Comparative Study of Ethno-Cultural Youth organized in 13 immigration-receiving countries, for example, suggests that first-generation migrant youth were generally equal to or better than their nonmigrant peers in psychological well-being (life satisfaction, self-esteem, mental health) and school adjustment and behavior; second-generation youth were largely indistinguishable from their national peers (Berry et al., 2006; Sam et al., 2006).

So it is particularly difficult at this stage to identify institutional settings and policies that promote well-being of immigrant youth in the domain of family and peer relationships, despite many valuable studies in specific contexts and settings. More open and less discriminatory attitudes and practices in the host country may be important in facilitating adaptation by immigrant youth, but it not easy to pin down their precise role, much less how policy might best be directed to bring about change.

Conclusions

Institutional settings and policies vary greatly across industrialized countries, so comparative analysis can seek to identify which settings and policies are most effective in promoting the well-being of immigrant youth. Recent studies and monitoring procedures in relation to well-being, social inclusion/exclusion, and child well-being provide a framework within which this can be set, distinguishing key dimensions. This chapter has sought to place some key findings from the disparate social science research literature on immigration and youth within that framework, dealing in turn with the domains of education, employment and earnings, economic resources and poverty, housing, and family and peer relationships.

To assess which institutional settings and policies are most effective, one needs to look at how similar immigrants fare in different countries, but that is very demanding in terms of information, in relation to institutions and policies, to outcomes, and most important to the migrants themselves and their backgrounds – treating immigrants as a homogenous group is highly misleading. Furthermore, whether migrant youth are doing better in terms of key outcomes in one country versus another in absolute terms is distinct from the "migrant penalty," which compares their outcomes with others in the country in question.

In discussing educational outcomes, traditional explanations emphasizing social background were seen to work rather well in explaining ethnic minority disadvantage; targeted programs aimed at migrants did not appear to be responsible for much of the difference in outcomes for migrant youth across countries, with the way the education system is structured in the first place being much more important. Though the comparative research available to support it is less well developed, this broad conclusion may hold across other domains as well. Structures that are unfavorable for the disadvantaged are also likely to handicap many immigrants, and strategies to improve the situation of those with limited educational and skills – for example directing resources toward schools in deprived neighborhoods or toward retraining and reintegration of the unemployed – will also benefit without targeting them explicitly. First generation migrants (and the "1.5" generation) may still face particular obstacles across the various domains, due for example to limited entitlements to social protection and to language and other socioeconomic and cultural barriers to integration. This provides a clear rationale for targeted support in language acquisition and schooling, for health and social services directed toward the special needs of migrants and aimed at promoting and facilitating appropriate utilization patterns, and for housing policies that prioritize access of recent migrants to rental or social housing. Antidiscrimination policies may be at least as important. Many countries have implemented stringent antidiscrimination legislation and education programs aimed at changing attitudes, and vigorous implementation on both fronts seems essential if outcomes for migrants from particular minority groups are to be improved. The conditions under which affirmative action does more good than harm for such groups need careful study.

In addition to the way welfare states are structured and treat people generally and how extensive and effective specific policies are for migrants, policies in relation to which migrants to accept and how illegal entrants are treated probably play a central role in the observed variation in outcomes for migrants across countries. There is a significant literature on the immigration policy of developed countries focused on how many are admitted and on what basis, including in Europe at the EU level (see for example Sainsbury, 2006), but linking this to how immigrants fare across those countries is a priority for future research. More generally, we have emphasized throughout this chapter that arriving at meaningful conclusions about the circumstances and causal processes affecting first- and second-generation immigrants is very demanding in terms of data. It requires first that first- and second-generation migrants be identified in general samples of the population large enough to support statistical inference, distinguished by ethnic group or origin. It requires that key outcomes be measured in a reliable and comprehensive fashion. Finally, both the factors hypothesized to affect those outcomes for everyone, and the specific factors in relation to migrant experience, context, and culture, need be measured. This is a tall order, and so it is not surprising that rigorous comparative studies – where all this has to be available across a number of countries, and with the variables measured in the same way – have only begun to emerge in recent years. They demonstrate the resources and time that must be devoted to getting such comparative studies right, and the benefits of doing so: They now provide us with a template for similar studies within the various domains and across them in the future.

REFERENCES

Abraído-Lanza, A. F., Chao, M. T., & Flórez, K. (2005). Do healthy behaviors decline with greater acculturation?: Implications for the Latino mortality paradox. *Social Science & Medicine, 61*, 1243–55.

Bassanini, A., & Saint-Martin, A. (2008). The price of prejudice: Labour market discrimination on the grounds of gender and ethnicity. *Employment Outlook*. OECD: Paris.

Ben-Arieh, A., & Frones, I. (Eds.). (2009). Indicators of children's well-being theory and practice in a multi-cultural perspective. *Social Indicators Research Series, Vol. 36*. Berlin: Springer.

Bénabou, R., Kramarz, F., & Prost, C. (2005). *The French zones d'education prioritaire: Much ado about nothing?* DP5085, CEPR: London.

Bendick, M. (1996). Discrimination against racial/ethnic minorities in access to employment in the United States: Empirical findings from situation testing. ILO International Migration Papers No. 12, International Labour Organisation: Geneva.

Berry, J., Phinney, J., Sam, D., & Vedder, P. (Eds.). (2006). *Immigrant youth in cultural transition: Acculturation, identity, and adaptation across national contexts*. Mahwah, NJ and London: Lawrence Erlbaum.

Bollini, P., & Siem, H. (1995). No real progress towards equity: Health of migrants and ethnic minorities on the eve of the year 2000. *Social Science and Medicine, 41*(6), 819–28.

Borjas, G. (1999). *Heaven's door: Immigration policy and the American economy*. Princeton, NJ: Princeton University Press.

Breen, R., & Jonsson, J. O. (2005). Inequality of opportunity in comparative perspective: Recent research on educational attainment and social mobility. *Annual Review of Sociology, 31*, 223–43.

Campbell, A., Converse, P., & Rodgers, W. (1976). *The quality of American life: Perceptions, evaluations, and satisfactions*. New York: Russell Sage.

Carlsson, M., & Rooth, D.-O. (2007). Evidence of ethnic discrimination in the Swedish labor market using experimental data. *Labour Economics, 14*, 716–29.

Carter, T. (2005). The influence of immigration on global city housing markets: The Canadian perspective. *Urban Policy and Research, 23*(3), 265–86.

Crul, M., & Vermeulen, H. (2003). The second generation in Europe. *International Migration Review, 37*(4), 965–86.

Cutler, D. M., & Glaeser, E. L. (1997). Are ghettos good or bad? *Quarterly Journal of Economics, 112*, 827–72.

Dustmann, C., Fabbri, F., Preston, I., & Wadsworth, J. (2003). Labour market performance of immigrants in the UK labour market. Home Office Online Report 05/03: London.

Edgar, B., Doherty, J., & Meert, H. (2004). *Immigration and homelessness in Europe*. Bristol: Policy Press.

Edin, P.-A., Frederiksson, P., & Aslund, O. (2000). Ethnic enclaves and the economic success of immigrants – Evidence from a natural experiment. WP 2000:9, IFAU – Office of Labour Market Evaluation, Stockholm.

Erikson, R., & Aberg, R. (Eds.). (1987). *Welfare in transition: Living conditions in Sweden 1968–1981*. Oxford: Clarendon Press.

Esser, H. (2004). Does the "new" immigration require a "new" theory of intergenerational integration? *International Migration Review, 38*(3), 1126–59.

European Commission. (2008). Child poverty and well-being in the EU: Current status and way forward. Social Protection Committee, Luxembourg: Office for Official Publications of the European Communities.

Fahey, T., Nolan, B., & Whelan, C. T. (2003). Monitoring quality of life in Europe. European Foundation for the Improvement of Living and Working Conditions, Office for Official Publications of the European Communities, Luxembourg.

Fase, W. (1994). *Ethnic Divisions in Western European Education*. Munster: Wasmann.

Federal Interagency Programme on Child and Family Statistics. (2008). America's children in brief – key national indicators of child well-being, 2008. Washington, DC: US Government Printing Office.

Fertig, M., & Schurer, S. (2007). Labour market outcomes of immigrants in Germany: The importance of heterogeneity and attrition bias. Discussion Paper No. 2915, IZA: Bonn.

Fleury, D. (2007). A study of poverty and working poverty among recent immigrants to Canada. Human Resources and Social Development Canada.

Gross, D. M. (1999). Three million foreigners, three million unemployed? Immigration and the French Labour Market, IMF Working Paper, n.124.

Hair, E. C., Moore, K. A., Hunter, D., & Kaye, J. W. (2001). Youth outcomes compendium. Washington, DC: Child Trends and the Edna McConnell Clark Foundation.

Harrison, M. (2005). Ethnicity, 'race' and policy issues. In P. Somerville and N. Sprigings, (Eds.), *Housing and social policy: Contemporary themes and critical perspectives.* (pp. 124–42) London: Routledge.

Hauser, R. M., Brown, B. V., & Prosser, W. R. (Eds.). (1997). *Indicators of children's well-being.* New York: Russell Sage Foundation.

Harvey B. (1994). *Homelessness in Europe.* European Network of Housing Research Conference, University of Glasgow: Glasgow.

Heath, A., & Birnbaum, Y. (2007). Explaining ethnic inequalities in educational attainment. *Ethnicities, 7(3)*, 291–305.

Heath, A. F., & Cheung, S. Y. (Eds.). (2007). Unequal chances: Ethnic minorities in western labour markets. *Proceedings of the British Academy.* Oxford: Oxford University Press.

Hernandez, D. J. (Ed.). (1999). *Children of immigrants: Health, adjustment and public assistance.* Washington, DC: National Academy Press.

Hernandez, D. J., & Charney, E. (1998). *From generation to generation: The health and well-being of children in immigrant families.* National Academies Press.

Hoynes, H., Page, M., & Stevens, A. H. (2006). Poverty in America: Trends and explanations. *Journal of Economic Perspectives, 20(1)*, 47–68.

Hyman, I., Vu, N., & Belser, M. (2000). Post-migration stresses among Southeast Asian refugee youth in Canada: A research note. *Journal of Comparative Family Studies, 31(2)*, 281–93.

Jasso, G., Massey, D., Rosenzweig, M., & Smith, J. (2004). Immigrant Health: Selectivity and Acculturation, WP04/23, Institute for Fiscal Studies: London.

Kahanec, M., & Zimmermann, K. (Eds.) (2009). *EU labor markets after post-enlargement migration.* Springer: Berlin.

Kazemipur, A., & Halli, S. (2001). Immigrants and "new poverty": The case of Canada. *International Migration Review, 35(4)*, 1129–56.

Kristen, C. (2008). Primary school choice and ethnic school segregation in German elementary schools. *European Sociological Review, 24(4)*, 495–510.

Laroche, M. (2000). Health status and health services utilization of Canada's immigrant and non-immigrant populations. *Canadian Public Policy, 26(1)*, 51–75.

Leduc, N., & Proulx, M. (2004). Patterns of health services utilization by recent immigrants. *Journal of Immigrant Health, 6(1)*, 15–27.

Lelkes, O. (2007). Poverty among migrants in Europe. Policy Brief, European Centre for Social Welfare Policy and Research: Vienna.

Levitt, P., & Waters, M. (Eds.). (2002). The changing face of home: The transnational lives of the second generation. Washington, DC: Russell Sage Foundation.

McDonald, J., & Kennedy, S. (2004). Insights into the "healthy immigrant effect": Health status and health service use of immigrants to Canada. *Social Science and Medicine, 59*, 1613–27.

McGinnity, F., Nelson, J., Lunn, P., & Quinn, E. (2009). Discrimination in recruitment: Evidence from a field experiment. Equality Authority and ESRI: Dublin.

McKennell, A. C., & Andrews, F. M. (1980). Model of cognition and affect in perceptions of well-being. *Social Indicators Research, 8*, 257–98.

Moore, K. A., Lippman, L., & Brown, B. (2004). Indicators of child well-being: The promise for positive youth development. *The Annals of the American Academy of Political and Social Science*, *591*(1), 125–45.

Musterd, A., & Ostendorf, W. (1998). *Urban segregation and the welfare state: Inequality and exclusion in western cities*. London: Routledge.

Musterd, S., & Deurloo, R. (2002). Unstable immigrant concentrations in Amsterdam: Spatial segregation and integration of newcomers. *Housing Studies*, *17*(3), 487–503.

OECD. (2008). Ending job Discrimination. Policy brief, OECD: Paris.

Parsons, C. A., & Smeeding, T. (Eds.). (2006). *Immigration and the transformation of Europe*. Cambridge: Cambridge University Press.

Portes, A., & Zhou, M. (1993). The new second generation: Segmented assimilation and its variants. *The Annals of the American Academy of Political and Social Science*, *530*, 74–96.

Portes, R., & Rumbaut, R. (2001). *Legacies: The story of the immigrant second generation*. Berkeley: University of California Press.

Pumariega, A., Rothe, E., & Pumariega, J. (2005). Mental health of immigrants and refugees. *Community Mental Health Journal*, *41*(5), 581–97.

Riach, P., & Rich, J. (2002). Field experiments of discrimination in the marketplace. *The Economic Journal*, *112*, F480–F518.

Sainsbury, D., (2006). Immigrants' social rights in comparative perspective: Welfare regimes, forms in immigration and immigration policy regimes. *Journal of European Social Policy*, *16*(3), 229–44.

Salant, T., & Lauderdale, D. (2003). Measuring culture: A critical review of acculturation and health in Asian immigrant populations. *Social Science and Medicine*, *57*, 71–90.

Sam, D. L., Vedder, P., Ward, C., & Hoarenczyk, G. (2006). Psychological and sociocultural adaptation of immigrant youth. In J. W. Berry, J. S. Phinney, D. L. Sam, and P. Vedder. (Eds.), *Immigrant youth in cultural transition: Acculturation, identity and adaptation across national contexts* (pp. 117–42). London: Lawrence Erlbaum.

Sanromá, E., Ramos, R., & Simón, H. (2009). Immigrant wages in the Spanish labour market: Does the origin of human capital matter? Discussion Paper No. 4157, IZA: Bonn.

Schnepf S. V. (2007). Immigrants' educational disadvantage: An examination across ten countries and three surveys. *Journal of Population Economics*, *20*(3), 527–45.

Sen, A. (1993). Capability and well-being. In M. Nussbaum and A. Sen (Eds.), *The quality of life*. Oxford: Clarendon Press.

   (2000), *Social Exclusion: Concept, Application and Scrutiny*, Social Development Papers, No. 1, Office of Environment and Social Development, Asian Development Bank: Manilla.

Shavit, Y., & Blossfeld, H.-P. (Eds.). (1993). *Persistent inequalities: A comparative study of educational attainment in thirteen countries*. Boulder Colorado: Westview Press.

Shavit, Y., & Müller, W. (Eds.). (1998). From school to work: A comparative study of educational qualifications and occupational destinations. Oxford: Clarendon Press.

Suárez-Orozco, C., & Suárez-Orozco, M. (1995). Transformations: Immigration, family life, and achievement motivation among Latino adolescents. Stanford University Press: Stanford, CA.

Suárez-Orozco, C., & Qin, D. B. (2006). Psychological and gendered perspectives on immigrant origin youth. *International Migration Review, 40*(1), 165–99.

UNICEF. (2007). Child poverty in perspective: An overview of child well-being in rich countries. Innocenti Report Card 7, UNICEF: Florence.

Van de Werfhorst, H., & van Tubergen. (2007). Postimmigration investment in education: A study of immigrants in the Netherlands. *Demography, 44*(4), 883–98.

Venema, H., Garretsen, H., & van der Maas, P. (1995). Health of migrants and migrant health policy, the Netherlands as an example. *Social Science and Medicine, 41*(60), 809–18.

Ward. C. (2008). The experiences of migrant youth: A generational analysis, Migrant and Refugee Youth Settlement and Social Inclusion Series, Department of Labour: Wellington.

Westin, C. (2003). Young people of migrant origin in Sweden. *International Migration Review, 37*(4), 987–1010.

Whiteford, P., & Adema, W. (2007). What works best in reducing child poverty: A benefit or work strategy? OECD Social, Employment and Migration Working Papers No. 51, Paris: OECD.

Zimmermann, K. (2005). *European Migration: What Do We Know?* Oxford: Oxford University Press.

Index